INTERPLAY:
The Process of Interpersonal Communication
TWELFTH EDITION

Ronald B. Adler
Lawrence B. Rosenfeld
Russell F. Proctor II

WITH

UNDERSTANDING HUMAN COMMUNICATION
TWELFTH EDITION

Ronald B. Adler
George Rodman
Athena du Pré

Source material from:
Adler, Rosenfeld, and Proctor II, *Interplay: The Process of Interpersonal Communication, 12th edition.*
978-0-19-982742-8

Adler, Rodman, and du Pré, *Understanding Human Communication, 12th edition.*
978-0-19-933432-2

Oxford New York
OXFORD UNIVERSITY PRESS

OXFORD

UNIVERSITY PRESS

Oxford University Press is a department of the University of Oxford. It furthers the University's
objective of excellence in research, scholarship, and education by publishing worldwide.

Oxford   New York
Auckland   Cape Town   Dar es Salaam   Hong Kong   Karachi
Kuala Lumpur   Madrid   Melbourne   Mexico City   Nairobi
New Delhi   Shanghai   Taipei   Toronto

With offices in
Argentina   Austria   Brazil   Chile   Czech Republic   France   Greece
Guatemala   Hungary   Italy   Japan Poland   Portugal   Singapore
South Korea   Switzerland   Thailand   Turkey   Ukraine   Vietnam

Published by Oxford University Press.
198 Madison Avenue, New York, New York 10016
http://www.oup.com

ISBN 978-0-19-021932-1

Contents

CHAPTER 3

Communication and the Self   64

CHAPTER 4

Perceiving Others   106

PART TWO: CREATING AND RESPONDING TO MESSAGES

CHAPTER 5

Language   140

CONTENTS

CHAPTER 8
Emotions 244

PART THREE: DIMENSIONS OF INTERPERSONAL RELATIONSHIPS

CHAPTER 9

Dynamics of Interpersonal Relationships 278

FEATURES

DARK SIDE OF COMMUNICATION: ABUSING THOSE WHO DISCLOSE 286

FOCUS ON RESEARCH: OPENING LINES: INITIATING ROMANTIC RELATIONSHIPS 288

AT WORK: SOCIAL CAPITAL AND CAREER ADVANCEMENT 296

FOCUS ON RESEARCH: REEL TO REAL?: RELATIONAL COMMUNICATION IN ROMANTIC COMEDIES 303

CHAPTER 12

Interpersonal Contexts: Friends, Family, and Intimate Relationships 382

FEATURES

AT WORK: CAN WOMEN BE COWORKERS AND FRIENDS? 388

FOCUS ON RESEARCH: FRIENDS WITH BENEFITS: THE COMMUNICATION CHALLENGES OF NOT-SO-CASUAL SEX 389

DARK SIDE OF COMMUNICATION: VIRTUALLY UNFAITHFUL: EMOTIONAL INFIDELITY IN CYBERSPACE 407

FOCUS ON RESEARCH: MAINTAINING MARRIAGES THROUGH FLIRTING 408

understanding human communication

Contents

CHAPTER 12 Organization and Support 534

CHAPTER 13 Informative Speaking 561

> Features

■ Preface

"This course is just common sense." Most teacher-scholars in our field have heard that refrain for years, both from students and laypersons.

Some of the concepts discussed in *Interplay* are indeed familiar. Listening is vital to personal and professional success. Respectful, supportive language gets better results than harsh words. Win-win conflict management benefits everyone involved. Just because students are aware of these truths, however, doesn't mean they can or do put them into practice. One of the goals of *Interplay* is to give readers strategies for effectively using skills they already recognize as valuable.

Not all of what's included in this textbook is "common sense." Some of the research findings cited in *Interplay* are counterintuitive. For instance, most laypeople don't know there's a downside to many positive traits such as self-esteem, self-monitoring, and empathy (see Chapters 1, 3, and 4). They aren't aware that using disclaimers such as "I don't mean to sound arrogant" actually leads others to perceive them as *more* arrogant (see Chapter 5). Few know that liars tend to make *more* eye contact and fidget *less* than non-liars (see Chapter 6). And it takes more than common sense to reconcile contradictory bits of received wisdom like "birds of a feather flock together" and "opposites attract" (see Chapter 9).

We hope *Interplay* will help students recognize that the process of interpersonal communication isn't as simple as it might first appear. Beyond understanding how scholarship informs everyday interaction, we have striven to show readers how research and theories can lead to more effective and satisfying relationships.

Basic Approach

This 12th edition of *Interplay* retains the proven approach that has served several hundred thousand students and professors for many years. The accessible writing style is based on the belief that even complicated ideas can be presented in a straightforward way. A variety of thought-provoking photos, sidebars, and cartoons make the subject more interesting and compelling than text alone can. And in terms of its scholarly grounding, this edition cites more than 1,500 sources, 34 percent of which are new to this edition. Research and theory aren't presented for their own sake, but rather to support insights about how the process of interpersonal communication operates in everyday life.

New in This Edition

While the overall structure of the book will be familiar to long-time users, several changes enhance its usability and keep the content up to date. There are two important changes in the chapter organization of the book:

- **New Chapter 2, "Interpersonal Communication in a Changing World,"** addresses the impact of social media on interpersonal relationships.

- **New Chapter 12, "Interpersonal Contexts,"** expands and consolidates the discussion of communication with those who are closest to us. The chapter includes a new discussion of communication in friendships and updated sections on communication in intimate relationships and families.

Many changes have been made to individual chapters to interpret the latest communication research and address changing communication practices. These include:

- The role of mediated communication in identity management and self-disclosure (Chapter 3)

- Distinctions between empathy and sympathy (Chapter 4)

- How deception is (and isn't) communicated through nonverbal communication (Chapter 6)

- The best ways to offer advice (Chapter 7)

- New coverage of emotional intelligence, reappraisal, and emotion labor (Chapter 8)

- Updates on relational stages (Chapter 9)

- Expanded discussion of John Gottman's "Four Horsemen of the Apocalypse," an assessment of problematic conflict behaviors (Chapter 11)

In addition to updating key chapter discussions, many boxes and sidebars have been added or revised to highlight contemporary issues and examples:

- New **At Work** boxes help readers apply scholarship to their careers. Topics include identity management in the workplace, the effects of swearing on the job, the role of touch in career success, and the value of cultivating social capital.

- Many **Focus on Research** boxes are new to this edition. They cover timely subjects such as the impact of overly casual e-mails, how people with disabilities assimilate into organizations, the effects of nonverbal poses on feelings of power, blogging as a means for social support, the relational messages in romantic comedies, and the role of flirting in marriage.

■ **Dark Side of Communication** sidebars address a variety of challenging topics. New to this edition is coverage of problems including the dangers of being overly connected in cyberspace, the incivility of hate speech, cyberbullying, and the hazards of jealousy.

■ **Media Clips** now use both television and films to illustrate communication concepts. Twenty of the sidebars are new to this edition, including *House, M.D.* (communication competence), *The Social Network* (cybercommunication), *What Not to Wear* (clothing and communication), *Yes Man* (debilitative emotions), *30 Rock* (conflict), and *Modern Family* (family communication).

Ancillaries

In addition to the text, a variety of ancillaries provide resources for both students and instructors.

For Students

■ A **Student Success Manual**, written by Leah Bryant of DePaul University, is packed with information that will help students master the course material. It includes a primer on effective study habits as well as chapter-specific material such as outlines, summaries, key terms, review questions (and answers), and critical thinking exercises.

■ *Now Playing: Learning Communication Through Film*, available as an optional printed product, looks at more than 60 contemporary and classic feature films through the lens of communication principles. Developed by Russell F. Proctor II and revised by Darin Garard of Santa Barbara City College, *Now Playing* illustrates a variety of both individual scenes and full-length films, highlighting concepts and offering discussion questions for a mass medium that is interactive, familiar, and easily accessible.

■ The **companion website** at www.oup.com/us/adler offers a wealth of resources including exercises, flashcards for key terms in the book, interactive self-tests, and links to a variety of communication-related websites, such as *Now Playing* online.

For Instructors

■ An enhanced **Instructor's Manual and Test Bank**, revised by Ellen Bremen and Shannon Proctor of Highline Community College, provides teaching tips, exercises, and test questions that will prove useful to both new and veteran instructors. The Instructor's Manual includes teaching strategies, course outlines, chapter exercises, discussion questions, and unit wind-ups. The comprehensive Test Bank offers approximately 100 class-tested exam questions per chapter in multiple-choice, true/false, essay, and matching formats.

▪ An **Instructor Resource CD with Computerized Test Bank**, available to adopters, includes the full Instructor's Manual and Test Bank, as well as computerized testing software and newly revised PowerPoint-based lecture presentations by Ellen Bremen of Highline Community College.

▪ **Instructor's Companion Website** at www.oup.com/us/adler is a password-protected site that features the Instructor's Manual, PowerPoint-based lecture slides, and links to supplemental materials and films.

▪ *Now Playing: Instructor's Edition*, an instructor-only print supplement, includes an introduction on how to incorporate film examples in class, more sample responses to the numerous discussion questions in the student edition of *Now Playing*, viewing guides, additional films, and references.

▪ Course cartridges for a variety of e-learning environments allow instructors to create their own course websites with the interactive material from the instructor and student companion websites. Contact your Oxford University Press representative for access.

Acknowledgments

The book you are reading wouldn't have been possible without the help of many talented people. We are grateful to the many colleagues whose suggestions have helped make this book a far better one:

Aurora Auter
University of Southwestern Louisiana

Heather Bixler
College of the Sequoias

Colleen Butcher
University of Florida

Katrina Eicher
Elizabethtown Community College

Karyn Friesen
Lone Star College-Montgomery

Gail Hankins
Wake Technical College

Meredith Harrigan
SUNY Geneseo

Kristin Haun
University of Tennessee

Tim Moreland
Catawba College

Mark Morman
Baylor University

Noreen Mysyk
North Central College

Tracey Powers
Central Arizona College

Laurie Pratt
Chaffey College

Elizabeth Ribarsky
University of Illinois-Springfield

Julie Simanski
Des Moines Community College

Renee Strom
Saint Cloud State University

Dennis Sutton
Grand Rapids Community College

Lindsay Timmerman
University of Wisconsin-Milwaukee

Gordon Young
Kingsborough Community College

Thanks are also due to Russell Collins and Mark Galbraith for their above-and-beyond insights.

Interplay continues to benefit from the contributions of these colleagues who helped shape the previous edition:

Marcanne Andersen
Anoka Ramsey Community College

Kathleen Czech
Point Loma Nazarene University

Kristin K. Froemling
Radford University

Darlene J. Geiger
Portland State University

Debra Gonsher
Bronx Community College

Em Griffin
Wheaton College

Lisa C. Hebert
Louisiana State University

Shaorong Huang
Raymond Walters College-University of Cincinnati

Beverly Merrill Kelley
California Lutheran University

Anastasia Kurylo
Marymount Manhattan College

Andrea Lambert
Northern Kentucky University

Phil Martin
North Central State College

Kelly Morrison
Michigan State University

Johance F. Murray
Hostos Community College/CUNY

Gretchen R. Norling
University of West Florida

Narissra Maria Punyanunt-Carter
Texas Tech University

Gregory W. Rickert
Lexington Community College

Jennifer A. Samp
University of Georgia

Debbie Sonandre
Tacoma Community College

Michael Wittig
Waukesha County Technical College

We salute the team of hardworking professionals at Oxford University Press. Mark Haynes, Editor; Thom Holmes and Danielle Christensen, Development Editors; Lisa Grzan, Managing Editor; Paula Schlosser and Betty Lew, Art Directors; Kate McClaskey, Editorial Assistant; and Caitlin Kaufman, intrepid Assistant Editor and photo researcher. We continue to value the legacy and friendship of Peter Labella. Our thanks also go to Deanna Hegle for her copyediting talents and Susan Monahan for crafting the useful indexes. Sherri Adler chose the variety of compelling photos that help make *Interplay* unique.

About the Authors

Ronald B. Adler is Professor Emeritus of Communication at Santa Barbara City College. He is coauthor of *Understanding Human Communication*, Eleventh Edition (OUP, 2012), *Looking Out, Looking In* (2011), and *Communicating at Work: Principles and Practices for Business and the Professions* (2010). In addition to his academic pursuits, Ron works with businesses and nonprofit agencies to improve communication among coworkers as well as with clients and the public.

Lawrence B. Rosenfeld is Professor of Communication Studies and Co-Chair of the Social-Behavioral Institutional Review Board, University of North Carolina at Chapel Hill. He is the author of articles appearing in journals in communication, education, social work, sport psychology, and psychology, and of books on small group, interpersonal, and nonverbal communication. His most recent book is *When Their World Falls Apart: Helping Families and Children Manage the Effects of Disasters* (NASW Press, 2010). In 2000, Lawrence received the Donald H. Eckroyd Award for Outstanding Teaching in Higher Education from the National Communication Association, and in 2006 received the Gerald M. Phillips Award for Applied Communication Research from the same national communication organization.

Russell F. Proctor II is Professor of Communication Studies at Northern Kentucky University. He primarily teaches courses in interpersonal communication and interviewing, and he won NKU's Outstanding Professor Award in 1997. In addition to his work on Interplay, he is also coauthor of *Looking Out, Looking In* (2011). Russ has written and presented extensively on the use of feature films as instructional tools in communication courses (including *Now Playing* for OUP).

Interpersonal Process

After studying the material in this chapter . . .

You should understand:

1. The needs that effective communication can satisfy.
2. Four insights from the communication model.
3. Five key principles of communication.
4. Four misconceptions about communication.
5. Quantitative and qualitative definitions of interpersonal communication.
6. The characteristics of competent communication.

You should be able to:

1. Identify examples of the physical, identity, social, and practical needs you attempt to satisfy by communicating.
2. Demonstrate how the communication model applies to your interpersonal communication.
3. Describe the degrees to which your communication is qualitatively impersonal and interpersonal, and describe the consequences of this combination.
4. Identify situations in which you communicate competently and those in which your competence is less than satisfactory.

E veryone communicates. Students and professors, parents and children, employers and employees, friends, strangers, and enemies—all communicate. We have been communicating with others from earliest childhood and will almost certainly keep doing so until we die.

Why study an activity you've done your entire life? There are at least three reasons (Morreale & Pearson, 2008). First, studying interpersonal communication will give you a new look at a familiar topic. For instance, in a few pages you will find that some people can go years—even a lifetime—without communicating in a truly interpersonal manner. In this sense, exploring human communication is rather like studying anatomy or botany—everyday objects and processes take on new meaning.

A second reason for studying the subject has to do with the staggering amount of time we spend communicating. For example, one survey (Nellermoe et al., 1999) revealed that business professionals spend 80 percent of their business day communicating with colleagues and clients. Online communication is just as pervasive as the face-to-face variety: One study showed that the majority of Internet users rely on e-mail (IT Facts, 2008), with most communicating online daily, and Twitter users satisfy their need for an informal sense of camaraderie by tweeting (Chen, 2011). Among teens, almost two-thirds have posted content online: creating personal websites, writing blogs, and posting online videos (Lenhart et al., 2007; Mesch & Talmud, 2010).

There is a third, more compelling reason for studying interpersonal communication. To put it bluntly, all of us could learn to communicate more effectively. In a nationwide survey, "lack of effective communication" was identified as the cause of relational breakups—including marriages—more often than any other reason, including money, relatives or in-laws, sexual problems, previous relationships, or children (National Communication Association, 1999). Ineffective communication is also a problem in the workplace. A group of senior executives cited lack of interpersonal skills as one of the top three skill deficits in today's workforce (Marchant, 1999). Poor communication can be physically dangerous: One study found that communication errors caused twice as many hospital admissions problems as practitioners' inadequate skills (Strachan, 2004), and another found that poor professional–patient communication was the primary problem in helping patients manage their own health care (Moffat et al., 2007).

If you pause now and make a mental list of communication problems you have encountered, you'll probably see that no matter how successful your relationships are at home, with friends, at school, and at work, there is plenty of room for improvement in your everyday life. The information that follows will help you improve the way you communicate with some of the people who matter most to you.

Why We Communicate

Research demonstrating the importance of communication has been around longer than you might think. Frederick II, emperor of the Holy Roman Empire from 1220 to 1250, was called *stupor mundi*—"wonder of the world"—by his admiring subjects. Along with his administrative and military talents, Frederick was a leading scientist of his time. A medieval historian described one of his dramatic, inhumane experiments:

> He bade foster mothers and nurses to suckle the children, to bathe and wash them, but in no way to prattle with them, for he wanted to learn whether they would speak the Hebrew language, which was the oldest, or Greek, or Latin, or Arabic, or perhaps the language of their parents, of whom they had been born. But he labored in vain because all the children died. For they could not live without the petting and joyful faces and loving words of their foster mothers. (Ross & McLaughlin, 1949, p. 366)

Fortunately, contemporary researchers have found less barbaric ways to illustrate the importance of communication. In one study of isolation, five participants were paid to remain alone in a locked room. One lasted for 8 days. Three held out for 2 days, one commenting "Never again." The fifth participant lasted only 2 hours (Schachter, 1959).

The need for contact and companionship is just as strong outside the laboratory, as individuals who have led solitary lives by choice or necessity have discovered. W. Carl Jackson, an adventurer who sailed across the Atlantic Ocean alone in 51 days, summarized the feelings common to most loners in a post-voyage interview:

> I found the loneliness of the second month almost excruciating. I always thought of myself as self-sufficient, but I found life without people had no meaning. I had a definite need for somebody to talk to, someone real, alive, and breathing. (Jackson, 1978)

You might claim that solitude would be a welcome relief from the irritations of everyday life. It's true that all of us need time by ourselves, often more than we get. On the other hand, each of us has a point beyond which we do not *want* to be alone. Beyond this point, solitude changes from a pleasurable to a painful condition. In other words, we all need people. We all need to communicate.

PHYSICAL NEEDS

Communication is so important that its presence or absence affects physical health. Recent studies confirm that people who process a negative experience by talking about it report improved life satisfaction, as well as enhanced mental and physical health, relative to those who think privately about it (Francis, 2003; Sousa, 2002). A study conducted with police officers found that being able to talk easily with colleagues and supervisors about work-related trauma was related to greater physical and mental health (Stephens & Long, 2000). A study of over 3,500 people ages 24–96 revealed that the more social contact we have, the higher the level of mental function (Ybarra et al., 2008). As little as 10 minutes of talking, face to face or by phone, improves memory and boosts intellectual function.

In extreme cases, communication can even become a matter of life or death. When he was a Navy pilot, U.S. Senator John McCain was shot down over North Vietnam and held as a prisoner of war for 6 years, often in solitary confinement. He describes how POWs set up clandestine codes in which they sent messages by tapping on walls to laboriously spell out words. McCain describes the importance of keeping contact and the risks that inmates would take to maintain contact with one another:

> The punishment for communicating could be severe, and a few POWs, having been caught and beaten for their efforts, had their spirits broken as their bodies were battered. Terrified of a return trip to the punishment room, they would lie still in their cells when their comrades tried to tap them up on the wall. Very few would remain uncommunicative for long. To suffer all this alone was less tolerable than torture. Withdrawing in silence from the fellowship of other Americans . . . was to us the approach of death. (McCain, 1999, p. 12)

Communication isn't just a necessity for prisoners of war. Evidence gathered by a host of medical researchers and social scientists (e.g., Braithwaite et al., 2010; Cole et al., 2007; Fitzpatrick & Vangelisti, 2001; Holt-Lunstad et al., 2010; Mendes de Leon, 2005; Parker-Pope, 2010; Uchino, 2004) shows that satisfying relationships can literally be a matter of life and death for people who lead normal lives. For example,

- A meta-analysis of nearly 150 studies and over 300,000 participants found that socially connected people—those with strong networks of family and friends—live an average of 3.7 years longer than those who are socially isolated.

- People with strong relationships have significantly lower risks of coronary disease, regardless of whether they smoke, drink alcoholic beverages, or exercise regularly.

- Divorced, separated, and widowed people are five to ten times more likely to need mental hospitalization than their married counterparts. Happily married people also have lower incidences of pneumonia, surgery, and cancer than single people. (It's important to note that the *quality* of the relationship is more important than the institution of marriage in these studies.)

▪ Pregnant women under stress and without supportive relationships have three times more complications than pregnant women who suffer from the same stress but have strong social support.

▪ Socially isolated people are four times more susceptible to the common cold than those who have active social networks.

▪ College students in committed relationships experience fewer mental health problems than those not in committed relationships.

Research like this demonstrates the importance of meaningful personal relationships, and it explains the conclusion of social scientists that communication is essential. Not everyone needs the same amount of contact, and the quality of communication is almost certainly as important as the quantity. Nonetheless, the point remains: Personal communication is essential for our well-being. To paraphrase a popular song, "People who need people" aren't "the luckiest people in the world": They're the *only* people!

IDENTITY NEEDS

Communication does more than enable us to survive. It is the way—indeed, the *major* way—we learn who we are (Fogel et al., 2002; Harwood, 2005). As you'll read in Chapter 3, our sense of identity comes from the way we interact with other people. Are we smart or stupid, attractive or ugly, skillful or inept? The answers to these questions don't come from looking in the mirror. We decide who we are based on how others react to us.

Deprived of communication with others, we would have no sense of identity. Consider the case of the famous "Wild Boy of Aveyron," who spent his early childhood without any apparent human contact. The boy was discovered in January 1800 while digging for vegetables in a French village garden. He could not speak, and he showed no behaviors one would expect in a social human. More significant than this absence of social skills was his lack of any identity as a human being. As author Roger Shattuck (1980, p. 37) put it, "The boy had no human sense of being in the world. He had no sense of himself as a person related to other persons." Only after the influence of a loving "mother" did the boy begin to behave—and, we can imagine, think of himself—as a human.

Contemporary stories support the essential role communication plays in shaping identity. In 1970, authorities discovered a 12-year-old girl (whom they called "Genie") who had spent virtually all her life in an otherwise empty, darkened bedroom with almost no human contact. The child could not speak and had no sense of herself as a person until she was removed from her family and "nourished" by a team of caregivers (Rymer, 1993).

Like Genie and the boy of Aveyron, each of us enters the world with little or no sense of identity. We gain an idea of who we are from the way others define us. As Chapter 3 explains, the messages we receive in early childhood are the strongest identity shapers, but the influence of others continues throughout life.

MEDIA CLIP

COMING IN FOR A LANDING: *UP IN THE AIR*

Ryan Bingham (George Clooney) is a corporate down-sizing consultant. He's hired by companies to fly into town and do the grim work of firing their employees. Bingham is good at what he does, and he does it a lot, living out of a suitcase as he jets from city to city. Although he has an apartment in Omaha, Bingham appears to have no real home. Or family. Or friends.

Ironically, Bingham's job is threatened when a new colleague, Natalie Keener (Anna Kendrick), suggests that firings could be accomplished more efficiently online. Bingham decides to prove her wrong, demanding that she accompany him on some in-person dismissals so she can see how heartless computer firings would be. Along the way, he begins to realize how heartless his own life has become. He slowly develops a friendship with Natalie, a romance with a fellow consultant, and a renewed relationship with sisters he had ignored for years.

By the film's end, it's clear that Bingham discovers that a life without meaningful interpersonal connections is a life that's not worth living—not even for all the frequent flyer miles in the world.

SOCIAL NEEDS

Besides helping define who we are, some social scientists have argued that communication is the principal way relationships are created (Duck & Pittman, 1994; Hubbard et al., 2009). For example, Julie Yingling (1994) asserts that children "talk friendships into existence." The same can be said for adult relationships: It's impossible to imagine how they could exist without communication, which satisfies a variety of needs such as giving and receiving affection, having fun, helping others and being helped, and giving us a sense of self-worth (Rubin et al., 1988). Because relationships with others are so vital, some theorists have gone so far as to argue that communication is the primary goal of human existence. Anthropologist Walter Goldschmidt (1990) calls the drive for meeting social needs "the human career."

There's a strong link between the quality of communication and the success of relationships. For example, children who grow up in strong conversation-oriented families report having more satisfying same-sex friendships and romantic relationships when they become adults (Koesten, 2004). Women in one study reported that "socializing" contributed more to a satisfying life than virtually any other activity, including relaxing, shopping, eating, exercise, television, or prayer (Kahneman et al., 2004).

Despite knowing that communication is vital to social satisfaction, evidence suggests that many people aren't very successful at managing their interpersonal relationships. For example, one study revealed that one quarter of the more than 4,000 adults surveyed knew more about their dogs than they did about their neighbors' backgrounds (Rochmis, 2000). Research also shows that the number of friendships is in decline. One widely recognized survey reported that in 1985, Americans had an average of 2.94 close friends. Twenty years later, that number had dropped to 2.08. It's worth noting that educated Americans reported having larger and more diverse networks. In other words, a higher education can enhance your relational life as well as your intellect.

PRACTICAL NEEDS

We shouldn't overlook the everyday, important functions communication serves. Communication is the tool that lets us tell the hairstylist to take just a little off the sides, direct the doctor to where it hurts, and inform the plumber that the broken pipe needs attention *now!*

Beyond these obvious needs, a wealth of research demonstrates that communication is an essential ingredient for success in virtually every career. (See the At Work box on this page.) On-the-job communication skills can even make the difference between life and death for doctors, nurses, and other medical practitioners. Researchers discovered that "poor communication" was the root of over 60 percent of reported medical errors—including death, serious physical injury, and psychological trauma (Joint Commission on Accreditation of Healthcare, 2008). Studies also show a significant difference between the communication skills of physicians who had no malpractice claims against them and doctors with previous claims (Rodriguez et al., 2008).

Communication is just as important outside of work. For example, married couples who are effective communicators report happier relationships than less skillful husbands and wives (Kirchler, 1988; Ridley et al., 2001)—a finding that has been supported across cultures (Rehman & Holtzworth-Munroe, 2007). In school, grade-point averages of college students are related positively to their communication competence (Hawken et al. 1991; Rubin & Graham, 1988); and school adjustment, dropout rate, and overall school achievement are highly related to students' having strong, supportive relationships (Buchanan & Bowen, 2008; Heard, 2007; Rosenfeld & Richman, 1999). And in medical settings, the outcomes of our interactions with a physician depend on the ability of both the doctor *and* patient to communicate effectively (Street, 2003).

AT WORK

Communication and Career Advancement

No matter what the field, research confirms what experienced workers already know—that communication skills are crucial in finding and succeeding in a job. The abilities to speak and listen effectively have been identified as the most important factors in helping graduating college students gain employment and advance in their careers: more important than technical competence, work experience, and academic background (Winsor et al., 1997). The National Association of Colleges and Employers identified "verbal communication skills" as the most important quality employers seek in job candidates (National Association of Colleges and Employers [NACE], 2010). "Employers consistently place communication skills at the top of the list of key skills," says Marilyn Mackes, NACE executive director.

Once you're hired, the need for communication skills is important in virtually every career. Engineers spend the bulk of their working lives speaking and listening, mostly in one-on-one and small-group settings (Darling & Dannels, 2003). Accounting professionals spend 80 percent of their time on the job communicating with others, individually and in groups (Nellermoe et al., 1999). Oral and written communication skills are also vital in the computer industry, according to Silicon Valley employers (Stevens, 2005). Writing in *The Scientist*, a commentator echoed this sentiment: "If I give any advice, it is that you can never do enough training around your overall communication skills" (Richman, 2002).

Psychologist Abraham Maslow (1968) suggests that human needs fall into five categories, each of which must be satisfied before we concern ourselves with the next one. As you read about each need, think about the ways in which communication is often necessary to satisfy it. The most basic needs are *physical:* sufficient air, water, food, and rest, and the ability to re-produce as a species. The second category of Maslow's needs involves *safety:* protection from threats to our well-being. Beyond physical and safety concerns are the *social* needs we have already mentioned. Next, Maslow suggests that each of us has the need for *self-esteem:* the desire to believe that we are worthwhile, valuable people. The final category of needs involves *self-actualization:* the desire to develop our potential to the maximum, to become the best person we can be.

The Communication Process

So far, we have talked about communication as if its meaning were perfectly clear. In fact, scholars have debated the definition of communication for years (Littlejohn, 2008). Despite their many disagreements, most would concur that at its essence, **communication** is about using messages to generate meanings (Korn et al., 2000). Notice how this basic definition holds true across a variety of contexts—public speaking, small groups, mass media, etc. Our goal in this section is to explain how messages and meanings are created in interpersonal communication, and to describe the many factors involved in this complex process.

A MODEL OF COMMUNICATION

As the old saying goes, "A picture is worth a thousand words." That's what scientists had in mind when they began creating models of the communication process in the 1950s. These early models were simplistic and usually better suited for explaining mass communication than the interpersonal variety. They characterized communication as a one-way, linear event—something that a sender "does" by encoding a message and delivering it to a passive receiver who decodes it. This one-way process resembles an archer (the sender) shooting an arrow (the message) at a target (the receiver). Even in interpersonal settings, this linear approach sometimes makes sense. If you labor over a letter or e-mail to get the tone just right before sending it, your message is primarily a one-way effort.

Later models represented communication more like a tennis game, with people sending messages to receivers who responded with verbal or nonverbal **feedback** that indicates a response to the previous message. A back-and-forth chain of text messages seems to fit this description pretty well.

Over time, though, communication theorists have developed increasingly sophisticated **transactional communication models** in an attempt to depict all the factors that affect human interaction. No model can completely represent the process of communication, any more than a map can capture everything about the neighborhood where you live. Still, the model in Figure 1.1 provides a starting point for explaining the insights and principles discussed in the next section.

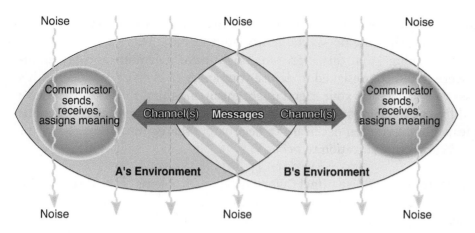

FIGURE 1.1 **Communication Model**

INSIGHTS FROM THE
TRANSACTIONAL COMMUNICATION MODEL

The model in Figure 1.1 reflects a number of important characteristics of transactional communication. As you read on, note how the following insights help explain the richness of this process.

Sending and Receiving Are Usually Simultaneous Some forms of interpersonal communication, such as e-mail, voice messages, or "snail mail" letters, aren't simultaneous: There's a delay between when they are sent and received (Chapter 2 will describe them as *asynchronous*). But in face-to-face interaction, it's hard to distinguish sender and receiver. Consider a few examples:

- A teacher explaining a difficult concept to a student after class

- A parent lecturing a teenager about the family's curfew rules

- A salesperson giving a customer information about a product

The natural impulse is to identify the teacher, parent, and salesperson as senders, while the student, teenager, and customer are receivers. Now imagine a confused look on the student's face; the teenager interrupting defensively; the customer blankly staring into the distance. It's easy to see that these verbal and nonverbal responses are messages being "sent," even while the other person is talking. Because it's often impossible to distinguish sender from receiver, our communication model replaces these roles with the more accurate term *communicator*. This term reflects the fact that—at least in face-to-face situations—people are simultaneously senders and receivers who exchange multiple messages.

Meanings Exist in and among People Messages, whether they are verbal or nonverbal, don't have meanings in themselves. Rather, meanings reside in the people who express and interpret them. Imagine that a friend says, "I'm sorry," after showing up several hours late to a date. There are several possible "meanings" that this expression might have: a genuine apology, an insincere statement designed to defuse your anger, or even a sarcastic jibe. It's easy to imagine that your friend might mean one thing and you might have a different interpretation of it. The possibility of multiple interpretations means that it is often necessary to negotiate a shared meaning in order for satisfying communication to occur.

Environment and Noise Affect Communication Problems often arise because communicators occupy different **environments** (sometimes called *contexts*): fields of experience that help them make sense of others' behavior. In communication terminology, environment refers not only to a physical location, but also to the personal experiences and cultural background that participants bring to a conversation. You can appreciate the influence of environments by thinking about your beliefs about an important topic like work, marriage, or government policies. Then imagine how your beliefs might be quite different if your personal history were different.

Notice how the model in Figure 1.1 shows that the environments of **A** and **B** overlap. This intersecting area represents the background that the communicators have in common. If this overlap didn't exist, communication would be difficult, if not impossible.

While similar environments often facilitate communication, different backgrounds can make effective communication more challenging. Consider just some of the factors that might contribute to different environments, and to challenges:

- **A** might belong to one ethnic group and **B** to another.
- **A** might be rich and **B** poor.
- **A** might be rushed and **B** have nowhere to go.
- **A** might have lived a long, eventful life, and **B** is young and inexperienced.
- **A** might be passionately concerned with the subject and **B** indifferent to it.

Another factor in the environment that makes communication difficult is what scientists call **noise**: anything that interferes with the transmission and reception of a message. Three types of noise can disrupt communication. *External noise* includes those factors outside the receiver that make it difficult to hear, as well as many other kinds of distractions. For instance, loud music in a bar or a jackhammer grinding in the street might make it hard for you to pay attention to another person. *Physiological noise* involves biological factors in the receiver that interfere with accurate reception: hearing loss, illness, and so on. *Psychological noise* refers to cognitive factors that make communication less effective. For instance, a woman who hears the word *gal* may become so irritated that she has trouble listening objectively to the rest of a speaker's message.

Channels Make a Difference Communication scholars use the term **channel** to describe the medium through which messages are exchanged. Along with face-to-face interaction, we have the option of using mediated channels such as phones, e-mail, and instant messages. The communication channel being used can affect the way a receiver responds to a message. For example, a typewritten love letter probably won't have the same effect as a handwritten expression of affection, and being fired from a job in person would feel different than getting the bad news in an e-mail.

Most people intuitively recognize that the selection of a channel depends in part on the kind of message they're sending. In one survey, Patrick O'Sullivan (2000) asked students to identify which channel they would find best for delivering a variety of messages. Most respondents said they would have little trouble sending positive messages face to face, but mediated channels had more appeal for sending negative messages (see also Feaster, 2010). Of course, the easiest channel for a message-sender to use might not be what's best for the message recipient. One survey of 1,000 cell phone users found that 45 percent had used their mobile device to end a relationship, usually by text (Mychalcewycz, 2009). Obviously, delivering bad news this way runs the risk of wounding and infuriating the person being dumped ("She didn't even have the guts to tell me to my face"). You'll read much more about social media in Chapter 2.

COMMUNICATION PRINCIPLES

In addition to the insights offered by the communication model, there are other principles that guide our understanding of communication.

Communication Is Transactional By **transactional**, we mean that communication is a dynamic process that the participants create through their interaction with one another.

Perhaps the most important consequence of communication's transactional nature is *the mutual influence that occurs when we interact*. To put it simply, communication isn't something we do *to* others; rather, it is an activity we do *with* them. In this sense, communication is rather like dancing—at least the kind of dancing we do with partners.

Like dancing, communication *depends on the behavior of a partner*. A great dancer who doesn't consider and adapt to the skill level of his or her partner can make both of them look bad. In communication and dancing, even two talented partners don't guarantee success. When two skilled dancers perform without coordinating their movements, the results feel bad to the dancers and look foolish to an audience.

Finally, relational communication—like dancing—is a unique creation that arises out of the way in which the partners interact. The way you dance probably varies from one partner to another because of its cooperative, transactional nature. Likewise, the way you communicate almost certainly varies with different partners.

Psychologist Kenneth Gergen (1991) captures the transactional nature of communication well when he points out how our success depends on interaction with others. As he says, "one cannot be 'attractive' without others who are attracted, a 'leader' without others willing to follow, or a 'loving person' without others to affirm with appreciation" (p. 158).

Communication Has a Content Dimension and a Relational Dimension Virtually all exchanges have content and relational dimensions. The **content dimension** involves the information being explicitly discussed: "Please pass the salt," "Not now, I'm tired," "You forgot to buy a quart of milk." In ad-

dition to this sort of obvious content, all messages also have a **relational dimension** (Dillard et al., 1999; Watzlawick et al., 1967) that expresses how you feel about the other person: whether you like or dislike the other person, feel in control or subordinate, feel comfortable or anxious, and so on. For instance, consider how many different relational messages you could communicate by simply saying "Thanks a lot" in different ways. You can appreciate the importance of communication's relational dimension by looking at the photo on this page. This image says as much about the relationship between boxer and trainer as it does about whatever they are discussing.

Sometimes the content dimension of a message is all that matters. For example, you may not care how the directory assistance operator feels about you as long as you get the phone number you're seeking. In a qualitative sense, however, the relational dimension of a message is often more important than the content under discussion. This explains why disputes over apparently trivial subjects become so important. In such cases we're not really arguing over whose turn it is to take out the trash or whether to play tennis or swim. Instead, we're disputing the nature of the relationship. Who's in control? How important are we to each other? Chapter 9 explores several key relational issues in detail.

Communication Can Be Intentional or Unintentional Some communication is clearly deliberate: You probably plan your words carefully before asking the boss for a raise or offering constructive criticism. Some scholars (e.g., Motley, 1990) argue that only intentional messages like these qualify as communication. However, others (e.g., Baxter & Montgomery, 1996; Buck & VanLear, 2002) suggest that even unintentional behavior is communicative. Suppose, for instance, that a friend overhears you muttering complaints to yourself. Even though you didn't intend for her to hear your remarks, they certainly did carry a message. In addition to these slips of the tongue, we unintentionally send many nonverbal messages. You might not be aware of your sour expression, impatient shifting, or sigh of boredom, but others view them nonetheless.

Even the seeming absence of a behavior has communicative value. Recall the times when you sent an e-mail or left a voice mail message and received no reply. You probably assigned some meaning to the nonresponse. Was the other person angry? Indifferent? Too busy to reply? Whether or not your hunch was correct, the point remains: All behavior has communicative value. "Nothing" never happens.

In *Interplay* we look at the communicative value of both intentional and unintentional behavior. This book takes the position that whatever you do—whether you speak or remain silent, confront or avoid, show emotion or keep a poker face—you provide information to others about your thoughts and feelings. In this sense, we are like transmitters that can't be shut off.

"*Let's stop this before we both say a lot of things we mean.*"

Communication Is Irreversible We sometimes wish that we could back up in time, erasing words or acts and replacing them with better alternatives. Unfortunately, such reversal is impossible. Sometimes, further explanation can clear up another's confusion or an apology can mollify another's hurt feelings, but other times no amount of explanation can erase the impression you have created. It is no more possible to "unreceive" a message than to "unsqueeze" a tube of toothpaste. Words said and deeds done are irretrievable.

Communication Is Unrepeatable Because communication is an ongoing process, an event cannot be repeated. The friendly smile that worked so well when meeting a stranger last week may not succeed with the person you encounter tomorrow. Even with the same person, it's impossible to re-create an event. Why? Because both you and the other person have changed. You've both lived longer. The behavior isn't original. Your feelings about each other may have changed. You need not constantly invent new ways to act around familiar people, but you should realize that the "same" words and behavior are different each time they are spoken or performed.

COMMUNICATION MISCONCEPTIONS

Now that we've described what communication is, we need to identify some things it is not. Avoiding these common misconceptions (adapted from McCroskey & Richmond, 1996) can save you a great deal of trouble in your personal life.

Not All Communication Seeks Understanding Most people operate on the implicit but flawed assumption that the goal of all communication is to maximize understanding between communicators. While some understanding is necessary for us to coordinate our interaction, there are some types of communication in which understanding, as we usually conceive it, isn't the primary goal. Consider, for example,

> *The social rituals we enact every day.* "How's it going?" you ask. "Great," the other person replies. The primary goal in exchanges like these is mutual acknowledgment of one another's existence and value (even if the person *isn't* feeling great). The unstated message is "I consider you important enough to notice." There's obviously no serious attempt to exchange information (Burnard, 2003).

> *Many attempts to influence others.* A quick analysis of most television commercials shows that they are aimed at persuading viewers to buy products, not to understand the content of the ad. In the same way, many of our attempts at persuading others to act as we want don't involve a desire to get the other person to understand what we want—just to comply with our wishes.

> *Deliberate ambiguity and deception.* When you decline an unwanted invitation by saying "I can't make it," you probably want to create the impression that the decision is really beyond your control. (If your goal were to be perfectly clear, you might say, "I don't want to get together. In fact, I'd rather do almost anything than accept your invitation.") As Chapter 3 explains in detail, we often lie or hedge our remarks precisely because we want to obscure our true thoughts and feelings.

More Communication Is Not Always Better While failure to communicate effectively can certainly cause problems, *too much* talking also can be a mistake. Sometimes excessive communication is simply unproductive, as when two people "talk a problem to death," going over the same ground again and again without making progress.

There are other times when talking too much actually aggravates a problem. We've all had the experience of "talking ourselves into a hole"—making a bad situation worse by pursuing it too far. As McCroskey and Wheeless (1976, p. 5) put it, "More and more negative communication merely leads to more and more negative results." In one study, college roommates revealed that thinking and talking about conflicts can actually increase relational problems (Cloven & Roloff, 1991). Even when relationships aren't troubled, less communication may be better than more. One study found that coworkers who aren't highly dependent on one another perform better when they don't spend a great deal of time talking together (Barrick et al., 2007). There are even times when *no* interaction is the best course. When two people are angry and hurt, they may say things they don't mean and will later regret. In such cases it's probably best to spend time cooling off, thinking about what to say and how to say it. Chapter 8 will help you decide when and how to share feelings.

Communication Will Not Solve All Problems Sometimes even the best-planned, best-timed communication won't solve a problem. For example, imagine that you ask an instructor to explain why you received a poor grade on a project you believe deserved top marks. The professor clearly outlines the reasons why you received the low grade and sticks to that position after listening thoughtfully to your protests. Has communication solved the problem? Hardly.

Sometimes clear communication is even the cause of problems. Suppose, for example, that a friend asks you for an honest opinion of an expensive outfit he just bought. Your clear and sincere answer, "I think it makes you look fat," might do more harm than good. Deciding when and how to self-disclose isn't always easy. See Chapter 3 for suggestions.

Effective Communication Is Not a Natural Ability Most people assume that communication is something that people can do without the need for training—rather like breathing. Although nearly everyone does manage to function passably without much formal communication training, most people operate at a level of effectiveness far below their potential. In fact, communication skills are rather like athletic ability. Even the most inept of us can learn to be more effective with training and practice, and even the most talented need to "keep in shape."

Interpersonal Communication Defined

Now that you have a better understanding of the overall process of human communication, it's time to look at what makes some types of communication uniquely interpersonal.

QUANTITATIVE AND QUALITATIVE DEFINITIONS

Scholars have characterized interpersonal communication in two ways (Redmond, 1995). Some definitions take a **quantitative** approach that defines interpersonal communication as any interaction between two people. Social scientists call two persons interacting a **dyad**, and they often use the adjective *dyadic* to describe this type of communication. So, in a quantitative sense, the terms *dyadic communication* and *interpersonal communication* can be used interchangeably. Using a quantitative definition, a salesclerk and customer or a police officer ticketing a speeding driver would be examples of interpersonal acts, whereas a teacher and class or a performer and audience would not.

Dyadic communication *is* different from the kind of interaction that occurs in larger groups (Lev-On & Chavez, 2010; Wilmot, 1995). In a group, participants can form coalitions to get support for their positions. In a dyad, though, partners must work matters out with each other. This difference explains why, when a task calls for competition, children prefer to play in

three-person groups, and if it calls for cooperation, they prefer to be in dyads (Benenson et al., 2000).

Despite the unique qualities of dyads, you might object to the quantitative definition of interpersonal communication. For example, consider a routine transaction between a salesclerk and customer, or the rushed exchange when you ask a stranger on the street for directions. Communication of this sort hardly seems the same as when you talk with a friend about a personal problem or share your experiences of a year in school with your family.

The impersonal nature of some two-person exchanges—the kind when you think, "I might as well have been talking to a machine"—has led many scholars to argue that quality, not quantity, is what distinguishes interpersonal communication. Using a **qualitative** approach, interpersonal communication occurs when people treat one another as unique individuals, regardless of the context in which the interaction occurs or the number of people involved. When quality of interaction is the criterion, the opposite of interpersonal communication is *impersonal* interaction, not group, public, or mass communication.

Several features distinguish qualitatively interpersonal communication from less personal exchanges. The first is *uniqueness*. Whereas impersonal exchanges are governed by the kind of social rules we learn from parents, teachers, and etiquette books, the way we communicate in a truly personal relationship is unlike our behavior with anyone else. In one relationship you might exchange good-natured insults, while in another you are careful never to offend your partner. Likewise, you might handle conflicts with one friend or family member by expressing disagreements as soon as they arise, whereas the unwritten rule in another relationship is to withhold resentments until they build up and then clear the air periodically. Communication scholar Julia Wood (2005b) coined the term "relational culture" to describe people in close relationships who create their own unique ways of interacting.

A second characteristic of qualitatively interpersonal communication is *irreplaceability*. Because interpersonal relationships are unique, they can't be replaced. This explains why we usually feel so sad when a close friendship or love affair cools down. We know that no matter how many other relationships fill our lives, none of them will ever be quite like the one that just ended.

Interdependence is a third characteristic of qualitatively interpersonal relationships. Here, the fate of the partners is connected. You might be able to brush off the anger, affection, excitement, or depression of someone you're not involved with interpersonally, but in an interpersonal relationship the other's life affects you. Sometimes interdependence is a pleasure, and at other times it is a burden. In either case, interdependence is a fact of life in qualitatively interpersonal relationships.

A fourth yardstick of qualitative interpersonal communication is *disclosure* of personal information. In impersonal relationships we don't reveal much about ourselves, but in many interpersonal ones communicators feel more comfortable sharing their thoughts and feelings. This doesn't mean that all interpersonal relationships are warm and caring or that all self-disclosure is positive. It's possible to reveal negative personal information: "I'm really mad at you!"

In impersonal communication we seek payoffs that have little to do with the people involved. You listen to professors in class or talk to potential buyers of your used car in order to reach goals that have little to do with developing personal relationships. By contrast, you spend time in qualitatively interpersonal relationships with friends, lovers, and others because of *intrinsic rewards* that come from your communication. It doesn't matter what you talk about: Developing the relationship is what's important.

Because interpersonal communication is characterized by the qualities of uniqueness, irreplaceability, interdependence, disclosure, and intrinsic rewards, it forms a small fraction of our interaction. The majority of our communication is relatively impersonal. We chat pleasantly with shopkeepers or fellow passengers on the bus or plane; we discuss the weather or current events with most classmates and neighbors; we deal with coworkers and teachers in a polite way; but considering the number of people with whom we communicate, interpersonal relationships are by far the minority.

The rarity of qualitatively interpersonal communication isn't necessarily unfortunate. Most of us don't have the time or energy to create personal relationships with everyone we encounter. Even with our closest relational partners, deeply personal conversations occur infrequently. In fact, the scarcity of interpersonal communication contributes to its value (Mehl et al., 2010). Like precious and one-of-a-kind artwork, qualitatively interpersonal communication is special because it is rare.

PERSONAL AND IMPERSONAL COMMUNICATION: A MATTER OF BALANCE

Now that the differences between qualitatively interpersonal and impersonal communication are spelled out, we need to ask some important questions. Is personal communication better than the impersonal variety? Is more personal communication the goal?

Most relationships aren't either personal or impersonal. Rather, they fall somewhere between these two extremes. Consider your own communication and you'll find that there is often a personal element in even the most impersonal situations. You might appreciate the unique sense of humor of a grocery checker or spend a few moments sharing private thoughts with the person cutting your hair. And even the most tyrannical, demanding, by-the-book boss might show an occasional flash of humanity.

When it comes to close relationships, there are certainly times when small talk isn't sufficient (Mehl et al., 2010). But just as there's a personal

⚫Ⓢⓔⓛⓕ-Ⓐⓢⓢⓔⓢⓢⓜⓔⓝⓣ

How Interpersonal Are Your Relationships?

Select three important relationships to assess. These might include your relationships with people at work or school, or with friends or family. For each relationship, respond to the following items:

1. To what extent is the relationship characterized by uniqueness? How much is this relationship one of a kind?

   LOW LEVEL OF UNIQUENESS   1   2   3   4   5   6   7   HIGHLY UNIQUE

2. To what extent is the relationship irreplaceable?

   VERY EASY TO REPLACE   1   2   3   4   5   6   7   VERY HARD TO REPLACE

3. To what extent are you and your relationship partner interdependent; that is, to what extent does one person's actions affect the other?

   LITTLE INTERDEPENDENCE   1   2   3   4   5   6   7   HIGH INTERDEPENDENCE

4. To what extent is communication in the relationship marked by high disclosure of personal information?

   LOW DISCLOSURE   1   2   3   4   5   6   7   HIGH DISCLOSURE

5. To what extent does the relationship create its own intrinsic rewards?

   REWARDS ARE EXTRINSIC   1   2   3   4   5   6   7   REWARDS ARE INTRINSIC

Based on your answers, decide how qualitatively interpersonal (or how impersonal) each of the relationships is. (If you have more 5s, 6s, and 7s in your answers, then your relationship is more interpersonal. If you have more 1s, 2s, and 3s, then the relationship is more impersonal.) How satisfied are you with your findings? What can you do to improve your level of satisfaction with these relationships?

element in many impersonal settings, there's also an impersonal side to our relationships with the people we care about most. In fact, most communication in even the closest relationships is comfortably mundane (see the Focus on Research box on page 19). Small talk is especially valuable in long-distance relationships where communication is mostly sustained online (Tong & Walther, 2011b). Being able to discuss mundane topics like daily activities and the weather helps normalize a relationship that would otherwise feel much different from one nurtured by everyday contact.

Along with small talk, there are occasions when we don't want to be personal: when we're distracted, tired, busy, or just not interested. In fact,

FOCUS ON RESEARCH

Maintaining Relationships through Daily Conversations

What can researchers learn from analyzing 172 hours of couples' daily conversations about mundane topics such as pets, television shows, and weekend plans? According to Jess Alberts and her colleagues, the routine talk that makes up much of everyday life is an important tool that helps couples maintain their relationships.

The research team took on the laborious task of taping, transcribing, and coding the daily interactions of 10 satisfied couples in long-term relationships. They found that more than 40 percent of the couples' conversations involved self-reports (e.g., "I had lunch today with the rep on my new account") or observations ("That clock is slow"). The researchers concluded that relational partners play important roles as "audiences for the articulation of one's experiences and thoughts." In other words, people want and expect their partners to provide a listening ear.

The couples talked about more than just themselves. For example, they discussed other people in their lives (friends, family, colleagues) and television shows (often while watching television together). Time was also spent discussing household tasks and upcoming plans. Were many of these interactions mundane and routine? Certainly. Were they unimportant? Hardly. Alberts and her colleagues concluded that these apparently mundane conversations are "necessary types of interaction for relationship maintenance that form the bedrock on which the relationship is built."

Alberts, J. K., Yoshimura, C. G., Rabby, M., & Loschiavo, R. (2005). Mapping the topography of couples' daily conversation. *Journal of Social and Personal Relationships, 22,* 299–322.

interpersonal communication is rather like rich food—it's fine in moderation, but too much can make you uncomfortable.

The blend of personal and interpersonal communication can shift in various stages of a relationship. The communication between young lovers who talk only about their feelings may change as their relationship develops. Several years later their communication has become more routine and ritualized, and the percentage of time they spend on personal, relational issues drops while the conversation about less intimate topics increases. Chapter 9 discusses how communication changes as relationships pass through various stages, and Chapter 3 describes various theories of self-disclosure. As you read this information, you will see even more clearly that while interpersonal communication can make life worth living, it isn't possible or desirable all the time.

Communication Competence

"What does it take to communicate better?" is probably the most important question to ask as you read this book. Answering it has been one of the leading challenges for communication scholars. While all the answers aren't in yet, research has identified a great deal of important and useful information about communication competence.

COMMUNICATION COMPETENCE DEFINED

Defining **communication competence** isn't as easy as it might seem. Although scholars continue to debate a precise definition, most agree that competent communication is both *effective* and *appropriate* (Spitzberg, 2000). To understand these two dimensions, consider how you might handle everyday communication challenges such as declining an unwanted invitation or communicating about a friend's annoying behavior. In cases like these, *effective* communication would get the results you want. *Appropriate* communication would do so in a way that, in most cases, enhances the relationship in which it occurs (Wiemann et al., 1997). You can appreciate the importance of both appropriateness and effectiveness by imagining approaches that would satisfy one of these criteria but not the other. Effectiveness without appropriateness might achieve your goals, but leave others unhappy. Conversely, appropriateness without effectiveness might leave others content but you frustrated. With the goal of balancing effectiveness and appropriateness, the following paragraphs outline several important characteristics of communication competence.

There Is No Single "Ideal" or "Effective" Way to Communicate Your own experience shows that a variety of communication styles can be effective. Some very successful communicators are serious, while others use humor; some are gregarious, while others are quieter; and some are more straightforward, while others hint diplomatically. Just as there are many kinds of beautiful music or art, there are many kinds of competent communication. Furthermore, a type of communication that is competent in one setting might be a colossal blunder in another, and what one person thinks is competent may be seen by another as incompetent (Dunleavy & Martin, 2010). The joking insults you routinely trade with one friend might offend a sensitive family member, and last Saturday night's romantic approach would probably be out of place at work on Monday morning. This means that there can be no surefire list of rules or tips that will guarantee your success as a communicator.

Flexibility is especially important when members of different cultures meet. Some communication skills seem to be universal (Ruben, 1989). Every culture has rules that

---

MEDIA CLIP

EFFECTIVE BUT NOT ALWAYS APPROPRIATE: *HOUSE M.D.*

No one at Princeton-Plainsboro Teaching Hospital would deny that Dr. Gregory House (Hugh Laurie) is an excellent physician. His sharp mind and keen analytical skills help him make diagnoses that often save lives. House's colleagues marvel at his ability to solve baffling medical cases, so they seek out and heed his advice.

On the other hand, House's interpersonal skills leave something to be desired. He is typically gruff, blunt, rude, and condescending. As a result, House often alienates his supervisors, students, and even the patients he's trying to serve. In terms of communication competence, he is long on effectiveness but short on appropriateness. If House engaged in more self-monitoring and expressed more empathy, he would be a better communicator and probably have more friends. But then again, this TV show wouldn't be nearly as entertaining.

require speakers to behave appropriately, for example. But the definition of what kind of communication is appropriate in a given situation varies considerably from one culture to another (Arasaratnam, 2007; Ulrey, 2001). On an obvious level, customs like belching after a meal or appearing nude in public that might be appropriate in some parts of the world would be considered outrageous in others. But there are more subtle differences in competent communication. For example, qualities like self-disclosure and straight talking that are valued in the United States are likely to be considered overly aggressive and insensitive in many Asian cultures, where subtlety and indirectness are considered important (Kim et al., 1998; Yeh, 2010). We'll discuss the many dimensions of intercultural competence in Chapter 2.

"How much you puttin' in?"

Competence Is Situational Because competent behavior varies so much from one situation and person to another, it's a mistake to think that communication competence is a trait that a person either possesses or lacks (Spitzberg, 1991). It's more accurate to talk about *degrees* or *areas* of competence.

You and the people you know are probably quite competent in some areas and less so in others. For example, you might deal quite skillfully with peers, while feeling clumsy interacting with people much older or younger, wealthier or poorer, more or less attractive than yourself. In fact, your competence may vary from situation to situation. This means it's an overgeneralization to say, in a moment of distress, "I'm a terrible communicator!" It's more accurate to say, "I didn't handle this situation very well, but I'm better in others."

Competence Can Be Learned To some degree, biology is destiny when it comes to communication competence (Teven et al., 2010). Some research suggests that certain personality traits predispose people toward particular competence skills (Hullman et al., 2010). For instance, those who are agreeable and conscientious by nature find it easier to be appropriate, and harder to be (and become) assertive and effective.

Fortunately, biology isn't the only factor that shapes how we communicate. Communication competence is, to a great degree, a set of skills that anyone can learn (Fortney et al., 2001). For instance, people with high communication apprehension often benefit from communication skills training (Ayres & Hopf, 1993; Dwyer, 2000). Skills training has also been shown to help communicators in a variety of professional fields (Brown et al., 2010; Hyvarinen et al., 2010; Kuntze et al., 2009). Even without systematic training, it's possible to develop communication skills through the processes of observation and trial and error. We learn from our own successes and failures, as well as from observing other models—both positive and negative. And, of course, it's our hope that you will become a more competent communicator as a result of putting the information in this book to work.

CHARACTERISTICS OF COMPETENT COMMUNICATION

Despite the fact that competent communication varies from one situation to another, scholars have identified several common denominators that characterize effective communication in most contexts.

A Large Repertoire of Skills As we've already seen, good communicators don't use the same approach in every situation. They know that sometimes it's best to be blunt and sometimes tactful; that there is a time to speak up and a time to be quiet.

The chances of reaching your personal and relational goals increase with the number of options you have about how to communicate. For example, if you want to start a conversation with a stranger, your chances of success increase as you have more options available (Kelly & Watson, 1986). All it might take to get the conversational ball rolling is a self-introduction. In other cases, seeking assistance might work well: "I've just moved here. What kind of neighborhood is the Eastside?" A third strategy is to ask a question about some situational feature: "I've never heard this band before. Do you know anything about them?" You could also offer a sincere compliment and follow it up with a question: "Great shoes! Where did you get them?"

Many people with disabilities have learned the value of having a repertoire of options available to manage unwanted offers of help (Braithwaite & Eckstein, 2003). Some of those options include performing a task quickly, before anyone has the chance to intervene; pretending not to hear the offer; accepting a well-intentioned invitation, to avoid seeming rude or ungrateful; using humor to deflect a bid for help; declining a well-intentioned offer with thanks; and assertively refusing help from those who won't take no for an answer.

Just as a golfer has a wide range of clubs to use for various situations, a competent communicator has a large array of behaviors from which to choose.

Adaptability Having a large repertoire of possible behaviors is one ingredient of competent communication, but you have to be able to choose the *right* one for a particular situation (Hullman, 2007). Effective communication means selecting appropriate responses for each situation—and for each recipient. The Focus on Research sidebar on page 23 describes how some college students don't adapt their messages when e-mailing instructors, creating a negative impression.

Ability to Perform Skillfully Once you have chosen the appropriate way to communicate, you have to perform that behavior effectively (Burleson, 2007). In communication, as in other activities, practice is the key to skillful performance. Much of the information in *Interplay* will introduce you to new tools for communicating, and the Skill Builder activities at the end of each chapter will help you practice them.

Involvement Not surprisingly, effective communication occurs when the people care about one another and the topic at hand (Cegala et al., 1982). Rod Hart suggests that this involvement has several dimensions (adapted

F⊕CUS ON RESEARCH

How to (NOT) Antagonize Your Professor: Adapting E-Messages

Research shows that out-of-classroom communication (OCC) usually strengthens teacher–student bonds and improves learning. Most OCC exchanges used to take place in hallways and offices, but now they often occur online through e-mails. A research team led by Keri Stephens investigated whether the writing style of student e-messages has an impact on their effectiveness.

The researchers asked college and university instructors to evaluate overly casual e-mails from students. These less-than-formal messages included a lack of openings/closings, incorrect punctuation and grammar, and shortcuts such as using "4" instead of "for." The findings aren't surprising. They include:

- Highly casual e-mails lower instructors' appraisals of the students who sent them.
- Instructors are far less likely to comply with requests made in overly casual messages, compared with e-mails that are written more formally.
- Two violations that particularly bother instructors are e-mails not signed by the message sender and messages that include shortcuts such as "RU" instead of "are you."

Failing to adapt your message to the recipient runs the risk that your requests will backfire. This is important not only for student–instructor emails, but also in every interpersonal interaction.

Stephens, K. K., Houser, M. L., & Cowan, R. L. (2009). R U able to meat me: The impact of students' overly casual email messages to instructors. *Communication Education, 58*, 303–326.

here from Knapp & Vangelisti, 2006). It includes commitment to the other person and the relationship, concern about the message being discussed, and a desire to make the relationship clearly useful.

Empathy/Perspective Taking People have the best chance of developing an effective message when they understand and empathize with the other person's point of view (Lobchuk, 2006; Sorensen, 2009). Since others aren't always good at expressing their thoughts and feelings clearly, the ability to imagine how an issue might look from another's perspective suggests why empathy is such an important communication skill. Not only does it help you understand others, but it also provides information to develop strategies about how to best influence them. Empathy is such an important element of communicative competence that researcher Mark Redmond (1989, p. 594) flatly states that "by definition, a person cannot produce a message that is empathic that is not also communicatively competent."

Cognitive Complexity Cognitive complexity is the ability to construct a variety of different frameworks for viewing an issue. Imagine that a longtime friend seems to be angry with you. One possible explanation is that your friend is offended by something you've done. Another possibility is that something has happened in another part of your friend's life that is upsetting. Or perhaps nothing at all is wrong, and you're just being overly sensitive.

Researchers have found that a large number of constructs for interpreting the behavior of others leads to greater "conversational sensitivity,"

increasing the chances of acting in ways that will produce satisfying results (Burleson & Caplan, 1998; Burleson, Hanasono, Bodie, Holmstrom, Rack, et al., 2009). Not surprisingly, research also shows a connection between cognitive complexity and empathy (Joireman, 2004). The relationship makes sense: The more ways you have to understand others and interpret their behaviors, the greater is the likelihood that you can see and communicate about the world from their perspective.

Dark Side of Communication
EXCESSIVE SELF-MONITORING DISCOURAGES INTIMACY

Although self-monitoring is generally an element of competent communication, some research suggests that paying *too much* attention to how you present yourself can have a dark side. One study revealed that high self-monitors often experience less intimacy, satisfaction, and commitment in their romantic relationships than people who aren't so strategic. On reflection, these results make sense: Communicators who are overly concerned with managing impressions often hide what they really think and feel—hardly a recipe for intimacy.

As a rule of thumb, self-monitoring is a valuable skill in less personal interactions and in the early stages of close relationships. Over time, however, romantic relationships can profit from communication that is a bit less guarded, crafted, and scrutinized.

Wright, C. N., Holloway, A., & Roloff, M. E. (2007). The dark side of self-monitoring: How high self-monitors view their romantic relationships. *Communication Reports, 20,* 101–114.

Self-Monitoring Psychologists use the term **self-monitoring** to describe the process of paying close attention to one's own behavior and using these observations to shape the way one behaves. Self-monitors are able to detach a part of their consciousness to observe their behavior from a detached viewpoint, making observations such as

> "I'm making a fool out of myself."
>
> "I'd better speak up now."
>
> "This approach is working well. I'll keep it up."

It's no surprise that self-monitoring generally increases one's effectiveness as a communicator (Day et al., 2002; Turnley & Bolino, 2001). The President's Council of Economic Advisers maintain that greater "self-awareness, self-monitoring, and self control" will help students be more successful when they enter the job market ("Preparing the Workers of Today," 2009, p. 10). The ability to ask yourself the question "How am I doing?" and to change your behavior if the answer isn't positive is a tremendous asset for communicators. People with poor self-monitoring skills often blunder through life, sometimes succeeding and sometimes failing, without the detachment to understand why.

How does your behavior as an interpersonal communicator measure up against the standards of competence described in this chapter? Like most people, you will probably find some areas of your life that are very satisfying and others that you would like to change. As you read on in this book, realize that the information in each chapter offers advice that can help your communication become more productive and rewarding.

Although the qualities described here do play an important role in communicative competence, they can be ineffective when carried to excess (Spitzberg, 1994). As the "Dark Side" box on page 24 shows, too much self-monitoring can be a problem in close relationships. Even in less personal contexts, an excessive concern for appearance ("How do I sound?," "How am I doing?") overshadows the need to be faithful to one's true beliefs. Likewise, an excess of empathy and cognitive complexity can lead you to see all sides of an issue so well that you're incapable of acting. In other words, there is a *curvilinear relationship* among most of the elements described in these pages: Both a deficiency and an excess can lead to incompetent communication.

Summary

Communication is important for a variety of reasons. Besides satisfying practical needs, meaningful communication contributes to physical health, plays a major role in defining our identity, and forms the basis for our social relationships.

Communication is the use of messages to generate meanings. It is a complex process that can be represented in a communication model. The model presented in this chapter depicts how interpersonal communicators usually send and receive messages simultaneously. The meaning of these messages resides in the people who exchange them, not in the messages themselves. Environment and noise affect communication, as do the channels we choose for sending our messages.

A variety of principles help explain how interpersonal communication operates. Communication is transactional—that is, it's a dynamic process that people create through interaction. Messages can be intentional or unintentional, and they almost always have both a content and a relational dimension. Once expressed, messages cannot be withdrawn. Finally, communication is unrepeatable.

Interpersonal communication can be defined quantitatively (by the number of people involved) or qualitatively (by the nature of interaction between them). In a qualitative sense, interpersonal relationships are unique, irreplaceable, interdependent, and intrinsically rewarding. Qualitatively interpersonal communication is relatively infrequent, even in many close relationships.

To understand the communication process, it is important to recognize and avoid several common misconceptions. Despite the value of self-expression, more communication is not always better. In fact, there are occasions when more communication can increase problems. Sometimes total understanding isn't as important as we might think. Even at its best, communication is not a panacea that will solve every problem. Effective communication is not a natural ability. While some people have greater aptitude at communicating, everyone can learn to interact with others more effectively.

Communication competency is the ability to be both effective and appropriate—that is, to get desired results from others in a manner that maintains the relationship on terms that are acceptable to everyone. There is no single ideal way to communicate: Flexibility and adaptability are characteristics of competent communicators, as are skill at performing behaviors, involvement with others, empathy and perspective taking, cognitive complexity, and self-monitoring. The good news is, communication competency can be learned.

Key Terms

- Channel (11)
- Cognitive complexity (23)
- Communication (8)
- Communication competence (20)
- Content dimension (of a message) (12)
- Dyad (15)
- Environment (10)
- Feedback (8)
- Noise (external, physiological, and psychological) (10)
- Qualitative (interpersonal communication) (16)
- Quantitative (interpersonal communication) (15)
- Relational dimension (of a message) (12)
- Self-monitoring (24)
- Transactional communication model (8)

Activities

1. Invitation to Insight

How much time do you spend communicating? Conduct an informal study to answer this question by keeping a 2-day log of your activities. Based on your findings, answer the following questions:

    a. What percentage of your waking time is spent speaking and listening to others?

   b. Using the explanation on pages 15–17, describe what percentage of
      your entire communication is qualitatively interpersonal.
   c. How satisfied are you with your findings? How would you like to
      change your everyday communication?

2. Critical Thinking Probe

As you read in this chapter, communication is transactional in nature: something we do *with* others and not *to* them. How does face-to-face communication differ from computer social media, such as e-mail? Are they equally
transactional?

3. Invitation To Insight

How competent are you as a communicator? You can begin to answer this
question by interviewing people who know you well: a family member,
friend, or fellow worker, for example. Interview different people to determine if you are more competent in some relationships than others, or in
some situations than others.
   a. Describe the characteristics of competent communicators outlined
      on pages 20–25 of this chapter. Be sure your interviewee under-
      stands each of them.
   b. Ask your interviewee to rate you on each of the observable qualities.
      (It won't be possible for others to evaluate internal characteristics,
      such as cognitive complexity and self-monitoring.) Be sure this evalu-
      ation reflects your communication in a variety of situations: It's likely
      you aren't uniformly competent—or incompetent—in all of them.
   c. If your rating is not high in one or more areas, discuss with your
      partner how you could raise it.

4. Skill Builder

Knowing how you want to communicate isn't the same as being able to
perform competently. The technique of behavior rehearsal provides a way
to improve a particular communication skill before you use it in real life.
Behavior rehearsal consists of four steps:
   a. Define your goal. Begin by identifying the way you want to behave.
   b. Break the goal into the behaviors it involves. Most goals are made
      up of several verbal and nonverbal parts. You may be able to identify
      these parts by thinking about them yourself, by observing others, by
      reading about them, or by asking others for advice.
   c. Practice each behavior before using it in real life. You can practice a
      new behavior by rehearsing it alone and then with others before you
      put it into action. Another approach is to picture yourself behaving
      in new ways. This mental image can boost effectiveness.
   d. Try out the behavior in real life. You can increase the odds of success
      if you follow two pieces of advice when trying out new communica-
      tion behaviors: Work on only one subskill at a time, and start with
      easy situations. Don't expect yourself suddenly to behave flawlessly
      in the most challenging situations. Begin by practicing your new
      skills in situations in which you have a chance of success.

CHAPTER

2

Interpersonal Communication in a Changing World
Culture and Social Networking

After studying the material in this chapter . . .

You should understand:

1. The prevalence and importance of intercultural and co-cultural communication in today's world.
2. The role of perception in intercultural communication.
3. Five key values that help shape a culture's communication norms.
4. The factors that shape a culture's verbal codes, nonverbal codes, and decoding of messages.
5. The attitudes, knowledge, and skills required for intercultural communication competence.
6. How social media differ from face-to-face interaction.
7. The advantages and drawbacks of mediated relationships.

You should be able to:

1. Identify the range and significance of intercultural and co-cultural contacts you are likely to experience.
2. Describe a set of cultural values, norms, and codes different from yours that could result in different cultural communication patterns.
3. Develop a strategy for interacting with people of cultural backgrounds different from your own by applying guidelines for intercultural competence.
4. Choose the approach—mediated channel or face-to-face—that has the best chance for success in a given situation.
5. Evaluate the optimal balance of face-to-face communication and social media in your important relationships and, as necessary, develop a plan for achieving that balance.
6. Use feedback from people familiar with your communication patterns to assess how competently you follow guidelines for competent online communication.

Over a half-century ago, Marshall McLuhan (1962) coined the metaphor of the world as a "global village" where members of every nation are connected by communication technology. Just like members of a traditional village, McLuhan suggested, the affairs and fates of the occupants of planet Earth are connected—for better or worse. This analysis has proven to be increasingly true in the years since McLuhan introduced it.

Thanks to the growth in communication technology, even stay-at-homes have access to virtually the entire world, and commerce has changed in ways that would have been unimaginable just a generation ago. International telephone service is affordable and efficient. The Internet allows users around the world to share information with one another instantaneously, at a cost no greater than exchanging computer messages with someone in the same town. Organizations span the globe, and their members form virtual teams that "meet" in cyberspace.

In this chapter we will explore how communication operates in a networked world where members of different cultures interact.

Interpersonal Communication in a Diverse World

When people from different backgrounds interact, they face a set of challenges different from those that arise when members of the same culture communicate (Stier & Kjellin, 2010; Williams & Johnson, 2011). With understanding and effort, those challenges can be managed and even leveraged to make communication richer and more rewarding.

FUNDAMENTALS OF CULTURE

Before going any further, we need to clarify two important concepts: *culture* and *intercultural communication*. We also need to look at what distinguishes intercultural communication from interpersonal communication.

Culture and Co-Culture Defining **culture** isn't an easy task. A survey of scholarly literature conducted over 60 years ago revealed 500 definitions, phrasings, and uses of the concept (Kroeber & Kluckholn, 1952). For our purposes, Larry Samovar and his colleagues (2007) offer a clear and comprehensive definition of *culture:* "the language, values, beliefs, traditions, and customs people share and learn."

This definition shows that culture is, to a great extent, a matter of *perception* and *definition.* When you identify yourself as a member of a culture, you must not only share certain characteristics, but you must also recognize yourself and others like you as possessing these features and see others who don't possess them as members of different categories. For example, eye color doesn't seem like a significant factor in distinguishing "us" from "them," while skin color plays a more important role, at least in some cases. It's not hard to imagine a society where the opposite were true. Social scientists use the label **in-groups** to describe groups with which we identify and **out-groups** to label those that we view as different (Frings & Abrams, 2010; Quist & Jørgensen, 2010). Cultural membership contributes to every person's **social identity**—the part of the self-concept that is based on membership in groups. Your answer to the question "Who are you?" would probably include social categories such as your ethnicity and nationality.

Social scientists use the term **co-culture** to describe the perception of membership in a group that is part of an encompassing culture (Orbe & Spellers, 2005). Co-cultures in North American society include categories based on

- age (e.g., teens, senior citizens)
- race/ethnicity (e.g., African American, Latino)
- sexual orientation (e.g., homosexual, transsexual)
- nationality (e.g., immigrants from a particular country, expatriates)
- geographic region (e.g., Southerners, Midwesterners)
- physical disability (e.g., wheelchair users, persons who are deaf)
- religion (e.g., Church of Jesus Christ of Latter Day Saints, Muslim)
- activity (e.g., biker, gamer)

Members of co-cultures often develop unique patterns of communication. For example, gangs fit the definition of a co-culture: Members have a well-defined identity, both among themselves and in the outside world. This sense of belonging is often reflected in distinctive language and nonverbal markers, such as clothing, tattoos, and hand signals (National Youth Violence Prevention Resource Center, 2007; U.S. Department of Justice, 2002). Other co-cultures also have distinctive communication patterns. True to an enduring stereotype, people from New York City are typically more assertive than those from the Upper Midwest (Sigler et al., 2008). And many

FOCUS ON RESEARCH

Fitting In: People with Disabilities and Organizational Cultures

People with physical disabilities represent about 15 percent of the U.S. population. Researchers Marsha Cohen and Susan Avanzino investigated how members of this co-culture manage the challenges of integrating into organizational cultures where they are in the minority. They interviewed 24 people with a variety of physical disabilities and job positions, asking about their experiences with employers and coworkers.

The participants described several strategies for integrating into the culture of their organizations. One is *assimilation*—adapting and conforming to the dominant (nondisabled) group. This involves deemphasizing differences and in some cases staying quiet about disabilities (one participant said, "The less you tell about your disability, the better off you are"). A second strategy, *accommodation*, takes a different approach. It involves acknowledging one's disability and asking for ways that it be accommodated. It can also include educating others about disabilities and actively dispelling misperceptions. A few opted for *separation*, distancing themselves from nondisabled people and banding together with people from their co-culture. The latter approach was the least common and viewed as least productive.

The participants in this study did not all use the same strategies. Some were more comfortable with accommodation; others with assimilation. But one value they all share is that they don't want to be defined by their disabilities. The authors provide this summary (p. 300):

> With many voices and different backgrounds and experiences, the participants in this study are stating: "We are people first."

Cohen, M., & Avanzino, S. (2010). We are people first: Framing organizational assimilation experiences of the physically disabled using co-cultural theory. *Communication Studies, 61,* 272–303.

first-generation college students have characteristics of a co-culture, as they censor their speech with classmates and professors to avoid calling attention to their status, and with family members to avoid threatening and alienating them (Orbe & Groscurth, 2004).

Membership in co-cultures can be a source of enrichment and pride. But when the group is stigmatized by others, being connected with a co-culture isn't always so fulfilling. For instance, Patrice Buzzanell (1999) describes how members of underrepresented groups are disadvantaged in employment interviews, where the rules are established by the dominant culture. Studies of Jamaican children (Ferguson & Cramer, 2007) and Latino children (Golash-Boza & Darity, 2008) indicate that skin color influences self-identification and self-esteem. In other cases, co-cultures voluntarily embrace the chance to distinguish themselves from society at large—such as teens creating slang that is understood only by members of their in-group. Some scholars (e.g., Kimmel, 2008; Tannen, 2003; Wood, 2009) and writers in the popular press (e.g., Gray, 2008) have even characterized men and women as belonging to different co-cultures because their communication styles are so different. As you read this chapter, you will notice that many of the communication challenges that arise between members of different cultures also operate when people from different co-cultures interact.

Intercultural Communication Having defined culture, we can go on to define **intercultural communication** as the process that occurs when members of two or more cultures or co-cultures exchange messages in a manner that is influenced by their different cultural perceptions and symbol systems, both verbal and nonverbal (Samovar et al., 2007).

Since all of us belong to many groups (ethnic, economic, interest-based, age, etc.), you might be asking yourself whether there is any communication that *isn't* intercultural or at least co-cultural. The answer to this question is "yes," for two reasons. First, even in an increasingly diverse world, there are still plenty of relationships in which people share a basically common background. The Irish marchers in a St. Patrick's Day parade, the suburban-bred group of men who play poker every other Friday night, and the members of a college sorority or fraternity are likely to share fundamentally similar personal histories and, therefore, have similar norms, customs, and values.

Second, even when people with different cultural backgrounds communicate, those differences may not be important. David may be a Jewish male whose ancestors came from Eastern Europe while Lisa is a third-generation Japanese person whose parents are practicing Christians, but they have created a life together that usually is more significant than their differences, and that leaves them able to deal comfortably with those differences when they do arise.

Rather than classifying some exchanges as intercultural and others as free from cultural influences, it's more accurate to talk about *degrees* of cultural significance (Lustig & Koester, 2005). Encounters can fit along a spectrum of "interculturalness." At the "most intercultural" end are situations where differences between the backgrounds and beliefs of communicators are high. A traveler visiting a new country for the first time with little knowledge of local society would be an obvious example. At the "least intercultural" end of the spectrum fall exchanges where cultural differences make little difference. A student from Los Angeles who attends a small liberal arts college in the Midwest might find life somewhat different, but the adjustment would be far less difficult than that for the international traveler. In between these extremes falls a whole range of encounters in which culture plays varying roles.

Note that intercultural communication (at least as we'll use the term here) doesn't always occur when people from different cultures interact. The cultural backgrounds, perceptions, and symbol systems of the participants must have a significant impact on the exchange before we can say that culture has made a difference. Social scientists use the term **salience** to describe how much weight we attach to a particular person or phenomenon. Consider a few examples where culture has little or no salience:

- A group of preschool children is playing together in a park. These 3-year-olds don't recognize the fact that their parents may come from different countries, or even that they don't speak the same language. At this point we wouldn't say that intercultural communication is taking place. Only when cultural factors become salient (diet, sharing, or parental discipline, for example) do the children begin to think of one another as different.

- Members of a school basketball team—some Asian, some black, some Latino, and some white—are intent on winning the league championship. During a game, cultural distinctions aren't salient. There's plenty of communication, but it isn't fundamentally intercultural. Away from their games, they might notice some fundamental differences in the way members of each group communicate.

- A husband and wife were raised in homes with different religious traditions. Most of the time their religious heritage makes little difference, and the partners view themselves as a unified couple. Every so often, however—perhaps during the holidays or when meeting members of each other's family—the different backgrounds are more salient. At those times we can imagine the partners feeling quite different from each other— thinking of themselves as members of separate cultures.

Interpersonal and Intercultural Communication What is the relationship between intercultural communication and interpersonal relationships? William Gudykunst and Young Kim (2002) suggest that interpersonal and intercultural factors combine to form a two-by-two matrix in which the importance of interpersonal communication forms one dimension and intercultural significance forms the second one (Figure 2.1). This model shows that some interpersonal transactions (for example, a conversation between two siblings who have been raised in the same household) have virtually no intercultural elements. Other encounters (such as a traveler from Senegal trying to get directions from a Ukrainian taxi driver in New York City) are almost exclusively intercultural, without the personal dimensions that we have discussed throughout this book.

Still other exchanges—the most interesting ones for our purposes— contain elements of both intercultural and interpersonal communication. This range of encounters is broad in the global village: Business people from different backgrounds try to wrap up a deal; U.S. born and immigrant

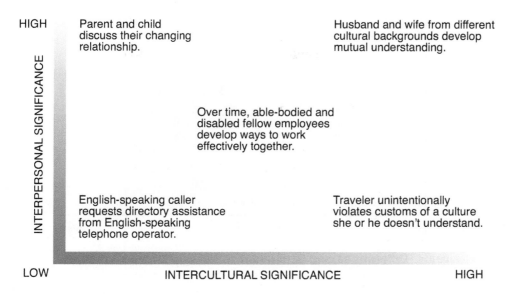

FIGURE 2.1 Some Possible Interactions among Interpersonal and Intercultural Dimensions of Person-to-Person Communication

children learn to get along in school; health care educators seek effective ways to serve patients from around the world; neighbors from different racial or ethnic backgrounds look for ways to make their streets safer and cleaner; suburban-bred teachers seek common ground with inner-city students—the list seems almost endless.

Cultural Differences as Generalizations The following pages spell out a variety of ways communication varies from one culture to another. While these variations can sometimes be significant, it's important to remember that cultural practices aren't *totally* different: People from varied backgrounds often share enough common ground to make relationships work. When all the physical and social attributes of human beings are added up, there are far more similarities than differences among the people of the world.

Moreover, there are sometimes greater differences *within* cultures than *between* them. Consider the matter of formality as an example: By most measures, U.S. culture is far more casual than many others. But Figure 2.2 shows that there may be more common ground between a formal American and a casual member of a formal culture than there is between two Americans with vastly differing levels of formality. Furthermore, within every culture, members display a wide range of communication styles. For instance, while most Asian cultures tend to be collectivistic, many members of those cultures would identify themselves as individualists. For these reasons, it's important to remember that generalizations—even when accurate and helpful—don't apply to every member of a group.

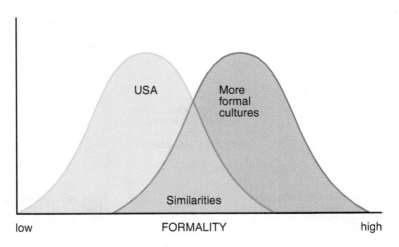

FIGURE 2.2 Differences and Similarities within and between cultures
Adapted from Trompenaars, F. (1994). *Riding the waves of culture.* New York: McGraw-Hill/Irwin, p. 28.

CULTURAL VALUES AND NORMS

Some cultural influences on communication are obvious. However, some far less visible values and norms can shape how members of cultures think and act (Gudykunst & Matsumoto, 1996). In this section we look at five of these subtle yet vitally important values and norms that shape the way members of a culture communicate. Unless communicators are aware of these differences, they may see people from other cultures as unusual—or even offensive—without realizing that their apparently odd behavior comes from following a different set of beliefs and unwritten rules about the "proper" way to communicate.

High versus Low Context Anthropologist Edward Hall (1959) identified two distinct ways that members of various cultures deliver messages. A **low-context culture** uses language primarily to express thoughts, feelings, and ideas as directly as possible. To low-context communicators, the meaning of a statement lies in the words spoken. By contrast, a **high-context culture** relies heavily on subtle, often nonverbal cues to maintain social harmony. Rather than upsetting others by speaking directly, communicators in these societies learn to discover meaning from the context in which a message is delivered: the nonverbal behaviors of the speaker, the history of the relationship, and the general social rules that govern interaction between people.

There are many examples of how context and culture affect communication. People in high-context India tend to disclose less private information in online discussions than low-context Germans; they also use more emoticons, reflecting the higher importance of nonverbal communication in their culture (Pflug, 2011). A study in which expressions of appreciation were examined found that in the low-context culture of the United States, people rely about evenly on verbal and nonverbal methods of expressing themselves, while people in the high-context culture of China favor non-verbal over verbal ones (Bello et al., 2010). Table 2.1 summarizes some key differences in how people from low- and high-context cultures use language.

Mainstream culture in the United States, Canada, Northern Europe, and Israel falls toward the low-context end of the scale. Longtime residents generally value straight-talk and grow impatient with "beating around the bush." By contrast, most Asian and Middle Eastern cultures fit the high-context pattern and can be offended by the bluntness of low-context communication styles.

In many Asian societies, for example, maintaining harmony is important, so communicators avoid speaking directly if that threatens another person's "face," or dignity. For this reason, communicators raised in Japanese or Korean cultures are less likely than Americans to offer a clear "no" to an undesirable request.

To members of high-context cultures, communicators with a low-context style can appear overly talkative, lacking in subtlety, and redundant. On the other hand, to people from low-context backgrounds, high-context communicators often seem unexpressive, or even dishonest. It is easy to see how the clash between directness and indirectness can aggravate problems between straight-talking, low-context Israelis and their Arab neighbors, whose high-context culture stresses smooth interaction. Israelis might view their Arab counterparts as evasive, while the Arabs might perceive the Israelis as insensitive and blunt.

TABLE 2.1 High-Context and Low-Context Communication Styles

LOW-CONTEXT CULTURES (e.g., Germany, Scandinavia, most English-speaking countries)	HIGH CONTEXT (e.g., most Southern European, Middle Eastern, Asian, and Latin American countries)
Majority of information is carried in explicit verbal messages, with less focus on the situational context.	Important information carried in contextual cues, such as time, place, relationship, situation. Less reliance on explicit verbal messages.
Self-expression is valued. Communicators state opinions and desires directly and strive to persuade others to accept their own viewpoint.	Relational harmony is valued and maintained by the indirect expression of options. Communicators abstain from saying "no" directly.
Clear, eloquent speech is considered praiseworthy. Verbal fluency is admired.	Communicators talk "around" the point, allowing the others to fill in the missing pieces. Ambiguity and use of silence is admired.

Adapted from Adler, R. B., & Elmhorst, J. (2008). *Communicating at work: Principles and practices for business and the professions* (9th ed., p. 31). New York: McGraw-Hill.

Individualism versus Collectivism Some cultures value the individual, while others place greater emphasis on the group. Members of an **individualistic culture** view their primary responsibility as helping themselves, whereas communicators in **collectivistic cultures** feel loyalties and obligations to an in-group: one's extended family, community, or even the organization one works for (Triandis, 1995). Individualistic cultures also are characterized by self-reliance and competition, whereas members of a collectivistic culture are more attentive to and concerned with the opinions of significant others. The consequences of a culture's individualistic–collectivistic orientation are so powerful that some scholars (e.g., Kim & Chu, 2011; Merkin & Ramadan, 2010; Nguyen et al., 2010) have labeled it as the most fundamental dimension of cultural differences. Table 2.2 summarizes some differences between individualistic and collectivistic cultures.

Members of individualistic cultures tend to view themselves in terms of what they *do*, while people in collectivistic cultures are more likely to define themselves in terms of group membership. For instance, members of several cultures were asked to answer the question "Who am I?" 20 times (DeAngelis, 1992). North Americans were likely to answer by giving individual factors ("I am athletic"; "I am short"). By contrast, members of more collectivistic societies—Chinese, Filipinos, Japanese, and some South Americans, for example—responded in terms of their relationships with others ("I am a father"; "I am an employee of XYZ Corporation").

TABLE 2.2 The Self in Individualistic and Collectivistic Cultures

INDIVIDUALISTIC CULTURES (e.g., USA, Canada, UK)	COLLECTIVISTIC CULTURES (e.g., Pakistan, Indonesia, Ecuador)
Self is separate, unique individual; should be independent, self-sufficient.	People belong to extended families or in-groups; "we" or group orientation.
Individual should take care of himself or herself and immediate family.	Person should take care of extended family before self.
Many flexible group memberships; friendships based on shared interests and activities.	Emphasis is on belonging to a very few permanent in-groups, which have a strong influence over the person.
Reward is for individual achievement and initiative; individual decision making is encouraged; individual credit and blame are assigned.	Reward is for contribution to group goals and well-being; cooperation with in-group members; group decision making is valued; credit and blame are shared.
High value on autonomy, change, youth, individual security, equality.	High value on duty, order, tradition, age, group security, status, and hierarchy.

Adapted by Sandra Sudweeks from Triandis, H. C. (1990). Cross-cultural studies of individualism and collectivism. In J. Berman (Ed.), *Nebraska symposium on motivation* (pp. 41-133). Lincoln: University of Nebraska Press; and Hall, E. T. (1959). *Beyond culture.* New York: Doubleday

The difference between individualistic and collectivistic cultures also shows up in the level of comfort or anxiety their respective members feel when communicating. In societies where the need to conform is great, there is a higher degree of communication apprehension. For example, as a group, residents of China, Korea, and Japan exhibit a significantly higher degree of anxiety about speaking out in public than do members of individualistic cultures such as the United States and Australia (Berry, 2007; Klopf, 1984). It's important to realize that different levels of communication apprehension don't mean that shyness is a "problem" in some cultures. In fact, just the opposite is true: In these societies reticence is valued. When the goal is to avoid being "the nail that sticks out," it's logical to feel nervous when you make yourself appear different by calling attention your way. A self-concept that includes "assertive" might make a Westerner feel proud, but in much of Asia it would more likely be cause for shame.

Power Distance For members of democratic societies, the principle embodied in the U.S. Declaration of Independence that "all men [and women] are created equal" is so fundamental that we accept it without question. However, not all cultures share this belief. Some operate on the assumption that certain groups of people (an aristocracy or an economic class, for example) and some institutions (such as a church or the government) have the right to control the lives of individuals. Geert Hofstede (1984) coined the term **power distance** to describe the degree to which members of a society accept an unequal distribution of power.

Cultures with low power difference believe in minimizing distinctions between various social classes. Rich and poor, educated and uneducated groups may still exist, but there is a pervasive belief in low power difference cultures that one person is as good as another regardless of his or her station in life. Low power difference cultures also support the notion that challenging authority is acceptable— even desirable. Members aren't necessarily punished for raising questions about the status quo. According to Hofstede's research, U.S. and Canadian societies have relatively low power distance, though not the lowest in the world. Austria, Denmark, Israel, and New Zealand proved to be the most egalitarian countries. At the other end of the spectrum are countries with a high degree of power distance: Philippines, Mexico, Venezuela, India, and Singapore.

The degree of power distance in a culture is reflected in key relationships (Lustig & Koester, 1999; Santilli & Miller, 2011). Children who are raised in cultures with high power difference are expected to obey their parents and other authority figures to a degree that would astonish most children raised in the United States or Canada. Power automatically comes with age in many countries. For example, the Korean language has separate terms for *older brother, oldest brother, younger sister, youngest sister,* and so on. Parents in cultures with low power distance don't expect the same degree of unquestioning obedience. They are not surprised when children ask "Why?" when presented with a request or demand.

On-the-job communication is different in low- and high-power-distance societies (A. Cohen, 2007). In countries with higher degrees of power distance, employees have much less input into the way they perform their work. In fact, workers from these cultures are likely to feel uncomfortable when given freedom to make their own decisions or when a more egalitarian boss asks for their opinion: They prefer to view their bosses as benevolent decision makers. The reverse is true when management from a culture with an egalitarian tradition tries to do business in a country whose workers are used to high power distance. They can be surprised to find that employees do not expect much say in decisions and do not feel unappreciated when they aren't consulted. They may regard dutiful, submissive, respectful employees as lacking initiative and creativity—traits that helped them gain promotions back home. Given these differences, it's easy to understand why multinational companies need to consider fundamental differences in communication values and behavior when they set up shop in a new country.

Uncertainty Avoidance The desire to resolve uncertainty seems to be a trait shared by people around the world (Berger, 1988). While uncertainty may be universal, cultures have different ways of coping with an unpredictable future. Hofstede (2003; Merkin, 2006) uses the term **uncertainty avoidance** to reflect the degree to which members of a culture feel threatened by ambiguous situations and how much they try to avoid them. He developed an uncertainty avoidance index (UAI) to measure differing degrees of uncertainty avoidance around the world. Residents of some countries (including Singapore, Great Britain, Denmark, Sweden, Hong Kong, and the United States) proved to be relatively unthreatened by change, while others (such as natives of Belgium, Greece, Japan, and Portugal) found new or ambiguous situations discomfiting.

A culture's degree of uncertainty avoidance is reflected in the way its members communicate. In countries that avoid uncertainty, deviant people and ideas are considered dangerous, and intolerance is high (Samovar & Porter, 2004). People in these cultures are especially concerned with security, so they have a strong need for clearly defined rules and regulations. By contrast, people in a culture that is less threatened by the new and unexpected are more likely to tolerate—or even welcome—people who don't fit the norm.

When a mainstream North American who is relatively comfortable with change and novelty spends time with someone from a high UAI culture such as Japan, both communicators may find the other behaving in disconcerting ways. The North American is likely to view the Japanese as rigid and overly controlled, while the Japanese would probably regard the North American as undisciplined, overly tolerant, and generally lacking self-control. On the other hand, if the communicators understand how their cultural conditioning affects their style, then they are more likely to understand, and maybe even learn from, the other's different style.

Achievement versus Nurturing The term **achievement culture** describes societies that place a high value on material success and a focus on the task at hand, while **nurturing culture** is a descriptive term for cultures that regard the support of relationships as an especially important goal.

There are significant differences in how people from an achievement culture like the United States and those from a nurturing culture like the Netherlands voice their opinions (van den Bos et al., 2010). In achievement cultures—which emphasize outperforming others—those who see themselves as highly capable feel more empowered to voice their opinions, and are satisfied when they can do so. By contrast, in nurturing cultures—which emphasize helping—those who see themselves as *less* capable feel valued as important group members and feel more satisfied when they have the opportunity to voice their opinions.

As you think about the cultural values described here, you may realize that they don't just arise between people from different countries. In today's increasingly multicultural society, people from different cultural backgrounds are likely to encounter one another "at home," in the country they share. Consider the United States and Canada in the new millennium: Native Americans; Latinos from the Caribbean, Mexico, and South America; Middle Easterners; and Asians from China, Japan, Korea, Vietnam, and other countries mingle with first-generation and longtime residents whose ancestors came from Europe. This is a cultural mixture that often seems less like a melting pot than a salad bowl, in which the many "ingredients" retain much of their own identity.

CODES AND CULTURE

At this point, you probably have a healthy appreciation for the challenges that arise when two or more people try to communicate with one another. These challenges become even greater when the communicators use different verbal and nonverbal communication systems.

Verbal Codes Although there are remarkable similarities between the world's many languages (Whaley, 1997), they also differ in important respects that affect the way their speakers communicate with one another and with speakers of other tongues. The following sections outline some of those factors.

Language and Identity If you live in a culture where everyone speaks the same tongue, then language will have little noticeable impact on how you view yourself and others. But when some members of a society speak the dominant language and others speak a minority tongue, or when that second language is not prestigious, the sense of being a member of an out-group is strong. At this point the speaker of a nondominant language can react in one of two ways: either feel pressured to assimilate by speaking the "better" language, or refuse to accommodate to the majority language and maintain loyalty to the ethnic tongue (Giles et al., 1992). The impact of language on the self-concept is powerful. On one hand, the feeling is likely to be "I'm not as good as speakers of the native language," and on the other, the belief is "There's something unique and worth preserving in my language" (Bergman et al., 2008).

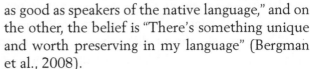

Even the names a culture uses to identify its members reflect its values and shape the way its members relate to one another. When asked to identify themselves, individualistic Americans, Canadians, Australians, and Europeans would probably respond by giving their first name, surname, street, town, and country. Many Asians do it the other way around (Servaes, 1989). If you ask Hindus for their identity, they will give you their caste and village and then their name. The Sanskrit formula for identifying oneself begins with lineage and goes on to state family and house, and ends with one's personal name (Bharti, 1985). The same collectivist orientation is reflected in Chinese written language, where the pronoun *I* looks very similar to the word for *selfish* (Samovar & Porter, 2004). The Japanese language has no equivalent to the English pronoun *I*. Instead, different words are used to refer to one's self depending on the social situation, age, gender, and other social characteristics (Gudykunst, 1993a).

Verbal Communication Styles Using language is more than just a matter of choosing a particular group of words to convey an idea. Each language has its own unique style that distinguishes it from others. Matters like the amount of formality or informality, precision or vagueness, and brevity or detail are major ingredients in speaking competently. When a communicator tries to use the verbal style from one culture in a different one, problems are likely to arise.

Gudykunst (2005) describes three important types of cultural differences in verbal style. One is *directness* or *indirectness*. We have already discussed how low-context cultures use language primarily to express thoughts, feelings, and ideas as clearly, directly, and logically as possible, while high-context cultures may speak less directly, using language to maintain social harmony.

Another way in which language styles can vary across cultures is in terms of whether they are *elaborate* or *succinct*. For instance, speakers of Arabic commonly use language that is much more rich and expressive than normally found in English. Strong assertions and exaggerations that would sound ridiculous in English are a common feature of Arabic. This contrast in linguistic style can lead to misunderstandings between people from different backgrounds.

Succinctness is most extreme in cultures where silence is valued. In many Native American cultures, for example, the favored way to handle ambiguous social situations is to remain quiet (Ferraro, 2008). When you contrast this silent style to the talkativeness that is common when people first meet in mainstream American cultures, it's easy to imagine how the first encounter between an Apache or Navajo and a European American might be uncomfortable for both people.

A third way that languages differ from one culture to another involves *formality* and *informality*. One guidebook for British readers who want to understand how Americans communicate describes the openness and informality that characterizes U.S. culture:

> Visitors may be overwhelmed by the sheer exuberant friendliness of Americans, especially in the central and southern parts of the country. Sit next to an American on an airplane and he will immediately address you by your first name, ask "So—how do you like it in the States?," explain his recent divorce in intimate detail, invite you home for dinner, offer to lend you money, and wrap you in a warm hug on parting. This does not necessarily mean he will remember your name the next day. Americans are friendly because they just can't help it; they like to be neighbourly and want to be liked. (Faul, 1994, pp. 3–4)

The informal approach that characterizes communication in countries like the United States is quite different from the great concern for propriety in many parts of Asia and Africa (Bjørge, 2007). Formality isn't so much a matter of using correct grammar as of defining social relationships. For example, there are different degrees of formality for speaking with old friends, nonacquaintances whose background one knows, and complete strangers. One sign of being a learned person in Korea is the ability to use language that recognizes these relational distinctions. When you contrast these sorts of distinctions with the casual friendliness many North Americans use even when talking with complete strangers, it's easy to see how a Korean might view American communicators as boorish and how an American might see Koreans as stiff and unfriendly.

Nonverbal Codes Many elements of nonverbal communication are shared by all humans, regardless of culture (Matsumoto, 2006; Schiefenhövel, 1997). For instance, people of all cultures convey messages through facial expressions and gestures. Furthermore, some of these physical displays have the same meaning everywhere. Crying is a universal sign of unhappiness or pain, and smiles signal friendly intentions. (Of course, smiles and tears may be insincere and manipulative, but their overt meanings are similar and constant in every culture.)

Despite nonverbal similarities, the range of differences in nonverbal behavior is tremendous. For example, the meaning of some gestures varies from one culture to another. Consider the use of gestures such as the "OK" sign made by joining thumb and forefinger to form a circle. This gesture is a cheery affirmation to most Americans, but it has very different meanings in other parts of the world (Knapp & Hall, 2006). In France and Belgium it means "you're worth zero," in Japan it means "money," and in Greece and Turkey it is an insulting or vulgar sexual invitation. Given this sort of cross-cultural ambiguity, it's easy to visualize how an innocent tourist from the United States could wind up in serious trouble overseas without understanding why.

Less obvious cross-cultural differences can damage relationships without the communicators ever recognizing exactly what has gone wrong (Beaulieu, 2004; Hall, 1959). Anglo-Saxons use the largest zone of personal space, followed by Asians. People from the Mediterranean and Latinos use the closest distance. It is easy to visualize the awkward advance and retreat pattern that might occur when two diplomats or businesspeople from these cultures meet. The Middle Easterner would probably keep moving forward to close the gap that feels so wide, while the North American would continually back away. Both would probably feel uncomfortable without knowing why.

Like distance, patterns of eye contact vary around the world. A direct gaze is considered appropriate for speakers in Latin America, the Arab world, and southern Europe. On the other hand, Asians, Indians, Pakistanis, and northern Europeans gaze at a listener peripherally or not at all. In either case, deviations from the norm are likely to make a culturally uneducated listener uncomfortable. You'll read much more about cultural differences in nonverbal communication in Chapter 6.

Decoding Messages As you'll see in Chapter 4, attribution is the process of making sense of another person's behavior. Attribution is an unavoidable part of communicating: We have to form some sort of interpretation of what others' words and actions mean. But most behavior is so ambiguous that it can be interpreted in several ways. Furthermore, the usual tendency is to stick to the first attribution one makes. It's easy to see how this quick, sloppy attribution process can lead to making faulty interpretations—especially when communicators are from different cultural backgrounds.

In Table 2.3, a supervisor from the United States invites a subordinate from Greece to get involved in making a decision (Triandis, 1975, pp. 42–43). Since U.S. culture ranks relatively low on power distance, the supervisor

TABLE 2.3 Culture Affects Attributions

BEHAVIOR	ATTRIBUTION
American: How long will it take you to finish the report?	American: I asked him to participate.
Greek: I do not know. How long should it take?	Greek: His behavior makes no sense. He is the boss. Why doesn't he tell me?
	American: He refuses to take responsibility.
	Greek: I asked him for an order.
American: You are in the best position to analyze time requirements.	American: I press him to take responsibility for his own actions.
Greek: Ten days.	Greek: What nonsense! I better give him an answer.
American: Take fifteen. It is agreed you will do it in fifteen days?	American: He lacks the ability to estimate time; this estimate is totally inadequate.
Greek: These are my orders. Fifteen days.	American: I offer a contract.
American: Where is the report?	American: I am making sure he fulfills his contract.
Greek: It will be ready tomorrow.	Greek: He is asking for the report.
	(Both understand that it is not ready.)
American: But we agreed that it would be ready today.	American: I must teach him to fulfill an agreement.
The Greek hands in his resignation.	Greek: The stupid, incompetent boss! Not only did he give me wrong orders, but he does not appreciate that I did a thirty-day job in sixteen days.
The American is surprised.	Greek: I can't work for such a man.

SELF-ASSESSMENT

What Is Your Intercultural Sensitivity?

A series of statements concerning intercultural communication follow. There are no right or wrong answers. Imagine yourself interacting with people from a wide variety of cultural groups, not just one or two. Record your first impression to each of the following statements by indicating the degree to which you agree or disagree, using the following scale.

5 STRONGLY AGREE **4** AGREE **3** UNCERTAIN **2** DISAGREE **1** STRONGLY DISAGREE

_____ 1. I enjoy interacting with people from different cultures.

_____ 2. I think people from other cultures are narrow-minded.

_____ 3. I am pretty sure of myself in interacting with people from different cultures.

_____ 4. I find it very hard to talk in front of people from different cultures.

_____ 5. I always know what to say when interacting with people from different cultures.

_____ 6. I can be as sociable as I want to be when interacting with people from different cultures.

_____ 7. I don't like to be with people from different cultures.

_____ 8. I respect the values of people from different cultures.

_____ 9. I get upset easily when interacting with people from different cultures.

_____ 10. I feel confident when interacting with people from different cultures.

_____ 11. I tend to wait before forming an impression of people from different cultures.

_____ 12. I often get discouraged when I am with people from different cultures.

_____ 13. I am open-minded to people from different cultures.

_____ 14. I am very observant when interacting with people from different cultures.

encourages input from the employee. In Greece, however, the distance between bosses and their subordinates is much greater. Therefore, the Greek employee wants and expects to be told what to do. After all, it's the boss's job to give orders. Table 2.3 shows how the differing cultural beliefs shape both figures' attributions of the other's messages.

Culturally based attributions don't just occur between members of different nationalities. Even different use of dialects or accents by native-born

_____ 15. I often feel useless when interacting with people from different cultures.

_____ 16. I respect the ways people from different cultures behave.

_____ 17. I try to obtain as much information as I can when interacting with people from different cultures.

_____ 18. I would not accept the opinions of people from different cultures.

_____ 19. I am sensitive to my culturally distinct counterpart's subtle meanings during our interaction.

_____ 20. I think my culture is better than other cultures.

_____ 21. I often give positive responses to my culturally different counterpart during our interaction.

_____ 22. I avoid those situations where I will have to deal with culturally distinct persons.

_____ 23. I often show my culturally distinct counterpart my understanding through verbal or nonverbal cues.

_____ 24. I have a feeling of enjoyment toward differences between my culturally distinct counterpart and me.

SCORING:
To determine your score, begin by reverse-coding items 2, 4, 7, 9, 12, 15, 18, 20, and 22 (if you indicated 5, reverse-code to 1, if you indicated 4, reverse-code to 2, and so on). Higher scores indicate a greater probability of intercultural communication competence.

Sum items 1, 11, 13, 21, 22, 23, and 24 _____ Interaction Engagement (range is 7–35)
Sum items 2, 7, 8, 16, 18, and 20 _____ Respect for Cultural Differences (6–30)
Sum items 3, 4, 5, 6, and 10 _____ Interaction Confidence (5–25)
Sum items 9, 12, and 15 _____ Interaction Enjoyment (3–15)
Sum items 14, 17, and 19 _____ Interaction Attentiveness (3–15)
Sum of all the items = _____ (24–120, with a midpoint of 48)

Permission to use courtesy of Guo-Ming Chen. Chen, G. M., & Starosta, W. J. (2000). The development and validation of the Intercultural Sensitivity Scale. *Human Communication, 3,* 1-14.

members of the same country can affect a listener's evaluation of a speaker. Most cultures have a "standard dialect," which is spoken by high-status opinion leaders. For the most part, people who use the standard dialect are judged as being competent, intelligent, industrious, and confident (Ng & Bradac, 1993). By contrast, nonstandard speakers are likely to be rated less favorably. The likely attribution is "this person doesn't even speak correctly. There must be something wrong with him or her."

DEVELOPING INTERCULTURAL COMMUNICATION COMPETENCE

What distinguishes competent and incompetent intercultural communicators? The rest of this chapter focuses on answering this question. But before we get to the answers, take a moment to complete the Self-Assessment on pages 46–47 to evaluate your intercultural communication sensitivity.

To a great degree, interacting successfully with strangers calls for the same ingredients of general communicative competence outlined in Chapter 1. It's important to have a wide range of behaviors and to be skillful at choosing and performing the most appropriate ones in a given situation. A genuine concern for others plays an important role. Cognitive complexity and the ability to empathize also help, although empathizing with someone from another culture can be challenging (DeTurk, 2001). Finally, self-monitoring is important, since the need to make midcourse corrections in your approach is often necessary when dealing with people from other cultures.

But beyond these basic qualities, communication researchers have worked long and hard to identify qualities that are unique, or at least especially important, ingredients of intercultural communicative competence (Arasaratnam, 2007; Hajek & Giles, 2003).

Motivation and Attitude The desire to communicate successfully with strangers is an important start. For example, people high in willingness to communicate with people from other cultures report a greater number of friends from different backgrounds than those who are less willing to reach out (Kassing, 1997; Massengill & Nash, 2009). But desire alone isn't sufficient (Arasaratnam, 2006). Some other ways of thinking—called "culture-general"—are essential when dealing with people from other backgrounds (Samovar et al., 2007). These culture-general attitudes are necessary when communicating competently with people from any background that is different from one's own.

Tolerance for Ambiguity As noted earlier, one of the most important concerns facing communicators is their desire to reduce uncertainty about one another (Berger, 1988; Gibbs et al., 2011). When we encounter communicators from different cultures, the level of uncertainty is especially high. Consider the basic challenge of communicating in an unfamiliar language.

Pico Iyer (1990, pp. 129–130) captures the ambiguity that arises from a lack of fluency when he describes his growing friendship with Sachiko, a Japanese woman he met in Kyoto:

> I was also beginning to realize how treacherous it was to venture into a foreign language if one could not measure the shadows of the words one used. When I had told her, in Asuka, *"Jennifer Beals ga suki-desu. Anata mo"* ("I like Jennifer Beals—and I like you"), I had been pleased to find a way of conveying affection, and yet, I thought, a perfect distance. But later I looked up suki and found that I had delivered an almost naked protestation of love. . . .
>
> Meanwhile, of course, nearly all her shadings were lost to me. . . . Once, when I had to leave her house ten minutes early, she said, "I very sad," and another time, when I simply called her up, she said, "I very happy"—and I began to think her unusually sensitive, or else prone to bold and violent extremes, when really she was reflecting nothing but the paucity of her English vocabulary. . . . Talking in a language not one's own was like walking on one leg; when two people did it together, it was like a three-legged waltz.

Competent intercultural communicators accept—even welcome—this kind of ambiguity. Iyer (1990, pp. 220–221) describes the way the mutual confusion he shared with Sachiko actually helped their relationship develop:

> Yet in the end, the fact that we were both speaking in this pared-down diction made us both, I felt, somewhat gentler, more courteous, and more vulnerable than we would have been otherwise, returning us to a state of innocence.

Without a tolerance for ambiguity, the mass of often confusing and sometimes downright incomprehensible messages that bombard intercultural sojourners would be impossible to manage. Some people seem to come equipped with this sort of tolerance, while others have to cultivate it. One way or the other, that ability to live with uncertainty is an essential ingredient of intercultural communication competence (Gudykunst, 1993b).

Open-Mindedness Being comfortable with ambiguity is important, but without an open-minded attitude a communicator will have trouble interacting competently with people from different backgrounds. To understand open-mindedness, it's helpful to consider three traits that are incompatible with it. **Ethnocentrism** is an attitude that one's own culture is superior to others. An ethnocentric person thinks—either privately or openly—that anyone who does not belong to his or her in-group is somehow strange, wrong, or even inferior. Travel writer Rick Steves (n.d.) describes how an ethnocentric point of view can interfere with respect for other cultural practices:

> We [Americans] consider ourselves very clean, but when we take baths, we use the same water for soaking, cleaning, and rinsing. (We wouldn't wash our dishes that way.) The Japanese, who use clean water for every step of the bathing process, might find our ways strange or even disgusting. People

49

meDIa CLIP

OPENING A CLOSED DOOR:
GRAN TORINO

Cantankerous widower Walt Kowalski (Clint Eastwood) spends much of his time nursing a seemingly endless string of beers and grudges as he watches Hmong families transform his Detroit neighborhood from an all-white enclave into a Southeast Asian Laotian community.

Walt's prejudices are a product of the time and place where he grew up. They are aggravated by memories of fighting in the Korean War, and by his buddies who speak the same language of intolerance. His racism is reinforced when a neighborhood boy named Thao (Bee Vang) attempts to steal his prized possession, a lovingly maintained 1972 Ford Gran Torino.

Walt's ignorance slowly dissolves as he defends, and gradually befriends, Thao's family when they come under assault by a Hmong gang. His transformation from racist to loyal friend is an object lesson in the power of knowledge to banish intolerance.

in some cultures blow their nose right onto the street. They couldn't imagine doing that into a small cloth, called a hanky, and storing it in their pocket to be used again and again. . . .

Too often we judge the world in terms of "civilized" and "primitive." I was raised thinking the world was a pyramid with the US on top and everyone else was trying to get there. I was comparing people on their ability (or interest) in keeping up with us in material consumption, science, and technology. . . .

Over the years, I've found that if we measure cultures differently (maybe according to stress, loneliness, heart attack rates, hours spent in traffic jams, or family togetherness), the results stack up differently. It's best not to fall into the "rating game." All societies are complex and highly developed in their own way.

Ethnocentrism leads to an attitude of **prejudice**—an unfairly biased and intolerant attitude toward others who belong to an out-group. (Note that the root term in *prejudice* is "prejudge.") An important element of prejudice is stereotyping. Stereotypical prejudices include the obvious exaggerations that all women are emotional, all men are sex-crazed and insensitive goons, all older people are out of touch with reality, and all immigrants are welfare parasites. Stereotyping can even be a risk when it comes to knowledge of cultural characteristics like individualism or collectivism. Not all members of a group are equally individualistic or collectivistic. For example, a close look at Americans of European and Latin descent showed differences within each group (Oetzel, 1998). Some Latinos were more independent than some European Americans, and vice versa. Open-mindedness is especially important in intercultural work teams (Matveev, 2004). Chapter 4 has more to say about stereotyping.

Knowledge and Skill Attitude alone isn't enough to guarantee success in intercultural encounters. Communicators need to possess enough knowledge of other cultures to know what approaches are appropriate. The ability to "shift gears" and adapt one's style to the norms of another culture or co-culture is an essential ingredient of communication competence (Kim et al., 1996; Self, 2009).

How can a communicator acquire the culture-specific information that leads to competence? One important element is what Stella Ting-Toomey (1999) and others label as *mindfulness*—awareness of one's own behavior and that of others. Communicators who lack this quality blunder through intercultural encounters *mindlessly*, oblivious of how their own behavior may confuse or offend others, and how behavior that they consider weird may be simply different.

Charles Berger (1979) suggests three strategies for moving toward a more mindful, skillful style of intercultural communication.

- *Passive observation* involves noticing what behaviors members of a different culture use and applying these insights to communicate in ways that are most effective.

- *Active strategies* include reading, watching films, and asking experts and members of the other culture how to behave, as well as taking academic courses related to intercultural communication and diversity.

- *Self-disclosure* involves volunteering personal information to people from the other culture with whom you want to communicate. One type of self-disclosure is to confess your cultural ignorance: "This is very new to me. What's the right thing to do in this situation?" This approach is the riskiest of the three described here, since some cultures may not value candor and self-disclosure as much as others. Nevertheless, most people are pleased when strangers attempt to learn the practices of their culture, and they are usually more than willing to offer information and assistance.

Social Media in a Changing World

Until a generation ago, face-to-face communication was essential to starting and maintaining most, if not all, personal relationships. Other channels existed: The telephone (in an era of expensive long-distance rates and less-than-perfect technology) might have worked during temporary absences, and postal correspondence helped bridge the gap until the people involved could reconnect in person. Nonetheless, interpersonal communication seemed to require physical proximity.

Now things are different. Obviously, face-to-face communication is still vitally important; but technology plays a key role in starting and maintaining relationships. The term that collectively describes all the channels that make remote personal communication possible is **social media.** You're using social media when you text message with friends or coworkers; send a tweet; exchange e-mails, texts, and instant messages; and when you use

social networking websites like Facebook. The number of social media technologies has exploded in the past few decades, giving communicators today an array of choices that would have amazed someone from a previous era.

By the beginning of 2010, almost 75 percent of Americans under age 30 used social networking sites (Lenhart & Purcell, 2010), and the number is almost as high in many other countries (Global Publics Embrace Social Networking, 2010). By contrast, about 40 percent of those thirty and older were social networkers, and the fastest growth in social networking has come from users 74 and older, where use increased fourfold from 4 percent to 16 percent (Zickuhr, 2010).

CHARACTERISTICS OF SOCIAL MEDIA

In many ways, mediated and face-to-face communication are similar. Both include the same elements described in Chapter 1—messages, channels, noise, etc. Both are used to satisfy the same physical, identity, social, and practical needs outlined on pages 4–8. Despite these similarities, communication by social media differs from the in-person variety in some important ways.

Message Richness Social scientists use the term **richness** to describe the abundance of nonverbal cues that add clarity to a verbal message. As you'll read in Chapter 6, face-to-face communication is rich because it abounds with nonverbal messages that give communicators cues about the meanings of one another's words, and it offers hints about their feelings (Surinder & Cooper, 2003). By comparison, social media are much leaner for conveying information.

To appreciate how message richness varies by medium, imagine you haven't heard from a friend in several weeks and you decide to ask, "Is anything wrong?" Your friend replies, "No, I'm fine." Would that response be more or less descriptive depending on whether you received it via text message, over the phone, or in person?

You almost certainly would be able to tell a great deal more from a face-to-face response because it would contain a richer array of cues: facial expressions, vocal tone, and so on. By contrast, a text message contains only words. The phone message—containing vocal cues but no visual ones—would probably fall somewhere in between.

Because most mediated messages are leaner than the face-to-face variety, they can be harder to interpret with confidence. Irony and attempts at humor can easily be misunderstood, so as a receiver it's important to clarify your interpretations before jumping to conclusions. Adding phrases such as "just kidding" or emoticons like :(can help your lean messages become richer, but the potential for your sincerity being interpreted as sarcasm still exists. As a sender, think about how to send unambiguous messages so you aren't misunderstood.

The leanness of social media messages presents another challenge. Without nonverbal cues, online communicators can create idealized—and sometimes unrealistic—images of one another. As we'll discuss in Chapters 3 and 6, the absence of nonverbal cues allows communicators to manage their identities carefully. After all, it's a world without bad breath, unsightly blemishes, or stammering responses. Such conditions encourage participants to engage in what Joseph Walther (1996) calls *hyperpersonal* communication, accelerating the discussion of personal topics and relational development beyond what normally happens in face-to-face interaction. This may explain why communicators who meet online sometimes have difficulty shifting to a face-to-face relationship (see the Focus on Research box on page 55).

Synchronicity Synchronous communication is two-way and occurs in real time. In-person communication is synchronous, as are phone conversations. By contrast, **asynchronous communication** occurs when there's a time gap between when a message is sent and when it's received. E-mail and voice mail messages are asynchronous. So are "snail mail" letters, and Twitter postings.

The asynchronous nature of most mediated messages makes them fundamentally different from synchronous communication. Most obviously, asynchronous messages give you the choice of not responding at all: You can ignore most problematic text messages without much fallout. That isn't a good option if the person who wants an answer gets you on the phone or confronts you in person.

Even if you want to respond, asynchronous media give you the chance to edit your reply. You can mull over different wording, or even ask others for advice about what to say. On the other hand, delaying a response to an asynchronous message can send a message of its own, intentionally or not ("I wonder why she hasn't texted me back?").

Dark Side of Communication
ALONE TOGETHER

Social scientist Sherry Turkle has made a career of studying how technologies shape who we are and how we relate to one another. After 15 years of research and hundreds of interviews, she argues that the "always on, always connected" nature of our world has changed the way we interact. Instead of a life enriched by a small number of meaningful relationships, we now have scores or even hundreds of superficial ones. We count as "friends" people we barely know on Facebook, and we increasingly communicate with those closest to us in 140 characters or less via texting, IM, and tweeting. Turkle argues that this overabundance of superficial contacts offers the "illusion of companionship."

It isn't the frequency or brevity of mediated messages that Turkle finds dangerous and depressing. It's the way these forms of communication make us less willing to engage in closer, deeper, more personal relationships. She describes young children who lavish attention on increasingly sophisticated electronic toys. She worries about teens who are uncomfortable with the immediacy and unpredictability of phone conversations, and who spend more time crafting online identities than talking in person with others. She tells familiar tales about working adults who ignore their families to stay in touch with others via the Internet.

"We don't need to reject or disparage technology," Turkle says. "We need to put it in its place." She urges us to stop multitasking, at least once in a while. To turn off our devices. To ask ourselves who really matters, and to spend quality time communicating in depth with those people.

Turkle, S. (2011). *Alone together: Why we expect more from technology and less from each other.* New York: Basic Books.

Permanence What happens in a face-to-face conversation is transitory. By contrast, the text and video you send via hard copy or social media channels can be stored indefinitely and forwarded to others. The permanence of digital messages can be a plus. You can save and share the smartphone photos of your once-in-a-lifetime encounter with a celebrity. And if your boss e-mails saying it's okay to come in late on Monday morning, you're covered if she later complains about your tardy arrival.

There can also be a downside to the enduring nature of digital messages. It's bad enough to blurt out a private thought or lash out in person, but at least there's no permanent record of your indiscretion. By contrast, a regrettable text message, e-mail, or web posting can be archived virtually forever. Even worse, it can be retrieved and forwarded in ways that can only be imagined in your worst nightmares. The best advice, then, is to take the same approach with mediated messages that you do in person: Think twice before saying something you might later regret. As one writer (Bennehum, 2005) put it, "Old e-mail never dies."

SOCIAL MEDIA AND RELATIONAL QUALITY

At first glance, social media might seem inferior to face-to-face interaction. As noted earlier, it lacks the rich array of nonverbal cues that are available in person. One observer put it this way: "E-mail is a way to stay in touch, but you can't share a coffee or a beer with somebody on e-mail or give them a hug" (Nie & Erbring, 2000, p. 19).

"Cyberpessimists" argue that there's a dark side to relying on mediated channels. (For a review, see DeAndrea et al., 2010.) Some critics describe how the almost hypnotic attraction of an Internet connection discourages a sense of community (e.g., Putnam, 2000). Others claim that the "always on" nature of today's communication technology leads to more superficial relationships. (See the Dark Side box on page 54.)

Some research supports this position. A few older studies showed that heavy Internet users spend less time talking in person and on the phone with friends and family members (Bower, 1998; Nie, 2001). Even worse, excessive Internet use has been linked with depression, loneliness, and problems at school and work (Moody, 2001).

Despite claims like these, a growing body of research suggests that social media can be rich and satisfying (Walther & Ramirez, 2010). One survey revealed that social networking sites usually don't replace offline relationships as much as extend them (Kujath, 2011). For example, in one study, regular Internet users were 20 percent more likely to communicate daily with a relative or a friend, and 66 percent of them said their contact with friends increased because of e-mail (Horrigan et al., 2001).

Even more significant than the amount of communication that occurs online is its quality. Couples who talk frequently via cell phone feel more loving, committed, and confident about their relationship (Jin &

FOCUS ON RESEARCH

Less Can Be More: When Online Partners Meet in Person

Imagine meeting someone online—in a chat room, on a blog, or through a social networking site like Facebook. After interacting for months using various technologies (e-mail, texting), you find yourself wondering whether getting together in person would enhance your growing relationship. The answer, according to a recent study, might surprise you.

Communication researchers Artemio Ramirez and Shuangyue Zhang placed over 800 previously unacquainted college students into two-person "virtual partnerships." Over a 9-week period, the partners were required to complete a series of tasks together. Some of the duos communicated only online, with no face-to-face contact. Others began their work online but later met in person to finish their tasks. The researchers wanted to know whether "modality switching"—that is, moving from online to face-to-face communication—would affect the way the partners thought and felt about one another.

The findings: Partners who communicated exclusively online actually felt greater intimacy and social attraction to one another than those who met in person. For those who did meet face to face, the longer they delayed getting together, the lower their attraction when they finally met in person. The researchers explained that in online-only relationships, "idealization and heightened expectations can occur"—and that face-to-face meetings sometimes lead to a chilly dose of reality.

These findings raise a cautionary note for communicators who meet online and look forward to their relationship's flourishing in person. While some relationships can handle the transition, this study suggests there are risks involved—and that success is hardly guaranteed.

Ramirez, A., & Zhang, S. (2007). When online meets offline: The effect of modality switching on relational communication. *Communication Monographs, 74*, 287–310.

Peña, 2010). In long-distance relationships, partners who use social media to stay in touch report greater levels of intimacy (Gunn & Gunn, 2000) and higher levels of trust (Dainton & Aylor, 2002). Almost 60 percent of American teenagers say that their use of the Internet helps their relationships with their friends, and almost a third report that it helps them make new friends (Lenhart et al., 2010). And finally, participants who have both in-person and electronic contact with friends are less lonely than their counterparts who have fewer ways of keeping in touch (Baiocco et al., 2011).

There are several reasons why mediated channels can increase both the amount and quality of interpersonal communication (Barnes, 2003). For one thing, it makes communication easier. Busy schedules and long distances can make quality time in face-to-face contact difficult or impossible. The challenge of finding time is especially tough for people who are separated by long distances and multiple time zones. In relationships like this, the asynchronous nature of e-mail provides a way to share information that otherwise would be difficult. Online chat is another way to keep in touch: Discovering that a friend or relative is logged on and starting a conversation is "like walking down the street and sometimes running into a friend," said one computer consultant (Marriott, 1998).

Sociolinguist Deborah Tannen (1994b, p. 52) offers one example of how social media transformed the quality of a relationship:

> E-mail deepened my friendship with Ralph. Though his office was next to mine, we rarely had extended conversations because he is shy. Face to face he mumbled so, I could barely tell he was speaking. But when we both got on e-mail, I started receiving long, self-revealing messages; we poured our hearts out to each other. A friend discovered that e-mail opened up that kind of communication with her father. He would never talk much on the phone (as her mother would), but they have become close since they both got on line.

Experiences like these help explain why Steve Jobs, the cofounder of Apple Computer, suggested that personal computers be renamed "*inter*-personal computers."

COMMUNICATING COMPETENTLY WITH SOCIAL MEDIA

Like face-to-face communication, mediated interaction can seem natural and almost effortless. But despite its apparent ease, there's potential for trouble unless you proceed mindfully. The following guidelines will help.

Be Careful What You Post A quick scan of social networking home pages shows that many users post text and images about themselves that could prove embarrassing in some contexts: "Here I am just before my DUI arrest"; "This is me in Cancun on spring break." This is not the sort of information most people would be eager to show a prospective employer or certain family members.

As a cautionary tale about how your digital goofs can haunt you, consider the case of Kevin Colvin, a young intern at a Boston bank who e-mailed his boss saying "something came up at home" and he would need to miss a few days of work. A Facebook search by his boss revealed a photo showing Kevin's true location during the absence: an out-of-town Halloween party with the missing intern dressed in a fairy costume, complete with wings and wand. Besides seeing his pixie-like image plastered over the web, Kevin found that his indiscretion was not a brilliant career move. (To see the photo and read the boss's reaction, type the words "Kevin" and "cool wand" into your search engine.)

Some incautious posts can go beyond being simply amusing. One example is the practice of "sexting"—sharing explicit photos of one's self or others via mediated channels. One survey revealed that 10 percent of young adults between the ages of 14 and 24 have texted or e-mailed a nude or partially nude image of themselves to someone else, and 15 percent have received such pictures or videos of someone else they know (Lenhart, 2009). Perhaps even more disturbing, 8 percent reported that they had received a nude or partially nude image of someone they knew from a third party (MTV, 2009). The impulsive message or post that seems harmless at the time can haunt you for a lifetime.

MEDIA CLIP — ONLINE BUT DISCONNECTED: *THE SOCIAL NETWORK*

In this character study, Facebook creator Mark Zuckerberg (Jesse Eisenberg) is portrayed as a genius at computer programming and meeting the needs of the marketplace. At the same time, he is a disaster in the domain of personal relationships.

Film critic Roger Ebert called Zuckerberg's character "a heat-seeking missile in search of his own goals." He insults and humiliates his girlfriend Erica (Rooney Mara) and betrays his best friend Eduardo Saverin (Andrew Garfield). He builds an empire but lives in an isolated world of his own creation, indifferent to the feelings of those around him.

The irony of Zuckerberg's successes and failures offer a parable for our times. Mastering communication technology is no guarantee of interpersonal competence. On the relational front, success must come the old-fashioned way. Meaningful relationships can't be reduced to bits, bytes, and dollars.

Be Considerate The word "etiquette" calls to mind old-fashioned rules that have little to do with today's world. But whatever you call them, mostly unspoken rules of conduct still keep society running smoothly. We don't shove or cut in waiting lines. We return others' greetings, say "please" and "thanks," and (mostly) let others speak without cutting them off. By acting appropriately, we feel good about ourselves, and we're more effective in getting our needs met.

Communication by social media calls for its own rules, which some refer to as "netiquette." Here are a few.

Respect Others' Need for Undivided Attention If you've been texting, IMing, and e-mailing since you could master a keypad, it might be hard to realize that some people are insulted when you divide your attention between your in-person conversational partner and distant contacts. As one observer put

AT WORK

Choosing a Communication Channel

A generation ago, choosing which communication channel to use on the job wasn't very complicated. If a face-to-face conversation wasn't desirable or possible, you either mailed a letter or used the telephone. Today's communicators have many more options. If you want to put your thoughts in writing, you can use e-mail, fax, text messaging, instant messaging ... or the traditional pen-and-paper approach. If you want to speak, you can use a landline telephone, a cell phone, or an Internet-based system such as Skype.

Sometimes the choice of a medium is a no-brainer. If a customer says "phone me while I'm on the road," you know what to do. If your boss only responds to e-mails, then it would be foolish to use any other approach. But in many other situations, you have several options available. The table below outlines the advantages and drawbacks of the most common ones. Choosing the best channel can make a real difference in your success. In one survey (Lengel & Daft, 1988), managers who were identified as most "media sensitive" were almost twice as likely as their less-savvy peers to receive top ratings in performance reviews.

	SYNCHRONIZATION	RICHNESS OF INFORMATION CONVEYED	SENDER'S CONTROL OVER MESSAGE	CONTROL OVER RECEIVER'S ATTENTION	EFFECTIVENESS FOR DETAILED MESSAGES
Face-to-Face	Synchronous	High	Moderate	Highest	Weak
Telephone, Teleconferencing, and Videoconferencing	Synchronous	Moderate	Moderate	Moderate	Weak
Voice Mail	Asynchronous	Moderate	High	Low	Weak
E-mail	Asynchronous	Low	High	Low	High
Instant Messaging	Almost synchronous	Low	High	Varies	Weak
Text Messaging and Twitter	Varies	Low	High (given briefness of message)	Low	Good for brief messages
Hard Copy (e.g., handwritten or typed message)	Asynchronous	Low	High	Low	High

Adapted from Adler, R. B., & Elmhorst, J. (2010). *Communicating at work: Principles and practices for business and the professions* (10th ed., p. 29). New York: McGraw-Hill.

it, "While a quick log-on may seem, to the user, a harmless break, others in the room receive it as a silent dismissal. It announces: 'I'm not interested'" (Bauerlein, 2009).

Chapter 7 has plenty to say about the challenges of listening effectively when you are multitasking. Even if you think you can understand others while dealing with communication media, it's important to realize that they may perceive you as being rude.

Keep Your Tone Civil If you've ever posted a snide comment on a blog, shot back a nasty reply to a text or instant message, or forwarded an embarrassing e-mail, you know that it's easier to behave badly when the recipient of your message isn't right in front of you.

The tendency to transmit messages without considering their consequences is called **disinhibition**, and research shows it is more likely in mediated channels than in face-to-face contact (Watts, 2007). Sometimes communicators take disinhibition to the extreme, blasting off angry—even vicious—e-mails, text messages, and blogs. The common term for these outbursts is *flaming*. In text-based forms of social media, flaming includes profanity, all capital letters, excessive exclamation points, and question marks (Turnage, 2007). Here is the account of one writer who was the target of an obscenity-filled e-mail:

> No one had ever said something like this to me before, and no one could have said this to me before: in any other medium, these words would be, literally, unspeakable. The guy couldn't have said this to me on the phone, because I would have hung up and not answered if the phone rang again, and he couldn't have said it to my face, because I wouldn't have let him finish. . . . I suppose the guy could have written me a nasty letter: he probably wouldn't have used the word "rectum," though, and he probably wouldn't have mailed the letter; he would have thought twice while he was addressing the envelope. But the nature of e-mail is that you don't think twice. You write and send. (Seabrook, 1994, p. 71)

In some online communities, flaming is part of the culture, and is a way to instruct or correct a member who has misstated facts or abused the group's rules. But in most contexts, it's hard to find a justification for flaming.

Flaming isn't the only type of mediated harassment. Ongoing "cyberbullying" has become a widespread phenomenon, often with dire consequences (Bauman, 2011). More than 4 in 10 teens report being the target of online harassment—and the problem is international in scope (Huang & Chou, 2010). Recipients of cyberbullying often feel helpless and scared, to such a degree that one report found they are eight times more likely to carry a weapon to school than other students. There are several reported cases in the United States where a victim of cyberbullying committed suicide (Ybarra & Mitchell, 2007), which is sobering in light of reports that 81 percent of cyberbullies admit their only reason for bullying is because "it's funny" (National Crime Prevention Council, 2007).

One way to behave better in asynchronous situations is to ask yourself a simple question before you send, post, or broadcast: Would you deliver the same message to the recipient in person? If your answer is no, then you might want to think before hitting the "enter" key.

Be Mindful of Bystanders If you spend even a little time in most public spaces, you're likely to encounter communicators whose use of technology interferes with others: Restaurant patrons whose phone voices intrude on your conversation, pedestrians who are more focused on their handheld device than on avoiding others, or people in line who are trying to pay the cashier and talk on their cell phone at the same time. If you aren't bothered by this sort of behavior, it can be hard to feel sympathetic with others who are offended by it. Nonetheless, this is another situation where the "platinum rule" applies: Consider treating others the way *they* would like to be treated.

Balance Mediated and Face Time Being connected 24/7 can steal time from in-person communication. But research confirms what commonsense suggests: "face time" is still important (Vitak et al., 2011).

Overuse of social media can range from slightly abnormal to borderline obsessive. It's tempting to use the term "addict" to describe someone who spends an unhealthy amount of time online. Whether or not the label is technically accurate, there's plenty of evidence that becoming hooked on the web can be harmful to emotional and relational health (Junghyun & Haridakis, 2008; Ko et al., 2005).

So what is the happy medium? There's no simple answer, but there are a couple of tests to keep in mind. If your loved ones hint—or directly tell you—that they would like more face time with you, it's probably wise to heed their request. And if you find that technological devices are subtracting from, rather than adding to, your interpersonal relationships, it might be time to monitor and limit your social media.

Summary

The growing diversity of American culture and the increased exposure to people from around the world make an understanding of intercultural communication essential.

When members of different cultures interact, their values can affect interaction in ways that may be felt but not understood. These values include an emphasis on high- or low-context communication, individualism or collectivism, high or low power distance, relatively more or less avoidance of uncertainty, and either achievement or nurturing.

The codes that are used by members of a culture are often the most recognizable factors that shape communication between people from different backgrounds. Verbal codes include language spoken and the worldview created by it, as well as verbal communication style. Nonverbal codes also differ significantly, as do the attributions that cultural conditioning generate.

Intercultural communicative competence involves four dimensions: motivation and attitude, tolerance for ambiguity, open-mindedness, and knowledge and skill.

Social media differ from the face-to-face variety in several noteworthy ways: They are typically less rich, often asynchronous, and can be permanent. Social media do pose risks for relationships; but when used mindfully, they can enhance them. This chapter offers several guidelines for using social media with due caution and consideration. Following them can help relational communication thrive, as well as increasing the effectiveness of one's identity management.

Key Terms

- Achievement culture (41)
- Asynchronous communication (53)
- Co-culture (31)
- Collectivistic culture (38)
- Culture (31)
- Disinhibition (59)
- Ethnocentrism (49)
- High-context culture (36)
- Individualistic culture (38)
- In-group (31)
- Intercultural communication (33)
- Low-context culture (36)
- Nurturing culture (41)
- Out-group (31)
- Power distance (39)
- Prejudice (50)
- Richness (52)
- Salience (33)
- Social identity (31)
- Social media (51)
- Synchronous communication (53)
- Uncertainty avoidance (40)

Activities

1. Invitation to Insight

What in-groups do you belong to? You can best answer this question by thinking about whom you regard as belonging to out-groups. Based on your observations, consider the criteria you use to define in- and out-groups. Do you rely on race? Ethnicity? Age? Lifestyle? How do your judgments about in- and out-group membership affect your communication with others?

2. Critical Thinking Probe

Identify one of your important interpersonal relationships. Consider how that relationship might be different if you and your partner adopted values and norms that were opposite from the ones you already hold. For example, if your communication is low context, how would things be different if you shifted to a high-context style? If you are tolerant of uncertainty, what might happen if you avoided any surprises? Based on your answers, consider the advantages and disadvantages of the cultural values and norms you hold. Think about the pros and cons of cultures that have differing values and norms.

3. Ethical Challenge

Some cultural differences seem charming. However, others might seem alien—even inhumane. Explore the question of whether there are (or should be) any universal norms of behavior by identifying what rights and practices, if any, should be prohibited or honored universally.

4. Skill Builder

Use the criteria on pages 48–51 to evaluate your intercultural communication competence. Identify one culture with which you currently interact or could interact with in the future. Collect information on communication rules and norms in that culture through library research and personal interviews. Based on your findings, describe the steps you can take to communicate more effectively with the culture's members.

5. Invitation to Insight

Send the same message to four friends, but use a different medium for each person. For example, ask the question "How's it going?" Use the following media:

- e-mail
- instant message
- text message
- telephone

Notice how each response differs and what that may say about the nature of the medium.

6. Invitation to Insight

Construct a diary of the ways you use social media in a 3-day period. For each instance when you use social media (e-mail, social networking website, phone, Twitter, etc.), describe

    a. The kind(s) of social media you use
    b. The nature of the communication (e.g., "Wrote on friend's Facebook wall," "Reminded roommate to pick up dinner on the way home")
    c. The reason you chose that medium for that particular message

Based on your observations, describe the types of media you use most often and why you chose them. Do you think some of your messages could have been more effective if you had used a different medium?

Communication and the Self

After studying the material in this chapter . . .

You should understand:

1. The subjective nature of the self-concept and the communicative influences that shape it.
2. How it is possible to change one's self-concept.
3. The nature and extent of identity management.
4. How and why we engage in self-disclosure, and its benefits and risks.
5. The alternatives to self-disclosure.

You should be able to:

1. Describe the influence others have had on shaping your self-concept and the influence you have had on others.
2. Explain the steps you can take to change undesirable elements of your self-concept.
3. Describe the differences between your perceived self and various presenting selves and outline the identity management strategies you use.
4. Explain how the social penetration and Johari Window models represent the level of self-disclosure in one of your relationships.
5. Outline the potential benefits and risks of disclosing in a selected situation.
6. Compose responses to a situation that reflect varying degrees of candor and equivocation.

Who are you? Before reading on, take a few minutes to try a simple experiment. First, make a list of the 10 words or phrases that describe the most important features of who you are. Some of the items on your list may involve social roles: student, son or daughter, employee, and so on. Or you could define yourself through physical characteristics: fat, skinny, tall, short, beautiful, ugly. You may focus on your intellectual characteristics: smart, stupid, curious, inquisitive. Perhaps you can best define yourself in terms of moods, feelings, or attitudes: optimistic, critical, energetic. Or you could consider your social characteristics: outgoing, shy, defensive. You may see yourself in terms of belief systems: pacifist, Christian, vegetarian, libertarian. Finally, you could focus on particular skills (or lack of them): swimmer, artist, carpenter. In any case, choose 10 words or phrases that best describe you, and write them down.

Next, choose the one item from your list that is the most fundamental to who you are and copy it on another sheet of paper. Then pick the second most fundamental item and record it as number two on your new list. Continue ranking the 10 items until you have reorganized them all.

Communication and the Self-Concept

The list you created in the exercise you just completed offers clues about your **self-concept**: the relatively stable set of perceptions you hold of yourself. One way to understand self-concept is to imagine a special mirror that not only reflects physical features, but also allows you to view other aspects of yourself—emotional states, talents, likes, dislikes, values, roles, and so on. The reflection in that mirror would be your self-concept.

Any description of your self-concept that you constructed in this exercise is only a partial one. To make it complete, you'd have to keep adding items until your list ran into hundreds of words. Of course, not every dimension of your self-concept list is equally important. For example, the most significant part of one person's self-concept might consist of social roles, whereas for another it might be physical appearance, health, friendships, accomplishments, or skills.

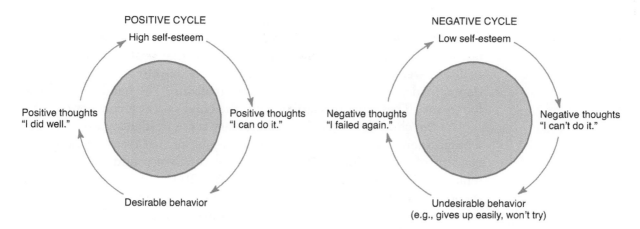

FIGURE 3.1 The Relationship between Self-Esteem and Communication Behavior

Adapted from Johnson, H. M. (1998). *How do I love me?* (3rd ed.). Salem, WI: Sheffield, pp. 3, 5.

Self-esteem is the part of the self-concept that involves evaluations of self-worth. A communicator's self-concept might include being quiet, argumentative, or serious. His or her self-esteem would be determined by how he or she feels about these qualities.

High or low self-esteem has a powerful effect on communication behavior, as Figure 3.1 shows. People who feel good about themselves have positive expectations about how they will communicate (Baldwin & Keelan, 1999). These feelings increase the chance that communication will be successful, and successes contribute to positive self-evaluations, which reinforce self-esteem. Of course, the same principle can work in a negative way with communicators who have low self-esteem.

Although high self-esteem has obvious benefits, it doesn't guarantee interpersonal success (Baumeister, 2005; Baumeister et al., 2003). People with high levels of self-esteem may *think* they make better impressions on others and have better friendships and romantic lives, but neither impartial observers nor objective tests verify these beliefs. It's easy to see how people with an inflated sense of self-worth could irritate others by coming across as condescending know-it-alls, especially when their self-worth is challenged (vanDellen et al., 2010; Vohs & Heatherton, 2004). Moreover, people with low self-esteem have the potential to change their self-appraisals (more on that later in this chapter). The point here is that positive self-evaluations can often be the starting point for positive communication with others.

HOW THE SELF-CONCEPT DEVELOPS

Researchers generally agree that the self-concept does not exist at birth (Rochat, 2001). An infant lying in a crib has no notion of self, no notion—even if verbal language were miraculously made available—of how to answer the question "Who am I?" At about 6 or 7 months, the child begins to recognize "self" as distinct from surroundings. If you've ever watched children at this age, you've probably marveled at how they can stare with great fascination at a foot, hand, and other body parts that float into view, almost as if they were strange objects belonging to someone else. Then the connection is made, almost as if the child were realizing "The hand is me," "The foot is me." These first revelations form the child's earliest concept of self.

As the child develops, this rudimentary sense of identity expands into a much more complete and sophisticated picture that resembles the self-concept of adults. This evolution is almost totally a product of social interaction (Schmidt, 2006; Weigert & Gecas, 2003). Two complementary theories describe how interaction shapes the way individuals view themselves: reflected appraisal and social comparison (Burkitt, 1992; Sedikides & Skowronski, 1995).

Reflected Appraisal Before reading on, try the following exercise: Either by yourself or aloud with a partner, recall someone you know or once knew who helped enhance your self-concept by acting in a way that made you feel accepted, worthwhile, important, appreciated, or loved. This person needn't have played a crucial role in your life, as long as the role was positive. Often one's self-concept is shaped by many tiny nudges as well as a few giant shoves. For instance, you might recall a childhood neighbor who took a special interest in you or a grandparent who never criticized or questioned your youthful foolishness.

After thinking about this supportive person, recall someone who acted in either a big or small way to diminish your self-esteem. For instance, you may have had a coach who criticized you in front of the team, or a teacher who said or implied that you wouldn't amount to much.

F⊕CUS ON RESEARCH

Body Image and the Pressure to Be Perfect

It's the rare viewer who hasn't felt at least a little inadequate after seeing the handsome faces and sculpted bodies that populate so many films, TV shows, and advertisements. But not everyone is affected to the same degree by images of unattainable beauty. Communication researcher Pavica Sheldon wanted to know why some college students are particularly susceptible to media comparisons that result in negative self-appraisals.

Sheldon found that mere exposure to media doesn't reduce self-esteem. Rather, perfectionistic tendencies and negative social comparisons are often triggered by messages from family and friends. Students who suffered the most from comparing themselves to media images answered affirmatively to survey items such as "I have noticed a strong message from my friends to have a thin body," and "I've felt pressure from my family to lose weight."

These findings show how interpersonal messages play a vital role in social comparison. Our self-evaluations are often based on standards that have been communicated to us by significant others.

Sheldon, P. (2010). Pressure to be perfect: Influences on college students' body esteem. *Southern Communication Journal, 75,* 277-298.

After thinking about these two types of people, you should begin to see that everyone's self-concept is to some degree a **reflected appraisal**: a mirroring of the judgments of those around her or him. To the extent that you have received supportive messages, you have learned to appreciate and value yourself. To the degree that you have received critical signals, you are likely to feel less valuable, lovable, and capable (Felson, 1985; Jaret et al., 2005). Your self-concept can be seen, at least in part, as a reflection of the messages you've received throughout your life.

Social scientists use the term **significant other** to describe a person whose evaluations are especially influential. Messages from parents, of course, are an early and important influence on the self-concept. Supportive parents are more likely to raise children with healthy self-concepts. By contrast, parents with poor, negative, or deviant self-concepts tend to have unhappy children who view themselves in primarily negative ways (Fitts, 1971; Salimi et al., 2005), communicate less effectively (Huang, 1999), and go on to have unsatisfying relationships (Vangelisti & Crumley, 1998). Interestingly, if one parent has a good self-concept and the other a poor self-concept, the child is most likely to choose the parent with the more positive self-concept as a model. If neither parent has a strong self-concept, the child may seek an adult outside the family with whom to identify.

Along with family, the messages from many other significant others shape our self-concept (Hergovitch et al., 2002). A teacher from long ago, a special friend or relative, someone you dated, or even a barely known acquaintance whom you respected can all leave an imprint on how you view yourself—sometimes for better, sometimes for worse (Rill et al., 2009).

As we grow older, the power of messages from significant others remains (Voss et al., 1999). Some social scientists have coined the phrase "Michelangelo phenomenon" to describe the way significant others sculpt one another's self-concepts (Righetti et al., 2010; Rusbult et al., 2009). Romantic partners, people on the job, friends, and many others can speak and act in ways that have a profound effect on the way we view ourselves.

You might argue that not every part of your self-concept is shaped by others, that there are certain objective facts recognizable by self-observation alone. After all, nobody needs to tell you whether you are taller than others, speak with an accent, have curly hair, and so on. Indeed, some features of the self are immediately apparent. But the *significance* we attach to them—that is, the rank we assign them in the hierarchy of our list and the interpretation we give them—depends greatly on the opinions of others.

Social Comparison So far, we have looked at the way others' messages shape the self-concept. In addition to using these messages, we form our self-image by the process of **social comparison**: evaluating ourselves in terms of how we compare with others (Johnson & Stapel, 2010). We decide whether we are superior or inferior and similar or different by comparing ourselves to what social scientists call **reference groups**—those people we use to evaluate our own characteristics. You might feel ordinary or inferior in terms of talent, friendships, or attractiveness if you compare yourself with an inappropriate reference group (Pahl & Eiser, 2007). For instance, studies have

shown that young women who regularly compare themselves with ultra-thin media models develop negative appraisals of their own bodies, in some cases leading to eating disorders (Harrison & Hefner, 2006; Krcmar et al., 2008). Men, too, who compare themselves to media-idealized male physiques, evaluate their bodies negatively (Strong, 2005). People also use others' online profiles as points of comparison, and they may feel less attractive and successful after doing so (Haferkamp & Kramer, 2010). Even popular TV makeover shows—with their underlying message of "you must improve your appearance"—can lead viewers to view themselves negatively (Kubic & Chory, 2007).

To some degree, we're in control of whom we choose for comparison. It's possible to seek out people with whom we compare favorably. This technique may bring to mind a search for a community of idiots in which you would appear as a genius, but there are healthier ways of changing your standards for comparison. For instance, you might decide that it's foolish to constantly compare your athletic prowess with professionals or campus stars, your looks with movie idols, and your intelligence with members of Phi Beta Kappa. Once you place yourself alongside a truly representative sample, your self-concept may become more realistic.

CHARACTERISTICS OF THE SELF-CONCEPT

Now that you have a better idea of how your self-concept has developed, we can take a closer look at some of its characteristics.

The Self-Concept Is Subjective The way we view ourselves may be at odds with others' perceptions—and often with the observable facts. For instance, people are notoriously bad judges of their own communication skills. In one study, there was no relationship between the subjects' self-evaluations as interpersonal communicators, public speakers, or listeners and their observed ability to perform well in any of these areas (Carrell & Willmington, 1996). In another study (Myers, 1980), a random sample of men was asked to rank themselves on their ability to get along with others. Defying mathematical laws, all subjects—every last one—put themselves in the top half of the population. Sixty percent rated themselves in the top 10 percent of the population, and an amazing 25 percent believed they were in the top 1 percent. The men had similarly lofty appraisals of their leadership and athletic abilities. Other research shows that these perceptions of superiority tend to increase over time (Kanten & Teigen, 2008).

There are several reasons why some people have a level of self-esteem that others would regard as unrealistically favorable. First, a self-estimation might be based on obsolete information. Perhaps your jokes used to be well received, or your grades were high, or your work was superior, but now the facts have changed. Self-esteem might also be excessively favorable due to distorted feedback from others. A boss may claim to be an excellent manager because assistants pour on false praise in order to keep their jobs. A child's inflated ego may be based on the praise of doting parents. A third reason is that we may simply ignore our negative qualities. One study found that online daters often have a "foggy mirror"—that is, they see themselves more positively than others do (Ellison et al., 2006). This leads to inflated self-descriptions that don't always match what an objective third party might say about them.

There are also times when we view ourselves more harshly than the facts warrant. We have all experienced a temporary case of the "uglies," convinced we look much worse than others say that we really appear. Research confirms what common sense suggests—people are more critical of themselves when they are experiencing these negative moods than when they are feeling more positive (Sturman & Mongrain, 2008), and may even feel they don't deserve good things to happen to them (Wood et al., 2009). While everyone suffers occasional bouts of low self-esteem, some people suffer from long-term or even permanent states of excessive self-doubt and criticism (Gara et al., 1993). It's easy to understand how this chronic condition can influence the way these people approach and respond to others.

What are the reasons for such excessively negative self-evaluations? As with unrealistically high self-esteem, one source for an overabundance of self-put-downs is obsolete information. A string of past failures in school or with social relations can linger to haunt a communicator long after they have occurred. Similarly, we've known slender students who still think of themselves as fat, and clear-complexioned people who still behave as if they were acne ridden.

Distorted feedback also can lead to low self-esteem. Growing up in an overly critical family is one of the most common causes of a negative self-image. In other cases, the remarks of cruel friends, uncaring teachers, excessively demanding employers, or even memorable strangers can have a lasting effect. As you read earlier, the impact of significant others and reference groups in forming a self-concept can be great, and their effect on your self-esteem can be just as great.

Along with obsolete information and distorted feedback, another cause for low self-esteem is the myth of perfection that is common in our society.

From the time most of us learn to understand language, we are exposed to fairy-tale models who appear to be perfect at whatever they do. Unfortunately, many parents perpetuate the myth of perfection by refusing to admit that they are ever mistaken or unfair. Children, of course, accept this perfectionist façade for a long time, not being in a position to dispute the wisdom of such powerful beings. From the behavior of the adults around them comes the clear message: "A well-adjusted, successful person has no faults." We'll have a great deal to say about perfection and other irrational ideas, both later in this chapter and in Chapter 8.

A final reason people often sell themselves short is also connected to social expectations. Curiously, the perfectionist society to which we belong rewards those people who downplay the strengths we demand they possess (or pretend to possess). We term these people "modest" and find their behavior agreeable. On the other hand, we consider some of those who honestly appreciate their own strengths to be "braggarts" or "egotists," confusing them with the people who boast about accomplishments they do not possess (Miller et al., 1992). This convention leads most of us to talk freely about our shortcomings while downplaying our accomplishments. It's all right to proclaim that you're miserable if you have failed to do well on a project, but it's seen as boastful to express your pride at a job well done.

A Healthy Self-Concept Is Flexible People change. From moment to moment, we aren't the same. We wake up in the morning in a jovial mood and turn grumpy before lunch. We find ourselves fascinated by a conversational topic one moment, then suddenly lose interest. You might be a relaxed conversationalist with people you know but at a loss for words with strangers. The self-concepts of most communicators react to these changes ("I'm patient at work," "I'm not patient at home"), and these changes affect self-esteem ("I'm not as good a person at home as I am in the office").

As we change in these and many other ways, our self-concept must also change in order to stay realistic. An accurate self-portrait today would not be exactly the same as the one we had a year ago, a few months ago, or even yesterday. This does not mean that you change radically from day to day. The fundamental characteristics of your personality will stay the same for years, perhaps for a lifetime. After the age of 30, most people's self-concept doesn't change radically, at least not without a conscious effort, such as psychotherapy (Klimstra et al. 2010; Updegraff et al., 2010). However, it is likely that in important ways you are changing—physically, intellectually, emotionally, and spiritually.

The Self-Concept Resists Change A realistic self-concept should reflect the way we change over time, but the tendency to resist revision of our self-perception is strong. Once a communicator fastens onto a self-concept, the tendency is to seek out people who confirm it. Numerous studies (e.g., Stets & Cast, 2007; Swann et al., 2003) have shown that both college students and married couples with high self-esteem seek out partners who view them favorably, while those with low self-esteem are more inclined to interact with people who view them unfavorably. This tendency to seek information that conforms to an existing self-concept has been labeled **cognitive conservatism** (Greenwald, 1995; Kihlstrom & Klein, 1994).

We are understandably reluctant to revise a favorable self-concept. If you were a thoughtful, romantic partner early in a relationship, it would be hard to admit that you might have become less considerate and attentive lately. Likewise, if you used to be a serious student, acknowledging that you have slacked off isn't easy.

Curiously, the tendency to cling to an outmoded self-perception holds even when the new image would be more favorable. We can recall scores of attractive, intelligent students who still view themselves as the gawky underachievers they were in the past. The tragedy of this sort of cognitive conservatism is obvious. People with unnecessarily negative self-esteem can become their own worst enemies, denying themselves the validation they deserve and need to enjoy satisfying relationships.

Once the self-concept is firmly rooted, only a powerful force can change it. At least four requirements must be met for an appraisal to be regarded as important (Bergner & Holmes, 2000; Dehart et al, 2010; Gergen, 1971).

■ The person who offers a particular appraisal must be *someone we see as competent to offer it*. Parents satisfy this requirement extremely well because as young children we perceive that our parents know so much about us—sometimes more than we know about ourselves.

■ *The appraisal must be perceived as highly personal.* The more the other person seems to know about us and adapts what is being said to fit us, the more likely we are to accept judgments from this person.

■ The appraisal must be *reasonable in light of what we believe about ourselves*. If an appraisal is similar to one we give ourselves, we will believe it; if it is somewhat dissimilar, we will probably still accept it; but if it is completely dissimilar, we will probably reject it.

■ Appraisals that are *consistent* and *numerous* are more persuasive than those that contradict usual appraisals or those that occur only once. As long as only a *few* students yawn in class, a teacher can safely disregard them as a reflection on his or her teaching ability. In like manner, you could safely disregard the appraisal of the angry date who tells you in no uncertain terms what kind of person behaves as you did. Of course, when you get a second or third similar appraisal in a short time, the evaluation becomes harder to ignore.

THE SELF-FULFILLING PROPHECY AND COMMUNICATION

Self-concept is such a powerful influence on the personality that it not only determines how you see yourself in the present but also can actually affect your future behavior and that of others. Such occurrences come about through a phenomenon called the self-fulfilling prophecy.

73

A **self-fulfilling prophecy** occurs when a person's expectations of an event, and her or his subsequent behavior based on those expectations, make the outcome more likely to occur than would otherwise have been true (Snyder & Klein, 2005; Watzlawick, 2005). A self-fulfilling prophecy involves four stages:

1. Holding an expectation (for yourself or for others)

2. Behaving in accordance with that expectation

3. The expectation coming to pass

4. Reinforcing the original expectation

Let's use a slightly exaggerated example to illustrate the concept. One morning you read your horoscope, which offers the following prediction: "Today you will meet the person of your dreams, and the two of you will live happily ever after." Assuming you believe in horoscopes, what will you do? You'll probably start making plans to go out on the town that night in search of your "dream person." You'll dress up, groom yourself well, and carefully evaluate every person you encounter. You'll also be attentive, charming, witty, polite, and gracious when you end up meeting your "dream candidate." As a result, that person is likely to be impressed and attracted to you—and lo and behold, the two of you end up living happily ever after. Your conclusion? That horoscope sure had it right!

Upon closer examination, the horoscope—which helped create the Stage 1 expectation—really wasn't the key to your success. While it got the ball rolling, you would still be single if you had stayed home that evening. Stage 2—going out on the town and acting charming—was what led your "dream person" to be attracted to you, bringing about the positive results (Stage 3). While it's tempting to credit the horoscope for the outcome (Stage 4), it's important to realize that *you* were responsible for bringing the prediction to pass—hence the term *self-fulfilling* prophecy.

The horoscope story is fictional, but research shows that self-fulfilling prophecies operate in real-life situations. To see how, read on.

Types of Self-Fulfilling Prophecies There are two types of self-fulfilling prophecies. Self-imposed prophecies occur when your own expectations influence your behavior. You've probably had the experience of waking up in a cross mood and saying to yourself, "This will be a bad day." Once you made such a decision, you may have acted in ways that

"I don't sing because I am happy. I am happy because I sing."

74

made it come true. If you avoid the company of others because you expect they had nothing to offer, your suspicions would have been confirmed—nothing exciting or new is likely to happen. On the other hand, if you approach the same day with the idea that it could be a good one, this expectation may well be met. Smile at people, and they're more likely to smile back. Enter a class determined to learn something, and you probably will—even if it's how not to instruct students! In these cases and other similar ones, your attitude has a great deal to do with what you see and how you behave.

Research has demonstrated the power of self-imposed prophecies. In one study, communicators who believed they were incompetent proved less likely than others to pursue rewarding relationships and more likely to sabotage their existing relationships than did people who were less critical of themselves (Kolligan, 1990). Research also suggests that communicators who feel anxious about giving speeches seem to create self-fulfilling prophecies about doing poorly, which causes them to perform less effectively (MacIntyre & Thivierge, 1995). On the other hand, students who perceive themselves as capable achieve more academically (Zimmerman, 1995).

A second category of self-fulfilling prophecies occurs when one person's expectations govern another's actions (Blank, 1993)—whether those expectations are positive (the Pygmalion effect) or negative (the Golem effect; Jussim et al., 2009; Reynolds, 2007). The classic example was demonstrated by Robert Rosenthal and Lenore Jacobson (1968) in a study they described in their book *Pygmalion in the Classroom*. The experimenters told teachers that 20 percent of the children in a certain elementary school showed unusual potential for intellectual growth. The names of the 20 percent were drawn by means of a table of random numbers—much as if they were drawn out of a hat. Eight months later these unusual or "magic" children showed significantly greater gains in IQ than did the remaining children, who had not been singled out for the teachers' attention. The change in the teachers' behavior toward these allegedly "special" children led to changes in their intellectual performance. Among other things, the

meDIa CLIP   MEASURING UP (OR DOWN): *SHE'S OUT OF MY LEAGUE*

Kirk (Jay Baruchel) is just an average, ordinary guy, according to his own estimation and the appraisals of others. By chance, he meets and gets to know Molly (Alice Eve), who is regarded as a perfect "10" by all who behold her physical beauty. As Kirk considers pursuing a romantic relationship with Molly, he gets warned repeatedly that he's venturing "out of his league."

The movie illustrates many of the concepts discussed in this chapter. Reflected appraisals and social comparisons are in evidence in Kirk's conversations with his buddies. In one memorable scene, the guys rank each other's attractiveness on a 1–10 scale (they determine Kirk is a 5). And Kirk's relatively low self-esteem, especially when it comes to dating women, turns into a self-fulfilling prophecy. His lack of confidence leads him to engage in awkward behaviors that, while humorous for the audience, threaten to sabotage the goal he's pursuing.

The fact that our culture uses attractiveness rating scales and talks about "leagues" makes it clear that how we see ourselves is strongly influenced by the appraisals of, and comparisons with, significant others in our lives.

teachers gave the "smart" students more time to answer questions, and provided more feedback to them. These children did better not because they were any more intelligent than their classmates, but because their teachers—significant others—communicated the expectation that they could.

Notice that it isn't just the observer's *belief* that creates a self-fulfilling prophecy for the person who is the target of the expectations. The observer must *communicate that belief* verbally or nonverbally in order for the prediction to have any effect. If parents have faith in their children but the kids aren't aware of that confidence, they won't be affected by their parents' expectations. If a boss has concerns about an employee's ability to do a job but keeps those worries to herself, the subordinate won't be influenced. In this sense, the self-fulfilling prophecies imposed by one person on another are as much a communication phenomenon as a psychological one.

CHANGING YOUR SELF-CONCEPT

You've probably begun to realize that it is possible to change an unsatisfying self-concept. In the next sections we discuss some methods for accomplishing such a change.

Have Realistic Expectations It's important to realize that some of your dissatisfaction might come from expecting too much of yourself. Nobody is able to handle every conflict productively, to be totally relaxed and skillful in conversations, to ask perceptive questions all the time, or to be 100 percent helpful when others have problems. Expecting yourself to reach such unrealistic goals is to doom yourself to unhappiness at the start.

It's important to judge yourself in terms of your own growth and not against the behavior of others. Rather than feeling miserable because you're not as talented as an expert, realize that you probably are a better, wiser, or more skillful person than you used to be and that this growth is a legitimate source of satisfaction. Perfection is fine as an ideal, but you're being unfair to yourself if you actually expect to reach it.

Have a Realistic Perception of Yourself One source of low self-esteem is inaccurate self-perception. As you've already read, such unrealistic pictures

sometimes come from being overly harsh on yourself, believing that you're worse than the facts indicate. Of course, it would be foolish to deny that you could be a better person than you are, but it's also important to recognize your strengths. A periodic session of "bragging"—acknowledging the parts of yourself with which you're pleased and the ways you've grown—is often a good way to put your strengths and shortcomings into perspective.

Unrealistically low self-esteem also can come from the inaccurate feedback of others. Workers with overly critical supervisors, children with cruel "friends," and students with unsupportive teachers are all prone to suffer from low self-esteem due to excessively negative feedback. If you fall into this category, it's important to seek out supportive people who will acknowledge your assets as well as point out your shortcomings. Doing so is often a quick and sure boost to your self-esteem.

Have the Will to Change Often we say we want to change but aren't willing to do the necessary work. In such cases the responsibility for not growing rests squarely on your shoulders. At other times we maintain an unrealistic self-concept by claiming that we "can't" be the person we'd like to be, when in fact we're simply not willing to do what's required (we'll discuss the fallacy of helplessness and ridding yourself of "can't" statements in Chapter 8). You can change in many ways, but only if you are willing to put out the effort.

Have the Skill to Change Trying is often not enough. There are times when you would change if you knew how to do so.

First, you can seek advice—from books such as this one and other printed sources. You also can get advice from instructors, counselors, and other experts, as well as from friends. Of course, not all the advice you receive will be useful, but if you read widely and talk to enough people, you have a good chance of learning the things you want to know.

A second method of learning how to change is to observe models—people who handle themselves in the ways you would like to master. It's often been said that people learn more from models than in any other way, and by taking advantage of this principle you will find that the world is full of teachers who can show you how to communicate more successfully. Become a careful observer. Watch what people you admire do and say, not so you can copy them but so you can adapt their behavior to fit your own personal style.

At this point you might be overwhelmed by the difficulty of changing the way you think about yourself and the way you act. Remember, we never said that this process would be easy (although it sometimes is). But even when change is difficult, it's possible if you are serious. You don't need to be perfect, but you *can* change your self-concept and raise your self-esteem, and, as a result, your communication—*if you choose to.*

Presenting the Self: Communication as Identity Management

So far, we've described how communication shapes the way communicators view themselves. We will now turn the tables and focus on the topic of **identity management**—the communication strategies people use to influence how others view them. In the following pages you will see that many of our messages are aimed at creating desired impressions.

PUBLIC AND PRIVATE SELVES

To understand why identity management exists, we have to discuss the notion of self in more detail. So far, we have referred to the "self" as if each of us had only one identity. In truth, each of us possesses several selves, some private and others public (Fenigstein, 2009). These selves are often quite different.

The **perceived self** is the person you believe yourself to be in moments of honest self-examination. The perceived self may not be accurate in every respect. For example, you might think you are much more (or less) intelligent than an objective test would measure. Accurate or not, the perceived self is powerful because we believe it reflects who we are. We can call the perceived self "private" because you are unlikely to reveal all of it to another person. You can verify the private nature of the perceived self by thinking of elements of your self-perception that you would not disclose. For example, you might be reluctant to share some feelings about your appearance ("I think I'm rather unattractive"), your goals ("The most important thing to me is becoming rich"), or your motives ("I care more about myself than about others").

In contrast to the perceived self, the **presenting self** is a public image—the way we want to appear to others. In most cases the presenting self we seek to create is a socially approved image: diligent student, loving partner, conscientious worker, loyal friend, and so on. Sociologist Erving Goffman (1959, 1971) used the word **face** to describe this socially approved identity, and he coined the term **facework** to describe the verbal and nonverbal ways in which we act to maintain our own presenting image and the images of others. He argued that each of us can be viewed as a kind of playwright who creates roles that we want others to believe, as well as the performer who acts out those roles.

Goffman suggested that each of us maintains face by putting on a *front* when we are around others whom we want to impress. In contrast, behavior in the *back region*—when we are alone—may be quite different. You can recognize the difference between front and backstage behavior by recalling a time when you observed a driver, alone in her or his car, behaving in ways that would never be acceptable in public. All of us engage in backstage ways of acting that we would never exhibit in front of others. Just recall how you behave in front of the bathroom mirror when the door is locked, and you will appreciate the difference between public and private behavior. If you knew someone was watching, would you behave differently?

CHARACTERISTICS OF IDENTITY MANAGEMENT

Now that you have a sense of what identity management is, we can look at some characteristics of this process (Locher, 2010).

We Strive to Construct Multiple Identities It is an oversimplification to suggest we use identity management strategies to create just one identity. In the course of even a single day, most people play a variety of roles: "respectful student," "joking friend," "friendly neighbor," and "helpful worker," to suggest just a few. We even play a variety of roles around the same person. As you grew up, you almost certainly changed characters as you interacted with your parents. In one context you acted as the responsible adult ("You can trust me with the car!") and at another time you were the helpless child ("I can't find my socks!"). At some times—perhaps on birthdays or holidays—you were a dedicated family member, and at other times you may have played the role of rebel. Likewise, in romantic relationships we switch among many ways of behaving, depending on the context: friend, lover, business partner, scolding critic, apologetic child, and so on. Each of us constructs multiple identities, many of which may be independent of each other, and some of which may even conflict with one another (Spears, 2001). For example, some student-athletes experience tension when the roles of student and athlete seem to have incompatible demands (Yopyk & Prentice, 2005).

Identity Management Is Collaborative As we perform like actors trying to create a front, our "audience" is made up of other actors who are trying to create their own characters. Identity-related communication is a kind of process theater in which we improvise scenes where our character reacts with others. Good-natured teasing only works if the other person appreciates your humor and responds well. (Imagine how your kidding would fall flat if somebody didn't get or enjoy the joking.) Likewise, being a successful romantic can only succeed if the object of your affections plays his or her part.

Identity Management Can Be Deliberate or Unconscious There's no doubt that sometimes we are highly aware of managing impressions. Most job interviews and first dates are clear examples of deliberate identity management. But in other cases we unconsciously act in ways that are really small public performances. For example, experimental participants expressed facial disgust in reaction to eating sandwiches laced with a supersaturated solution of saltwater only when there was another person present; when they were alone, they made no faces upon eating the same snack (Brightman et al., 1975). Another study showed that communicators engage in facial mimicry (such as smiling or looking sympathetic in response to another's message) only in face-to-face settings, when their expressions can be seen by the other person. When they are speaking over the phone and their reactions cannot be seen, they do not make the same expressions (Chovil, 1991). Studies like these suggest that most of our behavior is aimed at sending messages to others—in other words, identity management.

Despite the claims of some theorists, it seems an exaggeration to suggest that *all* behavior is aimed at making impressions. Young children certainly aren't strategic communicators. A baby spontaneously laughs when pleased and cries when sad or uncomfortable, without any notion of creating an impression in others. Likewise, there are almost certainly times when we, as adults, act spontaneously. But when a significant other questions the presenting self we try to portray, the likelihood of acting to prop it up increases.

People Differ in Their Degree of Identity Management As you read in Chapter 1, some people are much more aware of their identity management behavior than others. There are certainly advantages to being a high self-monitor (Hamachek, 1992). People who pay attention to themselves are generally good "people-readers" who can adjust their behavior to get the desired reaction from others. Also, high self-monitors are more likely than low self-monitors to cope by seeking the help of others (Büyükşahin, 2009). Along with the advantages, there are some potential drawbacks to being an extremely high self-monitor (Wright et al., 2007). Their analytical nature may prevent them from experiencing events completely, since a portion of their attention will always be viewing the situation from a detached position. High self-monitors' ability to act makes it difficult to tell how they are really feeling. In fact, because high self-monitors change roles often, they may have a hard time knowing *themselves* how they really feel.

By now it should be clear that neither extremely high nor low self-monitoring is the ideal. There are some situations when paying attention to yourself and adapting your behavior can be useful, and other times when reacting without considering the effect on others is a better approach. This need for a range of behaviors demonstrates once again the notion of communicative competence outlined in Chapter 1—flexibility is the key to successful relationships.

WHY MANAGE IMPRESSIONS?

Why bother trying to shape others' opinions? Sometimes we create and maintain a front to follow *social rules*. As children we learn to act politely, even when bored. Likewise, part of growing up consists of developing a set of manners for various occasions, such as meeting strangers, attending school, and going to church. Young children who haven't learned all the dos and don'ts of polite society often embarrass their parents by behaving inappropriately ("Mommy, why is that man so fat?"), but by the time they enter school, behavior that might have been excusable or even amusing just isn't acceptable. Good manners are often aimed at making others more comfortable. For example, able-bodied people often mask their discomfort upon encountering someone who is disabled by acting nonchalant or stressing similarities between themselves and the disabled person (Coleman & DePaulo, 1991).

Social rules govern our behavior in a variety of settings. For example, it would be impossible to keep a job without meeting certain expectations. Salespeople are supposed to treat customers with courtesy. Employees need to appear reasonably respectful when talking to the boss. Some forms of clothing would be considered outrageous at work. By agreeing to take on a job, you are signing an unwritten contract that dictates you will present a certain face at work, whether or not that face reflects the way you might be feeling at a particular moment.

Even when social rules don't dictate the proper way to behave, we often manage impressions for a second reason: to accomplish *personal goals*. You might, for example, dress up for

AT WORK

Identity Management in the Workplace

Some advisors encourage workers to "Just be yourself" on the job. But there are times when disclosing certain information about your personal life can damage your chances for success (Fleming & Sturdy, 2009). This is especially true for people with "invisible stigmas"—traits that run the risk of being viewed unfavorably (Ragins, 2008).

Many parts of a worker's identity have the potential to be invisible stigmas: Religion (evangelical Christian, Muslim), sexual orientation (gay, lesbian, bisexual), health (bipolar, HIV positive). What counts as a stigma to some people (liberal, conservative) might be favored in another organization (Ragins & Singh, 2007).

As you consider how to manage your identity at work, take the following into account:

- Proceed with caution. In an ideal world, it would be safe to reveal ourselves without hesitation. But in real life, total candor can have consequences, so it may be best to move slowly.

- Assess the organization's culture. If your workplace seems supportive of differences—and especially if it appears to welcome people like you—then revealing more of yourself may be safe.

- Consider the consequences of not opening up. Keeping an important part of your identity secret can also take an emotional toll (Pachankis, 2007). If staying quiet is truly necessary, you may be better off finding a more welcoming place to work.

- Test the waters. If you have a trusted colleague or manager, think about revealing yourself to that person and asking advice about whether and how to go further. But realize that secrets can be leaked, so be sure the person you approach can keep confidences.

a visit to traffic court in the hope that your front (responsible citizen) will convince the judge to treat you sympathetically. You might be sociable to your neighbors so they will agree to your request that they keep their dog off your lawn. To achieve success in some organizations, gay and lesbian employees may manage their sexual identity three different ways (Button, 2004): create a false heterosexual identity, avoid the issue of sexuality altogether, or integrate a gay or lesbian identity into the work context. In cases like these, personal goals may influence how professional impressions are managed. (See the At Work sidebar on this page for more on this.)

Identity management sometimes aims at achieving *relational goals*. For instance, you might act more friendly and lively than you feel upon meeting a new person so that you will appear likable. You might smile and preen to show the attractive stranger at a party that you would like to get better acquainted. In situations like these, you aren't being deceptive as much as "putting your best foot forward."

All these examples show that it is difficult—perhaps even impossible—*not* to create impressions. After all, you have to send some sort of message. If you don't act friendly when meeting a stranger, you have to act aloof, indifferent, hostile, or in some other manner. If you don't act businesslike, you have to behave in an alternative way: casual, goofy, or whatever. Often the question isn't whether or not to present a face to others; it's only which face to present.

HOW DO WE MANAGE IMPRESSIONS?

How do we create a public face? In an age in which technology provides many options for communicating, the answer depends in part on the communication channel chosen.

Face-to-Face Identity Management In face-to-face interaction, communicators can manage their front in three ways: manner, appearance, and setting. *Manner* consists of a communicator's words and nonverbal actions. Chapters 5 and 6 will describe in detail how what you say and do creates impressions. Since you have to speak and act, the question isn't whether your manner sends a message; rather, it's whether these messages will be intentional.

A second dimension of identity management is *appearance*—the personal items people use to shape an image. Sometimes clothing is part of creating a professional image. A physician's white lab coat and a police officer's uniform set the wearer apart as someone special. In the business world, a tailored suit creates a very different impression than a rumpled outfit. Off the job, clothing is just as important. We choose clothing that sends a message about ourselves: "I'm stylish," "I'm sexy," "I'm athletic," and a host of other possible messages.

A final way to manage impressions is through the choice of *setting*—physical items we use to influence how others view us. In modern Western society, the car is a major part of identity management. This explains why many people lust after cars that are far more expensive and powerful than they really need. A sporty convertible or fancy imported sedan doesn't just get drivers from one place to another; it also makes statements about the kind of people they are. The physical setting we choose and the way we arrange it is another important way to manage impressions. What colors do you choose for the place you live? What artwork is on your walls? What music do you play? If possible, we choose a setting that we enjoy, but in many cases we create an environment that will present the desired front to others. Even the cell phone brand we use and the ringtones we choose communicate something about us (Lobet-Maris, 2003)—which leads to the next topic.

Identity Management in Social Media Most of the preceding examples involve face-to-face interaction, but identity management is just as pervasive and important in other types of communication. At first glance, social media seem to limit the potential for identity management. Instant messaging and e-mail, for example, appear to lack the "richness" of other channels. They don't convey the tone of your voice, postures, gestures, or facial expressions. Recently, though, communication scholars have begun to recognize that what is missing in mediated messages can actually be an advantage for communicators who want to manage the impressions they make (Hancock & Dunham, 2001). John Suler (2002, p. 455) puts it this way:

> One of the interesting things about the Internet is the opportunity it offers people to present themselves in a variety of different ways. You can alter your style of being just slightly or indulge in wild experiments with your identity by changing your age, history, personality, and physical appearance, even your gender. The username you choose, the details you do or don't indicate about yourself, the information presented on your personal web page, the persona or avatar you assume in an online community—all are important aspects of how people manage their identity in cyberspace.

E-mailers and instant messengers can choose the desired level of clarity or ambiguity, seriousness or humor, logic or emotion. Unlike face-to-face communication, electronic correspondence allows a sender to say difficult things without forcing the receiver to respond immediately, and it permits the receiver to ignore a message rather than give an unpleasant response. Options like these show that social media can serve as a tool for identity management at least as well as the face-to-face variety (Renner & Schütz, 2008; Suler, 2002; Tong & Walther, 2011b).

Like other forms of online communication, "broadcasting" on the Internet is also a tool for managing one's identity. Blogs, personal web pages, and profiles on social networking websites such as Facebook and MySpace all provide opportunities for their creators to manage their identities (Mehdizadeh, 2010; Salimkhan et al., 2010). Consider how featuring or withholding the following kinds of information affects how others might regard your online profile: age, personal photo, educational or career accomplishments, sexual orientation, job title, personal interests, personal philosophy and religious beliefs, and organizations to which you belong. You can easily think of a host of other kinds of material that could be included or excluded, and the effect that each would have on how others regard you.

Viewing your online presence as a neutral third party can be a valuable identity management exercise. Enter your name in a search engine and see what pops up. You may decide it's time to engage in what researchers call "reputation management" (Madden & Smith, 2010). "Search engines and social media sites now play a central role in building one's identity online," says Pew Internet researcher Mary Madden. "Many users are changing privacy settings on profiles, customizing who can see certain updates and deleting unwanted information about them that appears online."

"I loved your E-mail, but I thought you'd be older."

IDENTITY MANAGEMENT AND HONESTY

At first, identity management might sound like an academic label for manipulation or phoniness. There certainly are situations where people misrepresent themselves to gain the trust of others (Buller & Burgoon, 1996; Whitty, 2007). A manipulative date who pretends to be affectionate in order to gain sexual favors is clearly unethical and deceitful. So are job applicants who lie about their academic records to get hired or salespeople who pretend to be dedicated to customer service when their real goal is to make a quick buck. Lindsy Van Gelder (1996) reports "the strange case of the electronic lover" in which a male computer bulletin board user misrepresented himself as a female therapist named Joan to women who were seeking counseling.

Deception in cyberspace is common. In one survey, 27 percent of respondents had engaged in deceptive behaviors while online (Lenhart et al., 2001), and a diary study found that 22 to 25 percent of mediated interactions involve deception (George & Robb, 2008). A quarter of teens have pretended to be a different person online, and a third confess they have given false information about themselves while e-mailing, instant messaging, or game playing. Even the selection of an avatar can involve deception (Galanxhi & Nah, 2007). And a surprising number of people represent themselves as members of the opposite sex (Samp et al., 2003; Turkle, 1996).

Interviewees in one study (Toma et al., 2008) acknowledged the delicate task of balancing an ideal online identity against the "real" self behind their profile. Many admitted they sometimes fudged facts about themselves—using outdated photos or "forgetting" information about their age, for instance. But respondents were less tolerant when prospective dates posted inaccurate identities. For example, one date-seeker expressed resentment upon learning that a purported "hiker" hadn't hiked in years.

THE PROMISE AND PERILS OF ONLINE RELATIONSHIPS: *CATFISH*

Twentysomething New York photographer Nev Schulman is flattered and intrigued when a bright 8-year old Michigan girl named Abby begins sending him fan mail and paintings based on his work. Nev and Abby strike up a long-distance friendship via e-mail, Facebook, and phone. Soon the artist is also exchanging messages with Abby's family and friends.

Nev's brother Ariel and friend Henry are filmmakers, and they begin documenting Nev's adventures in cyberspace. The narrative becomes more intriguing when Nev falls into an online romance with Abby's older sister Megan, even though the two haven't met in person.

The most gripping parts of this documentary reveal what happens when the three New Yorkers take a road trip to Michigan to finally meet the family that has occupied a major part of their thoughts and time. Without spilling too many details, it's enough to say that the surprising ending to this story dramatizes ethical questions about identity management, self-disclosure, and relational development in mediated relationships.

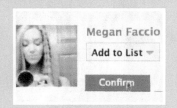

These examples raise important ethical questions about identity management. Is it okay to omit certain information in an online dating service in an attempt to put your best foot forward? In a job interview, is it legitimate to act more confident and reasonable than you really feel? Likewise, are you justified in acting attentive in a boring conversation out of courtesy to the other person? Is it sometimes wise to use false names and information on the Internet for your protection and security? Situations like these suggest that managing impressions doesn't necessarily make you a liar. In fact, it is almost impossible to imagine how we could communicate effectively without making decisions about which front to present in one situation or another.

Each of us has a repertoire of faces—a cast of characters—and part of being a competent communicator is choosing the best role for a situation. Imagine yourself in each of the following situations, and choose the most effective way you could act, considering the options:

- You offer to teach a friend a new skill, such as playing the guitar, operating a computer program, or sharpening up a tennis backhand. Your friend is making slow progress with the skill, and you find yourself growing impatient.

- You've been corresponding for several weeks with someone you met online, and the relationship is starting to turn romantic. You have a physical trait that you haven't mentioned.

- At work you face a belligerent customer. You don't believe that anyone has the right to treat you this way.

In each of these situations—and in countless others every day—you have a choice about how to act. It is an oversimplification to say that there is only one honest way to behave in each circumstance and that every other response would be insincere and dishonest. Instead, identity management involves deciding which face—which part of yourself—to reveal.

Disclosing the Self: What to Reveal?

What we choose to disclose about ourselves is an important component of identity management. So what constitutes self-disclosure? You might argue that aside from secrets, it's impossible *not* to make yourself known to others. After all, every time you open your mouth to speak, you're revealing your tastes, interests, desires, opinions, beliefs, or some other bit of information about yourself. In addition, Chapter 6 will describe how each of us communicates nonverbally even when we're not speaking.

If every verbal and nonverbal behavior in which you engage is self-revealing, how can self-disclosure be distinguished from any other act of communication? Psychologist Paul Cozby (1973) offers an answer. He suggests that in order for a communication act to be considered self-disclosing, it must (1) contain personal information about the sender, (2) the sender must communicate this information verbally, and (3) another person must be the target. Put differently, the subject of self-disclosing communication is the *self,* and information about the self is *purposefully communicated to another person.*

Although this definition is a start, it ignores the fact that some messages intentionally directed toward others are not especially revealing. For example, telling an acquaintance "I don't like clams" is quite different from announcing "I don't like you." Let's take a look at several factors that further distinguish self-disclosure from other types of communication.

Honesty It almost goes without saying that true self-disclosure has to be honest. It's not revealing to say "I've never felt this way about anyone before" to every Saturday night date, or to preface every lie with the statement "Let me be honest. . . ."

As long as you are honest and accurate to the best of your knowledge, communication can qualify as an act of self-disclosure. On the other hand, painting an incomplete picture of yourself (telling only part of what's true) is not genuine disclosure. We'll talk more about the relationship between honesty and disclosure later in this chapter.

Depth A self-disclosing statement is generally regarded as being personal—containing relatively "deep" rather than "surface" information. Of course, what is personal and intimate for one person may not be for another. You might feel comfortable admitting your spotty academic record, short temper, or fear of spiders to anyone who asks, whereas others would be embarrassed to do so. Even basic demographic information, such as age, can be extremely revealing for some people.

Availability of Information Self-disclosing messages must contain information that the other person is not likely to know at the time or be able to obtain from another source. For example, describing your conviction for a drunk-driving accident might feel like an act of serious disclosure because the information concerns you, is offered intentionally, is honest and accurate, and is considered personal. However, if the other person could obtain that information elsewhere without much trouble—from a glance at the morning newspaper or from various gossips, for example—your communication would not be especially self-disclosing.

Context of Sharing Sometimes the self-disclosing nature of a statement comes from the setting in which it is uttered. For instance, relatively innocuous information about family life seems more personal when a student shares it with the class (Myers, 1998), when an athlete tells it to her coach (Officer & Rosenfeld, 1985), or when it's shared online (Stritzke et al., 2004).

We can summarize our definitional tour by saying that **self-disclosure** (1) has the self as subject, (2) is intentional, (3) is directed at another person, (4) is honest, (5) is revealing, (6) contains information generally unavailable from other sources, and (7) gains much of its intimate nature from the context in which it is expressed.

Although many acts of communication may be self-revealing, this definition makes it clear that few of our statements may be classified as self-disclosure. Most conversations—even among friends—focus on everyday mundane topics and disclose little or no personal information (Dindia et al., 1997). Even partners in intimate relationships don't talk about personal matters with a high degree of frequency. (See the Focus on Research sidebar in Chapter 1, p. 19.)

MODELS OF SELF-DISCLOSURE

Now that we've defined self-disclosure, let's take a look at two models that help us better understand how self-revelations operate in our relationships with others.

Degrees of Self-Disclosure: The Social Penetration Model Social psychologists Irwin Altman and Dalmas Taylor (Taylor & Altman, 1987) describe two ways in which communication can be more or less disclosing. Their **social penetration model** is pictured in Figure 3.2. The first dimension of self-disclosure in this model involves the breadth of information volunteered—the range of subjects being discussed. For example, the breadth of disclosure in your relationship with a fellow worker will expand as you begin revealing information about your life away from the job, as well as

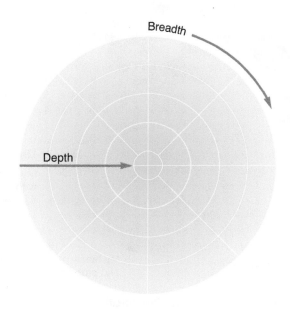

FIGURE 3.2 Social Penetration Model

on-the-job details. The second dimension of disclosure is the depth of the information being volunteered—the shift from relatively impersonal messages to more personal ones.

Depending on the breadth and depth of information shared, a relationship can be defined as casual or intimate. In a casual relationship, the breadth may be great, but not the depth. A more intimate relationship is likely to have high depth in at least one area. The most intimate relationships are those in which disclosure is great in both breadth and depth. Altman and Taylor (1973) see the development of a relationship as a progression from the periphery of their model to its center, a process that typically occurs over time. Each of your personal relationships probably has a different combination of breadth of subjects and depth of revelation. Figure 3.3 pictures a student's self-disclosure in one relationship.

One way to classify the depth of disclosure is to look at the types of information that can be revealed. *Clichés* are ritualized, stock responses to social situations—virtually the opposite of self-disclosure: "How are you doing?" "Fine." Although hardly revealing, clichés can serve as a valuable kind of shorthand that makes it easy to keep the social wheels greased.

Another kind of message involves communicating *facts*. Not all factual statements qualify as self-disclosure. To qualify they must fit the criteria of being intentional, significant, and not otherwise known: "This isn't my first try at college. I dropped out a year ago with terrible grades." Disclosing personal facts like these often signals a desire to move a relationship to a new level of intimacy.

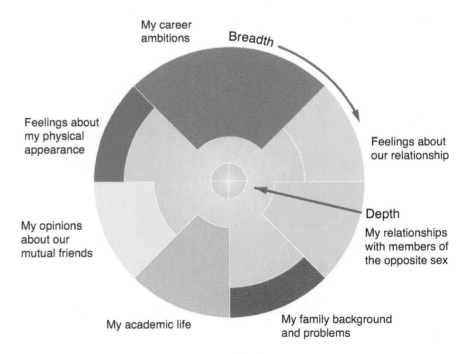

FIGURE 3.3 **Sample Model of Social Penetration**

Opinions can be a kind of self-disclosure since they often reveal more about a person than facts alone do. Every time you offer a personal opinion, you are giving others valuable information about yourself.

The fourth level of self-disclosure—and usually the most revealing one—involves the expression of *feelings*. At first glance, feelings might appear to be the same as opinions, but there's a big difference. "I don't think you're telling me about what's on your mind" is an opinion. Notice how much more we learn about the speaker by looking at three different feelings that could accompany this statement: "I don't think you're telling me what's on your mind . . .

and I'm suspicious."

and I'm angry."

and I'm hurt."

Awareness of Self-Disclosure: The Johari Window Model Another way to illustrate how self-disclosure operates in communication is to look at a model called the **Johari Window**, developed by Joseph Luft and Harry Ingham (Janas, 2001; Luft, 1969).

Imagine a frame that contains everything there is to know about you: your likes and dislikes, your goals, your secrets, your needs—everything. This frame could be divided into information you know about yourself and things you don't know. It could also be split into things others know about you and things they don't know. Figure 3.4 reflects these divisions.

Part 1 represents the information of which both you and the other person are aware. This part is your *open area*. Part 2 represents the *blind area*: information of which you are unaware but that the other person knows. You learn about information in the blind area primarily through feedback from others. Part 3 of the Johari Window represents your *hidden area*:

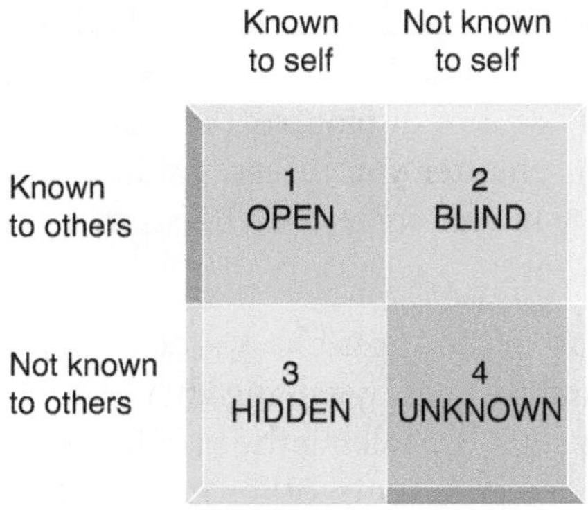

FIGURE 3.4 Johari Window

Luft, J. *Group process: An introduction to group dynamics.* © 1963, 1970 by Joseph Luft. Used with permission of Mayfield Publishing Company.

information that you know but aren't willing to reveal to others. Items in this hidden area become public primarily through self-disclosure, which is the focus of this section. Part 4 of the Johari Window represents information that is *unknown* to both you and to others. At first the unknown area seems impossible to verify. After all, if neither you nor others know what it contains, how can you be sure it exists at all? We can deduce its existence because we are constantly discovering new things about ourselves. For example, it is not unusual to discover that you have an unrecognized talent, strength, or weakness. Items move from the unknown area into the open area when you share your insight, or into the hidden area, where it becomes a secret.

The relative size of each area in our personal Johari Windows changes from time to time according to our moods, the subject we are discussing, and our relationship with the other person. Despite these changes, a single Johari Window could represent most people's overall style of disclosure.

BENEFITS AND RISKS OF SELF-DISCLOSURE

By now it should be clear that neither all-out disclosure nor complete privacy is desirable. On one hand, relationships suffer when people keep important information from one another (Caughlin & Golish, 2002; Mashek & Sherman, 2004). On the other hand, revealing deeply personal information can threaten the stability—or even the survival—of a relationship. Communication researchers use the term **privacy management** to describe the choices people make to reveal or conceal information about themselves (Petronio, 2007). In the following pages we will outline both the benefits and risks of opening yourself to others.

Benefits of Self-Disclosure Modern culture, at least in the United States, places high value on self-disclosure (Marshall, 2008). The following are some reasons people disclose personal information:

Catharsis Sometimes you might disclose information in an effort to "get it off your chest." Catharsis can indeed relieve the burden of pent-up emotions (Pennebaker, 1997), whether face-to-face or online (Vilhauer, 2009), but when it's the *only* goal of disclosure, the results of opening up may not be good. Later in this chapter you'll read guidelines for disclosing that increase the odds that you can achieve catharsis in a way that helps, instead of harming relationships.

Self-Clarification It is often possible to clarify your beliefs, opinions, thoughts, attitudes, and feelings by talking about them with another person. This sort of gaining insight by "talking the problem out" occurs in many psychotherapies, but it also goes on in other relationships, ranging from good friends to interaction with bartenders or hairdressers.

Self-Validation If you disclose information with the hope of seeking the listener's agreement ("I think I did the right thing"), you are seeking validation of your behavior—confirmation of a belief you hold about yourself.

On a deeper level, this sort of self-validating disclosure seeks confirmation of important parts of your self-concept. For instance, self-validation is an important part of the "coming out" process through which gay people recognize their sexual orientation and choose to disclose this knowledge in their personal, family, and social lives (Han, 2001; Savin-Williams, 2001).

Reciprocity A well-documented conclusion from research is that one person's act of self-disclosure increases the odds that the other person will reveal personal information (Dindia, 2000b, 2002; Forgas, 2011). There is no guarantee that revealing personal information will trigger self-disclosures by others, but your own honesty can create a climate that makes the other person feel safer, and perhaps even obligated to match your level of candor ("I've been bored with our relationship lately" might get a response of "Wow, me too!"). Reciprocity applies online as well as in person: The number of mediated friendships a person has may be predicted by the amount of perceived reciprocity (Detenber et al., 2008). Reciprocity doesn't always occur on a turn-by-turn basis: Telling a friend today about your job-related problems might help her feel comfortable opening up to you later about her family history, when the time is right for this sort of disclosure.

Impression Formation Sometimes we reveal personal information to make ourselves more attractive, and research shows that this strategy seems to work. One study revealed that both men's and women's attractiveness was associated with the amount of self-disclosure in conversations (Stiles et al., 1996). Consider a couple on their first date. It's not hard to imagine how one or both partners might share personal information to appear more sincere, interesting, sensitive, or curious about the other person. The same principle applies in other situations. A salesperson might say, "I'll be honest with you" primarily to show that she is on your side.

Relationship Maintenance and Enhancement Research demonstrates that we like people who disclose personal information to us. In fact, the relationship between self-disclosure and liking works in several directions: We like people who disclose personal information to us; we reveal more about ourselves to people we like; and we tend to like others more after we have disclosed to them (Dindia, 2000b).

Appropriate self-disclosure is positively related to marital satisfaction (Hess et al., 2007; Rosenfeld & Bowen, 1991). Disclosing spouses give their relationships higher evaluations and have more positive expectations than do partners who disclose less (MacNeil & Byers, 2009). And a number of studies have demonstrated that increased self-disclosure can improve troubled marriages (Laurenceau et al., 2005; Waring, 1981). With the guidance of a skilled counselor or therapist, partners can learn constructive ways to open up.

Moral Obligation Sometimes we disclose personal information out of a sense of moral obligation. People who are HIV-positive, for example, are often faced with the choice of whether they should tell their health care providers and their partner. One study (Agne et al., 2000) found that patients typically did disclose their HIV status to their health care provider

SELF-ASSESSMENT

Analyzing Your Self-Disclosure Choices

PART 1: WHY YOU DISCLOSE

Use the following scale to indicate your reasons for self-disclosing. These reasons are likely to vary for each relationship you analyze, so you may choose to repeat this self-assessment more than once. Keep one relationship in mind as you complete the self-assessment.

1 = This is *definitely not* a reason I self-disclose.
2 = This is *probably not* a reason I self-disclose.
3 = I am *unsure* whether this is a reason I self-disclose.
4 = This is *probably* a reason I self-disclose.
5 = This is *definitely* a reason I self-disclose.

_____ 1. I disclose as a means to get something off my chest—to vent my feelings.

_____ 2. I disclose as a way to clarify my beliefs, feelings, opinions, and thoughts to use the other person as a "sounding board."

_____ 3. I disclose as a way to encourage the other person to talk to me.

_____ 4. I disclose certain pieces of information so as to create a particular impression of myself.

_____ 5. I disclose to keep the other person current with what is happening to me, so that our relationship "doesn't fall behind."

_____ 6. I disclose so I can get advice, support, or assistance from this person.

_____ 7. I disclose because I "owe it" to this person, feel obligated, because this person has the right to know.

_____ 8. I disclose to the other person because we care for each other, trust one another, and support one another.

PART 2: REASONS FOR NOT DISCLOSING

Use the following scale to identify your reasons for not disclosing personal information. As before, you may choose to repeat this self-assessment for each of your important relationships, but keep one relationship in mind for each evaluation.

1 = This is *definitely not* a reason I avoid self-disclosing.
2 = This is *probably not* a reason I avoid self-disclosing.
3 = I am *unsure* whether this is a reason I avoid self-disclosing.
4 = This is *probably* a reason I avoid self-disclosing.
5 = This is *definitely* a reason I avoid self-disclosing.

_____ 1. I can't find the opportunity to self-disclose.

_____ 2. I don't want to upset or hurt the person.

_____ 3. I can't think of a way to self-disclose.

_____ 4. The information I disclose might be used against me in some way.

_____ 5. I might be treated differently after I self-disclose.

_____ 6. I might not be understood.

_____ 7. My self-disclosure might hurt our relationship.

_____ 8. What I self-disclose might be told to people I would prefer not know.

_____ 9. I don't self-disclose because our relationship isn't close enough.

What are your most important or usual reasons for disclosing? What are your most important or usual reasons for not disclosing? What does this information reveal to you about how you use self-disclosure in your relationships, and the kinds of relationships you have?

because they felt it was the responsible thing to do for themselves (to help fight their illness) and to protect the provider. Another study (Derlega et al., 2000) found that people who are HIV-positive often see disclosing their status "as a duty" and as a way to educate the partner—as an obligation. Despite this prevailing belief, two decades of research has shown that 40 percent of persons testing positive for HIV did not reveal this result to their sexual partners (Allen at al., 2008).

Social Influence People sometimes reveal personal information to help others. This behavior is common in self-help groups such as Alcoholics Anonymous (Hegelson & Gottlieb, 2000). On a larger scale, one study revealed that guests who chose to self-disclose on a particular television talk show indicated that their primary motive was "evangelical": They felt a calling to address injustices and remedy stereotypes (Priest & Dominick, 1994).

Self-Defense Sometimes you may choose to self-disclose something before someone else discloses it for you. A review of the social influence literature by Williams and Dolnik (2001) suggests that self-disclosing negative or damaging information is frequently used as an adaptive social influence strategy called "stealing thunder."

Risks of Self-Disclosure While the benefits of disclosing are certainly important, opening up can also involve risks that make the decision to disclose a difficult and sometimes painful one (Afifi & Caughlin, 2007; Facebook: Nosko et al., 2010). The risks of self-disclosure fall into several categories (Greene et al., 2006; Rosenfeld, 2000).

Rejection In answering the question that forms the title of his book, *Why Am I Afraid to Tell You Who I Am?*, John Powell (1969) summed up the risks of disclosing: "I am afraid to tell you who I am because if I tell you who I am, you may not like who I am, and that's all I have." The fear of disapproval is powerful. Sometimes it is exaggerated and illogical, but there are real dangers in revealing personal information:

> A: I'm starting to think of you as more than a friend. To tell the truth, I think I love you.

> B: I think we should stop seeing one another.

Negative Impression Even if disclosure doesn't lead to total rejection, it can create a negative impression.

> A: You know, I've never had a relationship with a woman that lasted more than a month.

> B: Really? I wonder what that says about you.

Decrease in Relational Satisfaction Besides affecting others' opinions of you, disclosure can lead to a decrease in the satisfaction that comes from a relationship. Consider a scenario like this, where the incompatible wants and needs of each person become clear through disclosure:

> A: Let's get together with Wes and Joanne on Saturday night.
>
> B: To tell you the truth, I'm tired of seeing Wes and Joanne. I don't have much fun with them, and I think Wes is kind of a jerk.
>
> A: But they're my best friends!

Loss of Influence Another risk of disclosure is a potential loss of influence in the relationship. Once you confess a secret weakness, your control over how the other person views you can be diminished.

> A: I'm sorry I was so sarcastic. Sometimes I build myself up by putting you down.
>
> B: Is that it? I'll never let you get away with that again!

Loss of Control Revealing something personal about yourself means losing control of the information. What might happen if the person tells others what you disclosed, people you prefer not know, or who you would like to tell yourself?

> A: I never really liked Leslie. I agreed to go out because it meant a good meal in a nice restaurant.
>
> B: Really? Leslie would sure like to know that!

Hurt the Other Person Even if revealing hidden information leaves you feeling better, it might hurt others—cause them to be upset, for example. It's probably easy to imagine yourself in a situation like this:

> A: Well, since you asked, I have felt less attracted to you lately. I know you can't help it when your skin breaks out, but it is kind of a turnoff.
>
> B: I know! I don't see how you can stand me at all!

GUIDELINES FOR SELF-DISCLOSURE

Self-disclosure is a special kind of sharing that is not appropriate for every situation. Let's take a look at some guidelines that can help you recognize how to express yourself in a way that's rewarding for you and for the others involved (Greene et al., 2006).

Is the Other Person Important to You? There are several ways in which someone might be important. Perhaps you have an ongoing relationship deep enough so that sharing significant parts of yourself justifies keeping your present level of togetherness intact. Perhaps the person to whom you're considering disclosing is someone with whom you've previously related on a less personal level. Now you see a chance to grow closer, and disclosure may be the path toward developing that personal relationship.

Is the Risk of Disclosing Reasonable? Most people intuitively calculate the potential benefits of disclosing against the risks of doing so (Affifi & Steuber, 2009; Vangelisti et al., 2001). Even if the probable benefits are great, opening yourself up to almost certain rejection may be asking for trouble. For instance, it might be foolhardy to share your important feelings with someone you know is likely to betray your confidences or ridicule them. On the other hand, knowing that your partner will respect the information makes the prospect of speaking out more reasonable. This is true in both personal and professional relationships. See the At Work sidebar on page 81 for a discussion of the potential risks of revealing personal information on the job.

Is the Self-Disclosure Appropriate? Some people have trouble with what's popularly known as "TMI"—that is, sharing "too much information" (Alter & Oppenheimer, 2009). In general, it's wise not to divulge personal secrets with strangers, in classroom discussions, or on public Facebook postings, among other settings. Even students who appreciate self-disclosure from their teachers acknowledge that they don't want to hear too much, too often about their instructors' personal lives (Myers & Brann, 2009). Of course, it's also possible to *withhold* too much information—perhaps in a marital counseling session or at a doctor's appointment. The key is to recognize that there's a time and a place for engaging in, and refraining from, self-disclosure.

Dark Side of Communication

BATTLING ADDICTIONS THROUGH SELF-DISCLOSURE

Medical dictionaries define addiction as a habitual dependence on a substance or practice beyond one's voluntary control. There are two broad categories: substance addictions (e.g., alcoholism, drug abuse) and behavioral addictions (e.g., gambling, spending, sexual activity). Many addictive behaviors, such as eating disorders and self-harm, have both physical and psychological components.

Addictions are typically shrouded in secrecy. The people involved often mask or hide behaviors, sometimes with deception and lies. Self-disclosure, therefore, can play a key role in addiction recovery. Venerable organizations such as Alcoholics Anonymous have found that opening up with support groups, counselors, and loved ones is a vital part of the addiction healing process.

There are a variety of ways to disclose an addiction. One study found that it's easier for some to acknowledge addictions in same-sex groups. Another study showed that social media can help those with addictions disclose things they might not share in face-to-face interaction.

The battle to overcome an addiction is a tough one, and self-disclosure alone probably won't guarantee victory. Still, opening up to understanding and supportive others can be an important—and perhaps necessary—tool for achieving a healthier lifestyle.

Butler, S. F., Villapiano, A., & Malinow, A. (2009). The effect of computer-mediated administration on self-disclosure of problems on the Addiction Severity Index. *Journal of Addiction Medicine, 3,* 194–203.

Malpede, J. M. (2003). What is the experience of shame and the impact of self-disclosure on the healing process of women involved in a gender-specific addiction treatment program? *Dissertation Abstracts International: Section B: The Sciences and Engineering, 64*(1-B), 425.

Is the Disclosure Reciprocated? There's nothing quite as disconcerting as talking your heart out to someone, only to discover that the other person has yet to say anything to you that is half as revealing. You think to yourself, "What am I doing?" Unequal self-disclosure creates an unbalanced relationship, one with potential problems. This

F⊕CUS ON RESEARCH

Disclosing Identity Information—Offline vs. Online

From the time most of us were toddlers, we were warned to be cautious around strangers. Researchers Gustavo Mesch and Guy Beker wanted to explore whether this kind of watchfulness extended into adolescence, both in face-to-face communication and through social media. They used data from the Pew Internet and American Life Project to analyze how, and how much, teens disclosed "identity information" to strangers—details like name, school, e-mail address, phone number, and photos.

The researchers discovered a significant difference between adolescents' willingness to disclose in person and online. Both males and females were willing to reveal much more information about themselves through social media than in face-to-face settings. Not everyone disclosed equally: Older teens disclosed more information than younger ones, and there was a strong, positive correlation between the amount of time spent on the Internet and the amount of disclosure.

This study didn't explore the consequences of greater disclosure via social media. It's easy to hypothesize about both the risks and benefits of revealing personal information to people one hasn't ever seen, let alone met. As researchers learn more, the nature of such disclosures will become clearer.

Mesch, G. S., & Beker, G. (2010). Are norms of disclosure of online and offline personal information associated with the disclosure of personal information online? *Human Communication Research, 36,* 570–592.

doesn't mean that you are obliged to match another person's revelations on a tit-for-tat basis. What's important is that there is an appropriate balance of disclosure for maintaining each party's investment in the relationship.

Will the Effect Be Constructive? Self-disclosure can be a vicious tool if it's not used carefully. Every person has a psychological "beltline," and below that beltline are areas about which the person is extremely sensitive. It's important to consider the effects of your candor before opening up to others. Comments such as "I've always thought you were pretty unintelligent" or "Last year I made love to your best friend" may sometimes resolve old business and thus be constructive, but they also can be devastating—to the listener, to the relationship, and to your self-esteem.

ALTERNATIVES TO SELF-DISCLOSURE

While self-disclosure plays an important role in interpersonal relationships, it isn't the only type of communication available. To understand why complete honesty isn't always an easy or ideal choice, consider some familiar dilemmas:

- You have grown increasingly annoyed with some habits of the person you live with. You fear that bringing up this topic could lead to an unpleasant conversation and maybe even damage the relationship.

- Your friend, who is headed out the door for an important job interview, says, "I know I'll never get this job! I'm really not qualified, and besides I look terrible." You agree with your friend's assessment.

- You've just been given a large, extremely ugly lamp as a gift by a relative who visits your home often. How would you respond to the question, "Where will you put it?"

Although honesty is desirable in principle, it often has risky, potentially unpleasant consequences. It's tempting to sidestep situations where self-disclosure would be difficult, but examples like the ones you just read show that avoidance isn't always possible. Research and personal experience show that communicators—even those with the best intentions—aren't always completely honest when they find themselves in situations when honesty would be uncomfortable (Ennis et al., 2008; Scott, 2010). Four common alternatives to self-disclosure are silence, lying, equivocation, and hinting. We will take a closer look at each one.

Silence One alternative to self-disclosure is to keep your thoughts and feelings to yourself. As the cartoon on this page shows, there are many times when keeping information to yourself can seem like the best approach, both for you and the other person. One study showed that in the workplace, withholding information is often seen as a better alternative than lying or engaging in deception (Dunleavy et al., 2010).

You can get a sense of how much you rely on silence instead of disclosing by keeping a record of when you do and don't express your opinions. You're likely to find that withholding thoughts and feelings is a common approach for you.

Lying A **lie** is a deliberate attempt to hide or misrepresent the truth. Lying to gain unfair advantage over an unknowing victim seems clearly wrong, but

another kind of mistruth—the "benevolent lie"—isn't so easy to dismiss as completely unethical. **Benevolent lies** are defined (at least by the people who tell them) as not being malicious—and perhaps they are even helpful to the person to whom they are told. You can almost certainly recall times when you have been less than truthful in order to avoid hurting someone you care for.

Whether or not they are innocent, benevolent lies are certainly common. In several studies spanning four decades, a significant majority of people surveyed acknowledge that even in their closest relationships, there are times when lying is justified (DePaulo et al., 2009; Knapp, 2006). In one study, 130 subjects were asked to keep track of the truthfulness of their everyday conversational statements (Turner et al., 1975). Only 38.5 percent of these statements—slightly more than a

third—proved to be totally honest. Another study (DePaulo & Kashy, 1998) found that both community leaders and undergraduate students lied about once in every 10 conversations with people they were close to, such as romantic partners, best friends, and family members. More of the lies told to best friends and friends, however, were benevolent rather than self-serving, and the reverse was true of lies told to acquaintances and strangers, a finding replicated in a recent study (Ennis et al., 2008).

Most people think benevolent lies are told for the benefit of the recipient. For example, the majority of subjects in the DePaulo et al. (1996) study claimed such lying was "the right thing to do." Other research paints a less flattering picture of who benefits most from lying. One study found that of 322 lies recorded, 75.8 percent were for the benefit of the liar (Lippard, 1988). Less than 22 percent were for the benefit of the person hearing the lie, while a mere 2.5 percent were intended to aid a third person. Table 3.1 identifies various reasons for lying, adapted from Camden et al. (1984) and other studies cited in this section.

Not all lies are equally devastating. Feelings like dismay and betrayal are greatest when the relationship is most intense, the importance of the subject is high, and when there was previous suspicion that the other person

TABLE 3.1 Some Reasons for Lying

REASON	EXAMPLE
Save face for others	"Don't worry—I'm sure nobody noticed that stain on your shirt."
Save face for self	"I wasn't looking at the files—I was accidentally in the wrong drawer."
Acquire resources	"Oh, *please* let me add this class. If I don't get in, I'll never graduate on time!"
Protect resources	"I'd like to lend you the money, but I'm short myself."
Initiate interaction	"Excuse me, I'm lost. Do you live around here?"
Be socially gracious	"No, I'm not bored—tell me more about your vacation."
Avoid conflict	"It's not a big deal. We can do it your way. Really."
Avoid interaction	"That sounds like fun, but I'm busy Saturday night."
Leave taking	"Oh, look what time it is! I've got to run!"
Present a competent image	"Sure I understand. No problem."
Increase social desirability	"Yeah, I've done a fair amount of skiing."
Exaggeration	"You think *this* is cold? Let me tell you about how cold it was on that trip...."

wasn't being completely honest. Of these three factors, the importance of the information lied about proved to be the key factor in provoking a relational crisis (McCornack & Levine, 1990). We may be able to cope with "misdemeanor" lying, but "felonies" are a grave threat—often leading to the end of a relationship.

The lesson here is clear: Lying about major parts of your relationship can have the gravest of consequences. If preserving a relationship is important to you, then honesty—at least about important matters—really does appear to be the best policy.

Equivocation Lying isn't the only alternative to self-disclosure. When faced with the choice between lying and telling an unpleasant truth, communicators can—and often do—equivocate. **Equivocal language** has two or more equally plausible meanings.

The value of equivocation becomes clear when you consider the alternatives. Consider the dilemma of what to say when you've been given an unwanted present—an ugly painting, for example—and the giver asks what you think of it. How can you respond? On the one hand, you need to choose between telling the truth and lying. At the same time, you have a choice of whether to make your response clear or vague. Figure 3.5 displays these choices.

A study by Sandra Metts and her colleagues (1992) shows how equivocation can save face in difficult situations. Several hundred college students were asked how they would turn down unwanted sexual overtures from a person whose feelings were important to them: a close friend, a prospective

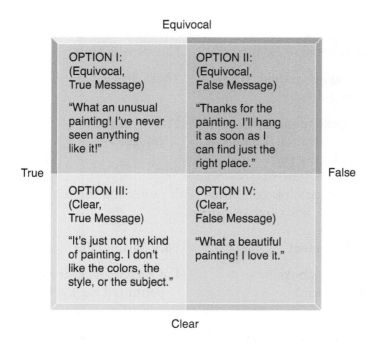

FIGURE 3.5 Dimensions of Truthfulness and Equivocation

date, or a dating partner. The majority of students chose a diplomatic re-action ("I just don't think I'm ready for this right now") as being more face-saving and comfortable than a direct statement like "I just don't feel sexually attracted to you." The diplomatic reaction seemed sufficiently clear to get the message across, but not so blunt as to embarrass or humiliate the other person. As Bavelas et al. (1990, p. 171) put it, "Equivocation is neither a false message nor a clear truth, but rather an alternative used precisely when both of these are to be avoided."

The underlying point of equivocal messages is often not lost on their re-cipients. Renee Edwards and Richard Bello (2001; Bello & Edwards, 2005) explored how receivers interpreted equivocal statements, such as telling a friend that his or her speech was "interesting" instead of saying "You messed up." Besides regarding the equivocal statements as more polite, they had no trouble discerning the intended meaning—that the speech was poor, to use our example.

Given the advantages of equivocation, it's not surprising that most people usually will choose to equivocate rather than tell a lie. In a series of experiments, subjects chose between telling a face-saving lie, the truth, and equivocating (Bavelas et al., 1990). Only 6 percent chose the lie, and be-tween 3 and 4 percent chose the hurtful truth. By contrast, over 90 percent chose the equivocal response. People may say they prefer truth-telling to equivocating, but given the choice, they usually finesse the truth (Robinson et al., 1998).

Hinting Hints are more direct than equivocal statements. Whereas an equivocal message isn't necessarily aimed at changing another's behavior, a hint seeks to get the desired response from the other person. As Michael Motley (1992) suggests, some hints are designed to save the receiver from embarrassment:

Direct Statement	Face-Saving Hint
You're too overweight to be ordering dessert.	These desserts are terribly overpriced.
I'm too busy to continue with this conversation. I wish you would let me go.	I know you're busy; I'd better let you go.

Other hints are less concerned with protecting the receiver than with saving the sender from embarrassment:

Direct Statement	Face-Saving Hint
Please don't smoke here; it bothers me.	I'm pretty sure that smoking isn't permitted here.
I'd like to invite you out for lunch, but I don't want to risk a "no" answer to my invitation.	Gee, it's almost lunch time. Have you ever eaten at that new Italian restaurant around the corner?

The success of a hint depends on the other person's ability to pick up the unexpressed message. Your subtle remarks might go right over the head of an insensitive receiver, or one who chooses not to respond to them. If this happens, you still have the choice to be more direct. If the costs of a straightforward message seem too high, you can withdraw without risk.

The Ethics of Evasion It's easy to see why people often choose hints, equivocations, and benevolent lies instead of complete self-disclosure. These strategies provide a way to manage difficult situations that is easier than the alternatives for both the speaker and the receiver of the message. In this sense, successful liars, equivocators, and hinters can be said to possess a certain kind of communicative competence. On the other hand, there *are* times when honesty is the right approach, even if it's painful. At times like these, evaders could be viewed as lacking either the competence or the integrity to handle a situation effectively.

Are hints, benevolent lies, and equivocations ethical alternatives to self-disclosure? Some of the examples in these pages suggest the answer is a qualified "yes." Many social scientists and philosophers agree. For example, researchers David Buller and Judee Burgoon (1994) argue that the morality of a speaker's motives for lying ought to be judged, not the deceptive act itself. Another approach is to consider whether the effects of a lie will be worth the deception. Ethicist Sissela Bok (1978) offers some circumstances where deception may be justified: doing good, avoiding harm, and protecting a larger truth. One example is when a patient asks, "How am I doing?"; if a nurse perceives that telling the truth could be harmful, it would violate the obligation to "do good and avoid harm," and honesty would be less important than caring (Tuckett, 2005). Perhaps the right questions to ask, then, are whether an indirect message is truly in the interests of the receiver and whether this sort of evasion is the only effective way to behave. Bok suggests another way to check the justifiability of a lie: Imagine how others would respond if they knew what you were really thinking or feeling. Would they accept your reasons for not disclosing?

Summary

The self-concept is a relatively stable set of perceptions individuals hold about themselves. It begins to develop soon after birth, being shaped by the appraisals of significant others and by social comparisons with reference groups. The self-concept is subjective and can vary substantially from the way a person is perceived by others. Although the self may evolve over time, the self-concept resists change.

A self-fulfilling prophecy occurs when a person's expectations of an event and subsequent behavior influence the event's outcome. One type of prophecy consists of predictions by others, while another category is self-imposed. It is possible to change one's self-concept in ways that lead to more effective communication.

Identity management consists of an individual's strategic communication designed to influence others' perceptions. Identity management aims at presenting one or more faces to others, which may be different from private, spontaneous behavior that occurs outside of others' presence. Some communicators are high self-monitors who are highly conscious of their own behavior, while others are less aware of how their words and actions affect others. Communicating through mediated channels can enhance a person's ability to manage impressions. Since each person has a variety of faces that she or he can reveal, choosing which one to present is a central concern of competent communicators.

Self-disclosure consists of honest, revealing messages about the self that are intentionally directed toward others. Disclosing communication contains information that is generally unavailable via other sources.

The percentage of messages that are truly self-disclosing is relatively low. A number of factors govern whether a communicator will be judged as being a high- or low-level discloser.

Two models for describing self-disclosure are the social penetration model and the Johari Window model. The social penetration model describes two dimensions of self-disclosure: breadth and depth. The Johari Window illustrates the amount of information that an individual reveals to others, hides, is blind to, and is unaware of.

Communicators disclose personal information for a variety of reasons. There also are several reasons to choose not to self-disclose, some of which serve primarily the interests of the nondiscloser, and others of which are intended to benefit the target. When deciding whether or not to disclose, communicators should consider a variety of factors detailed in the chapter.

Four alternatives to revealing self-disclosures are silence, lies (both benevolent and self-serving), equivocations, and hints. These may be ethical alternatives to self-disclosure; however, whether they are or not depends on the speaker's motives and the effects of the deception.

Key Terms

- Benevolent lie (97)
- Cognitive conservatism (73)
- Equivocal language (99)
- Face (78)
- Facework (78)
- Identity management (77)
- Johari Window (89)

- Lie (97)
- Perceived self (78)
- Presenting self (78)
- Privacy management (90)
- Reference groups (69)
- Reflected appraisal (69)
- Self-concept (66)
- Self-disclosure (87)
- Self-esteem (67)
- Self-fulfilling prophecy (74)
- Significant other (69)
- Social comparison (69)
- Social penetration model (87)

Activities

1. Invitation to Insight/Ethical Challenge

Choose someone with whom you have an important interpersonal relationship, and explore how you influence each other's self-concepts.

a. Interview your partner to discover how your words and deeds influence his or her self-concept. Identify specific incidents to illustrate these influences, and discuss which specific parts of the self-concept you have affected.

b. Now share with your partner how his or her behaviors have affected your self-concept. Again, be specific about identifying the incidents and the parts of your self-concept that were affected.

c. Once you recognize the power you have to shape another's self-concept, ask yourselves what responsibility each of you has to treat the other person in a supportive manner when you are faced with delivering a potentially critical message.

d. Based on the information exchanged so far, discuss whether you are satisfied with the way you have affected each other's self-concepts. Identify any ways you could communicate more effectively.

2. Invitation to Insight

What reference groups do you use to define your self-concept? You can recognize your social comparison groups by answering several questions:

a. Select one area in which you compare yourself to others. In what area is the comparison made? (For example, is the comparison based on wealth, intelligence, or social skill?)

b. In the selected area, ask yourself, "Which people am I better or worse than?"

c. In the selected area, ask yourself, "Which people am I the same as or different from?"

What is the effect of using these groups as a basis for judging yourself? How might you view yourself differently if you used other reference groups as a basis for comparison?

3. Invitation to Insight

Describe two incidents in which self-fulfilling prophecies you have imposed on yourself have affected your communication. Explain how each of these predictions shaped your behavior, and describe how you might have behaved differently if you had made a different prediction. Next, describe two incidents in which you imposed self-fulfilling prophecies on others. What effect did your prediction have on these people's actions?

4. Skill Builder

Identify one communication-related part of your self-concept you would like to change. Use the guidelines on pages 76–77 to describe how you could make that change.

    a. Decide whether your expectations for change are realistic. Don't expect to become a new person: Becoming a *better* one should be enough.

    b. Recognize your strengths as well as your shortcomings. You may not be as bad as you think you are!

    c. Decide whether you are willing to make the necessary effort to change. Good intentions are an important start, but hard work also is necessary.

    d. Develop a specific plan to change the way you behave. You may want to consult books and experts as well as observe models to gain a clear idea of your new goals and how to achieve them.

5. Ethical Challenge

You can gain a clearer sense of the ethical implications of impression management by following these directions:

    a. Make a list of the different presenting selves you try to communicate at school or work, to family members, to friends, and to various types of strangers—in either face-to-face communication or via social media.

    b. Which of these selves are honest, and which are deceptive?

    c. Are any deceptive impressions you try to create justified? What would be the consequences of being completely candid in the situations you have described?

    d. Based on your answers to these questions, develop a set of guidelines to distinguish ethical and unethical impression management.

6. Ethical Challenge

Recall three recent situations in which you used each of the following evasive approaches: benevolent lying, equivocating, and hinting. Write an anonymous written description of each situation on a separate sheet of paper. Submit the cases to a panel of "judges" (most likely fellow students), who will use the criteria of justifiable motives and desirable effects to evaluate the morality of this deception. Invite the "judges" to consider how they would feel if they knew someone used these evasive approaches with them.

7. Skill Builder

Use the guidelines on pages 94–96 to develop one scenario in which you *might* reveal a self-disclosing message. Create a message of this type, and use the information in this chapter to discuss the risks and benefits of sharing the message.

CHAPTER

4

Perceiving Others

CHAPTER OUTLINE ▪ ▪ ▪ ▪

After studying the material in this chapter . . .

You should understand:

1. The difference between first- and second-order realities, and how the processes of selection, organization, interpretation, and negotiation affect a communicator's perception of others.
2. How physiological, psychological, social, and cultural factors lead communicators to perceive one another and other phenomena differently.
3. The common tendencies in perception that can sometimes lead to misperceptions.
4. The value of empathy in interpersonal communication and relationships.

You should be able to:

1. Describe the factors that shape your perceptions of important people and events, and explain how these and other factors could lead another person to perceive the same people and events differently.
2. Describe an interpersonal issue from the other person's point of view, showing how and why the other person experiences the issue differently.
3. Use perception checking to clarify your understanding of another person's point of view.

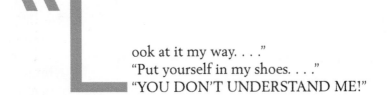

ook at it my way. . . ."
"Put yourself in my shoes. . . ."
"YOU DON'T UNDERSTAND ME!"

Statements like these reflect one of the most common communication challenges. We can talk to (or at) one another until we're hoarse and exhausted, yet we still don't really understand one another. Research confirms this fact: Typical dyads can interpret and explain only 25–50 percent of each other's behavior accurately (Spitzberg, 1994), and spouses consistently overestimate the degree to which they agree with their partners (Fletcher & Kerr, 2010; Sillars et al., 1994). Some communication scholars (e.g., Eisenberg & Goodall, 2001) have suggested complete understanding could lead to more disagreement and dissatisfaction, not smoother relationships. Nonetheless, failing to share each other's view of the world can leave us feeling isolated and frustrated, despairing that our words don't seem able to convey the depth and complexity of what we think and feel.

Just like the boxes in Figure 4.1, virtually every interpersonal situation can be seen from many points of view. Take a minute to study that figure. How many ways can you discover to view this image? If you only see one or two, keep looking. (You can see at least four ways of viewing the image by looking at Figure 4.2.) If making quick and accurate sense of simple drawings is a difficult task, imagine the challenge involved in trying to understand the perspectives of other human beings, who are far more complex and multidimensional.

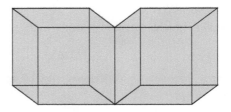

FIGURE 4.1 **Two Cubes Touching**

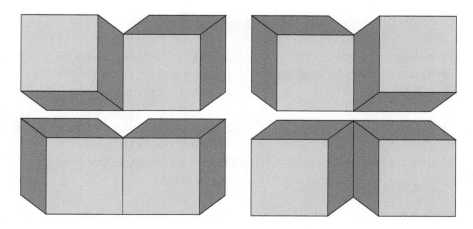

FIGURE 4.2 **Four Sets of Two Cubes Touching**

This chapter provides tools for communicating in the face of perceptual differences. It begins by explaining that reality is constructed through communication. Then it introduces some of the many reasons why the world appears so different to each of us. After examining the perceptual factors that make understanding so difficult, we will look at tools for bridging the perceptual gap.

The Perception Process

How do our perceptions affect our communication with others? We begin to answer these questions by taking a look at the way we make sense of the world.

REALITY IS CONSTRUCTED

Most social scientists agree that the world we know isn't "out there." Rather, we create our reality with others through communication (DeCapua, 2007; O'Brien, 2005). This may seem hard to accept until we recognize that there are two levels of reality, which have been labeled "first-order" and "second-order" (Nardone & Watzlawick, 2005; Watzlawick, 1984, 1990). **First-order realities** are physically observable qualities of a thing or situation. For example, the fact that your grandmother wrapped you in a big hug would be obvious to any observer. Likewise, there probably wouldn't be an argument about what word was uttered if a friend called you a "bonehead." By contrast, **second-order realities** involve our *attaching meaning* to first-order things or situations. Second-order realities don't reside in objects or events, but rather in our minds.

Life runs most smoothly when we share second-order realities:

First-order reality:	Your grandma gives you a hug.
Shared second-order reality:	It's appropriate for grandparents to hug their grandchildren.
First-order reality:	A job interviewer asks you how your day has been going.
Shared second-order reality:	This is a reasonable question for the situation.

Communication becomes more problematic when we have different second-order realities. For example

First-order reality:	Your friend calls you a "bonehead."
Your second-order reality:	Your friend is being critical.
Friend's second-order reality:	The remark was an affectionate joke.
First-order reality:	A job interviewer asks whether you are married.
Your second-order reality:	The question has nothing to do with the job and is inappropriate.
Interviewer's second-order reality:	The interviewer is trying to make conversation.

As the cartoon below shows, communication problems arise when we don't share second-order realities. This is especially true when we don't realize that these views of the world are personal constructions, not objective facts. This chapter explores many of the factors that cause us to experience and make sense of the world in different ways. Perhaps more importantly, it introduces you to some communication tools that can help bridge the gap between differing perceptions, and in so doing improve relationships.

STEPS IN THE PERCEPTION PROCESS

We attach meanings to our experiences in four steps: selection, organization, interpretation, and negotiation.

Selection Since we're exposed to more input than we can possibly manage, the first step in perception is the **selection** of which data we will attend to. There are several factors that cause us to notice some messages and ignore others.

Stimuli that are *intense* often attract our attention. Something that is louder, larger, or brighter stands out. This explains why—other things being equal—we're more likely to remember extremely tall or short people and why someone who laughs or talks loudly at a party attracts more attention (not always favorable) than do more quiet guests.

Repetitious stimuli, repetitious stimuli, repetitious stimuli, repetitious stimuli, repetitious stimuli, repetitious stimuli also attract attention.* Just as a quiet but steadily dripping faucet can come to dominate our awareness, people to whom we're frequently exposed become noticeable.

Attention is also frequently related to *contrast* or *change* in stimulation. Put differently, unchanging people or things become less noticeable. This principle offers an explanation (excuse?) for why we take consistently wonderful people for granted when we interact with them frequently. It's only when they stop being so wonderful or go away that we appreciate them.

Later in this chapter, we'll look at a variety of other factors—physiological, psychological, social, and cultural—that lead us to pay attention to certain people and events while ignoring others.

Organization After selecting information from the environment, we must arrange it in some meaningful way in order to make sense of the world. We call this stage **organization**. The raw sense data we perceive can be organized in more than one way. (See Figure 4.2 for a visual example of this principle.) We do this by using *perceptual schema*, cognitive frameworks that allow us to give order to the information we have selected (Macrae & Bodenhausen, 2001).

We use four types of schema to classify others (Andersen, 1999; Freeman & Ambady, 2011). As you read about each category, think about how you use it to organize your perceptions.

Physical constructs classify people according to their appearance: beautiful or ugly, fat or thin, young or old, and so on.

---

* The graphic demonstrations of factors influencing perception in this and the following paragraphs are borrowed from Coon (2009).

Role constructs use social position, such as student, attorney, wife.

Interaction constructs focus on social behavior: friendly, helpful, aloof, or sarcastic, for example.

Psychological constructs refer to internal states of mind and dispositions: confident, insecure, happy, neurotic, and so on.

Once we have selected an organizing scheme to classify people, we use that scheme to make generalizations about members of the groups who fit our categories. For example, if you are especially aware of a person's sex, you might be alert to the differences between the way men and women behave or the way they are treated. You might even misremember or distort information that doesn't fit with your beliefs on the subject (Frawley, 2008). If religion plays an important part in your life, you might think of members of your faith differently than you do others. If ethnicity is an important issue for you, you probably tune into the differences between members of various ethnic groups. There's nothing wrong with generalizations about groups as long as they are accurate. In fact, it would be impossible to get through life without them. But faulty overgeneralizations can lead to problems of stereotyping, which you'll read about in a few pages.

Perceptual differences don't just involve the general categories we use to classify others. We also can organize specific communication transactions in different ways, and these differing organizational schemes can have a powerful effect on our relationships. Communication theorists have used the term **punctuation** to describe the determination of causes and effects in a series of interactions (Watzlawick et al., 1967; Wood, 2010). You can begin to understand how punctuation operates by visualizing a running quarrel between a husband and wife. The husband accuses the wife of being a nag, while she complains that he is withdrawing from her. Notice that the order in which each partner punctuates this cycle affects how the dispute looks. The husband begins by blaming the wife: "I withdraw because you nag." The wife organizes the situation differently, starting with the husband: "I nag because you withdraw." Once the cycle gets rolling, it is impossible to say which accusation is accurate, as Figure 4.3 indicates. The answer depends on how the sequence is punctuated.

Anyone who has seen two children argue about "who started it" can understand that haggling over causes and effects isn't likely to solve a conflict. In fact, the kind of finger pointing that goes along with assigning blame will probably make matters worse (Caughlin & Huston, 2002). Rather than argue about whose punctuation of an event is correct, it's far more productive to recognize that a dispute can look different to each person and then move on to the more important question of "What can we do to make things better?"

Interpretation Once we have selected and organized our perceptions, we interpret them in a way that makes some sort of sense. **Interpretation** plays a role in virtually every interpersonal act. Is the person who smiles at you

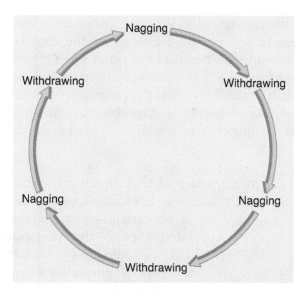

FIGURE 4.3 The way a communication sequence is punctuated affects its perceived meaning. Which comes first, the nagging or the withdrawing?

across a crowded room interested in romance or simply being polite? Is a friend's kidding a sign of affection or irritation? Should you take an invitation to "drop by any time" literally or not?

There are several factors that cause us to interpret a person's behavior in one way or another. *Relational satisfaction* is a powerful one: The behavior that seems positive when you are happy with a partner might seem completely different when the relationship isn't satisfying (Luo et al., 2010). For example, couples in unsatisfying relationships are more likely than satisfied partners to blame one another when things go wrong (Bradbury & Fincham, 1990; Manusov, 1993).

Expectation is another factor that shapes our interpretations (Burgoon & Burgoon, 2001). For instance, if you go into a conversation expecting a hostile attitude, you're likely to hear a negative tone in the other person's voice—even if that tone isn't there (Hample et al., 2007). We'll talk more about how expectations affect perception later in this chapter.

A third factor that influences interpretations is *personal experience*. For instance, if you've been taken advantage of by landlords in the past, you might be skeptical about an apartment manager's assurances that careful housekeeping will ensure the refund of your cleaning deposit.

Assumptions about human behavior also influence interpretations. Do you assume people are lazy, dislike work, avoid responsibility, and must be coerced to do things, or do you believe people exercise self-direction and self-control, possess creativity, and seek responsibility? Imagine the differences in a boss who assumes workers fit the first description versus one who assumes they fit the second (Neuliep, 1996; Sager, 2008).

Although we have talked about selection, organization, and interpretation separately, these three phases of perception can occur in differing sequences. For example, a parent's or babysitter's past interpretations (such as "Jason is a troublemaker") can influence future selections (his behavior becomes especially noticeable) and the organization of events (when there's a fight, the assumption is that Jason started it). As with all communication, perception is an ongoing process in which it is hard to pin down beginnings and endings.

Negotiation In Chapter 1 you read that meaning is created both *in* and *among* people. So far our discussion has focused on the inner components of perception—selection, organization, and interpretation—that take place in each individual's mind. Now we need to examine the part of our sense-making that occurs *among* people. The process by which communicators influence each other's perceptions through communication is known as **negotiation**.

One way to explain negotiation is to view interpersonal communication as the exchange of stories. Scholars call the stories we use to describe our personal worlds **narratives** (Allan et al., 2002; Langellier & Peterson, 2006). Just as the boxes in Figure 4.1 on page 108 can be viewed in several ways, virtually every interpersonal situation can be described by more than one narrative. These narratives often differ in their casting of characters as "heroes" and "villains" (Aleman, 2005). For instance, consider a conflict between a boss and employee. If you ask the employee to describe the situation, she might depict the manager as a "heartless bean counter" while she sees herself as a worker who "always gets the job done." The manager's narrative might cast the roles quite differently: the "fair boss" versus the "clock watcher who wants to leave early." Similarly, children may say their parents are too controlling, while the parents talk about their children as irresponsible and naïve. Stepmothers and mothers-in-law who see themselves as "helpful" might be portrayed as "meddlesome" in the narratives of stepdaughters and daughters-in-law (Christian, 2005; Sandel, 2004).

MEDIA CLIP

THE POWER OF A SHARED NARRATIVE: *LARS AND THE REAL GIRL*

Lars (Ryan Gosling) is a kind and decent but painfully shy 27-year-old. By choice, he lives alone in a garage and avoids conversation and contact with others as much as possible.

Everyone in his small, close-knit town is stunned when Lars introduces his new girlfriend, Bianca—an anatomically correct silicone mannequin. Understandably worried about Lars' mental health, his brother and sister-in-law seek the help of their family doctor, who advises them to play along with his delusion and to see what happens. Soon the entire town buys into the shared narrative that Bianca and Lars are a real couple. Bianca volunteers at the local hospital, "reads" stories to schoolchildren, and even wins a seat on the school board.

While this plot might seem farfetched, critics and moviegoers have agreed that this tender drama-comedy showcases the power of a community to support one of its own. The obvious fiction they conspire to construct takes on its own reality, illustrating how communication can be a powerful tool for creating shared narratives.

"I know what you're thinking, but let me offer a competing narrative."

When our narratives clash with those of others we can either hang on to our own point of view and refuse to consider anyone else's (usually not productive), or try to negotiate a narrative that creates at least some common ground.

Shared narratives provide the best chance for smooth communication. For example, romantic partners who celebrate their successful struggles against relational obstacles are happier than those who don't have this shared appreciation (Flora & Segrin, 2000). Likewise, couples that agree about the important turning points in their relationships are more satisfied than those who have different views of which incidents were most important (Baxter & Pittman, 2001).

Shared narratives don't have to be accurate to be powerful (Martz et al., 1998). Couples who report being happily married after 50 or more years seem to collude in a relational narrative that doesn't always jibe with the facts (Miller et al., 2006). They agree that they rarely have conflict, although objective analysis reveals that they have had their share of disagreements and challenges. Without overtly agreeing to do so, they choose to blame outside forces or unusual circumstances for problems, instead of attributing responsibility to one another. They offer the most charitable interpretations of one another's behavior, believing that their spouse acts with good intentions when things don't go well. They seem willing to forgive, or even forget transgressions. Examining this research, Judy Pearson (2000) asks:

> Should we conclude that happy couples have a poor grip on reality? Perhaps they do, but is the reality of one's marriage better known by outside onlookers than by the players themselves? The conclusion is evident. One key to a long happy marriage is to tell yourself and others that you have one and then to behave as though you do! (p. 186)

Influences on Perception

How we select, organize, interpret, and negotiate data about others is influenced by a variety of factors. Some of our perceptual judgments are affected by physiology, others by cultural and social factors, and still others by psychological factors.

PHYSIOLOGICAL INFLUENCES

Sometimes differing perspectives come from our physical environment and the ways that our bodies differ from others.

The Senses The differences in how each of us sees, hears, tastes, touches, and smells stimuli can affect interpersonal relationships (Clark, 2000). Consider a few examples arising from physiological differences:

"Turn down that radio! It's going to make me go deaf."
"It's not too loud. If I turn it down, it will be impossible to hear it."

"It's freezing in here."
"Are you kidding? We'll suffocate if you turn up the heat!"

"Why don't you pass that truck? The highway is clear for half a mile."
"I can't see that far, and I'm not going to get us killed."

Age Older people view the world differently than younger ones because of a greater scope and number of experiences. Developmental differences also shape perceptions. Developmental psychologists (Piaget, 1952; Steinberg, 2010) describe ways in which younger children are incapable of performing mental feats that are natural to the rest of us. Until they approach the age of seven, for example, they aren't able to take another person's point of view. This fact helps explain why youngsters often seem egocentric, selfish, and uncooperative. A parent's exasperated "Can't you see I'm too tired to play?" just won't make sense to a 4-year-old full of energy, who imagines that everyone else must feel the same.

Health and Fatigue Recall the last time you came down with a cold, flu, or some other ailment. Health can have a strong impact on how you relate to others. It's good to realize that someone else may be behaving differently because of illness. In the same way, it's important to let others know when you feel ill so they can give you the understanding you need.

Likewise, fatigue can affect relationships. When you've been working long hours or studying late for an exam, the world can seem quite different than when you are well rested. People who are sleep deprived, for example, perceive time intervals as longer than they really are. So the 5 minutes you're waiting for a friend to show up may seem longer, leaving you feeling more impatient than you otherwise would be (Miró et al., 2003).

Hunger Your own experience probably confirms that being hungry (and getting grumpy) or having overeaten (and getting tired) affects how we interact with others. For example, a study by Katherine Alaimo and her colleagues (2001) found that teenagers who reported that their family did not get enough food to eat were almost three times as likely to have been suspended from school, almost twice as likely to have difficulty getting along with others, and four times as likely to have no friends. While the exact nature of the causes and effects in this study are hard to pin down, one thing is clear: Hunger can affect our perception and communication.

Biological Cycles Are you a "morning person" or a "night person"? Each of us has a daily cycle in which all sorts of changes constantly occur, including variations in body temperature, sexual drive, alertness, tolerance to stress, and mood (Koukkari & Sothern, 2006). These cycles can affect the way we relate toward each other. For example, Jeffrey Larson and his associates (1991) discovered that couples with mismatched waking and sleeping patterns (e.g., an evening person and a morning person) reported significantly more conflict, less sexual intimacy, and less time spent conversing on important topics than couples with matched sleeping patterns.

Neurobehavioral Challenges Some differences in perception are rooted in neurology. For instance, people with ADHD (attention-deficit-hyperactivity disorder) are easily distracted from tasks and have difficulty delaying gratification (Goldstein, 2008; Tripp et al., 2007). It's easy to imagine how those with ADHD might find a long lecture boring and tedious, while other audience members are fascinated by the same lecture (Von Briesen, 2007). Also, young women with ADHD are more likely to have conflicts with their mothers and have fewer romantic relationships than those without ADHD (Babinski et al., 2011). People with bipolar disorder experience significant mood swings in which their perceptions of events, friends, and even family members shift dramatically. The National Institute of Mental Health (2008) estimates that between 5 million and 7 million Americans are affected by these two disorders alone—and there are many other psychological conditions that influence people's perceptions.

MEDIA CLIP "DIFFERENT . . . NOT LESS": *TEMPLE GRANDIN*

It's clear that something is different about teenaged Temple Grandin (played by Claire Danes). As she steps off an airplane into Arizona's furnace-like summer heat, we perceive the world as she does. Sounds and images are chaotic and intensified to an almost unbearable level. Sudden movements are frightening. Grandin's awkward stature and too-loud voice soon make it clear that she occupies a place on the autism scale.

With the support of a devoted mother and caring teachers, Temple grows into a successful adult despite the prejudices and ignorance of the 1960s. Her love for large animals and her heightened sensitivity to their feelings leads to her life's work as a university professor and consultant, designing humane ways of managing livestock. She claims that her professional success is due in part to her hypersensitivity to the behavior and emotions of animals.

This true story reminds us that perceiving the world in unique ways can lead to triumphs as well as challenges. As Grandin's mother puts it, people with disabilities are "different, but not less."

For more information about Temple Grandin's life and work, see her website at www.templegrandin.com

PSYCHOLOGICAL INFLUENCES

Along with physiology, our psychological state also influences the way we perceive others.

Mood Our emotional state strongly influences how we view people and events, and therefore how we communicate (Avramova et al., 2010; Forgas & Bower, 2001). An early experiment using hypnotism dramatically demonstrated the influence of mood on perception (Lebula & Lucas, 1945). Each subject was shown the same series of six pictures, each time having been put in a different mood. The descriptions of the pictures differed radically depending on the emotional state of the subject. For example, these are descriptions by one subject in various emotional states while describing a picture of children digging in a swampy area:

> *Happy mood:* "It looks like fun, reminds me of summer. That's what life is for, working out in the open, really living—digging in the dirt, planting, watching things grow."

> *Anxious mood:* "They're going to get hurt or cut. There should be someone older there who knows what to do in case of an accident. I wonder how deep the water is."

> *Critical mood:* "Pretty horrible land. There ought to be something more useful for kids of that age to do instead of digging in that stuff. It's filthy and dirty and good for nothing."

Such evidence shows that our judgments often say more about our own emotional state than about the other people involved.

Although there's a strong relationship between mood and happiness, it's not clear which comes first: the perceptual outlook or the amount of relational satisfaction. There is some evidence that perception leads to satisfaction rather than the opposite order (Fletcher et al., 1987). In other words, the attitude/expectation we bring to a situation shapes our level of happiness or unhappiness. Once started, this process can create a spiral. If you're happy about your relationship, you will be more likely to interpret your partner's behavior in a charitable way. This, in turn, can lead to greater happiness. Of course, the same process can work in the opposite direction. One study revealed that spouses who felt uncertain about the status of their marriage saw relational threats in conversations their partners had with strangers that seemed quite ordinary to outsiders (Knobloch et al., 2007).

One remedy to serious distortions—and unnecessary conflicts—is to monitor your own moods. If you're aware of being especially critical or sensitive, you can avoid overreacting to others.

Self-Concept Another factor that influences perception is self-concept (Hinde et al., 2001). For example, the recipient's self-concept has proven to be the single greatest factor in determining whether people who are being teased interpret the teaser's motives as being friendly or hostile, and whether they respond with comfort or defensiveness (Alberts et al., 1996). Children who have a low opinion of themselves are more likely to see themselves as victims of bullying, both in their classrooms and in cyberspace (Katzer et al., 2009). As discussed in Chapter 3, the way we think and feel about ourselves strongly influences how we interpret others' behavior.

SOCIAL INFLUENCES

Within a culture, our personal point of view plays a strong role in shaping perceptions. Social scientists have developed **standpoint theory** to describe how a person's position in a society shapes her or his view of society in general, and of specific individuals (Litwin & Hallstein, 2007; Wood, 2005a). Standpoint theory is most often applied to the difference between the perspectives of privileged social groups and people who have less power, and to the perspectives of women and men (Dougherty, 2001). Unless one has been disadvantaged, it can be difficult to imagine how the world might look to someone who has been treated badly because of race, ethnicity, gender, biological sex, sexual orientation, or socioeconomic class. After some reflection, though, you probably can understand how being marginalized can make the world seem like a very different place.

Sex and Gender Roles Physiological and psychological differences aren't the only factors that shape the differing perceptions of men and women. Personal experiences and social expectations also are powerful. Examples abound: women and men judge the same behaviors quite differently. Men tend to rate verbal and nonverbal behaviors as more flirtatious and seductive than do women (La France et al., 2009). Women react differently depending on their age and marital status (Hanzal et al., 2008). As you will read in the At Work box on page 120, some types of behavior men find innocuous have been judged as being harassing by women (Dougherty, 2001; Ohse & Stockdale, 2008). Not surprisingly, much of the difference comes from experience: Women who report having been harassed are more likely to find harassment in subsequent interactions (Singer, 1998). Experience isn't the only factor, though: Younger women are more likely to perceive harassment than older ones who, presumably, have a different set of expectations about what kinds of communication are and aren't appropriate. Also, attitudes play a role: People who disapprove of socializing and dating between coworkers are more likely to perceive harassment than those who accept this sort of relationship (Solomon & Williams, 1997).

"How is it gendered?"

119

Early theorizing by Sandra Bem (1974) suggested that stereotypical masculine and feminine behaviors are not opposite poles of a single continuum, but rather two separate sets of behavior. With this view, a person—regardless of her or his biological sex—can act in a masculine manner or a feminine manner, or exhibit both types of characteristics. The masculine–feminine dichotomy, then, is replaced with four **psychological sex types**, including masculine, feminine, **androgynous** (combining masculine and feminine traits), and undifferentiated (neither masculine nor feminine). The word **gender** is a shorthand term for psychological sex type. Combining the four psychological sex types with the traditional biological sex types produces four categories for men: masculine males, feminine males, androgynous males, and undifferentiated males; and four categories for women: masculine females, feminine females, androgynous females, and undifferentiated females. Although there are women and men who fit into all of the categories, in general, people see themselves as either sex-typed (masculine male/feminine female) or androgynous (Choi et al. 2009).

Each of these eight combined psychological/biological sex types perceives interpersonal relationships differently. For example, masculine males tend to see their interpersonal relationships as opportunities for competitive interaction, as opportunities to win something. Feminine females typically see their interpersonal relationships as opportunities to be nurturing, to express their feelings and emotions. Androgynous males and females, on the other hand, probably differ little in their perceptions of their interpersonal relationships. For example, feminine females and androgynous individuals, both male and female, give more sympathy to grieving people than do masculine males (Versalle & McDowell, 2004–2005).

Androgynous individuals tend to see their relationships as opportunities to behave in a variety of ways, depending on the nature of the relationships themselves, the context in which a particular relationship takes place, and the myriad other variables affecting what might constitute appropriate behavior. These variables are usually ignored by the sex-typed masculine males and feminine females, who have a smaller repertoire of behaviors.

AT WORK

Sexual Harassment and Perception

Almost 50 years after the U.S. Civil Rights Act prohibited it, sexual harassment in the workplace remains a problem. Complaints of unwanted sexual advances and a hostile work environment have cost employers almost $50 million annually in recent years (Equal Employment Opportunity Commission, 2010).

Scholars have tried to understand why complaints of harassment persist when the law clearly prohibits behavior that creates a "hostile work environment." They have discovered that while clear-cut examples of hostile sexism do exist, differing perceptions help explain many other incidents.

Not surprisingly, what constitutes harassment depends on one's sex (Ohse & Stockdale, 2008): Women are more likely than men to rate a behavior as hostile and/or offensive. Perhaps more surprisingly, younger people (both men and women) are less likely than older people to regard a scenario as sexual harassment.

Along with age and sex, cultural background helps shape perceptions of harassment (Fiedler & Blanco, 2006). People from cultures with high power distance (see Chapter 2, pages 39–40) are less likely to perceive harassment than those from places with low power distance.

Findings like these may not excuse harassment, but they do help explain it. The more members of an organization understand one another's perceptions, the better the odds that unpleasant and unfortunate feelings of harassment will arise.

Occupational Roles The kind of work we do also governs our view of the world. Imagine five people taking a walk through a park. One, a botanist, is fascinated by the variety of trees and plants. The zoologist is on the lookout for interesting animals. The third, a meteorologist, keeps an eye on the sky, noticing changes in the weather. The fourth, a psychologist, is totally unaware of the goings-on of nature, concentrating instead on the interaction among the people in the park. The fifth, a pickpocket, quickly takes advantage of the others' absorption to collect their wallets. There are two lessons in this little story: The first, of course, is to watch your wallet carefully. The second is that our occupational roles frequently govern our perceptions.

Perhaps the most dramatic illustration of how occupational roles shape perception occurred in the early 1970s. Stanford psychologist Philip Zimbardo (1971, 2007) recruited a group of well-educated, middle-class young men. He randomly chose 11 to serve as "guards" in a mock prison set up in the basement of Stanford's psychology building. He issued the guards uniforms, handcuffs, whistles, and billy clubs. The remaining 10 participants became "prisoners" and were placed in rooms with metal bars, bucket toilets, and cots.

Zimbardo let the guards establish their own rules for the experiment. The rules were tough: no talking during meals and rest periods and after lights out. They took head counts at 2:30 A.M. Troublemakers received short rations.

Faced with these conditions, the prisoners began to resist. Some barricaded their doors with beds. Others went on hunger strikes. Several ripped off their identifying number tags. The guards reacted to the rebellion by clamping down hard on protesters. Some turned sadistic, physically and verbally abusing the prisoners. The experiment was scheduled to go on for two weeks, but after six days Zimbardo realized that what had started as a simulation had become too intense. It seems that *what* we are is determined largely by society's designation of *who* we are.

Relational Roles Think back to the "Who am I?" list you made in Chapter 3 (page 66). It's likely your list included roles you play in relation to others: daughter, roommate, spouse, friend, and so on. Roles like these don't just define who you are—they also affect your perception.

Take for example the role of parent. As most new mothers and fathers will attest, having a child alters the way they see the world. They might perceive their crying baby as a helpless soul in need of comfort, while nearby strangers have a less charitable appraisal. As the child grows, parents often pay more attention to the messages in the child's environment. One father we know said he never noticed how much football fans curse and swear until he took his 6-year-old to a game with him. In other words, his role as father affected what he heard and how he interpreted it.

The roles involved in romantic love can also dramatically affect perception. These roles have many labels: partner, spouse, boyfriend/girlfriend, sweetheart, and so on. There are times when your affinity biases the way you perceive the object of your affection. You may see your sweetheart as more attractive than other people do, and perhaps you overlook some faults that others notice (Segrin et al., 2009; Swami & Furnham, 2008). Your romantic role can also change the way you view others. One study found that when people are in love, they view other romantic candidates as less attractive than they normally would (Gonzaga et al., 2008).

Perhaps the most telltale sign of the effect of "love goggles" is when they come off. Many people have experienced breaking up with a romantic partner and wondering later, "What did I ever see in that person?" The answer—at least in part—is that you saw what your relational role led you to see.

CULTURAL INFLUENCES

Culture influences selection, organization, interpretation, and negotiation, and exerts a powerful influence on the way we view others' communication. For example, when making judgments of emotion, Japanese tend to focus more on vocal cues, whereas Dutch tend to focus more on facial expressions (Tanaka et al., 2010). Even beliefs about the very value of talk differ from one culture to another (Dailey et al., 2005; Giles, Coupland, et al., 1992). Western cultures tend to view talk as desirable and use it for social purposes as well as to perform tasks. Silence has a negative value in these cultures. It is likely to be interpreted as lack of interest, unwillingness to communicate, hostility, anxiety, shyness, or a sign of interpersonal incompatibility. Westerners are uncomfortable with silence, which they find embarrassing and awkward.

FOCUS ON RESEARCH

Ethnicity Shapes Perceptions

Common wisdom suggests that we're known by the company we keep. Daryl Wout, Mary Murphy, and Claude Steele wanted to see if this principle operates when it comes to evaluating new acquaintances based on ethnicity.

The researchers asked black students to form impressions of fellow students based on social networking profiles. Some of the experimental subjects viewed profiles of a white student with a racially diverse social network, while others saw the profile of a white student with only white friends. Researchers then asked the subjects to guess how the person whose profile they had just viewed would likely perceive them if they were to meet.

Results showed that the black college students did indeed expect to be regarded more favorably by white students whom they believed already had ethnically diverse networks of friends than by those whose social groups were not ethnically diverse.

It's not unreasonable to assume that people who already have a diverse group of friendships are likely to be open to meeting more people from different backgrounds. But it's also possible that students with homogenous social networks would welcome the chance to broaden their circle of friends. Expecting rejection from people who don't have diverse friends is a mistake that can create a self-fulfilling prophecy.

Wout, D. A., Murphy, M. C., & Steele, C. M. (2010). When your friends matter: The effect of white students' racial friendship networks on meta-perceptions and perceived identity contingencies. *Journal of Experimental Social Psychology, 46,* 1035–1041.

On the other hand, Asian cultures tend to perceive talk quite differently. For thousands of years, Asian cultures have discouraged the expression of thoughts and feelings. Silence is valued, as Taoist sayings indicate: "In much talk there is great weariness" or "One who speaks does not know; one who knows does not speak." Unlike Westerners, who are uncomfortable with silence, Japanese and Chinese people believe that remaining quiet is the proper state when there is nothing to be said. To Asians, a talkative person is often considered a show-off or a fake.

It's easy to see how these different views of speech and silence can lead to communication problems when people from different cultures meet. Both the "talkative" Westerner and the "silent" Asian are behaving in ways they believe are proper, yet each may view the other with disapproval and mistrust. Only when they recognize the different standards of behavior can they adapt to one another, or at least understand and respect their differences.

The valuing of talk isn't the only way culture shapes perceptions. Author Anne Fadiman (1997) explains why Hmong immigrants from the mountains of Laos preferred their traditional shamanistic healers, called *txiv neeb*, to American doctors—and perceived their behaviors very differently:

> A *txiv neeb* might spend as much as eight hours in a sick person's home; doctors forced their patients, no matter how weak they were, to come to the hospital, and then might spend only twenty minutes at their bedsides. *Txiv neebs* were polite and never needed to ask questions; doctors asked about their sexual and excretory habits. *Txiv neebs* could render an immediate diagnosis; doctors often demanded samples of blood (or even urine or feces, which they liked to keep in little bottles), took X rays, and waited for days for the results to come back from the laboratory—and then, after all that, sometimes they were unable to identify the cause of the problem. *Txiv neebs* never undressed their patients; doctors asked patients to take off all their clothes, and sometimes dared to put their fingers inside women's vaginas. *Txiv neebs* knew that to treat the body without treating the soul was an act of patent folly; doctors never even mentioned the soul. (p. 33)

Perceptual differences don't just occur between residents of different countries. Within a single national culture, regional and ethnic co-cultures can create very different realities. In a fascinating series of studies, Peter Andersen and colleagues (1990) discovered that climate and geographic latitude were remarkably accurate predictors of communication predispositions. People living in southern latitudes of the United States were found to be more socially isolated, less tolerant of ambiguity, higher in self-esteem, more likely to touch others, and more likely to verbalize their thoughts and feelings than their northern counterparts. This sort of finding helps explain why communicators who travel from one part of a country to another find that their old patterns of communicating don't work as well in their new location. A southerner whose relatively talkative, high-touch style seemed completely normal at home might be viewed as pushy and aggressive in a new, northern home.

Culture plays an important role in our ability to understand the perspectives of others. Research shows that people raised in individualist cultures, which value independence, are often less adept at perspective taking than those from collectivist cultures, which value interdependence. In one study, Chinese and American players were paired together in a communication game that required the participants to take on the perspective of their partners (Wu & Keysar, 2007). In all measures, the collectivist Chinese had greater success in perspective taking than did their American counterparts. This isn't to suggest that one cultural orientation is better than the other; it only shows that culture shapes the way we perceive, understand, and empathize with others.

Common Tendencies in Perception

By now it's obvious that many factors distort the way we interpret the world. Social scientists use the term **attribution** to describe the process of attaching meaning to behavior. We attribute meaning to both our own actions and to the actions of others, but we often use different yardsticks. Research has uncovered several perceptual tendencies that may lead to inaccurate attributions.

WE MAKE SNAP JUDGMENTS

Our ancestors often had to make quick judgments about whether strangers were likely to be dangerous, and there are still times when this ability can be a survival skill (Flora, 2004). But there are many cases when judging others without enough knowledge or information can get us into trouble. In the most serious cases, innocent people are gunned down by shooters who make inaccurate snap decisions about "intruders" or "enemies." On a more personal level, most of us have felt badly misjudged by others who made unfavorable snap judgments about us. If you've ever been written off by a potential employer in the first few minutes of an interview, or have been unfairly rebuffed by someone you just met, then you know the feeling.

Despite the risks of rash decision making, in some circumstances people can make surprisingly good choices in the blink of an eye (Gladwell, 2004). The best snap judgments come from people whose decisions are based on expertise and experience. For example, psychologist John Gottman (1994) can watch a couple talking for just 12 minutes and predict with 90 percent accuracy whether they will still be married in 15 years.

Sometimes even nonexperts can be good at making split-second decisions. For example, students who watched a silent, 2-second video of a professor they never met and were asked to rate the teacher's effectiveness came up with ratings very similar to those of students who were in the professor's class for a semester (Ambady & Rosenthal, 1993). And many people who have tried the technique called "speed dating" are able to use physically observable traits to determine in just a few minutes whether a person they have just met will become a romantic partner (Kurzban & Weeden, 2005).

Snap judgments become particularly problematic when they are based on **stereotyping**—exaggerated beliefs associated with a categorizing system. Stereotypes, which people automatically make on "primitive categories" like race, sex, and age (Nelson, 2005), may be founded on a kernel of truth, but they go beyond the facts at hand and make claims that usually have no valid basis.

Three characteristics distinguish stereotypes from reasonable generalizations. The first involves *categorizing others on the basis of easily recognized but not necessarily significant characteristics.* For example, perhaps the first thing you notice about a person is his or her skin color—but that may not be nearly as significant as the person's intelligence or achievements. The second feature that characterizes stereotypes is *ascribing a set of characteristics to most or all members of a group.* For example, you might unfairly assume that all older people are doddering or that all men are insensitive to women's concerns (Hummert, 2011). Finally, stereotyping involves *applying the generalization to a particular person.* Once you believe all old people are geezers or all men are jerks, it's a short step to considering a particular senior citizen as senile or a particular man as a sexist pig.

Stereotypes can plague interracial communication (Buttny, 1997; Hughes & Baldwin, 2002). Surveys of college student attitudes show that many blacks characterize whites as "demanding" and "manipulative," while many whites describe blacks as "loud" and "ostentatious." Many black women report having been raised with stereotypical characterizations of whites (e.g., "most whites cannot be trusted"). One black college professor reported a personal story revealing a surprising set of stereotypical assumptions from a white colleague. "As the only African American at a university-sponsored party for faculty a few years ago, I was appalled when a white professor (whom I had just met) asked me to sing a Negro spiritual" (Hecht et al., 1993). Although it's possible that behavior like this can be motivated by a desire to be friendly, it is easy to see how it can be insensitive and offensive.

By adulthood, we tend to engage in stereotyping frequently, effortlessly, and often unconsciously (Zenmore et al., 2000). Once we create and hold stereotypes, we seek out isolated behaviors that support our inaccurate beliefs. For example, men and women in conflict with each other often remember only behaviors of the opposite sex that fit their stereotypes (Allen, 1998). They then point to these behaviors—which might not be representative of how the other person typically behaves—as "evidence" to suit their stereotypical and inaccurate claims: "Look! There you go criticizing me again. Typical for a woman!"

Farcus

by David Waisglass
Gordon Coulthart

© 1993 Farcus Cartoons

WAISGLASS/COULTHART

www.farcus.com

"There are two types of people in this world ... those who generalize, and those who don't."

One way to avoid the kinds of communication problems that come from excessive stereotyping is to "decategorize" others, giving yourself a chance to treat people as individuals instead of assuming that they possess the same characteristics as every other member of the group to which you assign them.

WE CLING TO FIRST IMPRESSIONS

Snap judgments can be dangerous because we tend to cling to them—whether or not they're correct. If our impressions are accurate, they can be useful ways of deciding how to respond best to people in the future. However, problems arise when our initial assessments are inaccurate; for once we form an opinion of someone, we tend to hang onto it and make any conflicting information fit our image.

Social scientists have coined the term **halo effect** to describe the tendency to form an overall positive impression of a person on the basis of one positive characteristic. Most typically, the positive impression comes from physical attractiveness, which can lead people to attribute all sorts of other virtues to the good-looking person (Dion et al., 1972; van Leeuwen & Macrae, 2004). For example, employment interviewers rate mediocre but attractive job applicants higher than their less attractive candidates (Watkins & Johnston, 2000). The first impression can also come from something you're told about a person. For example, in one study (Pentok-Voak et al., 2007), women who were told that a man liked children perceived him as more attractive and social.

Once we form a first impression—whether it's positive or negative—we tend to seek out and organize our impressions to support that opinion. Psychologists use the term **confirmation bias** to describe this process. For example, experimental subjects asked more suspicious questions when they believed that a suspect had been cheating on a task (Hill et al., 2008). The same bias occurs in job interviews: once a potential employer forms a positive impression, the tendency is to ask questions that confirm the employer's image of the applicant (Dougherty et al., 1994). The interviewer might ask leading questions aimed at supporting her positive views ("What lessons did you learn from that setback?"), interpret answers in a positive light ("Ah, taking time away from school to travel was a good idea!"), encourage the applicant ("Good point!"), and sell the company's virtues ("I think you would like working here"). Likewise, applicants who create a negative first impression are operating under a cloud that may be impossible to dispel.

The power of first impressions is also important in personal relationships. A study of college roommates found that those who had positive initial impressions of each other were likely to have positive subsequent interactions, manage their conflicts constructively, and continue living together (Marek et al., 2004). The converse was also true: Roommates who got off to a bad start tended to spiral negatively. This reinforces the wisdom and importance of the old adage, "You never get a second chance to make a first impression."

WE JUDGE OURSELVES MORE
CHARITABLY THAN WE DO OTHERS

While we may evaluate others critically, we tend to judge ourselves in the most generous terms possible (Farah & Atoum, 2002; McClure et al., 2011; Pal, 2007). Social scientists have labeled this tendency **self-serving bias**. On the one hand, when others suffer, we often blame the problem on their personal qualities. On the other hand, when we're the victims we find explanations outside ourselves (Floyd, 2000; Sedikides et al., 1998). Consider a few examples:

- When *they* botch a job, we think they weren't listening well or trying hard enough; when *we* make the mistake, the problem was unclear directions or not enough time.

- When *she* lashes out angrily, we say she's being moody or too sensitive; when *we* blow off steam, it's because of the pressure we've been under.

- When *he* gets caught speeding, we say he should have been more careful; when *we* get the ticket, we deny we were driving too fast or say, "Everybody does it."

- When *she* uses profanity, it's because of a flaw in her character; when *we* swear, it's because the situation called for it (Young, 2004).

- If *he* wins the lottery, we predict he'll make many negative changes to his life; if *we* win the lottery, changes we make to our lives will be positive (Nelson & Beggan, 2004).

Not surprisingly, self-serving bias is especially common in troubled relationships. In one study (Schütz, 1999), couples in conflict were more likely

FOCUS ON RESEARCH

Does Honesty Hurt? Receivers Say "Yes," Senders Say "No"

An old song claims that "You always hurt the one you love." Communication scholar Shuangyue Zhang explored this notion in a series of studies that examine honest but hurtful (HBH) messages in romantic relationships.

In one experiment, Zhang asked over 500 subjects to describe the impact of painfully honest messages. Lovers were much more likely to rate candid messages as hurtful when they were on the receiving end. When they were senders, they didn't even remember delivering many HBH messages to their partner. When confronted with these HBH messages, senders rated their own messages as more honest and constructive than did the partners on the receiving end.

Zhang's research confirms that we do often hurt the people we care most about—and that a self-serving bias prevents us from recognizing the effect of our words.

Zhang, S. (2009). Sender-recipient perspectives of honest but hurtful evaluative messages in romantic relationships. *Communication Reports, 22,* 89-101.

to blame their partner for the problem than to accept responsibility for their role in the problem. The researchers point out that these results came from couples dealing with ordinary relational challenges. They observe that self-serving bias is likely to be even stronger in troubled relationships.

When people are aware of both the positive and negative characteristics of another person, they tend to be more influenced by the undesirable traits (Baumeister et al., 2001; Kellermann, 1989). This attitude sometimes makes sense. If the negative quality clearly outweighs any positive ones, you would be foolish to ignore it. For example, a surgeon with shaky hands and a teacher who hates children would be unsuitable for their jobs, whatever their virtues. But much of the time it's a bad idea to pay excessive attention to negative qualities and overlook good ones.

WE ARE INFLUENCED BY OUR EXPECTATIONS

Suppose you took a class and were told in advance that the instructor is terrific. Would this affect the way you perceive the teacher? Research shows that it almost certainly would. In one study, students who read positive comments about instructors on a website viewed those teachers as more credible and attractive than did students who were not exposed to the same comments (Edwards et al., 2007).

Expectations don't always lead to more positive appraisals. There are times when we raise our expectations so high that we are disappointed with the events that occur. If you are told that someone you are about to meet is extremely attractive, you may create a picture in your mind of a professional model, only to be let down when the person doesn't live up to your unrealistic expectations. What if you had been told that the person isn't very good looking? In that case, you might have been pleasantly surprised by the person's appearance, and perhaps you would rate the person's attractiveness more positively. The point is, our expectations influence the way we see others, both positively and negatively—and may lead to self-fulfilling prophecies (DiPaola et al., 2010).

The knowledge that expectations influence our perceptions is important when making decisions about others. Many professions require that manuscripts submitted to journals be evaluated through "blind review"—that is, the person submitting the manuscript is not allowed to offer identifying information that might influence the evaluator's appraisal. In the same way, you can probably think of times when it would be wise to avoid advance information about another person so that you perceive the person as neutrally as possible.

WE ARE INFLUENCED BY THE OBVIOUS

Being influenced by what is most obvious is understandable. As you read earlier, we select stimuli from our environment that are noticeable—that is, intense, repetitious, unusual, or otherwise attention grabbing. The problem is that the most obvious factor is not necessarily the only cause—or the most significant one—of an event. For example

- When two children (or adults, for that matter) fight, it may be a mistake to blame the one who lashes out first. Perhaps the other one was at least equally responsible, teasing or refusing to cooperate.

- You might complain about an acquaintance whose malicious gossiping or arguing has become a bother, forgetting that by putting up with that kind of behavior you have been at least partially responsible.

- You might blame an unhappy work situation on the boss, overlooking other factors beyond her control, such as a change in the economy, the policy of higher management, or demands of customers or other workers.

These examples show that it is important to take time to gather all the facts before arriving at a conclusion.

WE ASSUME OTHERS ARE LIKE US

We commonly imagine that others possess the same attitudes and motives that we do (Human & Biesanz, 2011). The frequently mistaken assumption that others' views are similar to our own applies in a wide range of situations. For example

- You've heard a slightly raunchy joke that you found funny. You assume that it won't offend a friend. It does.

- You've been bothered by an instructor's tendency to get off the subject during lectures. If you were a professor, you'd want to know if you were creating problems for your students; so you decide that your instructor will probably be grateful for some constructive criticism. Unfortunately, you're wrong.

- You lost your temper with a friend a week ago and said some things you regret. In fact, if someone said those things to you, you would consider the relationship finished. Imagining that your friend feels the same way, you avoid making contact. In fact, your friend feels that he was partly responsible and has avoided you because he thinks you're the one who wants to end things.

These examples show that others don't always think or feel the way we do and that assuming similarities can lead to problems. Sometimes you can find out the other person's real position by asking directly, sometimes by checking with others, and sometimes by making an educated guess after you've thought the matter out. All these alternatives are better than simply assuming everyone would react the way you do.

We don't always fall into the kind of perceptual tendencies described in this section. Sometimes, for instance, people *are* responsible for their misfortunes, or our problems *are not* our fault. Likewise, the most obvious interpretation of a situation may be the correct one. Nonetheless, a large amount of research has shown again and again that our perceptions of others are often distorted in the ways we have described. The moral, then, is clear: Don't assume your perceptions are accurate or unbiased.

Synchronizing Our Perceptions

After reading this far, you can appreciate how out of synch our perceptions of one another can be. It's easy to understand how these mismatched perceptions can interfere with our communication. What we need, then, are tools to help others understand our perceptions and for us, in turn, to understand theirs. The following section introduces two such tools.

PERCEPTION CHECKING

With the likelihood for perceptual errors so great, it's easy to see how a communicator can leap to the wrong conclusion and make inaccurate assumptions. Consider the defense-arousing potential of incorrect accusations like these:

> "Why are you mad at me?" (Who said I was?)
>
> "What's the matter with you?" (Who said anything was the matter?)
>
> "Come on now. Tell the truth." (Who said I was lying?)

Even if your interpretations are correct, these kinds of mind-reading statements are likely to generate defensiveness. The skill of **perception checking** provides a better way to check and to share your interpretations (Hansen et al., 2002). A complete perception check has three parts:

1. A description of the behavior you noticed;
2. Two possible interpretations of the behavior;
3. A request for clarification about how to interpret the behavior.

Perception checks for the preceding three examples would look like this:

> "When you stomped out of the room and slammed the door [behavior], I wasn't sure whether you were mad at me [first interpretation] or just in a hurry [second interpretation]. How did you feel? [request for clarification]"

"You haven't laughed much in the last couple of days [behavior]. It makes me wonder whether something's bothering you [first interpretation] or whether you're just being quiet [second interpretation]. What's up? [request for clarification]"

"You said you really liked the job I did [behavior], but there was something about your voice that made me think you may not like it [first interpretation]. Maybe it's just my imagination, though [second interpretation]. How do you really feel? [request for clarification]"

Perception checking is a tool to help us understand others accurately instead of assuming that our first interpretation is correct. Because its goal is mutual understanding, perception checking is a cooperative approach to communication. Besides leading to more accurate perceptions, it signals an attitude of respect and concern for the other person, saying, in effect, "I know I'm not qualified to judge you without some help."

Sometimes an effective perception check won't need all of the parts listed in the preceding example to be effective:

"You haven't dropped by lately. Is anything the matter?" [single interpretation].

"I can't tell whether you're kidding me about being cheap or if you're serious [behavior combined with interpretations]. Are you mad at me?"

"Are you sure you don't mind driving? I can use a ride if it's no trouble, but I don't want to take you out of your way" [request for clarification comes first; no need to describe behavior].

The straightforward approach of perception checking has the best chance of working in what Chapter 2 identifies as *low-context cultures*, ones in which members use language as clearly and logically as possible. The dominant cultures of North America and Western Europe fit into this category, and members of these groups are most likely to appreciate the kind of straight talking that perception checking embodies. On the other hand, members of *high-context cultures* (more common in Latin America and Asia) value social harmony over clarity. High-context communicators are more likely to regard candid approaches like perception checking as potentially embarrassing, preferring instead less direct ways of understanding one another. Thus, a "let's get this straight" perception check might work well with a European American manager who was raised to value clarity, but it could be a serious mistake with a Mexican American or Asian American boss who has spent most of his or her life in a high-context culture.

Along with clarifying meaning, perception checking can sometimes be a face-saving way to raise an issue without directly threatening or attacking the other person. Consider these examples:

"Are you planning on doing those dishes later, or did you forget that it's your turn?

"Am I boring you, or do you have something else on your mind?"

In the first case you might have been quite confident that the other person had no intention of doing the dishes, and in the second that the other person was bored. Even so, a perception check is a less threatening way of pointing out their behavior than direct confrontation. Remember—one element of competent communication is the ability to choose the best option from a large repertoire, and perception checking can be a useful strategy at times.

BUILDING EMPATHY

Perception checking can help you decode messages more accurately, but it doesn't provide enough information for us to claim that we fully understand another person. For example, a professor who uses perception checking might learn that a student's reluctance to ask questions is due to confusion and not lack of interest. This information would be helpful, but imagine how much more effective the professor would be if she could get a sense of how it feels to be confused, and consider how the material that is so familiar to her appears to the student who is examining it for the first time. Likewise, parents whose perception checks reveal that their teenager's outlandish behavior grows from a desire to be accepted by others don't necessarily understand (or perhaps recall) what it feels like to crave that acceptance.

Empathy Defined What we need, then, to understand others more completely is **empathy**—the ability to re-create another person's perspective, to experience the world from his or her point of view (Breithaupt, 2011). It is impossible to achieve total empathy, but with enough effort and skill, we can come closer to this goal (Krause, 2010; Long et al., 1999).

As we'll use the term here, empathy has three dimensions (Stiff et al., 1988; Watt, 2007). On one level, empathy involves *perspective taking*—the ability to take on the viewpoint of another person. This understanding requires a suspension of judgment so that for the moment you set aside your own opinions and take on those of the other person. Besides cognitive understanding, empathy also has an affective dimension— what social scientists term *emotional contagion*. In everyday language, emotional contagion means that we experience the same feelings that others have. We know their fear, joy, sadness, and so on. A third ingredient of empathy is a genuine *concern* for the welfare of the other person. Not only do we think and feel as others do, but we have a sincere interest in their well-being. Full empathy requires both intellectual understanding of the other person's position and an affective understanding of the other's feelings (Kerem et al., 2001).

It's easy to confuse empathy with sympathy, but the concepts are different. With sympathy,

"How would you feel if the mouse did that to you?"

you view the other person's situation from your point of view. With empathy, you view it from the other person's perspective. Consider the difference between sympathizing and empathizing with an unwed mother or a homeless person. When you sympathize, your feelings focus on the other person's confusion, joy, or pain. When you empathize, the experience becomes your own, at least for the moment. Note that empathy doesn't require you to agree with the other person. You can empathize with difficult relatives or rude strangers without endorsing their behavior.

There's a physiological basis for empathy. Brain scans reveal that neural firing patterns that register our own thoughts and feelings are in many cases identical to those that register thoughts and feelings about others (Lombardo et al., 2010). This explains empathy on the biochemical level: It's possible to feel others' experiences in the same way we feel our own.

Besides *imagining* how another person feels, another way to gain empathy is to *physically experience* the same reality. Since body melds only occur in science fiction, simulations are the closest we can get to another person's reality. Stanford University communication researchers Nick Yee and Jeremy Bailenson (2006) created an "immersive virtual environment" in which college-age subjects took on the identity of an elderly "avatar," viewing themselves as a walking, speaking character of advanced age. Other subjects inhabited avatars of young people. After only a few minutes of self-observation and conversation with a research assistant, the students took a variety of tests to measure their attitudes toward the elderly. Subjects who had just acted as elderly people displayed significantly more positive attitudes toward the aged than did those whose avatars were more youthful.

Dark Side of Communication

WHEN EMPATHY GOES OVERBOARD

After reading these pages, you might think that there's no such thing as too much empathy. But both social and cognitive science tell us otherwise. Therapists have recognized that couples and families can become too connected with one another's experiences. When this happens, they lose track of their individual identities.

Enmeshment (sometimes called *fusion*) is the opposite of emotional detachment. Whereas detached family members are emotionally distant, enmeshed members lose track of where "I" ends and "you" begins. For example, think about parents who are so caught up in their children's lives that they become emotionally spent. Or imagine someone who stays in a failed relationship out of excessive concern for his or her partner's feelings.

Some neuroscientists suggest that enmeshment occurs when the part of the brain that processes empathy becomes overactive. When this happens, we become too involved in the emotional lives of those we care about, creating problems for both them and ourselves.

Lamm, C., Batson, C. D., & Decety, J. (2007). The neural substrate of human empathy: Effects of perspective-taking and cognitive appraisal. *Journal of Cognitive Neuroscience, 19*, 42–58.

The Value of Empathy The recipient of empathy receives several payoffs (Sezov, 2002; Swart et al., 2011). The first is increased *self-esteem*. Others usually respond to your point of view with judgments such as "That's right . . ." or "No, it's not that way at all. . . ." An empathic response is different: It suggests the listener is willing to accept you as you are, without any evaluations. It's flattering to find that someone is interested enough in your position to hear you out without passing judgment. The act of being understood also can be very *comforting*, whether or not the other person's reflections offer any additional help. When others empathize, a common thought is "I'm not alone." Finally, the target of empathy learns to *trust* the empathizer in a way that probably would not be otherwise possible.

Empathy and Ethics The "golden rule" of treating others as we want to be treated points to the clear relationship between the ability to empathize and the ethical principles that enable society to function in a manner that we consider civilized (Rifkin, 2009). Martin Hoffman (1991) and Frans de Waal (2008, 2009) have cited research showing the link between empathy and ethical altruism. Bystanders who feel empathy for victims are more likely to intervene and offer help than those who are indifferent. On a larger scale, studies have revealed a relationship between feelings of empathy and the willingness of people to favor the moral principle that resources should be allocated according to people's needs (Batson et al., 1995).

A look at criminal behavior also demonstrates the link between empathy and ethics. Typically, people who commit the most offensive crimes against others, such as rape and child abuse, are not inhibited by any sense of how their offenses affect the victims (Clements et al., 2007; Goleman, 1995). New treatments attempt to change behavior by instilling the ability to imagine how others are feeling (Day et al., 2010; Wade & Worthington, 2005). These programs have offenders read emotional descriptions of crimes similar to the ones they have committed and watch videotapes of victims describing what it was like to be assaulted. They also write accounts of what their offense must have felt like to the victim, read these stories to others in therapy groups, and even experience simulated reenactments of the crime in which they play the role of the victim. Through strategies like these, therapists try to help offenders develop the ethical compass that makes it more difficult to be indifferent to causing pain in others.

Requirements for Empathy Empathy may be valuable, but it isn't always easy to achieve. In fact, research shows that it's hardest to empathize with people who are radically different from us: in age, sex, socioeconomic status, intelligence, and so forth (Cronkhite, 1976; Samovar et al., 2010). In order to make such perceptual leaps, you need to develop several skills and attitudes: open-mindedness, imagination, and commitment.

Perhaps the most important characteristic of an empathic person is the ability and disposition to be *open-minded*—to set aside for the moment your own beliefs, attitudes, and values and to consider those of the other person (Herfst et al., 2008). Open-mindedness is especially difficult when the other person's position is radically different from your own. The temptation is to think (and sometimes say) "That's crazy!," "How can you believe that?," or "I'd do it this way. . . ."

Being open-minded is often difficult because people confuse *understanding* another's position with *accepting* it. These are quite different matters. To understand why a friend disagrees with you, for example, doesn't mean you have to give up your position and accept hers.

ⓈⒺⓁⒻ-ⒶⓈⓈⒺⓈⓈⓂⒺⓃⓉ

Empathy in Friendships

This instrument can help you determine the degree to which empathy is part of your friendships. Think of one of your close personal friendships and, with that friendship in mind, respond to each statement according to how much you agree with it.

If you agree completely, mark the statement **4**.
If you agree a great deal but not completely, mark the statement **3**.
If you agree somewhat, mark the statement **2**.
If you agree very little, mark the statement **1**.
If you do not agree, mark the statement **0**.

_____ 1. I understand what my friend says.

_____ 2. I understand how my friend feels.

_____ 3. I appreciate what my friend's experiences feel like to her or him.

_____ 4. I try to see things through my friend's eyes.

_____ 5. I ask my friend questions about what his or her experiences mean to him or her.

_____ 6. I ask my friend questions about what she or he is thinking.

_____ 7. I ask my friend questions about how he or she is feeling.

_____ 8. My friend understands what I say.

_____ 9. My friend understands how I feel.

_____ 10. My friend appreciates what my experiences feel like to me.

_____ 11. My friend tries to see things through my eyes.

_____ 12. My friend asks me questions about what my experiences mean to me.

_____ 13. My friend asks me questions about what I'm thinking.

_____ 14. My friend asks me questions about how I'm feeling.

SCORING:

Add your scores for items 1–7: This figure represents your perception of your empathy for your friend.
Add your scores for items 8–14: This represents your perception of your friend's empathy for you.

Each sum can range from 0 to 28. The higher the sum, the greater the empathy.
Now have your friend respond to the items, and compare your answers. The results might well contribute to greater empathy in your relationship.

Being open-minded often isn't enough to allow empathy. You also need enough *imagination* to be able to picture another person's background and thoughts (Decety, 2005). A happily married or single person needs imagination to empathize with the problems of a friend considering divorce. A young person needs it to empathize with a parent facing retirement. A teacher needs it to understand the problems facing students, just as students can't be empathic without trying to imagine how their instructor feels.

Because empathizing is often difficult, a third necessary quality is *commitment*, a sincere desire to understand another person. Listening to unfamiliar, often confusing information takes time and isn't always fun. If you aim to be empathic, be willing to face the challenge.

By now, you can see the tremendous challenges that face us when we want to understand one another. Physiological distortion, psychological interference, and social and cultural conditioning all insulate us from our fellow human beings. But the news isn't all bad: With a combination of determination and skill, we can do a better job of spanning the gap that separates us and, as a result, enjoy more satisfying interpersonal relationships.

Summary

Many communication challenges arise because of differing perceptions. The process of interpersonal perception is a complex one, and a variety of factors cause each person's view of reality to vary.

The reality we perceive is constructed through communication with others. First-order realities involve things and events that are tangible; second-order realities are the meanings we assign to those things and events. Interpersonal perception involves four phases: selection, organization, interpretation, and negotiation. A number of influences can affect how we perceive others' behavior. Physiological factors include our senses, age, health, fatigue, hunger, and biological cycles. Psychological factors such as mood and self-concept also have a strong influence on how we regard others. In addition, social influences such as sex and gender roles and occupational roles play an important part in the way we view those with whom we interact. Finally, cultural influences shape how we recognize and make sense of others' words and actions.

Our perceptions are often affected by common perceptual tendencies. We tend to make snap judgments and cling to first impressions, even if they are mistaken. We are more likely to blame others than ourselves for misfortunes. We are influenced by our expectations. We also are influenced by obvious stimuli, even if they are not the most important factors. Finally, we assume others are similar to us.

One way to coordinate our interpretations with others is through perception checking. Instead of jumping to conclusions, communicators who check their perceptions describe the behavior they noticed, offer two equally plausible interpretations, and ask for clarification from their partner.

Empathy is the ability to experience the world from another person's perspective. There are three dimensions to empathy: perspective taking, emotional involvement, and concern for the other person. Empathy has benefits for both the empathizer and the recipient. Some evidence suggests that there may be hereditary influences on the ability to empathize but that this ability can be developed with practice. Requirements for empathy include open-mindedness, imagination, and commitment.

Key Terms

- Androgynous (120)
- Attribution (124)
- Confirmation bias (126)
- Empathy (132)
- First-order realities (109)
- Gender (120)
- Halo effect (126)
- Interpretation (112)
- Narrative (114)
- Negotiation (114)
- Organization (111)
- Perception checking (130)
- Psychological sex type (120)
- Punctuation (112)
- Second-order realities (109)
- Selection (111)
- Self-serving bias (127)
- Standpoint theory (119)
- Stereotyping (125)

Activities

1. Critical Thinking Probe

Complete the following sentences:

a. Women _____

_____

b. Men _____

_____

    c. Latinos _____

    _____

    d. European Americans _____

    _____

    e. African Americans _____

    _____

    f. Older people _____

    _____

Now ask yourself the degree to which each of your responses was a stereotype and/or a generalization. Is it possible to make generalizations about these groups? How could your answers to these questions change the way you perceive and respond to people in these groups?

2. Invitation to Insight

You can get a better appreciation of the importance of punctuation by using the format pictured in Figure 4.3 to diagram the following situations:

    a. A father and daughter are growing more and more distant. The daughter withdraws because she interprets her father's coolness as rejection. The father views his daughter's aloofness as a rebuff and withdraws further.

    b. The relationship between two friends is becoming strained. One jokes to lighten up the tension, and the other becomes more tense.

    c. A couple is on the verge of breaking up. One partner frequently asks the other to show more affection. The other withdraws physical contact.

Explain how each of these situations could be punctuated differently by each participant. Next, use the same procedure to identify how an event from your experience could be punctuated in at least two different ways. Describe the consequences of failing to recognize the plausibility of each of these punctuation schemes.

3. Invitation to Insight

Choose one of the following situations, and describe how it could be perceived differently by each person. Be sure to include the steps of selection, organization, and interpretation. What might their narratives sound like as they negotiate their perceptions? List any relevant physiological, psychological, social, and cultural influences, as well as suggesting how the communicators' self-concepts might have affected their perceptions.

    a. A customer complains to a salesperson about poor service in a busy store.

    b. A parent and teenager argue about the proper time for returning home after a Saturday night date.

    c. A quiet student feels pressured when called upon by an instructor to speak up in class.

    d. A woman and a man argue about whether to increase balance in the workplace by making special efforts to hire employees from underrepresented groups.

4. Invitation to Insight

Pages 124–130 of this chapter outline several common perceptual tendencies. Describe instances in which you committed each of them, and explain the consequences of each one. Which of these perceptual tendencies are you most prone to make, and what are the potential results of making it? How can you avoid these tendencies in the future?

5. Skill Builder

Improve your perception-checking ability by developing complete perception-checking statements for each of the following situations. Be sure your statements include a description of the behavior, two equally plausible interpretations, and a request for verification.

    a. You made what you thought was an excellent suggestion to your boss. He or she said, "I'll get back to you about that right away." It's been 3 weeks, and you haven't received a response yet.

    b. You haven't received the usual weekly phone call from your family in over a month. Last time you spoke, you had an argument about where to spend the holidays.

6. Skill Builder

You can develop your empathy skills by putting yourself in the shoes of someone with whom you have an interpersonal relationship. With that person's help, describe *in the first person* how the other person views an issue that is important to him or her. In other words, try as much as possible to become that person and see things from his or her perspective. Your partner will be the best judge of your ability to make this perceptual jump, so use his or her feedback to modify your account. After completing the exercise, describe how your attempt changed the way you might relate to the other person.

After studying the material in this chapter . . .

You should understand:

1. The symbolic nature of language.
2. That meanings are in people, not words.
3. The types of rules that govern the use of language.
4. How language affects worldview.
5. The influence of language on identity, credibility and status, affiliation, power, and attitudes about sexism and racism.
6. The factors that influence precision and vagueness in language.
7. The language patterns that reflect a speaker's level of responsibility for his or her statements.
8. Three forms of disruptive language.
9. Varying positions about the relationship between gender and language.

You should be able to:

1. Identify cases in which you have attributed meanings to words instead of people.
2. Analyze a real or potential misunderstanding in terms of semantic or pragmatic rules.
3. Describe how principles presented in the section of this chapter titled "The Impact of Language" operate in your life.
4. Construct a message at the optimal level of specificity or vagueness for a given situation.
5. Construct statements that acknowledge your responsibility for the content of messages.
6. Rephrase disruptive statements in less inflammatory terms.
7. Identify similarities and differences in male and female language use, and provide explanations for such differences.

Stanford University professor Lera Boroditsky (2009) often begins her undergraduate lectures by asking students which cognitive faculty they would least want to lose. Most choose vision, and a few pick hearing. Almost no one mentions language.

Boroditsky suggests that this is an oversight. After all, she reasons, people who lack the ability to see or hear can still have rich and satisfying lives. "But what would your life be like if you had never learned a language?" she wonders. "Could you still have friends, get an education, hold a job, start a family? Language is so fundamental to our experience, so deeply a part of being human, that it's hard to imagine life without it" (p. 116).

Language is arguably the most essential component of human communication. In this chapter we explore the relationship between words and ideas. We describe some important characteristics of language and show how these characteristics affect our day-to-day communication. We outline several types of troublesome language and show how to replace them with more effective kinds of speech. Finally, we look at the degree to which gender influences the way we use language.

The Nature of Language

We begin our survey by looking at some features that characterize all languages. These features explain both why language is such a useful tool and why it can be so troublesome.

LANGUAGE IS SYMBOLIC

Words are arbitrary symbols that have no meaning in themselves. For example, the word *five* is a kind of code that represents the number of fingers on your hand only because we agree that it does. As Bateson and Jackson (1964) point out, "There is nothing particularly five-like in the number 'five'" (p. 271). To a speaker of French, the symbol *cinq* would convey the same meaning; to a computer, the same value would be represented by the electronically coded symbol *00110101*.

Even sign language, as "spoken" by most deaf people, is symbolic in nature and not the pantomime it might seem (Tolar et al., 2008). Because this form of communication is symbolic and not literal, there are hundreds of different sign languages used around the world that have evolved independently, whenever significant numbers of deaf people have come in contact (Meir et al., 2010). These distinct languages include American Sign Language, Mexican Sign Language, British Sign Language, French Sign Language, Danish Sign Language, Chinese Sign Language, and Australian Aboriginal and Mayan sign languages—and communicating across different sign languages can be as difficult as it is across different spoken languages (Quinto-Pozos, 2008).

LANGUAGE IS RULE-GOVERNED

The only reason symbol-laden languages work at all is that people agree on how to use them. The linguistic agreements that make communication possible can be codified in rules. Languages contain several types of rules. **Phonological rules** govern how sounds are combined to form words. For instance, the words *champagne, double,* and *occasion* have the same meaning in French and English, but are pronounced differently because the languages have different phonological rules.

Whereas phonological rules determine how spoken language sounds, **syntactic rules** govern the way symbols can be arranged. Notice that the following statements contain the same words, but the shift in syntax creates quite different meanings:

Whiskey makes you sick when you're well.
Whiskey, when you're sick, makes you well.

Although most of us aren't able to describe the syntactic rules that govern our language (Parisse, 2005), it's easy to recognize their existence when they are violated. A humorous example is the way the character Yoda speaks in the *Star Wars* movies. Phrases such as "the dark side are they" or "your father he is" often elicit a chuckle because they bend syntactical norms. Sometimes, however, apparently ungrammatical speech is simply following a different set of syntactic rules, reflecting regional or co-cultural dialects. Linguists believe it is crucial to view such dialects as *different* rather than *deficient* forms of English (Wolfram & Schilling-Estes, 2005).

Semantic rules also govern our use of language. Whereas syntax deals with structure, semantics governs the meaning of statements. Semantic rules are what make it possible for us to agree that "bikes" are for riding and "books" are for reading, and they help us know whom we will

"What part of oil lamp next to double squiggle over ox don't you understand?"

encounter when we use restrooms marked "men" and "women." Without semantic rules, communication would be impossible: Each of us would use symbols in unique ways, unintelligible to others.

Semantic rules help us understand the meaning of individual words, but they often don't explain how language operates in everyday life. Consider the statement "Let's get together tomorrow." The semantic meaning of the words in this sentence is clear enough, yet the statement could be taken in several ways. It could be a request ("I hope we can get together"), a polite command ("I want to see you"), or an empty cliché ("I don't really mean it"). We learn to distinguish the accurate meanings of such speech acts through **pragmatic rules** that tell us what uses and interpretations of a message are appropriate in a given context.

When pragmatic rules are understood by all players in the language game, smooth communication is possible. For example, one rule specifies that the relationship between communicators plays a large role in determining the meaning of a statement. Our example, "I want to see you," is likely to mean one thing when uttered by your boss and another entirely when it comes from your lover. Likewise, the setting in which the statement is made plays a role. Saying "I want to see you" will probably have a different meaning at the office than the same words uttered at a cocktail party—although the nonverbal behaviors that accompany a statement help us decode its meaning.

People in individual relationships create their own sets of pragmatic rules. Consider the use of humor: The teasing and jokes you exchange with gusto with one friend might be considered tasteless or offensive in another relationship. For instance, imagine an email message typed in CAPITAL LETTERS and filled with CURSE WORDS, INSULTS, NAME-CALLING, and EXCLAMATION MARKS!!! How would you interpret such a message? An outside observer might consider this an example of "flaming" and be appalled, when in fact the message might be a fun-loving case of "verbal jousting" between buddies (O'Sullivan & Flanagin, 2003). If you have a good friend whom you call by a less-than-tasteful nickname as a term of endearment, then you understand the concept. Keep in mind, however, that those who aren't privy to your relationship's pragmatic rules are likely to

TABLE 5.1 Pragmatic Rules Govern the Use and Meaning of a Statement

Notice how the same message ("You look very pretty today") takes on a different meaning depending on which of a variety of rules are used to formulate and interpret it.

	BOSS	EMPLOYEE
Content Actual words	"You look very pretty today."	
Speech Act The intent of a statement	Compliment an employee	Unknown
Relational Contract The perceived relationship between communicators	Boss who treats employees like family members	Subordinate employee, dependent on boss's approval for advancement
Episode Situation in which the interaction occurs	Casual conversation	Possible come-on by boss?
Life Script Self-concept of each communicator	Friendly guy	Woman determined to succeed on own merits
Cultural Archetype Cultural norms that shape a member's perceptions and actions	Middle-class American	Working-class American

Adapted from Pearce, W. B., & Cronen, V. (1980). *Communication, action, and meaning.* New York: Praeger. Used by permission.

misunderstand you, so you'll want to be wise about when and where to use these personal codes.

The *coordinated management of meaning* (CMM) theory describes some types of pragmatic rules that operate in everyday conversations. It suggests that we use rules at several levels to create our own messages and interpret others' statements (Moore & Lauters, 2008; Pearce, 2005). Table 5.1 uses a CMM framework to illustrate how two people might wind up confused because they are using different rules at several levels. In situations like this, it's important to make sure that the other person's use of language matches yours before jumping to conclusions about the meaning of his or her statements (Dougherty et al., 2009). The skill of perception checking described in Chapter 4 can be a useful tool at times like these.

LANGUAGE IS SUBJECTIVE

If the rules of language were more precise and if everyone followed them, we would suffer from fewer misunderstandings. You have an hour-long argument about "feminism" only to discover that you were using the term in different ways and that you really were in basic agreement. You tease a friend in what you mean to be a playful manner, but he takes you seriously and is offended.

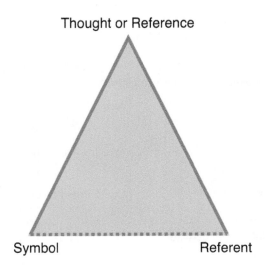

Thought or Reference

Symbol   Referent

FIGURE 5.1 **Ogden and Richards' Triangle of Meaning**

These problems occur because people attach different meanings to the same message. Ogden and Richards (1923) illustrated this point graphically in their well-known "triangle of meaning" (see Figure 5.1). This model shows that there is only an indirect relationship—indicated by a broken line—between a word and the thing or idea it represents.

The Ogden and Richards model is oversimplified in that not all words refer to physical "things" or referents. For instance, some referents are abstract ideas (such as *love*), while others (like *angry* or *exciting*) aren't even nouns. Despite these shortcomings, the triangle of meaning is useful since it clearly demonstrates an important principle: *Meanings are in people, not words.* Hence, an important task facing communicators is to establish a common understanding of the words they use to exchange messages. In this sense, communication—at least the effective kind—requires us to negotiate the meaning of our language (Duck, 1994; Fine & Beim, 2007). This brings us back to a familiar theme: Meaning is both *in* and *among* people.

LANGUAGE AND WORLDVIEW

For almost 150 years, theorists have put forth the notion of **linguistic relativism:** that the worldview of a culture is shaped and reflected by the language its members speak (Boroditsky, 2009; Deutscher, 2010). For instance, bilingual speakers seem to think differently when they change languages (Barner et al., 2009; Giles & Franklyn-Stokes, 1989). In one study, French Americans were asked to interpret a series of pictures. When they spoke in French, their descriptions were far more romantic and emotional than when they used English to describe the same kind of images. Likewise, when students in Hong Kong were asked to complete a values test, they expressed more traditional Chinese values when they answered in Cantonese than when they spoke in English. In Israel, both Muslim and Jewish students saw bigger distinctions between their group and "outsiders" when using their native language than when they spoke in English, a neutral tongue. Examples like these show the power of language to shape cultural identity—sometimes for better and sometimes for worse.

The best-known declaration of linguistic relativism is the **Sapir–Whorf hypothesis**, formulated by Benjamin Whorf, an amateur linguist, and anthropologist Edward Sapir (Tohidian, 2009; Whorf, 1956). Following Sapir's theoretical work, Whorf found that the language spoken by Hopi Native Americans represented a view of reality that is dramatically different from most tongues. For example, the Hopi language makes no distinction between nouns and verbs. Therefore, the people who speak it describe the entire world as being constantly in process. Whereas English speakers use nouns to characterize people or objects as being fixed or constant, the Hopi language represents them more as verbs, constantly changing. In this sense, English represents the world rather like a collection of snapshots, whereas Hopi reflects a worldview that is more like a motion picture.

Some languages contain terms that have no English equivalents (Rheingold, 1988; Wire, 2010). For example, consider a few words in other languages that have no simple translation in English:

- *Nemawashi* (Japanese): the process of informally feeling out all the people involved with an issue before making a decision

- *Lagniappe* (French/Creole): an extra gift given in a transaction that wasn't expected by the terms of a contract

- *Lao* (Mandarin): respectful term used for older people, showing their importance in the family and in society

- *Dharma* (Sanskrit): each person's unique, ideal path in life and the knowledge of how to find it

- *Koyaanisquatsi* (Hopi): nature out of balance; a way of life so crazy it calls for a new way of living

- *Jayus* (Indonesian): a joke told so poorly and that is so boring that the listener cannot help but laugh

"You'll have to phrase it another way. They have no word for 'fetch.'"

It's possible to imagine concepts like these without having specific words to describe them; but linguistic relativism suggests that the terms do shape the thinking and actions of people who use them. Thus, speakers of a language that includes the notion of *lao* would probably be more inclined to treat its older members respectfully, and those who are familiar with *lagniappe* might be more generous. As author David Malouf (2003, p. 44) observes,

> It is all very well to regard language as simply "a means of communication. . . . " But for most of us it is also a machine for thinking; and what can be thought and felt . . . is different, both in quality and kind, from one language to the next.

The Impact of Language

Besides simply describing the world, language can have a strong effect on our perceptions and how we regard one another. In the following pages we examine some of the many ways language can impact our lives.

NAMING AND IDENTITY

"What's in a name?" Juliet asked rhetorically. If Romeo had been a social scientist, he would have answered, "A great deal." Research has demonstrated that names are more than just a simple means of identification: They shape the way others think of us, the way we view ourselves, and the way we act (Lieberson, 2000).

For more than a century, researchers have studied the impact of rare and unusual names on the people who bear them (Christenfeld & Larsen, 2008). Early studies claimed that people with non-normative names suffered everything from psychological and emotional disturbance to failure in college. More recent studies have shown that people often have negative appraisals not only of unusual names, but also of unusual name spellings (Mehrabian, 2001). Of course, what makes a name (and its spelling) unusual changes with time. In 1900, the 20 most popular names for baby girls included Bertha, Mildred, and Ethel. By 2010, top 20 names included Madison, Addison, and Alyssa—names that would have been highly unusual a century earlier (Social Security Administration, 2011).

Some people regard unique names as distinctive rather than unusual. You can probably think of four or five unique names—of celebrities, sports stars, or even personal friends—that make the person easily recognizable and memorable. Sometimes the choice of unique names is connected with cultural identity. For example, in recent decades a large percentage of names given to African American babies have been distinctively black (Fryer & Levitt, 2004). In California, over 40 percent of black girls born recently have names that not a single white baby born in the entire state was given. Researchers suggest that distinctive names like these are a symbol of solidarity with the African American community. Conversely, choosing a less distinctive name can be a way of integrating the baby into the majority culture.

Names aren't just a reflection of ethnic identity: They can also be an indicator of status. Steven Levitt and Stephen Dubner (2005) used Census data to show the link between children's names and socioeconomic status. Once a name catches on among high-income, highly educated parents, it starts working its way down the socioeconomic ladder as it is bestowed on children of parents with less education and lower income. Thus, it's possible to speculate about the socioeconomic status of people once you know their name and date of birth.

AFFILIATION

Along with expressing ideas and feelings, speech can be a way of building and demonstrating solidarity with others.

An impressive body of research has demonstrated that communicators who want to show affiliation with one another adapt their speech in a variety of ways, including their choice of vocabulary, rate of talking, number and placement of pauses, and level of politeness (Aune & Kikuchi, 1993; Giles, Mulac, et al., 1992). In one study, the likelihood of mutual romantic interest increased when conversation partners' use of pronouns, articles, conjunctions, prepositions, and negations matched (Ireland et al., 2011). The same study revealed that when couples used similar language styles while instant messaging, the chances of their relationship continuing increased by almost 50 percent. The researchers speculate that unconscious language-style matching relates to how much each is paying attention to what the other says.

Close friends and lovers often develop a set of special terms that serve as a way of signifying their relationship (Bell & Healey, 1992; Dunleavy & Booth-Butterfield, 2009). Using the same vocabulary serves to set these people apart from others, reminding themselves and the rest of the world of their relationship. The same process works among members of larger groups, ranging from street gangs to military personnel. Communication researchers call the process of adapting one's speech style to match that of others with whom the communicator wants to identify **convergence**.

When two or more people feel equally positive about one another, their linguistic convergence will be mutual. But when communicators want or need approval, they often adapt their speech to accommodate the other person's style, trying to say the "right thing" or speak in a way that will help them fit in. We see this process when immigrants who want to gain the reward of material success in a new culture strive to master the host language. Likewise, employees who seek advancement tend to speak more like their superiors, supervisors adopt the speech style of managers, and managers converge toward their bosses. One study (Baruch & Jenkins, 2006) even showed that adopting the swearing patterns of bosses and coworkers can help people feel connected on the job. (See the At Work sidebar on page 154 for a discussion of this topic.)

The principle of speech accommodation works in reverse, too. Communicators who want to set themselves apart from others adopt the strategy of **divergence**, speaking in a way that emphasizes their differences. For example, members of an ethnic group, even though fluent in the dominant language, might use their own dialect as a way of showing solidarity with one another—a sort of "we're proud of our heritage" strategy. The same can occur across age lines, such as teens who adopt the slang of subcultures other than their own to show divergence with adults and convergence with their peers (Reyes, 2005). Of course, communicators need to be careful about when—and when not—to converge their language with others. Most of us can remember the embarrassment of hearing a parent use youthful slang and thinking, "You're too old to be saying that." On a more serious level, using ethnic/racial epithets when you're not a member of that in-group may be inappropriate and even offensive. One of the pragmatic goals of divergence is the creation of norms about who has the "right" to use certain words and who does not. (See the Media Clip on page 154 for an example of this issue.)

POWER

Communication researchers have identified a number of language patterns that add to or detract from a speaker's power to influence others. Notice the difference between these two statements:

> Excuse me, sir. I hate to say this, but I . . . uh . . . I guess I won't be able to turn in the assignment on time. I had a personal emergency and . . . well . . . it was just impossible to finish it by today. I'll have it in your mailbox on Monday, OK?

> I won't be able to turn in the assignment on time. I had a personal emergency and it was impossible to finish it by today. I'll have it in your mailbox on Monday.

Whether or not the instructor finds the excuse acceptable, it's clear that the second one sounds more confident, whereas the tone of the first is apologetic and uncertain. Table 5.2 identifies several **powerless speech mannerisms** illustrated in the statements you just read. A number of studies have shown that speakers whose talk is free of these mannerisms are rated as more competent, dynamic, and attractive than speakers who sound powerless (Ng & Bradac, 1993; Reid & Ng, 1999). The effects of powerful versus powerless speech styles also are apparent on employment interview outcomes: a powerful speech style results in more positive attributions of competence and employability than a powerless one (Parton et al., 2002). Even a single type of powerless speech mannerism, such as hedges, appears to make a person appear less authoritative or socially attractive (Hosman & Siltanen, 2006). If the person who uses powerless speech has high credibility to start with,

TABLE 5.2 Examples of Less Powerful Language

TYPE OF USAGE	EXAMPLE
Hedges	"I'm kinda disappointed . . ." "I think we should ..." "I guess I'd like to ..."
Hesitations	"Uh, can I have a minute of your time?" "Well, we could try this idea ..." "I wish you would—er—try to be on time."
Polite forms	"Excuse me, sir ..."
Tag questions	"It's about time we got started, isn't it?" "Don't you think we should give it another try?"
Disclaimers	"I probably shouldn't say this, but ..."

Adapted from Adler, R. B., & Elmhorst, J. (2010). *Communicating at work: Principles and practices for business and the professions* (10th ed., p. 29). New York: McGraw-Hill.

the powerless language seems to have less of an effect on how she or he is perceived (Blankenship & Craig, 2007).

Powerful speech that gets the desired results in mainstream North American and European culture doesn't succeed everywhere with everyone (Samovar & Porter, 2004). In Japan, saving face for others is an important goal, so communicators there tend to speak in ambiguous terms and use hedge words and qualifiers. In most Japanese sentences the verb comes at the end of the sentence so the "action" part of the statement can be postponed. Traditional Mexican culture, with its strong emphasis on cooperation, also uses hedging to smooth over interpersonal relationships. By not taking a firm stand with their speech mannerisms, Mexicans believe they will not make others feel ill at ease. The Korean culture represents yet another group of people who prefer "indirect" (for example, *perhaps, could be*) over "direct" speech.

Even in North American culture, simply counting the number of powerful or powerless statements won't always reveal who has the most control in a relationship. Social rules often mask the real distribution of power. A boss who wants to be pleasant might say to a secretary, "Would you mind getting this file?" In truth, both boss and secretary know this is an order and not a request, but the questioning form makes the medicine less bitter. Sociolinguist Deborah Tannen (1994a, p. 101) describes how politeness can be a face-saving way of delivering an order:

> I hear myself giving instructions to my assistants without actually issuing orders: "Maybe it would be a good idea to . . . ;" "It would be great if you could . . . " all the while knowing that I expect them to do what I've asked right away. . . . This rarely creates problems, though, because the people who work for me know that there is only one reason I mention tasks— because I want them done. I *like* giving instructions in this way; it appeals to my sense of what it means to be a good person . . . taking others' feelings into account.

F⊕CUS ON RESEARCH

"I Don't Mean to Antagonize You, But ..."

We use disclaimers to ward off a negative reaction by distancing ourselves from the unwelcome remarks we're about to utter. For example, you might preface a critical message by saying, "I don't mean to sound judgmental, but ..." and then go on to express your disapproval.

Disclaimers lower a speaker's credibility and attractiveness, which is why they are classified as a form of powerless speech (See Table 5.2). Despite this disadvantage, it might be worth using them if the payoff is preserving a positive relationship. To explore whether this trade-off of power for harmony is a valid option, a research team led by Amani El-Alayli explored whether disclaimers can, in fact, inoculate a speaker from the disapproval for delivering an unwelcome message.

The researchers found that disclaimers actually *increase* negative judgments about precisely the qualities the speaker is trying to downplay. For instance, the disclaimer "I don't mean to sound arrogant ..." followed by a high-handed comment led subjects to regard the speaker as *more* arrogant. Disclaimers involving other negative qualities, such as laziness and selfishness, produced similar results.

It seems that disclaimers backfire because they sensitize listeners to look for—and find—precisely the qualities that the speaker is trying to disavow.

El-Alayli, A., Myers, C. J., Petersen, T. L., & Lystad, A. L. (2008). "I don't mean to sound arrogant, but ..." The effects of using disclaimers on person perception. *Personality and Social Psychology Bulletin, 34,* 130–143.

As the proceeding quotation suggests, high-status speakers—especially higher-status women, according to Tannen—often realize that politeness is an effective way to get their needs met while protecting the dignity of the less-powerful person. The importance of achieving both content and relational goals helps explain why a mixture of powerful and polite speech is usually most effective (Geddes, 1992). The key involves adapting your style to your conversational partner (Loyd et al., 2010). If the other person is likely to perceive politeness as weakness, it may be necessary to shift to a more powerful speaking style. Conversely, if the person sees powerful speech as rude and insensitive, it might be best to use a more polite approach. As always, competent communication requires flexibility and adaptability.

SEXISM AND RACISM

Sexist language "includes words, phrases, and expressions that unnecessarily differentiate between females and males *or* exclude, trivialize, or diminish" either sex (Parks & Roberton, 2000, p. 415). This type of speech can affect the self-concepts of women and men, which is why one author (Lillian, 2007) argues that it is a form of hate speech. Suzanne Romaine (1999) offers several examples of how linguistic terms can subtly stereotype men and women. To say that a woman *mothered* her children focuses on her nurturing behavior, but to say that a man *fathered* a child talks only about his biological role. We are familiar with terms like *working mother,* but there is no term *working father* because we assume (perhaps inaccurately) that men are the breadwinners.

Beyond just stereotyping, sexist language can stigmatize women. For example, the term *unmarried mother* is common, but we do not talk about *unmarried fathers* because for many people there is no stigma attached to this status for men. Whereas there are over 200 English words for promiscuous women, there are only 20 for men (Piercey, 2000). Perhaps that's why "attitude towards women" is a significant predictor of attitudes regarding nonsexist language (Parks & Roberton, 2008). Education and perspective taking are also positively related to mindsets about inclusive language.

There are at least two ways to eliminate sexist language (Lei, 2006; Rakow, 1992). The first circumvents the problem altogether by eliminating sex-specific terms or substituting neutral terms. For example, using the plural *they* eliminates the

"Sorry, Chief, but of course I didn't mean 'bimbo' in the pejorative sense."

ⓈⒺⓁⒻ-ⒶⓈⓈⒺⓈⓈⓂⒺⓃⓉ

Sexist Language*

Respond to each of the following statements by indicating the extent to which you agree with it:

5 STRONGLY AGREE **4** AGREE **3** UNCERTAIN **2** DISAGREE **1** STRONGLY DISAGREE

_____ 1. Women who think that being called a "chairman" is sexist are misinterpreting the word "chairman."

_____ 2. When people use the term "man and wife," the expression is not sexist if the users don't mean it to be.

_____ 3. The elimination of sexist language is an important goal.

_____ 4. Sexist language is related to sexist treatment of people in society.

_____ 5. When teachers talk about the history of the United States, they should change expressions, such as "our forefathers," to expressions that include women.

_____ 6. The English language will never be changed because it is too deeply engrained in the culture.

SCORING:
Add your responses to the six statements, making sure to reverse-score statements 1, 2, and 6 (if you indicated 5, change it to 1; change 4 to 2; change 2 to 4; and change 1 to 5; 3 remains 3) = _____. Scores can range from 6 to 30, and scores that are approximately 24 and higher reflect a negative attitude toward sexist language.

*This Self-Assessment contains 6 of the 21 items on the Inventory of Attitudes Toward Sexist/Nonsexist Language-General, developed by Parks and Roberton (2000).

MEDIA CLIP   DIVIDE OR UNITE:
THE N WORD

It is possibly the most inflammatory word in American culture—so much so that the letter *N* is substituted for the actual word in most public discussions of the term. But as this documentary shows, the "N word" has many and varied meanings, ranging from a degrading slur to a term of endearment. A host of scholars and celebrities (including Chris Rock, Whoopi Goldberg, George Carlin, Ice Cube, and Quincy Jones) discuss and debate when, where, how, by whom, and even whether the "N word" should be used.

The film offers a vivid illustration of how pragmatic rules and linguistic convergence/divergence operate in interpersonal and intercultural communication. It also shows how failing to know and abide by cultural meanings and rules can lead to significant misunderstandings and conflict.

necessity for *he, she, she and he,* or *he and she.* When no sex reference is appropriate, you can substitute neutral terms. For example: *mankind* may be replaced with *humanity, human beings, human race,* and *people; man-made* may be replaced with *artificial, manufactured,* and *synthetic; manpower* may be replaced with *labor, workers,* and *workforce;* and *manhood* may be replaced with *adulthood.* In the same way, *Congressmen* are *members of Congress; firemen* are *firefighters; chairmen* are *presiding officers, leaders,* and *chairs; foremen* are *supervisors; policemen* and *policewomen* are both *police officers;* and *stewardesses* and *stewards* are both *flight attendants.* Of course, some terms refer to things that could not possibly have a sex— so, for example, a *manhole* is a *sewer lid.*

The second method for eliminating sexism is to mark sex clearly—to heighten awareness of whether the reference is to a female or a male. For example, rather than substitute "chairperson" for "chairman," use the terms chairman and chairwoman to specify whether the person is a man or a woman. (Note, also, that there is nothing sacred about putting he before she; in fact, putting *she, her,* and *hers* after *he, him,* and *his,* without changing the order, continues to imply that males are the more important sex and should come first.)

While sexist language usually defines the world as made up of superior men and inferior women, **racist language** reflects a worldview that classifies members of one racial group as superior and others as inferior (Asante, 2002). Not all language that might have racist overtones is deliberate. For example, the connotations of many words favor whites over people of color, as noted by Aaron Smith-McLallen and his colleagues (2006):

> In the United States and many other cultures, the color white often carries more positive connotations than the color black. . . . Terms such as "Black Monday," "Black Plague," "black cats," and the "black market" all have negative connotations, and literature, television, and movies have traditionally portrayed heroes in white and villains in black. The empirical work of John E. Williams and others throughout the 1960s demonstrated that these positive and negative associations with the colors black and white, independent of any explicit connection to race, were evident among white and black children as young as 3 years old . . . as well as among adults. (pp. 47–48)

An obvious step toward eliminating racist language is to make sure your communication is free of offensive labels and slurs—even those "innocent" uses of racist language that are not meant to be taken seriously but are used to maintain relationship solidarity (Guerin, 2003). Some troublesome language will be easy to identify, while other problematic speech will be more subtle. For instance, you may be unaware of using racial and ethnic modifiers when describing others, such as "black professor" or "Pakistani merchant" (or modifiers identifying sex, such as "female doctor" or "male secretary"). Modifiers like these usually aren't necessary, and they can be subtle indicators of racism/sexism. If you wouldn't typically use the phrases "white professor," "European American merchant," "male doctor," or "female secretary," then modifiers that identify race and sex might be indicators of attitudes and language that need to be changed.

Uses (and Abuses) of Language

By now, it's apparent that language can shape the way we perceive and understand the world. Next we will look at some specific types of usage and explore both the value and the potential problems that can arise.

PRECISION AND VAGUENESS

Most people assume that the goal of language is to make our ideas clear to one another. When clarity *is* the goal, we need language skills to make our ideas understandable to others. Sometimes, however, we want to be less than perfectly clear. The following pages point out some cases where vagueness serves useful purposes as well as cases where perfect understanding is the goal.

Ambiguous Language **Ambiguous language** consists of words and phrases that have more than one commonly accepted definition. Some ambiguous language is amusing, as the following newspaper headlines illustrate:

Police Begin Campaign to Run Down Jaywalkers

Teacher Strikes Idle Kids

20-Year Friendship Ends at the Altar

Many misunderstandings that arise from ambiguity are trivial. We recall eating dinner at a Mexican restaurant and ordering a "tostada with beans." Instead of being served a beef tostada with beans on the side, we were surprised to see the waiter bring us a plate containing a tostada *filled* with beans. As with most such misunderstandings, hindsight showed that the phrase *tostada with beans* has two equally correct meanings.

Other misunderstandings involving ambiguous messages can be more serious. A nurse gave one of her patients a scare when she told him that he "wouldn't be needing" his robe, books, and shaving materials anymore. The patient became quiet and moody. When the nurse inquired about the odd behavior, she discovered that the poor man had interpreted her statement to mean he was going to die soon. In fact, the nurse meant he would be going home shortly.

For another example of ambiguous language, consider the word *love*. J. A. Lee (1973; see also Berscheid, 2006) points out that people commonly use that term in six very different ways: *eros* (romantic love), *ludus* (game-playing love), *storge* (friendship love), *mania* (possessive, dependent love), *pragma* (logical love), and *agape* (all-giving, selfless love). These boil down to two basic notions (Fehr & Broughton, 2001): passionate love (intense arousal, attraction, and emotions) and companionate love (a bond of trust, caring, and respect). Imagine the conflicts that would occur between a couple who sincerely pledged their love to one another, each with a different kind of love in mind. We can imagine them asking one another, "If you really love me, why are you acting like this?" without realizing that each of them views the relationship differently (e.g., Olson, 2003).

It's difficult to catch and clarify every instance of ambiguous language. For this reason, the responsibility for interpreting statements accurately rests in large part with the receiver. Feedback of one sort or another—for example, paraphrasing and questioning—can help clear up misunderstandings: "You say you love me, but you want to see other people. In my book, 'love' is exclusive. What about you?"

Despite its obvious problems, ambiguous language has its uses (Eisenberg, 2007). For example, when a hospital system defined the nursing role of "care coordinator" in a strategically ambiguous way, some nurses were excited and exhilarated by the challenge of crafting a new role (Miller et al., 2000). As discussed in Chapter 3, using language that is open to several interpretations can help you avoid the kind of honesty and clarity that can embarrass both the speaker and listener. For

Dark Side of Communication
THE INCIVILITY OF HATE SPEECH

Sooner or later, you're bound to hear the slur. It may disparage an ethnic group, or perhaps a religion. The insult could be sexist or focus on sexual orientation. Whatever the subject, remarks like this can be called hate speech.

In many countries, hate speech is a crime. In the United States, even the vilest insults are protected by the First Amendment to the Constitution, as long as they don't incite immediate violence. (Private institutions such as employers or schools can constitutionally impose their own codes of conduct.)

Johns Hopkins University professor P.M. Forni argues that just because hateful language is legal doesn't make it right. He has dedicated his career to encouraging civility. He documents the physical and emotional toll that uncivil exchanges take on both the attacker and target. On a larger scale, Forni maintains that "vigorous civility is necessary for the survival of society as we know it."

To rephrase a well-known children's taunt, "Sticks and stones may break my bones, but words can *surely* hurt me." The next time you hear—or are tempted to use—hateful words, consider the toll they take on interpersonal relationships and a quest toward a more civil society.

Forni, P. M. (2010, July 23). Why civility is necessary for society's survival. *Dallasnews.com*. Retrieved from http://www.dallasnews.com/opinion/sunday-commentary/20100723-p.m.-forni-why-civility-is-necessary-for-society_s-survival.ece Dr. Forni's Civility Web Site: http://krieger.jhu.edu/civility

example, if a friend proudly shows you a newly completed painting and asks your opinion about it, you might respond equivocally by saying, "Gee, it's really unusual. I've never seen anything like it," instead of giving a less ambiguous but more hurtful response such as "This may be the ugliest thing I've ever seen!" See the discussion of euphemism on page 159 for more information on the value of ambiguity.

Abstraction High-level **abstractions** are convenient ways of generalizing about similarities between several objects, people, ideas, or events. Figure 5.2 is an **abstraction ladder** that shows how to describe the same phenomenon at various levels of abstraction.

We use higher-level abstractions all the time. For instance, rather than saying "Thanks for washing the dishes," "Thanks for vacuuming the rug," and "Thanks for making the bed," it's easier to say "Thanks for cleaning up." In such everyday situations, abstractions are a useful kind of verbal shorthand.

Like ambiguity, high-level abstractions also can help communicators find face-saving ways to avoid confrontations and embarrassment by being deliberately unclear (Eisenberg, 1984; Eisenberg & Witten, 1987). If a friend apologizes for arriving late for a date, you can choose to brush off the incident instead of making it an issue by saying "Don't worry. It wasn't the end of the world"—a true statement, but less specific than saying "To tell you the truth, I was mad at the time, but I've cooled off now." If your boss asks your opinion of a new idea that you think is weaker than your own approach but you don't want to disagree, you could respond with a higher-level abstraction by saying "I never thought of it that way."

FIGURE 5.2 Abstraction Ladder

A boss gives feedback to an employee about career advancement at various levels of specificity.

MEDIA CLIP

EVADING THE OBVIOUS: *DOUBT*

Sister Aloysius (Meryl Streep) begins to have doubts about everyone's favorite priest, Father Flynn (Philip Seymour Hoffman), who seems to have become inappropriately close with one of his pupils. Father Flynn's only defense is accusing the Sister of fact-opinion confusion, and pointing out that her use of accusatory language breaches the traditional power roles of the church.

Throughout the movie, Flynn and other characters rely on evasive language in their attempts to refute the Sister's accusations. In the movie's most dramatic scene, the young boy's mother (Viola Davis) uses euphemisms and evasive language to explain to the Sister that she knows that Father Flynn is molesting her son. The film illustrates how linguistic hedging makes it possible to steer clear of lying without telling the truth.

Although vagueness does have its uses, highly abstract language can cause several types of problems. At the most basic level, the vagueness of some abstract language makes it hard to understand the meaning of a message. Overly abstract language can also lead to stereotyping. Imagine someone who has had one bad experience and, as a result, blames an entire group: "Marriage counselors are worthless"; "New Yorkers are all rude"; or "Men are no good." Overly abstract expressions like these can cause people to think in generalities, ignoring uniqueness.

Besides narrowing your own options, excessively abstract language also can confuse others. Telling the hairstylist "not too short" or "more casual" might produce the look you want, or it might lead to an unpleasant surprise, just as telling the boss "Having several ideas to test is better than having just one" might give her the impression you like her idea.

You might assume that abstract statements will soften the blow of critical messages, but research suggests that isn't always the case. People who use vague language to describe others' negative actions are rated as less likeable than those who use concrete language (Douglas & Sutton, 2010). It seems a person describing another's negative behavior in abstract terms is assumed to have a hidden agenda. By contrast, using abstract language to describe the positive behaviors of others results in a more favorable impression of the describer.

Overly abstract language can lead to problems of a more serious nature. For instance, accusations of sexual assault can arise because one person claims to have said "no" when the other person insists no such refusal was ever conveyed. In response to this sort of disagreement, specific rules of sexual conduct have become more common in work and educational settings. Perhaps the best-known code of this type is the one developed at Antioch College (2006) in Ohio. The policy uses low-level abstractions to minimize the chances of anyone claiming confusion about a partner's willingness. For example, the code states:

- If sexual contact and/or conduct is not mutually and simultaneously initiated, then the person who initiates sexual contact/conduct is

158

responsible for getting verbal consent of the other individual(s) involved.

- Verbal consent [for sexual activity] should be obtained with each new level of physical and/or sexual behavior. . . . Asking "Do you want to have sex with me?" is not enough. The request for consent must be specific to each act.

- If someone has initially consented but then stops consenting during a sexual interaction, she/he should communicate withdrawal of consent verbally (example: saying "no" or "stop") and/or through physical resistance (example: pushing away). The other individual(s) must stop immediately.

Some critics have ridiculed rules like these as being unrealistically legalistic and chillingly inappropriate for romantic relationships. Whatever their weaknesses, the Antioch code illustrates how low-level abstractions can reduce the chances of a serious misunderstanding. Specific language may not be desirable or necessary in many situations, but in an era when misinterpretations can lead to accusations of physical assault, it does seem to have a useful place.

You can make your language—and your thinking—less abstract and more clear by learning to make *behavioral descriptions* of your problems, goals, appreciations, complaints, and requests. We use the word *behavioral* because such descriptions move down the abstraction ladder to describe the specific, observable objects and actions we're thinking about. Table 5.3 (page 160) shows how behavioral descriptions are much more clear and effective than vague, abstract statements.

Euphemism Euphemisms (from a Greek word meaning "to use words of good omen") are innocuous terms substituted for blunt ones. A euphemism avoids a direct, literal reference to an event (such as "She died"), substituting terms describing its consequences ("She's no longer with us"), related events ("She took her last breath"), metaphors ("She jumped the last hurdle"), or other, more abstract associations (McGlone et al., 2006). Euphemisms are typically used to soften the impact of information that might be unpleasant. It's easy to imagine how a relational breakup might be easier to handle with the explanation, "I'm not ready for commitment," than with "I want to date other people." We tend to use euphemisms more when talking with people of higher status, probably as a way to avoid offending them (Makin, 2004). When choosing how to broach difficult subjects, the challenge is to be as kind as possible without sacrificing either your integrity or the clarity of your message.

Relative Language Relative language gains meaning by comparison. For example, do you attend a large or a small school? This depends on what you compare it to. Alongside a campus such as Ohio State University, with more than 60,000 students, your school may look small, but compared with a smaller institution, it may seem quite large. Relative words such as fast

TABLE 5.3 Abstract and Behavioral Descriptions

	ABSTRACT DESCRIPTION	BEHAVIORAL DESCRIPTION			REMARKS
		WHO IS INVOLVED	IN WHAT CIRCUMSTANCES	SPECIFIC BEHAVIORS	
Problem	I'm no good at meeting strangers.	People I'd like to date	At parties and in school	I think, "They'd never want to date me." Also, I don't originate conversations.	Behavioral description more clearly identifies thoughts and behaviors to change.
Goal	I'd like to be more assertive.	Telephone and door-to-door solicitors	When I don't want the product or can't afford it	Instead of apologizing, I want to keep saying "I'm not interested" until they go away.	Behavioral description clearly outlines how to act; abstract description doesn't.
Appreciation	"You've been a great boss."	(no clarification necessary)	When I've needed to change my schedule because of school exams or assignments	"You've rearranged my hours cheerfully."	Give both abstract and behavioral descriptions for best results.
Complaint	"I don't like some of the instructors around here."	Professors A and B	In class, when students ask questions the professors think are stupid	They either answer in a sarcastic voice (you might demonstrate) or accuse us of not studying hard enough.	If talking to A or B, use only behavioral description. With others, use both abstract and behavioral descriptions.
Request	"Quit bothering me!"	You and your friends, X and Y	When I'm studying for exams	"Instead of asking me again and again to party with you, I wish you'd accept my comment that I need to study tonight."	Behavioral description will reduce defensiveness and make it clear that you don't always want to be left alone.

and slow, smart and stupid, short and long are clearly defined only through comparison.

Using relative terms without explaining them can lead to communication problems. Have you ever responded to someone's question about the weather by saying it was warm, only to find out the person thought it was cold? Have you followed a friend's advice and gone to a "cheap" restaurant, only to find that it was twice as expensive as you expected? Have

160

classes you heard were "easy" turned out to be hard? The problem in each case resulted from failing to link the relative word to a more measurable term.

One way to make words more measurable is to turn them into numbers. Health care practitioners have learned that patients often use vague wording when describing their pain: "It hurts a little"; "I'm pretty sore." The use of a numeric pain scale can give a more precise response—and lead to a better diagnosis (Prentice, 2005). When patients are asked to rank their pain from 1 to 10, with 10 being the most severe pain they've ever experienced, the number 7 is much more concrete and specific than "It aches a bit." The same technique can be used when asking people to relate anything from the movies they've seen to their job satisfaction.

Static Evaluation "Mark is a nervous guy." "Karen is short-tempered." "You can always count on Wes." Descriptions or evaluations that use the word *is* contain a **static evaluation**—the usually mistaken assumption that people or things are consistent and unchanging. Instead of labeling Mark as permanently and completely nervous, it would probably be more accurate to outline the situations in which he behaves nervously: "Mark acts nervously until you get to know him." The same goes for Karen, Wes, and the rest of us: We are more changeable than the way static, everyday language describes us.

Edward Sagarian (1976) writes about an unconscious language habit that imposes a static view of others. Why is it, he asks, that we say, "He has a cold" but say, "He is a convict" or a genius, a slow learner, or any other set of behaviors that are also not necessarily permanent? Sagarian argues that such linguistic labeling leads us to typecast others and in some cases forces them to perpetuate behaviors that could be changed.

General semanticist Alfred Korzybski (1933; see Levinson, 2010) suggested the linguistic device of *dating* to reduce static evaluation. He proposed adding a subscript whenever appropriate to show the transitory nature of a referent. For example, a teacher might write the following as an evaluation of a student: "Susan$_{May\ 12}$ had difficulty cooperating with her classmates." Although the actual device of subscripting is awkward in writing and impractical in conversation, the idea it represents can still be used. Instead of saying "I'm shy," a more accurate statement might be "I haven't approached any new people since I moved here." The first statement implies that your shyness is an unchangeable trait, rather like your height, while the second one suggests that you are capable of changing.

THE LANGUAGE OF RESPONSIBILITY

Besides providing a way to make the content of a message clear or obscure, language reflects the speaker's willingness to take responsibility for her or his beliefs, feelings, and actions. This acceptance or rejection of responsibility says a great deal about the speaker, and it can shape the tone of a relationship. To see how, read on.

"It" Statements Notice the difference between the sentences of each set:

"It bothers me when you're late."
"I'm worried when you're late."

"It's nice to see you."
"I'm glad to see you."

"It's a boring class."
"I'm bored in the class."

As their name implies, **"it" statements** replace the personal pronoun *I* with the less immediate construction *it's*. By contrast, **"I" language** clearly identifies the speaker as the source of a message. Communicators who use "it" statements avoid responsibility for ownership of a message, instead attributing it to some unidentified body. This habit isn't just imprecise; more important, it's an unconscious way to avoid taking a position. You can begin to appreciate the increased directness of "I" language by trying to use it instead of the less direct and more evasive "it" statements in your own conversations.

"But" Statements Statements that take the form "X-but-Y" can be quite confusing. A closer look at the **"but" statement** explains why. *But* has the effect of canceling the thought that precedes it:

"You're really a great person, but I think we ought to stop seeing each other."
"You've done good work for us, but we're going to have to let you go."
"This paper has some good ideas, but I'm giving it a grade of *D* because it's late."

"Buts" *can* be a face-saving strategy worth using at times. When the goal is to be absolutely clear, however, the most responsible approach will deliver the central idea without the distractions that can come with "but" statements. Breaking statements like the foregoing into two sentences and explaining each one as necessary lets you acknowledge both parts of the statement without contradicting yourself.

"I," "You," and "We" Language We've already seen that "I" language is a way of accepting responsibility for a message. **"You" language** is quite different. Like other forms of evaluative language, it expresses a judgment of the other person. Positive judgments ("You look great today!") rarely cause problems, but notice how each of the following critical "you" statements implies that the subject of the complaint is doing something wrong:

"You left this place a mess!"
"You didn't keep your promise!"
"You're really crude sometimes!"

It's easy to see why "you" language can arouse defensiveness. A "you" statement implies that the speaker is qualified to judge the target—not an idea that most listeners are willing to accept, even when the evaluation is correct.

162

"I" language provides a more accurate and less provocative way to express a complaint (Kubany et al., 1992; Winer & Majors, 1981). "I" language shows that the speaker takes responsibility for the accusation by describing his or her reaction to the other's behavior without making any judgments about its worth. Communicators who use these kinds of I-messages engage in **assertiveness**—clearly expressing their thoughts, feelings, and wants (Alberti & Emmons, 2008).

A complete "I" statement has three parts: It describes (1) the other person's behavior, (2) your feelings, and (3) the consequences the other's behavior has for you:

> "I get embarrassed [feeling] when you talk about my bad grades in front of our friends [behavior]. I'm afraid they'll think I'm stupid [consequence]."
> "When you didn't pick me up on time this morning [behavior], I was late for class and wound up getting chewed out by the professor [consequences]. That's why I got so angry [feeling]."
> "I haven't been very affectionate [consequence] because you've hardly spent any time with me in the past few weeks [behavior]. I'm confused [feeling] about how you feel about me."

When the chances of being misunderstood or getting a defensive reaction are high, it's a good idea to include all three elements in your "I" message. In some cases, however, only one or two of them will get the job done:

> "I went to a lot of trouble fixing this dinner, and now it's cold. Of course I'm annoyed!" (The behavior is obvious.)
> "I'm worried because you haven't called me up." ("Worried" is both a feeling and a consequence in this statement.)

As the "Cathy" cartoon on this page suggests, even the best-constructed and best-delivered "I" message won't always receive a nondefensive response

(Bippus & Young, 2005). As Thomas Gordon (1970) points out, "nobody welcomes hearing that his behavior is causing someone a problem, no matter how the message is phrased" (p. 145). Furthermore, "I" language in large doses can start to sound egotistical (Proctor, 1989). Research shows that self-absorbed people, also known as "conversational narcissists," can be identified by their constant use of first-person singular pronouns (Raskin & Shaw, 1988; Vangelisti et al., 1990). For this reason, "I" language works best in moderation.

One way to avoid overuse of "I" language is to consider the pronoun *we*. **"We" language** implies that the issue is the concern and responsibility of both the speaker and receiver of a message. Consider a few examples:

> "We have a problem. We can't seem to talk about money without fighting."
> "We aren't doing a very good job of keeping the apartment clean, are we?"
> "We need to talk to your parents about whether we'll visit them for the holidays."

It's easy to see how "we" language can help build a constructive climate. It suggests a kind of "we're in this together" orientation, a component of

TABLE 5.4 Pronoun Uses and Their Effects

PRONOUN	PROS	CONS	RECOMMENDATION
"I" Language	■ Takes responsibility for personal thoughts, feelings, and wants. ■ Less defense-provoking than evaluative "you" language.	■ Can be perceived as egotistical, narcissistic, and self-absorbed.	■ Use descriptive "I" messages in conflicts when the other person does not perceive a problem. ■ Combine "I" with "we" language in conversations.
"We" Language	■ Signals inclusion, immediacy, cohesiveness, and commitment.	■ Can speak improperly for others.	■ Combine with "I" language, particularly in personal conversations. ■ Use in group settings to enhance sense of unity. ■ Avoid when expressing personal thoughts, feelings, and wants.
"You" Language	■ Signals other-orientation, particularly when the topic is positive.	■ Can sound evaluative and judgmental, particularly during confrontations.	■ Use "I" language during confrontations. ■ Use "you" language when praising or including others.

what is known as *verbal immediacy* (Turman, 2008). Couples who use "we" language are more satisfied and manage conflict better than those who rely more heavily on "I" and "you" pronouns (Seider et al., 2009). On the other hand, using the pronoun "we" can be presumptuous since you are speaking for the other person as well as for yourself. It's easy to imagine someone responding to the statement "We have a problem . . . " by saying "Maybe *you* have a problem, but don't tell me *I* do!"

As Table 5.4 summarizes, all three pronouns—*I, you*, and *we*—have their advantages and drawbacks. Given this fact, what advice can we give about the most effective pronouns to use in interpersonal communication? A study by Russell Proctor and James Wilcox (1993) offers an answer. The researchers found that "I"/"we" combinations (for example, "I think that we . . . " or "I would like to see us . . . ") were strongly endorsed by college students, particularly for confrontational conversations in romantic relationships. Richard Slatcher and his associates (2008) came to a similar conclusion: There is value in both "I" and "we" messages in relational communication, as these pronouns demonstrate both autonomy and connection (see Chapter 9, pages 295–300, for a discussion of these relational dialectics).

Since too much of any pronoun comes across as inappropriate, combining pronouns is generally a good idea. If your "I" language reflects your position without being overly self-absorbed, your "you" language shows concern for others without judging them, and your "we" language includes others without speaking for them, you will probably come as close as possible to the ideal mix of pronouns.

AT WORK

Swearing on the Job

Swearing serves a variety of communication functions (Jay & Janschewitz, 2008). It's a way to express emotions and to let others know how strongly you feel. It can be a compliment ("that was #$&@ing terrific!") or the worst of insults. Swearing can offend and alienate, but it can also build solidarity and be a term of endearment.

Communication researchers Danette Johnson and Nicole Lewis (2010) investigated the effects of swearing in work settings. Not surprisingly, they found that the more formal the situation, the more negative the appraisal. The chosen swear word also made a difference: "F-bombs" were rated as more inappropriate than other less-volatile terms. Perhaps most important, when hearers were caught by surprise by a speaker's swearing, they were likely to deem the person as incompetent.

Despite these findings, Stanford University professor Robert Sutton (2010) notes that choosing *not* to swear can actually violate the norms of some organizations. Moreover, he maintains that swearing on rare occasions can be effective for the shock value. (The fact that Sutton authored a book called *The No Asshole Rule* suggests he practices what he preaches.)

But even Sutton adds a cautionary note about swearing on the job: "If you are not sure, don't do it." The rules of interpersonal competence apply: Analyze and adapt to your audience, and engage in self-monitoring. And when in doubt, err on the side of restraint.

DISRUPTIVE LANGUAGE

Not all linguistic problems come from misunderstandings. Sometimes people understand one another perfectly and still wind up in conflict. Of course, not all disagreements can, or should be, avoided. But eliminating three harmful linguistic habits from your communication repertoire can minimize the kind of clashes that don't need to happen, allowing you to save your energy for the unavoidable and important struggles.

Fact–Opinion Confusion **Factual statements** are claims that can be verified as true or false. By contrast, **opinion statements** are based on the speaker's beliefs. Unlike matters of fact, they can never be proven or disproven. Consider a few examples of the difference between factual and opinion statements:

Fact	Opinion
It rains more in Seattle than in Portland.	The climate in Portland is better than in Seattle.
Kareem Abdul-Jabbar is the all-time leading scorer in the National Basketball Association.	Kareem is the greatest basketball player in the history of the game!
The United States is the only industrialized country without universal health care.	The quality of life in the United States is lower than in any other industrial country when it comes to health care.

When factual and opinion statements are set side by side like this, the difference between them is clear. In everyday conversation, however, we often present our opinions as if they were facts, and in doing so we invite an unnecessary argument. For example:

"That was a dumb thing to say!"
"Spending that much is a waste of money!"
"You can't get a fair shake in this country unless you're a white male."

Notice how much less antagonistic each statement would be if it were prefaced by a qualifier such as "In my opinion . . . " or "It seems to me. . . . "

Fact–Inference Confusion Labeling your opinions can go a long way toward relational harmony, but developing this habit won't solve all linguistic problems. Difficulties also arise when we confuse factual statements with **inferential statements**—conclusions arrived at from an interpretation of evidence.

Arguments often result when we label our inferences as facts:

A: Why are you mad at me?

B: I'm not mad at you. Why have you been so insecure lately?

A: I'm not insecure. It's just that you've been so critical.

B: What do you mean, "critical"? I haven't been critical. . . .

Instead of trying to read the other person's mind, a far better course is to identify the observable behaviors (facts) that have caught your attention and to describe the interpretations (inferences) that you have drawn from them. After describing this train of thought, ask the other person to comment on the accuracy of your interpretation:

> "When you didn't return my phone call [fact], I got the idea that you're mad at me [inference]. Are you [question]?"
> "You've been asking me a lot lately whether I still love you [fact], and that makes me think you're feeling insecure [inference]. Is that right [question]?"

Evaluative Language Evaluative language (sometimes also called *"emotive language"*) seems to describe something but really announces the speaker's attitude toward it (Armstrong, 2005; Defour, 2008; Harding, 2007; Richards, 1948). If you approve of a friend's roundabout approach to a difficult subject, you might call her "tactful"; if you don't like it, you might accuse her of "beating around the bush." Whether the approach is good or bad is more a matter of opinion than of fact, although this difference is obscured by evaluative language.

You can appreciate how evaluative words are really editorial statements when you consider these examples:

If You Approve, Say	If You Disapprove, Say
thrifty	cheap
traditional	old-fashioned
extrovert	loudmouth
cautious	coward
progressive	radical
information	propaganda
eccentric	crazy

Gender and Language

So far we have discussed language usage as if it were identical for both women and men. Are there differences between male and female language use? If so, how important are they?

EXTENT OF GENDER DIFFERENCES

Given the obvious physical differences between the sexes and the differences in how men and women are regarded in most societies, it's not surprising that the general public has been captivated by the topic of gender differences in language use. Some people believe that men and women communicate in significantly different ways, while others find far more similarities than differences. We'll outline two approaches that represent two different sides in the gender and language debate.

Approach 1: Significant Differences In 1992, John Gray argued that men and women are so fundamentally different that they might as well have come from separate planets. In his best-selling book *Men Are from Mars, Women Are from Venus*, he claimed that

> men and women differ in all areas of their lives. Not only do men and women communicate differently but they think, feel, perceive, react, respond, love, need, and appreciate differently. They almost seem to be from different planets, speaking different languages and needing different nourishment. (p. 5)

Gray's work is based largely on anecdotes and conjecture and lacks scholarly support. However, social scientists have acknowledged that there are some significant differences in the way men and women behave socially (Palomares, 2008; Wood, 2009). This has led some scholars to describe males and females as members of distinct cultures, with their differences arising primarily from socialization rather than biology. The best known advocate of this "two-culture" theory is sociolinguist Deborah Tannen (1990, 1994, 2001). She suggests that men and women grow up learning different rules about how to speak and act.

In support of the two-culture hypothesis, communication researcher Anthony Mulac (2006) reports that men are more likely than women to speak in sentence fragments ("Nice photo."). Men typically talk about themselves with "I" references ("I have a lot of meetings") and use judgmental language. They are also more likely to make directive statements. By contrast, Mulac found that female speech is more tentative, elaborate, and emotional. For instance, women's sentences are typically longer than men's. Women also make more reference to feelings and use intensive adverbs ("He's *really* interested") that paint a more complete verbal picture than the characteristically terse masculine style. In addition, female speech is often less assertive. It contains more statements of uncertainty ("It seems to be . . . "), hedges ("We're *kind of* set in our ways."), and tag questions ("Do you think so?"). Some theorists have argued that such differences cause women's speech to be less powerful than men's (although the use of less powerful speech may be seen as more inclusive).

Approach 2: Minor Differences Despite the differences in the way men and women speak, the link between sex and language use isn't as clear-cut as it might seem. One analysis of over 1,200 research studies found that only 1 percent of variance in communication behavior resulted from sex differences (Canary & Hause, 1993). An analysis of 30 studies looking at power differences in women's and men's speech found that differences were small and, for the most part, not important (Timmerman, 2002). Other studies have found no significant difference between male and female speech in use of qualifiers such as "I guess" or "this is just my opinion," tag questions, and vocal fluency (Grob et al., 1997; Nemati & Bayer, 2007; Zahn, 1989). And the popular myth that women are more talkative than men doesn't

F⊕CUS ON RESEARCH

Sex Differences in Instant Messages

You're working at your computer when an instant message (IM) pops onto your screen. If you paid attention only to the message's content without looking at the sender's name, could you guess the person's sex? According to one study, the answer is "probably"—if you know what to look for.

Annie Fox and her colleagues recruited 35 college students and gave them tools for recording their IM exchanges. Participants were asked to select six of their IM conversations—three with men and three with women—and to submit them to the researchers for analysis.

The results showed that messages written by women were more expressive than ones composed by men. They were more likely to contain laughter ("hehe") emoticons (smiley faces), emphasis (italics, boldface, repeated letters), and adjectives. However, a number of other variables—such as questions, words per turn, and hedges—revealed no significant sex differences.

The verdict is similar to other research discussed in this chapter. While there are differences in the language styles of men and women, they aren't as drastic as some might think.

Fox, A. B., Bukatko, D., Hallahan, M., & Crawford, M. (2007). The medium makes a difference: Gender similarities and differences in instant messaging. *Journal of Language and Social Psychology, 26,* 389-397.

hold up under scientific scrutiny—researchers have found that men and women speak roughly the same number of words per day (Mehl et al., 2007).

In one study, Kristen Precht (2008) compared women's and men's use of "stance" words—the expression of attitude, emotion, certainty, doubt, and commitment—by analyzing 900,000 words of informal conversation in social and work settings. She found no differences between the sexes in their use of many types of words—for example, opinion and attitude words (e.g., "amazing," "happy," "funny," and "interesting"); certainty, doubt, and factuality words (e.g., "of course," "right?," and "sure"); emphatic words (e.g., "absolutely" and "never"); and hedges (e.g., "almost" and "usually"). Only expletives (e.g., "cool," "damn," and "wow") showed a significant difference between men and women. (Men use more of them.)

In light of the considerable similarities between the sexes and the relatively minor differences, communication researcher Kathryn Dindia (2006) suggests that the "men are from Mars, women are from Venus" claim should be replaced by the metaphor that "men are from North Dakota, women are from South Dakota."

ACCOUNTING FOR GENDER DIFFERENCES

By now you might be confused by what seem like contradictory views of how large and important the differences are between male and female speech. A substantial body of research helps reconcile some of the apparent contradictions by pointing out factors other than communicator sex that influence language use.

Occupation can trump gender as an influence on speaking style. As an example, male and female athletes communicate in similar ways (Sullivan, 2004). Male day care teachers' speech to their students resembles the language of female teachers more closely than it resembles the language of fathers at home (Gleason & Greif, 1983). Female farm operators, working in a male-dominated world, reproduce the masculinity that spells success for their male counterparts, swearing and talking "tough as nails" (Pilgeram, 2007). A close study of trial transcripts showed that the speaker's experience on the witness stand and occupation had more to do with language use than did biological sex (O'Barr, 1982; Waara & Shaw, 2006).

Another factor that trumps sex differences is *power*. For instance, in gay and lesbian relationships, the conversational styles of partners reflect power differences in the relationship (e.g., who is earning more money) more than the biological sex of the communicators (Steen & Schwartz, 1995). There are also few differences between the way men and women use powerful speech (specifically, threats) when they have the same amount of bargaining strength in a negotiation (Scudder & Andrews, 1995). Findings like this suggest that characteristically feminine speech has been less a function of gender or sex than of women's historically less powerful positions in some parts of the social world.

Summary

Language is both a marvelous communication tool and the source of many interpersonal problems. Every language is a collection of symbols governed by a variety of rules. Because of its symbolic nature, language is not a precise vehicle: Meanings rest in people, not in words themselves. Finally, the very language we speak can shape our worldview.

Besides conveying meanings about the content of a specific message, language both reflects and shapes the perceptions of its users. Terms used to name people influence the way they are regarded. Language also reflects the level of affiliation communicators have with each other. In addition, language patterns reflect and shape a speaker's perceived power. Language reflects and influences sexist and racist attitudes.

When used carelessly, language can lead to a variety of interpersonal problems. The level of precision or vagueness of messages can affect a receiver's understanding of them. Both precise messages and vague, evasive messages have their uses in interpersonal relationships, and a competent communicator has the ability to choose the optimal level of precision for the situation at hand. Language also acknowledges or avoids the speaker's acceptance of responsibility for his or her positions, and competent communicators know how to use "I," "you," and "we" statements to accept the optimal level of responsibility and relational harmony. Some language habits—confusing facts with opinions or inferences and using emotive terms—can lead to unnecessary disharmony in interpersonal relationships.

The relationship between biological sex and language is a complex one. While some writers in the popular press have argued that men and women are radically different and thus speak different languages, this position isn't supported by scholarship. A growing body of research suggests that what differences do exist are relatively minor in light of the similarities between the sexes. Many of the language differences that first appear to be sex-related may actually due to other factors such as occupation and interpersonal power.

Key Terms

- Abstraction (157)
- Abstraction ladder (157)
- Ambiguous language (155)
- Assertiveness (163)
- "But" statement (162)
- Convergence (149)
- Divergence (150)
- Evaluative language (167)
- Euphemism (159)
- Factual statement (166)
- "I" language (162)
- Inferential statement (166)
- "It" statement (162)
- Linguistic relativism (146)
- Opinion statement (166)
- Phonological rules (143)
- Powerless speech mannerisms (150)
- Pragmatic rules (144)
- Racist language (154)
- Relative language (159)
- Sapir–Whorf hypothesis (147)
- Semantic rules (143)
- Sexist language (152)
- Static evaluation (161)
- Syntactic rules (143)
- "We" language (163)
- "You" language (162)

Activities

1. Invitation to Insight
For each of the following scenes, describe one syntactic, one semantic, and one pragmatic rule:
   a. Asking an acquaintance out for a first date.
   b. Declining an invitation to a party.
   c. Responding to a stranger who has just said "excuse me" after bumping into you in a crowd.

2. Invitation to Insight
Recall an incident in which you were misunderstood. Explain how this event illustrated the principle "Meanings are in people, not words."

3. Ethical Challenge
The information about the impact of language on pages 148–155 shows how the words a communicator chooses can shape others' perceptions. Create two scenarios for each type of linguistic influence in the following list. The first should describe how the type of influence could be used constructively, and the second should describe an unethical application of this knowledge.
   a. Naming and identity
   b. Affiliation
   c. Power
   d. Sexism and racism

4. Invitation to Insight
Because meanings reside in people and not in words, one way to understand the nature of offensive language is to explore the reactions of people who may be offended by words that others speak or write without malice. Explore this by interviewing several people from various groups who perceive themselves to be marginalized because of factors such as religion, ethnicity, sexual orientation, gender, or political philosophy. Ask your subjects what language, if any, they find offensive and what interpretation they place on such language. Based on your findings, explore ways in which you and others could adapt speech to get across ideas in a way that is less likely to offend others.

5. Skill Builder
Translate the following into behavioral language:
   ■ An abstract goal for improving your interpersonal communication (for example, "Be more assertive" or "Stop being so sarcastic").
   ■ A complaint you have about another person (for instance, that he or she is "selfish" or "insensitive").

In both cases, describe the person or people involved, the circumstances in which the communication will take place, and the precise behaviors involved. What difference will using the behavioral descriptions be likely to make in your relationships?

6. Invitation to Insight

Are there ever situations in your life when it is appropriate to be less clear and more vague? Use the information on pages 156–159 to answer this question and to decide whether vagueness is the most competent approach to the situation.

7. Skill Builder

You can develop your skill at delivering "I" and "we" messages by following these steps:

    a. Visualize situations in your life when you might have sent each of the following messages:

        "You're not telling me the truth!"

        "You only think of yourself!"

        "Don't be so touchy!"

        "Quit fooling around!"

        "You don't understand a word I'm saying!"

    b. Write alternatives to each statement, using "I" language.

    c. Think of three "you" statements you could make to people in your life. Transform each of these statements into "I" and "we" language, and rehearse them with a classmate.

8. Invitation to Insight

What roles do the types of disruptive language described on pages 165–167 play in your life? Recall incidents when you have confused facts and opinions, confounded facts and inferences, and used emotive language. Discuss the consequences of each type of language use, and describe how the results might have been different if you had used language more carefully.

9. Invitation to Insight

Some authors believe that differences between male and female communication are so great that they can be characterized as "men are from Mars, women are from Venus." Other researchers believe the differences aren't nearly so dramatic and would describe them as "men are from North Dakota, women are from South Dakota." Which approach seems more accurate to you? Offer experiences from your life to support your point of view.

After studying the material in this chapter . . .

You should understand:

1. The distinguishing characteristics of nonverbal communication.
2. The functions that nonverbal communication can serve.
3. The various ways in which nonverbal messages are communicated.

You should be able to:

1. Describe your nonverbal behavior in any situation.
2. Identify nonverbal behavior that creates/maintains relationships, regulates interaction, influences others, conceals/deceives, or manages identity.
3. Monitor and manage your nonverbal cues in ways that achieve your goals.
4. Share appropriately your interpretation of another's nonverbal behavior.

P eople don't always say what they mean . . . but their body gestures and movements tell the truth!

Will he ask you out? Is she encouraging you?

Know what is really happening by understanding the secret language of body signals. You can:

Improve your sex life . . .

Pick up your social life . . .

Better your business life . . .

Read Body Language so that you can penetrate the personal secrets, both of intimates and total strangers . . .

Does her body say that she's a loose woman?

Do his eyes say that he's interested in you?

Do her facial expressions say that she's a manipulator?

Does the way he's standing say that he's a player?

Unless you've been trapped in a lead mine or doing fieldwork in the Amazon Basin, claims like these are probably familiar to you. Almost every pharmacy, supermarket, and airport book rack has its share of "body language" paperbacks. They promise that, for only a few dollars and with a fifth-grade reading ability, you can learn secrets that will change you from a fumbling social failure into a self-assured mind reader who can uncover a person's deepest secrets at a glance.

Observations like these are almost always exaggerations or fabrications. Don't misunderstand: There *is* a scientific body of knowledge about nonverbal communication, and it *has* provided many fascinating and valuable clues to human behavior. That's what this chapter is about. It's unlikely the next few pages will turn you instantly into a rich, sexy, charming communication superstar, but don't go away. Even without glamorous promises, a quick look at some facts about nonverbal communication shows that it's an important and valuable field to study—and that nonverbal skills are worth acquiring (Riggio, 2006).

Nonverbal Communication Defined

If *non* means "not" and *verbal* means "with words," then it seems logical that *nonverbal communication* would involve "communication without words." This definition is an oversimplification, however, because it fails to distinguish between *vocal* communication (by mouth) and *verbal* communication (with words). Some nonverbal messages have a vocal element. For example, the words "I love you" have different meanings depending on the way they are spoken. Furthermore, some nonspoken forms of communication, including sign languages used in the deaf community, are actually linguistic and not really nonverbal in the sense most social scientists use the term. Therefore, a better definition of **nonverbal communication** is "messages expressed by nonlinguistic means."

These nonlinguistic messages are important because what we *do* often conveys more meaning than what we *say*. Psychologist Albert Mehrabian (1972) claimed that 93 percent of the emotional impact of a message comes from a nonverbal source, whereas only a paltry 7 percent is verbal. Anthropologist Ray Birdwhistell (1970) described a 65–35 percent split between actions and words, respectively. Although social scientists have disputed these figures and the relative importance of verbal versus nonverbal cues (e.g., Gore, 2009; Lapakko, 1997), the point remains: Nonverbal communication contributes a great deal to shaping perceptions.

You might ask how nonverbal communication can be so powerful. At first glance, it seems as if meanings come from words. To answer this question, recall a time when you observed speakers of an unfamiliar language communicating. Although you couldn't understand the words being spoken, there were plenty of clues that gave you an idea of what was going on in the exchange. By tuning into their facial expressions, postures, gestures, vocal tones, and other behaviors you probably could make assumptions about the way the communicators felt about one another at the moment and got some ideas about the nature of their relationship. Researchers (summarized in Knapp & Hall, 2010) have found that subjects who hear content-free speech—ordinary speech that has been electronically manipulated so that the words are unintelligible—can consistently recognize the emotion being expressed, as well as identify its strength.

Characteristics of Nonverbal Communication

The many types of nonverbal communication share some characteristics. As Table 6.1 shows, these characteristics are quite different from verbal, linguistic means of communication. We now take a look at four fundamental characteristics of nonverbal communication.

177

TABLE 6.1 Some Differences between Verbal and Nonverbal Communication

VERBAL COMMUNICATION	NONVERBAL COMMUNICATION
Mostly voluntary and conscious	Often unconscious
Usually content-oriented	Usually relational
Can be clear or vague	Inherently ambiguous
Primarily shaped by culture	Primarily shaped by biology
Discontinuous/intermittent	Continuous
Single channel (words only)	Multichanneled

Adapted from p. 16 of Andersen, P. A. (1999). *Nonverbal communication: Forms and functions.* Mountain View, CA: Mayfield.

ALL BEHAVIOR HAS COMMUNICATIVE VALUE

Some theorists suggest that *all* nonverbal behavior communicates information. They argue that it is impossible *not* to communicate. You can understand the impossibility of noncommunication by considering what you would do if someone told you not to communicate any messages at all. What would you do? Close your eyes? Withdraw into a ball? Leave the room? You can probably see that even these behaviors communicate messages that mean you're avoiding contact. One study (DePaulo, 1992) took just this approach. When communicators were told not to express nonverbal clues, others viewed them as dull, withdrawn, uneasy, aloof, and deceptive.

The impossibility of not communicating is significant because it means that each of us is a kind of transmitter that cannot be shut off. No matter what we do, we send out messages that say something about ourselves and our relationships with others. If, for instance, others were observing you now, what nonverbal clues would they get about how you're feeling? Are you sitting forward or reclining back? Is your posture tense or relaxed? Are your eyes wide open, or do they keep closing? What does your facial expression communicate now? Can you make your face expressionless? Don't people with expressionless faces communicate something to you? Even uncontrollable behaviors can convey a message. You may not intend to show that you're embarrassed, but your blushing can still be a giveaway. Of course, not all behaviors (intentional or not) will be interpreted correctly: Your trembling hands might be taken as a sign of nervousness when you're really just shivering from the cold. But whether or not your behavior is intentional, and whether or not it is interpreted accurately, all nonverbal behavior has the potential to create messages.

Although nonverbal behavior reveals information, reviews of research show we aren't always conscious of what we and others are communicating nonverbally (Byron, 2008; Choi et al., 2005; Lakin, 2006). In one study, less than a quarter of experimental participants who had been instructed

to show increased or decreased liking of a partner could describe the non-verbal behaviors they used (Palmer & Simmons, 1995). Furthermore, just because communicators are nonverbally expressive doesn't mean that others will tune in to the abundance of unspoken messages that are available.

NONVERBAL COMMUNICATION IS PRIMARILY RELATIONAL

Some nonverbal messages serve utilitarian functions. For example, a police officer directs the flow of traffic, or a team of street surveyors uses hand motions to coordinate their work. But nonverbal communication also serves in a far more common (and more interesting) series of *social* functions.

Nonverbal communication allows us to demonstrate the kind of relationships we have—or want to have—with others (Burgoon & Le Poire, 1999). You can appreciate this fact by thinking about the wide range of ways you could behave when greeting another person. You could wave, shake hands, nod, smile, clap the other person on the back, give a hug, or avoid all contact. Each one of these behaviors sends a message about the nature of your relationship with the other person.

Nonverbal messages perform another valuable social function: They convey emotions that we may be unwilling or unable to express, or ones we may not even be aware of. In fact, nonverbal communication is much better suited to expressing attitudes and feelings than it is ideas. You can prove this for yourself by imagining how you could express each item on the following list nonverbally:

1. "I'm tired."

2. "I'm in favor of capital punishment."

3. "I'm attracted to another person in the group."

4. "I think prayer in the schools should be allowed."

5. "I'm angry at someone in this room."

This experience shows that, short of charades, ideas (such as statements 2 and 4) don't lend themselves to nonverbal expressions nearly as well as attitudes and feelings (statements 1, 3, and 5). This explains why it's possible

179

to understand the attitudes or feelings of others, even if you aren't able to understand the subject of their communication.

Despite their inherent leanness (see Chapter 2, pages 52–53), even text-based messages such as e-mail, instant messaging, and cell phone texting can include clues that come automatically in face-to-face communication. The most obvious way to represent nonverbal expressions in type is with emoticons, keyboard characters like these:

:-)	Basic smile. Most commonly used to indicate humorous intent ("no offense intended").
;-)	Wink and grin. Sometimes used to indicate sarcasm or for saying "Don't hit me for what I just said."
:-(	Frown.
:-I	Indifference.
:-@	Screaming, swearing, very angry.
:-||	Disgusted, grim.
:~-(	Crying.
:-/ or :-\	Skeptical.
:-O	Surprised, yelling, realization of an error ("Oops!").

Just like true facial expressions, emoticons can clarify the meaning that isn't evident from words alone (Derks et al., 2007). For example, see how each graphic below creates a different meaning for the same statement:

- You are driving me crazy

- You are driving me crazy

- You are driving me crazy

NONVERBAL COMMUNICATION IS AMBIGUOUS

Chapter 5 pointed out how some language can be ambiguous. (For example, the statement, "That nose piercing really makes you stand out," could be a compliment or a criticism, and the vague statement, "I'm almost done," could mean you have to wait a few minutes or an hour.) Most nonverbal behavior has the potential to be even more ambiguous than verbal statements like these. To understand why, consider how you would interpret silence from your companion during an evening together. Think of all the possible meanings of this nonverbal behavior: warmth, anger, preoccupation, boredom, nervousness, thoughtfulness—the possibilities are many.

The ambiguity of nonverbal behavior was illustrated when one supermarket chain tried to emphasize its customer-friendly approach by instructing employees to smile and make eye contact with customers. Several clerks filed grievances when some customers mistook the service-with-a-smile approach as sexual come-ons. As this story suggests, nonverbal cues are much more ambiguous than verbal statements when it comes to expressing a willingness to become physically involved (La France, 2010; Lim & Roloff, 1999).

Because nonverbal behavior is so ambiguous, caution is wise when you are responding to nonverbal cues. Rather than jumping to conclusions about the meaning of a sigh, smile, slammed door, or yawn, it's far better to use the kind of perception-checking approach described in Chapter 4. "When you yawned, I got the idea I might be boring you. But maybe you're just tired. What's going on?" The ability to consider more than one possible interpretation for nonverbal behavior illustrates the kind of cognitive complexity that Chapter 1 identified as an element of communication competence. Popular advice on the subject notwithstanding, it's usually not possible to read a person like a book.

NONVERBAL COMMUNICATION IS INFLUENCED BY CULTURE AND GENDER

Cultures have different nonverbal languages as well as verbal ones (Matsumoto & Yoo, 2005). Fiorello LaGuardia, legendary mayor of New York from 1933 to 1945, was fluent in English, Italian, and Yiddish. Researchers who watched films of his campaign speeches with the sound turned off found that they could tell which language he was speaking by the changes in his nonverbal behavior (Birdwhistell, 1970).

Some nonverbal behaviors—called **emblems**—are culturally understood substitutes for verbal expressions. Nodding the head up and down is an accepted way of saying "yes" in most cultures. Likewise, a side-to-side head shake is a nonverbal way of saying "no," and a shrug of the shoulders is commonly understood as meaning "I don't know" or "I'm not sure." Remember, however, that some emblems—such as the thumbs-up gesture— vary from one culture to another (it means "Good job!" in the United States, the number 1 in Germany, and the number 5 in Japan). Most North Americans would say the hand gesture in the photo on this page means "Okay." But to a Buddhist it signifies acceptance of the world as it is. (In other parts of the world, its meaning is vulgar.)

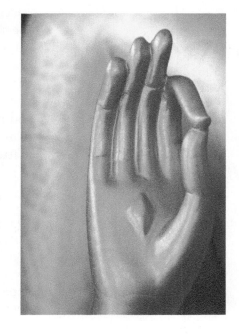

Despite differences like these, some nonverbal behaviors are universal. Certain expressions have the same meanings around the world. Smiles and laughter are a universal signal of positive emotions, for example, while the same sour expressions convey displeasure in every culture. Charles Darwin believed that expressions like these are the result of evolution, functioning as survival mechanisms that allowed early humans to convey emotional states before the development of language. The innateness of some facial expressions becomes even more clear when we examine the behavior of children born deaf and blind (Eibl-Eibesfeldt, 1972; see also Magnusson, 2006). Despite a lack of social learning, these children display a broad range of expressions. They smile, laugh, and cry in ways virtually identical to seeing and hearing infants.

While nonverbal expressions like these may be universal, the way they are used varies widely around the world (Matsumoto, 2006). In some cultures, display rules discourage the overt demonstration of feelings like happiness or anger. In other cultures, the same feelings are perfectly appropriate. Thus, a Japanese person might appear much more controlled and placid than an Arab, when in fact their feelings might be identical. It's important to note that the *culture* in which people live is far more important than their *nationality* or *ethnicity*. For example, the facial expressions of Japanese nationals and Japanese Americans differ in ways that reflect their cultural backgrounds (Marsh et al., 2003).

Sex also influences nonverbal communication—and with rare exceptions, differences between sexes hold true across cultures (Knapp & Hall, 2010). In general, females are more nonverbally expressive than males, and they are better at interpreting others' nonverbal behavior. More specifically, research summarized by Judith Hall (2006b) shows that, compared to men, women

- Smile more
- Use more facial expression
- Use more head, hand, and arm gestures (but less expansive gestures)
- Touch others more
- Stand closer to others
- Are more vocally expressive
- Make more eye contact

Despite these differences, men's and women's nonverbal communication patterns have a good deal in common (Dindia, 2006; Hall, 2006a). Differences like the ones noted above are noticeable, but they are outweighed by the similar rules we follow in most dimensions of nonverbal behavior. You can prove this by imagining what it would be like to use radically different nonverbal rules: standing only an inch away from others, sniffing strangers, or tapping people's foreheads to get their attention. Moreover, male-female nonverbal differences are less pronounced in conversations involving gay and lesbian participants (Knöfler & Imhof, 2007). Gender and culture certainly have an influence on nonverbal style, but the differences are often a matter of degree rather than kind.

Functions of Nonverbal Communication

Now that you understand what nonverbal communication is, we need to explore the functions it serves in relationships. As you'll read, nonverbal cues play several important roles in the way we relate with others.

CREATING AND MAINTAINING RELATIONSHIPS

As you will read in Chapter 9, communication is our primary means for beginning, maintaining, and ending relationships. Nonverbal behavior plays an important role during every relational stage.

Consider the importance of nonverbal communication during the very first stage of a relationship. When we first meet another person, our initial goal is to reduce our uncertainty about her or him (Berger, 1987, 2011). We ask ourselves questions like, "Would I like to know this person better?" and "Is this person interested in me?" One of the first ways we answer these questions is by observing nonverbal cues including facial expression, eye contact, posture, gesture, and tone of voice (Berger & Kellermann, 1994). This process occurs quite rapidly—often in a matter of seconds (Zebrowitz & Montepare, 2008).

At the same time we are sizing up others, we are providing nonverbal cues about our attitude toward them. We rarely share these thoughts and feelings overtly. Imagine how odd it would be to say or hear words like, "I'm friendly and relaxed" or "You look pretty interesting, but I won't pursue this unless you give me a sign that you're interested too." Messages like these are much more safely expressed via nonverbal channels. Of course, it's important to remember that nonverbal cues are ambiguous, and that you may be misinterpreting them (Mehrabian, 2008). In cases when you're considering moving the relationship forward, you may want to use the perception-checking skill outlined in Chapter 4 to verify your hunches.

Nonverbal cues are just as important in established, ongoing relationships, where they both create and signal the emotional climate. For example, nonverbal displays of affection—such as sitting close, holding hands, winks and gazes—are strongly connected to satisfaction and commitment in romantic relationships (Horan & Booth-Butterfield, 2010). In families, nonverbal cues offer a clear sign of relational satisfaction (Rogers, 2001), as well as who controls interaction and decision making (Aronsson & Cekaite, 2011; Brumark, 2010). On the job, supervisors who offer nonverbal cues of liking can increase subordinates' job motivation, job satisfaction, and liking of their boss (Richmond & McCroskey, 2000).

You can test the power of nonverbal behavior in relationships for yourself. First, observe the interaction of people in relationships without paying attention to their words. Watch couples or families in restaurants or other public places. Focus on fellow employees in the workplace. Observe professors and their students interacting in and outside of class. See how parents treat their children, and vice versa. You are likely to see a multitude of cues that suggest the quality of each relationship. Chances are good that you could make educated guesses about whether the people you're watching are satisfied with each other—and whether their relationship is beginning, maintaining, or ending.

REGULATING INTERACTION

Nonverbal **regulators** are cues that help control verbal interaction. The best example of such regulation is the wide array of turn-taking signals in

SELF-ASSESSMENT

Nonverbal Immediacy Behaviors

Most communication researchers agree that *nonverbal immediacy*—the display of involvement signaled by physical closeness, eye contact, movement, and touch—is an important ingredient of communication competence. You can measure your immediacy by completing this self-assessment. Indicate the degree to which you believe each statement applies to you.

Use the following 5-point measure as you apply each statement to yourself:

1 = NEVER   2 = RARELY   3 = OCCASIONALLY   4 = OFTEN   5 = VERY OFTEN

_____ 1. I use my hands and arms to gesture while talking to people.

_____ 2. I touch others on the shoulder or arm while talking to them.

_____ 3. I use a monotone or dull voice while talking to people.

_____ 4. I look over or away from others while talking to them.

_____ 5. I move away from others when they touch me while we are talking.

_____ 6. I have a relaxed body position when I talk to people.

_____ 7. I frown while talking to people.

_____ 8. I avoid eye contact while talking to people.

_____ 9. I have a tense body position while talking to people.

_____ 10. I sit close or stand close to people while talking with them.

_____ 11. My voice is monotonous or dull when I talk to people.

_____ 12. I use a variety of vocal expressions when I talk to people.

_____ 13. I gesture when I talk to people.

everyday conversation (Wiemann & Knapp, 2008). Three nonverbal signals that indicate a speaker has finished talking and is ready to yield to a listener are (1) changes in vocal intonation—a rising or falling in pitch at the end of a clause, (2) a drawl on the last syllable or the stressed syllable in a clause, and (3) a drop in vocal pitch or loudness when speaking a common expression such as "you know."

Eye contact is another way of regulating verbal communication (Bavelas et al., 2002). In conversations, the person listening typically looks more

_____ 14. I am animated when I talk to people.

_____ 15. I have a bland facial expression when I talk to people.

_____ 16. I move closer to people when I talk to them.

_____ 17. I look directly at people while talking to them.

_____ 18. I am stiff when I talk to people.

_____ 19. I have a lot of vocal variety when I talk to people.

_____ 20. I avoid gesturing while I am talking to people.

_____ 21. I lean toward people when I talk to them.

_____ 22. I maintain eye contact with people when I talk to them.

_____ 23. I try not to sit or stand close to people when I talk with them.

_____ 24. I lean away from people when I talk to them.

_____ 25. I smile when I talk to people.

_____ 26. I avoid touching people when I talk to them.

SCORING:
Step 1. Start with a score of 78. To that, add the scores from the following items: 1, 2, 6, 10, 12, 13, 14, 16, 17, 19, 21, 22, and 25.
Step 2. Add the scores from the following items: 3, 4, 5, 7, 8, 9, 11, 15, 18, 20, 23, 24, and 26.
Total Score = Step 1 minus Step 2. (Scores can range from a low of 26 to a high of 130.)

Men and women differed in their self-evaluations using this scale, with women perceiving themselves as engaging in more nonverbal immediacy behaviors then men. College-age women had an average score of 102, with most scores between 91 and 113. College-age men had an average score of 93.8, with most scores between 83 and 105.

Richmond, V. P., McCroskey, J. C., & Johnson, A. D. (2003). Development of the Nonverbal Immediacy Scale (NIS): Measures of self- and other-perceived nonverbal immediacy. *Communication Quarterly, 51,* 504–517.

at the speaker than the reverse. When the speaker seeks a response, he or she signals by looking at the listener, creating a brief period of mutual gaze called a "gaze window." At this point, the listener is likely to respond with a nod, "uh-huh," or other reaction, after which the speaker looks away and continues speaking. Children (and some socially insensitive adults) have not learned all the subtle signals of such turn taking. Through a rough series of trial and error, children finally learn how to "read" other people well enough to avoid interrupting.

INFLUENCING OTHERS

How we look, act, and sound can be more important in meeting our goals than the words we speak. The influence of nonverbal behavior comes in many forms. It can capture attention, show or increase liking, generate power, and boost credibility (Cesario & Higgins, 2008; Kopacz, 2006). Sometimes deliberately and sometimes without thought, we use nonverbal behaviors in ways that get others to satisfy our wants and needs. For example, people are more willing to do our bidding when we look them directly in the eye (Segrin, 1993), wear high-status clothing (Bushman, 1988), use open body postures (Burgoon et al. 1990), touch them (Guéguen et al., 2010), and behave in a friendly, upbeat way (Kleman, 2008). That's why job seekers are coached to offer firm handshakes (Stewart et al., 2008) and smile often and genuinely (Krumhuber et al., 2009) to help influence employers to hire them.

CONCEALING/DECEIVING

We may value and honor the truth, but the majority of messages we exchange are not completely truthful. Sometimes we keep silent, sometimes we hedge, and sometimes we downright lie. As you read in Chapter 3, not all deception is self-serving or malicious: Much of it is aimed at saving the "face" of the communicators involved. For example, you might pretend to have a good time at a family celebration or business event, even though you are bored senseless. Likewise, you might act graciously when socializing with someone you'd rather never see again. In situations like these and many others, it's easy to see how nonverbal factors can make the face-saving deception either succeed or fail.

Some people are better at hiding deceit than others. High self-monitors are usually better at hiding their deception than communicators who are less self-aware (Burgoon et al., 1994), and raters judge highly expressive liars as more honest than those who are more subdued (Burgoon et al., 1995). Not surprisingly, people whose jobs require them to act differently than they feel, such as actors, lawyers, diplomats, and salespeople, are more successful at deception than the general population (Riggio & Friedman, 1983).

Communication scholars Judee Burgoon and Tim Levine (2010) have studied deception detection for years. In their review of decades of

"I knew the suspect was lying because of certain telltale discrepancies between his voice and non verbal gestures. Also his pants were on fire."

research on the subject, they came up with what they call "Deception Detection 101"—three findings that have been supported time and again in studies. They are:

- We are accurate in detecting deception only slightly more than half the time—in other words, only a shade better than what we could achieve with a coin flip.

- We overestimate our abilities to detect others' lies—in other words, we're not as good at catching deception as we think we are.

- We have a strong tendency to judge others' messages as truthful—in other words, we want to believe people wouldn't lie to us (which biases our ability to detect deceit).

As one writer put it, "There is no unique telltale signal for a fib. Pinocchio's nose just doesn't exist, and that makes liars difficult to spot" (Lock, 2004, p. 72). Moreover, some popular prescriptions about liars' nonverbal behaviors simply aren't accurate (Guerrero & Floyd, 2006). For instance, conventional wisdom suggests that liars avert their gaze and fidget more than nonliars. Research, however, shows just the opposite: Liars often sustain *more* eye contact and fidget *less*, in part because they believe that to do otherwise might look deceitful. Popular characterizations of "scientific" lie detection aren't helpful, either. One experiment (Levine, 2009) found that viewers who watched the television show *Lie To Me* (in which the lead character attempts to catch liars) were actually *worse* at detecting lies than nonviewers, in part because the show focused on nonverbal cues and ignored important verbal content.

Despite the challenges, there are some clues that may reveal less-than-totally-honest communication (Ekman, 2009). For example, deceivers typically make more speech errors than truth-tellers: stammers, stutters, hesitations, false starts, and so on. Vocal pitch often rises when people

TABLE 6.2 Circumstances in Which a Deceiver Leaks Nonverbal Clues to Deception

DECEPTION CLUES ARE MORE LIKELY WHEN THE DECEIVER
Wants to hide emotions being felt at the moment
Feels strongly about the information being hidden
Feels apprehensive or guilty about the deception
Gets little enjoyment from being deceptive
Has not had time to rehearse the lie in advance
Knows there are severe punishments for being caught

Based on research summarized in P. Ekman. (2009). *Telling lies: Clues to deceit in the marketplace, politics, and marriage* (4th ed.). New York: W W Norton.

MEDIA CLIP MANAGING IDENTITY FOR ROMANCE: *HITCH*

Alex "Hitch" Hitchens (Will Smith) is a New York "date doctor" who teaches men how to romance the women of their dreams. His latest client is Albert Brenneman (Kevin James), a nerdy accountant who needs to improve his style to win the affections of the wealthy and beautiful Allegra Cole (Amber Valletta).

Hitch coaches Albert on a variety of nonverbal behaviors, including how to walk, stand, and dance, so that Albert can attract his dream woman. Despite the importance of self-presentation, Hitch's own love life shows that romantic success depends on more than manipulating a few nonverbal cues.

tell lies, and liars pause longer before offering answers than do truth-tellers (Sporer & Schwandt, 2007; Vrij et al., 2000). Perhaps most significantly—because it's a physiological reaction that's not easily controlled—liars' pupils tend to dilate because of the arousal associated with fib-telling (Vrij, 2006). That's why many professional poker players wear sunglasses to hide what their eyes might reveal. Table 6.2 outlines some conditions under which liars are likely to betray themselves with these sorts of clues.

The bottom line is that nonverbal cues offer important information for detecting deception, but most lies aren't detected through snap judgments of a facial expression or a shift in posture. Instead, people who suspect a lie tend to collect a variety of clues (including information from third parties and physical evidence) over a period of days, weeks, or even longer (Park et al., 2002). Jumping to conclusions based on limited information isn't wise communication, and it may lead to relational difficulties. Handle this material about deception detection with care and good judgment.

MANAGING IDENTITY

Chapter 3 (see pages 77–85) explained that one major goal of communicating is identity management: getting others to view us as we want to be seen. In many cases, nonverbal cues can be more important than verbal messages in creating impressions (DePaulo, 1992; Zuckerman et al., 1999), and a positive impression seems to be associated with consistency between our verbal and nonverbal behavior (Weisbuch et al., 2010). To appreciate how we manage impressions via nonverbal means, consider what happens when you meet strangers you would like to know better. Instead of projecting your image verbally ("Hi! I'm attractive, friendly, and easygoing"), you behave in ways that will present this identity. For example, you might dress fashionably, smile a lot, and perhaps try to strike a relaxed pose.

There are several ways of managing identity nonverbally. Sandra Metts and Erica Grohskopf (2003) reviewed professional trade journal articles on constructing good impressions and found examples of each of the following categories (their examples are in parentheses in the following list):

- *Manner* refers to the way we act: How we deliberately stand and move, the way we control facial expressions, and the adjustments we make in our voice. ("Stand tall and walk proudly"; "When meeting others, make direct eye contact and use a firm but friendly handshake.")

- *Appearance* involves the way we dress, the artifacts we wear, hair, makeup, scents, and so on. ("Dress how you wish to be remembered: with assurance, some spark of originality, and in a way that makes you feel comfortable and confident.")

- *Setting* involves the physical items we surround ourselves with: personal belongings, vehicles, and even the place we live. ("Mat and frame awards and certificates and display them in your office.")

Types of Nonverbal Communication

So far, we've talked about the role nonverbal communication plays in our interpersonal relationships. Now it's time to look at the many types of nonverbal communication.

BODY MOVEMENT

A primary way we communicate nonverbally is through the physical movement of our bodies: our posture, gestures, eye contact, facial expressions, and so on. Social scientists use the term **kinesics** to describe the study of how people communicate through bodily movements. We'll break them down by category, although these various features usually work in combination with each other.

Face and Eyes The face and eyes are probably the most noticeable parts of the body. However, the nonverbal messages they send are not always the easiest to read. The face is a tremendously complicated channel of expression to interpret, for several reasons.

First, it's hard to describe the number and kind of expressions commonly produced by the face and eyes. For example, researchers have found that there are at least 8 distinguishable positions of the eyebrows and forehead, 8 more of the eyes and lids, and 10 for the lower face (Ekman & Friesen, 1974a, 1975). When you multiply this complexity by the number of emotions we experience, you can see why it would be almost impossible to compile a dictionary of facial expressions and their corresponding emotions.

The significance of the face in interpersonal communication can be seen in the many phrases that allude to it. We talk about "saving face"; needing some "face time"; maintaining a "poker face"; and "facing our fears." That's because, according to Knapp and Hall (2010), the face may well be "the primary source of communicative information next to human speech" (p. 293).

A central component of facial expression is eye behavior. The study of how the eyes can communicate is sometimes known as **oculesics**. Gazes

"Spare a little eye contact?"

and glances are usually signals of the looker's interest. However, the *type* of interest can vary. Sometimes, as mentioned earlier, looking is a conversational turn-taking signal that says, "I'm finished talking. Now it's your turn." Gazing also is a good indicator of liking (Schotter et al., 2010). Sometimes, eye contact *reflects* liking that already exists, and at other times it actually creates or *increases* liking—hence the expression "making eyes." In other situations, eye contact indicates interest, but not attraction or approval, such as when a teacher glares at a rowdy student or a police officer "keeps an eye on" a suspect.

In addition to influencing verbal responses, research by Stephen Davis and Jamie Kieffer (1998; see also Kleman, 2008) details at least one effect of eye contact on an important nonverbal behavior: tipping. They found that customers in both small towns and urban areas leave larger tips when their servers (whether male or female) maintain eye contact with them. The authors speculate that good eye contact makes the atmosphere of the restaurant friendlier, and makes the customers feel as if they are dining at home. The At Work sidebar on page 193 discusses how touch can help achieve some of these same goals. That's not a coincidence: Research suggests there's a relationship between eye *contact* (note that word) and touching (Knapp & Hall, 2010).

Posture To appreciate the communicative value of body language, stop reading for a moment and notice how you're sitting. What does your position say nonverbally about how you feel? Are there any other people near you now? What messages do you get from their present posture? By paying attention to the postures of those around you, as well as to your own, you'll find another channel of nonverbal communication that reveals how people feel about themselves and others.

The English language indicates the deep links between posture and communication. English is full of expressions that tie emotional states with body postures:

> "I won't take this lying down!"

> "Stand on your own two feet."

> "Take a load off your back."

> "You're all wrapped up in yourself."

> "Don't be so uptight!"

Phrases like these show an awareness of posture, even if it's often unconscious. The main reason we miss most posture messages is that they

F⊕CUS ON RESEARCH

Power Posing

It's no surprise that commanding postures reflect self-confidence. But a team of researchers from Columbia and Harvard universities has discovered that bold postures can actually make people feel more self-assured.

The researchers assigned 42 participants to strike and maintain either high-power or low-power poses for two minutes. Lab tests showed that high-power posers experienced testosterone increases and lowered cortisol, both of which are linked to physiological empowerment. They also made bolder bets when given the chance to gamble after posing.

The results suggest that a change in posture can actually improve confidence and performance in communication contexts that include job interviews, public speeches, standing up to a boss, and taking risks that can lead to success. The researchers believe people can "fake it 'til they make it" by practicing powerful poses prior to an event and letting their feelings and behaviors follow.

Carney, D. R., Cuddy, A .J., & Yap, A. J. (2010). Power posing: Brief nonverbal displays affect neuroendocrine levels and risk tolerance. *Psychological Science, 21*, 1363–1368.

aren't too obvious. It's seldom that people who feel weighed down by a problem hunch over dramatically. When we're bored, we usually don't lean back and slump enough to embarrass the person with whom we're bored. In interpreting posture, then, the key is to look for small changes that might be shadows of the way people feel.

Some body language *can* be dramatic. Research shows that expansive poses—hands on hips, feet propped on a desk, or hawk-like stances—are signs of power and status (Hall et al., 2005). The Focus on Research sidebar on this page describes how adopting these poses can actually alter how we feel about ourselves.

Gestures Gestures are a fundamental element of communication—so fundamental, in fact, that people who have been blind from birth use them (Bruce et al., 2007). Gestures are sometimes intentional—for example, a cheery wave or thumbs-up. In other cases, however, our gestures are unconscious. Occasionally an unconscious gesture will consist of an unambiguous emblem, such as a shrug that clearly means "I don't know." More often, however, there are several possible interpretations to gestures. A group of ambiguous gestures consists of what we usually call *fidgeting*—movements in which one part of the body grooms, massages, rubs, holds, pinches, picks, or otherwise manipulates another part. Social scientists call these behaviors **manipulators**. Social rules may discourage us from performing more manipulators in public, but people still do so without noticing.

Research reveals what common sense suggests—that an increased use of manipulators is often a sign of discomfort (Ekman & Friesen, 1974b). But not *all* fidgeting signals uneasiness. People also are likely to use manipulators when relaxed. When they let their guard down (either alone or with friends), they will be more likely to fiddle with an earlobe, twirl a strand of hair, or clean their fingernails.

The amount and type of gesturing a person uses can be a measure of power and status (Andersen, 1999). For example, people who gesture more are rated by observers as being in positions of control and power, whereas those who gesture less are judged by observers as being subordinate. Head bowing is generally perceived as a submissive gesture and head raising as a dominant gesture (Mignault & Chaudhuri, 2003). Head nodding occurs more often when speaking with a person of higher status than of equal status; for example, a student nods more when talking with a professor than with another student (Helweg-Larsen et al., 2004). And pointing is judged by observers as one indicator of power, since it implies at least some ability to order other people around.

Gestures can produce a wide range of reactions in receivers. In many situations, the right kinds of gestures can increase persuasiveness (Maricchiolo et al., 2009), for example, increasing hand and arm movements, leaning forward, fidgeting less, and keeping limbs open all make a speaker more effective at influencing others. Even more interesting is the fact that persuasiveness increases when one person mirrors another's movements (Van Swol, 2003). When persuader and audience are reasonably similar, reciprocating the other person's gestures has a positive effect, whereas acting in a contrary manner is likely to have the opposite result (Sanchez-Burks et al., 2009).

As with almost any nonverbal behavior, the context in which gestures occur makes all the difference in the results they produce. Animated movements that are well received in a cooperative social setting may seem like signals of aggression or attempts at domination in a more competitive setting. Fidgeting that might suggest deviousness in a bargaining session could be appropriate when you offer a nervous apology in a personal situation. In any case, trying to manufacture insincere, artificial gestures (or any other nonverbal behaviors) will probably backfire. A more useful goal is to recognize the behaviors you find yourself spontaneously delivering and to consider how they reflect the attitudes you already feel.

TOUCH

Social scientists use the term **haptics** to distinguish the study of touching. Contemporary research confirms the value of touch for infants (Feldman et al., 2010; Field, 2003). Studies at the University of Miami's School of Medicine, for example, have shown that premature babies grow faster and gain more weight when massaged (Field, 2007). The same institute's researchers demonstrated that massage can help premature children gain weight, make colicky children sleep better, and boost the immune function of cancer and HIV patients. Massage helps newborn babies thrive, and it also helps depressed mothers of newborns feel better and smoothes the delivery process.

Touch also plays a large part in how we respond to others. For instance, in a laboratory task, participants evaluated partners more positively when they were touched (appropriately, of course) by them (Burgoon et al., 1992). Besides increasing liking, touch also boosts compliance. In a study by Chris

Kleinke (1977), participants were approached by a female confederate who requested that they return a dime left in the phone booth from which they had just emerged. When the request was accompanied by a light touch on the participant's arm, the probability that he or she would return the dime increased significantly. In a similar experiment (Willis & Hamm, 1980), participants were asked by a male or female confederate to sign a petition or complete a rating scale. Again, participants were more likely to cooperate when they were touched lightly on the arm.

Arguing that these small solicitations hardly get at the power of touch, Guéguen and Fischer-Lokou (2002) conducted an experiment in which confederates asked passersby to look after a large and very excited dog for 10 minutes so the owner could go into a pharmacy where animals were prohibited. In half of the cases, the passerby was touched during the request. Results confirmed that touch has a large effect on compliance: when touched, 55 percent agreed with the request, whereas only 35 percent in the no-touch condition agreed.

An additional power of touch is its on-the-job utility. Studies show that even fleeting touches on the hand or forearm can result in larger tips for restaurant servers (Crusco & Wetzel, 1984; Guéguen & Jacob, 2005). And a server who touches a patron's arm while suggesting a meal choice increases the probability of the patron's making the recommended choice (Guéguen et al., 2007). The effect extends to alcohol consumption: both women and men in taverns, whether in same-sex or different-sex dyads, increase their alcohol consumption when touched (appropriately, of course) by the server (Kaufman & Mahoney, 1999). For other examples of the power of touch on the job, see the At Work sidebar on this page.

In the United States, touching is generally perceived as more appropriate for women than for men (Derlega et al., 1989; Jones, 1986). Males touch their male friends less than they touch their female friends, and also less than females touch their female friends. Although women are generally more comfortable about touching than men, biological sex isn't the only factor that shapes contact. In general, the degree of touch comfort goes along with openness to expressing intimate feelings, an active interpersonal style, and satisfactory relationships (Fromme et al., 1989).

AT WORK

Touch and Career Success

The old phrase "keeping in touch" takes on new meaning once you understand the relationship between haptics and career effectiveness.

Some of the most pronounced benefits of touching occur in medicine and the health and helping professions. For example, patients are more likely to take their medicines when physicians give a slight touch while prescribing (Guéguen & Vion, 2009). Touch between therapists and clients has the potential to encourage a variety of beneficial changes: more self-disclosure, client self-acceptance, and better client–therapist relationships (Driscoll et al., 1988). In addition, patients with dementia who were administered hand massages, along with intermittent gentle touches on the arm and shoulder, decreased their anxiety and dysfunctional behavior (Kim & Buschmann, 1999).

Touch can also enhance success in sales and marketing. Customers in stores who were touched by a greeter spent more time shopping and bought more (Hornik, 1992). When an offer to try samples of a product is accompanied by a touch, customers are more likely to try the sample and buy the product (Smith et al., 1982).

Even athletes benefit from touch. One study of the National Basketball Association revealed that the touchiest teams had the most successful records, while the lowest scoring teams touched each other the least (Kraus et al., 2010).

It's important to note that too much contact can be annoying, harassing, and even downright creepy. But research confirms that *appropriate* professional contact can enhance your occupational success.

VOICE

Social scientists use the term **paralanguage** to describe the way a message is spoken. Vocal rate, pronunciation, pitch, tone, volume, and emphasis can give the same word or words many meanings. For example, note how many meanings come from a single sentence just by shifting the emphasis from one word to another:

This is a fantastic communication book.
(Not just any book, but *this* one in particular.)

This *is* a fantastic communication book.
(Without any doubt, this book is fantastic.)

This is a *fantastic* communication book.
(This book is superior, exciting.)

This is a fantastic *communication* book.
(The book is good as far as communication goes; it may not be so
  great as literature or as drama.)

This is a fantastic communication *book*.
(It's not a movie or music album; it's a book.)

There are many other ways we communicate paralinguistically—even through pauses. Consider two types of pauses that can lead to communication snags. The first is the *unintentional pause*—those times when people stop to collect their thoughts before deciding how best to continue their verbal message. It's no surprise that liars tend to have more unintentional pauses than truth-tellers, as they often make up stories on the fly (Guerrero & Floyd, 2006). When people pause at length after being asked a delicate question ("Did you like the gift I bought you?"), it might mean they're buying time to come up with a face-saving—and perhaps less-than-honest—response. A second type of pause is the *vocalized pause*. These range from **disfluencies** such as "um," "er," and "uh" to filler words such as "like," "okay," and "ya know." Vocalized pauses reduce a person's perceived credibility (Davis et al., 2006) and should thus be avoided—especially in job interviews (Latz, 2010).

The impact of paralinguistic cues is strong. For example, children are drawn more to playmates who—regardless of race—have similar speech styles than they are to students of the same race who speak differently (Kinzler et al., 2009). "Accent trumps race," as the authors' put it. In addition, listeners pay more attention to paralanguage than to the content of the words when asked to determine a speaker's attitudes (Burns & Beier, 1973) and emotions (Rodero, 2011). Furthermore, when vocal factors contradict a verbal message (as when a speaker shouts "I am *not* angry!"), listeners tend to judge the speaker's intention from the paralanguage, not the words themselves (Mehrabian & Weiner, 1967). Toward that end, it's important to pay attention to the paralinguistic messages you're sending. When first-year medical students watched videos of themselves and rated their doctor–patient communication, some of the primary shortcomings they noticed had to do with their paralanguage—particularly tone, rate, volume, and disfluencies (Zick et al., 2007).

Paralanguage can affect behavior in many ways, some of which are rather surprising. Studies by David Buller and Kelly Aune (1988, 1992) reveal that communicators are most likely to comply with requests delivered by speakers whose rate is similar to their own. However, speaking rate isn't constant. For example, it changes when a speaker's first message doesn't seem to get the desired results. Charles Berger and Patrick diBattista (1993) discovered that when communicators gave directions that weren't followed, the wording of their second attempts didn't change significantly. Instead, they simply slowed down and spoke louder.

Sarcasm is one approach in which we use emphasis, tone of voice, and length of utterance to change a statement's meaning to the opposite of its verbal message (Rockwell, 2007b). Experience this reversal yourself with the following three statements. First say them literally, and then say them sarcastically.

"You look terrific!"

"I really had a wonderful time on my blind date."

"There's nothing I like better than calves' brains on toast."

As with other nonverbal messages, people often ignore or misinterpret the vocal nuances of sarcasm. Members of certain groups—children, people with weak intellectual skills, poor listeners, people who have communication apprehension, and people with certain forms of brain damage—are more likely to misunderstand sarcastic messages than are others (Rockwell, 2007a; Shamay et al., 2002).

Young children in particular have difficulty making sense of mixed messages. In one study (Morton & Trehub, 2001),

Dark Side of Communication
ACCENTS AND STIGMAS

In the musical *My Fair Lady*, Professor Henry Higgins transforms Eliza Doolittle from a humble flower girl into a high-society woman by replacing her Cockney accent with an upper-crust British speaking style. Although the story (based on George Bernard Shaw's play *Pygmalion*) is fictional, the notion that we judge people by their accents is all too real.

Several decades of research show that judgments of attractiveness and status are strongly influenced by style of speech. In one study (Frumkin, 2007), jurors in the United States found testimony less believable when delivered by witnesses speaking with German, Mexican, or Middle Eastern accents. Not surprisingly, other research shows that speakers with nonnative accents feel stigmatized by the bias against them, often leading to a lower sense of belonging and more communication problems (Gluszek et al., 2011).

In another experiment (Bailey, 2003), researchers asked human resource professionals to rate the intelligence, initiative, and personality of job applicants after hearing a 45-second recording of their voices. The speakers with identifiable regional accents—Southern or New Jersey, for example—were recommended for lower-level jobs, while those with less pronounced speech styles were tagged for higher-level jobs that involved more public contact.

It's common knowledge that we shouldn't judge a book by its cover or people by superficial characteristics—but, unfortunately, we do so all the time. Remember when listening to people whose accent is different from yours to stay focused on what they're saying, not how they're saying it.

Bailey, R. W. (2003). Ideologies, attitudes, and perceptions. *American Speech, 88*, 115-142.

Frumkin, L. (2007). Influences of accent and ethnic background on perceptions of eyewitness testimony. *Psychology, Crime & Law, 13*, 317-331.

Gluszek, A., & Dovidio, J. F. (2010). Speaking with a nonnative accent: Perceptions of bias, communication difficulties, and belonging in the United States. *Journal of Language & Social Psychology, 29*, 224-234.

youngsters ages 4–8 years old were presented with a series of positive and negative statements. When positive statements (such as "Dad gave me a new bike for my birthday") were delivered in a sad tone of voice, the children gauged the speaker as happy because they paid attention to the words rather than the vocal cues. When negative statements were read in an upbeat tone, children interpreted the message as negative—again, relying more on the content than the paralanguage. There was a direct relationship between age and sensitivity to nonverbal cues, with the youngest children relying most heavily on the words spoken.

Communication through paralanguage isn't always intentional. Our voices often give us away when we're trying to create an impression different from our actual feelings. For example, you've probably had the experience of trying to sound calm and serene when you were really very nervous. Maybe your deception went along perfectly for a while—just the right smile, no telltale fidgeting of the hands, posture appearing relaxed—and then, without being able to do a thing about it, right in the middle of your relaxed comments, your voice squeaked! The charade was over.

In addition to reinforcing or contradicting messages, some vocal factors influence the way a speaker is perceived by others (Castelan-Cargile & Bradac, 2001). For example, surgeons whose voices were regarded as dominating and indifferent were more likely to be sued for malpractice than those with a less threatening vocal style (Ambady et al., 2002). Faster rates of speech and louder voices are generally perceived as more persuasive and

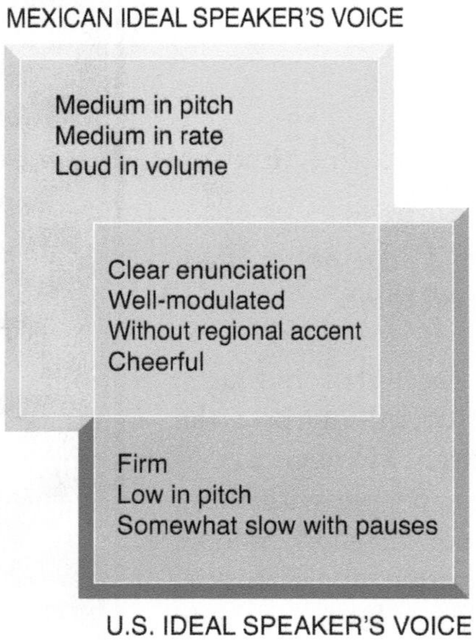

MEXICAN IDEAL SPEAKER'S VOICE

Medium in pitch
Medium in rate
Loud in volume

Clear enunciation
Well-modulated
Without regional accent
Cheerful

Firm
Low in pitch
Somewhat slow with pauses

U.S. IDEAL SPEAKER'S VOICE

FIGURE 6.1 A Comparison of the Ideal Speaker's Voice Types in Mexico and the United States

Reproduced from p. 62 of Valentine, C. A., & Saint Damian, B. (1988). Communicative power: Gender and culture as determinants of the ideal voice. In C. A. Valentine & N. Hoar (Eds.), *Women and communicative power: Theory, research, and practice* (pp. 42–68). Washington, DC: National Communication Association.

credible, although there's an upper limit to both (Knapp & Hall, 2010). Communicators with more attractive voices are rated more highly than those whose speech sounds less attractive (Francis & Wales, 1994; Zuckerman & Driver, 1989). Just what makes a voice attractive can vary. As Figure 6.1 shows, culture can make a difference. Surveys indicate that there are both similarities and differences between what Mexicans and U.S. citizens view as the "ideal" voice. Second-language learners have a hard time learning to speak without a noticeable accent, even after years or decades of living in a new culture. And even when accented speech is perfectly understandable, it can create discriminatory attitudes for some listeners (Felps et al., 2009). (See the Dark Side box on page 195 for more discussion of stigmas attached to accents.)

DISTANCE

Proxemics is the study of how communication is affected by the use, organization, and perception of space and distance. Each of us carries around a sort of invisible bubble of **personal space** wherever we go. We think of the area inside this bubble as our own—almost as much a part of us as our own bodies. Our personal bubbles vary in size according to the culture in which we were raised, the person we're with, and the situation. It's precisely the varying size of our personal space—the distance we put between ourselves and others—that gives a nonverbal clue to our feelings (Sommer, 2002).

D. Russell Crane (1987) and other researchers tested over 100 married couples, asking partners to walk toward one another and stop when they reached a "comfortable conversational distance." Then they gave each partner a battery of tests to measure their marital intimacy, desire for change, and potential for divorce. The researchers discovered that there was a strong relationship between distance and marital happiness. The average space between distressed couples was about 25 percent greater than that between satisfied partners. On average, the happy couples stood 11.4 inches apart, while the distance between unhappy spouses averaged 14.8 inches.

Preferred spaces are largely a matter of cultural norms (Beaulieu, 2004; Høgh-Olesen, 2008). For example, people living in hyperdense Hong Kong manage to live in crowded residential quarters that most North Americans would find intolerable (Chan, 1999). Looking at the distances that North American communicators use in everyday interaction, Edward Hall (1969) found four, each of which reflects a different way we feel toward others at a given time. By "reading" which distance people select, we can get some insight into their feelings.

Intimate Distance The first of Hall's zones begins with skin contact and ranges out to about 18 inches. We usually use **intimate distance** with people who are emotionally close to us, and then mostly in private situations—making love, caressing, comforting, protecting. By allowing people to move into our intimate distance, we let them enter our personal space. When we let them in voluntarily, it's usually a sign of trust: We've willingly lowered our defenses. On the other hand, when someone invades this most personal area without our consent, we usually feel threatened (especially when they're "in your face").

Personal Distance The second spatial zone, **personal distance**, ranges from 18 inches at its closest point to 4 feet at its farthest. Its closer phase is the distance at which most couples stand in public. If someone thought to be sexually attractive stands this near one partner at a party, the other partner is likely to become alert. This "moving in" often is taken to mean that something more than casual conversation is taking place. The far range of personal distance runs from about 2 1/2 to 4 feet. It's the zone just beyond the other person's reach. As Hall puts it, at this distance we can keep someone "at arm's length." His choice of words suggests the type of communication that goes on at this range: The contacts are still reasonably close, but they're much less personal than the ones that occur a foot or so closer.

Social Distance The third zone is **social distance**. It ranges from 4 to about 12 feet out. Within this zone, the distance between communicators can have a powerful effect on how we regard and respond to others. For example, students are more satisfied with teachers who reduce (at appropriate levels, of course) the distance between themselves and their classes. They also are more satisfied with the course itself and are more likely to follow the teacher's instructions (Hackman & Walker, 1990). Likewise, medical patients are more satisfied with physicians who use close physical proximity to convey warmth and concern (Conlee et al., 1993; Grant et al., 2000).

Public Distance **Public distance** is Hall's term for the farthest zone, running outward from 12 feet. The closer range of public distance is the one that most teachers use in the classroom. In the farther reaches of public space—25 feet and beyond—two-way communication is almost impossible. In some cases it's necessary for speakers to use public distance to reach a large audience, but we can assume that anyone who chooses to use it when more closeness is possible is not interested in a dialogue.

When our spatial bubble is invaded we experience stress, and we respond with *barrier behaviors*, strategies designed to create a barrier (or fix a broken one) between ourselves and other people (Evans & Wener, 2007; Kanaga & Flynn, 1981). Invade someone's personal space, and notice the reaction. At first the person is most likely simply to back away, probably without realizing what is happening. Next your partner might attempt to put an object between you, such as a desk, a chair, or some books clutched to the chest, all in an effort to get some separation. Then the other person will probably decrease eye contact (the "elevator syndrome," in which we can crowd in and even touch one another so long as we avoid eye contact). Furthermore, your reluctant partner might sneeze, cough, scratch, and exhibit any variety of behaviors to discourage your antisocial behavior. In the end, if none of these behaviors achieves the desired goal of getting some space between the two of you, the other person might leave or "counterattack," gently at first ("Move back, will you?"), then more forcefully (probably with a shove).

TERRITORIALITY

While personal space is the invisible bubble we carry around, the area that serves as an extension of our physical being, **territory**, remains stationary (Hidalgo & Hernandez, 2001). Robert Sommer (1969) watched students in a college library and found that there's a definite pattern for people who want to study alone. While the library was uncrowded, students almost always chose corner seats at one of the empty rectangular tables. After each table was occupied by one reader, new readers would choose a seat on the opposite side and at the far end, thus keeping the maximum distance between themselves and the other readers. One of Sommer's associates tried violating these "rules" by sitting next to and across from other female readers when more distant seats were available. She found that the approached women reacted defensively, signaling their discomfort through shifts in posture, gesturing, or moving away.

Consider how you would react if someone took "your" seat in one of your classes. Even though the chair isn't your possession, you probably have some sense of ownership about it (Kaya & Burgess, 2007). How you respond to perceived violations depends on *who* enters and uses your territory (a friend is less threatening than a stranger), *why* they do so (a "mistake" is less important than a "planned attack"), and *what* territory is entered or used (you may care more about a territory over which you have exclusive rights, such as your bedroom, than about a territory in a public area, such as your seat in class).

TIME

Social scientists use the term **chronemics** to describe the study of how humans use and structure time. The way we handle time can express both intentional and unintentional messages. Social psychologist Robert Levine (1988) describes several ways that time can communicate. For instance, in cultures like those of the United States, Canada, and northern Europe, which value time highly, waiting can be an indicator of status. "Important" people (whose time is supposedly more valuable than others) may be seen by appointment only, while it is acceptable to intrude without notice on lesser beings. To see how this rule operates, consider how natural it is for a boss to drop into a subordinate's office unannounced, while the employee would never intrude into the boss's office without an appointment. A related rule is that low-status people must never make more important people wait. It

FOCUS ON RESEARCH

It's About Time: The Costs of Delayed Responses

You receive an electronic message from someone in the business world—an e-mail from a potential employer, or an instant message from a colleague. Are there consequences for not responding in timely fashion? You bet, according to research by Yoram Kalman.

Kalman and his colleagues assessed perceptions of delayed responses to computer-mediated messages. In one study, job candidates who sent tardy replies to managers' e-mails or didn't respond at all lost credibility points (and presumably employment offers). In another study, members of virtual teams were regarded as less than trustworthy or even deceptive if they had long pauses in chat room conversations. By not responding promptly, the communicators sabotaged themselves—whether they realized it or not.

In a busy life, it's easy to delay or forget to respond to incoming messages. Nevertheless, it's important to remember that the way you manage time—as measured by the promptness of your responses—makes a statement about you.

Kalman, Y. M., & Rafaeli, S. (2011). Online pauses and silence: Chronemic expectancy violations in written computer-mediated communication. *Communication Research, 38,* 54–69.

Kalman, Y. M., Scissors, L. E., & Gergle, D. (2010). Chronemic aspects of chat, and their relationship to trust in a virtual team. *Proceedings of the 5th Mediterranean Conference on Information Systems,* Tel Aviv, Israel.

would be a serious mistake to show up late for a job interview, although the interviewer might keep you cooling your heels in the lobby. The Focus on Research sidebar on this page explains the importance of prompt responses in professional communication.

The use of time depends greatly on culture. In some cultures, punctuality is critically important, while in others it is barely considered (Levine & Norenzayan, 1999; Levine et al., 2008). Punctual U.S. mainlanders often report welcoming the laid-back Hawaiian approach to time. One psychologist discovered the difference between North and South American attitudes when teaching at a university in Brazil (Levine, 1988). He found that some students arrived halfway through a 2-hour class and that most of them stayed put and kept asking questions when the class was scheduled to end. A half hour after the official end of the period, the professor finally closed off discussion, since there was no indication that the students intended to leave. This flexibility of time is quite different from what is common in most North American colleges and universities!

Even within a culture, rules of time vary. Sometimes the differences are geographic. In New York City, the party invitation may say 9:00 P.M., but nobody would think of showing up before 10:30 P.M. In Salt Lake City, guests are expected to show up on time, or perhaps even a bit early. Even within the same geographic area, different groups establish their own rules about the use of time. Consider your own experience. In school, some instructors begin and end class punctually, while others are more casual. With some people, you feel comfortable talking for hours in person or on the phone, while with others time seems precious and not to be "wasted."

Time can be a marker not only of status and culture, but also of relationships. Research shows that the amount of time spent with a relational partner sends important messages about valuing that person (Andersen et al., 2006). In one study analyzing 20 nonverbal behaviors, "spending time together" was the most powerful predictor of both relational satisfaction and perceived interpersonal understanding (Egland et al., 1997).

PHYSICAL ATTRACTIVENESS

The importance of beauty has been emphasized in the arts for centuries. More recently, social scientists have begun to measure the degree to which physical attractiveness affects interaction between people (Lorenzo et al., 2010; Swami & Furnham, 2008). Women who are perceived as attractive have more dates, receive higher grades in college, persuade males with greater ease, and receive lighter court sentences (Knapp & Hall, 2010). Both men and women whom others view as attractive are rated as being more sensitive, kind, strong, sociable, and interesting than their less fortunate brothers and sisters—although higher self-esteem does not seem to be a by-product of all this positive regard (Mares et al., 2010). And more than 200 managers in a *Newsweek* survey admitted that attractive people get preferential treatment both in hiring decisions and on the job (Bennett, 2010).

The influence of attractiveness begins early in life (Dion, 1973). For example, preschoolers were shown photographs of children their own age and asked to choose potential friends and enemies. The researchers found that children as young as age 3 agreed as to who was attractive ("cute") and unattractive ("homely"). Furthermore, they valued their attractive counterparts—both of the same and the opposite sex—more highly. Also, preschool children rated by their peers as pretty were most liked, and those identified as least pretty were least liked. Children who were interviewed rated good-looking children as having positive social characteristics ("He's friendly to other children") and unattractive children negatively ("He hits other children without reason").

Teachers also are affected by students' attractiveness. Vicki Ritts and her colleagues (1992) found that physically attractive students are usually judged more favorably—more intelligent, friendly, and popular. Even the parents of attractive students benefit from their children's good looks: They

are judged by strangers as caring more about education than are parents of less attractive youngsters.

Fortunately, attractiveness is something we can control without having to call the plastic surgeon. If you aren't totally gorgeous or handsome, don't despair: Evidence suggests that, as we get to know more about people and like them, we start to regard them as better looking (Albada et al., 2002; Bazil, 1999). Moreover, we view others as beautiful or ugly not just on the basis of their "original equipment," but also on *how they use that equipment*. Posture, gestures, facial expressions, and other behaviors can increase the attractiveness of an otherwise unremarkable person. Finally, the way we dress can make a significant difference in the way others perceive us, as you'll now see.

CLOTHING

Besides protecting us from the elements, clothing is a means of nonverbal communication. One writer has suggested that clothing conveys at least 10 types of messages to others (Thourlby, 1978):

1. Economic level

2. Education level

3. Trustworthiness

4. Social position

5. Level of sophistication

6. Economic background

7. Social background

8. Educational background

9. Level of success

10. Moral character

We do make assumptions about people based on their style of clothing. For example, the way people are dressed affects judgments of their credibility. In one experiment sexual victims dressed in black were rated as less honest and more aggressive than those dressed in light colors (Vrij & Akehurst, 1999). Not surprisingly, the perception of a female actor's sexual intent increased when she wore more revealing clothes, although this effect was greater for men in the study (Koukounas & Letch, 2001). In another study, a man and a woman were stationed in a hallway so that anyone who wished to go by had to avoid them or pass between them. In one condition the conversationalists wore "formal daytime dress"; in the other, they wore "casual attire." Passersby behaved differently toward the couple, depending on the style of clothing: They responded positively to the well-dressed couple and showed more annoyance when the same people were casually dressed (Fortenberry et al., 1978).

Attire makes a difference in the classroom too. College students' perceptions of their graduate teaching associate's (GTA) expertise decreases as the GTA's attire becomes more casual. On the other hand, GTAs who dress casually are seen as more interesting, extroverted, and sociable than those who dress more formally (Morris et al., 1996; Roach, 1997). Dressing up may be more important for men than for women when it comes to perceptions of status. Observers rely more on women's nonverbal behavior as cues to their social position, whereas men are rated more on their attire (Mast & Hall, 2004).

Judgments based on what a person wears, like other perceptions, need to be made carefully. For example, while many Americans believe a *hijab*—a "veil" or "headscarf"—functions to oppress women, veiled women see their hijab as helping them define their Muslim identity, resist sexual objectification, and afford more respect (Droogsma, 2007). And while judgments of personality based on what someone wears may be accurate for a few dimensions, such as extraversion and religiosity, more information than clothing, such as facial expressions, is necessary (Naumann et al., 2009).

PHYSICAL ENVIRONMENT

We conclude our look at nonverbal communication by examining how physical settings, architecture, and interior design affect communication. Begin by recalling the different homes you've visited lately. Were some of these homes more comfortable to be in than others? Certainly a lot of your feelings were shaped by the people you were with, but there are some houses in which it seems impossible to relax, no matter how friendly the hosts. We've spent what seemed like endless evenings in what Knapp and Hall (2010) call "unliving rooms," where the spotless ashtrays, furniture coverings, and plastic lamp covers send nonverbal messages telling us not to touch anything, not to put our feet up, and not to be comfortable. People who live in such houses probably wonder why nobody ever seems to relax and enjoy themselves at their parties. One thing is quite certain: They don't understand that the environment they have created can communicate discomfort to their guests.

MAKING A FASHION STATEMENT: *WHAT NOT TO WEAR*

Does your style of dress affect how others perceive you? According to the television show *What Not to Wear*, the answer is a resounding yes. Hosts Stacy London and Clinton Kelley take poorly dressed "fashion victims" on a two-day shopping spree, aimed at transforming them into well-dressed and groomed versions of their former selves. The show demonstrates how a change in appearance can make a difference, both personally and professionally.

Besides illustrating the importance of nonverbal communication, most episodes illustrate how attire is related to Chapter 3's discussion of identity and self-presentation. The participants often admit that they dress poorly because of a skewed self-concept or a lack of self-esteem. Adopting a new wardrobe typically changes how they think and feel about themselves, and the impression they make on others.

There's nothing academic about *What Not to Wear*, but the show offers a good example of how attire and grooming can play a key role in self-perception and relationships.

The impressions that home designs communicate can be remarkably accurate. Edward Sadalla (1987) showed 99 students slides of the insides or outsides of 12 upper-middle-class homes and then asked them to infer the personality of the owners from their impressions. The students were especially accurate after glancing at interior photos. The decorating schemes communicated accurate information about the homeowners' intellectualism, politeness, maturity, optimism, tenseness, willingness to take adventures, family orientations, and reservedness. The home exteriors also gave viewers accurate perceptions of the owners' artistic interests, graciousness, privacy, and quietness.

Besides communicating information about the designer, an environment can also shape the kind of interaction that takes place in it. For example, students participating in a structured interview in a room with dim lighting were more relaxed, had a more favorable impression of the interviewer, and were more self-disclosing than those exposed to bright lighting (Miwa & Hanyu, 2006). In a classic experiment, participants working in a "beautiful" room were more positive and energetic than those working in "average" or "ugly" spaces (Maslow & Mintz, 1956). Inner-city adults and children who have access to landscaped public spaces interact in ways that are much more prosocial than do those who have to interact in more barren environments (Taylor et al., 1998)—just as elderly people in care homes report greater well-being when the home design allows viewing of nature and greenery (Burton & Sheehan, 2010). Public housing inner-city residents living in relatively barren buildings reported more mental fatigue, aggression, and violence than did their counterparts in buildings with nearby grass and trees (Kuo & Sullivan, 2001a, 2001b).

Students see professors who occupy well-decorated offices as being more credible than those occupying less attractive work areas (Teven & Comadena, 1996). Physicians have shaped environments to improve the quality of interaction with their patients. According to environmental psychologist Robert Sommer (1969), simply removing a doctor's desk made patients feel almost five times more at ease during office visits. Sommer also found that redesigning a convalescent ward of a hospital greatly increased the interaction between patients. In the old design, seats were placed shoulder to shoulder around the edges of the ward. By grouping the chairs around small tables so that patients faced each other at a comfortable distance, the amount of conversations doubled.

Summary

Nonverbal communication consists of messages expressed by nonlinguistic means. Nonverbal communication is pervasive; in fact, nonverbal messages are always available as a source of information about others. Most nonverbal behavior suggests messages about relational attitudes and feelings, in contrast to verbal statements, which are better suited to expressing ideas. Messages that are communicated nonverbally are usually more ambiguous than verbal communication.

Nonverbal communication serves many functions. It can help in the creating and maintaining of relationships. Nonverbal communication also serves to regulate interaction and to influence others. Nonverbal communication can be used to conceal or reveal deception. Finally, we use nonverbal cues to manage our identity and impressions with others.

Nonverbal messages can be communicated in a variety of ways: Through body movement (including the face and eyes, gestures, and posture), touch, voice, distance, territory, time, physical appearance, clothing, and environment. Culture plays a significant role in determining the rules and meanings for each of these factors.

Key Terms

- Chronemics (199)
- Disfluencies (194)
- Emblems (181)
- Haptics (193)
- Intimate distance (198)
- Kinesics (189)
- Manipulators (191)
- Nonverbal communication (177)
- Oculesics (189)
- Paralanguage (194)
- Personal distance (198)
- Personal space (197)
- Proxemics (197)
- Public distance (198)
- Regulators (183)
- Social distance (198)
- Territory (199)

Activities

1. Invitation to Insight
Demonstrate for yourself that it is impossible to avoid communicating nonverbally by trying *not* to communicate with a friend or family member. (You be the judge of whether to tell the other person about this experiment beforehand.) See how long it takes for your partner to inquire about what is going on and to report on what he or she thinks you might be thinking and feeling.

2. Critical Thinking Probe

Interview someone from a culture different from your own, and learn at least three ways in which nonverbal codes differ from the environment where you were raised. Together, develop a list of ways you could violate unstated but important rules about nonverbal behavior in your partner's culture in three of the following areas:

Eye contact
Posture
Gesture
Facial expression
Distance
Territory
Voice
Touch
Time
Clothing
Environmental design
Territory

Describe how failure to recognize different cultural codes could lead to misunderstandings, frustrations, and dissatisfaction. Discuss how awareness of cultural rules can be developed in an increasingly multicultural world.

3. Invitation to Insight

Using the videotape of a television program or film, identify examples of the following nonverbal functions:

Creating and maintaining relationships
Regulating interaction
Influencing others
Concealing or deceiving
Managing identity

If time allows, show these videotaped examples to your classmates.

4. Skill Builder

Sharpen your ability to distinguish between *observing* and *interpreting* nonverbal behaviors by following these directions:

Sit or stand opposite a partner at a comfortable distance. For a 1-minute period, report your observations of the other person's behavior by repeatedly completing the statement "Now I see (*nonverbal behavior*)." For example, you might report "Now I see you blinking your eyes . . . now I see you looking down at the floor . . . now I see you fidgeting with your hands. . . ." Notice that no matter what your partner does, you have an unending number of nonverbal behaviors to observe.

For a second 1-minute period, complete the sentence "Now I see (*nonverbal behavior*), and I think _____," filling in the blank with your interpretation of the other person's nonverbal behavior. For instance, you might say "Now I see you look away, and I think you're nervous about looking me in the eye . . . now I see you smiling and I think you're imagining that you agree with my interpretation. . . ." Notice that by clearly labeling your interpretation, you give the other person a chance to correct any mistaken hunches.

Repeat the first two steps, switching roles with your partner.

5. Invitation to Insight

Learn more about the nonverbal messages you send by interviewing someone who knows you well: a friend, family member, or coworker. Ask your interview participant to describe how he or she knows when you are feeling each of the following emotions, even though you may not announce your feelings verbally:

Anger or irritation

Boredom or indifference

Happiness

Sadness

Worry or anxiety

Which of these nonverbal behaviors do you display intentionally, and which are not conscious? Which functions do your nonverbal behaviors perform in the situations your partner described: creating/maintaining relationships, regulating interaction, influencing others, concealing/deceiving, and/or managing your identity?

6. Invitation to Insight

Explore your territoriality by listing the spaces you feel you "own," such as your parking space, parts of the place you live, and seats in a particular classroom. Describe how you feel when your territory is invaded and identify things you do to "mark" it.

7. Invitation to Insight

This activity requires you to observe how people use space in a particular setting and to note reactions to violations of spatial expectations. Select a supermarket, department store, college bookstore, or some other common setting in which people shop for things and then pay for them on a checkout line. Observe the interaction distances that seem usual between salesclerks and customers, between customers as they shop, and between customers in the checkout line.

   a. What are the average distances between the people you observed?

   b. How do people respond when one person comes too close to another or when one person touches another? How do people react to these violations of their space? How could they avoid violating each other's personal space?

   c. Try to observe people from a culture other than your own in this store. Describe their use of spatial distance. If this is not possible in the store, think back to a foreign film or a film that contains interaction between North Americans and people of another culture, as well as people from that same culture.

Listening
Receiving and Responding

After studying the material in this chapter . . .

You should understand:

1. The importance of listening.
2. The definition of listening.
3. Common myths that incorrectly suggest that listening is easy.
4. The habits of people who listen ineffectively.
5. The components of the listening process.
6. The differences among the listening responses introduced in this chapter.
7. The advantages and disadvantages of various listening styles.

You should be able to:

1. Identify the situations in which you listen mindfully and those when you listen mindlessly, and evaluate the appropriateness of each style.
2. Identify the circumstances in which you listen ineffectively, and the poor listening habits you use in these circumstances.
3. Identify the response styles you commonly use when listening to others.
4. Demonstrate a combination of listening styles you could use to respond effectively to another person.

T
he Grizzled army sergeant faced a roomful of new Signal Corps cadets about to begin their training as radio operators.

"The equipment is a snap to operate," he explained. "All you have to do to send a message is to push this button on the microphone, and your voice goes out to anyone who's tuned in. Go ahead . . . give it a try."

Each recruit picked up a microphone and began speaking. The sound of 30 amplified voices all transmitting at the same time created a loud, painful squeal.

"OK, soldiers," the sergeant announced. "You just learned the first principle of two-way radio communication. Any fool can send a message. The only way communication works is if you're willing and able to receive one, too."

The sergeant's lesson is a good one for every communicator. Speaking is important, but without listening, a message might as well never be sent. In this chapter you will learn just how important listening is in interpersonal communication. You will read about the many factors that make good listening difficult and find reasons for tackling those challenges. You will learn what really happens when listening takes place. Finally, you will read about a variety of listening responses that you can use to increase your own understanding, improve your relationships, and help others.

The Nature of Listening

When it comes to the subject of listening, plenty of people have advice on how to do it better, such as "close your mouth and open your ears." While such advice is a good start, simplistic prescriptions like these don't capture the complex nature of listening. We'll begin our exploration of this subject by describing the importance of listening in interpersonal communication.

THE IMPORTANCE OF LISTENING

How important is listening? If we use frequency as a measure, it ranks at the top of the list. Surveys (Barker et al., 1981; Emanuel et al., 2008) show that as much as 55 percent of college students' communication time is spent listening (see Figure 7.1). The business world yields similar numbers:

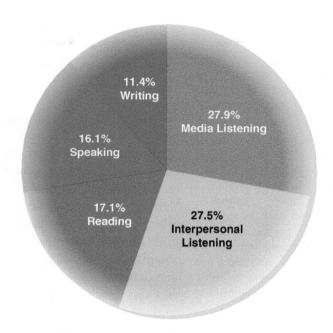

FIGURE 7.1 **Time Devoted to Communication Activities**

Emanuel, R., Adams, J., Baker, K., Daufin, E. K., Ellington, C., Fitts, E., Himsel, J., Holladay, L., & Okeowo, D. (2008). How college students spend their time communicating. *International Journal of Listening, 22,* 13-28.

Executives spend approximately 60 percent of their communication time listening (Brown, 1982; Steil, 1996). The At Work box on page 212 shows that workers not only listen a lot on the job, but that listening skills are highly valued.

The business world is not the only setting in which listening is vital. When a group of adults was asked to rank various communication skills according to their importance, listening topped the family/social list as well as the career list (Brownell & Wolvin, 2010; Wolvin, 1984). In committed relationships, listening to personal information in everyday conversations is considered an important ingredient of satisfaction (Prager & Buhrmester, 1998). John Gentile (2004) argues that listening to one another's personal narratives (see Chapter 4) is fundamental to our humanity and sense of well-being.

This chapter takes an in-depth look at the role of listening in interpersonal communication. We start by defining listening, and then we examine the many challenges that listeners face. After reviewing the components of listening, we spend the remainder of the chapter describing the variety of responses that a good listener can offer to a message-sender.

LISTENING DEFINED

So far we have used the term "listening" as if it needs no explanation. Actually, there's more to this concept than you might suspect. We define **listening**—at least the interpersonal type—as the process of receiving and responding to others' messages.

AT WORK

Listening on the Job

If you were asked to imagine the most talented communicators in the business world, it's likely that you would think about executives who are articulate, charismatic public figures. However, research shows that in the workplace, the ability to listen effectively is more important than public presentation skills. Numerous studies (summarized in Flynn et al., 2008) find listening to be the most important communication skill for entry-level workers, subordinates, supervisors, and managers on several dimensions: job and career success, productivity, upward mobility, communication training, and organizational effectiveness. Senior executives, students, and employers, when asked what skills are most important on the job, identified listening more often than any other ability, including technical competence, computer knowledge, creativity, and administrative talent (Gabric & McFadden, 2001; Landrum & Harrold, 2003).

Unfortunately, there's no connection between how well most communicators *think* they listen and how competent they really are in their ability to understand others. A study by Judi Brownell (1990) illustrates this point vividly. A group of managers in her study were asked to rate their listening skills. Astonishingly, not one of the managers described himself or herself as a "poor" or "very poor" listener, while 94 percent rated themselves as "good" or "very good." The favorable self-ratings contrasted sharply with the perceptions of the managers' subordinates, many of whom said their bosses' listening skills were weak.

As you'll soon read, some poor listening is inevitable. The good news is that listening can be improved through instruction and training (Lane et al., 2000; McNaughton et al., 2008).

Traditional approaches to listening focus on the reception of *spoken* messages. However, we've broadened the definition to include messages of all sorts because much of contemporary listening takes place through mediated channels, some of which involve the written word. Consider times you've said something like, "I was talking with a friend and she told me . . . "—and the conversation you recount actually took place via texting, e-mailing, or instant messaging. You'll read later in this chapter how social support can be offered in face-to-face communication, but also through blogs, Facebook posts, and other social media. We'll continue to focus on spoken messages in this chapter (beginning with our discussion of "hearing" below), but recognize that "listening" in contemporary society involves more than meets the ear.

Hearing versus Listening Listening and hearing aren't identical. **Hearing** is the process in which sound waves strike the eardrum and cause vibrations that are transmitted to the brain. Listening occurs when the brain reconstructs these electrochemical impulses into a representation of the original sound and then gives them meaning (Fernald, 2001; Robinshaw, 2007). Barring illness, injury, or cotton plugs, you can't stop hearing. Your ears will pick up sound waves and transmit them to your brain whether you want them to or not.

Listening, however, isn't automatic. Many times we hear but do not listen. Sometimes we automatically and unconsciously block out irritating sounds, such as a neighbor's lawn mower or the roar of nearby traffic. We also stop listening when we find a subject unimportant or uninteresting. Boring stories, television commercials, and nagging complaints are common examples of messages we may tune out.

Mindless Listening When we move beyond hearing and start to listen, researchers note that we process information in two very different ways (Chaiken & Trope, 1999; Todorov et al., 2002). Ellen Langer (1990) uses the terms "mindless" and "mindful" to describe these different ways of listening. **Mindless listening** occurs when we react to others' messages automatically

"You're not listening to what you're hearing."

and routinely, without much mental investment (Dumas, 2005). Words like "superficial" and "cursory" describe mindless listening better than terms like "ponder" and "contemplate."

While the term *mindless* may sound negative, this sort of low-level information processing is a potentially valuable type of communication, since it frees us to focus our minds on messages that require our careful attention (Burgoon et al., 2000). Given the number of messages to which we're exposed, it's impractical to listen carefully and thoughtfully 100 percent of the time. It's unrealistic to devote your attention to long-winded stories, idle chatter, or remarks you've heard many times before. The only realistic way to manage the onslaught of messages is to be "lazy" toward many of them (Griffin, 2006). In situations like these, we forgo careful analysis and fall back on the schemas—and sometimes the stereotypes—described in Chapter 4 to make sense of a message. If you stop right now and recall the messages you have heard today, it's likely that you processed most of them mindlessly.

Mindful Listening By contrast, **mindful listening** involves giving careful and thoughtful attention and responses to the messages we receive (Dumas, 2005). You tend to listen mindfully when a message is important to you, and also when someone you care about is speaking about a matter that is important to him or her. Think of how your ears perk up when someone starts talking about your favorite hobby, or how you tune in carefully when a close friend tells you about the loss of a loved one. In situations like these, you want to give the message-sender your complete and undivided attention.

EAR

EYES

UNDIVIDED
ATTENTION

HEART

FIGURE 7.2 **The Chinese characters that make up the verb "to listen"**

Sometimes we respond mindlessly to information that deserves—and even demands—our mindful attention. Ellen Langer's (1990) determination to study mindfulness began when her grandmother complained about headaches coming from a "snake crawling around" beneath her skull. The doctors quickly diagnosed the problem as senility—after all, they reasoned, senility comes with old age and makes people talk nonsense. In fact, the grandmother had a brain tumor that eventually killed her. The event made a deep impression on Langer (p. 3):

> For years afterward I kept thinking about the doctors' reactions to my grandmother's complaints, and about our reactions to the doctors. They went through the motions of diagnosis, but were not open to what they were hearing. Mindsets about senility interfered. We did not question the doctors; mindsets about experts interfered.

Most of our daily decisions about whether to listen mindfully don't have life-and-death consequences, but the point should be clear: There are times when we need to listen consciously and carefully to what others are telling us. That kind of mindful listening is the focus of the remainder of this chapter.

REASONS FOR LISTENING

There are several different reasons to listen, and each one requires a different set of attitudes and skills.

To Understand The most obvious reason for listening is *to understand and retain information.* You need to comprehend information from a lecture to earn the grade you're seeking. You have to understand your boss's feedback to succeed on the job. You want to grasp the advice from your coach so that you can do better in your favorite sport. Communication researchers use the term **listening fidelity** to describe the degree of congruence between what a listener understands and what the message sender was attempting to communicate (Fitch-Hauser et al., 2007; Powers & Witt, 2008).

Even people who are highly motivated to listen carefully often lack the skill to understand others' messages. For example, more than half of medical patients fail to grasp their doctors' instructions about medication and other treatments. Likewise, physicians often fail to understand their patients' concerns (Christensen, 2004; Scholz, 2005).

When the issue isn't a matter of personal concern, the lack of desire to understand others can be even stronger. Carl Trosset (1998) presented about 200 college students with a list of sensitive topics, such as "whether race is an important difference between people." Then the students were asked whether they thought it was possible to have an open exchange of ideas on these topics. The majority of students expressed little interest in wanting to understand others' views on these issues; they merely wanted to persuade others to see the world as they did.

Of course there's nothing wrong with advocating your strongly held beliefs, but one would assume that an equally valuable goal would be to learn something new. Yet only 5 of the 200 students in the study said they approached their conversations with what communication theorists Sonja Foss and Cindy Griffin (Foss & Foss, 2003; Lozano-Reich & Cloud, 2009) have called an *invitational* attitude: to learn more about perspectives other than their own.

To Evaluate A second type of listening involves *evaluating the quality of messages*—sometimes referred to as *critical listening* (Floyd & Clements, 2005). Being open-minded when trying to understand another person doesn't mean you should be gullible or naïve. If the facts don't line up in a friend's excuse, it's wise to be politely skeptical. When a salesperson makes a pitch, good shoppers evaluate the pros and cons. If someone's point of view doesn't seem logical, it may be necessary to challenge the claims. Of course, in all these cases it's best not to jump to hasty conclusions. The listening response skills of questioning and paraphrasing, discussed later in this chapter, can help ensure that you've understood another person's message before you evaluate it.

To Build and Maintain Relationships A third reason for listening is especially relevant for interpersonal communication: *building and maintaining relationships*. Research shows that effective listening "builds better relationships, and poor listening weakens relationships, or prevents relationships from developing at all" (Kaufmann, 1993, p. 4). In one survey, marital counselors identified "failing to take the other's perspective when listening" as one of the most frequent communication problems in the couples with whom they work (Vangelisti, 1994; see also Laurenceau et al., 2005). Roger McIntire (1999) argues that listening well is the first and most important habit parents need in order to build a good relationship with their children—a sentiment echoed for teachers and their students (Garforth, 2009). Listening is also vital for building relationships with clients in the health care industry (Davis et al., 2008) and in other businesses and organizations (Brunner, 2008; Gray, 2010).

To Help Others A fourth type of listening involves *helping others*, another important interpersonal skill. Listening is an essential tool professionals use to help their clients. Doctors, lawyers, teachers, managers, supervisors, clergy, and therapists must listen carefully so they can offer sound and appropriate assistance. Professionals aren't the only people we call on for help; we also seek the counsel of friends and family. When others listen to us with understanding and concern, we can gain different and useful perspectives for solving problems (Bender & Messner, 2003; Welch, 2003).

The Challenge of Listening

By now you can see that mindful listening is important. Even with the best intentions, though, listening carefully is a challenge. Now we'll take a look at some of the obstacles we need to overcome when we want to listen carefully.

LISTENING IS NOT EASY

Listening is more difficult than many realize. Consider the following common barriers.

Information Overload The sheer amount of information most of us encounter every day makes it impossible to listen carefully to everything we hear. We're bombarded with messages not only in face-to-face interaction, but also from the Internet, the media, cell phones, and various other sources (Arsenault, 2007). Given this barrage of information, it's virtually impossible for us to keep our attention totally focused for long. As a result, we often choose—understandably and sometimes wisely—to listen mindlessly rather than mindfully.

Personal Concerns A second reason we don't always listen carefully is that we're often wrapped up in personal concerns of more immediate importance to us than the messages others are sending (Golen, 1990; Nichols,

F⊕CUS ON RESEARCH

Divided Attention: Phoning While Driving

Cell phone use has increased exponentially in recent years, and so have traffic accidents related to phoning while driving. As a result, many states have instituted laws that restrict drivers from using handheld devices. In theory, hands-free phones should remedy the problem, but a study by scientists at Carnegie Mellon University shows that it's not that simple.

Experimental participants steered a vehicle along a curving virtual road, either undisturbed or while listening to sentences that they judged as true or false. Brain imaging revealed that mentally processing the spoken messages led to a decrease in driving accuracy. The findings show that language comprehension draws mental resources away from performance, even when the driver isn't holding a phone.

The researchers note that talking with a passenger in a car isn't as distracting as a cell phone conversation because the passenger is more likely to be aware of the competing demands for the driver's attention. Nevertheless, the verdict seems clear: Good listening requires full concentration—and so does good driving.

Just, M. A., Keller, T. A., & Cynkar, J. A. (2008). A decrease in brain activation associated with driving when listening to someone speak. *Brain Research, 1205,* 70-80.

2009). It's hard to pay attention to someone else when you're anticipating an upcoming test or thinking about the wonderful time you had last night. When we still feel that we have to pay attention to others while our focus is elsewhere, listening becomes mindless at best, and often a polite charade.

Rapid Thought Careful listening is also difficult because our minds are so active. Although we're capable of understanding speech at rates up to 600 words per minute (Versfeld & Dreschler, 2002), the average person speaks much more slowly—between 100 and 140 words per minute. Therefore, we have a lot of "spare time" to spend with our minds while someone is talking. The temptation is to use this time in ways that don't relate to the speaker's ideas, such as thinking about personal interests, daydreaming, planning a rebuttal, and so on. The trick is to use this spare time to understand the speaker's ideas better, rather than let your attention wander.

Noise Finally, our physical and mental worlds often present distractions that make it hard for us to pay attention. The sounds of other conversations, traffic, and music, as well as the kinds of psychological noise discussed in Chapter 1, all interfere with our ability to listen well. For example, research supports the commonsense suspicion that background noise, such as from a television set, reduces the ability of a communicator to understand messages (Armstrong et al., 1991; Jones et al., 2007). Also, fatigue or other forms of discomfort can distract us from paying attention to a speaker's remarks. For instance, consider how the efficiency of your listening decreases when you are seated in a crowded, hot, stuffy room full of moving people and other noises. In such circumstances, even the best intentions aren't enough to ensure cogent understanding.

ALL LISTENERS DO NOT RECEIVE THE SAME MESSAGE

When two or more people are listening to a speaker, we tend to assume that each hears and understands the same message. In fact, such uniform comprehension isn't the case. Recall our discussion of perception in Chapter 4, where we pointed out the many factors that cause each of us to perceive an event in a different manner. Physiological factors, social roles, cultural background, personal interests, and needs all shape and distort the raw data we hear into very different messages. It's no wonder that dyads typically achieve only 25 to 50 percent accuracy in interpreting or representing each other's behavior (Spitzberg, 1994). Our listening is always colored and limited by our unique, and fairly consistent, view of the world (Robins et al., 2004).

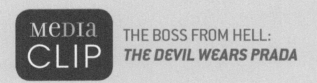

THE BOSS FROM HELL: *THE DEVIL WEARS PRADA*

Miranda Priestly (Meryl Streep) is every employee's nightmare. She's a self-centered, domineering, hard-driven boss who treats the people who work for her like slaves.

Priestly exemplifies every poor listening habit. She attends only to things that matter to her ("The details of your incompetence do not interest me") and does so insensitively ("Bore someone else with your questions"). Pseudolistening, defensive listening, and stage hogging? She does them all. She also interrupts, rolls her eyes when she doesn't like what she's hearing, and walks out on her subordinates in mid-conversation.

Priestly may be a successful businesswoman, but she fails on many other counts—especially as a listener.

POOR LISTENING HABITS

Most people possess one or more habits that keep them from understanding others' messages. As you read about the following poor listening behaviors, see which ones describe you.

Pseudolistening is only an imitation of the real thing. Pseudolisteners give the appearance of being attentive: They look you in the eye, and they may even nod and smile, but their minds are in another world.

When **stage hogging**, people are interested only in expressing their ideas and don't care about what anyone else has to say. These individuals allow you to speak from time to time, but only so they can catch their breath and use your remarks as a basis for their own babbling. Research on "conversational narcissism" (Vangelisti et al., 1990) shows that self-centered stage hogs ask questions, but not other-oriented, information-seeking ones. Rather, these conversational narcissists ask counterfeit questions to demonstrate their superiority and hold the floor (we talk more about counterfeit versus sincere questions later in this chapter). Research by Lisa Leit (2009) found that conversational narcissism characterizes as many as three quarters of marriages, with potentially devastating outcomes, such as spouses feeling invisible, and dialogue that does not allow the spouses to adapt to one another.

With **selective listening**, people respond only to the parts of a speaker's remarks that interest them, rejecting everything else. Unless and until you bring up one of these pet subjects, you might as well be talking to a tree.

People **filling in gaps** like to think that what they remember makes a whole story. These people manufacture information so that when they re-tell what they listened to, they can give the impression they "got it all." The message that's left is actually a distorted (not merely incomplete) version of the real message.

The habit of **insulated listening** is almost the opposite of selective lis-tening. Instead of looking for something, these listeners avoid it. Whenever a topic arises they'd rather not deal with, insulated listeners simply fail to hear or acknowledge it.

People who engage in **defensive listening** take innocent comments as personal attacks. It's fair to assume that many defensive listeners are suffer-ing from shaky self-images, and they avoid facing this by projecting their own insecurities onto others.

A person who engages in **ambushing** will listen carefully to you, but only be-cause he or she is collecting information that will be used to attack what you have to say. Needless to say, using this kind of strategy will justifiably initiate defensive-ness from the other person.

Components of Listening

By now, you can begin to see that there is more to listening than sitting quietly while another person speaks. In truth, listening —especially *mindful* listening—consists of five separate elements: hearing, attend-ing, understanding, remembering, and responding.

HEARING

As we have already discussed, hearing is the physiological aspect of listening. It is the nonselective process of sound waves impinging on the ear. Hearing is obviously vital to listening because it's the starting point of the process. It can be diminished by physiological disorders, background noise, or auditory fatigue, which is a tem-porary loss of hearing caused by continu-ous exposure to the same tone or loudness.

Dark Side of Communication

HEARING LOSS AND RELATIONAL STRESS

Over 22 million Americans have some form of impaired hearing. While hearing loss can be challenging for those who experience it, recent research suggests it can also affect their relationships. One survey explored the feelings of adults who have spouses with hearing loss. Nearly two thirds of the respondents said they feel an-noyed when their partner can't hear them clearly. Almost a quarter said that beyond just being annoyed, they felt ignored, hurt, or sad. Many of the respondents believe their spouses are in denial about their condition, which makes the problem even more frustrating.

Once a hearing problem has been diagnosed, it's often possible to treat it. If you suspect that you or someone you know might have a hearing loss, it's wise to have a physician or audiologist perform an examination. The results may lead to more satisfying relationships.

Williams, B. (2008, May 3). *Listen to this: Hearing problems can stress relationships*. Retrieved from http://www.healthyhearing.com/content/news/ Buying/Benefits/16759-Listen-to-this-hearing

Shafer, D. N. (2007). Hearing loss hinders relationships. *ASHA Leader, 12*(9), 5-7.

People who spend an evening at a rock concert or hearing fireworks may experience auditory fatigue and, if they are exposed often enough, permanent hearing loss (5.2 Million Young Americans, 2001). It's wise to heed the warnings of the Dark Side box on page 219 and protect your hearing—for your own sake as well as for the sake of your relationship partners.

ATTENDING

While hearing is a physiological process, **attending** is a psychological one, and it is part of the process of selection that we described in Chapter 4. As discussed earlier in this chapter, it's especially hard to focus on messages—even important ones—when we are bombarded by information. Face-to-

face messages come from friends, family, work, and school. Personal media—text messages, phone calls, e-mails, and instant messages—demand your attention. Along with these personal channels, we are awash in messages from the mass media. This deluge of communication has made the challenge of attending tougher than at any time in human history (Hansen, 2007).

We would go crazy if we attended to every thing we hear, so we filter out some messages and focus on others. Not surprisingly, we attend most carefully to messages when there's a payoff for doing so (Burleson, 2007). If you're planning to see a movie, you'll listen to a friend's description more carefully than you otherwise would. And when you want to get better acquainted with others, you'll pay careful attention to almost anything they say, in hopes of improving the relationship. If you care about another person's problems, you're more likely to attend thoughtfully to his or her laments.

As you read in Chapter 6, skillful communicators attend to both speakers' words and their nonverbal cues. If you asked a friend "How's it going?," you can easily imagine two ways he or she could answer "Fine": One set of nonverbal behaviors (big smile, enthusiastic vocal tone) would reinforce the verbal statement, while another (downcast eyes, slumped posture, dejected vocal tone) would contradict it. Some people are simply inattentive to nonverbal cues, but others suffer from a physiological syndrome called nonverbal learning disorder (Palombo, 2006). Due to a processing deficit in the right hemisphere of the brain, people with this disorder have trouble making sense of many nonverbal cues. Whether due to insensitivity or physiology, it's easy to see how failing to attend to nonverbal cues is a listening deficit.

Surprisingly, attending doesn't just help the listener: It also benefits the message-sender. Participants in one study viewed brief movie segments and then described them to listeners who varied in their degree of attentiveness to the speaker. Later on, the researchers tested the speakers' long-term recall of details from the movie segment. Those who had recounted the movie to attentive listeners remembered more details of the movie (Pasupathi et al., 1998).

One way to attend better to important messages is to screen out distractions. Some companies now hold "laptopless" meetings, prohibiting computer use that might distract participants (Guynn, 2008). You may be familiar with other public forums—including some classrooms—where cell phone interruptions are not welcome (Campbell, 2006). While new technology has greatly increased our ability to communicate with others, it's important to be mindful of when it intrudes on attentive listening.

"This requires both ears."

UNDERSTANDING

Paying attention—even close attention—to a message doesn't guarantee that you'll understand what's being said. **Understanding** is composed of several elements. First, of course, you must be aware of the syntactic and grammatical rules of the language. But beyond this basic ability, understanding a message depends on several other factors. One is your knowledge about the source of the message. Such background will help you decide, for example, whether a friend's insulting remark is a joke or a serious attack. The context of a message also helps you understand what's being said. A yawning response to your comments would probably have a different meaning at midnight than at noon.

Finally, understanding often depends on the listener's mental abilities. Generally speaking, the ability to make sense of messages is closely related to the listener's intelligence, including in children who are preschoolers (Bostrom & Waldhart, 1980; Florit et al., 2011). As early as 1948, Ralph Nichols related successful understanding to factors that included verbal ability, intelligence, and motivation. Timothy Plax and Lawrence Rosenfeld (1979; see also Villaume & Bodie, 2007) found that the personality traits of listeners also affect their ability to understand messages. People good at interpreting disorganized messages were especially secure, sensitive to others, and willing to understand the speaker. Listeners successful at understanding disorganized speech proved to be more insightful and versatile in their thinking.

REMEMBERING

The ability to recall information once we've understood it, or **remembering**, is a function of several factors: the number of times the information is heard or repeated, how much information there is to store in the brain, and whether the information may be "rehearsed" or not.

Early research on listening revealed that people remember only about half of what they hear immediately after hearing it, even when they listen mindfully (Barker, 1971). Within 2 months, 50 percent of the originally remembered portion is forgotten, bringing what we remember down to about 25 percent of the original message. However, this loss doesn't take 2 months: People start forgetting immediately (within 8 hours, the 50 percent remembered drops to about 35 percent). Of course, these amounts vary from person to person and depend on the importance of the information being recalled (Cowan & AuBuchon, 2008).

Whatever the particular amounts we remember may be, given the abundance of information we process every day in person and through mediated channels, the residual message (what we remember) is a small fraction of what we hear.

RESPONDING

All the steps we have discussed so far—hearing, attending, understanding, and remembering—are internal activities. A final part of the listening process involves **responding** to a message—giving observable feedback to the speaker (Bostrom, 1996). One study of 195 critical incidents in banking and medical settings showed that a major difference between effective and ineffective listening was the kind of feedback offered (Lewis & Reinsch, 1988). Good listeners showed that they were attentive by nonverbal behaviors such as keeping eye contact and reacting with appropriate facial expressions. Their verbal behavior—for example, answering questions and exchanging ideas—also demonstrated their attention. It's easy to imagine how other responses would signal less effective listening. A slumped posture, bored expression, and yawning send a clear message that you are not tuned in to the speaker.

Adding responsiveness to our listening model demonstrates a fact we discussed in Chapter 1, that communication is transactional in nature. Listening isn't just a passive activity. As listeners, we are active participants in a communication transaction. At the same time that we receive messages, we also send them.

Types of Listening Responses

Of the five components of listening described in the preceding section, it's responding that lets us know if others are truly tuned in to what we're saying (Maisel et al., 2008). Think for a moment of someone you consider a good listener. Why did you choose that person? It's probably because of the way she or he behaves while you are speaking: making eye contact and nodding when you're talking, staying attentive while you're telling an important story, reacting with an exclamation when you say something startling, expressing empathy and support when you're hurting, and offering another perspective or advice when you ask for it (Bippus, 2001). As Figure 7.3

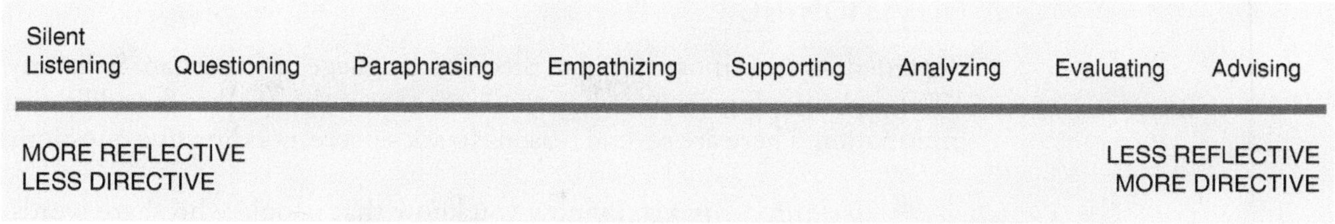

Silent Listening	Questioning	Paraphrasing	Empathizing	Supporting	Analyzing	Evaluating	Advising

MORE REFLECTIVE
LESS DIRECTIVE

LESS REFLECTIVE
MORE DIRECTIVE

FIGURE 7.3 Types of Listening Responses

illustrates, listening responses like these range from reflective feedback that invites the speaker to talk without concern of evaluation, to more directive responses that evaluate the speaker's messages. We spend the remainder of the chapter looking at each of these response styles in detail.

SILENT LISTENING

There are times when the best response is to say nothing. This is certainly true when you don't want to encourage a speaker to keep talking. For instance, recall times when a boss or instructor droned on and on when you needed to leave for an appointment, or instances when a friend retold the story of a love affair gone bad for what seemed like the tenth time. In situations like these, a verbal response would only encourage the speaker to continue—precisely the opposite reaction you would be seeking. The best response in these cases may be **silent listening**—staying attentive and nonverbally responsive without offering any verbal feedback.

Silent listening isn't just an avoidance strategy. It also can be the right approach when you are open to the other person's ideas but your interjections wouldn't be appropriate. If you are part of a large audience hearing a lecture, asking questions and offering comments would probably be disruptive. On a more interpersonal level, when a friend tells you a joke, butting in to ask for clarification ("There was a priest, a rabbi, and a *what?*") would probably spoil your friend's rhythm.

There are even times when silent listening can help others solve their problems. Sonia Johnson (1987; see also Smith, 2010) describes a powerful activity she calls "hearing into being." The process is simple: In brainstorming sessions, each participant has totally uninterrupted floor time. "When we are free to talk without threat of interruption, evaluation, and the pressure of time," notes Johnson, "we move quickly past known territory out into the frontiers of our thought" (p. 132). Johnson, who uses the technique in feminist seminars, reports that some women burst into tears when they first experience "hearing into being" because they are not used to being listened to so seriously and completely. Ask yourself: When was the last time you talked, uninterrupted, to an attentive partner for more than a few minutes? How would you like the chance to develop your ideas without pausing for another's comments? Silent listening is a response style that many of us could profit from using—and receiving—more often.

QUESTIONING

Regarded as "the most popular piece of language" (Goodman & Esterly, 1990), **questioning** occurs when the listener asks the speaker for additional information. There are several reasons to ask sincere, nondirective questions:

■ *To clarify meanings.* By now you know that people who share words do not always share meanings. Good listeners don't assume they know what their partners mean; they ask for clarification with questions such as these: "What did you mean when you said he had been 'unfair' to you?" "You said she's 'religious'—how do you define that term?" "You said you were going 'fast'—could you be more specific?" Of course, be sure to use an appropriate tone of voice when asking such questions, or else they might sound like an inquisition (Tracy, 2002).

■ *To learn about others' thoughts, feelings, and wants.* A caring listener may want to inquire about more than just "the facts." Opinions, emotions, needs, and even hopes are buried inside many messages; with sensitivity, a sincere question can draw these out. "What do you think about the new plan?"; "How did you feel when you heard the news?"; and "Were you hoping for something different?" are examples of such probes. When inquiring about personal information, it is usually best to ask **open questions** that allow a variety of extended responses rather than **closed questions** that only allow a limited range of answers. For instance, "How did you feel?" is an open question that allows a variety of responses, while "Did you feel angry?" is a closed question that requires only a yes or no answer (and may direct respondents toward feelings they weren't experiencing).

■ *To encourage elaboration.* People are sometimes hesitant to talk about themselves, or perhaps they aren't sure if others are interested. Remarks such as "Tell me more about that," "Try me again—I'm not sure I understand," and "Keep going—I'm following you" convey concern and involvement. Notice that none of these examples ends with a question mark. Unlike the television show *Jeopardy*, questioning responses need not be phrased in the form of a question. We can encourage elaboration simply by acknowledging that we are listening.

■ *To encourage discovery.* People in the helping professions—clergy, counselors, therapists, and so on—often ask questions to prod their clients into discovering solutions for their problems (Watts et al., 2005). "Playing counselor" can be a dangerous game, but there are times when you can use questions to encourage others to explore their thoughts and feelings. "So, what do you see as your options?" may prompt an employee to come up with creative problem-solving alternatives. "What would be your ideal solution?" might help a friend get in touch with various wants and needs. Most importantly, encouraging discovery rather than dispensing advice indicates you have faith in others' ability to think for themselves. This may be the most important message that you can communicate as an effective listener.

■ *To gather more facts and details.* Just because your conversational partner tells you something doesn't mean you understand the whole story. As long as your questions aren't intrusive (and you'll need to monitor others' nonverbal behavior to determine this), people often appreciate listeners who want to learn more. Questions such as "What did you do then?" and "What did she say after that?" can help a listener understand the big picture.

Not all questions are genuine requests for information. Whereas **sincere questions** are aimed at understanding others, **counterfeit questions** are really disguised attempts to send a message, not receive one. As such, they really fit better at the "more directive" end of the listening response continuum pictured in Figure 7.3 on page 223. It's also likely that they'll lead to a defensive communication climate, as discussed in Chapter 10.

Counterfeit questions come in several varieties:

■ *Questions that trap the speaker.* When your friend says, "You didn't like that movie, did you?" you're being backed into a corner. It's clear that your friend disapproves, so the question leaves you with two choices: You can disagree and defend your position, or you can devalue your reaction by lying or equivocating—"I guess it wasn't terrific." Consider how much easier it would be to respond to the sincere question, "What did you think of the movie?"

Adding a tag question such as "Did you?" or "Isn't that right?" to the end of a question can be a tip-off that the asker is looking for agreement, not information. While some listeners use these tag endings to confirm and facilitate understanding (Coates, 1986), our concern here is when tags are used to coerce agreement: "You said you'd call at five o'clock, but you forgot, didn't you?" Similarly, questions that begin with "Don't you" (such as "Don't you think she would make a good boss?") direct others toward a desired response. As a simple solution, changing "Don't you?" to "Do you?" makes the question less leading.

Leading questions not only signal what the desired answer is, they also affect memory, especially in children. David Bjorklund and his colleagues (2000) showed children and adults a video of a theft and then interviewed them several days later, using both leading and neutral questions. While the adults were unaffected by the type of question asked, the children who were asked leading questions had less accurate recall of the video than those who were asked free recall questions.

■ *Questions that make statements.* "Are you *finally* off the phone?" is more of a statement than a question—a fact unlikely to be lost on the targeted person. Emphasizing certain words also can turn a question into a statement: "You lent money to *Tony?*" We also use questions to offer advice. The person who asks, "Are you going to stand up to him and give him what he deserves?" has clearly stated an opinion about what should be done.

■ *Questions that carry hidden agendas.* "Are you busy Friday night?" is a dangerous question to answer. If you say "No," thinking the person has something fun in mind, you won't like hearing "Good, because I need some help moving my piano." Obviously, such questions are not designed to enhance understanding; they are setups for the proposal that follows. Other examples include "Will you do me a favor?" and "If I tell you what happened, will you promise not to get mad?" Because they are strategic rather than spontaneous, these questions are likely to provoke defensiveness (Gibb, 1961). Wise communicators answer questions that mask hidden agendas cautiously with responses such as "It depends" or "Let me hear what you have in mind before I answer."

■ *Questions that seek "correct" answers.* Most of us have been victims of question-askers who only want to hear a particular response. "Which shoes do you think I should wear?" can be a sincere question—unless the asker has a predetermined preference. When this happens, the asker isn't interested in listening to contrary opinions, and "incorrect" responses get shot down. Some of these questions may venture into delicate territory. "Honey, do you think I'm overweight?" is usually a request for a "correct" answer—and the listener must have a fair amount of discretion and good judgment to determine an appropriate response.

■ *Questions based on unchecked assumptions.* "Why aren't you listening to me?" assumes the other person isn't paying attention. "What's the matter?" assumes that something is wrong. As Chapter 4 explained, perception checking is a much better way of confirming assumptions. As you recall, a perception check offers a description of behavior and interpretations, followed by a sincere request for clarification: "When you kept looking over at the television, I thought you weren't listening to me, but maybe I was wrong. Were you paying attention?"

No question is inherently sincere or counterfeit, since the meaning and intent of any statement is shaped by its context. Moreover, a slight change in tone of voice or facial expression can turn a sincere question into a counterfeit one, and vice versa. Nonetheless, the types of questions in the preceding list are usually closer to statements than requests for information.

It's also worth noting that counterfeit questions aren't all bad: They can be powerful tools for making a point. Lawyers use them to get confessions in the courtroom (Cotterill, 2004), and journalists ask them to uncover concealed information. Our point is that they usually get in the way of effective listening and relationship building—after all, most people don't like feeling trapped or "grilled" in a conversation.

PARAPHRASING

Paraphrasing is feedback that restates, in your own words, the message you thought the speaker sent. You may wonder, "Why would I want to restate what's already been said?" Consider this simple exchange:

"Let's make plans to get together next weekend."
"So you want to chat next week to make plans for Saturday?"
"No, what I meant is that we should check our calendars now to see if we're free to go to the game on Sunday."

By paraphrasing, the listener learned that the speaker wanted to make plans now, not later—and that "weekend" meant Sunday, not Saturday. Note that the listener rephrased rather than repeated the message. In effective paraphrasing you restate what you think the speaker has said in your own words as a way of checking the meaning you've assigned to the message. It's important that you paraphrase, not "parrot-phrase." If you simply repeat the speaker's comments verbatim, you'll sound foolish or hard of hearing—and just as important, you still might misunderstand what's been said.

Types of Paraphrasing Statements Restating another person's message in a way that sounds natural can sometimes be a difficult skill to master. Here are three approaches to get you started:

1. Change the speaker's wording.

   Speaker: "Bilingual education is just another failed idea of bleeding-heart liberals."
   Paraphrase: "Let me see if I've got this right. You're mad because you think bilingual ed sounds good, but it doesn't work?"

2. Offer an example of what you think the speaker is talking about.
   When the speaker makes an abstract statement, you may suggest a specific example or two to see if your understanding is accurate.

   Speaker: "Lee is such a jerk. I can't believe the way he acted last night."
   Paraphrase: "You think those jokes were pretty offensive, huh?"

3. Reflect the underlying theme of the speaker's remarks.
   When you want to summarize the theme that seems to have run through another person's conversation, a complete or partial perception check is appropriate:

   Paraphrase: You keep reminding me to be careful. Sounds like you're worried that something might happen to me. Am I right?"

" WOOF, WOOF, WOOF – BUT I'M PARAPHRASING. "

227

There are several reasons why paraphrasing assists listening. First, as the preceding examples illustrate, paraphrasing allows you to find out if the message received is the message the sender intended. Second, paraphrasing often draws out further information from the speaker, much like questioning. (In fact, a good paraphrase often ends with a question such as, "Is that what you meant?") Third, paraphrasing is an ideal way to take the heat out of intense discussions. When conversations begin to boil, it is often because the people involved believe they aren't being heard. Rather than escalating the conflict, try paraphrasing what the other person says: "OK, let me be sure I understand you. It sounds like you're concerned about . . ." Paraphrasing usually short-circuits a defensive spiral because it assures the other person of your involvement and concern. When you take the time to restate and clarify a speaker's message, your commitment to mindful listening is hard to deny. For these and other reasons, we usually feel a sense of affinity for those who make the effort to paraphrase our messages (Weger et al., 2010).

There are two levels at which you can paraphrase messages. The first involves feedback of factual information; the second involves reflecting personal information.

Paraphrasing Factual Information Summarizing facts, data, and details is important during personal or professional conversations. "We've agreed that we'll take another few days to think about our choices and make a decision on Tuesday—right?" might be an effective way to conclude a business lunch. A questioning tone should be used; a listener wants to be sure that meaning has been shared. Even personal topics are sometimes best handled on a factual level: "So your main problem is that our friends take up all the parking spaces in front of your place. Is that it?" While this "neutral" response may be difficult when you are under attack, it helps to clarify facts before you offer your reaction. It is also a good idea to paraphrase instructions, directions, and decisions before acting on what you *think* has been said.

Paraphrasing Personal Information While restating factual information is relatively easy, it takes a sensitive ear to listen for others' thoughts, feelings, and wants. The "underlying message" is often the more important message, and effective listeners try to reflect what they hear at this level. Listening for thoughts, feelings, and wants addresses the cognitive (rational), affective (emotional), and behavioral (desired action) domains of human experience. Read the following statement as if a married, female friend is talking to you, and listen for all three components in her message:

> Bob has hardly been home all week—he's been so busy with work. He rushes in just long enough to eat dinner, then he buries himself at his desk until bedtime. Then he tells me today that he's going fishing Saturday with his buddies. I guess men are just like that—job first, play second, family third.

What is the speaker thinking, feeling, and wanting? Paraphrasing can help you find out: "Sounds like you're unhappy (feeling) because you think Bob's ignoring you (thought) and you want him to spend more time at home (want)." Recognize that you may not be accurate; the speaker might reply, "No, I really don't want him to spend more time at home—I just want him to pay attention to me when he's here." Recognize also that you could identify an entirely different think-feel-want set: "So you're frustrated (feeling) because you'd like Bob to change (want), but you think it's hopeless because men have different priorities (thought)." The fact that these examples offer such different interpretations of the same message demonstrates the value of paraphrasing.

Your paraphrases don't have to be as long as the examples in the preceding paragraph. It's often a good idea to mix paraphrasing with other listening responses. In many cases, you'll want to reflect only one or two of the think-feel-want components. The key is giving feedback that is appropriate for the situation and offering it in a way that assists the listening process. Because paraphrasing is an unfamiliar way of responding, it may feel awkward at first. If you start by paraphrasing occasionally and then gradually increase the frequency of such responses, you can begin to see the benefits of this method.

EMPATHIZING

Empathizing is a response style listeners use when they want to show that they *identify* with a speaker. As discussed in Chapter 4, empathy involves perspective taking, emotional contagion, and genuine concern. When listeners put the attitude of empathy into verbal and nonverbal responses, they engage in empathizing. Sometimes these responses can be quite brief: "Uh-huh," "I see," "Wow!" "Ouch!" "Whew!" "My goodness." In other cases, empathizing is expressed in statements like these:

"I can see that really hurts."
"I know how important that was to you."
"It's no fun to feel unappreciated."
"I can tell you're really excited about that."
"Wow, that must be rough."
"I think I've felt that way, too."
"Looks like that really made your day."
"This means a lot to you, doesn't it?"

MEDIA CLIP STYLES OF HELPFUL LISTENING: *IN TREATMENT*

This HBO series follows therapist Paul Weston (Gabriel Byrne) as he meets with a variety of clients. In a recent season, they included a childless workaholic who makes poor choices in men, a young student in denial about her serious illness, the 12-year-old who blames himself for his parents' divorce, and a seemingly confident CEO who suffers from panic attacks.

Paul's therapeutic manner includes all the listening responses described in this chapter. His genuine regard for each client and his skill show that these response styles don't need to sound formulaic, and that they can indeed be helpful.

Even statements like these may not fully capture the feeling of effective empathizing, which is not reducible to a technique or skill, but something that emerges from a relationship (Myers, 2000). Genuine empathizing ideally requires genuine identification with another person (Malle & Hodges, 2005).

Empathizing falls near the middle of the listening response continuum pictured in Figure 7.3. It is different from the more reflective responses at the left end of the spectrum, which attempt to gather information neutrally. It is also different from the more evaluative styles at the right end of the spectrum, which offer more direction than reflection. To understand how empathizing compares to other types of responses, consider these examples:

"So your boss isn't happy with your performance and you're thinking about finding a new job." (Paraphrasing)

"Ouch—I'll bet it hurt when your boss said you weren't doing a good job." (Empathizing)

"Hey, you'll land on your feet—your boss doesn't appreciate what a winner you are." (Supporting)

Notice that empathizing identifies with the speaker's emotions and perceptions more than paraphrasing does, yet offers less evaluation and agreement than supporting responses. In fact, it's possible to empathize with others while disagreeing with them. For instance, the response "I can tell that this issue is important to you" legitimizes a speaker's feelings without assenting to that person's point of view (note that it could be said to either a friend or a foe at a business meeting). Empathizing is therefore an important skill not only for interacting with people with whom you agree, but also for responding to those who see the world differently than you.

Perhaps a better way to explain empathizing is to describe what it *doesn't* sound like. Many listeners believe they are empathizing when, in fact, they are offering responses that are evaluative and directive—providing what has been called "cold comfort" (Burleson, 2003; Hample, 2006). Listeners are probably *not* empathizing when they display the following behaviors:

■ *Denying others the right to their feelings.* Consider this common response to another person's problem: "Don't worry about it." While the remark may be intended as a reassuring comment, the underlying message is that the speaker wants the person to feel differently. The irony is that the direction probably won't work—after all, it's unlikely that people can or will stop worrying just because you tell them to do so. Other examples of denying feelings are "It's nothing to get so upset about" and "That's a silly way to feel." Research shows that attempting to identify with others' emotions is more effective than denying their feelings and perspectives (Burleson & Samter, 1985, 1994).

■ *Minimizing the significance of the situation.* Think about the times someone said to you, "Hey, it's only _____." You can probably fill in the blank a variety of ways: "a game," "words," "a test," "a party." How did you react? You probably thought the person who said it just didn't understand. To someone who has been the victim of verbal abuse, the hurtful message wasn't "just words"; to a child who didn't get an invitation, it wasn't "just a party" (see Burleson, 1984); to a student who has flunked an important exam, it wasn't "just a test" (see Burleson & Samter, 1985). When you minimize the significance of someone else's experience, you aren't empathizing. Instead, you are interpreting the event from your perspective and then passing judgment—rarely a helpful response.

■ *Focus on yourself.* It can be tempting to talk at length about a similar experience you've encountered ("I know exactly how you feel. Something like that happened to me—let me tell you about it. . . .). While your intent might be to show empathy, research shows that such messages aren't perceived as helpful because they draw attention away from the distressed person (Burleson, 2008).

■ *Raining on the speaker's parade.* Most of the preceding examples deal with difficult situations or messages about pain. However, empathizing involves identifying with others' joys as well as their sorrows. Many of us can recall coming home with exciting news, only to be told "A 5 percent raise? That isn't so great." "An *A minus*? Why didn't you get an *A*?" "Big deal—I got one of those years ago." Taking the wind out of someone's sails is the opposite of empathizing.

Authors Florence Wolff and Nadine Marsnik (1993) believe that empathizing requires "fine skill and exquisite tuning to another's moods and feelings" (p. 100). Research suggests that cognitive complexity and flexibility are needed to offer these nonjudgmental, other-oriented responses (Applegate, 1990; Reid & Foels, 2010). Fortunately, research also indicates that the ability to offer such responses can be learned by both children and adults (Vancleave, 2008; Wei & Li, 2001). The exercises at the end of this chapter can offer you valuable practice in developing your skill as an empathic communicator.

SUPPORTING

So far, we have looked at listening responses that put a premium on being reflective and nonevaluative. However, there are times when other people want to hear more than a reflection of how *they* feel: They would like to know how *you* feel about *them*. **Supporting** responses reveal the listener's solidarity with the speaker's situation. Brant

Burleson (2003) describes supporting as "expressions of care, concern, affection, and interest, especially during times of stress or upset" (p. 552). There are several types of supportive responses:

Agreement	"Yeah, that class was tough for me too." "You're right—the landlord is being unfair."
Offers to help	"I'm here if you need me." "Let me try to explain it to him."
Praise	"I don't care what the boss said: I think you did a great job!" "You're a terrific person! If she doesn't recognize it, that's her problem."
Reassurance	"The worst part seems to be over. It will probably get easier from here." "I know you'll do a great job."
Diversion	"Let's catch a movie and get your mind off this." "That reminds me of the time we. . . ."

There's no question about the value of receiving support when faced with personal problems. "Comforting ability" and social support have been shown to be among the most important communication skills a friend—or a teacher, or a coach, or a parent—can have (Cunningham & Barbee, 2000; Robbins & Rosenfeld, 2001). Supportive responses can enhance the psychological, physical, and relational health of those who receive them (Jones & Wirtz, 2006). For example, support helps buffer the effects of aging (Fitzpatrick et al., 2005), anxiety and depression (Hatchett & Park, 2004), and even financial strain (Ramirez-Ponce, 2005). Evidence suggests that people who benefit from emotional support recover more quickly from injuries and disease, and may even live longer (Burleson, 2003).

Men and women differ in the way they act when the opportunity to support others arises. Women are more prone than men to give supportive responses when presented with another person's problem (Burleson et al., 2005; Hale et al., 1997) and are more skillful at composing and processing such messages (Burleson et al., 2009, 2011). In fact, women who *aren't* skillful at offering emotional support to their female friends run the risk of being shunned by their same-sex peers (Holmstrom et al., 2005). By contrast, men tend to respond to others' problems by offering advice, or by diverting the topic (Barbee et al., 1990; Derlega et al., 1994). In a study of sororities and fraternities, Woodward and his colleagues (1996) found that sorority women frequently respond with emotional support when asked to help; also, they rated their sisters as being better at listening nonjudgmentally, and on comforting and showing concern for them. Fraternity men, on the other hand, fit the stereotypical pattern of offering help by challenging their brothers to evaluate their attitudes and values. This may be due in part to societal norms that discourage men from offering sensitive emotional support (Burleson, 2005).

Although women and men may tend to offer different kinds of support, both sexes respond well to the same types of comforting messages. Both men and women feel most supported by messages that are highly personal, and which are delivered with nonverbal immediacy such as touching and maintaining eye contact (Jones & Burleson, 2003).

Even the most sincere supportive efforts don't always help. Mourners suffering from the recent death of a loved one often report that a majority of the statements made to them are unhelpful (Davidowitz & Myrick, 1984; Glanz, 2007). Most of these statements are advice: "You've got to get out more" and "Don't question God's will." Another frequent response is reassurance, such as, "She's out of pain now" and "Time heals all wounds." A study of bereaved parents found that these kinds of clichés actually do more harm than good (Toller, 2011). People who are grieving don't appreciate being told how to feel or what they should do. Instead, bereaved parents said they would feel more supported by the silent listening approach described on page 223. One mother who lost a child offered this recommendation for people who want to help a grieving friend:

> Go and be with them. You don't have to say anything, just say, "I don't know how you feel, but I'm here." Go sit down and just be with that person. What I wouldn't have given to have somebody come and knock on the door and stop in. (Toller, 2011, p. 26)

FOCUS ON RESEARCH

Blogging as Social Support for the Morbidly Obese

People who are morbidly obese—defined as being 100 pounds or more over a person's ideal weight or a body mass index of 40 or greater—represent about 5 percent of the U.S. population. They typically face serious health risks and are often victims of discrimination. When people in this category decide to lose weight, they often seek help from others facing similar battles. Researcher Amy Sanford investigated a contemporary medium for communicating about these shared challenges—blogging.

Sanford surveyed 50 morbidly obese people who blog about weight loss. She discovered that the communal nature of blogging makes it far more valuable than solo journaling. Blog sites become interactive communities where like-minded people share their struggles and offer each other affirming feedback. Comments like these capture the bloggers' feelings:

> "In the past I would try a diet, lose a little weight, get frustrated or bored and quit. Now that I've got the blog, quitting doesn't feel like an option."
> "When I have a bad week on the scale or a problem I don't know how to handle, all I have to do is write up an entry and post it on the blog. My readers are always full of good advice, comments and support."
> "I have never in my life felt so listened to, so empowered."

This study shows that supportive communication—whether offered in person or through mediated channels—is invaluable in helping people face their personal challenges.

Sanford, A. A. (2010). "I can air my feelings instead of eating them": Blogging as social support for the morbidly obese. *Communication Studies, 61*, 567–584.

As with the other helping styles, supporting can be beneficial, but only under certain conditions (Goldsmith & Fitch, 1997; Halone & Pecchioni, 2001):

- *Make sure your expression of support is sincere.* Phony agreement or encouragement is probably worse than no support at all, since it adds the insult of your dishonesty to whatever pain the other person is already feeling.

- *Be sure the other person can accept your support.* Sometimes people are so upset that they aren't ready or able to hear anything positive. When you know a friend is going through a difficult time, it's important not to be overly intrusive before that person is ready to talk and receive your support (Clark & Delia, 1997).

- *Focus on "here and now" rather than "then and there."* While it's sometimes true that "You'll feel better tomorrow," it sometimes isn't (you can probably remember times when you felt worse the next day). More importantly, focusing on the future avoids supporting in the present. Even if the prediction that "ten years from now, you won't even remember her name" proves correct, it gives little comfort to someone experiencing heartbreak today.

- *Make sure you're ready for the consequences.* Talking about a difficult event may reduce distress for the speaker but increase distress for the listener (Lewis & Manusov, 2009). Recognize that supporting another person is a worthwhile but potentially taxing venture.

© Mike Baldwin / Cornered

"There you go again, trying to solve my problems. I'm not asking you to do that. I just need you to listen."

ANALYZING

In **analyzing** a situation, the listener offers an interpretation of a speaker's message ("I think what's really bothering you is . . . "; "She's doing it because . . . "; or "Maybe the problem started when he . . . "). Interpretations are often effective in helping people who have problems seeing alternative meanings of a situation—meanings they would have never thought of without your assistance. Sometimes an analysis helps clarify a confusing problem, providing an objective understanding of the situation. Research suggests that analytic listeners are able to hear the concerns of emotionally upset others without experiencing similar emotions, which can be an advantage in problem solving (Weaver & Kirtley, 1995).

In other cases, an analysis can create more problems than it solves. There are two reasons why: First, your interpretation may not be correct, in which case the problem holder may become even more confused by accepting it. Second, even if your analysis is accurate, sharing it with the problem holder might not be useful. There's a chance that it will arouse defensiveness (analysis implies being superior and in a position to evaluate). Besides, the problem holder may not be able to understand your view of the problem without working it out personally.

How can you know when it's helpful to offer an analysis? There are several guidelines to follow:

- *Offer your interpretation in a tentative way rather than as absolute fact.* There's a big difference between saying "Maybe the reason is . . . " and insisting "This is the truth."

- *Your analysis ought to have a reasonable chance of being correct.* An inaccurate interpretation—especially one that sounds plausible—can leave a person more confused than before.

- *Make sure that the other person will be receptive to your analysis.* Even if you're completely accurate, your thoughts won't help if the problem holder isn't ready to consider them. Pay attention to the other person's verbal and nonverbal cues to see how your analysis is being received.

- *Be sure that your motive for offering an analysis is truly to help the other person.* It can be tempting to offer an analysis to show how brilliant you are or even to make the other person feel bad for not having thought of the right answer in the first place. Needless to say, an analysis offered under such conditions isn't helpful.

EVALUATING

An **evaluating** response appraises the sender's thoughts or behaviors in some way. The evaluation may be favorable ("That's a good idea" or "You're on the right track now") or unfavorable ("An attitude like that won't get you anywhere"). In either case, it implies that the person evaluating is in some way qualified to pass judgment on the speaker's thoughts or actions.

235

Sometimes negative evaluations are purely critical. How many times have you heard responses such as "Well, you asked for it!" or "I told you so!" or "You're just feeling sorry for yourself"? Although such comments can sometimes serve as a verbal slap that "knocks sense" into the problem holder, they usually make matters worse by arousing defensiveness in that person. After all, suggesting that someone is foolish or mistaken is an attack on the presenting image that most people would have a hard time ignoring or accepting.

Other times, negative evaluations are less critical. These involve what we usually call constructive criticism, which is intended to help the problem holder improve in the future. Friends give this sort of response about the choice of everything from clothing, to jobs, to friends. A common setting for constructive criticism is school, where instructors evaluate students' work in order to help them master concepts and skills. Even constructive criticism can arouse defensiveness because it may threaten the self-concept of the person at whom it is directed. Chapter 10 provides guidelines for offering constructive criticism in ways that protect the self-concept of the recipient.

ADVISING

When approached with another's problem, the most common reaction is **advising** (Notarius & Herrick, 1988). We're all familiar with advising responses: "If you're so unhappy, you should just quit the job"; "Just tell him what you think"; "You should take some time off."

Even though advice might be just what a person needs, there are several reasons why it often isn't helpful. First, it may not offer the best suggestion about how to act. There's often a temptation to tell others how you would behave in their place, but it's important to realize that what's right for one person may not be right for another. A related consequence of advising is that it often allows others to avoid responsibility for their decisions. A partner who follows a suggestion of yours that doesn't work out can always pin the blame on you. Finally, people often don't want advice: They may not be ready to accept it, and instead may simply need to talk out their thoughts and feelings.

Studies on advice giving (summarized in MacGeorge et al., 2008) offer the following important considerations when trying to help others:

- *Is the advice needed?* If the person has already taken a course of action, giving advice after the fact ("I can't believe you got back together with him") is rarely appreciated.

- *Is the advice wanted?* People generally don't value unsolicited advice. It's usually best to ask if the speaker is interested in hearing your counsel. Remember that sometimes people just want a listening ear, not solutions to their problems.

- *Is the advice given in the right sequence?* Advice is more likely to be received after the listener first offers empathizing, paraphrasing, and questioning responses to understand the speaker and the situation better.

- *Is the advice coming from an expert?* If you want to offer advice about anything from car purchasing to relationship managing, it's important to have experience and success in those matters. If you *don't* have expertise, it's a good idea to offer the speaker supportive responses, then encourage the person to seek out expert counsel.

- *Is the advisor a close and trusted person?* While sometimes we seek out advice from people we don't know well (perhaps because they have expertise), in most cases we value advice given within the context of a close and ongoing interpersonal relationship.

- *Is the advice offered in a sensitive, face-saving manner?* No one likes to feel bossed or belittled, even if the advice is good (Miczo & Burgoon, 2008). Remember that messages have both content and relational dimensions, and sometimes the unstated relational messages when giving advice ("I'm smarter than you"; "You're not bright enough to figure this out yourself") will keep people from hearing counsel.

WHICH STYLE TO USE?

By now, it should be clear that there are many ways to respond as a listener. You also can see that each style has advantages and disadvantages. This leads to the important question: Which style is best? There isn't a simple answer to this question. All response styles have the potential to help others accept their situation, feel better, and have a sense of control over their problems (Imhof, 2003; Young & Cates, 2004).

As a rule of thumb, it's probably wise to begin with responses from the left and middle of the listening response continuum: silent listening, questioning, paraphrasing, empathizing, and supporting. Once you've gathered the facts and demonstrated your interest and concern, it's likely that the speaker will be more receptive to (and perhaps even ask for) your analyzing, evaluating, and advising responses.

You can boost the odds of choosing the best style in each situation by considering three factors. First, think about the *situation*, and match your response to the nature of the problem. People sometimes need your advice. In other cases your encouragement and support will be most helpful, and in still other instances your analysis or judgment may be truly useful. And, as you have seen, there are times when your questioning and paraphrasing can help others find their own answer.

Besides considering the situation, you also should think about the *other person* when deciding which approach to use. It's important to be sure that the other person is open to receiving *any* kind of help. Furthermore, you need to be confident that you will be regarded as someone whose support is valuable. The same response that would be accepted with gratitude when it comes from one communicator can be regarded as unhelpful when it's offered by the wrong person (Clark et al., 1998; Sullivan, 1996).

It's also important to match the type of response you offer with the style of the person to whom it is directed (Bippus, 2001). One study found that highly rational people tend to respond more positively to advice than

ⓈⒺⓁⒻ-ⒶⓈⓈⒺⓈⓈⓂⒺⓃⓉ

Your Listening Responses

Learn more about your helping style by indicating how you would most likely respond to each of the statements below. Don't try to guess the "right" response: Choose the response that is closest to what you would probably say after hearing each statement.

1. "I think I understand the material, but I don't know where I stand in the course. I'm not sure what the instructor expects of me, and she doesn't tell me how I'm doing. I wish I knew where I stood."
   a) "Has your instructor ever given you any indication of what she thinks of your work?"
   b) "If I were you, I'd discuss it with her."
   c) "She's probably just trying to give everyone in the class a lot of freedom to do what they want to do."
   d) "It sounds like you're worried about your grade. Is that it?"
   e) "Don't take it so seriously. Most of the time in school you don't know where you stand."
   f) "I've had instructors like this, and I agree—it's frustrating!"
   g) "I've had teachers like that, and it's a lousy situation."

2. "The policy in the chemistry department is supposed to be to hire lab assistants from people in the advanced chem classes. And now I find that this person from a beginning class is getting hired. I had my eyes on that job; I've been working hard for it. I know I could be a terrific assistant if I had a chance."
   a) "I can tell how disappointed you are."
   b) "Why do you think they hired the person from the beginning class?"
   c) "If not getting the job means not having enough money to make it through the semester, I can help out with a loan."
   d) "Getting ahead is very important to you, and it sounds like you feel cheated that someone else got the job as lab assistant."
   e) "You should take some more chemistry classes to help you advance."
   f) "I told you not to get your hopes up."
   g) "You shouldn't complain—they probably hired the best person to be an assistant."

3. "I'm really tired of this. I'm taking more classes than anyone I know, and then on the same day three of my teachers tell me that there's another assignment due on top of what's already due. I've got so many people asking me to do things that I just can't keep up, and it bothers me. I like my teachers, and my classes are interesting, but I am getting overwhelmed."
   a) "With so many teachers asking you to do extra assignments, it's difficult for you to accomplish all of it, and the pressure gets you down."
   b) "Are all these requests from your teachers required work?"
   c) "You seem to be handling this overwhelming situation pretty well!"
   d) "You seem to have too much work. Why don't you talk it over with your teachers?"

e) "Yikes! Sounds like things are pretty hectic for you right now."
f) "You're probably overworked because you're not organized."
g) "Who told you to take so many classes?"

4. "My teacher tells the class that he would appreciate getting term projects as soon as possible to help him with grading. So I work like mad to get it completed and on his desk early. What's my reward for helping him out? Nothing! No thanks, no nothing. In fact, I think my project will sit on his desk until all the projects are handed in."
a) "How often do teachers do this to you?"
b) "Don't be a baby. You don't need a pat on the back for every good thing you do."
c) "You ought to tell him how you feel."
d) "You feel resentful because you think he's taking advantage of you?"
e) "I hate when teachers do that to us!"
f) "That may be so, but you did the right thing."
g) "I think your professor was trying to teach the value of doing work before the last minute."

5. "He used to be one of the guys until he was made the team's coach. Now, it's like he's not my friend anymore. I don't mind being told about my mistakes, but he doesn't have to do it in front of the rest of the team. Whenever I get the chance, he's going to get his!"
a) "How about going to dinner and relaxing tonight?"
b) "I'll bet that really upset you."
c) "To be told about your mistakes in front of the rest of the team is embarrassing, especially by a person you once considered a friend."
d) "If you didn't make so many mistakes, the coach wouldn't have to tell you about them."
e) "Why don't we talk it over with a few other people on the team and then go talk to him about this situation?"
f) "How often does he criticize you in front of the others?"
g) "Seems like he's on a power trip."

Listed below are the possible response types for each of the five situations. For example, if you indicated answer a in situation number 1, note that this is a "questioning response." If you indicated answer b, note that this is an "advising response." Do this for your five responses.

Questioning response: 1a, 2b, 3b, 4a, 5f
Advising response: 1b, 2e, 3d, 4c, 5e
Analyzing response: 1c, 2g, 3f, 4g, 5g
Paraphrasing response: 1d, 2d, 3a, 4d, 5c
Evaluating response: 1e, 2f, 3g, 4b, 5d
Supportive response: 1f (agreement support), 2c (offer-to-help support), 3c (praise support), 4f (reassurance support), 5a (diversion support)
Empathizing response: 1g, 2a, 3e, 4e, 5b

Do you have a particular way of responding? What does this tell you about how you listen, that is, the kinds of information you listen for? When is your typical way of responding most and least useful? What do you think is the most useful—needed—response in each of the five situations?

do more emotional people (Feng & Lee, 2010). Many communicators are extremely defensive and aren't capable of receiving analysis or judgments without lashing out. Still others aren't equipped to think through problems clearly enough to profit from questioning and paraphrasing. Sophisticated listeners choose a style that fits the person.

Finally, think about *yourself* when deciding how to respond. Most of us reflexively use one or two styles (did you notice this when you completed the Self-Assessment on pages 238–239?). You may be best at listening quietly, posing a question, or paraphrasing from time to time. Or perhaps you are especially insightful and can offer a truly useful analysis of the problem. Of course, it's also possible to rely on a response style that is *unhelpful*. You may be overly judgmental or too eager to advise, even when your suggestions aren't invited or productive. As you think about how to respond to another's problems, consider your weaknesses as well as your strengths.

Summary

Listening is both more frequent and less emphasized than speaking. Despite its relative invisibility, listening is at least as important as speaking. Research shows that good listening is vital for both personal and professional success.

Listening is the process of making sense of others' spoken messages. We listen to many messages mindlessly, but it's important to listen mindfully in a variety of situations. There are several reasons why we listen to others. At the most basic level, we listen to understand and retain information. Perhaps more importantly, we listen to build and maintain our interpersonal relationships. We may listen to help others, and also to evaluate their messages.

Most peoples' understanding of listening is based on poor listening habits and also on several misconceptions that communicators need to correct. Mindful listening is not easy; rather, it is a challenge that requires much effort and talent. Several barriers can hamper effective listening: personal concerns, information overload, rapid thought, and both internal and external noise. Even careful listening does not mean that all listeners will receive the same message. A wide variety of factors discussed in this chapter can result in widely varying interpretations of even simple statements.

Listening consists of several components: hearing, attending to a message, understanding the statement, recalling the message after the passage of time, and responding to the speaker. Listening responses are important because they let us know if others are truly tuned in to what we're saying. Listening responses can be placed on a continuum. More reflective/less directive responses include silent listening, questioning, paraphrasing, and empathizing. These put a premium on gathering information and showing interest and concern. Less reflective/more directive responses include supporting, analyzing, evaluating, and advising. These put a premium on offering input and direction. It is possible to use the "more reflective" listening responses to help people arrive at their own decisions without offering advice or evaluation. The most effective listeners use several styles, depending on the situation, the other person, and their own personal skills and motivation.

Key Terms

- Advising (236)
- Ambushing (219)
- Analyzing (235)
- Attending (220)
- Closed questions (224)
- Counterfeit questions (225)
- Defensive listening (219)
- Empathizing (229)
- Evaluating (235)
- Filling in gaps (219)
- Hearing (212)
- Insulated listening (219)
- Listening (211)
- Listening fidelity (215)
- Mindful listening (213)
- Mindless listening (212)
- Open questions (224)
- Paraphrasing (227)
- Pseudolistening (218)
- Questioning (224)
- Remembering (221)
- Responding (222)
- Selective listening (218)
- Silent listening (223)
- Sincere questions (225)
- Stage hogging (218)
- Supporting (231)
- Understanding (221)

Activities

1. Invitation to Insight

You can start to overcome bad listening habits by recalling specific instances when:

    a. you heard another person's message but did not attend to it.

    b. you attended to a message but forgot it almost immediately.

    c. you attended and remembered a message but did not understand it

accurately.
 d. you understood a message but did not respond sufficiently to convey your understanding to the sender.
For each situation, describe how you could have listened more effectively.

2. Invitation to Insight

Keep a 3-day journal of your listening behavior, noting the time you spend listening in various contexts. In addition, analyze your reasons for listening. Which goal(s) were you trying to achieve?
 a. To understand and retain information
 b. To build and maintain relationships
 c. To help
 d. To evaluate

3. Critical Thinking Probe

Communication problems can arise from factors that aren't easily observed. Based on your experience, decide which of the following steps in the listening process cause the greatest difficulties for you:
 a. Hearing
 b. Attending
 c. Understanding
 d. Remembering
 e. Responding
Discuss your findings with your friends, and develop a list of remedies that can help minimize listening problems in the areas you identified.

4. Skill Builder

Explore the benefits of silent listening by using a "Talking Stick." Richard Hyde (1993) developed this exercise from the Native American tradition of "council." Gather a group of people in a circle, and designate a particular item as the talking stick. Participants will then pass the stick around the circle. Participants may speak
 a. only when holding the stick;
 b. for as long as they hold the stick; and
 c. without interruption from anyone else in the circle.
When a member is through speaking, the stick passes to the left and the speaker surrendering the stick must wait until it has made its way around the circle before speaking again.
After each member of the group has had the chance to speak, discuss how this experience differs from more common approaches to listening. Decide how the desirable parts of this method could be introduced in everyday conversations.

5. Ethical Challenge

What responsibility do communicators have to listen as carefully and thoughtfully as possible to other speakers? Are there ever cases where the poor listening habits listed on pages 218–219 (for example, pseudolistening, stage hogging, and defensive listening) are justified? How would you feel if you knew that others weren't listening to you?

6. Skill Builder

Practice your ability to paraphrase in order to understand others by following these steps.

    a. Choose a partner, and designate one of yourselves as A and the other as B. Find a subject on which you and your partner seem to disagree—a personal dispute, a philosophical or moral issue, or perhaps a matter of personal taste.

    b. A begins by making a statement on the subject. B's job is to paraphrase the idea. In this step B should feed back only what he or she heard A say, without adding any judgment or interpretation. B's job here is simply to *understand* A—not to agree or disagree with A.

    c. A responds by telling B whether or not the response was accurate, and by making any necessary additions or corrections to clarify the message.

    d. B then paraphrases the revised statement. This process should continue until A is sure that B understands him or her.

    e. Now B and A reverse roles and repeat the procedure in steps a–d. Continue the conversation until both partners are satisfied that they have explained themselves fully and have been understood by the other person.

After the discussion has ended, consider how this process differed from typical conversations on controversial topics. Was there greater understanding here? Do the partners feel better about one another? Finally, ask yourself how your life might change if you used more paraphrasing in everyday conversations.

7. Skill Builder

Explore the various types of listening responses by completing the following steps.

    a. Join with two partners to form a trio. Designate members as A, B, and C.

    b. A begins by sharing a current, real problem with B. The problem needn't be a major life crisis, but it should be a real one. B should respond in whatever way seems most helpful. C's job is to categorize each response by B as silent listening, questioning, paraphrasing, empathizing, supporting, analyzing, evaluating, or advising.

    c. After a 4- to 5-minute discussion, C should summarize B's response styles. A then describes which of the styles were most helpful and which were not helpful.

    d. Repeat the same process two more times, switching roles so that each person has been in all of the positions.

    e. Based on their findings, the threesome should develop conclusions about what combination of response styles can be most helpful.

After studying the material in this chapter . . .

You should understand:

1. The four components of emotion.
2. The influence of culture and gender on emotional expressiveness and sensitivity.
3. The relationships among activating events, thoughts, emotions, and communication behavior.
4. Seven fallacies leading to unnecessarily debilitative emotions that can interfere with effective communication.
5. The steps in the rational-emotive approach for coping with debilitative emotions.

You should be able to:

1. Observe the physical and cognitive manifestations of some of the emotions you experience.
2. Label your own emotions accurately.
3. Identify the degree to which you express your emotions and the consequences of this level of expression.
4. Follow the guidelines in this chapter in deciding when and how to express your emotions in an important relationship.
5. Realize which of your emotions are facilitative and which are debilitative.
6. Identify the fallacious beliefs that have caused you to experience debilitative emotions in a specific situation.
7. In a specific situation, apply the rational-emotive approach to managing your debilitative emotions.

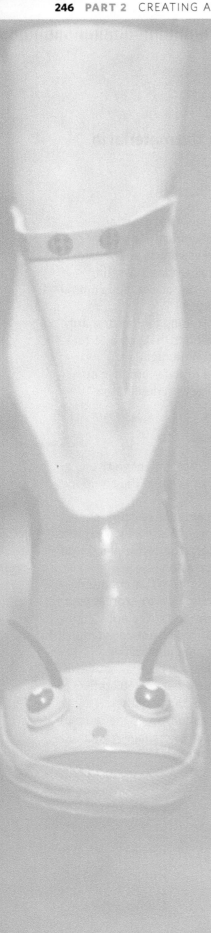

magine how different life would be if you lost your ability to experience emotions. An emotionless world would be free of boredom, frustration, fear, and loneliness. But the cost of such a pain-free existence would be the loss of emotions like joy, pride, excitement, and love. Few of us would be willing to make that sort of trade-off.

Daniel Goleman (1995) coined the term **emotional intelligence** to describe the ability to understand and manage one's own emotions and to be sensitive to others' feelings. Goleman maintains that cognitive ability is not the only way to measure one's talents, and that success in the world depends in great part on emotional intelligence. In support of that claim, studies show that emotional intelligence is positively linked with self-esteem and life satisfaction (Carmeli et al., 2009; Singh & Woods, 2008), healthy conflict communication (Smith et al., 2008), and effective workplace interactions (Kidwell et al., 2011; Ybarra et al., 2011).

Stop for a moment and try to identify someone you know who is emotionally intelligent. Perhaps it's a family member who is in touch with a wide range of feelings without being overwhelmed by them, or a boss who makes wise and rational choices even under stress. Now think of a person who might be lacking emotional intelligence. Maybe it's a colleague who is uptight and dismissive about honest human feelings, or a friend who blows up at the smallest inconvenience. And finally, assess your own emotional intelligence. How well do *you* understand and manage your emotions, and how sensitive are you to others' feelings? The Self-Assessment on page 247 can help you make that call.

Because emotions are such an important part of human communication, we will take a close look at them in the following pages. We will explore what feelings are, discuss the ways they are handled in contemporary society, and see how recognizing and expressing them can improve relationships. We will look at some guidelines that should give you a clearer idea of when and how to express your emotions constructively. Finally, we will explore a method for coping with troublesome, debilitating feelings that inhibit rather than help your communication.

ⓈⒺⓁⒻ-ⒶⓈⓈⒺⓈⓈⓂⒺⓃⓉ

Your Emotional Intelligence

To what extent is each of the following items true for you? Rate each one on a scale from 0 to 6, where 0 = "not at all true of me," 3 = "somewhat true of me," and 6 = "completely true of me."

NOT AT ALL TRUE OF ME   0   1   2   3   4   5   6   COMPLETELY TRUE OF ME

_____   1. I have no problem verbally expressing my emotions.

_____   2. I have little trouble "getting into" another person's emotions.

_____   3. I find it easy to regulate my emotions.

_____   4. It's easy for me to figure out what emotion I'm feeling.

_____   5. Generally, I have no trouble influencing the way other people feel.

_____   6. Usually, I'm able to empathize with others and experience their emotions.

_____   7. I'm able to control my emotions when I want to.

_____   8. I think frequently about my feelings.

_____   9. I understand why my emotions change.

_____   10. By looking at their facial expressions or listening to their tone of voice, I recognize the emotions people are experiencing.

Add your responses to items 1 through 10:   _____

Your score should give you an indication of your Emotional Intelligence. Scores range from 0 to 60, with those approximately 43 and higher indicative of greater Emotional Intelligence.

Adapted from: Cooper, A., & Petrides, K. V. (2010). A psychometric analysis of the Trait Emotional Intelligence Questionnaire-Short Form (TEIQue-SF) using item response theory. *Journal of Personality Assessment, 92*, 449–457.

Davies, K. A., Lane, A. M., Devonport, T. J., & Scott, J. A. (2010). Validity and reliability of a Brief Emotional Intelligence Scale (BEIS-10). *Journal of Individual Differences, 31*(4), 198–208.

What Are Emotions?

Suppose an extraterrestrial visitor asked you to explain emotions. How would you answer? You might start by saying that emotions are things that we feel. But this doesn't say much, for in turn you would probably describe feelings as synonymous with emotions. Social scientists generally agree that there are several components to the phenomena we label as an emotion (Baumeister, 2005; Planalp et al., 2006).

PHYSIOLOGICAL CHANGES

When a person has strong emotions, many bodily changes occur (Rochman & Diamond, 2008). For example, the physical components of fear include an increased heartbeat, a rise in blood pressure, an increase in adrenaline secretions, an elevated blood sugar level, a slowing of digestion, and a dilation of pupils. Marriage researcher John Gottman notes that symptoms like these also occur when couples are in intense conflicts (Gottman & Silver, 1999). He calls the condition "flooding" and has found that it impedes effective problem solving. Some of these changes are recognizable to the person having them. These physiological messages can offer a significant clue to your emotions once you become aware of them. A churning stomach or tense jaw can be a signal that something is wrong.

NONVERBAL REACTIONS

Not all physical changes that accompany emotions are internal. Feelings are often apparent by observable changes. Some of these changes involve a person's appearance, such as blushing or perspiring. Other changes involve behavior: a distinctive facial expression, posture, gestures, different vocal tone and rate, and so on. The Focus on Research sidebar on page 249 shows that these nonverbal reactions often become more pronounced under the influence of alcohol.

F⊕CUS ON RESEARCH

Emoting under the Influence

It's no surprise that alcohol affects emotional expression. Communication scholars Jennifer Samp and Jennifer Monahan studied what happens when communicators are "under the influence."

In one study, the researchers had 42 male teams play a guessing game. One teammate was randomly assigned to the drinking condition while the other remained sober. Trained coders rated the partners who drank as more emotionally expressive during the games, based on the players' nonverbal cues. These expressions included both positive emotions (such as excitement) and negative ones (such as anxiety).

In a follow-up study, Samp and Monahan turned their attention to communication about relationships. Partners in 44 heterosexual dyads were encouraged to talk about a hypothetical romantic infidelity. In half the groups, the male partner was sober; in the other half the men were legally drunk. Raters found that the drinkers expressed a wider range of emotions than their sober counterparts. Given the topic, it's not surprising that the emotions expressed by the drinkers were more negative than positive.

Findings like these confirm that alcohol is an "emotion-enhancer." These studies, and others cited by Samp and Monahan, show that the type of feelings communicated—positives or negatives—depend on the context. In some circumstances, alcohol can enhance emotional expression. In other cases, it can be extremely harmful. Before drinking and communicating, that's an important fact to remember.

Samp, J. A., & Monahan, J. L. (2007). Expressing under the influence: Alcohol consumption, nonverbal behavior, and performance. *Communication Research Reports, 24*, 79–86.

Samp, J. A., & Monahan, J. L. (2009). Alcohol-influenced nonverbal behaviors during discussions about a relationship problem. *Journal of Nonverbal Behavior, 33*, 193–211.

Although it's reasonably easy to tell when someone is feeling a strong emotion, it's more difficult to be certain exactly what that emotion might be. A slumped posture and sigh may be a sign of sadness, or it may signal fatigue. Likewise, widened eyes might indicate excitement, or they may be an outward sign of fear. As you learned in Chapter 6, nonverbal behavior is usually ambiguous, and it's dangerous to assume that it can be "read" with much accuracy.

Although we usually think of nonverbal behavior as the reaction to an emotional state, there may be times when the reverse is true—when nonverbal behavior *causes* emotions. Research shows that people can actually create emotional states by altering their facial expressions. When volunteers in one study were coached to smile, they reported feeling better, and when they altered their expressions to look unhappy, they felt worse than before (Kleinke et al., 1998). Previous research by Paul Ekman and his colleagues (1983; see also Levenson et al., 1990) produced similar results, with subjects feeling afraid, angry, disgusted, amused, sad, surprised, and contemptuous when they created facial expressions that mimicked those feelings. Clenching your fists can help you feel stronger (Schubert & Koole, 2009), and so can adopting power poses (see the At Work sidebar on page 254). As behavioral scientists like to say, it can be easier to act yourself into new ways of feeling than to feel yourself into new ways of acting.

There's also a connection between verbalizing emotions and nonverbal reactions. One study showed that participants who generated words associated with pride and disappointment experienced a change in posture (Oosterwijk et al., 2009). They unconsciously stood taller when talking about pride and slumped when using words for disappointment. The participants also experienced emotions associated with their words (e.g., feeling sad when speaking about disappointment). This reminds us that verbal and nonverbal expressions of emotion are often interconnected.

COGNITIVE INTERPRETATIONS

Although there may be instances when there is a direct connection between physical behavior and emotional states, in most situations the mind plays an important role in determining how we feel (Genov, 2001). As noted earlier, some physiological components of fear are a racing heart, perspiration, tense muscles, and elevated blood pressure. Interestingly enough, these symptoms are similar to the physical changes that accompany excitement, joy, and other emotions. In other words, if we were to measure the physical condition of someone having a strong emotion, we would have a hard time knowing whether that person was trembling with fear or quivering with excitement. For example, Stephen Mallalieu and his colleagues (2003) found that some athletes experiencing precompetition stress labeled their feelings in positive emotional terms and interpreted their emotion as facilitating their work, while other athletes experiencing the same stress labeled it negatively.

The recognition that the bodily components of most emotions are similar led some psychologists to conclude that the experience of fright, joy, or anger comes primarily from the labels—and the accompanying cognitive interpretations—we give to our physical symptoms (Kagan, 2007). Psychologist Philip Zimbardo (1977, p. 53) offers a good example of this principle:

> I notice I'm perspiring while lecturing. From that I infer I am nervous. If it occurs often, I might even label myself a "nervous person." Once I have the label, the next question I must answer is "Why am I nervous?" Then I start to search for an appropriate explanation. I might notice some students leaving the room, or being inattentive. I am nervous because I'm not giving a good lecture. That makes me nervous. How do I know it's not good? Because I'm boring my audience. I am nervous because I am a boring lecturer and I want to be a good lecturer. I feel inadequate. Maybe I should open a delicatessen instead. Just then a student says, "It's hot in here, I'm perspiring and it makes it tough to concentrate on your lecture." Instantly, I'm no longer "nervous" or "boring."

VERBAL EXPRESSION

As you read in Chapter 6, nonverbal behavior is a powerful way of communicating emotion. In fact, nonverbal actions are better at conveying attitudes than they are at expressing ideas, which may explain why people tend to express their emotions nonverbally rather than verbally (Planalp, 1998). But sometimes words are necessary to express feelings. Saying "I'm really angry" is clearer and probably more helpful than stomping out of the room, and "I'm feeling nervous" might help explain a pained expression on your face.

Some researchers believe there are several "basic" or "primary" emotions (Panksepp, 2007; Plutchik, 1984). However, there isn't much agreement among scholars about what those emotions are, or about what makes them "basic" (Cohen, 2005; Ortony & Turner, 1990). Moreover, emotions that are primary in one culture may not be primary in others, and some emotions may have no equivalent in other cultures (Ferrari & Koyama, 2002). For example, "shame" is a central emotion in the Chinese experience (Zhong et al., 2008), while it's much less central to most people from Western cultures. Despite this debate, most scholars acknowledge that *anger, joy, fear,* and *sadness* are common and typical human emotions.

We experience most emotions with different degrees of intensity—and we use specific emotion words to represent these differences. Figure 8.1 illustrates this point clearly. To say you're "annoyed" when a friend breaks an important promise, for example, would probably be an understatement. In other cases, people chronically overstate the strength of their feelings. To them, everything is "wonderful" or "terrible." The problem with this sort of exaggeration is that when a truly intense emotion comes along, they have no words left to describe it adequately. If chocolate chip cookies from the local bakery are "fantastic," how does it feel to fall in love?

The ability to communicate clearly about feelings has been characterized as part of "emotional intelligence," which we discussed earlier in this chapter. Social scientists have identified a wide range of problems that arise

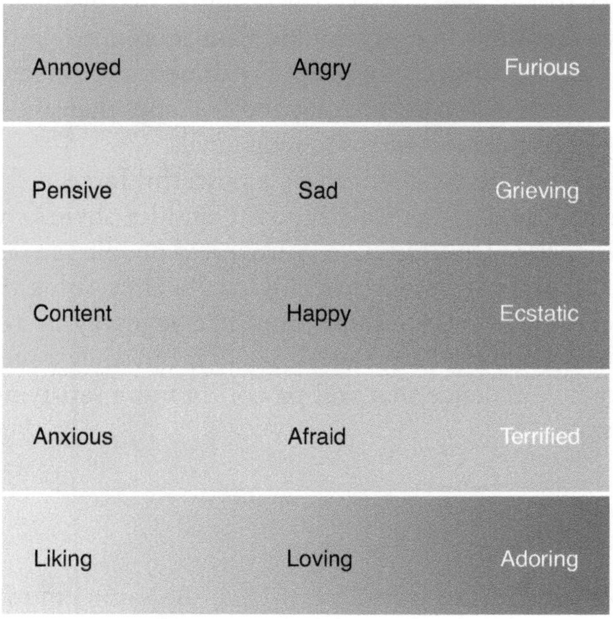

Annoyed	Angry	Furious
Pensive	Sad	Grieving
Content	Happy	Ecstatic
Anxious	Afraid	Terrified
Liking	Loving	Adoring

FIGURE 8.1 **Intensity of Emotions**

for people who aren't able to talk about emotions constructively, including social isolation, unsatisfying relationships, feelings of anxiety and depression, and misdirected aggression (Cherniss et al., 2006; Whiffen et al., 2007).

The way parents talk to their children about emotions has a powerful effect on the children's development. John Gottman and his associates (1997) identified two distinct parenting styles, "emotion coaching" and "emotion dismissing." They show how the coaching approach gives children skills for communicating about feelings in later life that lead to much more satisfying relationships. Children who grow up in families where parents dismiss emotions are at higher risk for behavior problems than those who are raised in families that practice emotion coaching (Lunkenheimer et al., 2007; Young, 2009). Later in this chapter you will find some guidelines for communicating effectively about emotions.

Influences on Emotional Expression

Each of us is born with the disposition to reveal our emotions, at least nonverbally. But over time, a wide range of differences develops in emotional expression. In the next few pages, we will look at some influences that shape how people communicate their feelings.

PERSONALITY

Science has established an increasingly clear relationship between personality and the way people experience and communicate emotions (Gross et al., 1998; McCroskey et al., 2004). For example, extroverted people report more positive emotions in everyday life than more introverted individuals (Lucas et al., 2008). Conversely, people with neurotic personalities—those with a tendency to worry, be anxious, and feel apprehensive—report more negative emotions than less neurotic individuals.

However, while personality can be a powerful force, it doesn't have to govern your communication satisfaction. Consider shyness, which can be seen as the opposite of extroversion. Introverted people can devise comfortable and effective strategies for reaching out, such as using the Internet to make contact. Online relationships shouldn't be a way to avoid in-person communication (Ebeling-Witte et al., 2007); but they can be a rewarding way to gain confidence that will pay off in more satisfying face-to-face relationships.

CULTURE

While people around the world experience the same emotions, the same events can generate quite different feelings in different cultures. The notion of eating snails might bring a smile of delight to some residents of France,

F⊕CUS ON RESEARCH

Saying "I Love You": Different Cultures, Different Rules

It's been said that love is the universal language. To the contrary, Richard Wilkins and Elisabeth Gareis found that saying "I love you" (or its equivalent in other languages) has very different meanings around the world.

Wilkins and Gareis surveyed college students from a variety of countries and cultures. They found significant differences about when, where, how often, and with whom the phrase "I love you" is used. The investigation revealed that Americans say "I love you" more frequently and with more people than do members of most other cultures. By contrast, Middle Easterners in the survey believed that "I love you" should only be expressed between spouses. They warned that American men who use the phrase casually with Middle Eastern women might be misinterpreted as making a marriage proposal. Participants from several other cultures (e.g., Eastern Europe, India, Korea) also reported saying "I love you" sparingly, believing that the power of expressing their love would be diminished if used too often.

Interestingly, many participants for whom English is a second language said they were more likely to make declarations of love in English than in their native tongues. That matches what other researchers found in a study of Mandarin-English bilinguals. Participants in that study said it's easier to express emotions in English because of more relaxed social constraints in English-speaking contexts. They also had stronger physiological responses to saying "I love you" in English than in Mandarin.

This line of research shows that while love may be a universal emotion, the rules for *communicating* that sentiment vary greatly from culture to culture.

Caldwell-Harris, C. L., Tong, J., Lung, W., & Poo, S. (in press). Physiological reactivity to emotional phrases in Mandarin-English bilinguals. *International Journal of Bilingualism.* Retrieved from http://www.bu.edu/psych/charris/papers/PhysReactMandarin.pdf

Wilkins, R., & Gareis, E. (2006). Emotion expression and the locution "I love you": A cross-cultural study. *International Journal of Intercultural Relations, 30*, 51–75.

though it would cause many North Americans to grimace in disgust. More to the point of this book, research has shown that fear of strangers and risky situations is more likely to frighten people living in the United States and Europe than those in Japan, while Japanese are more apprehensive about relational communication than are Americans and Europeans (Iwata et al., 2011; Ting-Toomey, 1991).

There are also differences in the degree to which people in various cultures display their feelings (Cole et al., 2002; Matsumoto, 2006). For example, social scientists have found support for the notion that people from warmer climates are more emotionally expressive than those who live in cooler places (Pennebaker et al., 1996). Over 2,900 respondents representing 26 nationalities reported that people from the southern part of their countries were more emotionally expressive than northerners. More specifically, communication researcher Christina Kotchemidova (2010) notes that the United States is known internationally as a "culture of cheerfulness." She cites a Polish author who describes U.S. expressiveness this way: "Wow! Great! How nice! That's fantastic! I had a terrific time! It was wonderful! Have a nice day! Americans. So damned cheerful" (p. 209).

Cultural background influences the way we interpret others' emotions as well as the way we express our own. In one experiment (Matsumoto,

1993), an ethnically varied group of students—European American, Latinos, African American, and Asian American—identified the type, intensity, and appropriateness of emotional expression in 56 photos representing eight social situations (e.g., alone, with a friend, in public, with someone of higher status). Results indicated that ethnicity led to considerable differences in the way subjects gauged others' emotional states. For example, blacks perceived the emotions in the photos as the most intense while Asian Americans perceived them as the least intense. Also, blacks reported a greater frequency of anger expressions than the other groups. Ethnicity also shaped ideas about appropriate rules for expressing one's own emotions. For example, European Americans perceived the display of emotions as more appropriate than did the other groups; Asian Americans perceived their display as least appropriate. These findings remind us that, in a multicultural society, one element of communicative competence is the ability to understand our own cultural filters when judging others' emotion-related behaviors.

One of the most significant factors influencing emotional expression is the position of a culture on the individualism-collectivism spectrum (Halberstadt & Lozada, 2011; Kim-Prieto & Eid, 2004). Members of collectivistic cultures (such as Japan and India) prize harmony among members of their "in-group" and discourage expression of any negative emotions that might upset relationships among people who belong to it. By contrast, members of highly individualistic cultures, like the United States and Canada, feel comfortable revealing their feelings to people with whom they are close. Individualists and collectivists also handle emotional expression with members of out-groups differently: Whereas individualists are quite frank about expressing negative emotions toward outsiders, collectivists are more likely to hide emotions

AT WORK

Emotion Labor on the Job

The rules for expressing emotions in the workplace are clearly different from those in personal life. In intimate relationships (at least in mainstream Western culture), it's often important to tell friends, family, and loved ones how you feel. In the workplace, however, it can be just as important to *conceal* emotions for the sake of clients, customers, coworkers, and supervisors—and also to protect your job.

Emotion labor—the process of managing and sometimes suppressing emotions—has been studied in a variety of occupational contexts. A few examples are

- If firefighters don't mask their emotions of fear, disgust, and stress, it impedes their ability to help the people whose lives they are trying to save. Emotion-management training is therefore vital for new firefighters (Scott & Myers, 2005).

- Correctional officers at two minimum-security prisons described the tension of needing to be "warm, nurturing, and respectful" to inmates while also being "suspicious, strong, and tough." The officers acknowledged that it's taxing to manage competing emotions and juggle conflicting demands (Tracy, 2005).

- Money is an emotion-laden topic, which means that financial planners often engage in emotion labor. Researchers concluded that "relationships and communication with clients may indeed be more central to the work of financial planners than portfolio performance reports and changes in estate tax laws" (Miller & Koesten, 2008, p. 23).

While some of these occupations deal with life-and-death situations, emotion management is equally important in less intensive jobs. For instance, most customer-service positions require working with people who may express their dissatisfaction in angry and inappropriate ways ("I hate this store—I'm never shopping here again!"). In situations like these, it's usually unwise to "fight fire with fire," even if that's your natural impulse. Instead, competent on-the-job communicators can use the listening, defense-reducing, and conflict-management skills described in Chapters 7, 10, and 11.

It's not always easy to manage emotions, especially when you're feeling fearful, stressed, angry, or defensive. Nevertheless, doing the work of emotion labor is often vital for success on the job.

such as disliking (Triandis, 1994). It's easy to see how differences in display rules can lead to communication problems. For example, individualistic North Americans might view collectivistic Asians as less than candid, whereas a person raised in Asia could easily regard North Americans as overly demonstrative.

GENDER

Even within our culture, gender roles often shape the ways in which men and women experience and express their emotions (Guerrero et al., 2006; Wester et al., 2002). For example, research suggests that women are faster than men at recognizing both positive and negative emotions from facial cues (Hampson et al., 2006), are better at recognizing multiple emotions (Hall & Matsumoto, 2004), and are more physiologically attuned to emotions than men (Canli et al., 2002).

Research on emotional expression suggests that there is also some truth in the cultural stereotype of the inexpressive male and the more demonstrative female. On the whole, women seem more likely than men to verbally and nonverbally express a wide range of feelings (Burgoon & Bacue, 2003; Palomares, 2008). One study showed that fathers mask their emotions more than mothers do, which led their children to have more difficulty reading their fathers' emotional expressions (Dunsmore et al., 2009). On the Internet, the same differences between male and female emotional expressiveness apply. For example, women are more likely to use emoticons to clarify their feelings (Brunet & Schmidt, 2010), whereas men are more likely to use emoticons sarcastically (Wolf, 2000). Women also express more affection on Facebook than do men (Mansson & Myers, 2011).

Whether on the Internet or in face-to-face conversations, men tend to be less emotionally expressive, particularly when it comes to revealing feelings of vulnerability, including fear, sadness, loneliness, and embarrassment. On the other hand, men are less bashful about revealing their strengths and positive emotions, and both sexes feel and express anger equally (Goldsmith & Fulfs, 1999). Moreover, research shows that some married men become more emotionally expressive later in life (Dickson & Walker, 2001).

SOCIAL CONVENTIONS AND ROLES

In mainstream U.S. society, the unwritten rules of communication discourage the direct expression of most emotions (Durik et al., 2006; Shimanoff,

"If I were a car, you could find the words."

MEDIA CLIP

SOCIAL RULES AND EMOTIONS: *MAD MEN*

In the 1960s, advertising was a glamour career and New York's Madison Avenue was the center of the action. The world was different in many ways. Many people smoked, even in elevators, and the two-martini lunch was commonplace. The executive suite was run by men. Casual sexual harassment, though no less distasteful than today, was often tolerated by the "girls" in the typing pool.

Relationships then evoked a wealth of emotions, but the rules for expressing those feelings were different. Women—whether at home or in the workplace—were expected to be deferential and positive. The ideal professional man was suave and unruffled. *Mad Men* makes it clear that social conventions masked a wealth of intense feelings about relationships. It also shows how important it seemed to avoid communicating about those feelings, and the costs of doing so.

It's easy to feel smug when looking back at what seems like such dated social conventions—until you wonder what people a half-century from now will think of us.

1984, 1985). Count the number of genuine emotional expressions you hear over a 2- or 3-day period ("I'm angry"; "I feel embarrassed") and you'll discover that such expressions are rare. People are generally comfortable making statements of fact and often delight in expressing their opinions, but they rarely disclose how they feel.

Not surprisingly, the emotions that people do share directly are usually positive ("I'm happy to say . . . "; "I really enjoyed . . . "). Communicators are reluctant to send messages that embarrass or threaten the "face" of others (Shimanoff, 1988). Scholars offer detailed descriptions of the ways contemporary society discourages expressions of anger. When compared to past centuries, North Americans today strive to suppress this "unpleasant" emotion in almost every context, including child rearing, the workplace, and personal relationships (Kotchemidova, 2010). One study of married couples (Shimanoff, 1985) revealed that the partners shared complimentary feelings ("I love you") or face-saving ones ("I'm sorry I yelled at you"). They also willingly disclosed both positive and negative feelings about absent third parties ("I like Fred"; "I'm uncomfortable around Gloria"). On the other hand, the husbands and wives rarely verbalized face-threatening feelings ("I'm disappointed in you") or hostility ("I'm mad at you").

Researchers use the term **emotion labor** to describe situations in which managing and even suppressing emotions is both appropriate and necessary. Studies show that emotion labor is an important component of many if not most occupations (see the At Work box on page 254 for specific examples).

Just as a muscle withers away when it is unused, our capacity to recognize and act on certain emotions decreases without practice. It's hard to cry after spending most of one's life fulfilling the role society expects of a man, even when the tears are inside (Cole & Spalding, 2009; Pollack, 1999). After years of denying anger, the ability to recognize that feeling takes real effort. For someone who has never acknowledged love for one's friends, accepting that emotion can be difficult indeed.

FEAR OF SELF-DISCLOSURE

In a society that discourages the expression of feelings, emotional self-disclosure can seem risky. For a parent, boss, or teacher whose life has been built on the image of confidence and certainty, it may be frightening to say, "I'm sorry. I was wrong."

Moreover, someone who musters up the courage to share feelings such as these still risks unpleasant consequences. Others might misunderstand: An expression of affection might be construed as a romantic invitation (Erbert & Floyd, 2004), and a confession of uncertainty might appear to be a sign of weakness. Another risk is that emotional honesty might make others feel uncomfortable. Finally, there's always a chance that emotional honesty could be used against you, either out of cruelty or thoughtlessness. Chapter 3 discussed alternatives to complete disclosure and suggests circumstances when it can be both wise and ethical to keep your feelings to yourself.

EMOTIONAL CONTAGION

Along with cultural rules, social roles, and self-induced fears, our emotions are also affected by the feelings of those around us through **emotional contagion**, the process by which emotions are transferred from one person to another (Dasborough et al., 2009; Hatfield et al., 1994). As Daniel Goleman (1995, p. 115) observed, "We catch feelings from one another as though they were some kind of social virus." There is evidence that students "catch" the mood of their teachers (Bakker, 2005), that husbands and wives influence each other's emotions directly (Goodman & Shippy, 2002), and that coworkers can affect each other's emotions—especially positive ones—with their online communications (Belkin, 2008).

Although people differ in the extent to which they're susceptible to emotional contagion (Lundqvist, 2008), most of us recognize the degree to which emotions are "infectious." You can probably recall instances in which being around a calm person leaves you feeling more at peace, or when your previously sunny mood was spoiled by contact with a grouch. Researchers have demonstrated that this process can occur quickly, and with little or no verbal communication. In one study (Sullins, 1991), two volunteers completed a survey that identified their moods. They spent 2 unsupervised minutes together, ostensibly waiting for the researcher to return to the room. At the end of that time, they completed another emotional survey. Time after time, the brief exposure resulted in the less expressive partner's moods coming to resemble the feelings of the more expressive one. If an expressive communicator can shape another person's feelings with so little input in such a short time, it's easy to understand how emotions can be even more "infectious" with prolonged contact (Du et al., 2011).

Guidelines for Expressing Emotions

A wide range of research supports the value of expressing emotions appropriately. At the most basic physiological level, people who know how to share their feelings are healthier than those who don't. On one hand, underexpression of feelings can lead to serious ailments. Inexpressive people—those who value rationality and self-control, try to control their feelings and impulses, and deny distress—are more likely to get a host of ailments, including cancer, asthma, and heart disease (Consedine et al., 2002; Quartana & Burns, 2010). On the other hand, people who are overly expressive also suffer physiologically. When people lash out verbally, their blood pressure jumps an average of 20 points, and in some people it increases by as much as 100 points (Mayne, 1999; Siegman & Snow, 1997). The key to health, then, is to learn how to express emotions *constructively*. In a few pages, you will find guidelines for this important communication skill.

Beyond the physiological benefits, another advantage of expressing emotions effectively is the chance of improving relationships (Graham et al., 2008; Kennedy-Moore & Watson, 1999). As Chapter 9 explains, self-disclosure is one path (though not the only one) to intimacy. Even on the job, many managers and organizational researchers are contradicting generations of tradition by suggesting that constructively expressing emotions can lead to career success as well as helping workers feel better (O'Neill, 2009; Zapf & Holz, 2006). Of course, the rules for expressing emotions on the job are usually stricter than those in personal relationships—especially when it comes to the expression of anger (Brescoll & Uhlmann, 2008; Kramer & Hess, 2002).

Despite its benefits, expressing emotions effectively isn't a simple matter (Fussell, 2002). It's obvious that showing every feeling of boredom, fear, anger, or frustration would get you in trouble. Even the indiscriminate sharing of positive feelings—love, affection, and so on—isn't always wise. On the other hand, withholding emotions can be personally frustrating and can keep relationships from growing and prospering.

The following suggestions can help you decide when and how to express your emotions. Combined with the guidelines for self-disclosure in Chapter 3, they can improve the effectiveness of your emotional expression.

RECOGNIZE YOUR FEELINGS

As you read earlier in this chapter, answering the question "How do you feel?" isn't as easy for some people as for others (Peper, 2000). Communication researchers Melanie Booth-Butterfield and Steven Booth-Butterfield (1998; see also Samter & Burleson, 2005) found that some people (whom they term "affectively oriented") are much more aware of their own emotional states and use information about those feelings when making important decisions. By contrast, people with a low affective orientation are usually unaware of their emotions, and tend to reject feelings as useful, important information. The researchers summarize studies showing a relationship between awareness of feelings and a wide range of valuable traits, including positive relationships between parents and children, the ability to comfort others, sensitivity to nonverbal cues, and even skillful use of humor. In other words, being aware of one's feelings is an important ingredient in skillful communication.

Beyond being *aware* of one's feelings, research shows that it's valuable to be able to *identify* one's emotions. Lisa Barrett and her colleagues (2001) found that college students who could pinpoint the negative emotions they experienced (such as "nervous," "angry," "sad," "ashamed," and "guilty") also had the best strategies for managing those emotions. Studies like this led Grewal and Salovey (2005) to conclude that the ability to distinguish and label emotions is a vital component of emotional intelligence.

As you read earlier in this chapter, there are a number of ways in which feelings become recognizable. Physiological changes can be a clear sign of your emotional state. Monitoring nonverbal behaviors is another excellent way to keep in touch with your feelings. You can also recognize your emotions by monitoring your thoughts, as well as the verbal messages you send to others. It's not far from the verbal statement "I hate this!" to the realization that you're angry (or bored, nervous, or embarrassed).

CHOOSE THE BEST LANGUAGE

Most people suffer from impoverished emotional vocabularies. Ask them how they're feeling and the response will almost always include the same terms: *good* or *bad*, *terrible* or *great*, and so on. Take a moment now and see how many feelings you can write down. After you've done your best, look at Table 8.1 on page 260 and see which ones you've missed from this admittedly incomplete list.

Many communicators think they are expressing feelings when, in fact, their statements are emotionally counterfeit. For example, it sounds emotionally revealing to say "I feel like going to a show" or "I feel we've been seeing too much of each other." But in fact, neither of these statements has any emotional content. In the first sentence the word *feel* really stands for an intention: "I *want* to go to a show." In the second sentence the "feeling" is really a thought: "I *think* we've been seeing too much of each other." You can recognize the absence of emotion in each case by adding a genuine word of feeling to it. For instance, "I'm *bored* and I want to go to a show" or "I think we've been seeing too much of each other and I feel *confined*."

"What's the word I want for that disposition of yours?"

TABLE 8.1   Descriptive Terms for Emotions

affectionate	foolish	preoccupied
afraid	forlorn	pressured
aggravated	frustrated	quiet
amazed	furious	regretful
ambivalent	glad	relieved
angry	glum	remorseful
annoyed	grateful	repulsed
anxious	guilty	resentful
apathetic	happy	restless
ashamed	hateful	sad
bashful	helpless	secure
bewildered	hopeful	sentimental
bored	hopeless	sexy
calm	horrible	shaky
comfortable	hurt	shocked
concerned	hyper	shy
confident	impatient	silly
confused	inhibited	smug
content	insecure	sorry
curious	irritable	stubborn
defensive	isolated	stupid
delighted	jealous	subdued
depressed	joyful	surprised
desperate	lazy	suspicious
detached	lonely	sympathetic
devastated	love-struck	tense
disappointed	loving	terrified
disgusted	mad	tired
disturbed	mean	touchy
eager	melancholy	trapped
ecstatic	miserable	uneasy
edgy	mortified	unsure
elated	nervous	useless
embarrassed	overwhelmed	vulnerable
empty	passionate	wacky
enthusiastic	peaceful	warm
excited	pessimistic	weak
exhausted	playful	weary
exhilarated	pleased	worried
fidgety	possessive	zany

Relying on a small vocabulary of feelings is as limiting as using only a few terms to describe colors. To say that the ocean in all its moods, the sky as it varies from day to day, and the color of your true love's eyes are all "blue" only tells a fraction of the story. Likewise, it's overly broad to use a term like *good* or *great* to describe how you feel in situations as different as earning a high grade, finishing a marathon, and hearing the words "I love you" from a special person.

There are several ways to express a feeling verbally:

- Through *single words:* "I'm angry" (or "excited," "depressed," "curious," and so on).

- By describing *what's happening to you metaphorically:* "My stomach is tied in knots," "I'm on top of the world."

- By describing *what you'd like to do:* "I want to run away," "I'd like to give you a hug," "I feel like giving up."

Finally, you can improve emotional expression by making it clear that your feeling is centered on a specific set of circumstances, rather than the whole relationship. Instead of saying "I resent you," say "I get resentful when you don't keep your promises." Rather than "I'm bored with you," say "I get bored when you talk about money."

SHARE MULTIPLE FEELINGS

Many times the feeling you express isn't the only one you're experiencing. For example, you might often express your anger but overlook the confusion, disappointment, frustration, sadness, or embarrassment that preceded it. To understand the importance of expressing multiple emotions, consider the following examples. For each one, ask yourself two questions: How would I feel? What feelings might I express?

- An out-of-town friend has promised to arrive at your house at 6 o'clock. When your guest hasn't arrived by 9 o'clock, you are convinced that a terrible accident has occurred. Just as you pick up the phone to call the police and local hospitals, your friend breezes in the door with an offhand remark about getting a late start.

- You and your companion have a fight just before leaving for a party. Deep inside, you know you were mostly to blame, even though you aren't willing to admit it. When you arrive at the party, your companion leaves you to flirt with several other attractive guests.

In situations like these you would probably feel several emotions. Consider the case of the overdue friend. Your first reaction to his arrival would probably be relief—"Thank goodness, he's safe!" But you would also be likely to feel anger—"Why didn't he phone to tell me he'd be late?" The second example would probably leave you with an even greater number of emotions: guilt at contributing to the fight, hurt and perhaps embarrassment at your friend's flirtations, and anger at this sort of vengefulness.

Despite the commonness of experiencing several emotions at the same time (Carofiglio et al., 2008), we often communicate only one feeling—usually, the most negative one. In both of the preceding examples you might show only your anger, leaving the other person with little idea of the full range of your feelings. Consider the different reaction you would get by describing *all* your emotions in these situations as well as others.

RECOGNIZE THE DIFFERENCE BETWEEN FEELING AND ACTING

Just because you feel a certain way doesn't mean you must always act on it. In fact, there is compelling evidence that people who act out angry feelings—even by hitting an inanimate punching bag—actually feel worse than those who experience anger without lashing out (Bushman et al., 1999). More to the point of this book, researchers have discovered that people who deal with negative feelings by venting them indiscriminately have above-average levels of anxiety in their interpersonal relationships (Jerome & Liss, 2005).

Recognizing the difference between feeling and acting can liberate you from the fear that getting in touch with certain emotions will commit you to some disastrous course of action. If, for instance, you think, "I'm so nervous about the interview that I want to cancel it and pretend that I'm sick," it becomes possible to explore why you feel so anxious and then work to remedy the problem. Pretending that nothing is the matter, on the other hand, will do nothing to diminish your anxiety, which can then block your chances for success.

ACCEPT RESPONSIBILITY FOR YOUR FEELINGS

As you'll soon read, people don't *make us* like or dislike them, and believing that they do denies the responsibility each of us has for our own emotions. It's important to make sure that your emotional expressions don't blame others for the way you feel (Bippus & Young, 2005). The "I" language described in Chapter 5 makes it clear that you own your feelings. For example, instead of saying "You're making me angry," it's more accurate to say, "I'm feeling angry." Instead of "You hurt my feelings," a more responsible statement is, "I feel hurt when you do that."

CHOOSE THE BEST TIME AND PLACE TO EXPRESS YOUR FEELINGS

Often the first flush of a strong feeling is not the best time to speak out. If you're awakened by the racket caused by a noisy neighbor, storming over to complain might result in your saying things you'll regret later. In such a case, it's probably wiser to wait until you have thought out carefully how you might express your feelings in a way that would be most likely to be heard.

Even after you've waited for the first flush of feeling to subside, it's still important to choose the time that's best suited to the message. Being rushed or tired or disturbed by some other matter is probably a good reason for postponing the expression of your feeling. Often, dealing with your emotions can take a great amount of time and effort, and fatigue or distraction will make it difficult to follow through on the matter you've started. In the same manner you ought to be sure that the recipient of your message is ready to hear you out before you begin.

There are also cases where you may choose never to express your feelings. Even if you're dying to tell an instructor that her lectures leave you bored to a stupor, you might decide it's best to answer her question "How's class going?" with an innocuous "OK." And even though you may be irritated by the arrogance of a police officer stopping you for speeding, the smartest approach might be to keep your feelings to yourself. In cases where you experience strong emotions but don't want to share them verbally (for whatever reason), writing out your feelings and thoughts has been shown to have mental, physical, and emotional benefits (Burton & King, 2008; Pennebaker, 2004).

Managing Difficult Emotions

Perceiving others more accurately isn't the only challenge communicators face. At times we view *ourselves* in a distorted way. These distorted self-perceptions can generate a wide range of feelings—insecurity, anger, and guilt, to name a few—that interfere with effective communication. To begin understanding how this process works, read on.

FACILITATIVE AND DEBILITATIVE EMOTIONS

We need to make a distinction between **facilitative emotions**, which contribute to effective functioning, and **debilitative emotions**, which hinder or prevent effective performance. A classic example of a debilitative emotion is **communication apprehension**—feelings of anxiety that plague some people at the prospect of communicating in an unfamiliar or difficult context, such as giving a speech, meeting strangers, or interviewing for a job. Not surprisingly, debilitative emotions like communication apprehension can lead to a variety of problems in personal, business, educational, and even medical settings (McCroskey, 2009).

The difference between facilitative and debilitative emotions often isn't one of quality so much as degree. For instance, a certain amount of anger or irritation can be constructive, since it often stimulates a person to improve the unsatisfying conditions. Rage, on the other hand, usually makes matters worse. The same is true for fear. A little bit of nervousness before a job interview may boost you just enough to improve your performance (mellow athletes or actors usually don't do well), but a job candidate who is inordinately anxious isn't likely to impress potential employers (Ayres & Crosby, 1995). One big difference, then, between facilitative and debilitative emotions is their *intensity*.

A second characteristic of debilitative feelings is their extended *duration*. Feeling depressed for a while after the breakup of a relationship or the

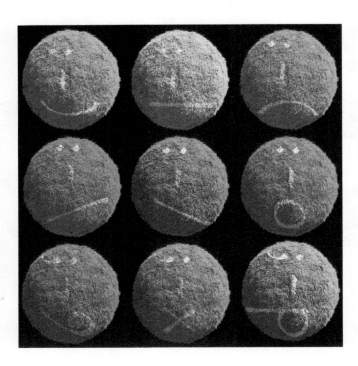

loss of a job is natural. Spending the rest of one's life grieving over the loss accomplishes nothing. In the same way, staying angry at someone for a wrong inflicted long ago can be just as punishing to the grudge holder as to the wrongdoer (Bushman et al., 2005). Social scientists call this **rumination**—recurrent thoughts not demanded by the immediate environment. For example, jealous lovers who dwell on imagined transgressions of their partners feel more distressed than necessary and act in counterproductive ways toward their partners (Carson & Cupach, 2000). Likewise, teenage girls who ruminate about problems with their friends have an increased risk of suffering from anxiety and depression (Rose et al., 2007). And sometimes ruminating can be used to sustain anger in preparation for retaliation—not a healthy approach (Knobloch-Westerwick & Alter, 2006).

THOUGHTS CAUSE FEELINGS

The goal, then, is to find a method for getting rid of debilitative feelings while remaining sensitive to the more facilitative emotions. Fortunately, such a method—termed a *rational-emotive* approach—does exist (Ellis, 2001, 2004; Neenan & Dryden, 2006). This reappraisal method is based on the idea that the key to changing feelings is to change unproductive cognitive interpretations. Let's see how it works.

For most people, emotions seem to have a life of their own. People wish they could feel calm when approaching strangers, yet their voices quiver. They try to appear confident when asking for a raise, but their eyes twitch nervously. Many people would say that the strangers or the boss *makes* them feel nervous, just as they would say that a bee sting causes them to feel pain:

Activating Event	→	Consequence
bee sting	→	physical pain
meeting strangers	→	nervous feelings

When looking at emotions in this way, people may believe they have little control over how they feel. However, the causal relationship between activating events and emotional discomfort (or pleasure) isn't as great as it seems. Cognitive psychologists and therapists argue that it is not events, such as meeting strangers or being jilted by a lover, that cause people to feel poorly, but rather the *beliefs they hold* about these events.

Albert Ellis tells a story that clarifies this point. Imagine yourself walking by a friend's house and seeing your friend come to a window and call you a string of vile names. (You supply the friend and the names.) Under the

circumstances, it's likely that you would feel hurt and upset. Now imagine that instead of walking by the house, you were passing a mental institution when the same friend, who was obviously a patient there, shouted the same offensive names at you. In this case, your reaction would probably be quite different; most likely, you'd feel sadness and pity.

In this story the activating event—being called names—was the same in both cases, yet the emotional consequences were very different. The reason for different feelings has to do with the pattern of thinking in each case. In the first instance you would most likely think that your friend was angry with you and that you must have done something terrible to deserve such a response. In the second case you would probably assume that your friend had experienced some psychological difficulty, so you would probably feel sympathetic. This example illustrates that people's *interpretations* of events determine their feelings:

Activating Event	→	**Thought or Belief**	→	**Consequences**
being called names	→	"I've done something wrong."	→	hurt, upset
being called names	→	"My friend must be sick."	→	pity, sympathy

The same principle applies in more common situations. For example, the words "I love you" can be interpreted in a variety of ways. They could be taken at face value, as a genuine expression of deep affection. They might also be decoded in a variety of other ways: for example, as an attempt at manipulation, a sincere but mistaken declaration uttered in a moment of passion, or an attempt to make the recipient feel better. It's easy to imagine how different interpretations of a statement like "I love you" can lead to different emotional reactions:

Event	→	**Thought**	→	**Feeling**
hearing "I love you"	→	"This is a genuine statement."	→	delight (perhaps)
hearing "I love you"	→	"She's (he's) just saying this to manipulate me."	→	anger

The key, then, to understanding and changing feelings lies in reappraising the event. This takes place through **self-talk** (Hatzigeorgiadis et al., 2009; Vocate, 1994)—the nonvocal, internal monologue that is our process of thinking. To understand how self-talk works, pay attention to the part of you that, like a little voice, whispers in your ear. Take a moment now and listen to what the voice is saying.

Did you hear the voice? It was quite possibly saying "What little voice? I don't hear any voices!" This little voice talks to you almost constantly:

"Better pick up a loaf of bread on the way home."
"I wonder when he's going to stop talking."
"It sure is cold today!"
"Are there two or four cups in a quart?"

At work or at play, while reading the paper or brushing our teeth, we all tend to talk to ourselves. This thinking voice rarely stops. It may fall silent for a while when you're running, riding a bike, or meditating, but most of the time it rattles on. Let's look now at how that voice sometimes processes thoughts in ways that need reappraising.

IRRATIONAL THINKING AND DEBILITATIVE EMOTIONS

This process of self-talk is essential to understanding the debilitative feelings that interfere with effective communication (E. D. Cohen, 2007). Many debilitative feelings come from accepting a number of irrational thoughts—we'll call them *fallacies* here—that lead to illogical conclusions and, in turn, to debilitating feelings. We usually aren't aware of these thoughts, which makes them especially powerful (Bargh, 1988).

The Fallacy of Perfection People who accept the **fallacy of perfection** believe that a worthwhile communicator should be able to handle any situation with complete confidence and skill. Although such a standard of perfection can serve as a goal and a source of inspiration (rather like

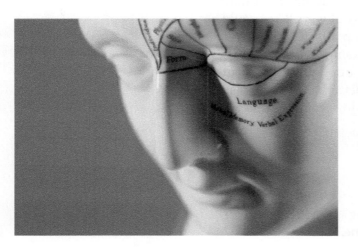

making a hole in one for a golfer), it's totally unrealistic to expect that you can reach or maintain this level of behavior. The truth is, people simply aren't perfect. Perhaps the myth of the perfect communicator comes from believing too strongly in novels, television, or films. In these media, perfect characters are often depicted—the perfect mate or child, the totally controlled and gregarious host, the incredibly competent professional. Although these fabrications are certainly appealing, real people will inevitably come up short compared to them.

People who believe that it's desirable and possible to be a perfect communicator come to think that people won't appreciate them if they are imperfect. Admitting mistakes, saying "I don't know," or sharing feelings of uncertainty or discomfort thus seem to be social defects. Given the desire to be valued and appreciated, these people are tempted at least to try to *appear* perfect. They assemble a variety of social masks, hoping that if they can fool others into thinking that they are perfect, perhaps they'll find acceptance. The costs of such deception are high. If others ever detect that this veneer of confidence is false, then the person hiding behind it is considered a phony. Even if the facade goes undetected, the performance consumes a great deal of psychological energy and diminishes the rewards of approval.

Not only can subscribing to the myth of perfection keep others from liking you, but it also acts as a force to diminish self-esteem. How can you like yourself when you don't measure up to your own standards?

You become more liberated each time you comfortably accept the idea that you are not perfect. For example, like everyone else, you sometimes have a hard time expressing yourself. Like everyone else, you make mistakes from time to time, and there is no reason to hide it. You are honestly doing the best you can to realize your potential, to become the best person you can be.

The Fallacy of Approval Another mistaken belief is based on the idea that it is vital—not just desirable—to obtain everyone's approval. Communicators who subscribe to the **fallacy of approval** go to incredible lengths to seek acceptance from others, even to the extent of sacrificing their own principles and happiness. Adherence to this irrational myth can lead to some ludicrous situations, such as feeling nervous because people you really don't like seem to disapprove of you, or feeling apologetic when you are not at fault.

The myth of approval is irrational. It implies that some people are more respectable and more likable because they go out of their way to please others. Often, this implication simply isn't true. How respectable are people who have compromised important values simply to gain acceptance? Are people highly regarded when they repeatedly deny their own needs as a means of buying approval? In addition, striving for universal acceptance is irrational because it is simply not possible.

Don't misunderstand: Abandoning the fallacy of approval doesn't mean living a life of selfishness. It's still important to consider the needs of others. It's also pleasant—one might even say necessary—to strive for the respect of certain people. The point is that the price is too high if you must abandon your own needs and principles in order to gain this acceptance.

The Fallacy of Should One huge source of unhappiness is the inability to distinguish between what *is* and what *should be*, or the **fallacy of should**. For instance, imagine a person who is full of complaints about the world:

"There should be no rain on weekends."
"People ought to live forever."
"Money should grow on trees."
"We should all be able to fly."

Beliefs such as these are obviously foolish. However pleasant such wishing may be, insisting that the unchangeable should be altered won't affect reality one bit. In each of these cases, the speaker *prefers* that people behave differently. Wishing that things were better is perfectly legitimate, and trying to change them is, of course, a good idea. However, it's unreasonable for people to insist that the world operate just as they want it to. Parents wish that their children were always considerate and neat. Teachers wish that their students were totally fascinated with their subjects and willing to study diligently. Consumers wish that inflation weren't such a problem. As the old saying goes, those wishes and a quarter (now you'd need much more) will get you a cup of coffee.

Becoming obsessed with shoulds yields three bad consequences. First, this preoccupation leads to unnecessary unhappiness. People who are constantly dreaming about the ideal are seldom satisfied with what they have. For instance, partners in a marriage who focus on the ways in which their mate could be more considerate, sexy, or intelligent may have a hard time appreciating the strengths that drew them together in the first place.

Second, the obsession keeps you from changing unsatisfying conditions. One employee, for example, constantly complains about the problems on the job: There should be better training, pay ought to be higher, the facilities should be upgraded, and so on. This person could be using the same energy to improve such conditions. Of course, not all problems have solutions, but when they do, complaining is rarely very productive. As one college manager puts it, "Rather than complain about the cards you are dealt, play the hand well."

Finally, this obsession tends to build a defensive climate in others. Imagine living around someone who insisted that people be more punctual, work harder, or refrain from using certain language. This kind of carping is obviously irritating. It's much easier to be around people who comment without preaching.

Rather than demanding that people behave the way you wish they would and feeling overly disappointed when they don't, it can be more realistic to think to yourself: "I *wish* she (he) would behave the way I want. It's probably reasonable to ask for change, but if the other person won't meet my expectations, I'm just setting myself up for disappointment if I expect change to happen."

The Fallacy of Overgeneralization The **fallacy of overgeneralization** occurs when a person bases a belief on a *limited amount of evidence.* Consider the following statements:

"I'm so stupid! I can't understand how to do my income tax."
"Some friend I am! I forgot my best friend's birthday."

In these cases people have focused on a single shortcoming as if it represented everything. Sometimes people forget that despite their difficulties, they have solved tough problems, and that although they can be forgetful, they're often caring and thoughtful.

A second, related category of overgeneralization occurs when we *exaggerate shortcomings:*

"You *never* listen to me."
"You're *always* late."
"I can't think of *anything.*"

Upon closer examination, such absolute statements are almost always false and usually lead to discouragement or anger. It's better to replace overgeneralizations with more accurate messages:

"You often don't listen to me."
"You've been late three times this week."
"I haven't had any ideas I like today."

The Fallacy of Causation People who live their lives in accordance with the **fallacy of causation** believe they should do nothing that can hurt or in any way inconvenience others because it will cause undesirable feelings. For example, you might visit friends or family out of a sense of obligation rather than a genuine desire to see them because, you believe, not to visit them will hurt their feelings. Did you ever avoid objecting to behavior that you found troublesome because you didn't want to cause anger? You may, on occasion, have pretended to be attentive—even though you were running late for an appointment and in a rush—because you didn't want a person to feel embarrassed for "holding you up." Then there were the times when you substituted praise for more honest negative responses in order to avoid causing hurt.

A reluctance to speak out in such situations often results from assuming that one person can cause another's emotions—that others, for example, are responsible for your feeling disappointed, confused, or irritated, or that you are responsible for others feeling hurt, angry, or upset. Actually, this assumption is incorrect. We may *act* in provocative ways, but each person is responsible for the way he or she *reacts.*

To understand why each person is responsible for his or her own feelings, consider how strange it sounds to suggest that people *make* you fall in love with them. Such a statement simply doesn't make sense. It would be more correct to say that people first act in one way or another; then you may or may not fall in love as a result of these actions.

In the same way, it's not accurate to say that people *make* you angry, upset, or even happy. Behavior that upsets or pleases one person might not bring any reaction from another. If you doubt this fact, think about people you know who respond differently to the same behaviors that you find so bothersome. (You may scream "Idiot!" when you're driving and someone switches lanes in front of you without signaling, while the person with you in the car may not even notice, or may notice but not care.) The contrast between others' reactions and yours shows that responses are determined more by our own temperament and thinking than by others' behavior.

MEDIA CLIP

FALLING TO FALLACIES: *YES MAN*

Carl Allen (Jim Carrey) is a man of many emotions—most of them negative. He's been depressed and lonely since a recent divorce, and he regularly rejects his friends' attempts to get him out of the house. His pattern is to say "no" to every invitation that comes his way—until he attends a motivational seminar that convinces him he needs to say "yes." To everything.

Allen's new approach leads to a host of counterintuitive choices, many of which are risky and dangerous (and of course amusing). The adventures that follow help him experience happiness, contentment, and love that otherwise might have escaped him.

However, feeling obligated to say "yes" comes with a price. Allen wrestles with some of the debilitative emotions described in this chapter as he subscribes to the fallacies of approval, shoulds, and helplessness. Ultimately, Allen realizes there's a time for yes and a time for no. He also learns that sound choices based on rational thinking are the best route to happiness.

One way to avoid the debilitative feelings that often accompany the fallacy of causation is to use responsible language, as discussed in Chapter 5. Instead of saying "He makes me so angry," reframe it as your reaction to the other person's behavior: "I don't like when he talks about me behind my back." Instead of saying, "I *had to* visit my parents this weekend; they gave me no option," take responsibility for your choices: "I decided to visit my parents this weekend, but I may choose differently next time." Taking ownership for your actions and reactions can often lead to a sense of empowerment.

The Fallacy of Helplessness The **fallacy of helplessness** suggests that forces beyond our control determine satisfaction in life. People with this outlook continually see themselves as victims:

> "There's no way a woman can get ahead in this society. It's a man's world, and the best thing I can do is to accept it."
>
> "I was born with a shy personality. I'd like to be more outgoing, but there's nothing I can do about that."
>
> "I can't tell my boss that she is putting too many demands on me. If I did, I might lose my job."

The error in such statements becomes apparent once a person realizes that few paths are completely closed. In fact, most "can't" statements may be more correctly restated in one of two ways.

The first is to say that you *won't* act in a certain way, that you choose not to do so. For instance, you may choose not to stand up for your rights or to follow unwanted requests, but it is usually inaccurate to claim that some outside force keeps you from doing so. The other way to rephrase a "can't" is to say that you *don't know how* to do something. Examples of such a situation include not knowing how to complain in a way that reduces defensiveness, or not being aware of how to conduct a conversation. Many difficulties a person claims can't be solved do have solutions: The task is to discover those solutions and to work diligently at applying them.

When viewed in this light, many "can'ts" are really rationalizations to justify an unwillingness to change. Research supports the dangers of helpless thinking. Lonely people, for example, tend to attribute their poor interpersonal relationships to uncontrollable causes (Marangoni & Ickes, 1989; Riggio & Kwong, 2009). "It's beyond my control," they think. Lonely people are more negative than nonlonely ones about ever finding a mate. Also, they expect their relational partners to reject them. Notice the self-fulfilling prophecy in this attitude: Believing that your relational prospects are dim can lead you to act in ways that make you an unattractive prospect. Once you persuade yourself that there's no hope, it's easy to give up trying. On the other hand, acknowledging that there is a way to change—even though it may be difficult—puts the responsibility for the predicament on your shoulders. Knowing that you can move closer to your goals makes it difficult to complain about the present. You *can* become a better communicator.

The Fallacy of Catastrophic Expectations Some fearful people operate on the assumption that if something bad can happen, it probably will. This is the **fallacy of catastrophic expectations**—a position similar to Murphy's Law. These statements are typical of such an attitude:

> "If I invite them to the party, they probably won't want to come."
> "If I speak up in order to try to resolve a conflict, things will probably get worse."
> "If I apply for the job I want, I probably won't be hired."
> "If I tell them how I really feel, they'll probably just laugh at me."

Once you start imagining terrible consequences, a self-fulfilling prophecy can begin to build. One study revealed that people who believed that their romantic partners would not change for the better were likely to behave in ways that contributed to the breakup of the relationship (Metts & Cupach, 1990). And people who have a "pessimism bias" often perceive threats in their relationships that are not apparent to outsiders, leading to relational dissatisfaction (Knoblach et al., 2007).

MINIMIZING DEBILITATIVE EMOTIONS

How can you overcome irrational thinking? Social scientists have developed a simple yet effective approach (E. D. Cohen, 2007; Ellis, 2001). When practiced conscientiously, it can help you cut down on the self-defeating thinking that leads to many debilitative emotions.

Monitor Your Emotional Reactions The first step is to recognize when you're having debilitative emotions. (Of course, it's also nice to be aware of pleasant feelings when they occur!) As we suggested earlier, one way to notice feelings is through physical stimuli: butterflies in the stomach, racing heart, hot flashes, and so on. Although such reactions might be symptoms of food poisoning, more often they reflect a strong emotion. You also can recognize certain ways of behaving that suggest your feelings: stomping instead of walking normally, being unusually quiet, and speaking in a sarcastic tone of voice are some examples.

It may seem strange to suggest that it's necessary to look for emotions—they ought to be immediately apparent. However, the fact is that we often suffer from debilitative feelings for some time without noticing them. For example, at the end of a trying day you've probably caught yourself frowning and realized that you've been wearing that face for some time without knowing it.

Remember the two key characteristics of debilitating emotions, intensity (they are *too* intense) and duration (they last *too* long), and use them to guide your assessment.

Note the Activating Event Once you're aware of how you're feeling, the next step is to figure out what activating event triggered your response. Sometimes it is obvious. If your sweetheart keeps calling you by the name of a former lover, you're likely to become upset. Research shows that dating couples can develop "social allergies" to each other, becoming hypersensitive about their partner's annoying behaviors (Cunningham et al., 2005). In these cases, it's easy to identify what triggers a given response. In other cases, however, the activating event isn't so apparent.

Sometimes there isn't a single activating event, but rather a series of small incidents that finally build toward a critical mass and trigger a debilitative feeling. This sort of thing happens when someone teases you over and over about the same thing, or when you suffer a series of small disappointments.

The best way to begin tracking down activating events is to notice the circumstances in which you have debilitative feelings. Perhaps they occur when you're around *specific people*. For example, you may feel tense or angry every time you encounter a person with whom you have struggled in the past. Until those issues are dealt with, feelings about past events can trigger debilitative emotions, even in apparently innocuous situations.

In other cases, you might discover that being around certain *types of individuals* triggers debilitative emotions. For instance, you might become nervous around people who seem more intelligent or self-confident than you are. In other cases, certain *settings* can stimulate unpleasant emotions: parties, work, school. Sometimes the *topic of conversation* is the factor that sets you off, whether politics, religion, sex, or some other subject. Maybe even the *information source* is part of the problem. For instance, research suggests that regularly checking a romantic partner's Facebook site can feed feelings of jealousy (Muise et al., 2009). That's because it offers access to ambiguous information that might not otherwise be available. Consider how easy it could be to misinterpret certain posts on your sweetheart's wall. (See the Dark Side sidebar on page 273 for more on jealousy.) Recognizing your activating events is an important step in minimizing debilitative emotions.

Record Your Self-Talk This is the point at which you analyze the thoughts that are the link between the activating event and your feelings. If you're serious about getting rid of debilitative emotions, it's important to actually write down your self-talk when first learning to use this method. Putting your thoughts on paper will help you see whether or not they make any sense.

Monitoring your self-talk might be difficult at first. This is a new skill, and any new activity seems awkward. If you persevere, however, you'll find you will be able to identify the thoughts that lead to your debilitative feelings. Once you get in the habit of recognizing this internal monologue, you'll be able to identify your thoughts quickly and easily.

Dispute Your Irrational Beliefs Social scientists refer to this process as **reappraisal**—rethinking the meaning of emotionally charged events in ways that alter their emotional impact (Berger & Lee, 2011). Research shows that reappraisal is vastly superior to suppressing one's feelings: It often leads to lower stress and increased productivity (Moore et al., 2008; Wallace et al., 2009). Reappraisal has both psychological and physiological benefits (Denson et al., 2011; Hopp et al., 2011), regardless of a person's age or culture (Goodman & Southam-Gerow, 2010; Haga et al., 2009).

Use the discussion of irrational fallacies on pages 266–271 to find out which of your internal statements are based on mistaken thinking. You can do this most effectively by following three steps. First, decide whether each belief you've recorded is rational or irrational. Next, explain why the belief does or doesn't make sense. Finally, if the belief is irrational, write down an alternative way of thinking that is more sensible and that can leave you feeling better when faced with the same activating event in the future.

After reading about this method for dealing with unpleasant emotions, some readers have objections:

"This rational-emotive approach sounds like nothing more than trying to talk yourself

Dark Side of Communication
WHEN JEALOUSY REARS ITS HEAD

You're at a party when your partner begins chatting with an attractive guest. At first you're unconcerned, but then you notice how long they've been talking. You begin to worry they might be flirting. Feelings of jealousy creep in. Now you have to decide what to do with those emotions.

Although jealousy can be an understandable reaction, it can also plague interpersonal relationships. In the scenario above, if the jealousy is warranted (they were indeed flirting), it often leads to personal insecurity and relational uncertainty. If the jealousy is unwarranted (there was no flirting), then the accused person is likely to feel defensive and angry. In either case, a relational transgression has occurred.

A flare-up of jealousy can happen for a variety of reasons. Perhaps you've been hurt in a previous relationship and now you're hypersensitive to any hint of a possible transgression. Or maybe your partner has been guilty of previous violations and you're justifiably suspicious. Research suggests that romantic partners who have high levels of relational commitment and satisfaction have lower levels of jealousy. The reason seems clear: A level of trust has been established, and so suspicion is low.

One way to explore the validity of your jealousy is to look for any of the self-defeating fallacies described on pages 266–271. If those aren't the issue, communication researchers suggest that civil discussions are the best method for addressing jealousy. The perception-checking method described on pages 271–274 may be useful: "I noticed you were talking a long time with at the party. Was it just a casual chat, or should I be concerned?" Of course, if you and your romantic partner are having these conversations on a regular basis, it may be a sign of larger relational problems.

Bevan, J. L. (2008). Experiencing and communicating romantic jealousy: Questioning the investment model. *Southern Communication Journal, 73*, 42-67.

Bevan, J. L., & Tidgewell, K. D. (2009). Relational uncertainty as a consequence of partner jealousy expressions. *Communication Studies, 60*, 305-323.

out of feeling bad." This accusation is totally correct. After all, since we talk ourselves into feeling bad, what's wrong with talking ourselves out of bad feelings, especially when they are based on irrational thoughts?

"The kind of disputing we just read sounds phony and unnatural. I don't talk to myself in sentences and paragraphs." There's no need to dispute your irrational beliefs in any special literary style. You can be just as colloquial as you want. The important thing is to clearly understand what thoughts led you into your debilitative feeling so you can clearly reappraise them. When the technique is new to you, it's a good idea to write or talk out your thoughts in order to make them clear. After you've had some practice, you'll be able to do these steps in a quicker, less formal way.

"This approach is too cold and impersonal. It seems to aim at turning people into cold-blooded, calculating, emotionless machines." This is simply not true. A rational thinker can still dream, hope, and love: There's nothing necessarily irrational about feelings like these. Rational people usually indulge in a bit of irrational thinking once in a while. But they usually know what they're doing. Like healthy eaters who occasionally treat themselves to a snack of junk food, rational thinkers occasionally indulge themselves in irrational thoughts, knowing that they'll return to their healthy lifestyle soon with no real damage done.

"This technique promises too much. There's no chance I could rid myself of all unpleasant feelings, however nice that might be." We can answer this by assuring you that rational-emotive thinking probably won't totally solve your emotional problems. What it can do is to reduce their number, intensity, and duration. This method is not the answer to all your problems, but it can make a significant difference—which is not a bad accomplishment.

Summary

Emotionally intelligent people are generally more effective communicators. Emotions have several dimensions. They are signaled by internal physiological changes, manifested by verbal and nonverbal reactions, and defined in most cases by cognitive interpretations.

There are several reasons why people do not verbalize many of the emotions they feel. Certain personality types respond to emotions more negatively than others. Some cultures encourage and others discourage the expression of emotions. Biological sex and gender roles also shape the way people experience and express emotions. Social rules discourage the expression of some feelings, particularly negative ones. Many social roles do not allow expression of certain feelings. Some people express emotions so rarely that they lose the ability to recognize when they are feeling them. Fear of the consequences of disclosing some emotions leads people to withhold expression of them. Finally, exposure to others' emotions can shape the way we feel ourselves, through the process of emotional contagion.

Since total expression of feelings is not appropriate for adults, several guidelines help define when and how to share emotions effectively. Self-awareness, clear language, and expression of multiple feelings are important, as is the ability to recognize the difference between feeling and acting. Willingness to accept responsibility for feelings instead of blaming them on others leads to better reactions. Choosing the proper time and place to share feelings is also important.

While some emotions are facilitative, other debilitative feelings inhibit effective functioning. Many of these debilitative emotions are caused by various types of irrational thinking. It is often possible to communicate more confidently and effectively by identifying troublesome emotions, identifying the activating event and self-talk that triggered them, and reappraising any irrational thoughts with a more logical analysis of the situation.

Key Terms

- Communication apprehension (263)
- Debilitative emotions (263)
- Emotional contagion (257)
- Emotional intelligence (246)
- Emotion labor (256)
- Facilitative emotions (263)
- Fallacy of approval (267)
- Fallacy of catastrophic expectations (271)
- Fallacy of causation (269)
- Fallacy of helplessness (270)
- Fallacy of overgeneralization (268)
- Fallacy of perfection (266)
- Fallacy of should (267)
- Reappraisal (273)
- Rumination (264)
- Self-talk (266)

Activities

1. Invitation to Insight

The Self-Assessment exercise on page 247 explored your "favorite" emotions without focusing on any particular relationship. What happens when you have a specific relationship in mind? Using the list of emotions in the Self-Assessment, complete the following steps:

    a. Focus on an important personal relationship.

b. Identify the few emotions that play the most important role for *you* in the relationship.

c. Identify the few emotions that you think play the most important role for the *other person* in the relationship.

d. Identify how you express each emotion you identified as most important for you. Focus on the frequency with which you express each feeling, the circumstances in which you express it, and the ways you express it.

e. Identify how the other person expresses each emotion you identified as most important for her or him. Focus on the frequency with which the other person expresses each feeling, the circumstances in which it is expressed, and how she or he expresses it.

f. What have you learned about yourself, the other person, and your relationship by conducting this analysis?

If possible, invite the other person to complete the same analysis and compare your results.

2. Skill Builder

Choose an important emotion you experience in one of your relationships. This relationship needn't be highly personal. You might, for example, focus on an employer, a professor, or a neighbor. Use the guidelines on pages 271–273 to determine whether and how you might express this emotion.

3. Ethical Challenge

According to the rational-emotive approach, we cause our own feelings by interpreting an event in one way or another. If this is true, it is a fallacy to claim we "make" others feel happy or sad. Do you accept this position? To what degree are you responsible for communicating in ways that "cause" others to feel happy or sad? Use a specific incident from your life to illustrate your answer.

4. Invitation to Insight

Explore whether you subscribe to the fallacy of helplessness by completing the following lists. Describe two important (to you) communication-related difficulties you have for each of the following: communicating with family members, people at school or at work, strangers, and friends. Use the following format for each difficulty:

I can't _____

because _____.

Now read the list, but with a slight difference. For each "can't," substitute the word "won't." Note which statements are actually "won'ts."

Read the list again, only this time substitute "I don't know how to" for your original "can't." Rewrite any statements that are truly "don't know hows," and decide what you could do to learn the skill that you presently lack.

Based on your experience, decide whether you subscribe to the fallacy of helplessness, and what you could do to eliminate this sort of debilitative thinking from your life.

5. Skill Builder

Choose an important situation in which you experience debilitative emotions that interfere with your ability to communicate effectively. Use the four steps on pages 271–274 to reappraise the rationality of your beliefs. Report on how the rational-emotive approach affects your communication in this important situation.

Dynamics of Interpersonal Relationships

After studying the material in this chapter . . .

You should understand:

1. The reasons people choose others as potential relational partners.
2. The stages of relational development and the characteristics of movement between them.
3. The dialectical tensions that can arise as communicators attempt to satisfy conflicting needs.
4. The ways content and relational messages are communicated in interpersonal relationships.
5. The strategies for repairing damaged relationships.

You should be able to:

1. Identify the bases of interpersonal attraction in one of your relationships.
2. Describe the current stage of an important personal relationship and the prospects for the relationship's moving to a different stage.
3. Identify the dialectical tensions that influence your communication goals, the strategies you use to manage these tensions, and alternative strategies you might consider using.
4. Describe ways to repair relationships that have been damaged.

"I'm looking for a meaningful relationship."
"Our relationship has changed lately."
"The relationship is good for both of us."
"This relationship isn't working."

Relationship is one of those words that people use all the time but have trouble defining. Even scholars who have devoted their careers to studying relationships don't agree on what the term means (Guerrero et al., 2007). Their definitions include words like "closeness," "influence," "commitment," and "intimacy"—but coming up with a single definition can be (as the old adage goes) like nailing Jell-O to a wall.

One useful way to distinguish interpersonal relationships from less personal ones is to look for the characteristics you read about in Chapter 1 (pages 15–19): uniqueness, irreplaceability, interdependence, disclosure, and rewards. Even the closest relationships don't always reflect all of these qualities, but, taken together, they are a good measure of where a relationship fits on the impersonal–interpersonal spectrum.

This chapter explores some of the dynamics that characterize interpersonal relationships and the communication that occurs within them. After reading it, you will see that relationships aren't fixed or unchanging. Rather, they can, and often do, change over time. In other words, a relationship is less a *thing* than a *process*. We'll look at why we form relationships, the dynamics of those relationships, and how to manage them.

Why We Form Relationships

Why do we form relationships with some people and not with others? Sometimes we have no choice: Children can't select their parents, and most workers aren't able to choose their colleagues. In many other cases, however, we seek out some people and actively avoid others.

Social scientists have collected an impressive body of research on interpersonal attraction (e.g., Luo & Zhang, 2009; Sprecher & Felmlee, 2008). The following are some of the factors they have identified that influence our choice of relational partners.

APPEARANCE

Most people claim that we should judge others on the basis of how they act, not how they look. However, the reality is quite the opposite (Mehrabian & Blum, 2003; Swami & Furnham, 2008). Appearance is especially important in the early stages of a relationship. In one study, a group of over 700 men and women were matched as blind dates, allegedly for a "computer dance." After the party was over, they were asked whether or not they would like to date their partners again. The result? The more physically attractive the person (as judged in advance by independent raters), the more likely he or she was seen as desirable. Other factors—social skills and intelligence, for example—didn't seem to affect the decision (Walster et al., 1966). In a more contemporary example, physical appearance seems to be the primary basis for attraction for speed daters (Luo & Zhang, 2009), and online daters routinely enhance their photographs and information about their height and weight to appear more attractive to potential suitors (Toma & Hancock, 2009). Online profile owners are also rated as more attractive when they have pictures of physically attractive friends on their sites (Antheunis & Schouten, 2011).

Although we might assume that attractive people are radically different from those who are less attractive, the truth is that we view the familiar as beautiful. Gül Günaydin and his colleagues (2011) found that women's snap judgments of unknown others who facially resemble a romantic partner are judged more favorably than unknown others who do not. In earlier research, Langlois and Roggman (1990) presented raters with two types of photos: Some were images of people from North European, Asian, and Latino backgrounds, while others were computer-generated images that combined the characteristics of several individuals. Surprisingly, the judges consistently preferred the composite photos of both men and women. When the features of eight individuals were combined into one image, viewers rated the picture as more attractive than the features of a single person or of a smaller combination of people.

Even if your appearance isn't beautiful by societal standards, consider these encouraging facts: First, after initial impressions have passed, ordinary-looking people with pleasing personalities are likely to be judged as attractive (Berscheid & Walster, 1978; Lewandowski et al., 2007), and perceived beauty can be influenced by traits such as liking, respect, familiarity, and social interaction (Albada et al., 2002; Singh et al. 2009). Second, physical factors become less important as a relationship progresses. In fact, as romantic relationships develop, partners create "positive illusions," viewing one another as more physically attractive over time (Barelds & Dijkstra, 2009). As one observer put it, "Attractive features may open doors, but apparently, it takes more than physical beauty to keep them open" (Hamachek, 1982, p. 59).

"Before the Internet, I just assumed I was the only one, and kept more or less to myself."

SIMILARITY

It's comforting to know someone who seems to like the same things you like, appears to have similar values, and may even be of the same race, economic class, or educational standing. The basis for this sort of relationship, commonly known as the *similarity thesis*, is the most frequently discussed and strongly supported determinant of relationship formation (Montoya et al., 2008; Morry et al., 2011). For example, the more similar a married couple's personalities are, the more likely they are to report being happy and satisfied in their marriage (Luo & Klohnen, 2005). Friends in middle and high school report being similar to each other in many ways, including having mutual friends, enjoying the same sports, liking the same social activities, and using (or not using) alcohol and cigarettes to the same degree (Aboud & Mendelson, 1998; Urberg et al., 1998). For adults, similarity is more important to relational happiness than even communication ability: Friends who have similarly low levels of communication skills are just as satisfied with their relationships as are friends having high levels of skills (Burleson & Samter, 1996).

There are several reasons why similarity is a strong foundation for relationships. First, similarities can be validating. The fact that another person shares your beliefs, tastes, and values is a form of ego support. One study described the lengths to which "implicit egotism" may unconsciously affect perceptions of attractiveness (Jones et al., 2004). Results showed that people are disproportionately likely to marry others whose first or last names resemble their own, and they're also attracted to those with similar birthdays and even sports jersey numbers.

Second, when someone is similar to you, you can make fairly accurate predictions—whether the person will want to eat at the Mexican restaurant or hear the concert you're so excited about. This ability to make confident predictions reduces uncertainty and anxiety (Duck & Barnes, 1992).

There's a third explanation for the similarity thesis. It may be that when we learn that other people are similar to us, we assume they'll probably like us, so we in turn like them. The self-fulfilling prophecy creeps into the picture again.

Similarity turns from attraction to dislike when we encounter people who are like us in many ways but who behave in a strange or socially offensive manner (Taylor & Mette, 1971). For instance, you have probably disliked people others have said were "just like you" but who talked too much, were complainers, or had some other unappealing characteristic. In fact, there is a tendency to have stronger dislike for similar but offensive people than for those who are offensive but different. One likely reason is that such people threaten our self-esteem, causing us to fear that we may be as unappealing as they are. In such circumstances, the reaction is often to put as much distance as possible between ourselves and this threat to our ideal self-image.

COMPLEMENTARITY

The old saying "opposites attract" seems to contradict the principle of similarity we just described. In truth, though, both are valid. Differences strengthen a relationship when they are *complementary*—when each partner's characteristics satisfy the other's needs. Research suggests that attraction to partners who have complementary temperaments might be rooted in biology (Fisher, 2007). In addition, some studies show that couples are more likely to be attracted to each other when one partner is dominant and the other passive (Swami & Furnham, 2008). Relationships also work well when the partners agree that one will exercise control in certain areas ("You make the final decisions about money") and the other will take the lead in different ones ("I'll decide how we ought to decorate the place"). Strains occur when control issues are disputed. One study shows that "spendthrifts and tightwads" are often attracted to each other, but their differences in financial management lead to significant conflict over the course of a relationship (Rick et al., 2011).

Studies that have examined successful and unsuccessful couples over a 20-year period show the interaction between similarities and differences (Klohnen & Luo, 2003). When partners are radically different, the dissimilar qualities that at first appear intriguing later become cause for relational breakups (Amodio & Showers, 2005; Felmlee, 2001). Partners in successful marriages were similar enough to satisfy each other physically and mentally, but were different enough to meet each other's needs and keep the relationship interesting. Successful couples find ways to keep a balance between their similarities and differences while adjusting to the changes that occur over the years (Shiota & Levenson, 2007).

MEDIA CLIP OPPOSITES ATTRACT: *STAR TREK*

Captain James T. Kirk and his right-hand man Spock are among popular culture's most iconic duos. Beginning with the *Star Trek* TV series in the 1960s, and through a series of movies that span into this millennium, Spock and Kirk are the yin and yang of science fiction heroes.

The two couldn't be more opposite. Kirk is a hot-headed, impetuous, hard-charging leader. Spock is an emotionless, rational, unflappable second-in-command. While they sometimes get on each other's nerves, they also realize how much they need each other's perspectives. Over the years, their complementarity leads to more than just a successful professional relationship. As Spock famously says to Kirk: "You are my superior officer. You are also my friend. I have been and always shall be yours."

REWARDS

Some relationships are based on an economic model called *exchange theory* (Stafford, 2008; Thibaut & Kelley, 1959). This approach suggests that we often seek out people who can give us rewards that are greater than or equal to the costs we encounter in dealing with them. Social exchange theorists define rewards as any outcomes we desire. They may be tangible (a nice place to live, a high paying job) or intangible (prestige, emotional support, companionship). Costs are undesirable outcomes: unpleasant work, emotional pain, and so on. A simple formula captures the social exchange explanation for why we form and maintain relationships:

$$\text{Rewards} - \text{Costs} = \text{Outcome}$$

According to social exchange theorists, we use this formula (often unconsciously) to calculate whether a relationship is a "good deal" or "not worth the effort," based on whether the outcome is positive or negative.

At its most blatant level, an exchange approach seems cold and calculating, but in some types of relationships it seems quite appropriate. A healthy business relationship is based on how well the parties help one another, and some friendships are based on an informal kind of barter: "I don't mind listening to the ups and downs of your love life because you rescue me when the house needs repairs." Even close relationships have an element of exchange. Friends and lovers often tolerate each other's quirks because the comfort and enjoyment they get make the less-than-pleasant times worth accepting. However, when one partner feels "underbenefited," it often leads to relational disruption or termination (DeMaris, 2007).

Costs and rewards don't exist in isolation: We define them by comparing a certain situation with alternatives. For example, consider a hypothetical woman, Gloria, who is struggling to decide whether to remain in a relationship with Raymond, her longtime boyfriend. Raymond does love Gloria, but he's not perfect: He has a hair-trigger temper, and he has become verbally abusive from time to time. Also, Gloria knows that Raymond was unfaithful to her at least once. In deciding whether or not to stay with Raymond, Gloria will use two standards.

The first standard is her **comparison level (CL)**—her minimum standard of what behavior is acceptable. If Gloria believes that relational partners have an obligation to be faithful and treat one another respectfully at all times, then Raymond's behavior will fall below her comparison level. This will be especially true if Gloria has had positive romantic relationships in the past (Merolla et al., 2004). On the other hand, if Gloria adopts a "nobody's perfect" standard, she is more likely to view Raymond's behavior as meeting or exceeding her comparison level.

Gloria also will rate Raymond according to her **comparison level of alternatives (CL_{alt})**. This standard refers to a comparison between the rewards she is receiving in her present situation and those she could expect to receive in others (Overall & Sibley, 2008). If, for example, Gloria doesn't want to be alone and she thinks, "If I don't have Raymond I won't have anyone," then her CL_{alt} would be lower than her present situation; but if she is confident that she could find a kinder partner, her CL_{alt} would be higher than the status quo.

Social exchange theorists suggest that communicators unconsciously use this calculus to decide whether to form and stay in relationships. At first this information seems to offer little comfort

"I'd like to buy everyone a drink. All I ask in return is that you listen patiently to my shallow and simplistic views on a broad range of social and political issues."

to communicators who are in unsatisfying relationships, such as when the partner's behavior is below the CL and there are no foreseeable alternatives (CL_{alt}). But there are other choices than being stuck in situations where the costs outweigh the rewards. First, you might make sure that you are judging your present relationship against a realistic comparison level. Expecting a situation to be perfect can be a recipe for unhappiness. (Recall the discussion of the "fallacy of shoulds" in Chapter 8.) If you decide that your present situation truly falls below your comparison level, you might explore whether there are other alternatives you haven't considered. And finally, the skills introduced throughout this book may help you negotiate a better relationship with the other person.

COMPETENCY

We like to be around talented people, probably because we hope their skills and abilities will rub off on us. On the other hand, we are uncomfortable around those who are too competent—probably because we look bad by comparison. Elliot Aronson and his associates demonstrated how competence and imperfection combine to affect attraction by having subjects evaluate tape recordings of candidates for a quiz program (summarized in Aronson, 2008). One was a "perfect" candidate who answered almost all the questions correctly and modestly admitted that he was an honor student, athlete, and college yearbook editor. The "average" candidate answered fewer questions correctly, had average grades, was a less successful athlete, and was a low-level member of the yearbook staff. Toward the end of half the tapes, the candidates committed a blunder, spilling coffee all over themselves. The remaining half of the tapes contained no such blunder. These, then, were the four experimental conditions: (1) a person with superior ability who blundered; (2) a person with superior ability who did not blunder; (3) an average person who blundered; and (4) an average person who did not blunder. The students who rated the attractiveness of these four types of people revealed an interesting and important principle of interpersonal attraction. The most attractive person was the superior candidate who blundered. Next was the superior person who did not blunder. Third was the average person who did not blunder. The least attractive person was the average person who committed the blunder. Aronson's conclusion was that we like people who are somewhat flawed because they remind us of ourselves.

PROXIMITY

As common sense suggests, we are likely to develop relationships with people with whom we interact frequently (Flora, 2005). In many cases, proximity leads to liking. For instance, we're more likely to develop friendships with close neighbors—whether near where we live or in adjacent seats in our classrooms (Back et al., 2008)—than with distant ones. Chances are also good that we'll choose a mate with whom we cross paths often. Proximity even has a role in social media, where sharing a portion of cyberspace—a chat room, or instant messaging connection, for example—constitutes virtual proximity (Baker, 2008; Levine, 2000). Facts like these are understandable when we consider that proximity allows us to get more information about other people and benefit from a relationship with them. Also, people in close proximity may be more similar to us than those not close—for example, if we live in the same neighborhood, odds are we share the same socioeconomic status.

Familiarity, on the other hand, can breed contempt. Evidence to support this fact comes from police blotters as well as university laboratories. Thieves frequently prey on nearby victims, even though the risk of being recognized is greater. Most aggravated assaults occur within the family or among close neighbors. The same principle holds in more routine contexts: You are likely to develop strong personal feelings, either positive or negative, toward others you encounter frequently.

Dark Side of Communication
ABUSING THOSE WHO DISCLOSE

As Chapter 3 explained (and as your own experience may confirm), self-disclosure has both benefits and risks. Revealing information about yourself can be a means for building and maintaining relationships. But those revelations can also leave you vulnerable.

In one study, college students described their levels of self-disclosure in an unpleasant dating relationship. The participants also reported on incidents of psychological abuse in the relationship: insulting and spiteful comments, false accusations, stomping out during conversations, and other demeaning behaviors.

Results showed that participants with strong self-disclosure orientations were also more frequently the targets of psychological abuse. The information these high-self-disclosers shared was often used against them. This doesn't mean that sharing personal information will always lead to problems. After all, the only subjects in this study were those reporting on unpleasant relationships. Still, the results raise a cautionary note: In a new relationship, the wisest course may be to reveal personal information cautiously until you are confident that you and your disclosures will be treated with respect.

Shirley, J. A., Powers, W. G., & Sawyer, C. R. (2007). Psychologically abusive relationships and self-disclosure orientations. *Human Communication, 10,* 289–301.

DISCLOSURE

Chapter 3 described how telling others important information about yourself can help build liking, both in person (Derlega et al., 1993; Dindia, 2002) and in mediated settings (Ledbetter et al., 2011). Sometimes the basis of this attraction comes from learning about ways we are similar, either in experiences ("I broke off an engagement myself") or in attitudes ("I feel nervous with strangers, too"). Self-disclosure also increases liking because it indicates regard. Sharing private information is a form of respect and trust—a kind of liking that we've already seen increases attractiveness.

Not all disclosure leads to liking. Research shows that the key to satisfying self-disclosure is reciprocity: getting back an amount and kind of information equivalent to that which you reveal (Dindia, 2000a). A second important ingredient in successful self-disclosure is timing. It's probably unwise to talk about your sexual insecurities with a new acquaintance or express your pet peeves to a friend at your birthday party. The information you reveal ought to be appropriate for the setting and stage of the relationship (Archer & Berg, 1978; Bowman, 2009). Finally, for the sake of self-protection, it's important to reveal personal information only when you are sure the other person is trustworthy (see the Dark Side box on this page).

Communication and Relational Dynamics

Even the most stable relationships vary from day to day and over longer periods of time. Communication scholars have attempted to describe and explain how communication creates and reflects the changing dynamics of relational interaction. The following pages describe two different characterizations of relational development and interaction.

DEVELOPMENTAL MODELS OF INTERPERSONAL RELATIONSHIPS

One of the best-known models of relational stages was developed by Mark Knapp (Knapp & Vangelisti, 2006; see also Avtgis et al., 1998; Mongeau & Henningsen, 2008), who broke the waxing and waning of relationships into 10 steps. Other researchers have suggested that in addition to coming together and coming apart, any model of relational communication ought to contain a third area, **relational maintenance**—communication aimed at keeping relationships operating smoothly and satisfactorily (we'll discuss relational maintenance in more detail in Chapter 12). Figure 9.1 shows how Knapp's 10 stages fit into this three-part view of relational communication. This model seems most appropriate for describing communication between romantic partners, but in some cases it can depict other types of close relationships. As you read the following section, consider how the stages could describe a long-term friendship (Johnson et al., 2004), a couple in love, or even business partners.

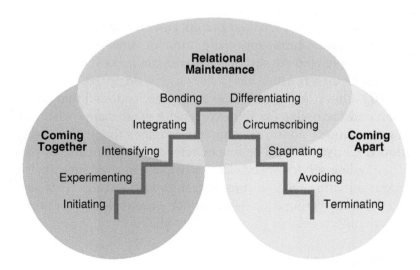

FIGURE 9.1 **Stages of Relationship Development**

Adapted from Mark L. Knapp & Anita L. Vangelisti, *Interpersonal communication and human relationships* (4th ed.). Published by Allyn & Bacon, Boston, MA. Copyright (c) 2000 by Pearson Education.

F CUS ON RESEARCH

Opening Lines: Initiating Romantic Relationships

Type the words "pick-up lines" into a web browser and you'll find dozens of sites filled with phrases designed to strike up a romantic relationship. These tips reflect the belief that men need to be suave and witty to initiate relationships with women they've just met. Keith Weber and his colleagues ran an experiment to see how these lines are perceived by both sexes.

The researchers created five videos set in a bar, where a man initiates a conversation with a woman. In each scenario, the man uses a different opening line: a direct introduction, an introduction by a friend (third-party introduction), a compliment (about the woman's attractiveness), a humor attempt (a comparison with a movie star), and a flippant cliché ("You must be tired because you've been running through my mind all day").

More than 600 college students (roughly equal numbers of men and women) rated the five opening lines. Third-party and direct introductions were rated as more appropriate than the other ways of initiating a conversation, and third-party introductions were rated as the most effective (with direct introductions a close second). The other three options were uniformly perceived as inappropriate and ineffective (the flippant introduction was rated least appropriate and effective).

The lesson is clear: When it comes to opening lines, keep it simple and straightforward—and skip the attempts to be suave and witty.

Weber, K., Goodboy, A. K., & Cayanus, J. L. (2010). Flirting competence: An experimental study on appropriate and effective opening lines. *Communication Research Reports, 27,* 184–191.

Initiating The goals in the **initiating** stage are to show that you are interested in making contact and to demonstrate that you are a person worth talking to. Communication during this stage is usually brief, and it generally follows conventional formulas: handshakes, remarks about innocuous subjects such as the weather, and friendly expressions. Such behavior may seem superficial and meaningless, but it is a way of signaling that you're interested in building some kind of relationship with the other person. It allows us to say, without saying, "I'm a friendly person, and I'd like to get to know you."

Initiating relationships—especially romantic ones—can be particularly difficult for people who are shy. Social media can make it easier for reticent people to strike up a relationship (Baker & Oswald, 2010; Sheeks & Birchmeier, 2007). One study of an online dating service found that participants who identified themselves as shy expressed a greater appreciation for the system's anonymous, nonthreatening environment than did non-shy users (Scharlott & Christ, 1995). The researchers found that many shy users employed the online service specifically to help them overcome their inhibitions about initiating relationships in face-to-face settings. This also helps explain why many young adults—shy or not—use social media sites such as Facebook to initiate relationships (Urista et al., 2009).

Experimenting After making contact with a new person, we generally begin the search for common ground. This search usually starts with the basics: "Where are you from? What's your major?" From there we look for other similarities: "You're a runner too? How many miles do you run a week?"

288

It usually doesn't take long for communicators who are interested in one another to move from initiating to **experimenting**. The shift seems to occur even more rapidly in cyberspace than in person (Pratt et al., 1999; Tidwell & Walther, 2002). People who develop relationships online begin asking questions about attitudes, opinions, and preferences more quickly than those in face-to-face contact. It probably helps that cybercommunicators can't see each others' nonverbal reactions—they don't have to worry about blushing, stammering, or looking away if they realize that they asked for too much information too quickly.

The hallmark of experimenting is small talk. We tolerate the ordeal of small talk because it serves several functions. First, it is a useful way to find out what interests we share with the other person. It also provides a way to "audition" the other person—to help us decide whether a relationship is worth pursuing. In addition, small talk is a safe way to ease into a relationship. You haven't risked much as you decide whether to proceed further. Finally, small talk does provide some kind of link to others. It's often better than being alone.

Social media, such as Facebook, may change the nature of this stage of relational development. As Katrina Shonbeck (2011) points out, information gathering that used to occur over a gradual period of self-disclosure could be done quickly:

> By perusing someone's social networking profile, I can, more often than not, learn many of the same things I'd learn from them during the first couple of dates without the other person being present. From what they disclose on the general information page, I can learn their relationship statuses, political preferences, favorite hobbies, music, books, and movies. By looking through their pictures and their wall, I can get a pretty good sense of the kinds of people they like to hang out with, what they like to do on weekends, their personal styles. (p. 398)

The kind of information we look for during the experimentation stage depends on the nature of the relationship we are seeking (Afifi & Lucas, 2008; Stewart et al., 2000). For example, both men and women who are seeking short-term relationships look for someone with an exciting personality and a good sense of humor. Qualities of being trustworthy and romantic become more important when people seek long-term relationships.

Of course, not all relational experiments are successful. You can probably remember an evening spent with a new friend or a first date in which you knew things were going nowhere before an hour had passed. Bowing out of such situations requires a measure of diplomacy and tact—but research shows it's easier to do so in online dating than in face-to-face encounters (Tong & Walther, 2011a).

Intensifying When a relationship begins **intensifying**, the kind of qualitatively interpersonal relationship defined in Chapter 1 starts to develop. In friendships, intensifying often includes participating in shared activities, hanging out with mutual friends, or taking trips together (Johnson et al., 2004). Dating couples use a wide range of strategies to communicate

that their relationship is intensifying (Tolhuizen, 1989). About a quarter of the time they express their feelings directly to discuss the state of the relationship, such as saying "I love you" (Brantley et al., 2002). More often they use less direct methods of communication: spending an increasing amount of time together, asking for support from one another, doing favors for the partner, giving tokens of affection, hinting and flirting, expressing feelings nonverbally, getting to know the partner's friends and family, and trying to look more physically attractive (Richmond et al., 1987).

The intensifying stage is usually a time of relational excitement and even euphoria. In friendships, it's about enthusiasm for having a new "BFF." For romantic partners, it's often filled with starstruck gazes, goose bumps, and daydreaming. As a result, it's a stage that's regularly depicted in movies and romance novels—after all, we love to watch lovers in love. The problem, of course, is that the stage doesn't last forever. Sometimes romantic partners who stop feeling goose bumps begin to question whether they're still in love, and friends begin to discover one another's flaws. While it's possible that the relationship isn't as good as it seems, it's equally likely that it has simply moved on to a different stage—such as integrating.

Integrating As the relationship strengthens, the individuals enter an **integrating** stage. They begin to take on an identity as a social unit. Invitations begin to come addressed to a couple. Social circles merge. The partners share each other's commitments: "Sure, we'll spend Thanksgiving with your family." Common property may begin to be designated—our apartment, our car, our song (Baxter, 1987). Partners develop their own personal idioms (Dunleavy & Booth-Butterfield, 2009) and forms of play (Baxter, 1992). They develop routines and rituals that reinforce their identity as a couple—jogging together, eating at a favorite restaurant, expressing affection with a goodnight kiss, and worshipping together (Afifi & Johnson, 1999; Bosson et al., 2006). As these examples illustrate, the stage of integrating is a time when we give up some characteristics of our former selves and become different people.

As we become more integrated with others, our sense of obligation to them grows (Korchmaros & Kenny, 2006; Roloff et al., 1988). We feel obliged to provide a variety of resources, such as class notes and money, whether or not the other person asks for them. When intimates do make requests of one another, they are relatively straightforward. Gone are the elaborate explanations, inducements, and apologies. In short, partners in an integrated relationship expect more from one another than they do in less intimate associations.

As integration increases and as we become more intimate, uncertainty about our relationship decreases: We become clearer about relationship norms, and about what behaviors are appropriate and inappropriate. In addition, our ability to influence each other's daily activities increases, such as the amount of time spent with friends and doing schoolwork (Solomon & Knobloch, 2001). Reducing uncertainty about our partner and the relationship enhances attraction and feelings of closeness (Knobloch & Solomon, 2002).

Bonding During the **bonding** stage, partners make symbolic public gestures to show the world that their relationship exists. These gestures can take the form of a contract between business partners or a license to be married. Bonding typically generates social support for the relationship. Custom and law impose certain obligations on partners who have officially bonded.

What constitutes a bonded, committed relationship is not always easy to define (Foster, 2008). Terms such as *common-law, cohabitation,* and *life partners* have been used to describe relationships that don't have the full support of custom and law but still involve an implicit or explicit bond. Nonetheless, given the importance of bonding in validating relationships and taking them to another level, it's not surprising that the gay and lesbian communities are striving to have legally sanctioned and recognized marriages.

For our purposes here, we'll define bonded relationships as those involving a significant measure of public commitment. These can include engagement or marriage, sharing a residence, a public ceremony, or a written or verbal pledge. The key is that bonding is the culmination of a developed relationship—the "officializing" of a couple's integration.

Relationships don't have to be romantic to achieve bonding. Consider, for instance, authors contracting to write a book together or a student being initiated into a sorority. As Lillian Rubin (1985) notes, in some cultures there are rituals for friends to mark their bonded status through a public commitment:

> Some Western cultures have rituals to mark the progress of a friendship and to give it public legitimacy and form. In Germany, for example, there's a small ceremony called *Duzen,* the name itself signifying the transformation in the relationship. The ritual calls for the two friends, each holding a glass of wine or beer, to entwine arms, thus bringing each other physically close, and to drink up after making a promise of eternal brotherhood with the word *Bruderschaft.* When it's over, the friends will have passed from a relationship that requires the formal *Sie* mode of address to the familiar *du.*

Bonding usually marks an important turning point in relationships. Up to now the relationship may have developed at a steady pace: Experimenting gradually moved into intensifying and then into integrating. Now, however, there is a spurt of commitment. The public display and declaration of exclusivity make this a critical period in the relationship.

Differentiating So far, we have been looking at the growth of relationships. Although some reach a plateau of development, going on successfully for as long as a lifetime, others pass through several stages of decline and dissolution. Even in the most committed relationships, partners often

291

find themselves needing to reestablish their individual identities in a stage Knapp calls **differentiating**. This transition often shows up in a couple's pronoun usage. Instead of talking about "our" weekend plans, differentiating conversations focus on what "I" want to do. Relational issues that were once agreed upon (such as "You'll be the breadwinner and I'll manage the home") now become points of contention: "Why am *I* stuck at home when I have better career potential than *you?*" The root of the term *differentiating* is the word *different*, suggesting that change plays an important role in this stage.

Differentiation also can be positive, for people need to be individuals as well as part of a relationship. Think, for instance, of young adults who want to forge their own unique lives and identity, even while maintaining their relationships with their families of origin (Skowron et al., 2009). And as the model on page 287 shows, differentiating is often a part of normal relational maintenance, in which partners manage the inevitable challenges that come their way. The key to successful differentiation is maintaining commitment to a relationship while creating the space for being individuals as well (we'll describe this later in the chapter as the connection-autonomy dialectic).

Circumscribing In the **circumscribing** stage, communication between partners decreases in quantity and quality. Subtle hints of dissatisfaction grow more evident. The good-natured teasing of the coming-together stages becomes more pointed and barbed (Dunleavy & Booth-Butterfield, 2009). Working later at the office, seeking less and less romance, and more and more arguing begin to form a pattern that is hard to ignore (Kellermann et al., 1991). Ironically, both partners in a circumscribed relationship still cooperate in one way: suppressing the true status of the relationship. They hide its decline from others and even from themselves (Vaughn, 1987). Restrictions and restraints characterize this stage, and dynamic communication becomes static. Rather than discuss a disagreement (which requires some degree of energy on both parts), members opt for withdrawal: either mental (silence or daydreaming and fantasizing) or physical (where people spend less time together). Circumscribing doesn't involve total avoidance, which comes later. Rather, it entails a shrinking of interest and commitment.

The word "circumscribe" comes from the Latin meaning "to draw circles around." Distinctions that emerged in the differentiating stage become more clearly marked and labeled: "my friends" and "your friends"; "my bank account" and "your bank account"; "my room" and "your room." As you'll soon read (on page 295), such distinctions can be markers of a healthy balance between individual and relational identity. They become a problem when there are clearly more areas of separation than integration in a relationship, or when the areas of separation seriously limit interaction, such as "my vacation" and "your vacation."

Stagnating If circumscribing continues, the relationship begins to stagnate. Members behave toward each other in old, familiar ways without much feeling. No growth occurs. The **stagnating** relationship is a hollow shell of its former self. We see stagnation in many workers who have lost enthusiasm for their job yet continue to go through the motions for years. The same sad event occurs for some couples who unenthusiastically have the same conversations, see the same people, and follow the same routines without any sense of joy or novelty.

Avoiding When stagnation becomes too unpleasant, people in a relationship begin to create distance between each other by **avoiding**. Sometimes they do it under the guise of excuses ("I've been sick lately and can't see you") and sometimes directly ("Please don't call me; I don't want to see you now"). In either case, by this point the handwriting is on the wall about the relationship's future.

Research by Jon Hess (2000) reveals that there are several ways we gain distance. One way is *expressing detachment*, such as avoiding the other person altogether, or zoning out. A second way is *avoiding involvement*, such as leaving the room, ignoring the person's questions, steering clear of touching, and being superficially polite. *Showing antagonism* is a third technique, which includes behaving in a hostile way and treating the other person as a lesser person. A fourth strategy is to *mentally dissociate* from the other person, such as by thinking about the other person as less capable, or as unimportant. A vicious cycle gets started when avoiding the other person: the more one person avoids the other, the greater the odds the other will reciprocate. And the more topics that are avoided, the less satisfactory is the relationship (Sargent, 2002).

Terminating Not all relationships end: Many partnerships, friendships, and marriages last for a lifetime once they're established. But many do deteriorate and reach the final stage of **terminating**. The process of terminating has its own distinguishable pattern (Battaglia et al., 1998; Conlan, 2008). Characteristics of this stage include summary dialogues of where the relationship has gone and the desire to dissociate. The relationship may end with a cordial dinner, a note left on the kitchen table, a phone call, or a legal document stating the dissolution. Depending on each person's feelings, this terminating stage can be quite short or it may be drawn out over time, with bitter jabs at each other. In either case, termination doesn't have to be totally negative. Understanding each other's investments in the relationship and needs for personal growth may dilute the hard feelings.

How do the individuals deal with each other after a romantic relationship has ended? The best predictor of whether the individuals will become friends after the relationship is terminated is whether they were friends before their romantic involvement (Metts et al., 1989). The way the couple splits up also makes a difference. It's no surprise to find that friendships are most possible when communication during the breakup was positive: expressions that there were no regrets for time spent together and other attempts to minimize hard feelings. When communication during termination is negative (manipulative, complaining to third parties), friendships are less likely.

Terminating a relationship is, for many people, a learning experience. Ty Tashiro and Patricia Frazier (2003) asked college students who recently had a romantic relationship breakup to describe the positive things they learned that might help them in future romantic relationships. Responses fell into four categories: "person positives," such as gaining self-confidence and that it's all right to cry; "other positives," such as learning more about what is desired in a partner; "relational positives," such as how to communicate better and how not to jump into a relationship too quickly; and "environment positives," such as learning to rely more on friends and how to better balance relationships and school work.

Limits of Developmental Models While Knapp's model offers insights into relational stages, it doesn't describe the ebb and flow of communication in every relationship. For instance, many relationships don't progress from one stage to another in a predictable manner as they develop and deteriorate. One study found that some terminated friendships did indeed follow a pattern similar to the one described by Knapp and pictured in Pattern One of Figure 9.2 (Johnson et al., 2004). However, several other patterns of development and deterioration were also identified, as seen in Patterns Two through Five.

Knapp's model suggests that a relationship exhibits only the most dominant traits of just one of the 10 stages at any given time. Despite this fact, elements of other stages are usually present. For example, two lovers deep in the throes of integrating may still do their share of experimenting ("Wow, I never knew that about you!") and have differentiating disagreements ("I

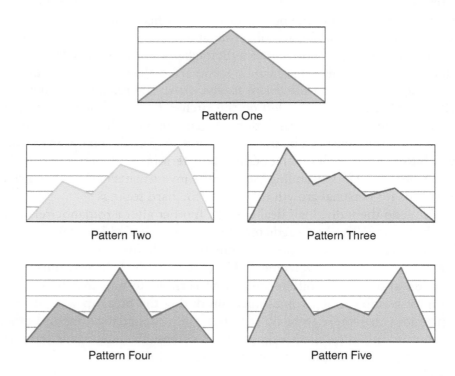

FIGURE 9.2 **Patterns of Relational Development and Deterioration**

Adapted from Johnson, A. J., Wittenberg, E., Haigh, M., Wigley, S., Becker, J., Brown, K., & Craig, E. (2004). The process of relationship development and deterioration: Turning points in friendships that have terminated. *Communication Quarterly, 52,* 54–67.

need a weekend to myself"). Likewise, family members who spend most of their energy avoiding each other may have an occasional good spell in which their former closeness briefly intensifies. The notion that relationships can experience features of both "coming together" and "coming apart" at the same time is explored in the following section on relational dialectics.

DIALECTICAL PERSPECTIVES ON RELATIONAL DYNAMICS

Not all theorists agree that relational stages are the best way to explain interaction in relationships. Some suggest that communicators grapple with the same kinds of challenges whether a relationship is brand new or has lasted decades. Their focus, then, is on the ongoing maintenance of relationships. They argue that communicators seek important but apparently incompatible goals. The struggle to achieve these goals creates **dialectical tensions**: conflicts that arise when two opposing or incompatible forces exist simultaneously.

Communication scholars including Leslie Baxter (Baxter, 2011; Baxter & Braithwaite, 2008) and William Rawlins (1992) have identified several dialectical forces that make successful communication challenging. They suggest that the struggle to manage these dialectical tensions creates the most powerful dynamics in relational communication. In the following pages we will discuss three influential dialectical tensions, which are summarized in Table 9.1. As the table shows, we experience dialectical challenges both *internally*, that is, within the relationship, and *externally* as we and our relational partners face other people whose desires clash with our own.

Integration versus Separation No one is an island. Recognizing this fact, we seek out involvement with others. But, at the same time, we are unwilling to sacrifice our entire identity to even the most satisfying relationship. The conflicting desires for connection and independence are embodied in the **integration-separation dialectic**. This set of apparently contradictory needs

TABLE 9.1 Dialectical Tensions

	DIALECTIC OF INTEGRATION-SEPARATION	DIALECTIC OF STABILITY-CHANGE	DIALECTIC OF EXPRESSION-PRIVACY
Internal Manifestations	Connection-Autonomy	Predictability-Novelty	Openness-Closedness
External Manifestations	Inclusion-Seclusion	Conventionality-Uniqueness	Revelation-Concealment

From Baxter, L. A. (1994). A dialogic approach to relationship maintenance. In D. J. Canary & L. Stafford (Eds.), *Communication and relational maintenance* (p. 240). San Diego, CA: Academic Press.

creates communication challenges that can show up both within a relationship and when relational partners face the world.

Internally, the struggle shows up in the **connection-autonomy dialectic**. We want to be close to others, but at the same time we seek independence. Sociolinguist Deborah Tannen (1986) captures the insoluble integration-separation dialectic nicely by evoking the image of two porcupines trying to get through a cold winter:

> They huddle together for warmth, but their sharp quills prick each other, so they pull away. But then they get cold. They have to keep adjusting their closeness and distance to keep from freezing and from getting pricked by their fellow porcupines—the source of both comfort and pain.
>
> We need to get close to each other to have a sense of community, to feel we're not alone in the world. But we need to keep our distance from each other to preserve our independence, so others don't impose on or engulf us. This duality reflects the human condition. We are individual and social creatures. We need other people to survive, but we want to survive as individuals.

Baxter (1994) describes the consequences for relational partners who can't successfully manage the conflicting needs for connection and autonomy. Some of the most common reasons for relational breakups involve failure of partners to satisfy one another's needs for connection: "We barely spent any time together"; "My partner wasn't committed to the relationship"; "We had different needs." But other relational complaints involve excessive demands for connection: "I was feeling trapped"; "I needed freedom." Perhaps not surprisingly, research suggests that in heterosexual romantic relationships, men often want more autonomy and women typically want more connection and commitment (Buunk, 2005; Feeney, 1999).

In accounts of relational turning points, both men and women in heterosexual romantic pairs cited the connection-autonomy dialectic as one of the most significant factors affecting their relationship (Baxter & Erbert, 1999). This dialectical tension was crucial in negotiating turning points related to commitment, conflict, disengagement, and reconciliation. Research also shows that managing the dialectical tension between connection and autonomy is as important during divorce as it is at the beginning of a marriage, as partners seek ways to salvage

AT WORK

Social Capital and Career Advancement

The old saying, "It isn't what you know, it's *who* you know," is at least somewhat true. *Social capital*, in part, refers to the potential benefits that come from belonging to one or more social networks. An impressive body of research confirms that robust personal networks can pay off in your career (Krebs, 2008).

People with high social capital are more likely to find good jobs quickly and be promoted early. They receive more positive performance evaluations from their bosses and earn larger bonuses. Social capital doesn't just benefit individuals. Group members who have rich and diverse personal networks enhance the performance of their teams, helping them generate more creative solutions and reach their goals more rapidly.

Along with contacts that you make and maintain through face-to-face and phone contact, online social networks can be a powerful tool for building and using social capital (Ellison et al., 2007). Business-oriented resources like LinkedIn can be helpful, as can "friends" on more general sites like Facebook. Within large organizations, company "intranets" can provide a way for employees to keep in touch.

Whatever their nature, social networks can go beyond their obvious value as sources of friendship, providing you with the resources that can make a critical difference in your career success.

and reconcile the unbreakable bonds of their personal history (including finances, children, and friends) with their new independence (Pam & Pearson, 1998).

Parents and children must deal constantly with the conflicting tugs of connection and autonomy. These struggles don't end when children grow up and leave home. Parents experience the mixed feelings of relief at their new freedom and longings to stay connected to their adult children. Likewise, grown children typically feel excitement at being on their own, and yet miss the bonds that had been taken for granted since the beginning of their lives (Blacker, 1999; Fulmer, 1999). We'll discuss these family dialectics further in Chapter 12.

It's important to emphasize that autonomy-connection tensions aren't necessarily a sign of a troubled relationship. Look again at Figure 9.1 on page 287. In that model, you'll see that Integrating and Bonding (connection), as well as Differentiating and Circumscribing (autonomy), fall in the circle labeled *relational maintenance*. Although descriptors such as "struggles" and "conflicts" can make dialectical tensions sound negative, it's best to see them as normal and manageable factors in maintaining healthy relationships.

The tension between integration and separation also operates externally, when people within a relationship struggle to meet the competing needs of the **inclusion-seclusion dialectic**. They struggle to reconcile a desire for involvement with the "outside world" with the desire to live their own lives, free of what can feel like interference from others. For example, when the end of a busy week comes, does a couple accept the invitation to a party (and sacrifice the chance to spend quality time with one another), or do they decline the invitation (and risk losing contact with valued friends)? Does a close-knit nuclear family choose to take a much anticipated vacation together (disappointing their relatives), or do they attend a family reunion (losing precious time to enjoy one another without any distractions)?

Stability versus Change Stability is an important need in relationships, but too much of it can lead to feelings of staleness. The **stability-change dialectic** operates both between partners and when they face others outside the relationship. Within a relationship, the **predictability-novelty dialectic** captures

THE DANGERS OF DIALECTICAL IMBALANCE: *CYRUS*

John (John C. Reilly) knows he's a lucky man when he strikes up a relationship with Molly (Marisa Tomei) after seven desperate years of singleness. There's just one problem—Molly's 21-year-old, live-at-home son Cyrus (Jonah Hill).

Cyrus has never outgrown his connection to his mom. Like John, we become increasingly creeped out by his jealous possessiveness. It soon becomes clear that Cyrus is out to destroy the bond between Molly and John so he won't have to share her affection.

Until the final moments of this serio-comedy, we don't know whether John will succeed in persuading mother and son to bring their autonomy-connection dialectic into better balance. What we do see clearly is how, in relationships, too much of a good thing can become a bad thing.

another set of tensions. While nobody wants a completely unpredictable relational partner ("You're not the person I married!"), humorist Dave Barry (1990, p. 47) exaggerates only slightly when he talks about the boredom that can come when husbands and wives know each other too well:

> After a decade or so of marriage, you know *everything* about your spouse, every habit and opinion and twitch and tic and minor skin growth. You could write a seventeen-pound book solely about the way your spouse eats. This kind of intimate knowledge can be very handy in certain situations— such as when you're on a TV quiz show where the object is to identify your spouse from the sound of his or her chewing—but it tends to lower the passion level of a relationship.

At an external level, the **conventionality-uniqueness dialectic** captures the challenges that people in a relationship face when trying to meet others' expectations as well as their own. On one hand, stable patterns of behavior do emerge that enable others to make useful judgments like "happy family" or "dependable organization." But those blanket characterizations can stifle people in relationships, who may sometimes want to break away from the expectations others hold of them. For example, playing the conventional role of "happy family" or "perfect couple" during a time of conflict can be a burden, when the couple feels the need to behave in less stereotypical ways.

Expression versus Privacy Disclosure is one characteristic of interpersonal relationships. Yet, along with the drive for intimacy, we have an equally important need to maintain some space between ourselves and others. These sometimes conflicting drives create the **expression-privacy dialectic**.

The internal struggle between expression and privacy shows up in the **openness-closedness dialectic**. What do you do in an intimate relationship when a person you care about asks an important question that you don't want to answer? "Do you think I'm attractive?" "Are you having a good time?" Your commitment to the relationship may compel you toward honesty, but your concern for the other person's feelings and a desire for privacy may lead you to be less than completely honest. Partners use a variety of strategies to gain privacy from each other (Burgoon et al., 1989; Petronio & Durham, 2008). For example, they may confront the other person directly and explain that they don't want to continue a discussion, or they may be less direct and offer nonverbal cues, change the topic, or leave the room. As you read in Chapter 3, there are both benefits and risks in self-disclosing.

The same conflicts between openness and privacy operate externally in the **revelation-concealment dialectic**. If you and a longtime fellow worker haven't been getting along, do you answer the boss's question, "How's it going?" honestly, or do you keep your disagreement to yourselves? If your family has had a run of bad (or good) financial luck and a friend asks to borrow (or lend) money, do you share your situation or keep quiet? If you're part of a lesbian couple but you're not sure your relationship will be endorsed by others, when and how do you go "public" with that information (Suter et al., 2006; Suter & Daas, 2007). All of these questions speak to tensions related to concealing versus revealing. These challenges have increased as social media such as Facebook make privacy boundaries more difficult to manage (Debatin et al., 2009).

For many couples, the revelation-concealment dialectic centers on decisions about how much news to share about their relationship. "Should we tell our friends that we're dating?" or "Is it time for you to meet my family?" are questions they might ask about sharing positive relational information with others. For some couples, however, the concealed news isn't so pleasant. Lara Dieckmann (2000) looked into the world of battered women and found that most of them wrestle with the dialectic of staying private or going public about the abuse in their relationships. A word that Dieckmann used to describe the women's experience is balance—the need to constantly juggle the competing demands of privacy and publicity, secrecy and disclosure, safety and danger. Telling others about partner abuse can be the first step in disengaging from a violent relationship, but it can also threaten a woman's self-esteem, security, and very life.

Although all of the dialectical tensions play an important role in managing relationships, some occur more frequently than others. In one study (Pawlowski, 1998), young married couples reported that connection-autonomy was the most frequent tension (30.8 percent of all reported contradictions). Predictability-novelty was second (occurring 21.7 percent of the time), and inclusion-seclusion was third (21.4 percent). Less common were tensions between openness-closedness (12.7 percent), conventionality-uniqueness (7.5 percent), and revelation-concealment (6 percent). Of all the dialectical tensions, connection-autonomy and openness-closedness seem to be the most important ones to manage, at least in romantic relationships (Baxter & Erbert 1999; Erbert, 2000).

Strategies for Managing Dialectical Tensions Managing the dialectical tensions outlined in these pages presents communication challenges (Duran et al., 2011; Prentice & Kramer, 2006). There are at least eight ways these challenges can be managed (Baxter & Braithwaite, 2006).

- *Denial* In the strategy of denial, communicators respond to one end of the dialectical spectrum and ignore the other. For example, a couple caught between the conflicting desires for stability and novelty might find their struggle for change too difficult to manage and choose to follow predictable, if unexciting patterns of relating to one another.

- *Disorientation* In this mode, communicators feel so overwhelmed and helpless that they are unable to confront their problems. In the face of dialectical tensions they might fight, freeze, or even leave the relationship. A couple who discovers soon after the honeymoon that living a "happily ever after" conflict-free life is impossible might become so terrified that they would come to view their marriage as a mistake.

299

- *Alternation* Communicators who use this strategy choose one end of the dialectical spectrum at some times, and the other end on different occasions. Friends, for example, might manage the connection-autonomy dialectic by alternating between times when they spend a large amount of time together and other periods when they live independent lives.

- *Segmentation* Partners who use this tactic compartmentalize different areas of their relationship. For example, a couple might manage the openness-closedness dialectic by sharing almost all their feelings about mutual friends with one another, but keeping certain parts of their past romantic histories private.

- *Balance* Communicators who try to balance dialectical tensions recognize that both forces are legitimate and try to manage them through compromise. As Chapter 11 points out, compromise is inherently a situation in which everybody loses at least a little of what he or she wants. A couple caught between the conflicting desires for predictability and novelty might seek balance by compromising with a lifestyle that is neither as predictable as one wants nor as surprise-filled as the other seeks—not an ideal outcome.

- *Integration* With this approach, communicators simultaneously accept opposing forces without trying to diminish them. Barbara Montgomery (1993) describes a couple who accept both the needs for predictability and novelty by devising a "predictably novel" approach: Once a week they would do something together that they had never done before. Similarly, Dawn Braithwaite and her colleagues (1998) found that stepfamilies often manage the tension between the "old family" and the "new family" by adapting and blending their family rituals.

- *Recalibration* Communicators can respond to dialectical challenges by reframing them so that the apparent contradiction disappears. Consider how a couple who felt hurt by one another's unwillingness to share parts of their past might redefine the secrets as creating an attractive aura of mystery instead of being a problem to be solved. The desire for privacy would still remain, but it would no longer compete with a need for openness about every aspect of the past.

- *Reaffirmation* This approach acknowledges that dialectical tensions will never disappear. Instead of trying to make them go away, reaffirming communicators accept—or even embrace—the challenges they present. The metaphorical view of relational life as a kind of roller-coaster reflects this orientation, and communicators who use reaffirmation view dialectical tensions as part of the ride.

Which of these strategies do you use to manage the dialectical tensions in your life? How successful is each one? Which strategies might serve your communication better? Generally speaking, the last three options above are seen as the most productive, and researchers suggest it's wise to make use of multiple strategies (Baxter & Montgomery, 1996). For example, broken-up couples report having used denial, alternation, and segmentation less than successfully, and they tended to rely on only one strategy rather than using the variety at their disposal (Sahlstein & Dun, 2008). Since dialectical tensions are a part of life, choosing how to communicate about them can make a tremendous difference in the quality of your relationships.

Communicating about Relationships

By now it is clear that relationships are complex, dynamic, and important. How do communicators address relational issues with one another?

CONTENT AND RELATIONAL MESSAGES

In Chapter 1 you read that every message has a *content* and a *relational* dimension. The most obvious component of most messages is their content—the subject being discussed. The content of statements like "It's your turn to do the dishes" or "I'm busy Saturday night" is obvious.

Content messages aren't the only information being exchanged when two people communicate. In addition, every message—both verbal and nonverbal—also has a second, relational dimension, which makes statements about how the communicators feel toward one another (Knobloch & Solomon, 2003; Watzlawick et al., 1967). These relational messages deal with one or more social needs: intimacy, affinity, respect, and control. Consider the two examples we just mentioned:

- Imagine two ways of saying "It's your turn to do the dishes," one that is demanding and another that is matter-of-fact. Notice how the different nonverbal messages make statements about how the sender views control in this part of the relationship. The demanding tone says, in effect, "I have a right to tell you what to do around the house," whereas the matter-of-fact one suggests, "I'm just reminding you of something you might have overlooked."

- You can easily imagine two ways to deliver the statement "I'm busy Saturday night," one with little affection and the other with much liking.

Like these messages, every statement we make goes beyond discussing the subject at hand and says something about the way the speaker feels about the recipient and their relationship. You can prove this fact by listening for the relational messages implicit in your own statements to others and theirs to you.

Most of the time we are unaware of the relational messages that bombard us every day. Sometimes these messages don't capture our awareness because they match our belief about the amount of control, liking, or intimacy that is appropriate in a relationship. For example, you probably won't be offended if your boss tells you to drop everything and tackle a certain job, because you agree that supervisors have the right to direct employees. However, if your boss delivered the order in a condescending, sarcastic, or abusive tone of voice, you would probably be offended. Your complaint wouldn't be with the order itself, but with the way it was delivered. "I may work for this company," you might think, "but I'm not a slave or an idiot. I deserve to be treated like a human being."

EXPRESSION OF RELATIONAL MESSAGES

Exactly how are relational messages communicated? As the boss-employee example suggests, they are usually expressed nonverbally. To test this fact for yourself, imagine how you could act while saying "Can you help me for a minute?" in a way that communicates each of the following relationships:

> superiority
> helplessness
> friendliness
> aloofness
> sexual desire
> irritation

Although nonverbal behaviors are a good source of relational messages, remember that they are ambiguous. The sharp tone you take as a personal insult might be due to fatigue, and the interruption you take as an attempt to ignore your ideas might be a sign of pressure that has nothing to do with you. Before you jump to conclusions about relational clues, it is a good idea to verify the accuracy of your interpretation with the other person: "When you cut me off, I got the idea you're angry at me. Is that right?"

Not all relational messages are nonverbal. Social scientists use the term **metacommunication** to describe messages that refer to other messages (Craig, 2005; Dindia & Baxter, 1987; Weder, 2008). In other words, metacommunication is communication about communication. Whenever we discuss a relationship with others, we are metacommunicating: "I wish we could stop arguing so much," or "I appreciate how honest you've been with me." Sooner or later, there are times when it becomes necessary to talk about what is going on between you and the other person. The ability to focus on the kinds of issues described in this chapter can be the tool for keeping your relationship on track.

Despite its importance, overt metacommunication isn't a common feature of most relationships (Fogel & Branco, 1997; Wilmot, 1995). In fact, there seems to be an aversion to it, even among many intimates (Bisson & Levine, 2009; Zhang & Stafford, 2008). When 90 people were asked to identify the taboo subjects in their

"She's texting me, but I think she's also subtexting me."

F⊕CUS ON RESEARCH

Reel to Real? Relational Communication in Romantic Comedies

Hollywood offers plenty of illustrations of interpersonal relationships, particularly in the genre of romantic comedies. Kimberly Johnson and Bjarne Holmes wanted to know what messages these movies send about communication in romantic relationships.

The researchers analyzed 40 popular romantic comedies released by major Hollywood studios over a 10-year period. They found 3,470 relationship-oriented incidents, which they organized into 103 categories and 16 relational themes. Here are a few of their findings and conclusions:

- Couples in noncommitted or nominally committed relationships were portrayed as more affectionate, expressive, and happy than married couples. The researchers expressed concern that this might lead viewers "to see marriage and romance as disparate entities."

- There seemed to be few if any negative consequences when relational transgressions occurred. As a result, the researchers suggested that viewers might underestimate the consequences that transgressions could have on their own relationships.

- Romantic comedies typically focus on the early stages of relationships, with all their accompanying excitement and passion. However, much of the couples' communication is representative of later stages of relationships, such as expressions of deep love and emotional support. This could lead viewers "to believe that characteristics of relationships that ordinarily take time to develop should be present early on."

The authors are quick to note that romantic comedies are designed to be entertaining, and that they must tell a relationship's story in two hours or less. As a result, they aren't necessarily designed to be realistic. Nevertheless, this study suggests that students of interpersonal communication might do well to view romantic comedies with a slightly critical eye—while still enjoying the films.

Johnson, K. R., & Holmes, B. M. (2009). Contradictory messages: A content analysis of Hollywood-produced romantic comedy feature films. *Communication Quarterly, 57,* 352-373.

personal relationships, the most frequent topics involved metacommunication (Baxter & Wilmot, 1985). For example, people were reluctant to discuss the state of their current relationships and the norms ("rules") that governed their lives together. Nevertheless, research shows that metacommunication can play a vital role in relational maintenance and repair (Becker et al., 2008). To learn how, read on.

Repairing Damaged Relationships

Sooner or later, even the most satisfying and stable relationships hit a bumpy patch. Some problems arise from outside forces: work, finances, competing relationships, and so on. At other times, problems arise from differences and disagreements within the relationship. Chapter 11 offers guidelines for dealing with these sorts of challenges.

A third type of relational problem comes from **relational transgressions**, when one partner violates the explicit or implicit terms of the relationship, letting the other one down in some important way.

TYPES OF RELATIONAL TRANSGRESSIONS

Table 9.2 lists some types of relational transgressions. Violations like these fall into different categories (Emmers-Sommer, 2003).

Minor versus Significant Some of the items listed in Table 9.2 aren't inherently transgressions, and in small doses they can actually aid relationships. For instance, a *little* distance can make the heart grow fonder, a *little* jealousy can be a sign of affection, and a *little* anger can start the process of resolving a gripe. In large and regular doses, however, these acts become serious transgressions that can damage personal relationships.

Social versus Relational Some transgressions violate *social rules* shared by society at large. For example, almost everyone would agree that ridiculing or humiliating a friend or family member in public is a violation of a fundamental social rule regarding saving others' face. Other rules are *relational* in nature—unique norms constructed by the parties involved. For instance, some families have a rule stating, "If I'm going to be more than a little bit late, I'll let you know so that you don't worry." Once such a rule exists, failure to honor it feels like a violation, even though outsiders might not view it as such.

Deliberate versus Unintentional Some transgressions are unintentional. You might reveal something about a friend's past without realizing that this disclosure would be embarrassing. Other violations, though, are intentional. In a fit of anger, you might purposely lash out with a cruel comment, knowing that it will hurt the other person's feelings.

TABLE 9.2 Some Types of Relational Transgressions

Lack of Commitment
  Failure to honor important obligations (e.g., financial, emotional, task-related)
  Self-serving dishonesty
  Unfaithfulness

Distance
  Physical separation (beyond what is necessary)
  Psychological separation (avoidance, ignoring)

Disrespect   Criticism (especially in front of third parties)

Problematic Emotions
  Jealousy
  Unjustified Suspicion
  Rage

Aggression
  Verbal hostility
  Physical violence

One-time versus Incremental The most obvious transgressions occur in a single episode: an act of betrayal, a verbal assault, or walking out in anger. But more subtle transgressions can occur over time. Consider emotional withdrawal: People have times when they retreat into themselves, and we usually give one another the space to do just that. But if the withdrawal slowly becomes pervasive, it becomes a violation of the fundamental rule in most relationships that partners should be available to one another.

STRATEGIES FOR RELATIONAL REPAIR

Research confirms the commonsense notion that a first step to repairing a transgression is to talk about the violation (Brandau-Brown & Ragsdale, 2008; Dindia & Baxter, 1987). Chapter 5 offers tips for sending clear, assertive "I-messages" when you believe you've been wronged ("I was really embarrassed when you yelled at me in front of everybody last night"). In other cases, you might be responsible for the transgression and want to raise it for discussion: "What did I do that you found so hurtful?" "Why was my behavior a problem for you?" Asking questions like these—and listening nondefensively to the answers—can be an enormous challenge. Chapter 7 offers guidelines for listening, and Chapter 10 provides tips about how to manage criticism.

Not surprisingly, some transgressions are harder to repair than others. One study of dating partners found that sexual infidelity and breaking up with the partner were the two least forgivable offenses (Bachman & Guerrero, 2006). The seriousness of the transgression and the relative strength of the relationship prior to the offense are the two most significant factors in whether forgiveness will be granted (Guerrero & Bachman, 2010).

For the best chance of repairing a seriously damaged relationship, an apology needs to be offered. *The Last Lecture* author Randy Pausch notes, "If you have done something wrong in your dealings with another person, it's as if there's an infection in your relationship. A good apology is like an antibiotic, a bad apology is like rubbing salt in the wound" (2008, p. 161). As the cartoon on page 306 illustrates, some apologies are less than sincere. An ideal apology contains these three elements (Kelley & Waldron, 2005; Villadsen, 2008):

- An explicit admission that the transgression was wrong: "I acted like a selfish jerk."

- A genuine acknowledgement of regret: "I'm really sorry. I feel awful for letting you down."

- Some type of compensation: "No matter what happens, I'll never do anything like that again."

An apology will be convincing only if the speaker's nonverbal behaviors match what is said. Even then, it may be unrealistic to expect immediate forgiveness. Sometimes, especially with severe transgressions, expressions of regret and promises of new behavior will only be accepted conditionally,

with a need for them to be demonstrated over time before the aggrieved party regards them as genuine (Merolla, 2008).

Given the challenges and possible humiliation involved in apologizing, is it worth the effort? Research suggests yes. Participants in one study consistently reported that they had more remorse over apologies they *didn't* offer than about those they did (Exline et al., 2007).

FORGIVING TRANSGRESSIONS

Many people think of forgiveness as a topic for theologians and philosophers. However, social scientists have found that forgiving others has both personal and relational benefits (Antonuccio & Jackson, 2009; McCullough et al., 2009). On a personal level, forgiveness has been shown to reduce emotional distress and aggression (Eaton & Struthers, 2006; Orcutt, 2006) as well as to improve cardiovascular functioning (Lawler et al., 2003). Interpersonally, extending forgiveness to lovers, friends, and family can often help restore damaged relationships (Waldron & Kelley, 2005). Moreover, most research shows that transgressors who have been forgiven are usually less likely to repeat their offenses than those who have not received forgiveness (Wallace et al., 2008; Whited et al., 2010).

Even when a sincere apology is offered, forgiving others can be difficult. Research shows that one way to improve your ability to forgive is to recall times when you have mistreated or hurt others in the past—in other words, to remember that you, too, have wronged others and needed their forgiveness (Exline et al., 2008; Takaku et al., 2001). Given that it's in our own best interest to be forgiving, communication researcher Douglas Kelley (1998) encourages us to remember these words from R. P. Walters: "When we have been hurt we have two alternatives: be destroyed by resentment, or forgive. Resentment is death; forgiving leads to healing and life" (p. 270).

Granting forgiveness to others can sometimes be done through nonverbal displays, such as replacing frowns with smiles or physical affection. More serious cases might require discussion and negotiation or even an explicit statement of forgiveness. The Self-Assessment on page 307 can help you recognize how you typically express forgiveness to others.

ⓈⒺⓁⒻ-ⒶⓈⓈⒺⓈⓈⓂⒺⓃⓉ

Forgiveness-Granting Strategies

Presented here is a list of behaviors a person might use to respond to someone seeking forgiveness. To what extent do you use each strategy? Rate each one on a scale from 0 to 7, where 0 = "never use," 3 or 4 = "use moderately," and 7 = "use extensively."

NEVER USE   0   1   2   3   4   5   6   7   USE EXTENSIVELY

_____ 1. I touch my partner in a way that communicates forgiveness.
_____ 2. I say I would forgive my partner if the offense never happened again.
_____ 3. I tell my partner it was no big deal.
_____ 4. I initiate discussion about the offense.
_____ 5. I put what happened aside so that we can resume our relationship.
_____ 6. The expression on my face says, "I forgive you."
_____ 7. I say I would forgive my partner only if things changed.
_____ 8. I tell my partner not to worry about it.
_____ 9. I discuss the offense with my partner.
_____ 10. I don't say anything but just do my best to restore our relationship.
_____ 11. I tell my partner, "I forgive you."

Add your responses to items 1 and 6:   _____   Nonverbal display of forgiveness
Add your responses to items 2 and 7:   _____   Conditional forgiveness
Add your responses to items 3 and 8:   _____   Minimize the consequences of the transgression
Add your responses to items 4 and 9:   _____   Discussion of the offense
Add your responses to items 5 and 10:   _____   Benevolent forgiveness
Record your response to item 11:   _____   Explicit, direct forgiveness

Your scores should give you an indication of which strategies you use most frequently.

Adapted from Waldron, V. R., & Kelley, D. L (2005). Forgiving communication as a response to relational transgressions. *Journal of Social and Personal Relationships, 22,* 723-742.

Paleari, F. G., Regalia, C., & Fincham, F. D. (2009). Measuring offence-specific forgiveness in marriage: The Marital Offence-Specific Forgiveness Scale (MOFS). *Psychological Assessment, 21,* 194-209.

Summary

There are several explanations for why we form relationships with some people and not with others. These explanations include appearance (physical attractiveness), similarity, complementarity, rewards, competency, proximity, and disclosure.

Some theorists argue that interpersonal relationships may go through as many as 10 stages of growth and deterioration. They suggest that communication may reflect more than one stage at a given time, although one stage will be dominant. Other models describe the dynamics of interpersonal communication in terms of dialectical tensions: mutually opposing, incompatible desires that can never be completely resolved. These dialectical tensions include integration-separation, stability-change, and expression-privacy.

Relational messages sometimes are expressed overtly via verbal metacommunication; however, more frequently they are conveyed nonverbally. Some relationships become damaged over time; others are hurt by relational transgressions. There are several strategies for repairing damaged relationships, with apologies and forgiveness being particularly important.

Key Terms

- Avoiding (293)
- Bonding (291)
- Circumscribing (292)
- Comparison level (CL) (284)
- Comparison level of alternatives (CL_{alt}) (284)
- Connection-autonomy dialectic (296)
- Conventionality-uniqueness dialectic (298)
- Dialectical tensions (295)
- Differentiating (292)
- Experimenting (289)
- Expression-privacy dialectic (298)
- Inclusion-seclusion dialectic (297)
- Initiating (288)
- Integrating (290)
- Integration-separation dialectic (295)
- Intensifying (289)
- Metacommunication (302)
- Openness-closedness dialectic (298)
- Predictability-novelty dialectic (297)
- Relational maintenance (287)
- Relational transgressions (303)
- Revelation-concealment dialectic (298)
- Stability-change dialectic (297)
- Stagnating (292)
- Terminating (293)

Activities

1. Critical Thinking Probe

Scholars have argued for years as to whether similarity ("Birds of a feather flock together") or complementarity ("Opposites attract") offers the best explanation for relational attraction and formation. Based on your own experience, which do you think is more valid? Are there cases where both are true? Offer examples to support your position.

2. Critical Thinking Probe

Some critics claim that Knapp's model of relational stages is better suited to describing romantic relationships than it is other types. Use a variety of romantic and nonromantic interpersonal relationships from your experience to evaluate the breadth of his model. If the model does not describe the developmental path of all types of interpersonal relationships, can you suggest alternative models?

3. Invitation to Insight

How do you manage the dialectical tensions in your important relationships? Is there a pattern to what you and the other person do, or does it depend on the type of relationship you have? Identify at least two dialectical tensions in two different relationships—one relationship, perhaps, with a person with whom you work closely, and the other with a romantic partner. How is each tension managed? Which approach do you and your partner tend to use (denial, disorientation, alternation, segmentation, balance, integration, recalibration, or reaffirmation)? What seem to be the conditions that determine which method you and your partner use?

4. Skill Builder

Identify three unexpressed relational messages in one or more of your interpersonal relationships.
  a. Describe how you could have used metacommunication to express each one. Consider skills you learned in other chapters, such as perception checking, "I" language, and paraphrasing.
  b. Discuss the possible benefits and drawbacks of this kind of metacommunication in each of the situations you identified. Based on your discussion here, what principles do you believe should guide your decision about whether and when to focus explicitly on relational issues?

5. Invitation to Insight

  a. Identify transgressions you have made in one important relationship. Describe whether these transgressions were social or relational, deliberate or unintentional, and one time or incremental. (If you think the relationship can handle it, consider asking the "victim" of your transgression to describe your behavior and its effects.)
  b. Consider (or ask the other person) whether it's necessary to repair your transgression. Examine the strategies described earlier, and decide how you could put them into action

Communication Climate

After studying the material in this chapter . . .

You should understand:

1. The definition of communication climate.
2. The importance of being valued and confirmed through communication.
3. The characteristics of confirming, disagreeing, and disconfirming messages.
4. The nature of positive and negative communication spirals.
5. The relationship between presenting self (face) and defensiveness.
6. The types of messages that are likely to create positive communication climates.
7. The various ways to transform negative communication climates.

You should be able to:

1. Identify confirming, disagreeing, and disconfirming messages and patterns in your own relationships.
2. Identify the parts of your presenting self (face) that you defend, and the consequences of doing so.
3. Create messages that are likely to build supportive rather than defensive communication climates.
4. Create appropriate nondefensive responses to real or hypothetical criticisms.

How would you describe your most important relationships? Fair and warm? Stormy? Hot? Cold? Just as physical locations have characteristic weather patterns, interpersonal relationships have unique climates, too. You can't measure the interpersonal climate by looking at a thermometer or glancing at the sky, but it's there nonetheless. Every relationship has a feeling, a pervasive mood that colors the goings-on of the participants.

What Is Communication Climate?

The term **communication climate** refers to the social tone of a relationship. A climate doesn't involve specific activities as much as the way people feel about each other as they carry out those activities. For example, consider two interpersonal communication classes. Both meet for the same length of time and follow the same syllabus. It's easy to imagine how one of these classes might be a friendly, comfortable place to learn, whereas the other could be cold and tense—even hostile. It's not the course content that differs—it's the way the people in the classroom feel about and treat each other (Johnson, 2009).

Just as every classroom has a unique climate, so does every relationship. Romances, friendships, and families—just like neighborhoods, cities, and countries—can be defined by their social tone. Another obvious context for observing climate's impact is the workplace, which may explain why the topic is so widely studied (Sopow, 2008; Yurtsever & de Rivera, 2010). Think for a moment: Have you ever held a job where backbiting, criticism, and suspicion were the norm? Or have you been lucky enough to work where the atmosphere was positive, encouraging, and supportive? If you've experienced both, you know what a difference climate makes. Other studies (e.g., Anderson et al., 2004) reinforce the fact that employees have a higher level of commitment at jobs in which they experience a positive communication climate, especially to their work group if not the organization as a whole (Bartels et al., 2008).

Like their meteorological counterparts, communication climates are shared by everyone involved. It's rare to find one person describing a relationship as open and positive while another characterizes it as cold and hostile. Also, just like the weather, communication climates can change over time. A relationship can be overcast at one time and sunny at another. Carrying the analogy to its conclusion, we should say that communication climate forecasting is not a perfect science. Unlike the weather, however, people can change their communication climates—and that's why it's important to understand them. We look at several climate issues in this chapter: how communication climates develop, how and why we respond defensively in certain climates, and what can be done to create positive climates and transform negative ones.

How Communication Climates Develop

Why does some communication create a positive climate while other behavior has the opposite effect? A short but accurate answer is that communication climate is determined by the degree to which people see themselves as *valued*. Communicators who perceive others as liking, appreciating, and respecting them react positively, whereas those who feel unimportant or abused react negatively. Social scientists use the term **confirming communication** to describe messages that convey valuing. In one form or another, confirming messages say "you exist," "you matter," and "you're important." By contrast, **disconfirming communication** signals a lack of regard. In one form or another, disconfirming messages say, "I don't care about you," "I don't like you," and "You're not important to me."

As we have stressed throughout this book, every message has a relational dimension along with its content. This means that we send and receive confirming and disconfirming messages virtually whenever we communicate. It isn't what we communicate about that shapes a relational climate as much as how we speak and act toward one another. Choosing not to speak to someone can also communicate disconfirmation. For example, one way employees nudge unwanted coworkers to quit their jobs is to avoid interaction with them, creating a chilly communication climate (Cox, 1999).

It's hard to overstate the importance of confirming messages and the impact of disconfirming ones. Children who lack confirmation suffer a broad range of emotional and behavioral problems (Osterman, 2001), while those who feel confirmed have more open communication with their parents, higher self-esteem, and lower levels of stress (Dailey, 2009, 2010; Schrodt et al., 2006). In the classroom, confirming communication by teachers has been shown to enhance student learning and participation while reducing negative behaviors (Goodboy & Myers, 2008). A confirming climate is also important in marriage, where it is the best predictor of marital satisfaction (Clarke, 1973; Veroff et al., 1998). Satisfied couples have a 5:1 ratio of positive to negative statements, while the ratio for dissatisfied partners is 1:1 (Gottman, 2003).

Like beauty, the decision about whether a message is confirming or disconfirming is in the eyes of the beholder. Consider, for example, times when you took a comment that might have sounded unsupportive to an outsider ("You turkey!") as a sign of affection within the context of your personal relationship. Likewise, a comment that the sender might have meant to be helpful ("I'm telling you this for your own good . . .") could easily be regarded as a disconfirming attack.

LEVELS OF MESSAGE CONFIRMATION

Figure 10.1 shows that the range of confirming and disconfirming communication includes several categories of messages, which are described in the following pages.

Confirming Messages There's no guarantee that others will regard even your best attempts at confirming messages the way you intend them, but research shows that three increasingly positive types of messages have the best chance of being perceived as confirming (Cissna & Sieberg, 2006).

Recognition The most fundamental act of confirmation is to recognize the other person. Recognition seems easy and obvious, yet there are many times when we do not respond to others on this basic level. Failure to call or visit a friend is a common example. So is failure to respond to an e-mail or text message. Likewise, avoiding eye contact can send a negative message. Consider what it's like when a store clerk or bank teller fails to nonverbally acknowledge that you're waiting for service. Of course, this lack of recognition may simply be an oversight. The clerk may be attending to other business, or the pressures of work and school may prevent you from staying in touch with your friend. Nonetheless, if the other person *perceives* you as avoiding contact, the message has the effect of being disconfirming.

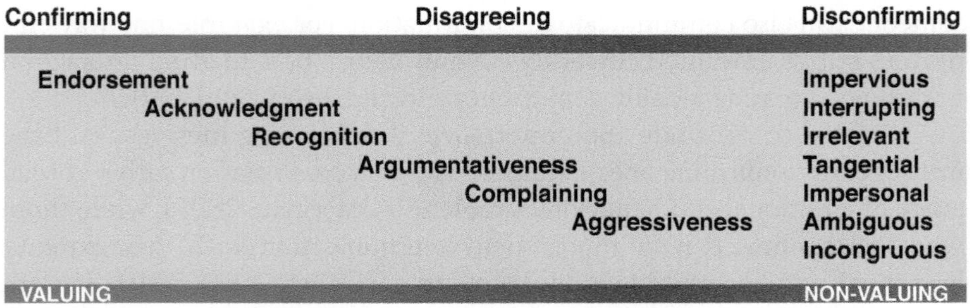

Confirming	Disagreeing	Disconfirming
Endorsement		Impervious
Acknowledgment		Interrupting
Recognition		Irrelevant
	Argumentativeness	Tangential
	Complaining	Impersonal
	Aggressiveness	Ambiguous
		Incongruous
VALUING		NON-VALUING

FIGURE 10.1 **Confirmation-Disconfirmation Continuum**

Acknowledgment Acknowledging the ideas and feelings of others is a stronger form of confirmation than simple recognition. Listening is probably the most common form of acknowledgment. Attending and responding to another person's words is one measure of your interest. Not surprisingly, employees give high marks to managers who solicit their opinions—even when the managers don't accept every suggestion (Allen, 1995). As you read in Chapter 7, reflecting the speaker's thoughts and feelings can be a powerful way to offer support when others have problems.

Endorsement Whereas acknowledgment communicates you are interested in another person, endorsement means that you agree with her or him or otherwise find her or him important. It's easy to see why endorsement is the strongest type of confirming message, since it communicates the highest form of valuing. The most obvious form of endorsement is agreeing ("You're right about that"), but it isn't necessary to agree completely with other people in order to endorse their message. You can probably find something in the message that you endorse. "I can see why you were so angry," you might reply to a friend, even if you don't approve of his or her outburst. Of course, direct praise ("Great job!") is a strong form of endorsement, one you can use surprisingly often once you look for opportunities to compliment others (Berg & DeJong, 2005). Nonverbal endorsement also can enhance the quality of a relational climate. For example, simple acts like maintaining eye contact and nodding while someone speaks can confirm the value of a speaker's idea. On a more intimate level, hugs and embraces can sometimes communicate endorsement in ways that words cannot.

Disagreeing Messages Between confirming and disconfirming lies a type of message that isn't always easy to categorize. A **disagreeing message** essentially says, "You're wrong." In its most constructive form, disagreement includes two of the confirming components we just discussed: recognition and acknowledgment. At its worst, a brutal disagreeing message can so devastate another person that the benefits of recognition and acknowledgment are lost. Because there are better and worse ways to disagree with others, disagreeing messages need to be put on a positive-to-negative scale. We do just that in this section as we discuss three types of disagreement: argumentativeness, complaining, and aggressiveness.

AT WORK

Take This Job and Love It

"Please describe your best workplace experience." Pamela Lutgen-Sandvik and her associates posed that question to 835 U.S. employees in an online survey. Some responded with a single phrase. Others wrote extended paragraphs. The researchers analyzed the comments in hopes of learning what creates an ideal workplace environment.

The two most frequently cited categories of positive on-the-job experiences had to do with *recognition* and *relationships*. Recognition can be as simple as a private word of praise or as significant as a public award. Being recognized helps workers "feel interpersonally significant, needed, unique, and particularly successful." Meaningful workplace relationships include coworker friendships and feeling like part of an organizational family. Social events (such as birthday celebrations or out-of-office gatherings) are typical in companies where members feel a strong sense of affinity and belonging.

These findings show that interpersonal communication plays a central role in positive organizational experiences. Professional achievements and financial rewards are important, but they are valued much more within an affirming workplace environment.

Lutgen-Sandvik, P., Riforgiate, S., & Fletcher, C. (2011). Work as a source of positive emotional experiences and the discourses informing positive assessment. *Western Journal of Communication, 75,* 2-27.

Argumentativeness Normally when we call a person "argumentative," we're making an unfavorable evaluation. However, the ability to create and deliver a sound argument is something we admire in lawyers, talk-show participants, letters to the editor, and political debates. Taking a positive approach to the term, communication researchers define **argumentativeness** as presenting and defending positions on issues while attacking positions taken by others (Infante & Rancer, 1996). Rather than being a negative trait, argumentativeness—at least in the United States—is sometimes associated with a number of positive attributes, such as enhanced self-concept (Rancer et al., 1992), leadership emergence (Limon & LaFrance, 2005), and communicative competence (Hsu, 2010). In the classroom, research shows a positive relationship between students' perceptions of their instructor as argumentative (not aggressive) and their motivation, learning, and satisfaction (Myers, 2002). You can assess your level of argumentativeness by completing the Self-Assessment on page 318.

The key for maintaining a positive climate while arguing a point is the *way* you present your ideas. It is crucial to attack issues, not people. In addition, a sound argument is better received when it's delivered in a supportive, affirming manner (Infante & Gorden, 1989). The supportive kinds of messages outlined on pages 325–333 show how it is possible to argue in a respectful, constructive way.

Complaining When communicators aren't prepared to argue, but still want to register dissatisfaction, they often complain. As is true of all disagreeing messages, some ways of **complaining** are better than others. Jess Alberts (1988, 1990) found that satisfied couples tend to offer behavioral complaints ("You always throw your socks on the floor"), while unsatisfied couples make more complaints aimed at personal characteristics ("You're a slob"). Personal complaints are more likely to result in an escalated conflict episode (Alberts & Driscoll, 1992). The reason should be obvious—complaints about personal characteristics attack a more fundamental part of the presenting self. Talking about socks deals with a habit that can be changed; calling someone a slob is a character assault that is unlikely to be forgotten when the conflict is over. Marriage researcher John Gottman (2000) has found that complaining is not a sign of a troubled relationship—in fact, it's usually healthy for spouses to get their concerns out in the open. However, when couples' communication is filled with disrespectful criticism, it is often a symptom of a marriage headed for divorce.

Aggressiveness The most destructive way to disagree with another person is through **aggressiveness**. Dominic Infante and his associates (1992, p. 116) define verbal aggressiveness as the tendency to "attack the self-concepts of other people in order to inflict psychological pain." Unlike argumentativeness, aggressiveness demeans the worth of others. Name calling, put-downs, sarcasm, taunting, yelling, badgering—all are methods of "winning" disagreements at others' expense.

It's no surprise that aggressiveness has been found to have a variety of serious consequences (Rancer & Avtgis, 2006). Research shows it is associated with physical violence in marriages (Infante et al., 1989), juvenile delinquency (Atkin et al., 2002; Straus & Field, 2003), lower self-esteem (Rill et al., 2009), depression (Lawrence et al., 2009), a negative climate in the workplace (Keashly & Neuman, 2009), lower organizational commitment (Houghton, 2001; Madlock & Kennedy-Lightsey, 2010)), occupational burnout (Avtgis & Rancer, 2008), and a negative climate in the classroom (Myers & Rocca, 2001; Thomas et al., 2011). As one example of aggression's effect on communication, Scott Myers and his colleagues (2007) found that students who perceive their instructor as verbally aggressive are less likely to ask questions, interact in the classroom, or seek out-of-class communication.

It's possible to send clear, firm messages that are assertive (standing up for yourself) rather than aggressive (putting others down). For instructions on creating assertive "I" statements, refer to Chapter 5. For details on win-win vs. win-lose approaches to conflict management, see Chapter 11. Later in this chapter, we'll provide tips on offering constructive criticism.

Disconfirming Messages Disconfirming messages are subtler than disagreeing ones but potentially more damaging. Disconfirming communication implicitly says, "You don't exist; you are not valued."

Disconfirming messages, unfortunately, are part of everyday life. While an occasional disconfirming message may not injure a relationship, a pattern of them usually indicates a negative communication climate. Sieberg and Larson (1971; see also Cissna & Sieberg, 2006) found it was easiest to identify disconfirming communication by observing *responses* to others' messages. They noted seven types of disconfirming responses.

Impervious Response An **impervious response** fails to acknowledge the other person's communicative attempt, either verbally or nonverbally. Impervious responses are especially common when adults and children communicate. Parents often become enraged when they are ignored by their children; likewise, children feel diminished when adults pay no attention to their questions, comments, or requests. Impervious responses also bother students, who, when ignored, report feeling that their self-esteem is being threatened (Sommer et al., 2001). Chapter 11 (page 360) describes the impact that impervious "stonewalling" can have on a relationship.

Dark Side of Communication
CYBERBULLYING: ELECTRONIC CHARACTER ASSASSINATION

It's bad enough to be ridiculed and humiliated by a known attacker. But cyberbullies hide behind a veil of anonymity, using e-mails, text messaging, social networking websites, blogging, and other communication technologies to ridicule, threaten, and lie about their victim. In a typical incident, one high schooler was stunned to discover that he was the subject of a web page titled "Welcome to the Page That Makes Fun of Dave Knight."

Cyberbullying is disturbingly common: About 15 percent of students report abusing someone else online, and twice as many report having been victims. The consequences of cyberbullying can be devastating. Online abuse leaves victims feeling angry, frustrated, sad, frightened, and embarrassed. Targets often respond with apathy and cheating in school, substance abuse, violence, and self-destructive behaviors. Perhaps the most infamous case is that of Megan Meier, a 13-year-old middle school student who committed suicide after a prolonged bullying campaign coordinated by the mother of a teenage neighbor who had parted ways with Megan.

Cases like these show that the climate created by cyberbullying is more than just chilly—it's downright cold and cruel.

Wade, A., & Beran, T. (2011). Cyberbullying: The new era of bullying. *Canadian Journal of School Psychology, 26,* 44-61.

SELF-ASSESSMENT

Argumentativeness and Verbal Aggression

The following items are from two instruments developed by Dominic Infante and his colleagues (Infante & Rancer, 1982; Infante & Wigley, 1986; see Kotowski et al., 2009). Use the following scale to indicate how true each statement is for you.

1 = Almost never true

2 = Rarely true

3 = Occasionally true

4 = Often true

5 = Almost always true

PART 1

_____   1. While in an argument, I worry that the person I am arguing with will form a negative impression of me.

_____   2. Arguing over controversial issues improves my intelligence.

_____   3. Once I finish an argument, I promise myself that I will not get into another.

_____   4. Arguing with a person creates more problems than it solves.

_____   5. I have a pleasant, good feeling when I win a point in an argument.

_____   6. When I finish arguing with someone I feel nervous and upset.

_____   7. I enjoy a good argument over a controversial issue.

_____   8. I have the ability to do well in an argument.

_____   9. I try to avoid getting into arguments.

_____   10. I enjoy defending my point of view on an issue.

Interrupting Response As its name implies, an **interrupting response** occurs when one person begins to speak before the other is through making a point.

> _Customer:_ I'm looking for an outfit I can wear on a trip I'm . . .
> _Salesperson:_ I've got just the thing. It's part wool and part polyester, so it won't wrinkle at all.

PART 2

_____ 1. I am extremely careful to avoid attacking individuals' intelligence when I attack their ideas.

_____ 2. When individuals are very stubborn, I use insults to soften the stubbornness.

_____ 3. I try to make people feel good about themselves, even when their ideas are stupid.

_____ 4. When people refuse to do a task I know is important, without good reason, I tell them they are unreasonable.

_____ 5. When people criticize my shortcomings, I take it in good humor and do not try to get back at them.

_____ 6. When people simply will not budge on a matter of importance, I lose my temper and say rather strong things to them.

_____ 7. I refuse to participate in arguments when they involve personal attacks.

_____ 8. I like poking fun at people who do things that are very stupid in order to stimulate their intelligence.

_____ 9. When an argument shifts to personal attacks, I try very hard to change the subject.

_____ 10. When I am not able to refute others' positions, I try to make them feel defensive in order to weaken their positions.

SCORING:

For Part 1, add your scores on items 2, 5, 7, 8, and 10. This is your tendency to approach argumentative situations. Now, add your scores on 1, 3, 4, 6, and 9. This is your tendency to avoid argumentative situations. To compute your argumentativeness score, subtract the second sum from the first. The higher your score, the greater your predisposition to be argumentative (the possible range is from 0 to 20, with a midpoint of 10).

For Part 2, sum the scores on the 10 items after reversing the scoring for items 1, 3, 5, 7, and 9 (i.e., 5 = 1, 4 = 2, 3 = 3, 2 = 4, and 1 = 5). This is your verbal aggressiveness score—the higher the score, the greater your tendency to be verbally aggressive (the possible range is 10 to 50, with a midpoint of 30).

C: Actually, wrinkling isn't that important. I want something that will work as a business outfit and . . .

S: We have a terrific blazer that you can dress up or down, depending on the accessories you choose.

C: That's not what I was going to say. I want something that I can wear as a business outfit, but it ought to be on the informal side. I'm going to . . .

S: Say no more. I know just what you want.

C: Never mind. I think I'll look in some other stores.

Irrelevant Response It is disconfirming to respond with an **irrelevant response**, making comments totally unrelated to what the other person was just saying.

A: What a day! I thought it would never end. First the car overheated and I had to call a tow truck, and then the computer broke down at work.

B: Listen, we have to talk about a present for Ann's birthday. The party is on Saturday, and I only have tomorrow to shop for it.

A: I'm really beat. You won't believe what the boss did. Like I said, the computer was down, and in the middle of that mess he decided he absolutely had to have the sales figures for the last 6 months.

B: I just can't figure what would suit Ann. She's been so generous to us, and I can't think of anything she needs.

A: Why don't you listen to me? I beat my brains out all day and you don't give a damn.

B: And you don't care about me!

Tangential Response Unlike the three behaviors just discussed, a **tangential response** does acknowledge the other person's communication. However, the acknowledgment is used to steer the conversation in a new direction. Tangents can come in two forms. One is the "tangential shift," which is an abrupt change in conversation. For example, a young boy runs into the house excited, showing his mother the rock he found. She says, "Wash you hands; that rock is dirty." In a "tangential drift" the speaker makes a token connection with what the other person is saying and then moves the conversation in another direction entirely. In the same scenario, the mother might look at the rock, say "Hmmm, nice rock," and then immediately add, "Go wash your hands before dinner."

Impersonal Response In an **impersonal response**, the speaker conducts a monologue filled with detached, intellectualized, and generalized statements. The speaker never really interacts with the other on a personal level.

Employee: I've been having some personal problems lately, and I'd like to take off early a couple of afternoons to clear them up.

Boss: Ah, yes. We all have personal problems. It seems to be a sign of the times.

Ambiguous Response An **ambiguous response** contains a message with more than one meaning. The words are highly abstract or have meanings private to the speaker alone.

>   *A:* I'd like to get together with you soon. How about Tuesday?
>   *B:* Uh, maybe so. Anyhow, see you later.
>
>   *C:* Are you mad at me?
>   *D:* I feel the same about you as I always do.

Incongruous Response An **incongruous response** contains two messages that seem to deny or contradict each other, one at the verbal level and the other at the nonverbal level.

>   *He:* Darling, I love you!
>   *She:* I love you too. (*giggles*)
>
>   *Teacher:* Did you enjoy the class?
>   *Student:* Yes. (*yawns*)

It's important to note again that disconfirming messages, like virtually every other type of communication, are a matter of perception. A message that might not be intended to devalue the other person can be interpreted as disconfirming. For example, your failure to return a phone call or respond to the e-mail of a friend might simply be the result of a busy schedule, but if the other person views the lack of contact as a sign that you don't value the relationship, the effect will be just as strong as if you had deliberately intended to convey a slight.

DEFENSIVENESS

It's no surprise that disconfirming and disagreeing messages can pollute a communication climate. Perhaps the most predictable reaction to a hostile or indifferent message is defensiveness.

The word *defensiveness* suggests protecting yourself from attack, but what kind of attack? Seldom when you become defensive is a physical threat involved. If you're not threatened by bodily injury, what *are* you guarding against? To answer this question, we need to talk more about notions of **presenting self** and **face**, both of which were introduced in Chapter 3. Recall that the presenting self consists of the physical traits, personality characteristics, attitudes, aptitudes,

"Go ask your search engine."

F⊕CUS ON RESEARCH

Saving Face While Delivering Bad News

It's never easy being the bearer of bad tidings. However, providing negative feedback is a "necessary evil" of being a supervisor, according to Catherine Kingsley Westerman and David Westerman. They conducted a study to learn how best to offer critical appraisals while saving face for both the boss and the employee.

Not surprisingly, research participants said that bad news from a supervisor was easier to take when it was offered with face-saving statements such as, "What was expected of you may not have been clear" and "You're on the right track and your work has potential." Phrases like these also led to more positive perceptions of the bosses who delivered them. In other words, critical appraisals couched with supportive comments helped save face for both parties.

The researchers also found that face-saving criticism is better received in face-to-face interaction than through email. It appears that when delivering tough news, a supervisor would do well to have a variety of verbal and nonverbal cues available—and that the "personal" approach is best.

Kingsley Westerman, C. Y., & Westerman, D. (2010). Supervisor impression management: Message content and channel effects on impressions. *Communication Studies, 61*, 585–601.

and all the other parts of the image you want to present to the world. Actually, it is a mistake to talk about a single face: We try to project different selves to different people. For instance, you might try to impress a potential employer with your seriousness but want your friends to see you as a joker.

When others are willing to accept and acknowledge important parts of our presenting image, there is no need to feel defensive. On the other hand, when others confront us with **face-threatening acts**—messages that we perceive as challenging the image we want to project—we are likely to resist what they say. **Defensiveness**, then, is the process of protecting our presenting self, our face.

You can understand how defensiveness operates by imagining what might happen if an important part of your presenting self were attacked. For instance, suppose an instructor criticized you for making a stupid mistake. Or consider how you would feel if a friend called you self-centered or your boss labeled you as lazy. You would probably feel threatened if these attacks were untrue. But your own experience will probably show that you sometimes respond defensively even when you know that others' criticism is justified. For instance, you have probably responded defensively at times when you *did* make a mistake, act selfishly, or cut corners in your work (Zhang & Stafford, 2008). In fact, we often feel most defensive when criticism is right on target (Becker et al., 2008; Stamp et al., 1992).

The topics that trigger defensiveness vary. Sometimes sensitive topics are personal. You might feel a strong need to protect your image of athletic skill or intelligence, while another person might be more concerned with appearing fashionable or funny. Some research suggests that defense-provoking topics can vary by sex. In one study, men interpreted messages about mental or physical errors (such as misfiling a file or tripping on a carpet) more defensively than women did. Males and females got equally defensive about messages about their clothes and hair, but women got more defensive about messages regarding weight (Futch & Edwards, 1999). And professional women report a variety of face-threatening interactions in the workplace, particularly with men in traditionally male occupations (Irizarry, 2004).

Who offers the potentially defense-arousing remark or criticism also matters. Matthew Hornsey and his colleagues (2002) conducted three experiments examining group members' responses to criticism from in-group (other Australians) and out-group (people from another country) members. They found that in-group criticisms were tolerated surprisingly well, while out-group criticisms were met with defensiveness—probably because in-group criticisms are seen as more legitimate and more constructive.

So far, we have talked about defensiveness as if it is only the responsibility of the person who feels threatened. If this were the case, then the prescription would be simple: Grow a thick skin, admit your flaws, and stop trying to manage impressions. This approach isn't just unrealistic—it also ignores the role played by those who send face-threatening messages. In fact, competent communicators protect others' face needs as well as their own. For example, the people college students judge as close friends are those who provide "positive face support" by endorsing the presenting image of others (Cupach & Messman, 1999). Skilled instructors carefully protect their students' presenting faces, especially when offering constructive criticism (Trees et al., 2009). This facework leads to less defensive responses from their students. Findings like this make it clear that defensiveness is *interactive:* all communicators contribute to the climate of a relationship.

As a practical example of these concepts, communication researcher Sarah Tracy (2002) analyzed emergency call-center interactions to understand better how and why these conversations sometimes turn into contentious struggles. Tracy concluded that callers become defensive when they perceive call-takers' questions to be face-threatening, and she offered suggestions for making the climate more supportive. For instance, changing a question from "Tell me if . . ." to "Can you tell me if . . ." adds only a few words—but those words soften the inquiry and make it more of a request than a demand. Changes like this take very little extra time, and they have the potential to keep the climate supportive rather than defensive—and in 911 calls, that's a small investment that can save a life.

CLIMATE PATTERNS

Once a communication climate is formed, it can take on a life of its own. The pattern can be either positive or negative. In one study of married couples, each spouse's response in conflict situations was found to be similar to the other's statement (Burggraf & Sillars, 1987). Conciliatory

	1 2 3 4 5 6 7 8 9 10 11 12 13 14 15 16 17 18 19 20 21 22 23 24 25 26 27 28 29 30 31	R	H	E
TAT	3 0 0 1 0 0 0 0 0 0 6 0 0 0 1 0 0 0 0 0 8 0 0 3 9 7 1 1 2 6 48	63	6	
TIT	3 0 0 1 0 0 0 0 0 0 6 0 0 0 1 0 0 0 0 0 8 0 0 3 9 7 1 1 2 6 48	63	6	

GAME CALLED ON ACCOUNT OF INFINITY

statements (for example, support, accepting responsibility, agreeing) were likely to be followed by conciliatory responses. Confrontive acts (for example, criticism, hostile questions, faultfinding) were likely to trigger an aggressive response. The same pattern held for other kinds of messages: Avoidance led to avoidance, analysis evoked analysis, and so on. This was also found in a study on disagreements of married couples (Newton & Burgoon, 1990). Video-taped interactions revealed that accusations from one partner triggered accusations in response, and that communication satisfaction was highest when both partners used supportive rather than accusatory tactics.

This reciprocal pattern can be represented as a **spiral** (Wilmot, 1987). Some spirals are negative. In poorly adjusted and abusive couples, for example, one spouse's complaint is likely to produce a countercomplaint or denial by the other (Sutter & Martin, 1999). Even among well-adjusted couples, negative communication is more likely to be reciprocated than positive; and once hostility is expressed, it usually escalates (Cahn, 1992). The cartoon on this page provides an amusing but sad image of how negative spirals can take on a life of their own.

Fortunately, spirals can also work in a positive direction. One confirming behavior can lead to a similar response from the other person, which in turn leads to further confirmation by the first person. However, whether positive or negative, spirals rarely go on indefinitely. When a negative spiral gets out of hand, the partners might agree to back off from their disconfirming behavior. "Hold on," one might say, "this is getting us nowhere." At this point there may be a cooling-off period, or the partners might work together more constructively to solve their problem (Becker et al., 2008). This ability to "rebound" from negative spirals and turn them in a positive direction is a hallmark of successful relationships (Gottman & Levenson, 1999). However, if the partners pass "the point of no return" and continue spiraling downward, the relationship may end. As you read in Chapter 1, it's impossible to take back a message once it has been sent, and some exchanges are so lethal that the relationship can't survive them. Positive spirals also have their limit: Even the best relationships go through rocky periods in which the climate suffers. However, the accumulated goodwill and communication ability of the partners can make these times less frequent and intense.

Creating Positive Climates

||||||||||||||||||||||||||||||||||||||||||||||||||||||||||||||||||||||||||||||||||||||||||||||||||||||||

Even the "best" message isn't guaranteed to create a positive climate. A comment of praise can be interpreted as sarcasm; an innocent smile can be perceived as a sneer; an offer to help can be seen as condescension. Because human communication is so complex, there aren't any foolproof words, phrases, or formulas for creating positive climates. Nonetheless, research suggests that there *are* strategies that can increase the odds of expressing yourself in ways that lead to positive relational climates—even when the message you're delivering is a tough one.

REDUCING DEFENSIVENESS

Several decades ago, psychologist Jack Gibb published a helpful study (1961, 2008) that isolated six types of defense-arousing communication and six contrasting behaviors that seem to reduce the level of threat and defensiveness. These "Gibb categories" are listed in Table 10.1. Gibb's findings have commonsense appeal and multiple applications. As a result, they've played an important part in communication textbooks, training seminars, journals, and research studies (e.g., Becker et al., 2008; Czech & Forward, 2010). We'll use them here to discuss how positive climates can be created by sending supportive rather than defense-provoking messages.

Evaluation versus Description The first type of defense-arousing message Gibb identified is **evaluation**. An evaluative message judges the other person, usually in a negative way. For instance, consider this message: "You don't care about me!" Evaluative messages like this possess several characteristics that make them so face-threatening. They judge what the other person is feeling rather than describing the speaker's thoughts, feelings, and wants. They don't explain how the speaker arrived at his or her conclusion, and they lack specifics. Furthermore, they're often phrased in the kind of

---

TABLE 10.1 The Gibb Categories of Defensive
and Supportive Behaviors

DEFENSIVE BEHAVIORS	SUPPORTIVE BEHAVIORS
1. Evaluation	1. Description
2. Control	2. Problem Orientation
3. Strategy	3. Spontaneity
4. Neutrality	4. Empathy
5. Superiority	5. Equality
6. Certainty	6. Provisionalism

defense-arousing "you" language described in Chapter 5. It's easy to understand why evaluative statements often trigger a defensive spiral.

Do the climate-threatening properties of evaluative messages mean that it's impossible to register a legitimate complaint? No: It simply means that you must be alert to more constructive ways to do so. **Description** is a way to offer your thoughts, feelings, and wants without judging the listener. Descriptive messages make documented observations that are specific and concrete. As we mentioned earlier when discussing complaining, description focuses on behavior that can be changed rather than on personal characteristics that cannot. In addition, descriptive messages often use "I" language, which tends to provoke less defensiveness than "you" language (Heydenberk & Heydenberk, 2007; Proctor & Wilcox, 1993). Contrast the evaluative "You don't care about me" with this more descriptive message: "I'm sorry that we don't spend as much time together as we did during the summer. When we don't talk during the week, I sometimes feel unimportant. Maybe we could set up a phone-call time on Wednesdays—that would mean a lot to me."

Let's look at more examples of the difference between evaluative and descriptive messages:

Evaluation	Description
You're not making any sense.	I don't understand the point you're trying to make.
You're inconsiderate.	I would appreciate it if you'd let me know when you're running late—I was worried.
That's an ugly tablecloth.	I'm not crazy about big blue stripes: I like something more subtle.

Note several characteristics of these descriptive messages. First, their focus is on the speaker's thoughts, feelings, and wants, with little or no judgment of the other person. Second, the messages address specific behaviors rather than making sweeping character generalizations (for example, "you don't care"). The messages also provide information about how the speaker arrived at these conclusions. Finally—and perhaps most important—notice that each of the descriptive statements is just as honest as their evaluative counterparts. Once you have learned to speak descriptively, you can be as direct and straightforward as ever, while avoiding personal attacks that can poison a climate.

Control versus Problem Orientation A second defense-provoking message involves some attempt to control another. **Controlling communication** occurs when a sender seems to be imposing a solution on the receiver with little regard for that person's needs or interests. The object of control can involve almost anything: where to eat dinner, how to spend a large sum of money, or whether to remain in a relationship. Whatever the situation, people who act in controlling ways create a defensive climate. None of us likes to feel that our ideas are worthless and that nothing we say will change other people's minds—yet this is precisely the attitude a controller communicates. Whether done with words, gestures, tone of voice, or through some other channel, whether control is accomplished through status, insistence on obscure or irrelevant rules, or physical power, the controller generates hostility wherever he or she goes. The unspoken message such behavior communicates is "I know what's best for you, and if you do as I say, we'll get along."

In **problem orientation**, however, communicators focus on finding a solution that satisfies both their own needs and those of the others involved. The goal here isn't to "win" at the expense of your partner but to work out some arrangement in which everybody feels like a winner. (Chapter 11 has a great deal to say about "win-win" problem solving as a way to find problem-oriented solutions.) Problem orientation is often typified by "we" language (see Chapter 5), which suggests the speaker is making decisions *with* rather than *for* other people (Seider et al., 2009). University chairpersons found to be most effective by members of their departments were best characterized as using few control communications and adopting a problem orientation (Czech & Forward, 2010).

Here are some examples of how some controlling and problem-orientation messages might sound:

Controlling	Problem Oriented
Get off the computer—now! I need to talk to you.	"I really need to talk soon. Can you take a break?"
There's only one way to handle this problem . . .	Looks like we have a problem. Let's work out a solution we can both live with.
Either you start working harder, or you're fired!	The production in your department hasn't been as high as I'd hoped. Any ideas on what we could do?

Strategy versus Spontaneity Gibb uses the word **strategy** to characterize defense-arousing messages in which speakers hide their ulterior motives. The terms *dishonesty* and *manipulation* reflect the nature of strategy. Even if the intentions that motivate strategic communication are honorable, the victim of deception who discovers the attempt to deceive is likely to feel offended at being played for a sucker. Even when giving help is involved, people rarely feel grateful for help given with an ulterior motive (Tsang, 2006).

As we discussed in Chapter 7, counterfeit questions are a form of strategic communication because they try to trap others into desired responses.

Many sales techniques are strategic, for they give customers limited information and then make it difficult to say no. This is not to say that all sales techniques are wrong or unethical, but most strategic ones aren't well-suited for interpersonal relationships. If you've ever gotten defensive when you thought a friend was doing a "sales job" on you, you understand the concept.

Spontaneity is the behavior that contrasts with strategy. Spontaneity simply means being honest with others rather than manipulating them. What it doesn't mean is blurting out what you're thinking as soon as an idea comes to you. As we discussed in Chapter 3, there are appropriate (and inappropriate) times for self-disclosure. You would undoubtedly threaten others' presenting selves if you were "spontaneous" about every opinion that crossed your mind. That's not what Gibb intended in using the term spontaneity. What he was after was setting aside hidden agendas that others both sense and resist. You can probably recall times when someone asked you a question and you suspiciously responded with "Hmmm . . . why do you want to know?" Your defensive antennae were up because you detected an underlying strategy. If the person had told you up front why he or she was asking the question, then your defenses probably would have been lowered. That's what we mean by spontaneity. Here are some examples:

Strategy	Spontaneity
What are you doing Friday after work?	I have a piano I need to move Friday after work. Can you give me a hand?
Have you ever considered another line of work?	I'm concerned about your job performance over the last year; let's set up a time to talk about it.
Ali and Kasey go out to dinner every week.	I'd like to go out for dinner more often.

This is a good place to pause and talk about larger issues regarding the Gibb model. First, Gibb's emphasis on being direct is better suited for a low-context culture like the United States, which values straight-talk, than for high-context cultures. Second, there are ways in which each of the communication approaches Gibb labels as "supportive" can be used to exploit others and, therefore, violate the spirit of positive climate building. For instance, consider spontaneity. Although it sounds paradoxical at first, spontaneity can be a strategy, too. Sometimes you'll see people using honesty in a calculating way, being just frank enough to win someone's trust or sympathy. This "leveling" is probably the most defense-arousing strategy of all because once we've learned someone is using frankness as a manipulation, there's almost no chance we'll ever trust that person again.

Neutrality versus Empathy Gibb used the term **neutrality** to describe a fourth behavior that arouses defensiveness. Probably a better word would be indifference. For example, 911 emergency telephone dispatchers are taught to be neutral in order to calm down the caller, but they shouldn't communicate indifference or a lack of caring (Shuler & Sypher, 2000). Using Gibb's terminology, a neutral attitude is disconfirming because it communicates a lack of concern for the welfare of another and implies that the other person isn't very important to you. This perceived indifference is likely to promote defensiveness because people do not like to think of themselves as worthless, and they'll protect a self-concept that sees them as worthwhile.

The poor effects of neutrality become apparent when you consider the hostility that most people have for the large, impersonal organizations with which they have to deal: "They think of me as a number instead of a person"; "I felt as if I were being handled by computers and not human beings." These common statements reflect reactions to being treated in an indifferent, neutral way.

The behavior that contrasts with neutrality is **empathy**. Gibb found that empathy helps rid communication of the quality of indifference. When people show that they care for the feelings of another, there's little chance that the person's self-concept will be threatened. Empathy means accepting another's feelings, putting yourself in another's place. This doesn't mean you need to agree with that person. By simply letting someone know about your care and respect, you'll be acting in a supportive way. Gibb noted the importance of nonverbal messages in communicating empathy. He found that facial and bodily expressions of concern are often more important to the receiver than the words used.

We addressed the concept of empathy in Chapter 4 and the skill of empathizing in Chapter 7; let's see what empathic messages look like when contrasted with neutral ones:

Neutrality	Empathy
This is what happens when you don't plan properly.	Ouch—looks like this didn't turn out the way you expected.
Sometimes things just don't work out. That's the way it goes.	I know you put a lot of time and effort into this project.
Don't get too excited—Everybody gets promoted sooner or later.	I'll bet you're pretty excited about the promotion.

Superiority versus Equality A fifth behavior creating a defensive climate involves **superiority**. A body of research describes how patronizing messages irritate receivers ranging from young students to senior citizens (Draper, 2005; Harwood et al., 1997). Any message that suggests "I'm better than you" is likely to arouse feelings of defensiveness in the recipients.

Many times in our lives we communicate with people who possess less talent or knowledge than we do, but it isn't necessary to convey an attitude of superiority in these situations. Gibb found ample evidence that many who have superior skills and talents are capable of projecting feelings of **equality** rather than superiority. Such people communicate that although they may have greater talent in certain areas, they see other human beings as having just as much worth as themselves.

ON EQUAL FOOTING: *THE KING'S SPEECH*

On the eve of World War II, Prince Albert Frederick Arthur George (Colin Firth) reluctantly ascends to the throne of England. The new king is paralyzed by a humiliating stutter that undermines his ability to rally the British Empire to resist the Nazi juggernaut.

After a series of prestigious but ineffective professionals fail to help, the King travels incognito to the basement flat of Australian speech coach Lionel Logue (Geoffrey Rush). Logue's approach is unconventional. He insists on addressing his royal client by his family nickname of "Bertie," saying that in therapy "it's better that we're equals."

At first, the King—a shy, aloof, but proud man—bridles at Logue's approach. But as the two men work together, two minor miracles happen. The King's speech becomes more fluent, and a lifelong friendship grows between commoner and monarch.

The King's Speech is a touching reminder that, in close relationships, mutual affection and respect are far more important than social roles.

Charles and Elizabeth Beck (1996) observe that equality is put to the test when a person doesn't have superior skills, yet is in a position of authority. Supervisors sometimes have less expertise in certain areas than their subordinates but believe it would be beneath them to admit it. Think for a moment: You've probably been in situations where you knew more about the subject than the person in charge—be it a boss, a teacher, a parent, or a salesperson—yet this person acted as if he or she knew more. Did you feel defensive? No doubt. Did that person feel defensive? Probably. You both were challenging each other's presenting self, so the climate most likely became hostile. A truly secure person can treat others with equality even when there are obvious differences in knowledge, talent, and status. Doing so creates a positive climate in which ideas are evaluated not on the basis of who contributed them, but rather on the merit of the ideas themselves.

What does equality sound like? Here are some examples:

Superiority	Equality
When you get to be in my position someday, *then* you'll understand.	I'd like to hear how the issue looks to you. Then I can tell you how it looks to me.
No, not that way! Let me show you how to do it right.	What if you tried it this way?
You really believe *that*?	Here's another way to think about it . . .

Certainty versus Provisionalism Have you ever run into people who are positive they're right, who know that theirs is the only or proper way of doing something, who insist that they have all the facts and need no additional information? If you have, you've met individuals who project the defense-arousing behavior Gibb calls **certainty**.

How do you react when you're the target of such certainty? Do you suddenly find your energy directed to proving the dogmatic individual wrong? If you do, you're reacting normally—if not very constructively.

Communicators who regard their own opinions with certainty while disregarding the ideas of others demonstrate a lack of regard for others. It's

"What do you mean 'Your guess is as good as mine'? My guess is a hell of lot <u>better</u> than your guess!"

likely the receiver will take the certainty as a personal affront and react defensively.

In contrast to dogmatic certainty is **provisionalism**, in which people may have strong opinions but are willing to acknowledge that they don't have a corner on the truth and will change their stand if another position seems more reasonable. Provisionalism often surfaces in a person's word choice. While certainty regularly uses the terms *can't, never, always, must,* and *have to,* provisionalism uses *perhaps, maybe, possibly, might,* and *may.* It's not that provisional people are spineless; they simply recognize that discussion is aided by open-minded messages. Katt and Collins (2009) found that when teachers use provisional language, it helps motivate students, and Winer and Majors (1981) found that provisional word choice does indeed enhance communication climate.

Let's look at some examples:

Certainty	Provisionalism
That will *never* work!	My guess is that you'll run into problems with that approach.
You'll hate that class! Stay away from it!	I didn't like that class very much; I'm not sure you would, either.
You won't get anywhere without a college education: Mark my words.	I think it's important to get that degree. I found it was hard to land an interview until I had one.

You've probably noticed a great deal of overlap among the various Gibb components—overlap confirmed by researchers (Forward & Czech, 2008). For instance, look at the final example under "Provisionalism." The statement is likely to create a positive climate, not only because it is provisional rather than certain, but also because it is descriptive rather than evaluative, problem-oriented rather than controlling, and equal rather than superior. You may also have noticed a tone underlying all of the supportive examples: *respect.* By valuing and confirming others—even if you disagree with them—you create a respectful climate that helps enhance a positive communication climate, both now and in future interactions. Communication scholars Sonja Foss and Cindy Griffin (1995) use the term *invitational rhetoric* to describe this sort of respectful approach that strives to understand others and invite them to see your point of view, rather than dominating them in defense-provoking ways. There are no guarantees of your achieving positive responses or outcomes, but by sending supportive messages, your odds for interpersonal success should improve.

OFFERING CONSTRUCTIVE CRITICISM

Gibb's supportive behaviors can work in a variety of situations, including times when you have a message that's likely to be taken as criticism. But along with being descriptive, problem-oriented, honest, empathic, egalitarian, and open-minded, you can exhibit attitudes and skills that are especially helpful when you want or need to offer constructive criticism.

Check Your Motives There are times when telling others what you think, feel, and want is primarily for *your* own good, not theirs. In those cases, it's more appropriate to use assertive "I" messages, described in Chapter 5 (pages 162–163).

Unlike criticism aimed at benefiting yourself, the goal of *constructive* criticism is to offer information that both helps the other person and preserves the relationship. It isn't about venting pent-up anger, unloading for catharsis, or trying to get even. Before offering constructive criticism, you would do well to check your motives to be sure you have the other person's interests in mind—or at the very least, that you're not motivated by ill will or revenge.

Choose a Good Time Although it's tempting to "teach someone a lesson" the moment they've done something that bothers you, that's often the worst time to do so. At those moments, both the other person's embarrassment and your frustration are probably running high. Marriage researcher John Gottman (Gottman & Silver, 1999) says that a "harsh startup" is a key predictor of conversations that turn into destructive fights, so getting off on the right foot is crucial. Ideally, it's best to wait for a time—or perhaps even arrange one—when both people can calmly and rationally discuss the issue of concern.

Buffer Negatives with Positives One way to start off on the right foot is to focus on positives. A popular approach for offering constructive criticism is known as the **sandwich (or hamburger)**

method (e.g., Just, 2007; Kohn & O'Connell, 2005; Yasir & Sajid, 2010). The idea is to sandwich your issue of concern between two positive comments. Here's an example in which one coworker approaches another:

- *Positive comment:* "It's been great being on the same shift the past few months. You're a hard worker and we've had a lot of fun."

- *Issue of concern:* "There's one thing, though: The past two weeks, you've showed up a half hour late almost every day. I know it's tough to get here early in the morning—for me, too—but it means that I end up doing both your work and mine, so we can open at noon."

- *Positive comment:* "I really hope we can figure out a way to resolve this because I want to keep working together on the same shift."

Research shows that buffering criticism with praise is effective because it helps the recipient perceive the comments as constructive and well intentioned (Hornsey et al., 2008). The same study showed that criticism is also better received when the message-sender acknowledges having similar shortcomings ("for me, too"). Doing so communicates Gibb's supportive climate components of equality and empathy.

It's important to note that methods like the sandwich can easily turn into hackneyed and insincere techniques. When that happens, they ring of Gibb's defensive components of strategy and control. For the sandwich approach to work, it's vital that the praise being offered is genuine—and that the criticism is a clear behavioral description. Moreover, if the *only* time you praise people is prior to criticizing them, they will likely grow leery of your positive comments, assuming the other shoe is about to drop (Kingsley Westerman & Westerman, 2010). Rather than viewing the sandwich method as a technique to use rigidly, it's better to understand and follow its underlying principle: Positive comments and praise make criticism easier to swallow. (See the Focus on Research sidebar on page 322 for further support of this principle.) As the well-known song accurately suggests, a spoonful of sugar *does* help the medicine go down.

Follow Up Constructive criticism shouldn't be a "hit-and-run" event. If the recipient makes positive changes as a result of your discussion, it's important to acknowledge them. Of course, it's also vital not to sound patronizing when doing so, which will likely generate a defensive response. Simple descriptions offered in supportive tones can go a long way toward reinforcing positive behaviors that enhance relationships:

"Thanks for being on time this week—it sure made things less crazy in the kitchen."
"I appreciate your forwarding me fewer e-mails—it helped me focus on the important ones you sent my way."
"Thanks for cutting back on the complaining—it makes a big difference for me."

Transforming Negative Climates

The world would be a happier place if everyone communicated supportively. But how can you respond nondefensively when others use evaluation, control, superiority, and all the other attacking behaviors Gibb identified? Despite your best intentions, it's difficult to be reasonable when you're faced with a torrent of criticism. Being attacked is hard enough when the critic is clearly being unfair, but it's often even more threatening when the judgments are on target. Despite the accuracy of your critic, the tendency is either to counterattack defensively with a barrage of verbal aggression or to withdraw nonassertively. Since these responses aren't likely to resolve a dispute, we need alternative ways of behaving. There are two such methods. Despite their apparent simplicity, they have proven to be among the most valuable skills communicators can learn.

SEEK MORE INFORMATION

The response of seeking more information makes good sense when you realize that it's foolish to respond to a critical attack until you understand what the other person has said (Gold & Castillo, 2010). Even comments that on first consideration appear to be totally unjustified or foolish often prove to contain at least a grain of truth and sometimes much more.

Many readers object to the idea of asking for details when they are criticized. Their resistance grows from confusing the act of *listening open-mindedly* to a speaker's comments with *accepting* them. Once you realize that you can listen to, understand, and even acknowledge the most hostile comments without necessarily accepting them, it becomes much easier to hear another person out. If you disagree with a speaker's objections, you will be in a much better position to explain yourself once you understand the criticism. On the other hand, after carefully listening to the other person's remarks, you might just see that they are valid, in which case you have learned some valuable information about yourself. In either case, you have everything to gain and nothing to lose by paying attention to the critic.

Of course, after years of instinctively resisting criticism, learning to listen to the other person will take some practice. To make matters clearer, here are several ways in which you can seek additional information from your critics.

Ask for Specifics Often the vague attack of a critic is virtually useless, even if you sincerely want to change. Abstract accusations such as "you're being unfair" or "you never help out" can be difficult to understand. In such cases it is a good idea to request more specific information from the sender. "What do I *do* that's unfair?" is an important question to ask before you can judge whether the accusation is correct. "When haven't I helped out?" you might ask before agreeing with or disputing the accusation.

If you already solicit specifics by using questions and are still accused of reacting defensively, the problem may be in the *way* you ask. Your tone of voice and facial expression, posture, or other nonverbal clues can give the same words radically different connotations. For example, think of how you could use the question, "Exactly what are you talking about?" to communicate either a genuine desire to know or your belief that the speaker is crazy. It's important to request specific information only when you genuinely want to learn more from the speaker; asking under any other circumstances will only make matters worse.

Guess about Specifics On some occasions even your sincere and well-phrased requests for specific details won't meet with success. Sometimes your critics won't be able to define precisely the behavior they find offensive. In these instances, you'll hear such comments as, "I can't tell you exactly what's wrong with your sense of humor—all I can say is that I don't like it." In other cases, your critics may know the exact behaviors they don't like, but for some reason they seem to get a perverse satisfaction out of making you struggle to figure them out. In instances like these, you can often learn more clearly what is bothering your critic by *guessing* at the specifics of a complaint. In a sense you become both detective and suspect, the goal being to figure out exactly what "crime" you have committed. Like the technique of asking for specifics, guessing must be done with goodwill if it's to produce satisfying results. You need to convey to the critic that for both of your sakes you're truly interested in finding out what is the matter. Once you have communicated this intention, the emotional climate generally becomes more comfortable because, in effect, both you and the critic are seeking the same goal.

MEDIA CLIP

EVERYONE'S A CRITIC: PERFORMANCE CONTESTS ON TV

Performance contests like *American Idol, Top Chef,* and *So You Think You Can Dance* have become a staple of television, both in the United States and around the world. These shows require contestants to put their talent on the line before a panel of judges who publicly critique their skills. Receiving criticism is always a challenge, but particularly so when a huge audience is watching.

Judges typically render their verdict in several ways. Some are blunt and judgmental ("That was awful!"). Others are broad and vague ("That didn't work"). The most helpful criticisms focus on specific behaviors and suggestions for change ("You would do better to focus less on being showy and more on executing perfectly").

On the receiving end, performers don't always respond well to suggestions. Many quickly defend themselves ("I thought I did just fine") or shift the blame ("I didn't choose the song"). Others follow principles described in this chapter, such as seeking more information or agreeing with the critic, hoping to improve their next performance.

Performance contests are designed for entertainment, not education—but from a communication perspective, they offer valuable lessons about giving and receiving criticism.

Here are some typical questions you might hear from someone guessing about the details of another's criticism:

"So you object to the language I used in writing the paper. Was my language too formal?"

"OK, I understand that you think the outfit looks funny. What is it that's so bad? Is it the color? Does it have something to do with the fit? The design?"

"When you say that I'm not doing my share around the house, do you mean that I haven't been helping enough with the cleaning?"

Paraphrase the Speaker's Ideas Another strategy is to draw out confused or reluctant speakers by paraphrasing their thoughts and feelings, using the reflective listening skills described in Chapter 7. Paraphrasing is especially good in helping others solve their problems—and since people generally criticize you because your behavior creates some problem for them, the method is especially appropriate at such times.

One advantage of paraphrasing is that you don't have to guess about the specifics of your behavior that might be offensive. By clarifying or amplifying what you understand critics to be saying, you'll learn more about their objections. A brief dialogue between a disgruntled customer and a store manager who is an exceptional listener might sound like this:

Customer: The way you people run this store is disgusting! I just want to tell you that I'll never shop here again.

Manager: (*reflecting the customer's feeling*) It seems that you're quite upset. Can you tell me your problem?

Customer: It isn't *my* problem; it's the problem your salespeople have. They seem to think it's a great inconvenience to help a customer find anything around here.

Manager: So you didn't get enough help locating the items you were looking for, is that it?

Customer: Help? I spent 20 minutes looking around in here before I even talked to a clerk. All I can say is that it's a lousy way to run a store.

Manager: So what you're saying is that the clerks seemed to be ignoring the customers?

Customer: No. They were all busy with other people. It just seems to me that you ought to have enough help around to handle the crowds that come in at this hour.

Manager: I understand now. What frustrated you the most was the fact that we didn't have enough staff to serve you promptly.

Customer: That's right. I have no complaint with the service I get once I'm waited on, and I've always thought you had a good selection here. It's just that I'm too busy to wait so long for help.

Manager: Well, I'm glad you brought this to my attention. We certainly don't want loyal customers going away mad. I'll try to see that it doesn't happen again.

This conversation illustrates two advantages of paraphrasing. First, the critic often reduces the intensity of the attack once the attacker realizes that the complaint is being heard. Criticism often grows from the frustration of unmet needs—which in this case was partly a lack of attention. As soon as the manager genuinely demonstrated interest in the customer's plight, the customer began to feel better and was able to leave the store relatively calmly. Of course, paraphrasing won't always mollify your critic, but even when it doesn't there's still another benefit that makes the technique worthwhile. In the sample conversation, for instance, the manager learned some valuable information by taking time to understand the customer. As you read earlier, even apparently outlandish criticism often contains at least a grain of truth, and thus a person who is genuinely interested in improving would be wise to hear it out—especially when the complaint is coming from a valued customer (Homburg & Fürst, 2007).

Ask What the Critic Wants Sometimes your critic's demand will be obvious:

"Turn down that music!"
"I wish you'd remember to tell me about phone messages."
"Would you clean up your dirty dishes *now?!*"

In other cases, however, you'll need to do some investigating to find out what the critic wants from you:

A: I can't believe you invited all those people over without asking me first!
B: Are you saying you want me to cancel the party?
A: No, I just wish you'd ask me before you make plans.

C: You're so critical! It sounds like you don't like *anything* about this paper.
D: But you asked for my opinion. What do you expect me to do when you ask?
C: I want to know what's wrong, but I don't just want to hear criticisms. If you think there's anything good about my work, I wish you'd tell me that too.

This last example illustrates the importance of accompanying your questions with the right nonverbal behavior. It's easy to imagine two ways D could have said, "What do you expect me to do when you ask?" One would show a genuine desire to clarify what C wanted, while the other would have been clearly hostile and defensive. As with all of the styles in this section, your responses to criticism have to be sincere in order to work.

Ask about the Consequences of Your Behavior As a rule, people complain about your actions only when some need of theirs is not being met. One way to respond to this kind of criticism is to find out exactly what troublesome consequences your behavior has for them. You'll often find that actions that seem perfectly legitimate to you cause some difficulty for your critic; once you have understood this, comments that previously sounded foolish take on a new meaning:

Neighbor A: You say that I ought to have my cat neutered. Why is that important to you?

Neighbor B: Because at night he picks fights with my cat, and I'm tired of paying the vet's bills.

Worker A: Why do you care whether I'm late to work?

Worker B: Because when the boss asks, I feel obligated to make up some story so you won't get in trouble, and I don't like to lie.

Husband: Why does it bother you when I lose money at poker? You know I never gamble more than I can afford.

Wife: It's not the cash itself. It's that when you lose, you're in a grumpy mood for 2 or 3 days, and that's no fun for me.

Ask What Else Is Wrong It might seem crazy to invite more criticism, but sometimes asking about other complaints can uncover the real problem:

A: Are you mad at me?

B: No, why are you asking?

A: Because the whole time we were at the picnic you hardly spent any time talking to me. In fact, it seemed like whenever I came over to where you were, you went off somewhere else.

B: Is anything else wrong?

A: Well, to be honest, I've been wondering lately if you're tired of me.

This example shows that asking if anything else bothers your critic isn't just an exercise in masochism. If you can keep your defensiveness in check, probing further can lead the conversation to issues that are the source of the critic's real dissatisfaction.

Soliciting more information from a critic sometimes isn't enough. For instance, what do you do when you fully understand the other person's objections and still feel a defensive response on the tip of your tongue? You know that if you try to protect yourself, you'll wind up in an argument; on the other hand, you simply can't accept what the other person is saying about you. The solution to such a dilemma is outrageously simple and is discussed in the following section.

AGREE WITH THE CRITIC

But, you protest, how can I honestly agree with comments I don't believe are true? The following pages will answer this question by showing that there's virtually no situation in which you can't honestly accept the other person's point of view and still maintain your position. To see how this can be so, you need to realize that there are several different types of agreement, one of which you can use in almost any situation (Michel, 2008).

Agree with the Truth Agreeing with the truth is easy to understand, though not always easy to practice. You agree with the truth when another person's criticism is factually correct:

> "You're right; I am angry."
> "I suppose I was just being defensive."
> "Now that you mention it, I did get pretty sarcastic."

Agreeing with the facts seems quite sensible when you realize that certain matters are indisputable. If you agree to be somewhere at 4:00 P.M. and don't show up until 5:00, you are late, no matter how good your explanation for tardiness is. If you've broken a borrowed object, run out of gas, or failed to finish a job you started, there's no point in denying the fact. In the same way, if you're honest you will have to agree with many interpretations of your behavior, even when they're not flattering. You do get angry, act foolishly, fail to listen, and behave inconsiderately. Once you rid yourself of the myth of perfection, it's much easier to acknowledge these truths.

If it's so obvious that the descriptions others give of your behaviors are often accurate, why is it so difficult to accept them without being defensive? The answer to this question lies in a confusion between agreeing with the *facts* and accepting the *judgment* that so often accompanies them. Most critics don't merely describe the action that offends them; they also evaluate it, and it's the evaluation that we resist:

> "It's silly to be angry."
> "You have no reason for being defensive."
> "You were wrong to be so sarcastic."

It's such judgments that we resent. By realizing that you can agree with—even learn from—the descriptive part of many criticisms and still not accept the accompanying evaluations, you'll often have a response that is both honest and nondefensive. A conversation between a teacher and a student illustrates this point:

> *Teacher:* Look at this paper! It's only two pages long, and it contains 12 misspelled words. I'm afraid you have a real problem with your writing.
> *Student:* You're right. I know I don't spell well at all.

T: I don't know what's happening in the lower grades. They just don't seem to be turning out people who can write a simple, declarative sentence.

S: You're not the first person I've heard say that.

T: I should think you'd be upset by the fact that after so much time in English composition classes you haven't mastered the basics of spelling.

S: You're right. It does bother me.

Notice that in agreeing with the teacher's comments the student did not in any way demean herself. Even though there might have been extenuating circumstances to account for her lack of skill, the student didn't find it necessary to justify her errors because she wasn't saddled with the burden of pretending to be perfect. By simply agreeing with the facts, she was able to maintain her dignity and avoid an unproductive argument.

Of course, in order to reduce defensiveness it's important that your agreement with the facts be honest and admitted without malice. It's humiliating to accept inaccurate descriptions, and maliciously pretending to agree with these only leads to trouble. You can imagine how unproductive the above conversation would have been if the student had spoken the same words in a sarcastic tone. Agree with the facts only when you can do so sincerely. Although it won't always be possible, you'll be surprised at how often you can use this simple response.

Agreeing with criticism is fine, but by itself it isn't an adequate response to your critic. For instance, once you've admitted to another that you are defensive, habitually late, or sarcastic, you can expect the other to ask what you intend to do about this behavior. Such questions are fair. In most cases it would be a mistake simply to understand another's criticism, to agree with the accusations, and then to go on behaving as before. Such behavior makes it clear that you have no concern for the speaker. The message that comes through is "Sure, now I understand what I've done to bother you. You're right, I have been doing it and I'll probably keep on doing it. If you don't like the way I've been behaving, that's tough!" Such a response might be appropriate for dealing with people you genuinely don't care about—manipulative solicitors, abusive strangers, and so on—but it is clearly not suitable for people who matter to you.

Before reading on, then, understand that responding nondefensively to criticism is only the *first* step in resolving the conflicts that usually prompt another's attack. In order to resolve your conflicts fully, you'll need to learn the conflict resolution skills described in Chapter 11.

Agree with the Odds Sometimes a critic will point out possible unpleasant consequences of your behavior:

"If you don't talk to more people, they'll think you're a snob."

"If you don't exercise more, you'll wind up having a heart attack one of these days."

"If you run around with that crowd, you'll probably be sorry."

Often such comments are genuinely helpful suggestions that others make for your own good. In other cases, however, they are really devices for manipulating you into behaving the way your critic wants you to. For instance, "If we go to the football game, you might catch cold" could mean "I don't want to go to the football game." "You'll probably be exhausted tomorrow if you stay up late" could be translated as "I want you to go to bed early." Chapter 11 will have more to say about such methods of indirect aggression, but for now it is sufficient to state that such warnings often generate defensiveness. A mother–son argument shows this outcome:

Mother: I don't see why you want to ride that motorcycle. You could wind up in an accident so easily. (*states the odds for an accident*)

Son: Oh, don't be silly. I'm a careful driver, and besides you know that I never take my bike on the freeway. (*denies the odds*)

M: Yes, but every time I pick up the paper I read about someone being hurt or killed. There's always a danger that some crazy driver will miss seeing you and run you off the road. (*states the odds of an injury*)

S: Oh, you worry too much. I always look out for the other driver. And besides, you have a lot better maneuverability on a motorcycle than in a car. (*denies the odds for an injury*)

M: I know you're careful, but all it takes is one mistake and you could be killed. (*states the odds for being killed*)

S: Somebody is killed shaving or taking a shower every day, but you don't want me to stop doing those things, do you? You're just exaggerating the whole thing. (*denies the odds for being killed*)

From this example you can see that it's usually counterproductive to deny another's predictions. You don't convince the critic, and your opinions stay unchanged as well. Notice the difference when you agree with the odds (though not the demands) of the critic:

M: I don't see why you want to drive that motorcycle. You could wind up in an accident so easily. (*states the odds for an accident*)

S: I suppose there is a chance of that. (*agrees with the odds*)

M: You're darned right. Every time I pick up the newspaper, I read about someone being hurt or killed. There's always a danger that some crazy driver will miss seeing you and run you off the road. (*states the odds for an injury*)

S: You're right; that could happen (*agrees with the odds*), but I don't think the risk is great enough to keep me off the bike.

M: That's easy for you to say now. Someday you could be sorry you didn't listen to me. (*states the odds for regret*)

S: That's true. I really might regret driving the bike someday—but I'm willing to take that chance. (*agrees with the odds*)

341

Notice how the son simply considers his mother's predictions and realistically acknowledges the chance that they might come true. While such responses might at first seem indifferent and callous, they can help the son avoid the pitfall of indirect manipulation. Suppose the conversation were a straightforward one in which the mother was simply pointing out to her son the dangers of motorcycle riding. He acknowledged that he understood her concern and even agreed with the possibility that her prediction could come true. If, however, her prediction were really an indirect way of saying "I don't want you to ride anymore," then the son's response would force her to clarify her demand so that he could deal with it openly. At this point they might be able to figure out a solution that lets the son satisfy his need for transportation and excitement and at the same time allows his mother to alleviate her concern.

In addition to bringing hidden agendas into the open for resolution, agreeing with the odds also helps you become aware of some possible previously unconsidered consequences of your actions. Instead of blindly denying the chance that your behavior is inappropriate, agreeing with the odds will help you look objectively at whether your course of action is in fact the best one. You might agree with your critic that you really should change your behavior.

Agree in Principle Criticism often comes in the form of abstract ideals against which you're unfavorably compared:

> "I wish you wouldn't spend so much time on your work. Relaxation is important too, you know."
> "You shouldn't expect so much from your kids. Nobody's perfect."
> "What do you mean, you're not voting? The government is only going to get better when people like you take more of an interest in it."
> "You mean you're still upset by that remark? You ought to learn how to take a joke better."

In cases like these, you can accept the principle upon which the criticism is based and still behave as you have been. After all, some rules do allow occasional exceptions, and people often are inconsistent. Consider how you might sincerely agree with the criticisms above without necessarily changing your behavior:

> "You're right. I am working hard now. It probably is unhealthy, but finishing the job is worth the extra strain to me."
> "I guess my expectations for the kids are awfully high, and I don't want to drive them crazy. I hope I'm not making a mistake."
> "You're right: If everybody stopped voting, the system would fall apart."
> "Maybe I *would* be happier if I could take a joke in stride. I'm not ready to do that, though, at least not for jokes like that one."

Agree with the Critic's Perception What about times when there seems to be no basis whatsoever for agreeing with your critics? You've listened carefully and asked questions to make sure you understand the objections, but the more you listen, the more positive you are that they are totally out of line: There is no truth to the criticisms, you can't agree with the odds, and you can't even accept the principle the critics are putting forward. Even here there's a way of agreeing—this time not with the critics' conclusions, but with their right to perceive things their way:

A: I don't believe you've been all the places you were just describing. You're probably just making all this up so that we'll think you're hot stuff.

B: Well, I can see how you might think that. I've known people who lie to get approval.

C: I want to let you know right from the start that I was against hiring you for the job. I think the reason you got it was because you're a woman.

D: I can understand why you'd believe that with all the antidiscrimination laws on the books. I hope that after I've been here for a while you'll change your mind.

E: I don't think you're being totally honest about your reasons for wanting to stay home. You say that it's because you have a headache, but I think you're avoiding Mary and Walt.

F: I can see why that would make sense to you since Mary and I got into an argument the last time we were together. All I can say is that I do have a headache.

Such responses tell critics that you're acknowledging the reasonableness of their perceptions, even though you don't agree or wish to change your behavior. This coping style is valuable, for it lets you avoid debates over who is right and who is wrong, which can turn an exchange of ideas into an argument. Notice the difference in the following scenes.

Disputing the perception:

A: I don't see how you can stand to be around Josh. The guy is so crude that he gives me the creeps.

B: What do you mean, crude? He's a really nice guy. I think you're just touchy.

A: Touchy! If it's touchy to be offended by disgusting behavior, then I'm guilty.

B: You're not guilty about anything. It's just that you're too sensitive when people kid around.

A: Too sensitive, huh? I don't know what's happened to you. You used to have such good judgment about people. . . .

Agreeing with the perception:

> *A:* I don't see how you can stand to be around Josh. The guy is so crude that he gives me the creeps.
>
> *B:* Well, I enjoy being around him, but I guess I can see how his jokes would be offensive to some people.
>
> *A:* You're damn right! I don't see how you can put up with him.
>
> *B:* Yeah. I guess if you didn't appreciate his humor, you wouldn't want to have much to do with him.

Notice how in the second exchange B was able to maintain his own position without attacking A's in the least. Such acceptance is the key ingredient for successfully agreeing with your critics' perceptions: Using acceptance, you clarify that you are in no way disputing their views. Because you have no intention of attacking your critics' views, your critics are less likely to be defensive.

All these responses to criticism may appear to buy peace at the cost of denying your feelings. However, as you can see by now, counterattacking usually makes matters worse. The nondefensive responses you have just learned won't solve problems or settle disputes by themselves. Nevertheless, they *will* make a constructive dialogue possible, setting the stage for a productive solution. How to achieve productive solutions is the topic of Chapter 11.

Summary

Communication climate refers to the social tone of a relationship. The most influential factor in shaping a communication climate is the degree to which the people involved see themselves as being valued and confirmed. Messages have differing levels of confirmation. We can categorize them as confirming, disagreeing, or disconfirming.

Confirming messages, which communicate "you exist and are valued," involve recognition, acknowledgment, or endorsement of the other party. Disagreeing messages, which communicate "you are wrong," use argumentativeness, complaining, or aggressiveness. Disconfirming messages, which communicate "you do not exist and are not valued," include responses that are impervious, interrupting, irrelevant, tangential, impersonal, ambiguous, or incongruous. Over time, these messages form climate patterns that often take the shape of positive or negative spirals.

Defensiveness is at the core of most negative spirals. Defensiveness occurs when individuals perceive that their presenting self is being attacked by face-threatening acts. We get particularly defensive about flaws that we don't want to admit and those that touch on sensitive areas. Both the attacker and the person attacked are responsible for creating defensiveness, since competent communicators protect others' face needs as well as their own.

Jack Gibb suggested a variety of ways to create a positive and nondefensive communication climate. These include being descriptive rather than evaluative, problem-oriented rather than controlling, spontaneous rather than strategic, empathic rather than neutral, equal rather than superior, and provisional rather than certain. When offering constructive criticism, it's important to check your motives, choose a good time, blend positive and negative comments, and follow up afterwards.

When faced with criticism by others, there are two alternatives to responding defensively: seeking additional information from the critic and agreeing with some aspect of the criticism. When performed sincerely, these approaches can transform an actual or potentially negative climate into a more positive one.

Key Terms

- Aggressiveness (316)
- Ambiguous response (321)
- Argumentativeness (316)
- Certainty (330)
- Communication climate (312)
- Complaining (316)
- Confirming communication (313)
- Controlling communication (326)
- Defensiveness (322)
- Description (326)
- Disagreeing message (315)
- Disconfirming communication (313)
- Empathy (329)
- Equality (330)
- Evaluation (325)
- Face (322)
- Face-threatening acts (322)
- Impersonal response (321)
- Impervious response (317)
- Incongruous response (321)
- Interrupting response (320)
- Irrelevant response (320)
- Neutrality (328)
- Presenting self (322)
- Problem orientation (327)
- Provisionalism (331)

- Sandwich method (332)
- Spiral (324)
- Spontaneity (328)
- Strategy (327)
- Superiority (330)
- Tangential response (320)

Activities

1. Invitation to Insight
Identify three personal relationships that matter to you. For each relationship,
    a. Come up with a weather phrase that describes the current climate of the relationship.
    b. Come up with a weather phrase that forecasts the climate of the relationship over the next year.
    c. Consider why you chose the phrases you did. In particular, identify how feeling valued and confirmed played a part in the climates you perceived and predicted.

2. Critical Thinking Probe
Mental health experts generally believe it is better to have others disagree with you than ignore you. Express your opinion on this matter, using specific examples from personal experiences to support your position. Next, discuss whether (and how) it is possible to disagree without being disconfirming.

3. Skill Builder
Develop your ability to communicate supportively instead of triggering defensive reactions in others. Restate each of the following evaluative "you" statements as descriptive "I" messages. Use details from your own personal relationships to create messages that are specific and personally relevant.
    a. "You're only thinking of yourself."
    b. "Don't be so touchy."
    c. "Quit fooling around!"
    d. "Stop beating around the bush and tell me the truth."
    e. "You're a slob!"

4. Ethical Challenge
Gibb argues that spontaneous rather than strategic communication reduces defensiveness. However, in some situations a strategic approach may hold the promise of a better climate than a completely honest message. Consider situations such as these:
    a. You don't find your partner very attractive. He or she asks, "What's the matter?"
    b. You intend to quit your job because you hate your boss, but you don't want to offend him or her. How do you explain the reasons for your departure?

c. You are tutoring a high school student in reading or math. The student is sincere and a hard worker, but is perhaps the most dull-witted person you have ever met. What do you say when the teenager asks, "How am I doing?"

Describe at least one situation from your experience where complete honesty increased another person's defensiveness. Discuss whether candor or some degree of strategy might have been the best approach in this situation. How can you reconcile your approach with Gibb's arguments in favor of spontaneity?

5. Invitation to Insight

Review the Gibb behaviors discussed on pages 325–332, and then answer the following questions:

    a. Which defense-provoking behavior do you find most annoying?

    b. Who in your life uses that behavior most often?

    c. What part of your presenting self is threatened by that behavior?

    d. How do you normally respond to that behavior?

    e. What behavior do you wish that person would use instead?

    f. How could you respond to avoid a negative spiral?

6. Skill Builder

Try your hand at offering constructive criticism in the following situations, using the sandwich method described on pages 332–333:

    a. Your partner rarely says "thank you" when you do favors for her or him.

    b. Your good friend wears unflattering clothing that embarrasses you in public

    c. Your sibling doesn't show up at important family events.

    d. Your coworker tells offensive jokes in front of customers.

7. Skill Builder

Practice your skill at responding nondefensively to critical attacks by following these steps:

    a. Identify five criticisms you are likely to encounter from others in your day-to-day communication. If you have trouble thinking of criticisms, invite one or more people who know you well to supply some real, sincere gripes.

    b. For each criticism, write one or more nondefensive responses using the alternatives on pages 334–344. Be sure your responses are sincere and that you can offer them without counterattacking your critic.

    c. Practice your responses, either by inviting a friend or classmate to play the role of your critics or by approaching your critics directly and inviting them to share their gripes with you.

Managing Conflict

After studying the material in this chapter . . .

You should understand:

1. The five elements of conflict.
2. That conflict is natural and inevitable.
3. The characteristics of functional and dysfunctional conflicts.
4. The differences between avoidance, accommodation, competition, compromise, and collaboration.
5. The influence of gender and culture on interpersonal conflict.
6. The ways individuals interact to create relational conflict systems.

You should be able to:

1. Recognize and accept the inevitability of conflicts in your life.
2. Identify the behaviors that characterize your dysfunctional conflicts and suggest more functional alternatives.
3. Identify the conflict styles you use most commonly and evaluate their appropriateness.
4. Describe the relational conflict system in one of your important relationships.
5. Use the win-win problem-solving approach to resolve an interpersonal conflict.

*O*nce upon a time, there was a world without conflicts. The leaders of each nation recognized the need for cooperation and met regularly to solve any potential problems before they could grow. They never disagreed on matters needing attention or on ways to handle these matters, and so there were never any international tensions, and of course there was no war.

Within each nation things ran just as smoothly. The citizens always agreed on who their leaders should be, so elections were always unanimous. There was no social friction among various groups. Age, race, and educational differences did exist, but each group respected the others, and all got along harmoniously.

Human relationships were always perfect. Strangers were always kind and friendly to each other. Neighbors were considerate of each other's needs. Friendships were always mutual, and no disagreements ever spoiled people's enjoyment of one another. Once people fell in love—and everyone did—they stayed happy. Partners liked everything about each other and were able to fully satisfy each other's needs. Children and parents agreed on every aspect of family life and never were critical or hostile toward each other. Each day was better than the one before.

Of course, everybody lived happily ever after.

This story is obviously a fairy tale. Regardless of what we may wish for or dream about, a conflict-free world just doesn't exist. Even the best communicators, the luckiest people, are bound to wind up in situations when their needs don't match the needs of others. Money, time, power, sex, humor, aesthetic taste, and a thousand other issues arise and keep us from living in a state of perpetual agreement.

For many people the inevitability of conflict is a depressing fact. They think that the existence of ongoing conflict means that there's little chance for happy relationships with others. Effective communicators know differently. They realize that although it's impossible to *eliminate* conflict, there are ways to *manage* it effectively. The skillful management of conflict can open the door to healthier, stronger, and more satisfying relationships, as well as to increased mental and physical health (Canary, 2003; Laursen & Pursell, 2009).

What Is Conflict?

Stop reading for a moment and make a list of as many different conflicts as you can think of that you've experienced personally. The list will probably show you that conflict takes many forms. Sometimes there's angry shouting, as when parents yell at their children. In other cases, conflicts involve restrained discussion, as in labor-management negotiations or court trials. Sometimes conflicts are carried on through hostile silence, as in the unspoken feuds of angry couples. Finally, conflicts may wind up in physical fighting between friends, enemies, or even total strangers.

Whatever forms they may take, all interpersonal conflicts share certain similarities. William Wilmot and Joyce Hocker (2010, p. 11) provide a thorough definition of conflict. They state that **conflict** is an expressed struggle between at least two interdependent parties who perceive incompatible goals, scarce resources, and interference from the other party in achieving their goals. The various parts of this definition can help you gain a better understanding of how conflict operates in everyday life.

EXPRESSED STRUGGLE

In order for conflict to exist, all the people involved must know that some disagreement exists. You may be upset for months because a neighbor's loud music keeps you awake at night, but no conflict exists until the neighbor learns about your problem. An expressed struggle doesn't have to be verbal. You can show your displeasure with someone without saying a word. A dirty look, the silent treatment, and avoiding the other person are all ways of expressing yourself. One way or another, both people must know that a problem exists before it fits our definition of conflict.

PERCEIVED INCOMPATIBLE GOALS

All conflicts look as if one person's gain would be another's loss. For instance, consider the neighbor whose music keeps you awake at night. It appears that someone has to lose: If the neighbor turns down the music, then he loses the enjoyment of hearing it at full volume; but if the neighbor keeps the volume up, then you're still awake and unhappy.

The goals in this situation really aren't completely incompatible—solutions do exist that allow both people to get what they want. For instance, you could achieve peace and quiet by closing your windows or getting the neighbor to close his. You might use a pair of earplugs, or perhaps the neighbor could get a set of earphones, which would allow the music to play at full volume without bothering anyone. If any of these solutions prove workable, then the conflict disappears.

Unfortunately, people often fail to see mutually satisfying answers to their problems. As long as they *perceive* their goals to be mutually exclusive, the conflict is real, albeit unnecessary.

PERCEIVED SCARCE RESOURCES

Conflicts also exist when people believe there isn't enough of something to go around: affection, money, space, and so on. Time is often a scarce commodity. As authors, teachers, and family men, the writers of this textbook are constantly in the middle of struggles about how to use the limited time we have at home. Should we work on this book? Spend time with our families? Enjoy the luxury of being alone? With only 24 hours in a day, we're bound to wind up in conflicts with our families, editors, students, colleagues, and friends—all of whom want more of our time than we have available to give.

INTERDEPENDENCE

However antagonistic they might feel, the people in a conflict are dependent upon each other. The welfare and satisfaction of one depends on the actions of another. If this were not true, then there would be no need for conflict, even in the face of scarce resources and incompatible goals. In fact, many conflicts remain unresolved because the people fail to understand their interdependence. One of the first steps toward resolving a conflict is to take the attitude that "we're all in this together."

INEVITABILITY

Conflicts are bound to happen, even in the best relationships. College students who kept diaries of their relationships reported that they take part in about seven arguments per

---

MEDIA CLIP

WORKING WITH, NOT AGAINST:
WIN WIN

At the outset of *Win Win*, everyone seems to be losing. Mike (Paul Giamatti) is a down-on-his luck lawyer and the coach of a winless high school wrestling team. Kyle (Alex Shaffer) is a runaway teenager who feels abandoned by his mother Cindy (Melanie Lynskey). She's a recovering drug addict who has recently lost her boyfriend. And her elderly father Leo (Burt Young) has been placed in assisted care against his will.

But each of these people has resources the others need, such as money, athletic talent, a house, and a home. At first, the characters try to gain these resources from each other through aggression or compromise. Ultimately, they recognize their interdependence and strive for mutually satisfying solutions. As its title suggests, the movie demonstrates that collaborative problem solving can help turn losing into winning.

week (Benoit & Benoit, 1987)—with some arguments "episodic" in nature and continuing off and on for a long time (Reznik & Roloff, 2011). Other surveys show that conflicts with friends are typical, with an average of one or two disagreements a day (Burk et al., 2009; Tuval-Mashiach & Shulman, 2006). Among families, conflict can be even more frequent. Researchers recorded dinner conversations for 52 families and found an average of 3.3 "conflict episodes" per meal (Vuchinich, 1987). This doesn't mean that families have "knock down, drag out" fights at the dinner table every night—but they regularly have disagreements and points of contention.

Since it is impossible to *avoid* conflicts, the challenge is to handle them effectively when they do arise. Decades of research show that people in both happy and unhappy relationships have conflicts, but that they perceive them and manage them in very different ways (Simon et al., 2008; Wilmot & Hocker, 2010). Unhappy couples argue in ways cataloged in this book as destructive. They are more concerned with defending themselves than with being problem-oriented. They fail to listen carefully to one another, have little or no empathy for their partners, use evaluative "you" language, and ignore each other's relational messages.

Many satisfied couples handle their conflicts more effectively. They recognize disagreements as healthy and know that conflicts need to be faced (Ridley et al., 2001; Segrin et al., 2009). While they may argue vigorously, they use skills like perception checking to find out what the other person is thinking, and they let the other person know that they understand the other side of the dispute (Canary et al., 1991). These people are willing to admit their mistakes, a habit that contributes to a harmonious relationship and also helps solve the problem at hand. With this in mind, let's take a closer look at what makes some conflicts more functional than others.

Functional and Dysfunctional Conflicts

Some bacteria are "good," aiding digestion and cleaning up waste, whereas others are "bad," causing infection. There are helpful forest fires, which clean out dangerous accumulations of underbrush, and harmful ones, which threaten lives and property. In the same way, some conflicts can be beneficial. They provide a way for relationships to grow by solving the problem at hand and often improving other areas of interaction. Other conflicts can be harmful, causing pain and weakening a relationship. Communication scholars usually describe harmful conflicts as dysfunctional and beneficial ones as functional (Canary & Messman, 2000; Gottman & Driver, 2005). In a **dysfunctional conflict**, the outcomes fall short of what is possible and have a damaging effect on the relationship. By contrast, participants in a **functional conflict** achieve the best possible outcome, even strengthening the relationship.

What makes some conflicts functional and others dysfunctional? Usually, the difference doesn't rest in the subject of the conflict, for it's possible to have good or poor results on almost any issue. Certain individual styles of communication can be more productive than others. In other cases, the success or failure of a conflict will depend on the method of resolution the communicators choose. We talk more about types of conflict resolution later in this chapter. Now, though, we describe some characteristics that distinguish functional from dysfunctional conflicts.

INTEGRATION VERSUS POLARIZATION

In a dysfunctional conflict, participants regard each other as polar opposites. They see themselves as "good" and the other person as "bad," their actions as "protective" and the other's as "aggressive," their behavior as "open and trustworthy" and the other's as "sneaky and deceitful." Researchers confirm

that in severe conflicts and dissatisfied relationships, married people see their spouses as more blameworthy than themselves (Sillars et al., 2000; Zinner, 2009). Robert Blake and Jane Mouton (1994) found that people engaged in this kind of polarization underestimate the commonalties shared with the other person and miss areas of agreement and goodwill.

By contrast, participants in a functional conflict recognize they are integrated—that they're in the difficult situation together. They don't think of the other person as necessarily "wrong" or "bad"; rather, they think of that person as a partner with whom to work. To use Gibb's language (see Chapter 10), they are *problem-oriented*, focused on solving the problem in a way that works for everybody rather than on controlling the other person. Integration is most likely when people in conflict appreciate each other's differences (Brown, 2004).

COOPERATION VERSUS OPPOSITION

Participants in a dysfunctional conflict see each other as opponents and view the other's gain as their loss: "If you win, I lose" is the attitude. This belief keeps partners from looking for ways to agree or finding solutions that can satisfy them both. People in opposition rarely try to redefine the situation in more constructive ways, and they seldom give in, even on noncritical issues (Deutsch, 2006).

A more functional approach recognizes that cooperation may bring about an answer that leaves everyone happy (Lewis, 2006). Even nations basically hostile to each other often recognize the functional benefits of cooperating. For example, although many member countries of the United Nations have clear-cut differences in certain areas, they work together to help alleviate world hunger and to encourage peaceful solutions to world conflict. Such cooperation is also possible in interpersonal conflicts. We'll have more to say about cooperative problem solving later in this chapter.

CONFIRMATION VERSUS DISCONFIRMATION

In functional conflicts, the people involved may disagree but they are not disagreeable. By using the supportive behaviors described on pages 325–332 in Chapter 10 (description instead of evaluation, provisionalism instead of certainty, etc.), it is possible to tackle the problem at hand without attacking the person with whom you share it. When partners treat one another with affection and without trying to dominate one another, relational satisfaction increases—even in the face of conflict (Ebesu-Hubbard, 2001; Weger, 2005).

AGREEMENT VERSUS COERCION

In destructive conflicts, the participants rely heavily on coercion to get what they want (Tuval-Mashiach & Shulman, 2006). "Do it my way, or else" is a threat commonly stated or implied in dysfunctional conflicts. Money, favors, friendliness, sex, and sometimes even physical coercion become tools for forcing the other person to give in. Needless to say, victories won with such power plays don't do much for a relationship.

More enlightened communicators realize that power plays are usually a bad idea, not only on ethical grounds but because they can often backfire. Rarely is a person in a relationship totally powerless; it's often possible to win a battle only to lose the war. One classic case of the dysfunctional consequences of using power to resolve conflicts occurs in families where authoritarian parents turn their children's requests into "unreasonable demands." It's easy enough to send 5-year-olds out of a room for some real or imagined misbehavior, but when they grow into teenagers they acquire many ways of striking back.

DE-ESCALATION VERSUS ESCALATION

In destructive conflicts, the problems seem to grow larger instead of smaller (Daitch, 2010; Kennedy & Pronin, 2008). As you read in Chapter 10, defensiveness is reciprocal: The person you attack is likely to strike back even harder. We've all seen a small incident get out of hand and cause damage out of proportion to its importance.

One clear sign of functional conflict is that in the long run the behaviors of the participants solve more problems than they create. We say "long run" because facing up to an issue instead of avoiding it will usually make life more difficult for a while. In this respect, handling conflicts functionally is rather like going to the dentist: You may find it a little (or even a lot!) painful for a short time, but you're only making matters worse if you don't face the problem.

FOCUSING VERSUS DRIFTING

In dysfunctional conflicts, the partners often bring in issues having little or nothing to do with the original problem. Take, for example, a couple having trouble deciding whether to spend the holidays at his or her parents' home. As they begin to grow frustrated at their inability to solve the dilemma, their interaction sounds like this:

A: Your mother is always trying to latch onto us!
B: If you want to talk about latching on, what about your folks? Ever since they loaned us that money, they've been asking about every dime we spend.
A: Well, if you could ever finish with school and hold down a decent job, we wouldn't have to worry about money so much. You're always talking about wanting to be an equal partner, but I'm the one paying all the bills around here.

You can imagine how the conversation would go from here. Notice how the original issue became lost as the conflict expanded. Such open-ended hostility is unlikely to solve any of the problems it brings up, not to mention its potential for creating problems that didn't even exist before.

One characteristic of communicators who handle conflict well is their ability to keep focused on one subject at a time. Unlike those dysfunctional battlers whom George Bach and Peter Wyden (1983) call "kitchen sink fighters," skillful communicators might say, "I'm willing to talk about how my parents have been acting since they made us that loan, but first let's settle the business of where to spend the holidays." In other words, for functional problem solving the rule is "one problem at a time."

FORESIGHT VERSUS SHORTSIGHTEDNESS

Shortsightedness can produce dysfunctional conflicts even when partners do not lose sight of the original issue. One common type of shortsightedness occurs when disputants try to win a battle and wind up losing the war. Friends might argue about who started a fight, but if you succeed in proving that you were "right" at the cost of the friendship, then the victory is a hollow one. In another type of shortsightedness, partners are so interested in defending

AT WORK

Third-Party Dispute Resolution

In a perfect world, people involved in disagreements would solve every problem themselves. But in real life, even the best intentions don't always lead to a satisfying conclusion. At times like these, a neutral third party can help.

The list of business disputes where a third party can help is long. It includes clashes between partners, contract disagreements, conflicts among team members, employee grievances, and consumer complaints. As these examples show, some conflicts occur between members of the same organization, while others involve the organization at odds with an outsider.

Third-party interventions can range from informal to legalistic. At the simple end of the spectrum, you and a colleague might ask a trusted coworker to help you work out a disagreement. In other cases, it may be useful to involve a trained mediator or facilitator who can help the disputants sort out issues and choose the best solution for themselves. In the most serious issues, parties may submit their grievances to an arbitrator or judge who will impose a decision. Whichever approach is used, it's important that a third party be neutral and unbiased to ensure a fair and effective outcome.

Whatever the form, third-party intervention can help bring closure to a dispute that would otherwise fester or explode.

Gent, S. E., & Shannon, M. (2011). Bias and effectiveness of third-party conflict management mechanisms. *Conflict Management and Peace Science, 28*, 124–144.

Wilmot, W. W., & Hocker, J. L. (2010). *Interpersonal conflict* (8th ed.). New York: McGraw-Hill.

their own solution to a problem that they overlook a different solution that would satisfy both their goals. A final type of shortsightedness occurs when one or both partners jump into a conflict without thinking about how they can approach the issue most constructively. In a few pages, we have more to say about preventing these last two types of shortsightedness.

Foresight is a feature of functional conflicts because it helps participants "pick their battles" wisely ("If I keep this up, I'm going to lose a friend—and I don't want that to happen"). It also helps partners see that their relationship is usually more important than the issue being disputed.

POSITIVE VERSUS NEGATIVE RESULTS

So far, we have looked at the differences between the *processes* of functional and dysfunctional conflicts. Now we will compare the *results* of these different styles.

Dysfunctional conflict typically has two consequences. First, no one is likely to get what was originally sought. In the short run, it may *look* as if one person might win a dispute while the other person loses, but today's victor is likely to suffer tomorrow at the hands of the original loser. Second, dysfunctional conflicts can threaten the future of a relationship. Family members, lovers, friends, neighbors, or fellow workers usually are bound together by webs of commitments and obligations that aren't easy to break. If they can't find satisfactory ways of resolving their differences, their connections will become strained and uncomfortable. Even when it is possible, dissolving a relationship in the face of a conflict is hardly a satisfying pattern.

In contrast to these dismal outcomes, functional conflicts have positive results. One benefit of skillfully handling issues is the reward of successfully facing a challenge. Finding a solution that works for you and the other person can leave partners feeling better about themselves and each other. Partners learn more about each other's needs and how they can be satisfied. Feelings are clarified. Backgrounds are shared. The relationship grows deeper and stronger. Of course, growth can occur in non-conflict situations too, but the point here is that dealing with problems can be an opportunity for getting to know each other better and appreciate each other more. Constructive conflict also provides a safe outlet for the feelings of frustration and aggression that are bound to occur. Without this kind of release, partners can build up a "gunnysack" of grudges that interfere with their everyday functioning and their goodwill toward one another.

Conflict Styles

Most people have "default" styles of handling conflict—characteristic approaches they take when their needs appear incompatible with what others want. While our habitual styles work sometimes, they may not work at all in other situations. What styles do you typically use to deal with conflict?

Find out by thinking about how two hypothetical characters—Chris and Pat—manage a problem.

Chris and Pat have been roommates for several years. Chris is a soccer fan and loves watching games with his friends at every opportunity. Their apartment has a large flat screen TV (owned by Chris) in the living room, and it has become a regular gathering spot for viewing. Pat doesn't mind watching an occasional game, but he's annoyed by what seems like endless TV (and endless houseguests). Chris thinks he ought to be able to watch his TV whenever he wants, with whomever he wants. The roommates have discussed the problem before, but they haven't been able to come up with a good solution. Here are five ways they could handle their conflict, representing five different conflict styles:

- Chris and Pat don't discuss the issue again—the prospect of fighting is too unpleasant. Chris has tried to cut back on watching with friends, but feels cheated. Pat keeps quiet, but when game time rolls around, his feelings of displeasure are obvious.

- Pat gives in, saying "Go ahead and watch all the soccer you want. I'll just go in the bedroom and listen to music." Pat hopes Chris and the other fans will take the hint and scale back their viewing.

- Chris tries to persuade Pat that watching more soccer will lead to a better understanding of the game, and that Pat will want to watch it more as a result. Pat tries to convince Chris that spending so much time watching TV isn't healthy. Both want the other person to give up and give in.

- The roommates agree to split the difference. Chris gets to watch any and every game at home, as long the friends don't come over. Chris gets soccer; Pat gets relative peace and quiet. Of course, Chris misses his friends and Pat must still endure hours of Chris's TV viewing.

- Chris and Pat brainstorm and discover other alternatives. For example, they decide that the fans could watch some games together at a local sports bar. They also realize that if each of Chris's friends could pitch in a modest sum, one of them could buy a large screen TV where they could watch some games (and avoid the sports bar costs). Pat also suggests that he and Chris could watch some non-sports TV together.

These approaches represent the five styles depicted in Figure 11.1, each of which is described in the following paragraphs.

AVOIDANCE (LOSE-LOSE)

Avoidance occurs when people nonassertively ignore or stay away from conflict. Avoidance can be physical (steering clear of a friend after having an argument) or conversational (changing the topic, joking, or denying that a problem exists).

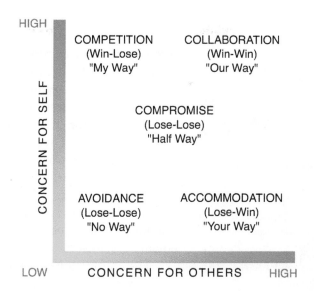

FIGURE 11.1 **Conflict Styles**

Adapted from Wilmot, W. W., & Hocker, J. L. (2010). *Interpersonal conflict* (8th ed.). New York: McGraw-Hill.

Avoidance reflects a pessimistic attitude about conflict. This approach reflects the belief that there is no good way to resolve the issue at hand. Avoiders usually believe it's easier to put up with the status quo than to face the problem head-on and try to solve it. In the case of Chris and Pat, avoidance means that, rather than having another fight, both of them will suffer in silence. Their solution illustrates how avoidance often produces lose-lose results.

Although avoiding important issues can keep the peace temporarily, it typically leads to unsatisfying relationships (Afifi et al., 2009; Caughlin & Golish, 2002). Partners of "self-silencers" report more frustration and discomfort when dealing with the avoiding partner than with those who face conflict more constructively (Harper & Welsh, 2007). Chronic misunderstandings, resentments, and disappointments pile up and contaminate the emotional climate. For this reason, we can say that avoiders have both a low concern for their own needs and for the interests of the other person, who is also likely to suffer from unaddressed issues (see Figure 11.1).

Despite its obvious shortcomings, avoidance isn't always a bad idea (Caughlin & Arr, 2004; Oduro-Frimpong, 2007). You might choose to avoid certain topics or situations if the risk of speaking up is too great, such as getting fired from a job you can't afford to lose, being humiliated in public, or even risking physical harm. You might also avoid a conflict if the relationship it involves isn't worth the effort. Even in close relationships, though, avoidance has its logic. If the issue is temporary or minor, you might let it pass. These reasons help explain why the communication of many happily married couples is characterized by "selectively ignoring" the other person's minor flaws (Segrin et al., 2009). This doesn't mean that a key to successful relationships is avoiding *all* conflicts. Instead, it suggests that it's smart to save energy for the truly important ones.

Dark Side of Communication

WHEN SILENCE ISN'T GOLDEN

"Silence is golden," says the well-known maxim. There certainly are times when keeping resentments to yourself can be a smart approach. But the "silent treatment"—acting aloof and nonresponsive when unhappy—is anything but golden. This form of passive aggression, which marriage researcher John Gottman calls "stonewalling," is a powerful predictor of divorce.

Why would anyone continue to use the silent treatment when a relational partner asks "Is anything wrong?" Communication researchers Courtney Wright and Michael Roloff explored this conundrum by asking 108 male and female students currently in romantic relationships two types of questions: First, about their commitment to the relationship, and second, about ways of expressing grievances with the other person.

The researchers found a link between commitment and stonewalling. Romantic partners with low levels of commitment use the silent treatment far more than do people who are strongly invested in their relationship. Partners with high levels of commitment would admit to being upset if asked about a relational problem. These findings led Wright and Roloff to agree with Gottman that stonewalling is a sign of a relationship that's in trouble.

Speaking up doesn't mean blasting your partner with criticism. As you read in Chapter 10, it's possible to express anger and complaints in ways that don't trigger defensiveness. In other words, it's constructive communication that's golden, not punishing silence.

Gottman, J. (1994). *Why marriages succeed or fail and how you can make yours last.* New York: Simon & Schuster.

Wright, C. N., & Roloff, M. E. (2009). Relational commitment and the silent treatment. *Communication Research Reports, 26*, 12-21.

ACCOMMODATION (LOSE-WIN)

Accommodation occurs when we allow others to have their own way rather than asserting our own point of view. Figure 11.1 depicts accommodators as having low concern for themselves and high concern for others, resulting in lose-win, "we'll do it your way" outcomes. In our hypothetical scenario, Pat accommodates to Chris by letting Chris watch soccer with his friends. It's a kind gesture by Pat, but he probably wishes Chris would be equally gracious.

The motivation of an accommodator plays a significant role in this style's effectiveness. If accommodation is a genuine act of kindness, generosity, or love, then chances are good that it will enhance the relationship. Most people appreciate those who "take one for the team," "treat others as they want to be treated," or "lose the battle to win the war." However, people are far less appreciative of those who habitually use this style to play the role of "martyr, bitter complainer, whiner, or saboteur" (Wilmot & Hocker, 2010).

We should pause here to mention the important role that culture plays in perceptions of conflict styles. People from high-context, collectivistic backgrounds (such as many Asian cultures) are likely to regard avoidance and accommodation as face-saving and noble ways to handle conflict (Lim, 2009; Oetzel & Ting-Toomey, 2003). In low-context, individualistic cultures (such as the United States), avoidance and accommodation are often viewed less positively. For instance, think of the many unflattering terms that North Americans use for people who give up or give in during conflicts ("pushover," "yes man," "doormat," "spineless"). As you will read later in this chapter, collectivistic cultures have virtuous words and phrases to describe these same traits. The point here is that all conflict styles have value in certain situations, and that culture plays a significant role in determining how each style is valued.

COMPETITION (WIN-LOSE)

The flip side of accommodation is **competition**, a win-lose approach to conflict that involves high concern for self and low concern for others. As Figure 11.1 shows, competition seeks to resolve conflicts "my way." When Chris and Pat make their cases about soccer and TV viewing, trying to get each other to concede, they are using a competitive approach.

Many North Americans default to a competitive approach because it's ingrained in their culture, as Laura Tracy (1991, p. 4) observes:

> Whether we like it or not, we live in a competitive society. Our economy is competitive by design, and as a nation, we see in competition a challenge to develop our resources and ourselves.

Just as competition can develop an economy, it can sometimes develop a relationship. Susan Messman and Rebecca Mikesell (2000) found that some men and women in satisfying dating relationships used competition to enrich their interaction. For example, some found satisfaction by competing in play (who's the better racquetball player?), in achievement (who gets the better job offer?), and in altruism (who's more romantic?). These satisfied couples developed a shared narrative (see Chapter 4) that defined competition as a measure of regard, quite different from conflict that signaled a lack of appreciation and respect. Of course, it's easy to see how these arrangements could backfire if one partner became a gloating winner or a sore loser. It's also easy to see how feeling like you've been defeated can leave you wanting to get even, creating a downward competitive spiral that degrades to a lose-lose relationship (Olson & Braithwaite, 2004; Singleton & Vacca, 2007).

If you feel your way is the best one, you may feel justified in trying to control the situation, but it's likely that the other person won't view your bid for control so charitably (Gross et al., 2004). The dark side of competition is that it often breeds aggression (Warren et al., 2005). Sometimes aggression is obvious, but at other times it can be more subtle. To understand how, read on.

Passive Aggression **Passive aggression** occurs when a communicator expresses dissatisfaction in a disguised manner. In the case of Pat and Chris, perhaps Pat runs the vacuum cleaner loudly during the soccer matches—or Chris makes sarcastic jokes about Pat not liking sports. Passive aggression can take the form of "crazymaking" (Bach & Wyden, 1983)—tactics designed to punish another person without direct confrontation. Crazymaking takes its name from the effect such behavior usually has on its target. There are a number of crazymaking ways to deal with conflict. One is through guilt: "Never mind. I'll do all the work myself [sigh]. Go ahead and have a good time. Don't worry about me [sigh]." Another crazymaker is when someone

"It's not enough that we succeed. Cats must also fail."

agrees with you to your face but has a different agenda behind your back—such as the teenager who says he'll clean his room, then doesn't do so as a means of getting back at the parent who grounded him. Some passive aggression is nonverbal: a loud sigh, a pained expression, or a disdainful laugh can get a message across. If the target of these messages asks about them, the passive aggressor can always deny the conflict exists. Even humor—especially sarcasm ("Gee, I can't *wait* to spend the weekend with your folks")—can be used as passive aggression (Bowes & Katz, 2011).

Direct Aggression A directly aggressive communicator lashes out to attack the source of displeasure. Dominic Infante (1987) identified nine types of **direct aggression:** character attacks, competence attacks, physical appearance attacks, maledictions (wishing the other bad fortune), teasing, ridicule, threats, swearing, and nonverbal emblems (fist shaking, waving arms, etc.). Like all types of relational communication, direct aggression has both verbal and nonverbal dimensions. In the case of Chris and Pat, the conflict might turn into an ugly shouting match, with denigrating comments about how only an "idiot" would or wouldn't like sports, TV viewing, or having friends over.

The results of direct aggression can have a severe impact on the target. There is a significant connection between verbal aggression and physical aggression (Atkin et al., 2002; Roberto et al., 2007). Even if the attacks never lead to blows, the psychological effects can be harmful, or even devastating. Recipients can feel embarrassed, inadequate, humiliated, hopeless, desperate, or depressed. These results can lead to decreased effectiveness in personal relationships (Muñoz-Rivas et al., 2007), on the job (Madlock & Kennedy-Lightsey, 2010), in the classroom (Martin et al., 2010), and in families (Doss et al., 2008). Verbal aggression can affect the relationship as well as the target. One aggressive remark can lead to an equally combative reaction, starting a destructive spiral that can expand beyond the original dispute and damage the entire relationship (Olson & Braithwaite, 2004; Turk & Monahan, 1999).

COMPROMISE (NEGOTIATED LOSE-LOSE)

A **compromise** gives both people at least some of what they want, although both sacrifice part of their goals. People usually settle for a compromise when it seems that partial satisfaction is the best they can hope for. In the case of Pat and Chris, they strike a "halfway" deal by letting Chris watch all the soccer he wants, as long as he doesn't invite friends to join him. Unlike avoidance, where both people lose because they don't address their problem, compromisers actually negotiate a lose-lose solution.

Although a compromise may be better than losing everything, this approach hardly seems to deserve the positive image it has with some people. In his valuable book on conflict resolution, Albert Filley (1975, p. 23) makes an interesting observation about our attitudes toward this method. Why is it, he asks, that if someone says, "I will compromise my values," we view the action unfavorably, yet we talk admiringly about people in a conflict who compromise to reach a solution? Although compromise may be the best

obtainable result in some conflicts, it's important to realize that both people in a dispute can often work together to find much better solutions. In such cases, *compromise* is a negative word.

Most of us are surrounded by the results of bad compromises. Consider a common example: the conflict between one person's desire to smoke cigarettes and another's need for clean air. The win-lose outcomes on this issue are obvious: Either the smoker abstains or the nonsmoker gets polluted lungs—neither option a very satisfying one. But a compromise in which the smoker gets to enjoy only a rare cigarette or must retreat outdoors and in which the nonsmoker still must inhale some fumes or feel like an ogre is hardly better. Both sides have lost a considerable amount of both comfort and goodwill. Of course, the costs involved in other compromises are even greater. For example, if a divorced couple haggles over custody in a way that leaves them bitter and emotionally scars their children, it's hard to say that anybody has won no matter what the outcome.

Some compromises do leave everyone satisfied. You and the seller might settle on a price for a used car that is between what the seller was asking and what you wanted to pay. While neither of you got everything you wanted, the outcome would still leave both of you satisfied. Likewise, you and your companion might agree to see a film that is the second choice for both of you in order to spend an evening together. As long as everyone is at least somewhat satisfied with an outcome, compromise can be an effective way to resolve conflicts. Catherine Sanderson and Kim Karetsky (2002) found that college students with a strong focus on intimacy goals were likely to engage in open discussion and compromise, show concern for their partner, and seek social support—and importantly, they were likely to successfully resolve the conflict. When compromises are satisfying and successful, it might be more accurate to categorize them as the final style we discuss: collaboration.

COLLABORATION (WIN-WIN)

Collaboration seeks win-win solutions to conflict. It involves a high degree of concern for both self and others, with the goal of solving problems not "my way" or "your way" but "our way." In the best case, collaborating can lead to a *win-win* outcome, where each person gets what she or he wants (Lewis, 2006).

363

As noted in the scenario, the brainstorming by Chris and Pat yields several collaborative options: Chris watching soccer with his friends at a sports bar, the friends buying a new TV, and/or Chris and Pat watching non-sports programs together. Perhaps you can think of other options as well. The key to true collaboration is whether Pat and Chris are happy with their decision and its outcomes.

In **win-win problem solving**, the goal is to find a solution that satisfies the needs of everyone involved. Not only do the partners avoid trying to win at each other's expense, but there's also a belief that working together can provide a solution in which all reach their goals without needing to compromise.

A few examples show how collaboration can lead to win-win outcomes:

- A boss and her employees get into a conflict over scheduling. The employees often want to shift the hours they're scheduled to work so that they can accommodate personal needs, whereas the boss needs to be sure that the operation is fully staffed at all times. After some discussion they arrive at a solution that satisfies everyone: The boss works up a monthly master schedule indicating the hours during which each employee is responsible for being on the job. Employees are free to trade hours among themselves, as long as the operation is fully staffed at all times.

- A conflict about testing arises in a college class. Due to sickness and other reasons, a certain number of students need to take exams on a makeup basis. The instructor doesn't want to give these students any advantage over their peers and also doesn't want to go through the task of making up a brand-new test for just a few people. After working on the problem together, instructor and students arrive at a win-win solution. The instructor will hand out a list of 20 possible exam questions in advance of the test day. At examination time, 5 of these questions are randomly drawn for the class to answer. Students who take makeup exams will draw from the same pool of questions at the time of their test. In this way, makeup students are taking a fresh test without the instructor having to create a new exam.

- A newly married husband and wife find themselves arguing frequently over their budget. The husband enjoys buying impractical and enjoyable items for himself and for the house, whereas the wife fears that such purchases will ruin their carefully constructed budget. Their solution is to set aside a small amount of money each month for "fun" purchases. The amount is small enough to be affordable yet gives the husband a chance to escape from their Spartan lifestyle. The wife is satisfied with the arrangement because the luxury money is now a budget category by itself, which gets rid of the "out of control" feeling that comes when her husband makes unexpected purchases. The plan works so well that the couple continues to use it even after their income rises, by increasing the amount devoted to luxuries.

ⓈⒺⓁⒻ-ⒶⓈⓈⒺⓈⓈⓂⒺⓃⓉ
Your Method of Conflict Resolution

Think of a relationship with someone with whom you interact regularly and with whom you engage in conflict (for example, a parent, sibling, roommate, close friend, spouse, partner, or lover). How do you usually respond to your conflict with this person? Indicate the degree to which you believe each statement below applies to you. Use the following 5-point measure as you apply each statement to yourself:

1 = NEVER   2 = RARELY   3 = OCCASIONALLY   4 = OFTEN   5 = VERY OFTEN

_____   1. I am usually firm in pursuing my goals.

_____   2. I attempt to deal with all of the other person's and my concerns.

_____   3. I try to find a compromise solution.

_____   4. I try to avoid creating unpleasantness for myself.

_____   5. It's important to me that others are happy, even if it comes at my expense.

_____   6. I try to win my position.

_____   7. I consistently seek the other's help in working out a solution.

_____   8. I give up some points in exchange for others.

_____   9. I try to postpone dealing with the issue.

_____   10. I might try to soothe the other's feelings and preserve our relationship.

_____   11. I press to get my points made.

_____   12. I try to integrate my concerns with the other person's concerns.

_____   13. I will let the other person have some of what she or he wants if she or he lets me have some of what I want.

_____   14. I sometimes avoid taking positions that would create controversy.

_____   15. I sometimes sacrifice my own wishes for the wishes of the other person.

_____   16. I try to show the other person the logic and benefits of my position.

_____   17. I tell the other person my ideas and ask for his or hers.

_____   18. I propose a middle ground.

_____   19. I try to do what is necessary to avoid tensions.

_____   20. I don't worry about my own concerns if satisfying them means damaging the relationship.

Add your responses to items 1, 6, 11, and 16. This is your **competition** score _____.
Add your responses to items 2, 7, 12, and 17. This is your **collaboration** score _____.
Add your responses to items 3, 8, 13, and 18. This is your **compromise** score _____.
Add your responses to items 4, 9, 14, and 19. This is your **avoidance** score _____.
Add your responses to items 5, 10, 15, and 20. This is your **accommodation** score _____.

Although such solutions might seem obvious when you read them here, a moment's reflection will show you that such cooperative problem solving is all too rare. People faced with these types of conflicts often resort to such styles as avoiding, accommodating, or competing, and they wind up handling the issues in a manner that results in either a win-lose or lose-lose outcome. As we pointed out earlier, it's a shame to see one or both partners in a conflict come away unsatisfied when they could both get what they're seeking by communicating in a win-win manner. Later in this chapter, you'll learn a specific process for arriving at collaborative solutions to problems.

Although a win-win approach sounds ideal, it is not always possible, or even appropriate. Collaborative problem solving can be quite time consuming, and some conflict decisions need to be made quickly. Moreover, many conflicts are about relatively minor issues that don't call for a great deal of creativity and brainstorming. As you'll see in the following section, there certainly will be times when compromising is the most sensible approach. You will even encounter instances when pushing for your own solution is reasonable. Even more surprisingly, you will probably discover that there are times when it makes sense to willingly accept the loser's role. Much of the time, however, good intentions and creative thinking can lead to outcomes that satisfy everyone's needs.

TABLE 11.1 Choosing the Most Appropriate Conflict Style

AVOIDANCE (LOSE-LOSE)	ACCOMMODATION (LOSE-WIN)	COMPETITION (WIN-LOSE)	COMPROMISE (NEGOTIATED LOSE-LOSE)	COLLABORATION (WIN-WIN)
When the issue is of little importance	When the issue is more important to the other person than it is to you	When the issue is not important enough to negotiate at length	When the issue is moderately important but not enough for a stalemate	When the issue is too important for a compromise
To cool down and gain perspective	When you discover you are wrong	When you are convinced that your position is right and necessary	When opponents are strongly committed to mutually exclusive goals	To merge insights with someone who has a different perspective on the problem
When the costs of confrontation outweigh the benefits	When the long-term cost of winning may not be worth the short-term gain	When there is not enough time to seek a win-win outcome	To achieve quick, temporary solutions to complex problems	To come up with creative and unique solutions to problems
	To build up credits for later conflicts	When the other person is not willing to seek a win-win outcome	As a backup mode when collaboration doesn't work	To develop a relationship by showing commitment to the concerns of both parties
	To let others learn by making their own mistakes	To protect yourself against a person who takes advantage of noncompetitive people		When a long-term relationship between you and the other person is important

Adapted from Wilmot, W. W., & Hocker, J. L. (2010). *Interpersonal conflict* (8th ed.), New York: McGraw-Hill.

WHICH STYLE TO USE?

Although collaborative problem solving might seem like the most attractive alternative to the other styles described in this chapter, it's an oversimplification to imagine that there is a single "best" way to respond to conflicts (Gross & Guerrero, 2000). Generally speaking, win-win approaches are preferable to win-lose and lose-lose solutions. But we've already seen that there are times when avoidance, accommodation, competition, and compromise are appropriate. Table 11.1 lists some of the factors to consider when deciding which style to use when facing a conflict.

A conflict style isn't necessarily a personality "trait" that carries across all situations. Wilmot and Hocker (2010) suggest that roughly 50 percent of the population change their style from one situation to another. As you learned in Chapter 1, this sort of behavioral flexibility is a characteristic of competent communicators. Several factors govern which style to use.

The Situation When someone clearly has more power than you, accommodation may be the best approach. If the boss tells you to "fill that order *now!*" you probably ought to do it without comment. A more competitive response ("Why don't you ask Karen to do it? She has less work than I do.") might state your true feelings, but it could also cost you your job.

The Other Person Although win-win is a fine ideal, sometimes the other person isn't interested in (or good at) collaborating. You probably know communicators who are so competitive that they put winning on even minor issues ahead of the well-being of your relationship. In such cases, your efforts to collaborate may have a low chance of success. Table 11.1 summarizes the pros and cons of each approach, taking into account the attitudes of the other person.

Your Goals When you want to solve a problem, it's generally good to be assertive (see Chapter 5 for information on creating assertive "I" messages). But there are other reasons for communicating in a conflict. Sometimes your overriding concern is to calm down an enraged or upset communicator. For example, tolerating an outburst from your crotchety and sick neighbor is probably better than standing up for yourself and triggering a stroke. Likewise, you might choose to sit quietly through the nagging of a family member rather than ruin Thanksgiving dinner. In other cases, your moral principles might compel an aggressive statement, even though it might not get you what you originally sought: "I've had enough of your racist jokes. I've tried to explain why they're so offensive, but you obviously haven't listened. I'm leaving!" Or your goal may be to be seen in a favorable way, in which case you may want to avoid being aggressive.

Conflict in Relational Systems

So far, we have been describing individual conflict styles. Even though the style you choose in a conflict is important, your approach isn't the only factor that will determine how a conflict unfolds. In reality, conflict is *relational*: Its character is usually determined by the way the people involved interact (Williams-Baucom et al., 2010; Wilmot & Hocker, 2010; Zarankin, 2008). For example, you might be determined to handle a conflict with your neighbors collaboratively, only to be driven to competition by their uncooperative nature or even to avoidance by their physical threats. Likewise, you might plan to hint to a professor that you are bothered by his apparent indifference but wind up discussing the matter in an open, assertive way in reaction to his constructive suggestion. Examples like these indicate that conflict isn't just a matter of individual choice. Rather, it depends on how the partners interact.

COMPLEMENTARY, SYMMETRICAL, AND PARALLEL STYLES

Partners in interpersonal relationships—and impersonal ones, too—can use one of three styles to manage their conflicts. In relationships with a **complementary conflict style**, the partners use different but mutually reinforcing behaviors. As Table 11.2 illustrates, some complementary styles are destructive, while others are constructive. In a **symmetrical conflict style**, both people use the same tactics. Some relationships are characterized by a **parallel conflict style**, which shifts between complementary and symmetrical patterns from one issue to another. Table 11.2 illustrates how the same conflict can unfold in very different ways, depending on whether the partners' communication is symmetrical or complementary. A parallel style would alternate between these two forms, depending on the situation.

Research shows that a complementary "fight-flight" style is common in many unhappy marriages. One partner—most commonly the wife—addresses the conflict directly, while the other—usually the husband—withdraws (Caughlin & Vangelisti, 2006). As discussed in Chapter 4, it's easy to see how this pattern can lead to a cycle of increasing hostility and

TABLE 11.2 Complementary and Symmetrical Conflict Styles

SITUATION	COMPLEMENTARY STYLES	SYMMETRICAL STYLES
Wife is upset because husband is spending little time at home.	Wife complains; husband withdraws, spending even less time at home. (Destructive complementarity)	Wife raises concern clearly and assertively, without aggression. Husband responds by explaining his concerns in the same manner. (Constructive symmetry)
Boss makes fun of employee in front of other workers.	Employee seeks out boss for private conversation, explaining why being the butt of public joking was embarrassing. (Constructive complementarity)	Employee maliciously "jokes" about boss at company party. (Destructive symmetry)
Parents are uncomfortable about teenager's new friends.	Parents express concerns. Teen dismisses them, saying "There's nothing to worry about." (Destructive complementarity)	Teen expresses concern that parents are being too protective. Parents and teen negotiate a mutually agreeable solution. (Constructive symmetry)

F CUS ON RESEARCH

Attachment Styles and Relational Conflict

Ever since Freud, psychologists have understood that who we are as adults is shaped by our earliest experiences. Attachment theorists believe that people who don't receive enough warmth, approval, and support as young children suffer a host of difficulties in their adult relationships. One set of challenges involves dealing with conflicts.

Researchers Rachel Domingue and Debra Mollen found that when both partners in a romantic relationship have secure attachment styles, they tend to communicate constructively during conflicts. By contrast, when both partners are insecure, they often fall into demand-withdraw or mutual avoidance patterns.

Communication scholars Craig Fowler and Megan Dillow discovered that expectations shape the way conflicts play out. Partners whose attachment styles reflect fears of abandonment and rejection "tend to enact conflict behaviors that increase the chances of their concerns becoming reality." In other words, their dismal expectations create dysfunctional self-fulfilling prophecies. By expecting the worst, they act in ways that create the realities they dread.

If one or both partners have attachment issues in a relationship, Domingue and Mollen believe that couples' therapy is the best avenue for change. That way, both people can learn communication skills to help make their conflict management patterns more constructive.

Domingue, R., & Mollen, D. (2009). Attachment and conflict communication in adult romantic relationships. *Journal of Social & Personal Relationships, 26,* 678–696.

Fowler, C., & Dillow, M. R. (2011). Attachment dimensions and the Four Horsemen of the Apocalypse. *Communication Research Reports, 28,* 16–26.

isolation, since each partner punctuates the conflict differently, blaming the other for making matters worse. "I withdraw because she's so critical," a husband might say. However, the wife wouldn't organize the sequence in the same way. "I criticize because he withdraws" would be her perception. Couples who use demand-withdraw patterns report being less than satisfied with their conflict discussions, and that their negotiations rarely produce change (McGinn et al., 2009).

Complementary styles aren't the only ones that can lead to problems. Some distressed relationships suffer from destructively symmetrical communication. If both partners treat one another with matching hostility, one threat and insult leads to another in an **escalatory spiral**. If the partners both withdraw from one another instead of facing their problems, a complementary **de-escalatory spiral** results, in which the satisfaction and vitality ebb from the relationship, leaving it a shell of its former self. (The Focus on Research sidebar on this page describes how individual attachment styles contribute to these relational patterns.)

As Table 11.2 shows, both complementary and symmetrical behavior can produce "good" results as well as "bad" ones. If the complementary behaviors are positive, then a positive spiral results, and the conflict stands a good chance of being resolved. This is the case in the second example in Table 11.2, in which the boss is open to hearing the employee's concerns, listening willingly as the employee talks. Here, a complementary talk-listen pattern works well.

Symmetrical styles also can be beneficial, as another look at the boss-employee example shows. The clearest example of constructive symmetry occurs when both people communicate assertively, listening to one another's concerns and working together to resolve them. Married couples who take this approach appraise their marriages more positively than any other type of couple (Ridley et al., 2001). The potential for this sort of solution occurs in the parent-teenager conflict in Table 11.2. With enough mutual respect and careful listening, both the parents and their teenager can understand one another's concerns and possibly find a way to give all three people what they want.

TOXIC CONFLICT: THE "FOUR HORSEMEN"

Some conflict styles are so destructive that they are almost guaranteed to wreak havoc on relationships. These toxic forms of communication include what John Gottman has called "The Four Horsemen of the Apocalypse" (Gottman, 1994; see also Fowler & Dillow, 2011; Holman & Jarvis, 2003).

Gottman has gathered decades of data about newlywed couples and their communication patterns. By observing their interactions, he has been able to predict with over 90 percent accuracy whether the newlyweds will end up divorcing. Here are the four destructive signs he looks for:

1. Criticism: These are attacks on a person's character. As you read in Chapters 5 and 10, there's a significant difference between legitimate complaints about behavior phrased in descriptive "I" language ("I wish you had been on time—we're going to be late to the movie") and critical character assaults stated as evaluative "you" messages ("You're so thoughtless—you never think of anyone but yourself").

2. Defensiveness: As Chapter 10 explained, defensiveness is a reaction that aims to protect one's presenting self by denying responsibility ("You're crazy—I never do that") and counterattacking ("You're worse about that than I am").

While some self-protection is understandable, problems arise when a person refuses to listen to or even acknowledge another's concerns.

3. Contempt: A contemptuous comment belittles and demeans. It can take the form of name-calling putdowns ("You're a real jerk") or sarcastic barbs ("Oh, *that* was brilliant"). Contempt can also be communicated nonverbally through dramatic eye rolls or disgusted sighs. (Try doing both of those at the same time and imagine how dismissing they can be).

4. Stonewalling: As you read on page 360, stonewalling occurs when one person in a relationship withdraws from the interaction, shutting down dialogue—and any chance of resolving the problem in a mutually satisfactory way. It sends a disconfirming "you don't matter" message to the other person. The Dark Side sidebar on page 360 describes stonewalling and withdrawal in greater detail.

Here's a brief exchange illustrating how the "four horsemen" can lead to a destructive spiral of aggression:

> "You overdrew our account again—can't you do *anything* right?" (Criticism)
>
> "Hey, don't blame me—you're the one who spends most of the money." (Defensiveness)
>
> "At least I have better math skills than a first-grader. Way to go, Einstein." (Contempt)
>
> "Whatever." (said while walking out of the room) (Stonewalling)

It's easy to see how this kind of communication can be destructive in any relationship, not just a marriage. It's also easy to see how these kinds of comments can feed off each other and develop into destructive conflict rituals, as we'll discuss now.

CONFLICT RITUALS

When people have been in a relationship for some time, their communication often develops into **conflict rituals**—unacknowledged but very real repeating patterns of interlocking behavior (Wilmot & Hocker, 2010). Consider a few common rituals:

- A young child interrupts his parents, demanding to be included in their conversation. At first the parents tell the child to wait, but he whines and cries until the parents find it easier to listen than to ignore the fussing. This pattern reoccurs whenever the child has a demand the parents hesitate to fulfill.

- A couple fights. One partner leaves. The other accepts blame for the problem and begs forgiveness. The first partner returns, and a happy reunion takes place. Soon they fight again and the pattern repeats.

- One friend is unhappy with the other. The unhappy person withdraws until the other asks what's wrong. "Nothing," the first replies. The questioning persists until the problem is finally out in the open. The friends then solve the issue and continue happily until the next problem arises, when the pattern repeats itself.

There's nothing inherently wrong with the interaction in many rituals (Olson, 2002). Consider the preceding examples. In the first, the child's whining may be the only way he can get the parent's attention. In the second, both partners might use the fighting as a way to blow off steam, and both might find that the joy of a reunion is worth the grief of the separation. The third ritual might work well when one friend is more assertive than the other.

Rituals can cause problems, though, when they become the *only* way relational partners handle their conflicts. As you learned in Chapter 1, competent communicators have a large repertoire of behaviors, and they are able to choose the most effective response for a given situation. Relying on one pattern to handle all conflicts is no more effective than using a screwdriver to handle every home repair, or putting the same seasoning in every dish you cook: What works in one situation isn't likely to succeed in many others. Conflict rituals may be familiar and comfortable, but they aren't the best way to solve the variety of conflicts that are part of any relationship.

Variables in Conflict Styles

By now you can see that every relational system is unique. The communication patterns in one family, business, or classroom are likely to be very different from any other. But along with the differences that arise in individual relationships, there are two powerful variables that affect the way people manage conflict: gender and culture. We now take a brief look at each of these factors and see how they affect the ways that conflict is managed.

GENDER

Some research suggests that men and women often approach conflicts differently (e.g., Archer, 2002; Gayle et al., 2002). Even in childhood, there is evidence that boys are (on average, of course) more likely to be aggressive, demanding, and competitive, while girls are more cooperative and accommodating. Studies of children from preschool to early adolescence have shown that boys try to get their way by ordering one another around: "Lie down." "Get off my steps." "Gimme your arm." By contrast, girls are more likely to make proposals for action that begin with the word *let's:* "Let's go find some." "Let's ask her if she has any bottles." "Let's move *these* out *first*" (Tannen, 1990; see also Noakes & Rinaldi, 2006). Whereas boys tell each other what role to take in pretend play ("Come on, be a doctor"), girls more commonly ask each other what role they want ("Will you be the patient for a few minutes?") or make a joint proposal ("We can both be doctors"). Furthermore, boys often make demands without offering an explanation ("Look, man, I want the Game Cube right now"). In contrast, girls often give reasons for their suggestions ("We gotta clean 'em first 'cause they got germs").

Adolescent girls use aggression in conflicts, but their methods are usually more indirect than those of boys. Whereas teenage boys often engage in verbal showdowns or even physical fights, teenage girls typically use gossip, backbiting, and social exclusion (Hess & Hagen, 2006; Underwood, 2003). This is not to suggest that girls' aggression is any less destructive than boys'. The movie *Mean Girls* (based on Rosalind Wiseman's book *Queen Bees and Wannabes*, 2003) offers a vivid depiction of just how injurious these indirect assaults can be on the self-concepts and relationships of young women.

Gender differences in dealing with conflict often persist into adulthood. Esin Tezer and Ayhan Demir (2001) studied the conflict behaviors late adolescents use with same-sex and opposite-sex peers. They found that compared to females, males use more competing behaviors with same-sex peers and more avoiding behaviors with opposite-sex peers. On the other hand, regardless of culture or the sex of the person with whom they are interacting, females are more likely than males to compromise (Holt & DeVore, 2005). Erica Woodin (2011, p. 332), analyzing the results of 64 studies that included more than 5,000 couples, found that "women tend to display more high-intensity behaviors (hostility, distress, and intimacy), whereas men tend to communicate in a less intense and more indirect manner during conflict (withdrawal and problem solving)."

A survey of college students reinforced stereotypes about the influence of gender in conflicts (Collier, 1991). Regardless of their cultural background, female students described men as being concerned with power and more interested in content than in relational issues. Sentences used to describe male conflict styles included, "The most important thing to males in conflict is their egos," "Men don't worry about feelings," and "Men are more direct." In contrast, women were described as being more concerned with maintaining the relationship during a conflict. Sentences used to describe female conflict styles included, "Women are better listeners," "Women try to solve problems without controlling the other person," and "Females are more concerned with others' feelings."

In contrast with this extreme view, another body of research suggests that the differences in how the two sexes handle conflict are rather small, and not at all representative of the stereotypical picture of aggressive men and passive women (Samter & Cupach, 1998; Woodin, 2011). As Woodin concluded, "men and women may be more similar than different in resolving conflict" (p. 332). People may *think* that there are greater differences in male and female ways of handling conflicts than actually exist (Allen, 1998). People who assume that men are aggressive and women accommodating may notice behavior that fits these stereotypes ("See how much he bosses her around? A typical man!"). On the other hand, behavior that doesn't fit these preconceived ideas (accommodating men, pushy women) goes unnoticed.

MEDIA CLIP

PRODUCING COOPERATION: *30 ROCK*

Liz Lemon (Tina Fey) is head writer of the fictional TV show *TGS with Tracy Jordan*. Almost everyone involved with the program—the cast, executives, writers, and staff—has a large ego and demanding personality. Lemon takes on responsibility for making sure this team of oddballs works together.

Lemon's conflict management style could be called "den mother." She placates, cajoles, accommodates, and harmonizes, working out compromises and occasionally even collaboration. It's clear that without her, the show would never survive. Liz may be a loveable, insecure neurotic with a catastrophic romantic life, but she is a highly effective conflict manager.

What, then, can we conclude about the influence of gender on conflict? Research has demonstrated that there are, indeed, some small but measurable differences in the two sexes. But, while men and women may have characteristically different conflict styles, the individual style of each communicator is more important than his or her sex in shaping the way he or she handles conflict.

CULTURE

People from most cultures prefer mutually beneficial resolutions to disagreements whenever possible (Cai & Fink, 2002). Nonetheless, the ways in which people communicate during conflicts do vary from one culture to another (Shearman et al., 2011; Ting-Toomey & Takai, 2006; van Meurs & Spencer-Oatey, 2010).

As you read in Chapter 2, the kind of straight-talking, assertive approach that characterizes many North Americans and Western Europeans is not the norm in other parts of the world. Assertiveness that might seem perfectly appropriate to a native of the United States or Canada would be rude and insensitive in many Asian countries (Ma & Jaeger, 2010; Samovar et al., 2010). Perhaps not surprisingly, members of individualistic cultures often choose competing as a conflict style more than those in collectivistic cultures, whereas members of collectivistic cultures prefer the styles of compromising and problem solving (Holt & DeVore, 2005; Lim, 2009).

Asian cultures tend to avoid confrontation, placing a premium on preserving and honoring the "face" of the other person. The Japanese notion of self-restraint is reflected in the important concept of *wa*, or harmony. This aversion to conflict is even manifested in the Japanese legal system. Estimates are that the Japanese only have one lawyer for every 10,000 people, while in the United States, a culture that values assertive behavior, there is one lawyer for every 50 people (Samovar et al., 2010).

The same attitude toward conflict prevails in China, where one proverb states, "The first person to raise his voice loses the argument." Among Chinese college students (in both the People's Republic and Taiwan), the three most common methods of persuasion used are "hinting," "setting an example by one's own actions," and "strategically agreeing to whatever pleases others" (Ma & Chuang, 2001). However, young adults in China favor collaborative problem solving more than do their elders, who prefer accommodating styles (Zhang et al., 2005).

Within the United States, the ethnic background of communicators plays a role in their ideas about conflict (Orbe & Everett, 2006). When a group of Mexican American and European American college students were asked about their views regarding conflict, some important differences emerged (Collier, 1991). For example, European Americans seem more willing to accept conflict as a natural part of relationships, while Mexican Americans describe the short- and long-term dangers of disagreeing. European Americans' willingness to experience conflicts may be part of their individualistic, low-context communication style of speaking directly and avoiding uncertainty. It's not surprising that people from cultures that emphasize harmony among people with close relationships tend to handle conflicts in less direct ways.

With differences like these, it's easy to imagine how two friends, lovers, or fellow workers from different cultural backgrounds might have trouble finding a conflict style that is comfortable for both of them.

Despite these differences, it's important to realize that culture isn't the only factor that influences the way people think about conflict or how they behave when they disagree. Some research (e.g., Beatty & McCroskey, 1997; Horwitz et al., 2010) suggests that our approach to conflict may be part of our biological makeup. Emotional intelligence (see Chapter 8) also plays a role: people high in emotional intelligence tend to use a collaborating conflict style, while those low in emotional intelligence tend to use an accommodating style (Morrison, 2008). Furthermore, scholarship suggests a person's self-concept is more powerful than his or her culture in determining conflict style (Bechtoldt et al., 2010; Ting-Toomey et al., 2001). For example, African Americans, Asian Americans, European Americans, and Latin Americans who view themselves as mostly independent of others are likely to use a direct, solution-oriented conflict style, regardless of their cultural heritage. Those who see themselves as mostly interdependent are likely to use a style that avoids direct confrontation. And those who see themselves as both independent and interdependent are likely to have the widest variety of conflict behaviors on which to draw.

Conflict Management in Practice

The collaborative conflict management style described earlier in this chapter may be unfamiliar to those who are used to handling conflict in other ways. As a result, collaboration sometimes requires more specific guidelines to put into practice. In an 11-year longitudinal study following a hundred couples who had conflict skills training, Kurt Hahlweg and Diana Richter (2010) found that *it works* for couples willing to focus on improving their relationships.

Win-win problem solving works best when it follows a seven-step approach that is based on plans developed by Deborah Weider-Hatfield (1981) and Ellen Raider and her colleagues (2006). Notice how many of the skills that have been discussed throughout this book are incorporated in this process.

1. Define your needs. Begin by deciding what you want or need. Sometimes the answer is obvious, as in our earlier example of the neighbor whose loud music kept others awake. In other instances, however, the apparent problem masks a more fundamental one. Consider an example: After dating for a few months, Elizabeth started to call Jim after they parted for the evening—a "goodnight call." Although the calling was fine with Jim at the beginning, he began to find it irritating after several weeks.

At first, Jim thought his aggravation focused on the nuisance of talking late at night when he was ready for sleep. More self-examination showed that his irritation centered on the relational message he thought Elizabeth's calls implied: that she was either snooping on Jim or was so insecure

FOCUS ON RESEARCH

Self-Fulfilling Prophecies Shape Conflict Outcomes

Think of someone you've considered confronting about a complaint or problem. Maybe it's a family member, friend, or romantic partner. As you imagine raising your issue of concern, how do you think the conversation will turn out? Do you anticipate a calm and rational discussion, or do you think it will degrade into a nasty fight?

Communication researchers Benjamin DiPaola and Michael Roloff discovered that what we expect to happen in a conflict can play a significant role in shaping the episode's outcome. They asked undergraduate students to recall a recent conflict conversation, and also to recall what they expected beforehand would happen during the discussion. Those who anticipated that their confrontations would not go well reported that the episodes were indeed emotionally upsetting, involved personal attacks, and subsequently interfered with their everyday lives. Those who approached their conflicts with positive expectations reported much less animosity in their conversations.

The researchers believe that a self-fulfilling prophecy was at work in these situations (see Chapter 3 for a discussion of this phenomenon). If you approach a conflict with negative expectations, you're likely to engage in the very behavior you feared would happen—and thus you inadvertently sabotage the outcome. The prescription appears clear: It's important to address conflicts with a positive attitude, envisioning the best rather than the worst. Your behavior in the conversation might depend on it.

DiPaola, B. M., & Roloff, M. E. (2010). College students' expectations of conflict intensity: A self-fulfilling prophecy. *Communication Quarterly, 58,* 59-76.

she needed constant assurances of his love. Once Jim recognized the true sources of his irritation, his needs became clear: (1) to have Elizabeth's trust and (2) to be free of her insecurities.

Because your needs won't always be clear, it's often necessary to think about a problem alone, before approaching the other person involved. Talking to a third person can sometimes help you sort out your thoughts. In either case, you should explore both the apparent content of your dissatisfaction and the relational issues that may lurk behind it.

2. Share your needs with the other person. Once you've defined your needs, it's time to share them with your partner. Two guidelines are important here: First, be sure to choose a time and place that is suitable. Unloading on a tired or busy partner lowers the odds that your concerns will be well received. Likewise, be sure you are at your best: Don't bring an issue up when your anger may cause you to say things you'll later regret, when your discouragement blows the problem out of proportion, or when you're distracted by other business. Making a date to discuss the problem—after dinner, over a cup of coffee, or even a day in advance—often can boost the odds of a successful outcome.

The second guideline for sharing a problem is to use the descriptive "I" language outlined in Chapter 5. Rather than implying blame, messages worded in this way convey how your partner's behavior affects you. Notice how Jim's use of the assertive message format conveys a descriptive, nonjudgmental attitude as he shares his concerns with Elizabeth: "When you call me after every date [sense data], I begin to wonder whether you're checking up on me [interpretation of Elizabeth's behavior]. I've also started to think that you're feeling insecure about whether I care about you and that you need lots of reassurance [more interpretation]. I'm starting to feel closed in by the calls [feeling], and I feel myself pulling back from you [consequence]. I don't like the way we're headed, and I don't think it's necessary. I'd like to know whether you are feeling insecure and to find a way that we can feel sure about each other's feelings without needing so much reassurance [intentions]."

In a tense situation, it may not be easy to start sharing your needs. Raider et al. (2006) recommend beginning with what they call *ritual sharing*, which is preliminary, casual conversation. The goal is to build rapport and establish common ground and, perhaps, to pick up information.

3. Listen to the other person's needs. Once your own wants and needs are clear, it's time to find out what the other person wants and needs. (Now the listening skills described in Chapter 7 and the supportive behaviors described in Chapter 10 become most important.) When Jim began to talk to Elizabeth about her telephoning, he learned some interesting things. In his haste to hang up the phone the first few times she called, he had given her the impression that he didn't care about her once the date was over. Feeling insecure about his love, she called as a way of getting attention and expressions of love from him.

Once Jim realized this fact, it became clear that he needed to find a solution that would leave Elizabeth feeling secure and at the same time relieve him of feeling pressured.

Arriving at a shared definition of the problem requires skills associated with creating a supportive and confirming climate. The ability to be non-judgmental, descriptive, and empathic is an important, support-producing skill. Both Jim and Elizabeth needed to engage in paraphrasing to discover all the details of the conflict.

When they're really communicating effectively, partners can help each other clarify what they're seeking. Truly believing that their happiness depends on each other's satisfaction, they actively try to analyze what obstacles need to be overcome.

4. Generate possible solutions. In the next step, the partners try to think of as many ways to satisfy both of their needs as possible. They can best do so by "brainstorming"—inventing as many potential solutions as they can. The key to success in brainstorming is to seek quantity without worrying about quality. The rule is to prohibit criticism of all ideas, no matter how outlandish they may sound. An idea that seems farfetched can sometimes lead to a more workable one. Another rule of brainstorming is that ideas aren't personal property. If one person makes a suggestion, the other should feel free to suggest another solution that builds upon or modifies the original one. The original suggestion and its offshoots are all potential solutions that will be considered later. Once

"Norman won't collaborate."

partners get over their possessiveness about ideas, the level of defensiveness drops and both people can work together to find the best solution without worrying about whose idea it is. (The supportive and confirming behaviors discussed in Chapter 10 are particularly important during this step.)

Jim and Elizabeth used brainstorming to generate solutions to their telephone problem. Their list consisted of continuing the calling but limiting the time spent on the phone, limiting the calls to a "once in a while" basis, Elizabeth's keeping a journal that could serve as a substitute for calling, Jim's calling Elizabeth on a "once in a while" basis, cutting out all calling, moving in together to eliminate the necessity for calling, getting married, and breaking up. Although some of these solutions were clearly unacceptable to both partners, they listed all the ideas they could think of, preparing themselves for the next step in win-win problem solving.

5. Evaluate the possible solutions and choose the best one. The time to evaluate the solutions is after they all have been generated, after the partners feel they have exhausted all the possibilities. In this step, the possible solutions generated during the previous step are evaluated for their ability to satisfy everyone's important goals. How does each solution stand up against the individual and mutual goals? Which solution satisfies the most goals? Partners need to work cooperatively in examining each solution and in finally selecting the best one.

It is important during this step to react spontaneously rather than strategically. Selecting a particular solution because the other person finds it satisfactory (an accommodation strategy), while seemingly a "nice" thing to do, is as manipulative a strategy as getting the other person to accept a solution satisfactory only to you (a win-lose strategy). Respond as you feel as solutions are evaluated, and encourage your partner to do the same. Any solution agreed upon as "best" has little chance of satisfying both partners' needs if it was strategically manipulated to the top of the list.

The solution Elizabeth and Jim selected as satisfying her need to feel secure, his need to be undisturbed before turning in, and their mutual goal of maintaining their relationship at a highly intimate level was to limit both the frequency and length of the calls. Also, Jim agreed to share in the calling.

6. Implement the solution. Now the time comes to try out the idea selected to see if it does, indeed, satisfy everyone's needs. The key questions to answer are *who* does *what* to *whom*, and *when*?

Before Jim and Elizabeth tried out their solution, they went over the agreement to make sure it was clear. This step proved to be important, for a potential misunderstanding existed. When will the solution be implemented? Should Elizabeth wait a few weeks before calling? Should Jim begin the calling? They agreed that Jim would call after their next date.

Another problem concerned their different definitions of length. How long is too long? They decided that more than a few minutes would be too long.

The solution was implemented after they discussed the solution and came to mutual agreement about its particulars. This process may seem awkward and time consuming, but both Elizabeth and Jim decided that without a clear understanding of the solution, they were opening the door to future conflicts.

Interestingly, the discussion concerning their mutual needs and how the solution satisfied them was an important part of their relationship's development. Jim learned that Elizabeth did, sometimes, feel insecure about his love; Elizabeth learned that Jim needed time to himself and that this need did not reflect on his love for her. Soon after implementing the solution, they found that the problem ceased to exist. Jim no longer felt the calls were invading his privacy, and Elizabeth, after talks with Jim, felt more secure about his love.

7. Follow up the solution. To stop after selecting and implementing a particular solution assumes any solution is forever, that time does not change things, that people remain constant, and that events never alter circumstances. Of course, this assumption is not the case: As people and circumstances change, a particular solution may lose or increase its effectiveness. Regardless, a follow-up evaluation needs to take place.

After you've tested your solution for a short time, it's a good idea to plan a meeting to talk about how things are going. You may find that you need to make some changes or even rethink the whole problem.

Reviewing the effects of your solution does not mean that something is wrong and must be corrected. Indeed, everything may point to the conclusion that the solution is still working to satisfy your needs and the mutually shared goal, and that the mutually shared goal is still important to both of you.

It is important at this stage in the win-win problem-solving process to be honest with yourself as well as with the other person. It may be difficult for you to say "We need to talk about this again," yet it could be essential if the problem is to remain resolved. Planning a follow-up talk when the solution is first implemented is important.

Elizabeth and Jim decided to wait one month before discussing the effects of their solution. Their talk was short, because both felt the problem no longer existed. Also, their discussions helped their relationship grow: They learned more about each other, felt closer, and developed a way to handle their conflicts constructively.

Summary

Despite wishes and cultural myths to the contrary, conflict is a natural and unavoidable part of any relationship. Since conflict can't be escaped, the challenge is how to deal with it effectively so that it strengthens a relationship rather than weakens it.

All conflicts possess the same characteristics: expressed struggle, perceived incompatible goals, perceived scarce resources, interdependence, and inevitability. Functional conflicts cope with these characteristics in very different ways from dysfunctional ones. Partners view one another as an integrated unit and not as opponents. They treat one another with respect, strive to cooperate instead of compete, and work to de-escalate the intensity of their conflict. They focus on rather than avoid the issues in dispute and seek positive, long-term solutions that meet each other's needs.

Communicators can respond to conflicts in a variety of ways: avoidance, accommodation, competition, compromise, or collaboration. Each of these approaches can be justified in certain circumstances. The way a conflict is handled isn't always the choice of a single person, since the communicators influence one another as they develop a relational conflict style. This style is also influenced by the partners' genders and the influences of their cultural backgrounds.

In most circumstances a collaborative, win-win outcome is the ideal, and it can be achieved by following the guidelines outlined in the last section of this chapter.

Key Terms

- Accommodation (360)
- Avoidance (358)
- Collaboration (363)
- Competition (361)
- Complementary conflict style (368)
- Compromise (362)
- Conflict (351)
- Conflict ritual (371)
- De-escalatory spiral (369)
- Direct aggression (362)
- Dysfunctional conflict (353)
- Escalatory spiral (369)
- Functional conflict (353)
- Parallel conflict style (368)
- Passive aggression (361)
- Symmetrical conflict style (368)
- Win-win problem solving (364)

Activities

1. Invitation to Insight
Even the best relationships have conflicts. Using the characteristics on pages 351–353, describe at least five conflicts in one of your important relationships. Then answer the following questions:
  a. Which conflicts involve primarily content issues? Which involve primarily relational issues?
  b. Which conflicts were one-time affairs, and which recur?

2. Invitation to Insight

From your recent experiences recall two conflict incidents, one functional and one dysfunctional. Then answer the following questions:
a. What distinguished these two conflicts?
b. What were the consequences of each?
c. How might the dysfunctional conflict have turned out differently if it had been handled in a more functional manner?
d. How could you have communicated differently to make the dysfunctional conflict more functional?

3. Skill Builder

Review the hypothetical conflict between Chris and Pat (page 358) and come up with examples (other than the ones mentioned in the text) of how they might use each of these conflict styles in their situation:
a. Avoidance
b. Accommodation
c. Competition
d. Compromise
e. Collaboration

In particular, see if you can come up with several collaborative, win-win solutions to their problem.

4. Invitation to Insight

Interview someone who knows you well. Ask your informant which personal conflict styles (avoidance, accommodation, etc.) you use most often and the effect each of these styles has on your relationship with this person. Based on your findings, discuss whether different behavior might produce more productive results.

5. Invitation to Insight

This activity will be most productive if you consult with several people with whom you share an interpersonal relationship as you answer the following questions:
a. Is your relational style of handling conflict complementary, symmetrical, or parallel? What are the consequences of this style?
b. What conflict rituals do you follow in this relationship? Are these rituals functional or dysfunctional? What might be better alternatives?

6. Skill Builder

To explore how the win-win approach might work in your life, try one of the following alternatives:
a. Use the steps on pages 375–379 to describe how you could manage a conflict by following the win-win approach. How could you try this approach in your personal life? What difference might such an approach make?
b. Try the win-win approach with a relational partner. What parts prove most helpful? Which are most difficult? How can you improve your relationship by using some or all of the win-win approach in future conflicts?

Interpersonal Contexts
Friends, Family, and Intimate Relationships

After studying the material in this chapter . . .

You should understand:

1. The various types of friendships.
2. The impact of gender on friendships.
3. How families are shaped and defined by communication.
4. How communication operates to create and maintain family systems.
5. The influence of gender, culture, and technology on communication in intimate relationships.

You should be able to:

1. Categorize your friendships according to certain characteristics.
2. Understand how you can improve the quality of communication in a specific friendship.
3. Describe the defining narratives, roles, rules, and patterns that involve communication in a specific family.
4. Evaluate the ways intimacy is expressed in a specific relationship.
5. Evaluate the quality of communication in a specific intimate relationship, and describe ways in which that relationship can be strengthened through more effective communication.

W hat relationships are most important to you? When researchers posed this question to several hundred college students, the answers were varied (Berscheid et al., 1989). Roughly half (47 percent) identified a romantic partner. About a third (36 percent) chose a friendship. Most of the rest (14 percent) cited a family member.

In this chapter, we'll look at how communication operates in the three contexts that most of us regard as central to our lives: Friendships, families, and intimate relationships. The information here builds on the concepts you learned in earlier chapters, but the focus here is on unique characteristics that shape communication in each type of relationship.

Communication in Friendships

Type the word "friendship" into a web browser along with one of these phrases: "in songs"; "in movies"; "in TV shows." You'll see that popular culture is filled with references to friends and friendship. In fact, you can probably think of several artistic tributes to friendship on your own without searching online. We depict and celebrate these special relationships because they are central to what it means to be human.

But what exactly is a friend? Scholars have offered many definitions of friendships (e.g., Bell, 1991; Bukowski et al., 2009; Fehr, 2000). Most of them include the notions that a **friendship** is a voluntary relationship that provides social support. Most importantly for our purposes, friendships are created, managed, and maintained through communication (Johnson et al., 2009; McEwan & Guerrero, 2010). Different types of friendships involve different levels of communication, as we'll explore now.

TYPES OF FRIENDSHIPS

Before reading further, take a moment to complete the Self-Assessment on the next page. Choose three friends from distinct parts of your life—perhaps an old neighborhood pal, someone from work, and your BFF ("best friend forever"). Next, rank these friends on the assessment scales. It's likely

---

SELF-ASSESSMENT
Analyzing Your Friendship Types

Select three of your personal friendships to assess. For each, respond to the following items:

1. How long have you maintained the friendship? How long do you think it will last?

   SHORT-TERM   1   2   3   4   5   LONG-TERM

2. Does your friendship primarily revolve around joint activities and hobbies, or do you spend time together just to enjoy each other's company?

   TASK-ORIENTED   1   2   3   4   5   MAINTENANCE-ORIENTED

3. How much do you tell your friend about yourself? Do you keep your conversations light and superficial, or do you share intimate details of your lives?

   LOW DISCLOSURE   1   2   3   4   5   HIGH DISCLOSURE

4. How much would you be willing to do for your friend? How quickly would you respond to a phone call or favor request from your friend?

   LOW OBLIGATION   1   2   3   4   5   HIGH OBLIGATION

5. How often do you have contact with your friend?

   INFREQUENT CONTACT   1   2   3   4   5   FREQUENT CONTACT

What are the similarities and differences in the communication of the friendships you assessed? Do these and your other friendships share common communication patterns? How satisfied are you with your findings? Do you want to change the types of friendships you tend to have? Why or why not?

---

that at least some characteristics of these three relationships are quite different, even though you would consider each to be a friend. Here's a closer look at several dimensions of communication in friendships.

Short Term vs. Long Term Friends come in and out of our lives for a variety of reasons. Some friendships last for years or even a lifetime, while others fade or end because of life changes (such as finishing high school, moving to a new location, or switching jobs). Although modern technologies have decreased the likelihood that a friendship will end because of a long-distance move (Utz, 2007), some falter or fail without face-to-face contact. Another reason some friendships may be short-term is due to a change in values (Solomon & Knafo, 2007). Perhaps you once had a group of friends with whom you enjoyed parties and nightlife, but as you grew out of that phase of your life, the mutual attraction waned.

Task Oriented vs. Maintenance Oriented Sometimes we choose friends because of shared activities: teammates in a softball league, coworkers, or fellow movie buffs. These types of friendships are considered task oriented if they primarily revolve around certain activities. On the other hand, maintenance-oriented friendships are grounded in mutual liking and social support, independent of shared activities. Of course these categories overlap: Some friendships are based in both joint activities and emotional support.

Low Disclosure vs. High Disclosure How much do you tell your friends about yourself? No doubt your level of disclosure differs from friend to friend. Some only know general information about you, while others are privy to your most personal secrets. The Social Penetration Model in Chapter 3 (pages 87–89) can help you explore the breadth and depth of your disclosure with your various friends.

Low Obligation vs. High Obligation There are some friends for whom we would do just about anything—no request is too big. We feel a lower sense of obligation to other friends, both in terms of what we would do for them and how quickly we would do it. Our closest friends usually get fast responses when they ask for a favor, give us a call, or even post on our Facebook wall.

Infrequent Contact vs. Frequent Contact You probably keep in close touch with some friends. Perhaps you work out, travel, socialize together, or Skype daily. Other friendships have less frequent contact—maybe an occasional phone call or e-message. Of course, infrequent contact doesn't always correlate with levels of disclosure or obligation. Many close friends may see each other only once a year, but they pick right back up in terms of the breadth and depth of their shared information.

　　After completing the self-assessment and reading this far, you can begin to see that the nature of communication can vary from one friendship to another. Furthermore, communication *within* a friendship can also change over time. Impersonal friendships can have sudden bursts of disclosure. The amount of communication can swing from more to less frequent. Low-obligation friendships can evolve into stronger commitments, and vice versa. In a few pages you'll read about types of communication that are common in virtually all good friendships. But for now, it's important to recognize that variety is a good thing.

FRIENDSHIPS, GENDER, AND COMMUNICATION

Not all friendships are created equal. Along with the differences described in the preceding pages, gender plays a role in how we communicate with friends.

Same-Sex Friendships Recall the first friend you ever had. If you're like most people, that person was probably the same sex as you. Many of the first close relationships outside the family are with same-sex friends (Bukowski et al., 1996).

In adolescence and adulthood, communication within same-sex friendships differs for men and women. Whereas women place a somewhat higher value on talking about personal matters as a measure of closeness, men are more likely to create and express closeness by doing things together—often in groups rather than in one-on-one interactions (Baumeister, 2005). In one study, more than 75 percent of the men surveyed said that their most meaningful experiences with friends came from shared activities (Swain, 1989). They reported that through shared activities they "grew on one another," developed feelings of interdependence, showed appreciation for one another, and demonstrated mutual liking. Likewise, men regarded practical help as a measure of caring. Findings like these show that, for many men, closeness grows from activities that don't always depend heavily on disclosure: A friend is a person who does things *for* you and *with* you.

Women tend to disclose personal information more than men, both in face-to-face relationships (Dindia & Allen, 1992; Rubin, 1983), and online (Bond, 2009). Activity 1 on page 410 will help you discover whether this research matches your own experience. Even without keeping records, you may be aware that the topics you talk and write about differ depending on the sex of the friend with whom you're communicating. Research suggests that sex differences like these seem to be stronger for friendships among heterosexuals than among homosexuals (de Vries and Megathlin, 2009).

MEDIA CLIP COMPANIONSHIP IN GROUPS: FLOCK COMEDIES

Although we typically think of friendship as a relationship between two people, you wouldn't know it from watching television. As critics have noted, TV friends are more likely to hang out in packs of three or more than in pairs (Brooks, 2010; Gabler, 2010). For several decades, groups have been the format for friendship; from *Friends* and *Sex in the City* to *How I Met Your Mother* and *The Big Bang Theory.*

Take a few moments to analyze the communication in your favorite flock comedy—and in your own flock. What are the friends' levels of contact, disclosure, and obligation, both to the group and its individual members? How do same-sex and cross-sex interactions affect the group's friendships? How well do the characters follow the expectations of successful friendships—and what happens when they don't?

Opposite-Sex Friendships Opposite-sex friendships offer a wealth of benefits (Sapadin, 1988; Werking, 1997). They give us a chance to see how the other half lives, and they offer a welcome contrast to the kinds of interaction that characterize communication with friends of the same sex. For men, this often means a greater chance to share emotions and focus on relationships. For women, it can be a chance to lighten up and enjoy banter without emotional baggage.

Opposite-sex friendships—at least for heterosexuals—present some challenges that don't exist among all-male or all-female companionships

AT WORK

Can Women Be Coworkers and Friends?

The studies cited in these pages suggest that female friendships are sometimes more open and closer than male friendships or cross-sex friendships. Nonetheless, a body of research suggests that on-the-job friendships between women can be problematic.

In one survey of over 1,000 nurses, three out of four reported being undermined by another woman in the workplace (Briles, 1999). Another study conducted for the American Management Association found that 95% of the female participants felt that other women had disrupted their careers at some point (Heim & Murphy, 2001).

This isn't to suggest that men don't sabotage others in the workplace—but they may not have the same assumptions about friendships on the job. Some scholars argue that high expectations play a role in women's feelings of being undermined in the workplace (Litwin & Hallstein, 2007). If the expectation is that female colleagues should become friends, then any behavior to the contrary may feel like betrayal.

(O'Meara, 1989). The most obvious is the potential for sexual attraction (Halatsis & Christakis, 2009). In one survey of 150 working professionals, over 60 percent noted that sexual tension was a factor in their relationship (Sapadin, 1988). While it's possible to have romance-free same-sex friendships, defining that sort of relationship can take effort. Some evidence suggests that opposite-sex friends communicate more online to keep the relationship platonic (Ledbetter et al., 2011). See the Focus on Research sidebar on the next page for more about sex and friendships.

When it comes to the potential for romance, heterosexual cross-sex friendships fit into one of four categories (Guerrero & Chavez, 2005). (We can assume the same holds true for same-sex friendships among gay men and lesbians.):

- *Mutual Romance*—both partners want the friendship to turn romantic

- *Strictly Platonic*—neither partner wants the friendship to turn romantic

- *Desires Romance*—one partner wants romance but fears the friend does not

- *Rejects Romance*—one partner does not want romance but thinks the friend does

Not surprisingly, the last two types of relationships are the most complicated. Guerrero and Chavez found that the less interested partner in these situations used strategies to communicate "no go" messages: less routine contact and activity, less flirtation, and more talk about outside romance.

Gender Considerations Biological sex isn't the only factor to consider when we examine different sorts of friendships. Another important consideration is *sex role* (see Chapter 4, page 119). For instance, a friendship between a masculine male and a feminine female might have very different properties than a friendship between a masculine female and a feminine male—even though these are both technically "cross-sex" relationships.

Sexual orientation is another factor that can shape friendships. Most obviously, for gay men and lesbians the potential for sexual attraction shifts from opposite- to same-sex relationships. But physical attraction aside,

F⊕CUS ON RESEARCH

Friends with Benefits: The Communication Challenges of Not-So-Casual Sex

It's more than casual sex and less than a committed relationship. "Friends with benefits" (FWB) is a popular term for nonromantic heterosexual friendships that include sexual activity. In separate studies conducted at different universities, nearly 60 percent of the students surveyed said they had participated in at least one FWB relationship.

Research conducted by Justin Lehmiller and his colleagues found that men and women are equally likely to be in FWB relationships—but often for different reasons. Whereas the majority of men viewed their relationships as primarily sexual, women were much more likely to be emotionally involved. The researchers concluded that in FWB relationships, women are typically more focused on being "friends" while men are more likely to be interested in the "benefits."

A study by communication researchers Melissa Bisson and Timothy Levine sheds additional light on the FWB experience. A common reason the surveyed students have FWBs is that those relationships offer trust and comfort while avoiding romantic commitment. However, a common concern for both men and women is that sexual activity might lead to unreciprocated desires for romantic commitment. Given this tension, it would seem logical that FWB partners would regularly discuss the status of their relationship—but the researchers found that FWBs routinely avoid explicit communication about this important topic. Bisson and Levine conclude that "FWB relationships are often problematic for the same reasons that they are attractive."

Bisson, M. A., & Levine, T. R. (2009). Negotiating a friends with benefits relationship. *Archives of Sexual Behavior, 38*, 66–73.

Lehmiller, J. J., VanderDrift, L. E., & Kelly, J. R. (2011). Sex differences in approaching friends with benefits relationships. *Journal of Sex Research, 48*, 275–284.

sexual orientation can still play a significant role in friendships. For example, many heterosexual women report that they value their friendships with gay men because (a) they often share interests, (b) the potential for romantic complications is small or nonexistent (Hopcke & Rafaty, 2001), and (c) the women feel more attractive (Bartlett et al., 2009).

COMMUNICATION IN SUCCESSFUL FRIENDSHIPS

Friendships come with a set of expectations about how to communicate. We rarely discuss these assumptions, and we often become aware of them only when they aren't met. Communication scholars have found that **expectancy violations**—instances when others don't behave as we assume they should—are the source of many relational problems (Afifi & Metts, 1998; Cohen, 2010). The following guidelines culled from two studies (Argyle & Henderson, 1984; Baxter, Dun, & Sahlstein, 2001) offer prescriptions on what most people expect from their friends. Although these guidelines are validated by research, they may seem like common sense. Nonetheless, it's likely you can judge the success of your friendships at least in part by seeing how closely you follow them.

Share Joys and Sorrows When you have bad news, you want to tell friends who will offer comfort and support. When a friend has good news, you want to hear about it and celebrate. When sharing sorrows and joys with friends, it's often important how quickly and in what order the news is delivered. The closer the friendship, the higher the expectation for sharing soon. Phrases like "How come you got a new job and I'm the last to find out?" suggest a violation has occurred.

Provide a Listening Ear As you read in Chapter 10, listening is an important type of confirming message. Paying attention—even when you aren't especially interested—is one way to show that you care about your friend. Chapter 7 describes a variety of responses you can offer to a friend to demonstrate that you're listening and understanding.

Maintain Confidences Betraying a confidence can injure, or even end, a friendship (Petronio, 2002). When you share personal information with a friend, you expect that person to be discrete about what you said—especially when the information could damage your reputation or other relationships.

Lend a Helping Hand The old saying "A friend in need is a friend indeed" is supported by studies showing that providing assistance is one of the most tangible markers of a friendship (MacGeorge et al., 2004; Semmer et al., 2008). Need a ride to the airport, some help on moving day, or a quick loan until payday? These are the kinds of things we expect from friends.

Stand Up for Each Other A loyal friend "has your back"—both when you're present and when you're not. Few things are more endearing than a friend who defends your rights, honor, and reputation.

Honor Pledges and Commitments "You can count on me" and "I'll be there for you" are common friendship sentiments. These pledges, however, need to be backed up with actions. Whether it's showing up on time, attending a scheduled event, or fulfilling an agreement about a shared task, it's vital for friends to live up to their promises and obligations.

Treat Each Other with Respect Sometimes we say the most hurtful things to people we care about the most (Vangelisti & Crumley, 1998; Zhang & Stafford, 2009). It's easy for banter in a friendship to slip into teasing that hurts and comments that sting. Good friends monitor their words and actions, making sure to communicate in ways that affirm the other person's dignity.

Have a Balanced Exchange Social exchange theory (page 284) tells us that the rewards of a relationship need to outweigh the costs. College students in one study identified "Don't take more than you give" as an important friendship rule (Baxter et al., 2001).

Value Both Connection and Autonomy Chapter 9 describes how all interpersonal relationships struggle with competing needs for both closeness and independence. In essence, we have a need to spend time with our friends and to spend time away from them. Allow your friends space to develop their own identity and nurture other relationships—and also the freedom to make choices that might not match your own.

Apologize and Forgive Sooner or later friends are bound to make the kinds of "relational transgressions" described in Chapter 9 (pages 304–305). As you read there, a good apology has several components, including *sincerely* expressing remorse, admitting wrongdoing, promising to behave better, and requesting forgiveness. When you're the one who has been wronged, granting forgiveness can help repair the friendship and leave you feeling better than holding a grudge (Bernstein, 2010; Merolla, 2008).

Communication in the Family

A few generations ago, "What is a family?" was an easy question to answer for most people. Common notions of a family in the Western world typically stressed shared residence, reproduction or adoption of children by different-sexed adults, and a "socially approved sexual relationship" (Murdock, 1965, p. 1). A more recent study of college students found that their definitions of family contained many of these same elements (Baxter et al., 2009). However, social scientists, lawyers, judges, theologians, and the public at large have grappled with much broader definitions as they ponder questions such as who the parents are when there is an egg or sperm donor, the rights of adoptive parents and adopted children, and whether homosexual couples can adopt a child.

After reviewing a century's worth of definitions, Kathleen Galvin and her colleagues (2007) define family broadly enough to include many types of relationships. According to them, a **family** is a system with two or more interdependent people who have a common history and a present reality, and who expect to influence each other in the future. With this broader definition in mind, communication scholars contend that families are defined primarily through their interaction rather than through biological relationship or kinship systems. To see how, read on.

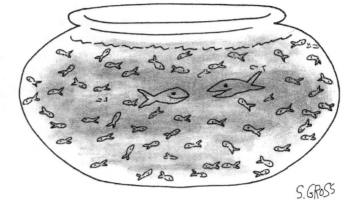

S. GROSS

"I guess we'd be considered a family. We're living together, we love each other, and we haven't eaten the children yet."

CREATING THE FAMILY THROUGH COMMUNICATION

Families are based on, formed, and maintained through communication (Noller & Fitzpatrick, 1993). It's through communication that family members create mental models of family life, and through communication those models endure over time and across generations (Vangelisti, 2004). The following sections describe several ways that communication shapes and constitutes the family.

Family Narratives Chapter 4 (pages 114–115) explained how shared narratives provide a storyline that keeps relationships operating harmoniously. Narratives are especially important in families, where they serve a variety of functions that include reinforcing shared goals, teaching moral values, and stressing family concerns (Galvin et al., 2007).

Family stories often have meaning that goes beyond the incident being recounted. Some might reflect beliefs about work ("I walked up the hill both ways, in the snow, barefoot"), family identity (e.g., stories related to immigrating to the United States), and warnings ("You don't want to end up like so-and-so, do you?"). Narratives may reflect a family's view of how members relate to one another: "We help each other a lot" or "We are proud of our heritage." Others reflect values about how to operate in the world: "It's impossible to be successful without a good education," or "It's our responsibility to help others less fortunate than ourselves." Even dysfunctional families can be united by a shared narrative: "What a hopeless bunch! We can never get along." One study showed that families who regularly engage in positive storytelling (focusing on achievements and using "we" language) have high levels of family functioning and satisfaction (Kellas, 2005).

Communication Rituals and Rules Rituals are another way family is created through communication (Baxter & Clark, 1996). Some rituals center on celebrations: special family meals, certain types of gifts, the post-Thanksgiving touch football game, and so on. Other rituals are part of everyday life: good-natured teasing about family members' quirks, or saying "I love you" at the end of every phone conversation.

Rituals aren't the only way that families create their own communication systems. As unique cultures, families also have their own rules about a variety of communication practices. Some communication rules are explicit: "If you're going to be more than a half hour late, phone home." Other rules aren't ever discussed, but they are just as important: "If Mom slams the door after coming home from work, wait until she's had time to relax before speaking to her." Some rules govern communication within the family (Caughlin & Petronio, 2004; Guerrero & Afifi, 1995). How far is it okay to push challenges of parental decisions? What kinds of language are allowed and forbidden? How much kidding and teasing are acceptable? Are there any forbidden topics?

Recent research by Leslie Baxter and Chitra Akkoor (2011) showed that some topics of conversation are allowed and encouraged while others are discouraged, if not off limits in most families. For example, both parents and children agreed that conversations about friendships and everyday matters were fine. On the other hand, topics related to sex, drinking, money, and how teens were doing academically fell into the second group.

Stepfamilies often have their own unique rules. Tamara Golish (2000) interviewed 115 adolescents and young adults in stepfamilies to learn about topics they tend to avoid with their parents and stepparents. Stepchildren reported more topic avoidance with their stepparents than with their parents. In particular, stepchildren say they often avoid "deep conversations" or talking about money and family issues with their stepparents. One factor affecting the comfort level in stepfamily communication is the type of parenting style used by the stepparents. Stepchildren feel more dissatisfied and avoid more topics with stepparents who are highly authoritarian (i.e., demanding and rigid). Interestingly, stepchildren also say they are dissatisfied with highly permissive stepparents.

Other rules—often explicit—govern communicating with people outside the family. Parents may tell a young child, "It's OK to talk with people you know, but don't talk to strangers when we're not around." Use of the Internet, which gives access to people and ideas outside the home, also is regulated by a host of rules (Papadakis, 2003). For example, parents can restrict the areas that can be visited online, as well as when (such as after homework is done) and how long the Internet can be accessed.

PATTERNS OF FAMILY COMMUNICATION

Whatever form families take, the communication that occurs within them shares some important characteristics, which we will examine now.

Families as Communication Systems Every family has its own unique ways of communicating. Despite these differences, all families are **systems** whose members interact with one another to form a whole. Families, like all systems, possess a number of characteristics that shape the way members communicate (Galvin et al., 2006; Lerner et al., 2002).

Family Members Are Interdependent If you touch one piece of a mobile, all the other parts will move in response. In the same way, one family member's feelings and behaviors affect all the other members. If, for example, one family member leaves home to marry, or a parent loses a job, or feuding siblings stop talking to one another, or a member wins the lottery, the system is no longer the same. Each event is a reaction to the family's history, and each event shapes future interaction.

A Family Is More Than the Sum of Its Parts Even if you knew each member separately, you still wouldn't understand the family system until you saw the members interact. When those members are together, new ways of communicating emerge (Whitchurch & Constantine, 1993). For instance, you may have known friends who turned into very different people when they became a couple. Maybe they became better as individuals—more confident, clever, and happy. Or perhaps they became more aggressive and

MEDIA CLIP

A CONTEMPORARY COMMUNICATION SYSTEM: *MODERN FAMILY*

The critically acclaimed TV sitcom *Modern Family* chronicles the misadventures of three households who are all part of the same extended clan.

As the title suggests, the diverse range of relationships in *Modern Family* would have been improbable in previous generations. The most traditional household includes cheerfully uncool dad Phil (Ty Burrell), over-stressed mom Claire (Julie Bowen), and their three very different children. Claire's father Jay (Ed O'Neill) is in a second marriage with Columbian wife Gloria (Sofia Vergara), who is half his age. They live with Manny (Rico Rodriguez), Gloria's son from a previous relationship. Claire's brother Mitchell (Jesse Tyler Ferguson) is in a committed relationship with his partner Cameron (Eric Stonestreet), and they have an adopted Vietnamese daughter.

Each episode of *Modern Family* illustrates the principles of family systems described in these pages. This series captures the rich, complicated, interdependent nature of relationships among partners, parents, children, grandparents, siblings, in-laws, step-cousins, and more.

defensive. Likewise, the nature of a couple's relationship is likely to change when a child arrives, and that family's interaction will change again with the arrival of each subsequent baby.

Families Have Systems within the Larger System Like boxes within boxes, families have subsystems (systems within the family). For example, a traditional family of four can have six communication subsystems with two people: mother and father, mother and son, mother and daughter, father and son, father and daughter, and daughter and son. If you add three-person subsystems to these six (e.g., mother, father, and daughter), the number of combinations is even greater. The nuclear family itself is a subsystem of larger suprasystems (systems of which the family is a part) that include aunts and uncles, cousins, grandparents, in-laws, and so on.

Openness and Conformity in the Family Ascan Koerner and Mary Ann Fitzpatrick (2002, 2006a) have identified two categories of rules about communication in the family: conversation and conformity. **Conversation orientation** involves the degree to which families favor an open climate of discussion of a wide array of topics. Families with a high conversation orientation interact freely, frequently, and spontaneously, without many limitations regarding topic or time spent interacting. They believe that this interaction is important in order to have an enjoyable and rewarding family life. Conversation-oriented families communicate with their children for relationally oriented motives, such as affection, pleasure, and relaxation (Barbato et al., 2003). Their conflict is characterized by integrating and compromising strategies (Sherman & Dumlao, 2008). On the other hand, members of families with a low conversation orientation interact less, and there is less exchange of private thoughts. It's no surprise that families with a strong conversation orientation regard communication as rewarding (Avtgis, 1999), and that children who grow up in

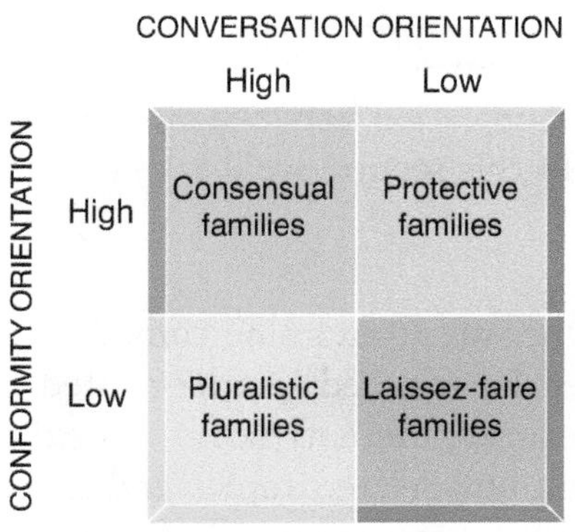

FIGURE 12.1 Conversation and conformity Orientations in Families

conversation-oriented families have a greater number of interpersonal skills in their later relationships (Koesten, 2004).

Conformity orientation refers to the degree to which family communication stresses uniformity of attitudes, values, and beliefs. High-conformity families seek harmony, conflict avoidance, interdependence, and obedience. They are often hierarchical, with a clear sense that some members have more authority than others—so it's not surprising that conflict in these families is characterized by avoiding and obliging strategies (Sherman & Dumlao, 2008). Conformity-oriented families communicate with their children for personal-influence motives (control and escape) and to show affection (Barbato et al., 2003). By contrast, communication in families with a low-conformity orientation is characterized by individuality, independence, and equality. The belief in such families is that individual growth should be encouraged, and that family interests should be subordinated to individual interests. Figure 12.1 displays the four types of families that result from crossing conversation orientation and conformity orientation.

Families high in both conversation orientation and conformity orientation are *consensual:* communication in these families reflects the tension between the pressure to agree and preserve the hierarchy, and an interest in open communication and exploration.

Families high in conversation orientation and low in conformity orientation are *pluralistic:* Communication in these families is open and unrestrained, with all family members' contributions evaluated on their own merits.

Families low in conversation orientation and high in conformity orientation are *protective:* Communication in these families emphasizes obedience to authority and the reluctance to share thoughts and feelings.

Families low in both conversation orientation and conformity orientation are *laissez-faire:* Communication in these families reflects family members' lack of involvement with each other, the fact that they are emotionally divorced, and that decision making is individual.

Which of these styles best represents your family? Which style would you *like* to be true of your family?

TYPES OF FAMILY RELATIONSHIPS

Within families, communication between different family members has distinct characteristics. In this section we'll take a brief look at some of these relationships.

Spouses/Partners One way to examine communication between partners is gender. As Chapter 4 explained, gender-related communication can be broken into four categories: Stereotypically *masculine* communication emphasizes instrumental, task-related topics and is low in expressive, emotional content. By contrast, stereotypically *feminine* communication is high in expressiveness and low in instrumentality. *Androgynous* communication is high in both emotional and instrumental messages, while *undifferentiated* communication is low in both instrumentality and expressiveness.

A three-year study of almost 200 heterosexual couples (married an average of 17 years) revealed that communication in about 38 percent of the relationships fit stereotypical gender roles: Wives focused more on emotional expressiveness, while husbands' messages were typically focused on task-related, instrumental topics (Helms et al., 2006). Communication among the remaining couples didn't follow gender stereotypes. About 37 percent of all the couples studied fit the undifferentiated category—low in both content and emotional expression. About a quarter of the sample fit the androgynous pattern, with communication high in both instrumentality and expressivity.

Is there a relationship between gender-type communication and the satisfaction of a couple? The Helms et al. research suggests the answer is "yes." Gender-typed pairs reported lower levels of satisfaction than androgynous pairs, with the lowest level of love and satisfaction reported for stereotypically feminine wives married to extremely masculine husbands.

Although androgynous couples fared best overall, the researchers also found that similarity was important. (Recall the discussion in Chapter 9 about similarity as a basis for attraction.) Couples with similar expressive and instrumental scores, such as found in undifferentiated couples, were about as satisfied as androgynous couples. By contrast, spouses with different expressive scores in a gender-typed couple feel less in love and less understood and have overall lower marital quality.

Sometimes spouses/partners handle their conflicts in destructive ways. For instance, physical and verbal aggression are inappropriate responses to conflict; however, the other extreme, ignoring a conflict, may be just as destructive to the family. For example, both husbands and wives feel less understood, and less satisfied with their marriages, when their partners respond to a conflict by withdrawing (Weger, 2005).

Parent-Child Family communication becomes more complex—and arguably more interesting and challenging—when children arrive on the scene. One study shows that the number of daily tasks in the average household jumps from 6 to 36 after the birth of a child (Huston & Vangelisti, 1995). In other words, children give parents much more to do and to talk about.

Describing parent-child communication in detail would take an entire book, but in the following paragraphs we'll preview some especially important dimensions.

Patterns of Interaction With the arrival of the first child, communication within the family becomes more complicated. Along with being a threesome, the members can form three very different dyads: Parent A and Parent B, Parent A and the child, and Parent B and the child. It's easy to see how any or all of these dyads can form coalitions that both enrich and complicate family communication.

The combinations are even more numerous when more children come along, and they can grow even more complex in nontraditional families (McBride, 2007; Murray, 2002). Consider a few examples: If a single parent is dating, how does that affect the way parent and child communicate? How does the parent's dating partner communicate with the child? In *blended families* (in which people who marry have children from a prior marriage), how do siblings who are blood-related interact with siblings who are not? How does age affect interaction, given that the family may now have children who are the same age? Do the parents interact with their blood-related children differently than with the other children? And what happens to family interaction when the parents in the blended family have a child of their own and a child who is blood-related to both of them?

Managing the Connection-Autonomy Dialectic As you read in Chapter 9 (pages 295–301), dialectical tensions arise in relationships when two opposing or incompatible forces exist simultaneously. The connection-autonomy dialectic is particularly challenging for families and their communication.

As children grow into adolescents, the "leave me alone" orientation becomes apparent. Teenagers who used to happily spend time with their parents now may groan at the thought of a family vacation, or even the notion of sitting down at the dinner table each evening. More time is spent alone or with friends. Often, answering the question "Who am I?" requires challenging family rules and beliefs, establishing powerful nonfamily relationships, and weakening family bonds. Through conflict, hopefully, an answer emerges; then, the adolescent can turn around and reestablish good relationships with family members.

Families who are most successful at negotiating this difficult period tend to be those with high flexibility who, for example, can change how they discipline and how they determine family roles. Adolescents are most likely to be healthy and well-adjusted when rules and roles can be discussed adult-to-adult with their parents, when they can explore alternative identities without excessive criticism, when their caring family relationships do not give way to conflict and abuse, and when they are encouraged to take responsibility for their lives. "The quality of the communication between parents and adolescents is a critical feature of all these tasks" (Noller, 1995, p. 106).

In families in the United States, it is common for children to leave the family—to be "launched"—when they are in their late teens or early 20s. Communication between parent and adolescent changes as the family adjusts to the dramatic alteration in family life. During this stage, the launched member needs to consider how to stay connected to the family: for example, how often to call home, whether to go home or not during vacations, and how to maintain open lines of communication with both parents.

With the launching of one of the children in the family, there are tasks for those "left behind." For example, the parents need to renegotiate their coupleness, and both the parents and the remaining children need to negotiate who takes on the roles filled by the launched family member. (If the launched member helped resolve conflicts among other people in the family, how will that happen now?)

Finally, communication between elderly parents and their adult children provides its own set of challenges. In many families, interaction comes full circle, as the children now provide for their frail, elderly parents, with the care they once received, while simultaneously meeting the obligations of their jobs and their own immediate families (Kees et al., 2007; Merrill, 1997).

Siblings The sibling relationship is most likely to be your longest family relationship. Like couples, siblings have identifiable communication strategies for maintaining their relationship. One study (Myers & Weber, 2004) revealed several categories of behaviors including *confirmation, humor, social support*, and *escape*. Sibling intimacy begins in early childhood, and the more positive the childhood, the closer siblings feel—although siblings generally remain involved with each other even if their early relationship was marked by family conflict.

Sibling relationships may be complex, but three dimensions of interaction explain a great deal of sibling-to-sibling communication: affection, hostility, and rivalry (Myers & Bryant, 2008; Tseung & Schott, 2004). Clare Stocker and Susan McHale (1992) found that siblings' indications of affection were positively related: If one had a great deal of affection for the other, the odds are the other returned the same feelings. Unlike affection, however, rivalry and hostility were unrelated to each other—one could be hostile or consider the other a rival, and the feelings may not be reciprocated. Interestingly, sibling relationships in a single-parent family—after separation and divorce—are more likely to be higher in both affection *and* hostility than in two-parent families (Noller, 2005).

Think about your interaction with your siblings over the years and you can probably identify many roles you played in each others' lives: playmate, confidant, friend, counselor, role model, and perhaps adversary. Research shows that sibling relationships can offer vital support throughout our lives

(Goetting, 1986; Rittenour et al., 2007), and thus it is important to maintain them through behaviors such as sharing tasks, expressing positivity, and offering assurances (Myers, 2003). Another way older siblings can nurture their relationships is by talking about their family: reminiscing about their childhood, crazy family events, and wild relatives. Sharing these stories holds the siblings together, as well as helps them clarify family events and validate their feelings and life choices (McGoldrick et al., 1999).

EFFECTIVE COMMUNICATION IN FAMILIES

Strive for Closeness While Respecting Boundaries Chapter 9 described the conflicting needs we all have for both integration and separation in our relationships, as well as for both expression and privacy. Nowhere are these opposing drives stronger than in families. We all know the importance of keeping close ties with our kin, although too much cohesion can be a problem. When cohesion is too high, a family may be **enmeshed**, that is, suffer from too much consensus, too little independence, and a very high demand for loyalty—all of which may feel stifling. At the other extreme, of course, members of families with too little cohesion may be **disengaged**—disconnected, with limited attachment or commitment to one another (Olson, 2000).

Families cope with these dialectical tensions by creating **boundaries**—limits a family sets on its members' actions. Communication researchers have devoted a good deal of attention to the importance of boundary management in interpersonal and family relationships (Petronio, 2000). The most obvious boundaries are physical (e.g., don't enter a bedroom without knocking if the door is closed; stay out of the garage when Dad is tinkering with the car). Other boundaries involve conversational topics, as discussed in the previous section. In some families, discussion of finances is off limits. In others, expression of certain emotions is restricted. Sex is one of the most-avoided topics with parents and stepparents (Golish & Caughlin, 2002).

In addition to governing what to talk about, boundaries can also dictate how topics are handled. In some families it is fine to persist if the first overture to discussion is rebuffed ("Come on, what's on your mind?"). In other families, privacy rules discourage this kind of persistence. While the particulars may differ, every family has communication boundaries—and newcomers would be wise to learn and heed those boundaries (consider the many television shows and movies that poke fun at in-laws violating each other's family rules).

The challenge families face is to define boundaries that include important kinds of relational communication while allowing members to have the privacy and freedom that everyone desires. Sometimes these boundaries need to be openly negotiated. At other times they are established through trial and error. In either case, healthy boundaries allow us to balance the opposing and equally important needs for connection and autonomy, for openness and closedness.

Strive for a Moderate Level of Adaptability A family experiences stress both from within (e.g., children get older and their needs change) and without (e.g., Mom loses her job). In the face of stresses like these, a healthy family needs to adapt the way it functions and how members deal with one another. To see how adaptability can help a family function, consider the stress a family experiences when a child reaches adolescence. As mentioned earlier, parents can begin to share control with their teenager as they negotiate issues like schedules, responsibilities, and rules. How does a family handle the stress of a family member who comes out as gay, lesbian, bisexual, or transsexual (GLBT)? Families high in adaptability report having more contact with the GLBT family member and with more GLBT acquaintances than low adaptability families (Reeves et al., 2010).

When adaptability is too high, the result may be a **chaotic family**: one that has erratic leadership or no leadership at all, dramatic shifts in roles, unclear roles, and impulsive decision making. When adaptability is too low, the result may be a **rigid family** with authoritarian leadership (usually in the hands of one person, the mother or father), strict discipline, roles that are inflexible, and unchanging rules. The extent to which a family is able to avoid these extremes in adaptability determines, to a large extent, how functional it is (Olson, 2000). Inasmuch as change is an inevitable fact of family life, it is important for healthy families to roll—at an appropriate level—with the changes that come their way.

Just as families cope with tensions related to cohesion by creating boundaries, families also create boundaries that regulate adaptability. For example, a rigid family might have strong topic boundaries and a lot of rules to make sure that who speaks to whom about what is carefully regulated. The goal is to make sure that the family hierarchy is maintained and lines of authority are clear. By contrast, a chaotic family is likely to have few if any rules in this area of family life. Similarly, a rigid family is likely to have many rules and clear boundaries regarding appropriate sex-role behavior, such as "the son mows the lawn" and "the daughter does the dishes," whereas in a chaotic family there may be no rules regarding who mows and who does the dishes.

Families generally function better if their levels of cohesion, conformity, and adaptability are moderate, rather than being extremely high or low (Olson & Lavee, 1989; Schrodt, 2005). It's easy to understand how too much cohesion, conformity, and adaptability could become stifling, and how too little could result in members drifting apart.

Encourage Confirming Messages Chapter 10 introduced the importance of confirming messages—ones that show in one way or another that we value the other person. Confirming messages from parents help satisfy a great many of their children's needs, such as the need for nurturance and respect. Kathleen Ellis (2002) looked at the different ways mothers and fathers communicate valuing and support to their children. She found that two highly confirming behaviors parents offer are (1) telling their children that they are unique and valuable as human beings, and (2) genuinely listening to their children when being told something of importance. Two highly disconfirming behaviors are (1) belittling their children, and (2) making statements that communicate that their ideas don't count: "Nobody asked for your opinion" or "What do you know about this anyway?" Confirming messages are just as important for teenagers as for young children. One study found a strong relationship between the amount of confirmation adolescents feel and the openness they exhibit in communication with their parents (Dailey, 2006).

Confirming communication is also important to successful marriages. Marital researcher John Gottman (2003) acknowledges that most couples aren't confirming in all of their communication—that would be unrealistic. The key, says Gottman, is having an appropriate ratio of positive-to-negative messages. His studies show that satisfied couples—and these include couples who fight with each other—consistently have a 5:1 ratio of positive-to-negative communication, with positive messages including features such as humor, empathizing, and expressions of affection.

Deal Constructively with Conflict As you read in Chapter 11, conflict is natural and inevitable. Conflict in families, however, is special because it occurs more often and may be more violent than in other relationships, whether between spouses/partners, parents and children, or between siblings (Koerner & Fitzpatrick, 2006b). In families, as in other relationships, the question isn't how to avoid conflict—that's impossible. Rather, the challenge is to engage in and resolve conflicts in a way that makes relationships stronger rather than weaker.

Sometimes families handle their conflicts in destructive ways. For instance, physical and verbal aggression are inappropriate responses to conflict; however, the other extreme, ignoring a conflict, may be just as destructive to the family. For example, both husbands and wives feel less understood, and less satisfied with their marriages, when their partners respond to a conflict by withdrawing (Weger, 2005).

Families can improve their communication by recognizing that family conflict should be dealt with. Placing conflict on the back burner, attempting to ignore it, smoothing it over, or denying that it exists creates tensions. The key to resolution lies in how the conflict is dealt with. There are several general principles of conflict management in the family.

Don't Sweat the Small Stuff There will always be differences of opinion and style in families. Many need attention, but others simply aren't worth bothering about. If it's not a big issue, it might be best to let it slide. (Of course, what constitutes a "big issue" is often a matter of perception.)

Focus on Manageable Issues Many big issues can be broken down into smaller, more manageable parts. For example, rather than arguing about a family member's "controlling personality," consider addressing specific problems: differing opinions about household neatness, the need to be informed about family plans, interference with your personal decisions, and so on.

Share Appreciations as Well as Gripes Along with addressing differences, let family members know that you appreciate them. As you read in Chapter 10, hearing an abundance of confirming messages makes it easier for us to hear negative information without feeling defensive and unappreciated.

Seek Win-Win Solutions Strong feelings that are not resolved in one conflict will probably resurface later in another. The guidelines for win-win problem solving in Chapter 11 can work well with family conflicts, especially when members realize that when one person is unhappy, all the others are likely to suffer. On the other hand, when all members contribute to and are satisfied with a solution to a family problem, it builds cohesion, trust, and good will.

Not all conflicts are resolvable, but just because a conflict is not resolvable does not mean that it needs to be a constant source of stress in the family. Conflicts regarding religious differences, in-laws, and even food preferences might never be resolved, but so long as the people with the problem engage in confirming as opposed to disconfirming behavior and fight fairly, the conflict does not have to reduce family commitment or satisfaction.

Based on his own research and a review of the literature on "excellent family communication," John Caughlin (2003) offers a list of standards college students have about what constitutes effective family communication. Several of these standards highlight the points discussed earlier and are good predictors of family satisfaction: Family members who communicate well provide each other with emotional support, express affection verbally and nonverbally, are polite to one another, and base discipline on clear rules.

Communication in Intimate Relationships

The musical group Three Dog Night said it well: One *can* be the loneliest number. For most of us, the desire to connect with others is a powerful force that leads us to seek out and form relationships. As Chapter 1 explained, strong attachments with others not only make us happier, they also can make us healthier and help us live longer.

In their book *Intimacy: Strategies for Successful Relationships*, C. Edward Crowther and Gayle Stone (1986) offer a reminder of just how important close relationships can be. As part of a study of people who were dying in hospices and hospitals in the United States and England, Crowther and Stone asked each person what mattered most in his or her life. Fully 90 percent of these terminally ill patients put intimate relationships at the top of the list. Similarly, Christopher Peterson (2006) summarizes research showing that close relationships "may be the *single most important* source of life satisfaction and emotional well-being, across different ages and cultures" (p. 261). With this in mind, let's take a closer look at what it means to have intimate relationships with others.

DIMENSIONS OF INTIMACY

Intimacy is a state of relational closeness that comes in many forms (Laurenceau & Kleinman, 2006; Lippert & Prager, 2001). One type is *emotional*: sharing important information and feelings. Chapters 3 and 8 described these kinds of self-disclosures in detail. Sometimes emotional intimacy comes from talking about feelings, such as acknowledging when you're hurt and embarrassed or saying "I love you." In other cases, emotional intimacy develops as a result of topics that are discussed—personal information, secrets, or delicate subjects. One such subject can be money, which has led some self-help authors to use the term *financial intimacy* to describe how couples need to be open, honest, and in sync on this important topic (Hayes, 2006; Orman, 2005).

Another form of intimacy is *physical*. Even before birth, the developing fetus experiences a kind of physical closeness with its mother that will never happen again: "Floating in a warm fluid, curling inside a total embrace, swaying to the undulations of the moving body and hearing the beat of the pulsing heart" (Morris, 1973, p. 7). As they grow up, fortunate children are continually nourished by physical intimacy: being rocked, fed, hugged, and held. As we grow older, the opportunities for physical intimacy are less regular, but still possible and important. Some physical intimacy is sexual, but this category also can include affectionate hugs, kisses, and even struggles. Companions who have endured physical challenges together—for example, in athletics or during emergencies—form a bond that can last a lifetime.

In other cases, intimacy comes from *intellectual* sharing (Cowan & Mills, 2004; Schaefer & Olson, 1981). Not every exchange of ideas counts as intimacy, of course. Talking about next week's midterm with your professor or classmates isn't likely to forge strong relational bonds. But when you engage another person in an exchange of important ideas, a kind of closeness develops that can be powerful and exciting.

Shared activities can provide a fourth way to emotional closeness (Radmacher & Azmitia, 2006; Wood & Inman, 1993). Not all shared activities lead to intimacy. You might work with a colleague for years without feeling any sort of emotional connection. But some shared experiences—struggling together against obstacles or living together as housemates are good examples—can create strong bonds. Play is one valuable form of shared activity. Leslie Baxter (1992) found that both same-sex friendships and opposite-sex romantic relationships were characterized by several forms of play. Partners invented private codes, fooled around by acting like other people, teased one another, and played games—everything from having punning contests to arm wrestling.

The amount and type of intimacy can vary from one relationship to another (Hoffman, 2010; Speicher, 1999). Some intimate relationships exhibit all four qualities: emotional disclosure, physical intimacy, intellectual exchanges, and shared activities. Other intimate relationships exhibit only one or two. Of course, some relationships aren't intimate in any way. Acquaintance, roommate, and coworker relationships may never become intimate. In some cases, even family members develop smooth but relatively impersonal relationships.

Despite the fact that no relationship is *always* intimate, living without *any* sort of intimacy is hardly desirable. For example, people who fear intimacy in dating relationships anticipate less satisfaction in a long-term relationship and report feeling more distant from even longtime dating partners. A great deal of evidence supports the conclusion that fear of intimacy can cause major problems in both creating relationships and sustaining them (Greenberg & Goldman, 2008; Vangelisti & Beck, 2007).

GENDER AND INTIMACY

Until recently, most social scientists believed that women were more concerned with and better than men at developing and maintaining intimate relationships (Impett & Peplau, 2006). Most research *does* show that women (taken as a group, of course) are more interested than men in achieving emotional intimacy (Eldridge & Christensen, 2002; Hoffman, 2010), more willing to make emotional commitments (Rusbult & Van Lange, 1996), and somewhat more willing to share their most personal thoughts and feelings (Dindia & Allen, 1992; Stafford et al., 2000), although the differences aren't as dramatic as most people believe (Dindia, 2000b, 2002).

But more recent scholarship has begun to show that emotional expression isn't the *only* way to develop close relationships (Floyd, 1996; Zorn & Gregory, 2005). As you read earlier in this chapter, men often experience and express intimacy through shared activities and by doing things for and with others. Of course, it's important not to assume that all men who value shared activities are reluctant to share feelings, or that doing things together isn't important to women. Recent scholarship offers convincing evidence that, in many respects, the meaning of intimacy is more similar than different for men and women (Goldsmith & Fulfs, 1999; Radmacher & Azmitia, 2006).

Whatever differences do exist between male and female styles of intimacy help explain some of the stresses and misunderstandings that can arise between the sexes. For example, a woman who looks for emotional disclosure as a measure of affection may overlook an inexpressive man's efforts to show he cares by doing favors or spending time with her. Fixing a leaky faucet or taking a hike may look like ways to avoid getting close, but to the man who proposes them, they may be measures of affection and bids for intimacy. Likewise, differing ideas about the timing and meaning of sex can lead to misunderstandings. Whereas many women think of sex as a way

to *express* an intimacy that has already developed, men are more likely to see it as a way to *create* that intimacy (Reissman, 1990). In this sense, the man who encourages sex early in a relationship or after a fight may not just be a testosterone-crazed lecher: He may view the shared activity as a way to build closeness. By contrast, the woman who views personal talk as the pathway to intimacy may resist the idea of physical closeness before the emotional side of the relationship has been discussed.

As with all research looking at women's and men's communication, it's important to realize that no generalization applies to every person. Furthermore, stereotypes are changing. For example, an analysis of prime-time television sitcoms revealed that male characters who disclose personal information generally receive favorable responses from other characters (Good et al., 2002). In addition, researchers Mark Morman and Kory Floyd (2002) note that a cultural shift is occurring in the United States in which fathers are becoming more affectionate with their sons than they were in previous generations—although some of that affection is still expressed through shared activities.

CULTURE AND INTIMACY

Historically, the notions of public and private behavior have changed dramatically (Adamopoulos, 1991; Gadlin, 1977). What would be considered intimate behavior today was quite public at times in the past. For example, in 16th-century Germany, the new husband and wife were expected to consummate their marriage upon a bed carried by witnesses who would validate the marriage! Conversely, in England as well as in colonial America, the customary level of communication between spouses was once rather formal—not much different from the way acquaintances or neighbors spoke to one another.

Today, the notion of intimacy varies from one culture to another (Adams et al., 2004; Marshall, 2008, 2010). In one study, researchers asked residents of Great Britain, Japan, Hong Kong, and Italy to describe their use of 33 rules that regulated interaction in social relationships (Argyle & Henderson, 1985). The rules governed a wide range of communication behaviors: everything from the use of humor, to handshaking, to the management of money. The results showed that the greatest differences between Asian and European cultures involved the rules for dealing with intimacy, including showing emotions, expressing affection in public, engaging in sexual activity, and respecting privacy.

While some of these distinctions continue to hold true, cultural differences in intimacy are becoming less prominent as the world becomes more connected through the media, travel, and technology. For instance, romance and passionate love were once seen as particularly "American" concepts of intimacy. However, recent evidence shows that men and women in a variety of cultures—individualist and collectivist, urban and rural, rich and poverty stricken—may be every bit as romantic as Americans (Hatfield & Rapson, 2006). These studies suggest that the large differences that once existed between Western and Eastern cultures may be fast disappearing.

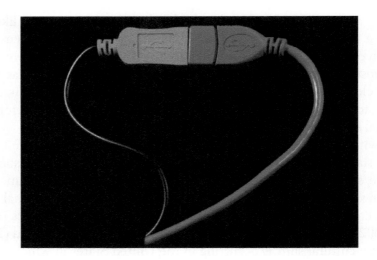

SOCIAL MEDIA AND INTIMACY

A few decades ago, it would have been hard to conceive that the words *computer* and *intimacy* could be positively linked. Computers were viewed as impersonal machines that couldn't transmit important features of human communication, such as facial expression, tone of voice, and touch. However, as Chapters 2 and 3 described, researchers now know that communication through social media can be just as personal as face-to-face (FtF) interaction. In fact, studies show that relational intimacy may develop more quickly through mediated channels than in FtF communication (Hian et al., 2004).

Your own experience probably supports these claims. The relative anonymity of chat rooms, blogs, and online dating services fosters a freedom of expression that might not occur in FtF meetings (Ben-Ze'ev, 2003), giving relationships a chance to get started. In addition, instant messaging, e-mailing, and text messaging offer more constant contact with loved ones than might otherwise be possible (Boase et al., 2006). The potential for developing and maintaining intimate relationships via computer is captured well by one user's comment (which has a fun double meaning): "I've never clicked this much with anyone in my life" (Henderson & Gilding, 2004).

This doesn't mean that all cyber-relationships are (or will become) intimate. Just as in face-to-face relationships, communicators choose varying levels of self-disclosure with their cyberpartners. Some online relationships are relatively impersonal; others are highly interpersonal. In any case, communication through social media is an important component in creating and maintaining intimacy in contemporary relationships.

COMMITMENT IN INTIMATE RELATIONSHIPS

How important is the role of commitment in intimate relationships? Sentiments like the following suggest an answer: "I'm looking for a committed relationship." "Our relationship didn't work because my partner wasn't committed." "I'm just not ready for commitment."

Relational commitment involves a promise—sometimes implied and sometimes explicit—to remain in a relationship and to make that relationship successful. Commitment is both formed and reinforced through communication. Table 12.1 spells out commitment indicators in romantic relationships.

As Table 12.1 indicates, words alone aren't a surefire measure of true commitment. Deeds are also important. Simply saying "You can count on me" doesn't guarantee loyalty. But without language, commitment may not be clear. For this reason, ceremonies formalizing relationships are an important way to recognize and cement commitment (see Chapter 9's discussion of "bonding" on page 291).

MAINTAINING INTIMATE RELATIONSHIPS

Just as gardens need tending, cars need tune-ups, and bodies need exercise, relationships need ongoing maintenance to keep them successful and satisfying. Maintenance-related communication aims to sustain the features that make the relationship successful and satisfying: enjoyment, love, commitment, trust, and so forth (Canary & Stafford, 1992; Sahlstein, 2004).

Even in long-distance relationships, it's possible to convey maintenance messages via mediated channels like texting, instant messaging, and social media websites (Tong & Walther, 2011a). In fact, some scholars suggest that interaction via social media is *more* effective than face-to-face interaction in improving the quality of a relationship (e.g., Walther, 1996, Walther & Ramirez, 2010). One reason text-based electronic channels are so effective is that lovers can craft their messages until they convey just the right expression of affection and immediacy (Walther, 2007). Also, edited messages allow communicators to present idealized versions of themselves, free of poor manners, stumbling speech, and other bad habits (Rabby & Walther, 2003). Of course, partners need to negotiate what constitutes acceptable online behavior—their "netiquette"—for maintaining their intimacy (Helsper & Whitty, 2010).

Dark Side of Communication

VIRTUALLY UNFAITHFUL: EMOTIONAL INFIDELITY IN CYBERSPACE

Infidelity has been a fact of life as long as romance has existed. In the digital age, some people are "virtually unfaithful," carrying on romantic relationships online. Researchers have begun to study whether mediated infidelity is as damaging as the in-person variety.

In an effort to learn about perceptions of "cybercheating," researcher Monica Whitty asked 234 university students to imagine how they would feel after discovering that a partner had developed an online romantic relationship. The majority of students—both men and women—believed that infidelity in an online relationship was just as much of a betrayal as cheating in person. In a later study, Branden Henline and his colleagues discovered that both men and women regarded emotional infidelity as *more* distressing than cheating sexually.

Research like this provides a warning about the dangers of online romance. Making emotional connections with someone in cyberspace—even if there's no physical involvement—can jeopardize committed face-to-face relationships.

Henline, B. H., Lamke, L. K., & Howard, M. D. (2007). Exploring perceptions of online infidelity. *Personal Relationships, 14,* 113–128.

Whitty, M. T. (2005). The realness of cybercheating: Men's and women's representations of unfaithful Internet relationships. *Social Science Computer Review, 23,* 57–67.

F⊕CUS ON RESEARCH

Maintaining Marriages through Flirting

It's a common perception—perhaps fostered by media depictions—that married couples have relatively little passion in their relationships. To use the language of relational stages (pages 287–294), the flirting and romantic energy of Experimenting and Intensifying go away once couples enter the Bonding stage. Or does it?

Communication researcher Brandi Frisby interviewed nine married couples to get a better understanding of flirting behaviors before and within marriage. In general, the couples said they flirt *more* now that they're married, but for different reasons than during courtship. When they were dating, couples used flirting primarily to explore the potential relationship and reduce uncertainty. After marriage, flirting became a means for building esteem, having fun, and engaging in relational maintenance. Here are a few of their descriptions:

- "I flirt with my husband to make him feel loved and important to me"
- "How we flirt now is by sharing personal jokes; it's nice having our own little private world within a crowd of people"
- "Once you are married you want some affirmation that we do still find one another attractive"

To use the language of relational dialectics (pages 295–299), it appears that flirting adds some novelty to the predictability of marital communication.

Frisby, B. N. (2009). "Without flirting, it wouldn't be a marriage": Flirtatious communication between relational partners. *Qualitative Research Reports in Communication, 10,* 55–60.

As you read in Chapter 1, communication involved in maintaining relationships may not always be exciting, but handling it effectively accounts for as much as 80 percent of the difference between satisfying and unsatisfying relationships (Weigel & Ballard-Reisch, 1999).

TABLE 12.1 Major Indicators of a Committed Romantic Relationship

- Providing affection
- Providing support
- Maintaining integrity
- Sharing companionship
- Making an effort to communicate regularly
- Showing respect
- Creating a relational future
- Creating a positive relational atmosphere
- Working on relationship problems together
- Reassuring one's commitment

Source: Weigel, D. J. (2008). Mutuality and the communication of commitment in romantic relationships. *Southern Communication Journal, 73,* 24–41.

Stafford and Canary (1991) identified five strategies for maintaining romantic relationships:

- *Positivity:* Keeping things pleasant by being polite, cheerful, and upbeat and also by avoiding criticism.

- *Openness:* Talking directly about the nature of the relationship and disclosing your personal needs and concerns.

- *Assurances:* Letting the other person know that he or she matters to you.

- *Sharing tasks:* Helping one another take care of life's chores and obligations.

- *Social networks:* Relying on friends and family to provide support and relief that helps relational partners understand and appreciate one another, as well as giving them other sources of companionship that take some load off of the relationship.

In successful relationships it's important for both partners to use relational maintenance strategies (Canary & Wahba, 2006). In heterosexual partnerships, both men and women do a roughly equal amount of relational maintenance work. Women contribute somewhat more effort in joint tasks—especially household chores—and they share personal thoughts and feelings more than men (Aylor & Dainton, 2004). As in most relational matters, the *perception* that both partners are working equally hard at maintaining the relationship is perhaps more important than the reality. When one partner feels like the other isn't doing his or her share, the relationship is headed for trouble (Canary & Stafford, 2001).

Summary

Friendships, families, and intimate relationships are three of the most important contexts of interpersonal communication. Several factors determine friendship types, such as length of the relationship, task/maintenance orientation, and degrees of disclosure, obligation, and contact. Sex and gender affect the way friends communicate with each other. Successful friendships follow a number of guidelines that help avoid expectancy violations.

Contemporary families have a variety of traditional and nontraditional arrangements. These arrangements are formed through the communication of narratives, rituals, and rules. Over time, families develop into systems, as members interact with one another to form a whole. Various subsystems—spouses/partners, parents and children, and siblings—have unique communication patterns.

Effective communication in families requires that members establish and maintain a moderate level of cohesion, and they do this by establishing appropriate boundaries. In addition, functional families are adaptable, managing change without too much rigidity or acquiescence. Members of healthy families encourage each other with confirming messages and strive for win-win solutions to their conflicts.

We also form relationships to achieve various forms of intimacy: emotional, physical, intellectual, and shared activities. Intimacy is influenced by gender and culture and can even take place through communication via social media. We often form relationships with others in quest of relational commitment, and those relationships require regular maintenance.

Key Terms

- Boundaries (399)
- Chaotic family (400)
- Conformity orientation (395)
- Conversation orientation (394)
- Disengaged family (399)
- Enmeshed family (399)
- Expectancy violation (389)
- Family (391)
- Friendship (384)
- Intimacy (402)
- Relational commitment (407)
- Rigid family (400)
- System (393)

Activities

1. Invitation to Insight
Analyze how gender affects communication in your friendships by keeping logs of communication in two relationships: One same sex, and the other opposite sex. For each incident in your log, record both the subject being discussed (e.g., school, finances) and the nature of the interaction (e.g., emotional expression, personal information, shared activities). Based on your findings, do you see a different pattern in communication with same- and opposite-sex friendships?

2. Invitation to Insight
Understand your own family system better by giving examples of each of the characteristics described on page 393:
   a. Interdependence of members

    b. How the family is more than the sum of its parts

    c. Family subsystems and suprasystems

    d. How environmental influences affect the family

3. Invitation to Insight

Describe an ongoing narrative in either your current family or your family of origin. Explain:

    a. The narrative

    b. When and how it is retold

    c. The way this narrative portrays your family

    d. The function the narrative serves

4. Invitation to Insight

What kinds of intimacy characterize your relationships? Answer the questions that follow as you think about your relationship with an important person in your life:

    a. What is the level of physical intimacy in your relationship?

    b. What intellectual intimacy do you share?

    c. How emotionally intimate are you? Is your emotional intimacy deeper in some ways than in others?

    d. What shared activities occupy an important role in this relationship?

    e. Has your intimacy level changed over time? If so, in what ways?

After answering these questions, ask yourself how satisfied you are with the amount of intimacy in this relationship. Identify any changes you would like to occur, and describe the steps you could take to make them happen.

■ Author Index

▪ Credits

Cartoons

||||||||||||||||||||||||||||||||||||||||||||||||||||||||||||||||||||||||||||||||||||||||||||

Page 332: © The New Yorker Collection 2004 Roz Chast from cartoonbank.com. All Rights Reserved.

Page 361: © The New Yorker Collection 1997 Leo Cullum from cartoonbank.com. All Rights Reserved.

Page 363: Calvin and Hobbes © 1993 Bill Waterson/ Dist. By Universal Uclick

Page 377: © The New Yorker Collection 2002 Robert Weber from cartoonbank.com. All Rights Reserved.

Page 391: © The New Yorker Collection 1993 Sam Gross from cartoonbank.com. All Rights Reserved.

Page 404: SALLY FORTH © King Features Syndicate.

Photos

Page 1: © Tim Pannell/Corbis

Page 12: Image Source/Getty Images

Page 16: Adam Gault/Getty Images

Page 28: © Nation Wong/Corbis

Page 33: iStockphoto.com/timsa

Page 39: Colin Anderson/GettyImages

Page 42: Punchstock/MIXA

Page 48: Peter Dazeley/Getty Images

Page 52: Fotolia/badahos

Page 64: Hola Images/Getty Images

Page 70: © Zak Kendal/cultura/Corbis

Page 71: Kent Mathews/Stone/Getty Images

Page 76: © iStockphoto.com/pixdeluxe

Page 78: Big Cheese Photo/Punchstock.com

Page 79: Bruce Gardner/Getty Images

Page 85: WIN-Initiative/Getty Images

Page 107: Dan Lim/Masterfile

Page 111: © HBSS/Corbis

Page 129: J. Scott Applewhite/AP Images

Page 140: © fstop/Corbis

Page 149: PureStock/JupiterImages

Page 155: Photos.com

Page 169: iStockPhoto.com/beemore

Page 174: AP Photo/Jeffrey Phelps

Page 177: Workbook Stock RM

Page 181: Cosmo Codina/Workbook Stock/ JupiterImages

Page 186: Frank Wing/Getty Images

Page 193: Altrendo Images/Getty Images

Page 197: © Eric Audras/PhotoAlto/Corbis

Page 208: Image Source/Getty Images

Page 215: James P. Blair/National Geographic Stock

Page 220: moodboard/Punchstock.com

Page 231: © Masterfile

Page 244: Ryan McVay/Getty Images

Page 248: fStop/Punchstock

Page 257: Darren Robb/Getty Images

Page 262: © Masterfile

Page 264: Shutterstock.com/Chernetskiy

Page 266: © Paul Hardy/Corbis

Page 278: Masterfile Royalty-Free

Page 290: © Masterfile

Page 298: Dirk Buwalda

Page 310: © Erproductions Ltd/Blend Images/Corbis

Page 313: © Photos.com

Page 322: © GoGo Images/JupiterImages

Page 327: © Franc Podgorsek/Istock Photo

Page 339: © iStockphoto.com/AlexanderNovikov

Page 348: Hans Neleman/Getty Images

Page 351: OJO Images via AP Images

Page 354: Punchstock.com/Imagemore

Page 370: Punchstock.com/Pixland

Page 382: © Veer

Page 390: ©2010 Jaime Monfort/Getty Images

Page 397: Geneva Palmer

Page 403: Punchstock.com/ImageSource

Page 406: © Antonio Pennisi/Fotolia

▪ Glossary

Abstraction ladder   A range of more abstract to less abstract terms describing an event or object.

Accommodation   A lose-win conflict style in which one person defers to the other.

Achievement culture   A culture that places a high value on the achievement of material success and a focus on the task at hand. Also termed "masculine" culture.

Advising (response)   A listening response in which the receiver offers suggestions about how the speaker should deal with a problem.

Aggressiveness   Verbal attacks that demean others' self-concept and inflict psychological pain.

Ambiguous language   Language consisting of words and phrases that have more than one commonly accepted definition.

Ambiguous response   A response with more than one meaning, leaving the other person unsure of the responder's position.

Ambushing   A style in which the receiver listens carefully in order to gather information to use in an attack on the speaker.

Analyzing (response)   A listening response in which the listener offers an interpretation of a speaker's message.

Androgynous   Possessing both masculine and feminine traits.

Argumentativeness   Presenting and defending positions on issues while attacking positions taken by others.

Assertiveness   Clearly and directly expressing one's thoughts, feelings, and wants to another person.

Asynchronous communication   Communication that occurs when there is a time gap between when a message is sent and when it is received.

Attending   A phase of the listening process in which the communicator focuses on a message, excluding other messages.

Attribution   The process of attaching meaning to another person's behavior.

Avoidance   A lose-lose conflict style in which people nonassertively ignore or stay away from conflict.

Avoiding   A relational stage immediately prior to terminating in which the partners minimize contact with one another.

Benevolent lie   A lie that is not considered malicious by the person who tells it.

Bonding   A stage of relational development in which the partners make symbolic public gestures to show that their relationship exists.

Boundaries   Limits that a family sets on its members' actions, such as what topics are permissible to discuss, how to discuss certain topics, and with whom family members may interact outside the family.

"But" statement   A statement in which the second half cancels the meaning of the first, for example, "I'd like to help you, *but* I have to go or I'll miss my bus."

Certainty   Dogmatically stating or implying that one's position is correct and others' ideas are not worth considering. Likely to arouse defensiveness, according to Gibb.

Channel   The medium through which a message passes from sender to receiver.

Chaotic family   A family that has erratic leadership or no leadership at all, dramatic shifts in roles, unclear roles, and impulsive decision making.

Chronemics   The study of how people use and structure time.

Circumscribing   A relational stage in which partners begin to reduce the scope of their contact and commitment to one another.

Closed questions   Questions that limit the range of possible responses, such as questions that seek a yes-or-no answer.

Co-culture   A group within an encompassing culture with a perceived identity.

Cognitive complexity   The ability to construct a variety of frameworks for viewing an issue.

Cognitive conservatism   The tendency to seek out information that conforms to an existing self-concept and to ignore information that contradicts it.

Collaboration   A win-win conflict style in which both people get what they want.

Collectivistic culture   A culture whose members feel loyalties and obligations to an in-group, such as an extended family, a community, and even a work organization.

Communication   The use of messages to generate meanings.

Communication apprehension   Feelings of anxiety that plague some people at the prospect of communicating in an unfamiliar or difficult context.

Communication climate   The emotional tone of a relationship between two or more individuals.

Communication competence   The ability to achieve one's goals in a manner that is personally acceptable and, ideally, acceptable to others.

Comparison level (CL)   The minimum standard of what behavior is acceptable from a relationship partner.

Comparison level of alternatives (CL$_{alt}$)   A comparison between the rewards one is receiving in a present situation and those one could expect to receive in others.

Competition   A win-lose conflict style in which one person wins at the other person's expense.

Complaining A disagreeing message that directly or indirectly communicates dissatisfaction with another person.

Complementary conflict style When partners in a conflict use different but mutually reinforcing behaviors.

Compliance-gaining strategy A tactic or plan used to persuade others to think or behave in a desired way.

Compromise A conflict style in which both people get only part of what they want because they sacrifice some of their goals.

Computer-mediated communication (CMC) Communication that occurs via computerized channels (e.g., e-mail, instant messaging, computer conferencing).

Confirmation bias The tendency to seek out and organize data that supports already existing opinions.

Confirming communication A message that expresses caring or respect for another person; the person is valued by the speaker.

Conflict ritual Repeating pattern of interlocking conflict behaviors.

Conflict An expressed struggle between at least two interdependent people who perceive incompatible goals, scarce rewards, and interference from the other person in achieving her or his goals.

Conformity orientation The degree to which family communication stresses uniformity of attitudes, values, and beliefs.

Connection-autonomy dialectic The tension between the need for integration and the need for independence in a relationship.

Content dimension The dimension of a message that communicates information about the subject being discussed. See *Relational dimension.*

Controlling communication According to Gibb, messages that attempt to impose some sort of outcome on another person, resulting in a defensive response.

Conventionality-uniqueness dialectic The tension between the need to behave in ways that conform to others' expectations and the need to assert one's individuality by behaving in ways that violate others' expectations.

Convergence The process of adapting one's speech style to match that of others with whom one wants to identify. See also *Divergence.*

Conversation orientation The degree to which families favor an open climate of discussion on a wide array of topics.

Counterfeit questions Questions that are disguised attempts to send a message rather than elicit information.

Culture According to Samovar, Porter, and McDaniel, "the language, values, beliefs, traditions, and customs people share and learn."

Debilitative emotions Emotions of high intensity and long duration that prevent a person from functioning effectively.

De-escalatory spiral A reciprocal communication pattern in which one person's nonthreatening behavior leads to reduced hostility by the other, with the level of hostility steadily decreasing. Opposite of *Escalatory spiral.*

Defensive listening A response style in which the receiver perceives a speaker's comments as an attack.

Defensiveness The attempt to protect a presenting image a person believes is being attacked.

Description Messages that describe a speaker's position without evaluating others.

Designated leader The person (or people) with official titles that indicate authority, for example, "manager."

Dialectical tensions Relational tensions that arise when two opposing or incompatible forces exist simultaneously.

Differentiating A relational stage in which the partners reestablish their individual identities after having bonded.

Direct aggression An expression of the sender's thoughts and/or feelings that attacks the position and dignity of the receiver.

Direct request A compliance-gaining strategy in which the communicator directly asks another person to meet his or her needs.

Disagreeing message A message that essentially communicates to another person, "You are wrong," and includes argumentativeness, complaining, and aggressiveness.

Disconfirming communication A message that expresses a lack of caring or respect for another person; the person is not valued by the speaker.

Disengaged family Families with too little cohesion, in which members have limited attachment or commitment to one another.

Disfluencies Nonlinguistic verbalizations, for example, *um, er, ah*.

Disinhibition Expressing messages without considering the consequences of doing so.

Divergence Speaking in a way that emphasizes difference from others. See also *Convergence*.

Downward communication Communication from managers to subordinates.

Dyad Two communicators who interact with one another.

Dysfunctional conflict Harmful conflict characterized by communication that is coercive, uncooperative, and unfocused, which often results in a win-lose outcome and a damaged relationship.

Emblems Deliberate nonverbal behaviors with precise meanings, known to virtually all members of a cultural group.

Emotional contagion The process by which emotions are transferred from one person to another.

Emotional intelligence The ability to understand and manage one's own emotions and to be sensitive to others' feelings.

Emotion labor Managing and even suppressing emotions when it is both appropriate and necessary to do so.

Empathizing (response) A listening response that conveys identification with a speaker's perceptions and emotions.

Empathy The ability to project oneself into another person's point of view in an attempt to experience the other's thoughts and feelings.

Enmeshed family Families with too much consensus, too little independence, and a very high demand for loyalty.

Environment Both the physical setting in which communication occurs and the personal perspectives of the people involved.

Equality A type of supportive communication described by Gibb, which suggests that the sender regards the receiver with respect.

Equivocal language Ambiguous language that has two or more equally plausible meanings.

Escalatory spiral A reciprocal communication pattern in which one person's attack leads to a counterattack by the other, with the level of hostility steadily increasing. Opposite of *De-escalatory spiral.*

Ethnocentrism An attitude that one's own culture is superior to that of others.

Euphemism A pleasant term substituted for a blunt one in order to soften the impact of unpleasant information.

Evaluating (response) A listening response that appraises a sender's thoughts or behaviors and implies that the person evaluating is qualified to pass judgment on the other.

Evaluation A message in which a sender judges a receiver in some way, usually resulting in a defensive response.

Evaluative language Language that conveys the sender's attitude rather than simply offering an objective description.

Expectancy violation An instance when others don't behave as we assume they should.

Experimenting An early stage in relational development, consisting of a search for common ground. If the experimentation is successful, the relationship progresses to intensifying. If not, it may go no further.

Expression-privacy dialectic The tension between the desire to be open and disclosive and the desire to be closed and private.

Face The image an individual wants to project to the world. See *Presenting self.*

Face-maintenance strategies Strategies that lead others to act in ways that reinforce the communicator's presenting self.

Face-threatening acts Behavior by another that is perceived as attacking an individual's presenting image, or face.

Facework Actions people take to preserve their own and others' presenting images.

Facilitative emotions Emotions that contribute to effective functioning.

Factual statement A statement that can be verified as true or false. See also *Inferential statement; Opinion statement.*

Fallacy of approval The irrational belief that it is vital to win the approval of virtually every person with whom a communicator interacts.

Fallacy of catastrophic expectations The irrational belief that the worst possible outcome will probably occur.

Fallacy of causation The irrational belief that emotions are caused by others and not by the person who has them.

Fallacy of helplessness The irrational belief that satisfaction in life is determined by forces beyond one's control.

Fallacy of overgeneralization Irrational beliefs in which (1) conclusions (usually negative) are based on limited evidence or (2) communicators exaggerate their shortcomings.

Fallacy of perfection   The irrational belief that a worthwhile communicator should be able to handle every situation with complete confidence and skill.

Fallacy of should   The irrational belief that people should behave in the most desirable way.

Family   A system with two or more interdependent people who have a common past history and a present reality and who expect to influence each other in the future.

Family of origin   The family in which a person grows up.

Feedback   A discernable response of a receiver to a sender's message. See Chapter 1 for a discussion of this concept's history and potential limitations.

Filling in gaps   A listening habit that involves adding details never mentioned by a speaker to complete a message.

First-order realities   The physically observable qualities of a thing or situation.

Formal communication   Interaction that follows officially established channels in an organization.

Friendship   A voluntary interpersonal relationship that provides social support.

Functional conflict   Beneficial conflict characterized by communication that is respectful, cooperative, and focused, which results in the resolution of a problem and the strengthening of a relationship.

Gender   Psychological sex-type.

Halo effect   The tendency to form an overall positive impression of a person on the basis of one positive characteristic.

Haptics   The study of touch in human communication.

Hearing   The first stage in the listening process, in which sound waves are received by a communicator.

High-context culture   A culture that relies heavily on verbal and nonverbal cues to maintain social harmony.

Horizontal communication   Communication between people who do not have direct supervisor-subordinate relationships.

"I" language   A statement that describes the speaker's reaction to another person's behavior without making judgments about its worth. See also *"You" language*.

Identity management   The communication strategies people use to influence how others view them.

Impersonal response   A disconfirming response that is superficial or trite.

Impervious response   A disconfirming response that ignores another person's attempt to communicate.

Inclusion-seclusion dialectic   The tension between a couple's desire for involvement with the "outside world" and their desire to live their own lives, free of what can feel like interference from others.

Incongruous response   A disconfirming response in which two messages, one of which is usually nonverbal, contradict one another.

Indirect appeal   A compliance-gaining strategy based on the hope that the other person will infer or assume the communicator's unexpressed intent.

Individualistic culture A culture in which people view their primary responsibility as helping themselves.

Inferential statement A statement based on an interpretation of evidence. See also *Factual statement; Opinion statement.*

Informal communication Communication based on friendship, shared personal or career interests, and proximity.

In-group A group with which an individual identifies herself or himself.

Initiating The first stage in relational development in which the interactants express interest in one another.

Insulated listening A style in which the receiver ignores undesirable information.

Integrating A relational stage in which the interactants begin to take on a single identity.

Integration-separation dialectic The tension between the desire for connection with others and the desire for independence.

Intensifying A relational stage following experimenting, in which the interactants move toward integration by increasing their amount of contact and the breadth and depth of their self-disclosure.

Intercultural communication Communication that occurs when members of two or more cultures or other groups exchange messages in a manner that is influenced by their different cultural perceptions and symbol systems.

Interpersonal communication, qualitative Communication in which people treat each other as unique individuals as opposed to objects.

Interpersonal communication, quantitative Communication between two people.

Interpretation The process of attaching meaning to sense data. Synonymous with decoding.

Interrupting response A disconfirming response in which one communicator interrupts another.

Intimacy A state achieved via intellectual, emotional, and/or physical closeness as well as via shared activities.

Intimate distance One of Hall's four distance zones, ranging from skin contact to 18 inches.

Irrelevant response A disconfirming response in which one communicator's comments bear no relationship to the previous speaker's ideas.

"It" statement A statement in which "it" replaces the personal pronoun "I," making the statement less direct and more evasive.

Johari Window A model that describes the relationship between self-disclosure and self-awareness.

Kinesics The study of body movements.

Lie A deliberate act of deception.

Linguistic relativism The notion that the language individuals use exerts a strong influence on their perceptions.

Listening The process of receiving and responding to others' messages.

Listening fidelity The degree of congruence between what a listener understands and what the message-sender was attempting to communicate.

Low-context culture A culture that uses language primarily to express thoughts, feelings, and ideas as clearly and logically as possible.

Manipulators Movements in which one part of the body grooms, massages, rubs, holds, fidgets with, pinches, picks, or otherwise manipulates another part.

Metacommunication Messages (usually relational) that refer to other messages; communication about communication.

Mindful listening Careful and thoughtful attention and responses to others' messages.

Mindless listening Reacting to others' messages automatically and routinely, without much mental involvement.

Narrative The stories we use to describe our personal worlds.

Negotiation A process in which two or more people discuss specific proposals in order to find a mutually acceptable agreement.

Networking The process of deliberately meeting people and maintaining contacts to get career information, advice, and leads.

Neutrality A defense-arousing behavior described by Gibb in which the sender expresses indifference toward a receiver.

Noise External, physiological, and psychological distractions that interfere with the accurate transmission and reception of a message.

Nonverbal communication Messages expressed by other than linguistic means.

Norm of reciprocity A social convention that obligates a communicator to return the favors extended by others.

Nurturing culture A culture that regards the support of relationships as an especially important goal. Also termed "feminine" culture.

Oculesics The study of how the eyes can communicate.

Open questions Questions that allow for a variety of extended responses.

Openness-closedness dialectic The tension between the desire to be honest and open and the desire for privacy.

Opinion statement A statement based on a speaker's beliefs. See also *Factual statement; Inferential statement*.

Organization The stage in the perception process that involves arranging data in a meaningful way.

Out-group A group that an individual sees as different from herself or himself.

Paralanguage Nonlinguistic means of vocal expression, for example, rate, pitch, and tone.

Parallel conflict style When partners in a conflict shift from complementary to symmetrical patterns from one conflict issue to another.

Paraphrasing Restating a speaker's thoughts and feelings in the listener's own words.

Passive aggression An indirect expression of aggression, delivered in a way that allows the sender to maintain a facade of kindness.

Perceived self The person we believe ourselves to be in moments of candor. It may be identical with or different from the presenting and desired selves.

Perception checking A three-part method for verifying the accuracy of interpretations, including a description of the sense data, two possible interpretations, and a request for confirmation of the interpretations.

Personal distance   One of Hall's four distance zones, ranging from 18 inches to 4 feet.

Personal space   The distance we put between ourselves and others.

Phonological rules   Rules governing the way in which sounds are pronounced in a language.

Power distance   The degree to which members of a society accept the unequal distribution of power among members.

Power   A source of influence, such as expert power.

Powerless speech mannerisms   Forms of speech that communicate to others a lack of power in the speaker: hedges, hesitations, intensifiers, and so on.

Pragmatic rules   Rules that govern interpretation of language in terms of its social context. See also *Semantic rules; Syntactic rules.*

Predictability-novelty dialectic   Within a relationship, the tension between the need for a predictable relational partner and one who is more spontaneous and less predictable.

Prejudice   An unfairly biased and intolerant attitude toward others who belong to an out-group.

Presenting self   The image a person presents to others. It may be identical with or different from the perceived and desired selves.

Privacy management   The choices people make to reveal or conceal information about themselves.

Problem orientation   A supportive style of communication described by Gibb in which the communicators focus on working together to solve their problems instead of trying to impose their own solutions on one another.

Provisionalism   A supportive style of communication described by Gibb in which a sender expresses open-mindeness to others' ideas and opinions.

Proxemics   The study of how people use space.

Pseudolistening   An imitation of true listening in which the receiver's mind is elsewhere.

Psychological sex type   When a person, regardless of her or his biological sex, can act in a masculine manner or a feminine manner or can exhibit strongly both types of characteristics (androgynous) or neither (undifferentiated); the word *gender* is a shorthand term for psychological sex type.

Public distance   One of Hall's four distance zones, extending outward from 12 feet.

Punctuation   The process of determining the causal order of events.

Qualitative interpersonal communication   Communication in which people treat each other as unique individuals as opposed to objects.

Quantitative interpersonal communication   Any interaction between two people.

Questioning (response)   A listening response in which the receiver seeks additional information from the sender.

Racist language   Language that classifies members of one racial group as superior and others as inferior.

Reappraisal Rethinking the meaning of emotionally charged events in ways that alter their emotional impact.

Reference groups Groups against which we compare ourselves, thereby influencing our self-concept and self-esteem.

Reflected appraisal The theory that a person's self-concept matches the way the person believes others regard him or her.

Regulators Nonverbal cues that help control verbal interaction.

Relational appeal Compliance-gaining strategy that relies on the target's relationship with the person making the request (e.g., "Help me because you're my friend").

Relational commitment A promise, explicit or implied, to remain in a relationship and to make that relationship successful.

Relational conflict style A pattern of managing disagreements that repeats itself over time.

Relational dimension The dimension of a message that expresses the social relationship between two or more individuals. See *Content dimension*.

Relational maintenance Communication aimed at keeping relationships operating smoothly and satisfactorily (e.g., behaving in a positive way, being open, and assuring your partner that you're committed to the relationship).

Relational transgression A violation of the explicit or implicit terms of a relationship, letting the partner down in some important way.

Relative language Words that gain their meaning by comparison.

Remembering A phase of the listening process in which a message is recalled.

Responding A phase of the listening process in which feedback occurs, offering evidence that the message has been received.

Revelation-concealment dialectic The tension between a couple's desire to be open and honest with the "outside world" and their desire to keep things to themselves.

Richness The quantity of nonverbal cues that accompany spoken messages.

Rigid family Families with authoritarian leadership, strict discipline, roles that are inflexible, and unchanging rules.

Rumination Recurrent thoughts not demanded by the immediate environment.

Salience The significance attached to a particular person or phenomenon.

"Sandwich" method Embedding an expression of concern between two positive comments.

Sapir-Whorf hypothesis The best-known declaration of linguistic relativism, formulated by Benjamin Whorf and Edward Sapir.

Second-order realities Perceptions that arise from attaching meaning to first-order things or situations. See *First-order realities*.

Selection A phase of the perception process in which a communicator attends to a stimulus from the environment. Also, a way communicators manage dialectical tensions by responding to one end of the dialectical spectrum and ignoring the other.

Selective listening A listening style in which the receiver responds only to messages that interest her or him.

Self-concept   The relatively stable set of perceptions each individual holds of herself or himself. See also *Self-esteem*.

Self-disclosure   The process of deliberately revealing information about oneself that is significant and that would not normally be known by others.

Self-esteem   The part of the self-concept that involves evaluations of self-worth. See *Self-concept*.

Self-fulfilling prophecy   The causal relationship that occurs when a person's expectations of an event and her or his subsequent behavior based on those expectations make the outcome more likely to occur than would otherwise have been true.

Self-monitoring   The process of attending to one's behavior and using these observations to shape the way one behaves.

Self-serving bias   The tendency to judge oneself in the most generous terms possible while being more critical of others.

Self-talk   The nonvocal, internal monologue that is our process of thinking.

Semantic rules   Rules that govern the meaning of language, as opposed to its structure. See *Syntactic rules; Pragmatic rules*.

Sexist language   Words, phrases, and expressions that unnecessarily differentiate between females and males or exclude, trivialize, or diminish either sex.

Significant other   A person whose opinion is important enough to affect one's self-concept strongly.

Silent listening   Staying attentive and nonverbally responsive without offering verbal feedback.

Sincere questions   Genuine attempts to elicit information from others.

Social comparison   Evaluating oneself in terms of or by comparison to others.

Social distance   One of Hall's four distance zones, ranging from 4 to 12 feet.

Social identity   The part of the self-concept that is based on membership in groups.

Social media   Mediated communication channels used primarily for personal reasons including text messaging, twitter, e-mail, instant messaging, and social networking services.

Social penetration model   A model that describes relationships in terms of their breadth and depth.

Spiral   A reciprocal communication pattern in which messages reinforce one another. See *Escalatory spiral; De-escalatory spiral*.

Spontaneity   A supportive communication behavior described by Gibb in which the sender expresses a message without any attempt to manipulate the receiver.

Stability-change dialectic   The tension between the desire to keep a relationship predictable and stable and the desire for novelty and change.

Stage hogging   A listening style in which the receiver is more concerned with making his or her own point than in understanding the speaker.

Stagnating   A relational stage characterized by declining enthusiasm and standardized forms of behavior.

Standpoint theory A body of scholarship that explores how one's position in a society shapes one's view of society in general and of specific individuals.

Static evaluation Treating people or objects as if they were unchanging.

Stereotyping Exaggerated beliefs associated with a categorizing system.

Strategy A defense-arousing style of communication described by Gibb in which a sender tries to manipulate or deceive a receiver.

Superiority A defense-arousing style of communication described by Gibb in which the sender states or implies that the receiver is not worthy of respect.

Supporting (response) A listening response in which the receiver reveals her or his solidarity with the speaker's situation.

Symmetrical conflict style Partners in a conflict use the same tactics.

Sympathy Feeling compassion for another person's emotions; entails less identification than *empathy.*

Synchronous communication Communication that occurs in real time.

Syntactic rules Rules that govern the ways symbols can be arranged, as opposed to the meanings of those symbols. See *Semantic rules; Pragmatic rules.*

System A group, such as a family, whose members interact with one another to form a whole.

Tangential response A disconfirming response that uses the speaker's remark as a starting point for a shift to a new topic.

Terminating The conclusion of a relationship, characterized by the acknowledgment of one or both partners that the relationship is over.

Territory A stationary area claimed by a person or animal.

Transactional The dynamic process in which communicators create meaning together through interaction.

Uncertainty avoidance The tendency of a culture's members to feel threatened by ambiguous situations, and how much they try to avoid them.

Understanding A stage in the listening process in which the receiver attaches meaning to a message.

Upward communication Communication from subordinates to their bosses.

Virtual teams Teams whose membership transcends the boundaries of location and time.

"We" language The use of first-person-plural pronouns to include others, either appropriately or inappropriately. Language implying that the issue being discussed is the concern and responsibility of both the speaker and the receiver of a message. See *"I" language; "You" language.*

Win-win problem solving An approach to conflict resolution in which people work together to satisfy all their goals.

"You" language A statement that expresses or implies a judgment of the other person. See *Evaluation; "I" language.*

■ References

5.2 million young Americans may have hearing problems. (2001, July 4). *The New York Times*, p. A11.

Aboud, F. E., & Mendelson, M. J. (1998). Determinants of friendship selection and quality: Developmental perspectives. In W. M. Bukowski & A. F. Newcomb (Eds.), *The company they keep: Friendship in childhood and adolescence* (pp. 87–112). New York: Cambridge University Press.

Adamopoulos, J. (1991). The emergence of interpersonal behavior: Diachronic and cross-cultural processes in the evolution of intimacy. In S. Ting-Toomey & F. Korzenny (Eds.), *Cross-cultural interpersonal communication* (pp. 155–170). Newbury Park, CA: Sage.

Adams, G., Anderson, S. L., & Adonu, J. K. (2004). The cultural grounding of closeness and intimacy. In D. Mashek & A. Aron (Eds.), *The handbook of closeness and intimacy* (pp. 321–339). Mahwah, NJ: Erlbaum.

Adler, R. B., & Elmhorst, J. M. (2008). *Communicating at work: Principles and practices for business and the professions* (9th ed.). New York: McGraw-Hill.

Adler, R. B., & Elmhorst, J. (2010). *Communicating at work: Principles and practices for business and the professions* (10th ed.). New York: McGraw-Hill.

Afifi, T. D., McManus, T., Steuber, K., & Coho, A. (2009). Verbal avoidance and dissatisfaction in intimate conflict situations. *Human Communication Research, 35,* 357–383.

Afifi, T. D., & Steuber, K. (2009). The Revelation Risk Model (RRM): Factors that predict the revelation of secrets and the strategies used to reveal them. *Communication Monographs, 76,* 144–176.

Afifi, W. A., & Caughlin, J. P. (2007). A close look at revealing secrets and some consequences that follow. *Communication Research, 33,* 467–488.

Afifi, W. A., & Johnson, M. L. (1999). The use and interpretation of tie signs in a public setting: Relationship and sex differences. *Journal of Social and Personal Relationships, 16,* 9–38.

Afifi, W. A., & Lucas, A. A. (2008). Information seeking in the initial stages of relational development. In S. Sprecher, A. Wenzel, & J. Harvey (Eds.), *Handbook of relationship initiation,* (pp. 135–151). New York: Psychology Press.

Afifi, W. A., & Metts, S. (1998). Characteristics and consequences of expectation violations in close relationships. *Journal of Social and Personal Relationships, 15,* 365–392.

Agne, R., Thompson, T. L., & Cusella, L. P. (2000). Stigma in the line of face: Self-disclosure of patients' HIV status to health care providers. *Journal of Applied Communication Research, 28,* 235–261.

Alaimo, K., Olson, C. M., & Frongillo, E. A. (2001). Food insufficiency and American school-aged children's cognitive, academic, and psychosocial development. *Pediatrics, 108,* 44–53.

Albada, K. F., Knapp, M. L., & Theune, K. E. (2002). Interaction Appearance Theory: Changing perceptions of physical attractiveness through social interaction. *Communication Theory, 12,* 8–40.

Alberti, R. E., & Emmons, M. L. (2008). *Your perfect right: Assertiveness and equality in your life and relationships* (9th ed.). San Luis Obispo, CA: Impact.

Alberts, J. K. (1988). An analysis of couples' conversational complaints. *Communication Monographs, 55,* 184–197.

Alberts, J. K. (1990). Perceived effectiveness of couples' conversational complaints. *Communication Studies, 40,* 280–291.

Alberts, J. K., & Driscoll, G. (1992). Containment versus escalation: The trajectory of couples' conversational complaints. *Western Journal of Communication, 56,* 394–412.

Alberts, J. K., Kellar-Guenther, U., & Corman, S. R. (1996). That's not funny: Understanding recipients' responses to teasing. *Western Journal of Communication, 60,* 337–357.

Alberts, J. K., Yoshimura, C. G., Rabby, M., & Loschiavo, R. (2005). Mapping the topography of couples' daily conversation. *Journal of Social and Personal Relationships, 22,* 299–322.

Aleman, M. W. (2005). Embracing and resisting romantic fantasies as the rhetorical vision on a SeniorNet discussion board. *Journal of Communication, 55*(1), 5–21.

Allan, J., Fairtlough, G., & Heinzen, B. (2002). *The power of the tale: Using narratives for organisational success.* Chichester, England: Wiley.

Allen, B., (1995). "Diversity" and organizational communication. *Journal of Applied Communication Research, 23,* 143–155.

Allen, M. (1998). Methodological considerations when examining a gendered world. In D. J. Canary & K. Dindia (Eds.), *Handbook of sex differences and similarities in communication* (pp. 427–444). Mahwah, NJ: Erlbaum.

Allen, M., Timmerman, L., Ksobiech, K., Valde, K., Gallagher, E. B., Hookham, L., et al., (2008). Persons living with HIV: Disclosure to sexual partners. *Communication Research Reports, 25,* 192–199.

Alter, A. L., & Oppenheimer, D. M. (2009). Suppressing secrecy through metacognitive ease: Cognitive fluency encourages self-disclosure. *Psychological Science, 20,* 1414–1420.

Altman, I., & Taylor, D. A. (1973). *Social penetration: The development of interpersonal relationships.* New York: Holt, Rinehart & Winston.

Ambady, N., LaPlante, D., Nguyen, T., Rosenthal, R., Chaumeton, N., & Levinson, W. (2002). Surgeons' tone of voice: A clue to malpractice history. *Surgery, 132,* 5–9.

Ambady, N., & Rosenthal, R. (1993). Half a minute: Predicting teacher evaluations from thin slices of nonverbal behavior and physical attractiveness. *Journal of Personality and Social Psychology, 64,* 431–441.

Amodio, D. M., & Showers, C. J. (2005). "Similarity breeds liking" revisited: The moderating role of commitment. *Journal of Social and Personal Relationships, 22,* 817–836.

Andersen, P. A. (1999). *Nonverbal communication: Forms and functions.* Palo Alto, CA: Mayfield.

Andersen, P. A., Guerrero, L. K., & Jones, S. M. (2006). Nonverbal behavior in intimate interactions and intimate relationships. In V. Manusov & M. L. Patterson (Eds.), *The Sage handbook of nonverbal communication* (pp. 259–278). Thousand Oaks, CA: Sage.

Andersen, P. A., Lustig, M. W., & Andersen, J. F. (1990). Changes in latitude, changes in attitude: The relationship between climate and interpersonal communication predispositions. *Communication Quarterly, 38,* 291–311.

Anderson, R. A., Corazzini, K. N., & McDaniel, R. R., Jr. (2004). Complexity science and the dynamics of climate and communication: Reducing nursing home turnover. *Gerontologist, 44,* 378–388.

Antheunis, M. L., & Schouten, A. P. (2011). The effects of other-generated and system-generated cues on adolescents' perceived attractiveness on social network sites. *Journal of Computer-Mediated Communication, 16,* 391–406.

Antioch College. (2006). *The Antioch College sexual offense prevention policy.* Retrieved from http:// antiochmedia.org/mirror/antiwarp/www .antioch-college.edu/Campus/sopp/index .html

Antonuccio, D., & Jackson, R. (2009). The science of forgiveness. In W. O'Donohue & S. R. Graybar (Eds.) *Handbook of contemporary psychotherapy: Toward an improved understanding of effective psychotherapy* (pp. 269–284). Thousand Oaks, CA: Sage.

Applegate, J. (1990). Constructs and communication: A pragmatic integration. In G. J. Neimeyer & R. A. Neimeyer (Eds.), *Advances in personal construct psychology* (pp. 203–230). Stamford, CT: JAI Press.

Arasaratnam, L. A. (2006). Further testing of a new model of intercultural communication competence. *Communication Research Reports, 23,* 93–99.

Arasaratnam, L. A. (2007). Research in intercultural communication competence. *Journal of International Communication, 13*(2), 66–73.

Archer, J. (2002). Sex differences in physically aggressive acts between heterosexual partners: A meta-analytic review. *Aggression and Violent Behavior, 7,* 313–351.

Archer, R., & Berg, J. (1978, November). To encourage intimacy, don't force it. *Psychology Today, 12,* 39–40.

Argyle, M., & Henderson, M. (1984). The rules of friendship. *Journal of Social and Personal Relationships, 1,* 211–237.

Argyle, M., & Henderson, M. (1985). The rules of relationships. In S. Duck & D. Perlman (Eds.), *Understanding personal relationships: An interdisciplinary approach* (pp. 63–84). Beverly Hills, CA: Sage.

Armstrong, E. (2005). Expressing opinions and feelings in aphasia: Linguistic options. *Aphasiology, 19,* 285–295.

Armstrong, G. B., Boiarsky, G. A., & Mares, M. L. (1991). Background television and reading performance. *Communication Monographs, 58,* 235–253.

Aronson, E. (2008). *The social animal* (10th ed.). New York: Worth.

Aronsson, K., & Cekaite, A. (2011). Activity contracts and directives in everyday family politics. *Discourse & Society, 22,* 137–154.

Arsenault, A. (2007, May). *Too much information?: Gatekeeping and information dissemination in a networked world.* Paper presented at the annual meeting of the International Communication Association, San Francisco.

Asante, M. K. (2002). Language and agency in the transformation of American identity. In W. F. Eadie & P. E. Nelson (Eds.), *The changing conversation in America: Lectures from the Smithsonian* (pp. 77–89). Thousand Oaks, CA: Sage.

Atkin, C. K., Smith, S. W., Roberto, A. J., Fediuk, T., & Wagner, T. (2002). Correlates of verbally aggressive communication in adolescents. *Journal of Applied Communication Research, 30,* 251–268.

Aune, R. K., & Kikuchi, T. (1993). Effects of language intensity similarity on perceptions of credibility, relational attributions, and persuasion. *Journal of Language and Social Psychology, 12,* 224–238.

Avramova, Y. R., Stapel, D. A., & Lerouge, D. (2010). Mood and context-dependence: Positive mood increases and negative mood decreases the effects of context on perception. *Journal of Personality and Social Psychology, 99,* 203–214.

Avtgis, T. A. (1999). The relationship between unwillingness to communicate and family communication patterns. *Communication Research Reports, 16,* 333–338.

Avtgis, T. A., & Rancer, A. S. (2008). The relationship between trait verbal aggressiveness and teacher burnout syndrome in K-12 teachers. *Communication Research Reports, 25,* 86–89.

Avtgis, T. A., West, D. V., & Anderson, T. L. (1998). Relationship stages: An inductive analysis identifying cognitive, affective, and behavioral dimensions of Knapp's relational stages model. *Communication Research Reports, 15,* 280–287.

Aylor, B., & Dainton, M. (2004). Biological sex and psychological gender as predictors of routine and strategic relational maintenance. *Sex Roles, 50,* 689–697.

Ayres, J., & Crosby, S. (1995). Two studies concerning the predictive validity of the personal report of communication apprehension in employment interviews. *Communication Research Reports, 12,* 145–151.

Ayres, J., & Hopf, T. (1993). *Coping with speech anxiety.* Norwood, NJ: Ablex.

Babinski, D. E., Pelham, W. E., Jr., Molina, B. S. G., Gnagy, E. M., Waschbusch, D. A., Yu, J., et al. (2011). Late adolescent and young adult outcomes of girls diagnosed with ADHD in childhood: An exploratory investigation. *Journal of Attention Disorders, 15,* 204–214.

Bach, G. R., & Wyden, P. (1983). *The intimate enemy: How to fight fair in love and marriage.* New York: Avon Books.

Bachman, G. F., & Guerrero, L. K. (2006). Forgiveness, apology, and communicative responses to hurtful events. *Communication Reports, 19,* 45–56.

Back, M. D., Schmukle, S. C., & Egloff, B. (2008). Becoming friends by chance. *Psychological Science, 19,* 439–440.

Baiocco, R., Laghi, F., Schneider, B. H., Dalessio, M., Amichai-Hamburger, Y., Coplan, R. J. Koszycki, D. & Flament., M. (2011). Daily patterns of communication and contact between Italian early adolescents and their friends. *Cyberpsychology, Behavior, and Social Networking, 14,* 467–471. doi: 10.1089/cyber.2010.0208

Bailey, R. W. (2003). Ideologies, attitudes, and perceptions. *American Speech, 88,* 115–142.

Baker, A. J. (2008). Down the rabbit hole: The role of place in the initiation and development of online relationships. In A. Barak (Ed.), *Psychological aspects of cyberspace: Theory, research, applications* (pp. 163–184). New York: Cambridge University Press.

Baker, L. R., & Oswald, D. L. (2010). Shyness and online social networking services. *Journal of Social & Personal Relationships, 27,* 873–889.

Bakker, A. B. (2005). Flow among music teachers and their students: The crossover of peak experiences. *Journal of Vocational Behavior, 66,* 26–44.

Baldwin, M. W., & Keelan, J. P. R. (1999). Interpersonal expectations as a function of self-esteem and sex. *Journal of Social and Personal Relationships, 16,* 822–833.

Barbato, C. A., Graham, E. E., & Perse, E. M. (2003). Communicating in the family: An examination of the relationship of family communication climate and interpersonal communication motives. *Journal of Family Communication, 3*(3), 123–148.

Barbee, P. P., Gulley, M. R., & Cunningham, M. R. (1990). Support seeking in personal relationships. *Journal of Social and Personal Relationships, 7,* 531–540.

Barelds, D., & Dijkstra, P. (2009). Positive illusions about a partner's physical attractiveness and relationship quality. *Personal Relationships, 16,* 263–283.

Bargh, J. A. (1988). Automatic information processing: Implications for communication and affect. In L. Donohew & H. E. Sypher (Eds.), *Communication, social cognition, and affect* (pp. 9–32). Hillsdale, NJ: Erlbaum.

Barker, L. L. (1971). *Listening behavior.* Englewood Cliffs, NJ: Prentice-Hall.

Barker, L. L., Edwards, R., Gaines, C., Gladney, K., & Holley, F. (1981). An investigation of proportional time spent in various communication activities by college students. *Journal of Applied Communication Research, 8,* 101–109.

Barner, D., Inagaki, S., & Li, P. (2009). Language, thought, and real nouns. *Cognition, 111,* 329–344.

Barnes, S. B. (2003). *Computer-mediated communication: Human-to-human communication across the Internet.* Boston: Allyn & Bacon.

Barrett, L. F., Gross, J., Christensen, T., & Benvenuto, M. (2001). Knowing what you're feeling and knowing what to do about it: Mapping the relation between emotion differentiation and emotion regulation. *Cognition and Emotion, 15,* 713–724.

Barrick, M. R., Bradley, B. H., Kristof-Brown, A. L., & Colbert, A. E. (2007). The moderating role of top management team interdependence: Implications for real teams and working groups. *Academy of Management Journal, 50,* 544–557.

Barry, D. (1990). *Dave Barry turns 40.* New York: Fawcett Columbine.

Bartels, J., Pruyn, A., De Jong, M., & Joustra, I. (2008). Multiple organizational identification levels and the impact of perceived external prestige and communication climate. *Journal of Organizational Behavior, 28,* 173–190.

Bartlett, N. H., Patterson, H. M., VanderLaan, D. P., & Vasey, P. L. (2009). The relation between women's body esteem and friendships with gay men. *Body Image, 6,* 235–241.

Baruch, Y., & Jenkins, S. (2006). Swearing at work and permissive leadership culture: When antisocial becomes social and incivility is acceptable. *Leadership & Organization Development Journal, 28,* 492–507.

Bateson, G., & Jackson, D. D. (1964). Some varieties of pathogenic organization. *Disorders of Communication* [Research Publications: Association for Research in Nervous and Mental Disease], *42*, 270–283.

Batson, C. D., Batson, J. G., Todd, R. M., Brummett, B. H., Shaw, L. L., & Aldeguer, C. M. R. (1995). Empathy and the collective good: Caring for one of the others in a social dilemma. *Journal of Personality and Social Psychology, 68*, 619–631.

Battaglia, D. M., Richard, F. D., Datteri, D. L., & Lord, C. G. (1998). Breaking up is (relatively) easy to do: A script for the dissolution of close relationships. *Journal of Social and Personal Relationships, 15*, 829–845.

Bauerlein, M. (2009, September 4). Why Gen-Y Johnny can't read nonverbal cues. *Wall Street Journal*. Retrieved from http://online.wsj.com/article/SB10001424052970203863204574348493483201758.html

Bauman, S. (2011). *Cyberbullying: What counselors need to know*. Alexandria, VA: American Counseling Association.

Baumeister, R. F. (2005). *The cultural animal: Human nature, meaning, and social life*. New York: Oxford University Press.

Baumeister, R. F., Bratslavsky, E., Finkenauer, C., & Vohs, K. D. (2001). Bad is stronger than good. *Review of General Psychology, 5*, 323–370.

Baumeister, R. F., Campbell, J. D., Krueger, J. I., & Vohs, K. D. (2003). Does high self-esteem cause better performance, interpersonal success, happiness, or healthier lifestyles? *Psychological Science in the Public Interest, 4*, 1–44.

Bavelas, J. B., Black, A., Chovil, N., & Mullett, J. (1990). *Equivocal communication*. Newbury Park, CA: Sage.

Bavelas, J. B., Coates, L., & Johnson, T. (2002). Listener responses as a collaborative process: The role of gaze. *Journal of Communication, 52*, 566–580.

Baxter, L. A. (1987). Symbols of relationship identity in relationship culture. *Journal of Social and Personal Relationships, 4*, 261–280.

Baxter, L. A. (1992). Forms and functions of intimate play in personal relationships. *Human Communication Research, 18*, 336–363.

Baxter, L. A. (1994). A dialogic approach to relationship maintenance. In D. J. Canary & L. Stafford (Eds.), *Communication and relational maintenance* (pp. 233–254). San Diego: Academic Press.

Baxter, L. A. (2011). *Voicing relationships: A dialogical perspective*. Thousand Oaks, CA: Sage.

Baxter, L. A., & Akkoor, C. (2011). Topic expansiveness and family communication patterns. *Journal of Family Communication, 11*, 1–20.

Baxter, L. A., & Braithwaite, D. O. (2006). Social dialectics: The contradictions of relating. In B. Whaley & W. Samter (Eds.), *Explaining Communication: Contemporary communication theories and exemplars* (pp. 305–324). Mahwah, NJ: Erlbaum.

Baxter, L. A., & Braithwaite, D. O. (2008). Relational dialectics theory. In L. A. Baxter & D. O. Braithwaite (Eds.), *Engaging theories in interpersonal communication: Multiple perspectives* (pp. 349–361). Thousand Oaks, CA: Sage.

Baxter, L. A., & Clark, C. L. (1996). Perceptions of family communication patterns and the enactment of family rituals. *Western Journal of Communication, 60*, 254–268.

Baxter, L. A., Dun, T., & Sahlstein, E. (2001). Rules for relating communicated among social network members. *Journal of Social and Personal Relationships, 18*, 173–200.

Baxter, L. A., & Erbert, L. A. (1999). Perceptions of dialectical contradictions in turning points of development in heterosexual romantic relationships. *Journal of Social and Personal Relationships, 16*, 547–569.

Baxter, L. A., Henauw, C., Huisman, D., Livesay, C., Norwood, K., Hua, S., Wolf, B., & Young, B. (2009). Lay conceptions of "family": A replication and extension. *Journal of Family Communication, 9*, 170–189.

Baxter, L. A., & Montgomery, B. M. (1996). *Relating: Dialogues and dialectics*. New York: Guilford Press.

Baxter, L. A., & Pittman, G. (2001). Communicatively remembering turning points of relational development in heterosexual romantic relationships. *Communication Reports, 14*, 1–17.

Baxter, L. A., & Wilmot, W. W. (1985). Taboo topics in close relationships. *Journal of Social and Personal Relationships, 2*, 253–269.

Bazil, L. G. D. (1999). The effects of social behavior on fourth- and fifth-grade girls' perceptions of physically attractive and unattractive peers. *Dissertation Abstracts International: Section B. Sciences and Engineering, 59*(8-B), 4533.

Beatty, M. J., & McCroskey, J. C. (1997). It's in our nature: Verbal aggressiveness as temperamental expression. *Communication Quarterly, 45,* 446–460.

Beaulieu, C. M. (2004). Intercultural study of personal space: A case study. *Journal of Applied Social Psychology, 34,* 794–805.

Bechtoldt, M. N., De Dreu, C. K. W., Nijstad, B. A., & Zapf, D. (2010). Self-concept clarity and the management of social conflict. *Journal of Personality, 78,* 539–574.

Beck, C. E., & Beck, E. A. (1996). The manager's open door and the communication climate. In K. M. Galvin & P. Cooper (Eds.), *Making connections: Readings in relational communication* (pp. 286–290). Los Angeles: Roxbury.

Becker, J. A. H., Ellevold, B., & Stamp, G. H. (2008) The creation of defensiveness in social interaction II: A model of defensive communication among romantic couples. *Communication Monographs, 75,* 86–110.

Belkin, L. Y. (2008). Emotional contagion in the electronic communication context in organizations. *Dissertation Abstracts International: Section A. Humanities and Social Sciences, 68*(9-A), 3940.

Bell, R. A. (1991). Gender, friendship, network density, and loneliness. *Journal of Social Behavior and Personality, 6,* 45–56.

Bell, R. A., & Healey, J. G. (1992). Idiomatic communication and interpersonal solidarity in friends' relational cultures. *Human Communication Research, 18,* 307–335.

Bello, R. S., Brandau-Brown, F. E., Zhang, S., & Ragsdale, J. D. (2010). Verbal and nonverbal methods for expressing appreciation in friendships and romantic relationships: A cross-cultural comparison. *International Journal of Intercultural Relations, 34,* 294–302.

Bello, R., & Edwards, R. (2005). Interpretations of messages: The influence of various forms of equivocation, face concerns, and sex differences. *Journal of Language and Social Psychology, 24,* 160–181.

Bem, S. L. (1974). The measurement of psychological androgyny. *Journal of Consulting and Clinical Psychology, 42,* 155–162.

Bender, S. L., & Messner, E. (2003). *Becoming a therapist: What do I say, and why?* New York: Guilford Press.

Benenson, J. F., Gordon, A. J., & Roy, R. (2000). Children's evaluative appraisals of competition in tetrads versus dyads. *Small Group Research, 31,* 635–652.

Bennehum, D. S. (2005, July). Old emails never die. Wired. Retrieved from http://www.wired.com/wired/archive/7.05/email_pr.html

Bennett, J. (2010, July 19). The beauty advantage: How looks affect your work, your career, your life. *Newsweek.* Retrieved from http://www.newsweek.com/2010/07/19/the-beauty-advantage.html

Benoit, W. L., & Benoit, P. J. (1987). Everyday argument practices of naive social actors. In J. Wenzel (Ed.), *Argument and critical practice: Proceedings of the fifth SCA/AFA conference on argumentation* (pp. 465–474). Annandale, VA: Speech Communication Association.

Ben-Ze'ev, A. (2003). Privacy, emotional closeness, and openness in cyberspace. *Computers in Human Behavior, 19,* 451–467.

Berg, I. K., & DeJong, P. (2005). Engagement through complimenting. *Journal of Family Psychotherapy, 16,* 51–56.

Berger, C. R. (1979). Beyond initial interactions: Uncertainty, understanding, and the development of interpersonal relationships. In H. Giles & R. St. Clair (Eds.), *Language and social psychology* (pp. 122–144). Oxford, England: Blackwell.

Berger, C. R. (1987). Communicating under uncertainty. In M. Roloff & G. Miller (Eds.), *Interpersonal processes: New directions in communication research* (pp. 39–62). Newbury Park, CA: Sage.

Berger, C. R. (1988). Uncertainty and information exchange in developing relationships. In S. Duck & D. F. Hay (Eds.), *Handbook of personal relationships: Theory, research and interventions* (pp. 239–255). New York: Wiley.

Berger, C. R. (2011). From explanation to application. *Journal of Applied Communication Research, 39,* 214–222.

Berger, C. R., & diBattista, P. (1993). Communication failure and plan adaptation: If at first you don't succeed, say it louder and slower. *Communication Monographs, 60,* 220–238.

Berger, C. R., & Kellermann, K. (1994). Acquiring social information. In J. M. Wiemann & J. A. Daly (Eds.), *Communicating strategically* (pp. 1–31). Hillsdale, NJ: Erlbaum.

Berger, C. R., & Lee, K. J. (2011). Second thoughts, second feelings: Attenuating the impact of threatening narratives through rational reappraisal. *Communication Research, 38,* 3–26.

Bergman, M. E., Watrous-Rodriguez, K. M., & Chalkley, K. M. (2008). Identity and language: Contributions to and consequences of speaking Spanish in the workplace. *Hispanic Journal of Behavioral Sciences, 30*(1), 40–68.

Bergner, R. M., & Holmes, J. R. (2000). Self-concepts and self-concept change: A status dynamic approach. *Psychotherapy: Theory, Research, Practice, Training, 37,* 36–44.

Bernstein, E. (2010, October 18). I'm very, very, very sorry . . . really? We apologize more to strangers than family, and why women ask for forgiveness more than men. *Wall Street Journal,* pp. D1, D2.

Berry, S. (2007). Personal report of intercultural communication apprehension. In R. A. Reynolds, R. Woods, & J. D. Baker (Eds.), *Handbook of research on electronic surveys and measurements* (pp. 364–366). Hershey, PA: Idea Group Reference/IGI Global.

Berscheid, E. (2006). Searching for the meaning of "love." In R. J. Sternberg & K. Weiss (Eds.), *The new psychology of love* (pp. 171–183). New Haven, CT: Yale University Press.

Berscheid, E., & Walster, E. H. (1978). *Interpersonal attraction* (2nd ed.). Reading, MA: Addison-Wesley.

Berscheid, E., Schneider, M., & Omoto, A. M. (1989). Issues in studying close relationships: Conceptualizing and measuring closeness. In C. Hendrick (Ed.), *Close relationships* (pp. 63–91). Newbury Park, CA: Sage.

Bevan, J. L. (2008). Experiencing and communicating romantic jealousy: Questioning the investment model. *Southern Communication Journal, 73,* 42–67.

Bevan, J. L., & Tidgewell, K. D. (2009). Relational uncertainty as a consequence of partner jealousy expressions. *Communication Studies, 60,* 305–323.

Bharti, A. (1985). The self in Hindu thought and action. In A. J. Marsella, G. DeVos, & F. L. K. Hsu (Eds.), *Culture and self: Asian and Western perspectives.* New York: Tavistock.

Bippus, A. M. (2001). Recipients' criteria for evaluating the skillfulness of comforting communication and the outcomes of comforting interactions. *Communication Monographs, 68,* 301–313.

Bippus, A. M., & Young, S. L. (2005). Owning your emotions: Reactions to expressions of self- versus other-attributed positive and negative emotions. *Journal of Applied Communication Research, 33,* 26–45.

Birdwhistell, R. L. (1970). *Kinesics and context.* Philadelphia: University of Pennsylvania Press.

Bisson, M. A., & Levine, T. R. (2009). Negotiating a friends with benefits relationship. *Archives of Sexual Behavior, 38,* 66–73.

Bjørge, A. K. (2007). Power distance in English lingua franca email communication. *International Journal of Applied Linguistics, 17*(1), 60–80.

Bjorklund, D. F., Cassel, W. S., Bjorklund, B. R., Brown, R. D., Park, C. L., & Ernst, K. (2000). Social demand characteristics in children's and adults' eyewitness memory and suggestibility: The effect of different interviewers on free recall and recognition. *Applied Cognitive Psychology, 14,* 421–433.

Blacker, L. (1999). The launching phase of the life cycle. In B. Carter & M. McGoldrick (Eds.), *The expanded family life cycle: Individual, family, and social perspectives* (3rd ed., pp. 287–306). Boston: Allyn & Bacon.

Blake, R. R., & Mouton, J. S. (1994). *The managerial grid.* Houston: Gulf Publishing.

Blank, P. D. (Ed.). (1993). *Interpersonal expectations: Theory, research, and applications.* Cambridge, England: Cambridge University Press.

Blakenship, K. L., & Craig, T. Y. (2007). Powerless language markers and the correspondence bias: Attitude confidence mediates the effects of tag questions on attitude attributions. *Journal of Language and Social Psychology, 26,* 28–47.

Boase, J., Horrigan, J. B., Wellman, B., & Rainie, L. (2006). The strength of Internet ties. *Pew Internet & American Life Project*. Retrieved from http://www.pewinternet.org/pdfs/PIP_Internet_ties.pdf

Bok, S. (1978). *Lying: Moral choice in public and private life*. New York: Pantheon.

Bond, B. J. (2009). He posted, she posted: Gender differences in self-disclosure on social network sites. *Rocky Mountain Communicator, 6*(2), 29–37.

Booth-Butterfield, M., & Booth-Butterfield, S. (1998). Emotionality and affective orientation. In J. C. McCroskey, J. A. Daly, M. M. Martin, & M. J. Beatty (Eds.), *Communication and personality: Trait perspectives* (pp. 171–190). Cresskill, NJ: Hampton.

Boroditsky, L. (2009). How does our language shape the way we think? In M. Brockman (Ed.), *What's next?: Dispatches on the future of science* (pp. 116–129). New York: Vintage.

Bosson, J. K., Johnson, A. B., Niederhoffer, K., & Swann, W. B., Jr. (2006). Interpersonal chemistry through negativity: Bonding by sharing negative attitudes about others. *Personal Relationships, 13*, 135–150.

Bostrom, R. N. (1996). Aspects of listening behavior. In O. Hargie (Ed.), *Handbook of communication skills* (2nd ed., pp. 236–259). London: Routledge.

Bostrom, R. N., & Waldhart, E. S. (1980). Components in listening behavior: The role of short-term memory. *Human Communication Research, 6*, 221–227.

Bower, B. (1998, September 12). Social disconnections on-line. *Science News, 154*, 168.

Bowes, A., & Katz, A. (2011). When sarcasm stings. *Discourse Processes, 48*, 215–236.

Bowman, J. M. (2009). The influences of attribution, context, and heterosexual self-presentation on perceived appropriateness of self-disclosure in same-sex male friendships. *Communication Research Reports, 26*, 215–227.

Bradbury, T. N., & Fincham, F. D. (1990). Attributions in marriage: Review and critique. *Psychological Bulletin, 107*, 3–33.

Braithwaite, D. O., & Eckstein, N. (2003). Reconceptualizing supportive interactions: How persons with disabilities communicatively manage assistance. *Journal of Applied Communication Research, 31*, 1–26.

Braithwaite, D. O., Baxter, L. A., & Harper, A. M. (1998). The role of rituals in the management of the dialectical tension of "old" and "new" in blended families. *Communication Studies, 49*, 101–120.

Brandau-Brown, F. E., & Ragsdale, J. D. (2008). Personal, moral, and structural commitment and the repair of marital relationships. *Southern Communication Journal, 73*, 68–83.

Brantley, A., Knox, D., & Zusman, M. E. (2002). When and why gender differences in saying "I love you" among college students. *College Student Journal, 36*, 614–615.

Breithaupt, F. (2011). How is it possible to have empathy? Four models. In P. Leverage, H. Mancing, R. Schweickert, & J. M. William (Eds.) *Theory of mind and literature* (pp. 273–288). West Lafayette, IN: Purdue University Press.

Brescoll, V. L., & Uhlmann, E. L. (2008). Can an angry woman get ahead? Status conferral, gender, and expression of emotion in the workplace. *Psychological Science, 19*, 268–275.

Brightman, V., Segal, A., Werther, P., & Steiner, J. (1975). Ethological study of facial expression in response to taste stimuli. *Journal of Dental Research, 54*, 141.

Briles, J. (1999), *Woman to woman 2000: Becoming sabotage savvy in the new millennium*. Far Hills, NJ: New Horizon Press.

Brooks, D. (2010, October 21). Flock comedies. *New York Times*. Retrieved from http://www.nytimes.com/2010/10/22/opinion/22brooks.html

Brown, J. R. (2004). Conflict, emotions and appreciation of differences. *Gestalt Review, 8*, 323–335.

Brown, L. (1982). *Communicating facts and ideas in business*. Englewood Cliffs, NJ: Prentice-Hall.

Brown, R. F., Bylund, C. L., Gueguen, J. A., Diamond, C., Eddington, J., & Kissane, D. (2010). Developing patient-centered communication skills training for oncologists: Describing the content and efficacy of training. *Communication Education, 59*, 235–248.

Brownell, J. (1990). Perceptions of effective listeners: A management study. *Journal of Business Communication, 27,* 401–415.

Brownell, J., & Wolvin, A. (2010). *What every student should know about listening.* Upper Saddle River, NJ: Pearson.

Bruce, S. M, Mann, A., Jones, C., & Gavin, M. (2007). Gestures expressed by children who are congenitally deaf-blind: Topography, rate, and function. *Journal of Visual Impairment & Blindness, 101,* 637–652.

Brumark, Å. (2010). Behaviour regulation at the family dinner table. The use of and response to direct and indirect behaviour regulation in ten Swedish families. *Journal of Child Language, 37,* 1065–1088.

Brunet, P. M., & Schmidt, L. A. (2010). Sex differences in the expression and use of computer-mediated affective language: Does context matter? *Social Science Computer Review, 28,* 194–205.

Brunner, B. R. (2008). Listening, communication and trust: Practitioners' perspectives of business/organizational relationships. *International Journal of Listening, 22,* 73–82.

Buck, R., & VanLear, C. A. (2002). Verbal and nonverbal communication: Distinguishing symbolic, spontaneous and pseudo-spontaneous nonverbal behavior. *Journal of Communication, 52,* 522–541.

Bukowski, W. M., Motzoi, C. C., & Meyer, F. (2009). Friendship as process, function, and outcome. In K. H. Rubin, W. M. Bukowski, & B. Laursen (Eds.), *Handbook of peer interactions, relationships, and groups* (pp. 217–231). New York: Guilford Press.

Bukowski, W., Newcomb, A., & Hartup, W. (1996). *The company they keep: Friendship in childhood and adolescence.* Cambridge, England: Cambridge University Press.

Buller, D. B., & Aune, K. (1988). The effects of vocalics and nonverbal sensitivity on compliance: A speech accommodation theory explanation. *Human Communication Research, 14,* 301–332.

Buller, D. B., & Aune, K. (1992). The effects of speech rate similarity on compliance application of communication accommodation theory. *Western Journal of Communication, 56,* 37–53.

Buller, D. B., & Burgoon, J. K. (1994). Deception: Strategic and nonstrategic communication. In J. A. Daly & J. M. Wiemann (Eds.), *Strategic interpersonal communication* (pp. 191–223). Hillsdale, NJ: Erlbaum.

Buller, D. B., & Burgoon, J. K. (1996). Interpersonal deception theory. *Communication Theory, 6,* 203–242.

Burggraf, C. S., & Sillars, A. L. (1987). A critical examination of sex differences in marital communication. *Communication Monographs, 54,* 276–294.

Burgoon, J. K., & Bacue, A. E. (2003). Nonverbal communication skills. In B. Burleson & J. O. Greene (Eds.), *Handbook of communication and social interaction skills* (pp. 179–219). Mahwah, NJ: Erlbaum.

Burgoon, J. K., & Burgoon, M. (2001). Expectancy theories. In W. P. Robinson & H. Giles (Eds.), *The new handbook of language and social psychology* (pp. 79–102). Sussex, England: Wiley.

Burgoon, J. K., Berger, C. R., & Waldron, V. R. (2000). Mindfulness and interpersonal communication. *Journal of Social Issues, 56,* 105–127.

Burgoon, J. K., Birk, T., & Pfau, M. (1990). Nonverbal behaviors, persuasion, and credibility. *Human Communication Research, 17,* 140–169.

Burgoon, J. K., Buller, D. B., & Guerrero, L. K. (1995). Interpersonal deception: IX. Effects of social skill and nonverbal communication on deception success and detection accuracy. *Journal of Language and Social Psychology, 14,* 289–311.

Burgoon, J. K., Buller, D. B., Guerrero, L. K., & Feldman, C. M. (1994). Interpersonal deception: VI. Effects of preinteractional and interactional factors on deceiver and observer perceptions of deception success. *Communication Studies, 45,* 263–280.

Burgoon, J. K., & Le Poire, B. A. (1999). Nonverbal cues and interpersonal judgments: Participant and observer perceptions of intimacy, dominance, and composure. *Communication Monographs, 66,* 105–124.

Burgoon, J. K., & Levine, T. R. (2010). Advances in deception detection. In S. W. Smith & S. R. Wilson (Eds.), *New directions in interpersonal communication research* (pp. 201–220). Thousand Oaks, CA: Sage.

Burgoon, J. K., Parrott, R., Le Poire, B. A., Kelley, D. L., Walther, J. B., & Perry, D. (1989). Maintaining and restoring privacy through different types of relationships. *Journal of Social and Personal Relationships, 6,* 131–158.

Burgoon, J. K., Walther, J., & Baesler, E. (1992). Interpretations, evaluations, and consequences of interpersonal touch. *Human Communication Research, 19,* 237–263.

Burk, W. J., Denissen, J., Van Doorn, M. D., Branje, S. J. T., & Laursen, B. (2009). The vicissitudes of conflict measurement: Stability and reliability in the frequency of disagreements. *European Psychologist, 14,* 153–159.

Burkitt, I. (1992). *Social selves: Theories of the social formation of personality.* Newbury Park, CA: Sage.

Burleson, B. R. (1984). Comforting communication. In H. Sypher & J. Applegate (Eds.), *Communication by children and adults: Social cognitive and strategic processes* (pp. 63–104). Beverly Hills, CA: Sage.

Burleson, B. R. (2003). Emotional support skill. In J. O. Greene & B. R. Burleson (Eds.), *Handbook of communication and social interaction skills* (pp. 551–594). Mahwah, NJ: Erlbaum.

Burleson, B. R. (2007). Constructivism: A general theory of communication skill. In B. B. Whaley & W. Samter (Eds.), *Explaining communication: Contemporary theories and exemplars* (pp. 105–128). Mahwah, NJ: Erlbaum.

Burleson, B. R. (2008). What counts as effective emotional support?" In M. T. Motley (Ed.), *Studies in applied interpersonal communication* (pp. 207–227). Thousand Oaks, CA: Sage.

Burleson, B. R., & Caplan, S. E. (1998). Cognitive complexity. In J. C. McCroskey, J. A. Daly, M. M. Martin, & M. J. Beatty (Eds.), *Communication and personality: Trait perspectives* (pp. 233–286). Cresskill, NJ: Hampton Press.

Burleson, B. R., Hanasono, L., Bodie, G., Holmstrom, A., McCullough, J., Rack, J., & Rosier, J. (2011). Are gender differences in responses to supportive communication a matter of ability, motivation, or both? Reading patterns of situation effects through the lens of a dual-process theory. *Communication Quarterly, 59,* 37–60.

Burleson, B. R., Hanasono, L., Bodie, G., Holmstrom, A., Rack, J., Rosier, J., & McCullough, J. (2009). Explaining gender differences in responses to supportive messages: Two tests of a dual-process approach. *Sex Roles, 61,* 265–280.

Burleson, B. R., Holmstrom, A. J., & Gilstrap, C. M. (2005). "Guys can't say that to guys": Four experiments assessing the normative motivation account for deficiencies in the emotional support provided by men. *Communication Monographs, 72,* 468–501.

Burleson, B. R., & Samter, W. (1985). Individual differences in the perception of comforting messages: An exploratory investigation. *Central States Speech Journal, 36,* 39–50.

Burleson, B. R., & Samter, W. (1994). A social skills approach to relationship maintenance. In D. J. Canary & L. Stafford (Eds.), *Communication and relationship maintenance: How individual differences in communication skills affect the achievement of relationship functions* (pp. 61–90). San Diego: Academic Press.

Burleson, B. R., & Samter, W. (1996). Similarity in the communication skills of young adults: Foundations of attraction, friendship, and relationship satisfaction. *Communication Reports, 9,* 127–139.

Burnard, P. (2003). Ordinary chat and therapeutic conversation: Phatic communication and mental health nursing. *Journal of Psychiatric and Mental Health Nursing, 10,* 678–682.

Burns, K. L., & Beier, E. G. (1973). Significance of vocal and visual channels for the decoding of emotional meaning. *Journal of Communication, 23,* 118–130.

Burton, C. M., & King, L. A. (2008). Effects of (very) brief writing on health: The two-minute miracle. *British Journal of Health Psychology, 13,* 9–14.

Burton, E., & Sheehan, B. (2010). Care-home environments and well-being: Identifying the design features that most affect older residents. *Journal of Architectural and Planning Research, 27,* 237–256.

Bushman, B. J. (1988). The effects of apparel on compliance: A field experiment with a female authority figure. *Personality and Social Psychology Bulletin, 14,* 459–467.

Bushman, B. J., Baumeister, R. F., & Stack, A. D. (1999). Catharsis, aggression, and persuasive influence: Self-fulfilling or self-defeating prophecies? *Journal of Personality and Social Psychology, 76,* 367–376.

Bushman, B. J., Bonacci, A. M., Pedersen, W. C., Vasquez, E. A., & Miller, N. (2005). Chewing on it can chew you up: Effects of rumination on triggered displaced aggression. *Journal of Personality and Social Psychology, 88,* 969–983.

Butler, S. F., Villapiano, A., & Malinow, A. (2009). The effect of computer-mediated administration on self-disclosure of problems on the Addiction Severity Index. *Journal of Addiction Medicine, 3,* 194–203.

Buttny, R. (1997). Reported speech in talking race on campus. *Human Communication Research, 23,* 477–506.

Button, S. B. (2004). Identity management strategies utilized by lesbian and gay employees: A quantitative investigation. *Group and Organizational Management, 29,* 470–494.

Buunk, A. P. (2005). How do people respond to others with high commitment or autonomy in their relationships? *Journal of Social and Personal Relationships, 22,* 653–672.

Büyükşahin, A. (2009). Impact of self-monitoring and gender on coping strategies in intimate relationships among Turkish university students. *Sex Roles, 60,* 708–720.

Buzzanell, P. M. (1999). Tensions and burdens in employment interviewing processes: Perspectives of non-dominant group members. *Journal of Business Communication, 36,* 143–162.

Byron, K. (2008). Carrying too heavy a load? The communication and miscommunication of emotion by email. *Academy of Management Review, 33,* 309–327.

Cahn, D. D. (1992). *Conflict in intimate relationships.* New York: Guilford Press.

Cai, D. A., & Fink, E. L. (2002). Conflict style differences between individualists and collectivists. *Communication Monographs, 69,* 67–87.

Caldwell-Harris, C. L., Tong, J., Lung, W., & Poo, S. (in press). Physiological reactivity to emotional phrases in Mandarin-English bilinguals. *International Journal of Bilingualism.* Retrieved from http://www.bu.edu/psych/charris/papers/PhysReactMandarin.pdf

Camden, C., Motley, M. T., & Wilson, A. (1984). White lies in interpersonal communication: A taxonomy and preliminary investigation of social motivations. *Western Journal of Speech Communication, 48,* 309–325.

Campbell, S. (2006). Perceptions of mobile phones in college classrooms: Ringing, cheating, and classroom policies. *Communication Education, 55,* 280–294.

Canary, D. (2003). Managing interpersonal conflict: A model of events related to strategic choices. In J. O. Greene & B. R. Burleson (Eds.), *Handbook of communication and social interaction skills* (pp. 515–549). Mahwah, NJ: Erlbaum.

Canary, D. J., & Hause, K. (1993). Is there any reason to research sex differences in communication? *Communication Quarterly, 41,* 482–517.

Canary, D. J., & Messman, S. J. (2000). Relationship conflict. In C. Hendrick & S. S. Hendrick (Eds.), *Close relationships: A sourcebook* (pp. 261–270). Thousand Oaks, CA: Sage.

Canary, D. J., & Stafford, L. (1992). Relational maintenance strategies and equity in marriage. *Communication Monographs, 59,* 243–267.

Canary, D. J., & Stafford, L. (2001). Equity in maintaining personal relationships. In J. H. Harvey & A. E. Wenzel (Eds.), *Close romantic relationships: Maintenance and enhancement* (pp. 133–150). Mahwah, NJ: Erlbaum.

Canary, D. J., & Wahba, J. (2006). Do women work harder than men at maintaining relationships? In K. Dindia & D. J. Canary (Eds.), *Sex differences and similarities in communication* (2nd ed.). Mahwah, NJ: Erlbaum.

Canary, D. J., Weger, H., Jr., & Stafford, L. (1991). Couples' argument sequences and their associations with relational characteristics. *Western Journal of Speech Communication, 55,* 159–179.

Canli, T., Desmond, J. E., Zhao, Z., & Gabrieli, J. D. E. (2002). Sex differences in the neural basis of emotional memories. *Proceedings of the National Academy of Sciences, 10,* 10789–10794.

Carmeli, A., Yitzhak-Halevy, M., Weisberg, J. (2009). The relationship between emotional intelligence and psychological wellbeing. *Journal of Managerial Psychology, 24,* 66–78.

Carney, D. R., Cuddy, A. J., & Yap, A. J. (2010). Power posing: Brief nonverbal displays affect neuroendocrine levels and risk tolerance. *Psychological Science, 21,* 1363–1368.

Carofiglio, V., de Rosis, F., & Grassano, R. (2008). Dynamic models of multiple emotion activation. In L. Cañamero & R. Aylett (Eds.), *Animating expressive characters for social interaction* (pp. 123–141). Amsterdam: John Benjamins.

Carrell, L. J., & Willmington, S. C. (1996). A comparison of self-report and performance data in assessing speaking and listening competence. *Communication Reports, 9,* 185–191.

Carson, C. L., & Cupach, W. R. (2000). Fueling the flames of the green-eyed monster: The role of ruminative thought in reaction to romantic jealousy. *Western Journal of Communication, 64,* 308–329.

Castelan-Cargile, A., & Bradac, J. J. (2001). Attitudes towards language: A review of speaker-evaluation research and a general process model. In W. B. Gudykunst (Ed.), *Communication yearbook 25* (pp. 347–382). Thousand Oaks, CA: Sage.

Caughlin, J. P. (2003). Family communication standards: What counts as excellent family communication and how are such standards associated with family satisfaction? *Human Communication Research, 29,* 5–40.

Caughlin, J. P., & Arr, T. D. (2004). When is topic avoidance unsatisfying? Examining moderators of the association between avoidance and dissatisfaction. *Human Communication Research, 30,* 479–513.

Caughlin, J. P., & Golish, T. D. (2002). An analysis of the association between topic avoidance and dissatisfaction: Comparing perceptual and interpersonal explanations. *Communication Monographs, 69,* 275–295.

Caughlin, J. P., & Huston, T. L. (2002). A contextual analysis of the association between demand/withdraw and marital satisfaction. *Personal Relationships, 9,* 95–119.

Caughlin, J. P., & Petronio, S. (2004). Privacy in families. In A. L. Vangelisti (Ed.), *Handbook of family communication* (pp. 379–412). Mahwah, NJ: Erlbaum.

Caughlin, J. P., & Vangelisti, A. L. (2006). Conflict in dating and marital relationships. In J. G. Oetzel & S. Ting-Toomey (Eds.), *The Sage handbook of conflict communication* (pp. 129–158). Thousand Oaks, CA: Sage.

Cegala, D. J., Savage, G. T., Brunner, C. C., & Conrad, A. B. (1982). An elaboration of the meaning of interaction involvement: Toward the development of a theoretical concept. *Communication Monographs, 49,* 229–248.

Cesario, J., & Higgins, E. T. (2008). Making message recipients "feel right": How nonverbal cues can increase persuasion. *Psychological Science, 19,* 415–420.

Chaiken, S., & Trope, Y. (Eds.). (1999). *Dual-process theories in social psychology.* New York: Guilford Press.

Chan, Y. K. (1999). Density, crowding, and factors intervening in their relationship: Evidence from a hyper-dense metropolis. *Social Indicators Research, 48,* 103–124.

Chen, G. M. (2011). Tweet this: A uses and gratifications perspective on how active twitter use gratifies a need to connect with others. *Computers in Human Behavior, 27,* 755–762.

Chen, G. M., & Starosta, W. J. (2000). The development and validation of the Intercultural Sensitivity Scale. *Human Communication, 3,* 1–14.

Cherniss, G., Extein, M., Goleman, D., & Weissberg, R. P. (2006). Emotional Intelligence: What does the research really indicate? *Educational Psychologist, 41,* 239–245.

Choi, N., Fuqua, D. R., & Newman, J. L. (2009). Exploratory and confirmatory studies of the structure of the Bem Sex Role Inventory short form with two divergent samples. *Educational and Psychological Measurement, 69,* 696–705.

Choi, Y. S., Gray, H. M., & Ambady, N. (2005). The glimpsed world: Unintended communication and unintended perception. In R. R. Hassin, J. S. Uleman, & J. A. Bargh (Eds.), *The new unconscious* (pp. 309–333). New York: Oxford University Press.

Chovil, N. (1991). Social determinants of facial displays. *Journal of Nonverbal Behavior, 15,* 141–154.

Christenfeld, N., & Larsen, B. (2008). The name game. *The Psychologist, 21,* 210–213.

Christensen, A. J. (2004). *Patient adherence to medical treatment regimens: Bridging the gap between behavioral science and biomedicine.* New Haven, CT: Yale University Press.

Christian, A. (2005). Contesting the myth of the "wicked stepmother": Narrative analysis of an online stepfamily support group. *Western Journal of Communication, 69,* 27–48.

Cissna, K. N., & Sieburg, E. (2006). Patterns of interactional confirmation and disconfirmation. In J. Stewart (Ed.), *Bridges not walls* (9th ed., pp. 429–439). Boston, MA: McGraw-Hill.

Clark, A. (2000). *A theory of sentience.* New York: Oxford University Press.

Clark, R. A., & Delia, J. G. (1997). Individuals' preferences for friends' approaches to providing support in distressing situations. *Communication Reports, 10,* 115–121.

Clark, R. A., Pierce, A. J., Finn, K., Hsu, K., Toosley, A., & Williams, L. (1998). The impact of alternative approaches to comforting, closeness of relationship, and gender on multiple measures of effectiveness. *Communication Studies, 49,* 224–239.

Clarke, F. P. (1973). *Interpersonal communication variables as predictors of marital satisfaction-dissatisfaction* (Doctoral dissertation, University of Denver, Denver, CO).

Clements, K., Holtzworth-Munroe, A., Schweinle, W., & Ickes, W. (2007). Empathic accuracy of intimate partners in violent versus nonviolent relationships. *Personal Relationships, 14,* 369–388.

Cloven, D. H., & Roloff, M. E. (1991). Sense-making activities and interpersonal conflict: Communicative cures for the mulling blues. *Western Journal of Speech Communication, 55,* 134–158.

Coates, J. (1986). *Women, men and language.* London: Longman.

Cohen, A. (2007). One nation, many cultures: A cross-cultural study of the relationship between personal cultural values and commitment in the workplace to in-role performance and organizational citizenship behavior. *Cross-Cultural Research: The Journal of Comparative Social Science, 41,* 273–300.

Cohen, E. D. (2007). *The new rational therapy: Thinking your way to serenity, success, and profound happiness.* Lanham, MD: Rowman & Littlefield.

Cohen, E. L. (2010). Expectancy violations in relationships with friends and media figures. *Communication Research Reports, 27,* 97–111.

Cohen, M. A. (2005). Against basic emotions, and toward a comprehensive theory. *Journal of Mind and Behavior, 26,* 229–254.

Cohen, M., & Avanzino, S. (2010). We are people first: Framing organizational assimilation experiences of the physically disabled using co-cultural theory. *Communication Studies, 61,* 272–303.

Cole, J., & Spalding, H. (2009). *The invisible smile: Living without facial expression.* New York: Oxford University Press.

Cole, P. M., Bruschi, C. J., & Tamang, B. L. (2002). Cultural differences in children's emotional reactions to difficult situations. *Child Development, 73,* 983–996.

Cole, S. W., Hawkley, L. C., Arevalo, J. M., Sung, C. Y., Rose, R. M., & Cacioppo, J. T. (2007). Social regulation of gene expression in human leukocytes. *Genome Biology, 8,* 189–201.

Coleman, L. M., & DePaulo, B. M. (1991). Uncovering the human spirit: Moving beyond disability and "missed" communications. In N. Coupland, H. Giles, & J. M. Wiemann (Eds.), *"Miscommunication" and problematic talk* (pp. 61–84). Newbury Park, CA: Sage.

Collier, M. J. (1991). Conflict competence within African, Mexican, and Anglo American friendships. In S. Ting-Toomey & F. Korzenny (Eds.), *Cross-cultural interpersonal communication* (pp. 132–154). Newbury Park, CA: Sage.

Conlan, S. K. (2008). Romantic relationship termination. *Dissertation Abstracts International:*

Section B. The Sciences and Engineering, 68(7-B), 4884.

Conlee, C., Olvera, J., & Vagim, N. (1993). The relationships among physician nonverbal immediacy and measures of patient satisfaction with physician care. *Communication Reports, 6,* 25–33.

Consedine, N. S., Magai, C., & Bonanno, G. A. (2002). Moderators of the emotion inhibition–health relationship: A review and research agenda. *Review of General Psychology, 6,* 204–228.

Coon, D. (2009). *Psychology: A modular approach to mind and behavior* (11th ed.). Boston: Cengage.

Cooper, A., & Petrides, K. V. (2010). A psychometric analysis of the Trait Emotional Intelligence Questionnaire–Short Form (TEIQue-SF) using item response theory. *Journal of Personality Assessment, 92,* 449–457.

Cotterill, J. (2004). Collocation, connotation, and courtroom semantics: Lawyers' control of witness testimony through lexical negotiation. *Applied Linguistics, 25,* 513–537.

Cowan, G., & Mills, R. D. (2004). Personal inadequacy and intimacy predictors of men's hostility toward women. *Sex Roles, 51,* 67–78.

Cowan, N., & AuBuchon, A. M. (2008). Short-term memory loss over time without retroactive stimulus interference. *Psychonomic Bulletin & Review, 15,* 230–235.

Cox, S. A. (1999). Group communication and employee turnover: How coworkers encourage peers to voluntarily exit. *Southern Communication Journal, 64,* 181–192.

Cozby, P. C. (1973). Self-disclosure: A literature review. *Psychological Bulletin, 79,* 73–91.

Craig, R. T. (2005). How we talk about how we talk: Communication theory in the public interest. *Journal of Communication, 55,* 659–667.

Crane, D. R. (1987). Diagnosing relationships with spatial distance: An empirical test of a clinical principle. *Journal of Marital and Family Therapy, 13,* 307–310.

Cronkhite, G. (1976). *Communication and awareness.* Menlo Park, CA: Cummings.

Crowther, C. E., & Stone, G. (1986). *Intimacy: Strategies for successful relationships.* Santa Barbara, CA: Capra Press.

Crusco, A. H., & Wetzel, G. G. (1984). The Midas Touch: Effects of interpersonal touch on restaurant tipping. *Personality and Social Psychology Bulletin, 10,* 512–517.

Cunningham, M. R., & Barbee, A. P. (2000). Social support. In C. Hendrick & S. S. Hendrick (Eds.), *Close relationships: A sourcebook* (pp. 273–285). Thousand Oaks, CA: Sage.

Cunningham, M. R., Shamblen, S. R., Barbee, A. P., & Ault, L. K. (2005). Social allergies in romantic relationships: Behavioral repetition, emotional sensitization, and dissatisfaction in dating couples. *Personal Relationships, 12,* 273–295.

Cupach, W. R., & Messman, S. J. (1999). Face predilections and friendship solidarity. *Communication Reports, 12,* 117–124.

Czech, K., & Forward, G. L. (2010). Leader communication: Faculty perceptions of the department chair. *Communication Quarterly, 58,* 431–457.

Dailey, R. M. (2006). Confirmation in parent–adolescent relationships and adolescent openness: Toward extending confirmation theory. *Communication Monographs, 73,* 434–458.

Dailey, R. M. (2009). Confirmation from family members: Parent and sibling contributions to adolescent psychosocial adjustment. *Western Journal of Communication, 73,* 273–299.

Dailey, R. M. (2010). Testing components of confirmation: How acceptance and challenge from mothers, fathers, and siblings are related to adolescent self-concept. *Communication Monographs, 77,* 592–617.

Dailey, R. M., Giles, H., & Jansma, L. L. (2005). Language attitudes in an Anglo-Hispanic context: The role of the linguistic landscape. *Language & Communication, 25*(1), 27–38.

Dainton, M., & Aylor, B. (2002). Routine and strategic maintenance efforts: Behavioral patterns, variations associated with relational length, and the prediction of relational characteristics. *Communication Monographs, 69,* 52–66.

Daitch, C. (2010). Dialing down distress: Affect regulation in intimate relationships. In M. Kerman (Ed.), *Clinical pearls of wisdom: Twenty one leading therapists offer their key insights* (pp. 144–154). New York: W. W. Norton.

Darling, A. L., & Dannels, D. P. (2003). Practicing engineers talk about the importance of talk: A report on the role of oral communication in the workplace. *Communication Education, 52,* 1–16.

Dasborough, M. T., Ashkanasy, N. M., Tee, E. Y. J., & Tse, H. H. M. (2009). What goes around comes around: How meso-level negative emotional contagion can ultimately determine organizational attitudes toward leaders. *The Leadership Quarterly, 20,* 571–585.

Davidowitz, M., & Myrick, R. (1984). Responding to the bereaved: An analysis of "helping" styles. *Death Education, 8,* 1–10.

Davies, K. A., Lane, A. M., Devonport, T. J., & Scott, J. A. (2010). Validity and reliability of a Brief Emotional Intelligence Scale (BEIS-10). *Journal of Individual Differences, 31*(4), 198–208.

Davis, J., Foley, A., Crigger, N., & Brannigan, M. C.. (2008). Healthcare and listening: A relationship for caring. *International Journal of Listening, 22,* 168–175.

Davis, M., Markus, K. A., & Walters, S. B. (2006). Judging the credibility of criminal suspect statements: Does mode of presentation matter?" *Journal of Nonverbal Behavior, 30,* 181–198.

Davis, S. F., & Kieffer, J. C. (1998). Restaurant servers influence tipping behavior. *Psychological Reports, 83,* 223–226.

Day, A., Casey, S., & Gerace, A. (2010). Interventions to improve empathy awareness in sexual and violent offenders: Conceptual, empirical, and clinical issues. *Aggression and Violent Behavior, 15,* 201–208.

Day, D. V., Schleicher, D. J., Unckless, A. L., & Hiller, N. J. (2002). Self-monitoring personality at work: A meta-analytic investigation of construct validity. *Journal of Applied Psychology, 87,* 390–401.

DeAndrea, D. C., Tong, S. T., & Walther, J. B. (2010). Dark sides of computer-mediated communication. In W. R. Cupach & B. H. Spitzberg (Eds.), *The dark side of close relationships II* (pp. 95–118). New York: Routledge.

DeAngelis, T. (1992, October). The "who am I" question wears a cloak of culture. *APA Monitor, 24,* 22–23.

Debatin, B., Lovejoy, J. P., Horn, A., & Hughes, B. N. (2009). Facebook and online privacy: Attitudes, behaviors, and unintended consequences. *Journal of Computer-Mediated Communication, 15,* 83–108.

DeCapua, A. (2007). The use of language to create realities: The example of Good Bye, Lenin! *Semiotica, 166*(1–4), 69–79.

Decety, J. (2005). Perspective taking as the royal avenue to empathy. In B. F. Malle & S. D. Hodges (Eds.), *Other minds: How humans bridge the divide between self and others* (pp. 143–157). New York: Guilford Press.

Defour, T. (2008). The speaker's voice: A diachronic study on the use of well and now as pragmatic markers. *English Text Construction, 1*(1), 62–82.

Dehart, T., Pelham, B., Fiedorowicz, L., Carvallo, M., & Gabriel, S. (2010). Including others in the implicit self: Implicit evaluation of significant others. *Self and Identity, 10*(1), 127–135.

DeMaris, A. (2007). The role of relationship inequity in marital disruption. *Journal of Social and Personal Relationships, 24,* 177–195.

Denson, T., Grisham, J., & Moulds, M. (2011). Cognitive reappraisal increases heart rate variability in response to an anger provocation. *Motivation & Emotion, 35,* 14–22.

De Vries, B., & Megathlin, D. (2009). The meaning of friendships for gay men and lesbians in the second half of life. *Journal of GLBT Family Studies, 5*(1–2), 82–98.

de Waal, F. B. M. (2008). Putting the altruism back into altruism: The evolution of empathy. *Annual Review of Psychology, 59,* 279–300.

de Waal, F. B. M. (2009). *The age of empathy: Nature's lessons for a kinder society.* New York: Random House.

DePaulo, B. M. (1992). Nonverbal behavior and self-presentation. *Psychological Bulletin, 3,* 203–243.

DePaulo, B. M., & Kashy, D. A. (1998). Everyday lies in close and casual relationships. *Journal of Personality and Social Psychology, 74,* 63–79.

DePaulo, B. M., Kashy, D. A., Kirkendol, S. E., & Wyer, M. M. (1996). Lying in everyday life. *Journal of Personality and Social Psychology, 70,* 779–795.

DePaulo, B. M., Morris, W. L., & Sternglanz, R. W. (2009). When the truth hurts: Deception in the name of kindness. In A. L. Vangelisti (Ed.), *Feeling hurt in close relationships* (pp. 167–190). New York: Cambridge University Press.

Derks, D., Bos, A. E. R., & von Grumbkow, J. (2007). Emoticons and social interaction on the Internet: The importance of social context. *Computers in Human Behavior, 23,* 842–849.

Derlega, V. J., Barbee, A. P., & Winstead, B. A. (1994). Friendship, gender, and social support: Laboratory studies of supportive interactions. In B. R. Burleson, T. L. Albrecht, & I. G. Sarson (Eds.), *Communication of social support: Message, interactions, relationships, and community* (pp. 136–151). Newbury Park, CA: Sage.

Derlega, V. J., Lewis, R. J., Harrison, S., Winstead, B. A., & Costanza, R. (1989). Gender differences in the initiation and attribution of tactile intimacy. *Journal of Nonverbal Behavior, 13,* 83–96.

Derlega, V. J., Metts, S., Petronio, S., & Margulis, S. T. (1993). *Self-disclosure.* Newbury Park, CA: Sage.

Derlega, V. J., Winstead, B. A., & Folk-Barron, L. (2000). Reasons for and against disclosing HIV-seropositive test results to an intimate partner: A functional perspective. In S. Petronio (Ed.), *Balancing the secrets of private disclosures* (pp. 71–82). Mahwah, NJ: Erlbaum.

Detenber, B. H., Wijaya, M., & Huiyi Go. (2008, May). *Blogging and online friendships: The role of self-disclosure and perceived reciprocity.* Paper presented at the Annual Meeting of the International Communication Association, Montreal, Quebec, Canada.

DeTurk, S. (2001). Intercultural empathy: Myth, competency, or possibility for alliance building? *Communication Education, 50,* 374–384.

Deutsch, M. (2006). Cooperation and competition. In M. Deutsch, P. T. Coleman, & E. C. Marcus, *The handbook of conflict resolution: Theory and practice* (2nd ed., pp. 23–42). Hoboken, NJ: Wiley.

Deutscher, G. (2010). *Through the language glass: Why the world looks different in other languages.* New York: Metropolitan Books.

Dickson, F. C., & Walker, K. L. (2001). The expression of emotion in later-life married men. *Qualitative Research Reports in Communication, 2,* 66–71.

Dieckmann, L. E. (2000). Private secrets and public disclosures: The case of battered women. In S. Petronio (Ed.), *Balancing the secrets of private disclosures* (pp. 275–286). Mahwah, NJ: Erlbaum.

Dillard, J. P., Solomon, D. H., & Palmer, M. T. (1999). Structuring the concept of relational communication. *Communication Monographs, 66,* 49–65.

Dindia, K. (2000a). Self-disclosure research: Advances through meta-analysis. In M. A. Allen, R. W. Preiss, B. M. Gayle, & N. Burrell (Eds.), *Interpersonal communication research: Advances through meta-analysis* (pp. 169–186). Mahwah, NJ: Erlbaum.

Dindia, K. (2000b). Sex differences in self-disclosure, reciprocity of self-disclosure, and self-disclosure and liking: Three meta-analyses reviewed. In S. Petronio (Ed.), *Balancing the secrets of private disclosures* (pp. 21–35). Mahwah, NJ: Erlbaum.

Dindia, K. (2002). Self-disclosure research: Knowledge through meta-analysis. In M. Allen & R. W. Preiss (Eds.), *Interpersonal communication research: Advances through meta-analysis* (pp. 169–185). Mahwah, NJ: Erlbaum.

Dindia, K. (2006). Men are from North Dakota, women are from South Dakota. In K. Dindia & D. J. Canary (Eds.), *Sex differences and similarities in communication* (2nd ed., pp. 3–18). Mahwah, NJ: Erlbaum.

Dindia, K., & Allen, M. (1992). Sex differences in self-disclosure: A meta-analysis. *Psychological Bulletin, 112,* 106–124.

Dindia, K., & Baxter, L. A. (1987). Strategies for maintaining and repairing marital relationships. *Journal of Social and Personal Relationships, 4,* 143–158.

Dindia, K., Fitzpatrick, M. A., & Kenny, D. A. (1997). Self-disclosure in spouse and stranger dyads: A social relations analysis. *Human Communication Research, 23,* 388–412.

Dion, K. K. (1973). Young children's stereotyping of facial attractiveness. *Developmental Psychology, 9,* 183–188.

Dion, K., Berscheid, E., & Walster, E. (1972). What is beautiful is good. *Journal of Personality and Social Psychology, 24,* 285–290.

DiPaola, B. M., Roloff, M. E., & Peters, K. M. (2010). College students' expectations of conflict intensity: A self-fulfilling prophecy. *Communication Quarterly, 58,* 59–76.

Domingue, R., & Mollen, D. (2009). Attachment and conflict communication in adult romantic relationships. *Journal of Social & Personal Relationships, 26,* 678–696.

Doss, B. D., Mitchell, A. E., & De la Garza-Mercer, F. (2008). Marital distress. In M. Hersen & J. Rosqvist (Eds.), *Handbook of psychological assessment, case conceptualization, and treatment: Vol. 1. Adults* (pp. 563–589). Hoboken, NJ: Wiley.

Dougherty, D. S. (2001). Sexual harassment as [dys]functional process: A feminist standpoint analysis. *Journal of Applied Communication Research, 29,* 372–402.

Dougherty, D. S., Kramer, M. W., Klatzke, S. R., & Rogers, T. K. K. (2009). Language convergence and meaning divergence: A meaning centered communication theory. *Communication Monographs, 76,* 20–46.

Dougherty, T., Turban, D., & Collander, J. (1994). Conforming first impressions in the employment interview. *Journal of Applied Psychology, 79,* 659–665.

Douglas, K. M., & Sutton, R. M. (2010). By their words ye shall know them: Language abstraction and the likeability of describers. *European Journal of Social Psychology, 40,* 366–374.

Draper, P. (2005). Patronizing speech to older patients: A literature review. *Reviews in Clinical Gerontology, 15,* 273–279.

Driscoll, M. S., Newman, D. L., & Seal, J. M. (1988). The effect of touch on the perception of counselors. *Counselor Education and Supervision, 27,* 344–354.

Droogsma, R. A. (2007). Redefining hijab: American Muslim women's standpoints on veiling. *Journal of Applied Communication Research, 35,* 294–319.

Du, J., Fan, X., & Feng, T. (2011). Multiple emotional contagions in service encounters. *Journal of the Academy of Marketing Science, 39,* 449–466.

Duck, S. (1994). Maintenance as a shared meaning system. In D. J. Canary & L. Stafford (Eds.), *Communication and relationship maintenance: How individual differences in communication skills affect the achievement of relationship functions* (pp. 45–60). San Diego: Academic Press.

Duck, S., & Barnes, M. K. (1992). Disagreeing about agreement: Reconciling differences about similarity. *Communication Monographs, 59,* 199–208.

Duck, S., & Pittman, G. (1994). Social and personal relationships. In M. L. Knapp & G. R. Miller (Eds.), *Handbook of interpersonal communication* (2nd ed., pp. 676–695). Newbury Park, CA: Sage.

Dumas, J. E. (2005). Mindfulness-based parent training: Strategies to lessen the grip of automaticity in families with disruptive children. *Journal of Clinical Child and Adolescent Psychology, 34,* 779–791.

Dunleavy, K. N., & Booth-Butterfield, M. (2009). Idiomatic communication in the stages of coming together and falling apart. *Communication Quarterly, 57,* 416–432.

Dunleavy, K. N., Chory, R. M., & Goodboy, A. K. (2010). Responses to deception in the workplace: Perceptions of credibility, power, and trustworthiness. *Communication Studies, 61,* 239–255.

Dunleavy, K. N., & Martin, M. M. (2010). Instructors' and students' perspectives of student nagging: Frequency, appropriateness, and effectiveness. *Communication Research Reports, 27,* 310–319.

Dunsmore, J., Her, P., Halberstadt, A., & Perez-Rivera, M. (2009). Parents' beliefs about emotions and children's recognition of parents' emotions. *Journal of Nonverbal Behavior, 33,* 121–140.

Duran, R. L., Kelly, L., & Rotaru, T. (2011). Mobile phones in romantic relationships and the dialectic of autonomy versus connection. *Communication Quarterly, 59,* 19–36.

Durik, A. M., Hyde, J. S., Marks, A. C., Roy, A. L., Anaya, D., & Schultz, G. (2006). Ethnicity and gender stereotypes of emotion. *Sex Roles, 54,* 429–445.

Dwyer, K. K. (2000). The multidimensional model: Teaching students to self-manage high communication apprehension by self-selecting treatments. *Communication Education, 49,* 72–81.

Eaton, J., & Struthers, C. W. (2006). The reduction of psychological aggression across varied interpersonal contexts through repentance and forgiveness. *Aggressive Behavior, 32*, 195–206.

Ebeling-Witte, S., Frank, M. L., & Lester, D. (2007). Shyness, Internet use, and personality. *Cyber-Psychology & Behavior, 10*, 713–716.

Ebesu-Hubbard, A. S. (2001). Conflict between relationally uncertain romantic partners: The influence of relational responsiveness and empathy. *Communication Monographs, 68*, 400–414.

Edwards, C., Edwards, A., Qingmei Q., & Wahl, S. T. (2007). The influence of computer-mediated word-of-mouth communication on student perceptions of instructors and attitudes toward learning course content. *Communication Education, 56*, 255–277.

Edwards, R., & Bello, R. (2001). Interpretations of messages: The influence of equivocation, face concerns, and ego involvement. *Human Communication Research, 27*, 597–691.

Egland, K. I., Stelzner, M. A., Andersen, P. A., & Spitzberg, B. S. (1997). Perceived understanding, nonverbal communication, and relational satisfaction. In J. E. Aitken & L. J. Shedletsky (Eds.), *Intrapersonal communication processes* (pp. 386–396). Annandale, VA: Speech Communication Association.

Eibl-Eibesfeldt, I. (1972). Similarities and differences between cultures in expressive movements. In R. A. Hinde (Ed.), *Nonverbal communication* (pp. 297–314). Oxford, England: Cambridge University Press.

Eisenberg, E. M. (1984). Ambiguity as strategy in organizational communication. *Communication Monographs, 51*, 227–242.

Eisenberg, E. M. (Ed.). (2007). *Strategic ambiguities: Essays on communication, organization and identity.* Thousand Oaks, CA: Sage.

Eisenberg, E. M., & Goodall, H., Jr. (2001). *Organizational communication* (3rd ed.). New York: Bedfort/St. Martin's.

Eisenberg, E. M., & Witten, M. G. (1987). Reconsidering openness in organizational communication. *Academy of Management Review, 12*, 418–426.

Ekman, P. (2009). *Telling lies: Clues to deceit in the marketplace, politics, and marriage* (4th ed.). New York: W. W. Norton.

Ekman, P., & Friesen, W. V. (1974a). Detecting deception from the body or face. *Journal of Personality and Social Psychology, 29*, 288–298.

Ekman, P., & Friesen, W. V. (1974b). Nonverbal behavior and psychopathology. In R. J. Friedman & M. N. Katz (Eds.), *The psychology of depression: Contemporary theory and research* (pp. 3–31). Washington, DC: Winston and Sons.

Ekman, P., & Friesen, W. V. (1975). *Unmasking the face: A guide to recognizing emotions from facial clues.* Englewood Cliffs, NJ: Prentice-Hall.

Ekman, P., Levenson, R. W., & Friesen, W. V. (1983, September). Autonomic nervous system activity distinguishes among emotions. *Science, 221*, 1208–1210.

El-Alayli, A., Myers, C. J., Petersen, T. L., & Lystad, A. L. (2008). "I don't mean to sound arrogant, but . . ." The effects of using disclaimers on person perception. *Personality and Social Psychology Bulletin, 34*, 130–143.

Eldridge, K. A., & Christensen, A. (2002). Demand-withdraw communication during couple conflict: A review and analysis. In P. Noller & J. A. Feeney (Eds.), *Understanding marriage: Developments in the study of couple interaction* (pp. 289–322). New York: Cambridge University Press.

Ellis, A. (2001). *Overcoming destructive beliefs, feeling and behaving: New directions for rational emotive behavior therapy.* Amherst, NY: Prometheus Books.

Ellis, A. (2004). Expanding the ABCs of rational emotive behavior therapy. In M. J. Mahoney, P. DeVito, D. Martin, & A. Freeman (Eds.), *Cognition and psychotherapy* (2nd ed., pp. 185–196). New York: Springer.

Ellis, K. (2002). Perceived parental confirmation: Development and validation of an instrument. *Southern Communication Journal, 67*, 319–334.

Ellison, N., Heino, R., & Gibbs, J. (2006). Managing impressions online: Self-presentation processes in the online dating environment. *Journal of Computer-Mediated Communication, 11*, 415–441.

Ellison, N. B., Steinfield, C., & Lampe, C. (2007): The benefits of Facebook "friends": Social capital and college students' use of online social network sites. *Journal of Computer-Mediated Communication, 12,* 1143–1168.

Emanuel, R., Adams, J., Baker, K., Daufin, E. K., Ellington, C., Fitts, E., Himsel, J., Holladay, L., & Okeowo, D. (2008). How college students spend their time communicating. *International Journal of Listening, 22,* 13–28.

Emmers-Sommer, T. M. (2003). When partners falter: Repair after a transgression. In D. J. Canary & M. Dainton (Eds.), *Maintaining relationships through communication* (pp. 185–205). Mahwah, NJ: Erlbaum.

Ennis, E., Vrij, A., & Chance, C. (2008). Individual differences and lying in everyday life. *Journal of Social and Personal Relationships, 25,* 105–118.

Equal Employment Opportunity Commission. (2010). *Sexual harassment charges EEOC & FEPAs combined: FY 1997–FY 2010.* Retrieved from http://www.eeoc.gov/eeoc/statistics/en forcement/sexual_harassment.cfm

Erbert, L. A. (2000). Conflict and dialectics: Perceptions of dialectical contradictions in marital conflict. *Journal of Social and Personal Relationships, 17,* 638–659.

Erbert, L. A., & Floyd, K. (2004). Affectionate expressions as face-threatening acts: Receiver assessments. *Communication Studies, 55,* 230–246.

Evans, G. W., & Wener, R. E. (2007). Crowding and personal space invasion on the train: Please don't make me sit in the middle. *Journal of Environmental Psychology, 27*(1), 90–94.

Exline, J. J., Baumeister, R. F., & Zell, L (2008). Not so innocent: Does seeing one's own capability for wrongdoing predict forgiveness? *Journal of Personality and Social Psychology, 94,* 495–515.

Exline, J. J., Deshea, L., & Holeman, V. T. (2007). Is apology worth the risk? Predictors, outcomes, and ways to avoid regret. *Journal of Social & Clinical Psychology, 26,* 479–504.

Fadiman, A. (1997). *The spirit catches you and you fall down.* New York: Farrar, Straus & Giroux.

Farah, A., & Atoum, A. (2002). Personality traits as self-evaluated and as judged by others. *Social Behavior and Personality, 30,* 149–156.

Faul, S. (1994). *The xenophobe's guide to the Americans.* Horsham, England: Ravette.

Feaster, J. C. (2010). Expanding the impression management model of communication channels: An information control scale. *Journal of Computer-Mediated Communication, 16,* 115–138.

Feeney, J. A. (1999). Issues of closeness and distance in dating relationships: Effects of sex and attachment style. *Journal of Social and Personal Relationships, 16,* 571–590.

Fehr, B. (2000). Adult friendship. In S. Hendrick & C. Hendrick (Eds.), *Close relationships: A Sourcebook* (pp. 71–82). Thousand Oaks, CA: Sage.

Fehr, B., & Broughton, R. (2001). Gender and personality differences in conceptions of love: An interpersonal theory analysis. *Personal Relationships, 8,* 115–136.

Feldman, R., Singer, M., & Zagoory, O. (2010). Touch attenuates infants' physiological reactivity to stress. *Developmental Science, 13,* 271–278.

Felmlee, D. H. (2001). From appealing to appalling: Disenchantment with a romantic partner. *Sociological Perspectives, 44,* 263–280.

Felps, D., Bortfeld, H., & Gutierrez-Osuna, R. (2009). Foreign accent conversion in computer assisted pronunciation training. *Speech Communication, 51,* 920–932.

Felson, R. B. (1985). Reflected appraisal and the development of self. *Social Psychology Quarterly, 48,* 71–78.

Feng, B., & Lee, K. J. (2010). The influence of thinking styles on responses to supportive messages. *Communication Studies, 61,* 224–238.

Fenigstein, A. (2009). Private and public self-consciousness. In M. R. Leary & R. H. Hoyle (Eds.), *Handbook of individual differences in social behavior* (pp. 495–511). New York: Guilford Press.

Ferguson, G. M., & Cramer, P. (2007). Self-esteem among Jamaican children: Exploring the impact of skin color and rural/urban residence. *Journal of Applied Developmental Psychology, 28,* 345–359.

Fernald, A. (2001). Hearing, listening, and understanding: Auditory development in infancy. In G. Bremner & A. Fogel (Eds.), *Blackwell handbook of infant development* (pp. 35–70). Malden, MA: Blackwell.

Ferrari, M., & Koyama, E. (2002). Meta-emotions about anger and amae: A cross-cultural comparison. *Consciousness and Emotion, 3,* 197–211.

Ferraro, G. (2008) *Cultural anthropology: An applied perspective* (7th ed.). Belmont, CA: Wadsworth.

Fiedler, A. M., & Blanco, R. I. (2006). The challenge of varying perceptions of sexual harassment: An international study. *Journal of Behavioral and Applied Management, 7,* 1274–1279.

Field, T. (2003). *Touch.* Cambridge, MA: MIT Press.

Field, T. (2007). *The amazing infant: Touch research institute at the university of Miami school of medicine.* Oxford, England: Blackwell.

Filley, A. C. (1975). *Interpersonal conflict resolution.* Glenview, IL: Scott, Foresman.

Fine, G. A., & Beim, A. (2007). Introduction: Interactionist approaches to collective memory. *Symbolic Interaction, 30,* 1–5.

Fisher, H. (2007, May–June). The laws of chemistry. *Psychology Today, 40,* 76–81.

Fitch-Hauser, M., Powers, W. G., O'Brien, K., & Hanson, S. (2007). Extending the conceptualization of listening fidelity. *International Journal of Listening, 21,* 81–91.

Fitts, W. H. (1971). *The self-concept and self-actualization.* Nashville, TN: Counselor Recordings and Tests.

Fitzpatrick, M. A., & Vangelisti, A. L. (2001). Communication, relationships, and health. In W. P. Robinson & H. Giles (Eds.), *The new handbook of language and social psychology* (2nd ed., pp. 505–530). New York: Wiley.

Fitzpatrick, T. R., Gitelson, R. J., Andereck, K. L., & Mesbur, E. S. (2005). Social support factors and health among a senior center population in Southern Ontario, Canada. *Social Work in Health Care, 40*(3), 15–38.

Fleming, P., & Sturdy, A. (2009). "Just be yourself!": Towards neo-normative control in organisations?" *Employee Relations, 31,* 569–583.

Fletcher, G. J. O., Fincham, F. D., Cramer, L., & Heron, N. (1987). The role of attributions in the development of dating relationships. *Journal of Personality and Social Psychology, 53,* 481–489.

Fletcher, G. J. O., & Kerr, P. S. G. (2010). Through the eyes of love: Reality and illusion in intimate relationships. *Psychological Bulletin, 136,* 627–658.

Flora, C. (2004a, Jan–Feb). Close quarters: Why we fall in love with the one nearby. *Psychology Today, 37,* 15–16.

Flora, C. (2004b, May–June). Snap judgments: The once-over—Can you trust first impressions? *Psychology Today, 37,* 60–64.

Flora, J., & Segrin, C. (2000). Relationship development in dating couples: Implications for relational satisfaction and loneliness. *Journal of Social and Personal Relationships, 17,* 811–825.

Florit, E., Roch, M., & Levorato, M. C. (2011). Listening text comprehension of explicit and implicit information in preschoolers: The role of verbal and inferential skills. *Discourse Processes, 48,* 119–138.

Floyd, J. J., & Clements, S. M. (2005). The vital importance of critical listening: An extended example. *International Journal of Listening, 19,* 39–50.

Floyd, K. (1996). Communicating closeness among siblings: An application of the gendered closeness perspective. *Communication Research Reports, 13,* 27–34.

Floyd, K. (2000). Attributions for nonverbal expressions of liking and disliking: The extended self-serving bias. *Western Journal of Communication, 64,* 385–404.

Flynn, J., Valikoski, T., & Grau, J. (2008). Listening in the business context: Reviewing the state of research. *International Journal of Listening, 22,* 141–151.

Fogel, A., & Branco, A. U. (1997). Metacommunication as a source of indeterminism in relationship development. In A. Fogel, M. C. D. P. Lyra, & J. Valsiner (Eds.), *Dynamics and indeterminism in developmental and social processes* (pp. 65–92). Hillsdale, NJ: Erlbaum.

Fogel, A., de Koeyer, I., Bellagamba, F., & Bell, H. (2002). The dialogical self in the first two years of life: Embarking on a journey of discovery. *Theory and Psychology, 12,* 191–205.

Forgas, J. P. (2011). Affective influences on self-disclosure: Mood effects on the intimacy and reciprocity of disclosing personal information.

Journal of Personality and Social Psychology, 100, 449–461.

Forgas, J. P., & Bower, G. H. (2001). Mood effects on person-perception judgments. In W. G. Parrott (Ed.), *Emotions in social psychology: Essential readings* (pp. 204–215). New York: Psychology Press.

Forni, P. M. (2010, July 23). Why civility is necessary for society's survival. *Dallasnews.com.* Retrieved from http://www.dallasnews.com/opinion/sunday-commentary/20100723-p.m.-forni-why-civility-is-necessary-for-society_s-survival.ece

Fortenberry, J. H., Maclean, J., Morris, P., & O'Connell, M. (1978). Mode of dress as a perceptual cue to deference. *Journal of Social Psychology, 104,* 131–139.

Fortney, S. D., Johnson, D. I., & Long, K. M. (2001). The impact of compulsive communicators on the self-perceived competence of classroom peers: An investigation and test of instructional strategies. *Communication Education, 50,* 357–373.

Forward, G., & Czech, K. (2008, November). *Why (most) everything you think you know about Gibb's climate theory may be wrong and what to do about it.* Paper presented at the conference of the National Communication Association, San Diego, CA.

Foss, S. K., & Foss, K. A. (2003). *Inviting transformation: Presentational speaking for a changing world* (2nd ed.). Long Grove, IL: Waveland.

Foss, S. K., & Griffin, C. L. (1995). Beyond persuasion: A proposal for an invitational rhetoric. *Communication Monographs, 62,* 2–18.

Foster, E. (2008). Commitment, communication, and contending with heteronormativity: An invitation to greater reflexivity in interpersonal research. *Southern Communication Journal, 73,* 84–101.

Fowler, C., & Dillow, M. R. (2011). Attachment dimensions and the Four Horsemen of the Apocalypse. *Communication Research Reports, 28,* 16–26.

Fox, A. B., Bukatko, D., Hallahan, M., & Crawford, M. (2007). The medium makes a difference: Gender similarities and differences in instant messaging. *Journal of Language and Social Psychology, 26,* 389–397.

Francis, J., & Wales, R. (1994). Speech a la mode: Prosodic cues, message interpretation, and impression formation. *Journal of Language and Social Psychology, 13,* 34–44.

Francis, L. E. (2003). Feeling good, feeling well: Identity, emotion, and health. In T. J. Owens & P. J. Burke (Eds.), *Advances in identity theory and research* (pp. 123–134). New York: Kluwer Academic/Plenum Publishers.

Frawley, T. (2008). Gender schema and prejudicial recall: How children misremember, fabricate, and distort gendered picture book information. *Journal of Research in Childhood Education, 22,* 291–303.

Freeman, J. B., & Ambady, N. (2011). A dynamic interactive theory of person construal. *Psychological Review, 118,* 247–279.

Frings, D., & Abrams, D. (2010). The effect of difference oriented communication on the subjective validity of an in-group norm: Doc can treat the group. *Group Dynamics: Theory, Research, and Practice, 14,* 281–291.

Frisby, B. N. (2009). "Without flirting, it wouldn't be a marriage": Flirtatious communication between relational partners. *Qualitative Research Reports in Communication, 10,* 55–60.

Fromme, D. K., Jaynes, W. E., Taylor, D. K., Hanold, E. G., Daniell, J., Rountree, J. R., & Fromme, M. (1989). Nonverbal behavior and attitudes toward touch. *Journal of Nonverbal Behavior, 13,* 3–14.

Frumkin, L. (2007). Influences of accent and ethnic background on perceptions of eyewitness testimony. *Psychology, Crime & Law, 13,* 317–331.

Fryer, R. G., & Levitt, S. D. (2004). The causes and consequences of distinctively black names. *Quarterly Journal of Economics, 119,* 767–805.

Fulmer, R. (1999). Becoming an adult: Leaving home and staying connected. In B. Carter & M. McGoldrick (Eds.), *The expanded family life cycle: Individual, family, and social perspectives* (3rd ed., pp. 215–230). Boston: Allyn & Bacon.

Fussell, S. R. (Ed.). (2002). *The verbal communication of emotions: Interdisciplinary perspectives.* Mahwah, NJ: Erlbaum.

Futch, A., & Edwards, R. (1999). The effects of sense of humor, defensiveness, and gender on the interpretation of ambiguous messages. *Communication Quarterly, 47,* 80–97.

Gabler, N. (2010, October 17). The social networks. *Los Angeles Times*. Retrieved from http://articles.latimes.com/2010/oct/17/entertainment/la-ca-tv-friendships-20101017

Gabric, D., & McFadden, K. L. (2001). Student and employer perceptions of desirable entry-level operations management skills. *Mid-American Journal of Business, 16*, 51–59.

Gadlin, H. (1977). Private lives and public order: A critical view of the history of intimate relations in the United States. In G. Levinger & H. L. Raush (Eds.), *Close relationships: Perspectives on the meaning of intimacy* (pp. 33–72). Amherst: University of Massachusetts Press.

Galanxhi, H., & Nah, F. F.-H. (2007). Deception in cyberspace: A comparison of text-only vs., avatar-supported medium. *International Journal of Human–Computer Studies, 65*, 770–783.

Galvin, K. M., Bylund, C. L., & Brommel, B. J. (2007). *Family communication: Cohesion and change* (7th ed.). Boston: Allyn & Bacon.

Galvin, K. M., Dickson, F. C., & Marrow, S. R. (2006). Systems theory: Patterns and w(holes) in family communication. In D. O. Braithwaite & L. A. Baxter (Eds.), *Engaging theories in family communication: Multiple perspectives* (pp. 309–324). Thousand Oaks, CA: Sage.

Gara, M. A., Woolfolk, R. L., Cohen, B. D., Goldston, R. B., & Allen, L. A. (1993). Perception of self and other in major depression. *Journal of Abnormal Psychology, 102*, 93–100.

Garforth, S. (2009). *Attention and listening in the early years*. London: Jessica Kingsley Publishers.

Gayle, B. M., Preiss, R. W., & Allen, M. A. (2002). A meta-analytic interpretation of intimate and nonintimate interpersonal conflict. In M. Allen, R. W. Preiss, B. M. Gayle, & N. Burrell (Eds.), *Interpersonal communication research: Advances through meta-analysis* (pp. 345–368). Mahwah, NJ: Erlbaum.

Geddes, D. (1992). Sex-roles in management: The impact of varying power of speech style on union members' perception of satisfaction and effectiveness. *Journal of Psychology, 126*, 589–607.

Genov, A. B. (2001). Autonomic and situational determinants of the subjective experience of emotion: An individual differences approach. *Dissertation Abstracts International: Section B. The Sciences and Engineering, 61*(9-B), 5043.

Gent, S. E., & Shannon, M. (2011). Bias and effectiveness of third-party conflict management mechanisms. *Conflict Management and Peace Science, 28*, 124–144.

Gentile, J. S. (2004). Telling the untold tales: Memory's caretaker. *Text and Performance Quarterly, 24*, 201–204.

George, J. F., & Robb, A. (2008). Deception and computer-mediated communication in daily life. *Communication Reports, 21*, 92–103.

Gergen, K. J. (1971). *The concept of self*. New York: Holt, Rinehart & Winston.

Gergen, K. J. (1991). *The saturated self: Dilemmas of identity in contemporary life*. New York: Basic Books.

Gibb, J. R. (1961). Defensive communication. *Journal of Communication, 11*, 141–148.

Gibb, J. R. (2008). Defensive communication. In C. D. Mortensen (Ed.), *Communication theory* (2nd ed., pp. 201–208). Piscataway, NJ: Transaction Publishers.

Gibbs, J. L., Ellison, N. B., & Lai, C.-H. (2011). First comes love, then comes Google: An investigation of uncertainty reduction strategies and self-disclosure in online dating. *Communication Research, 38*, 70–100.

Giles, H., & Coupland, N. (1991). *Language: Contexts and consequences*. Belmont, CA: Thomson Brooks/Cole.

Giles, H., Coupland, N., & Wiemann, J. M. (1992). "Talk is cheap . . ." but "my word is my bond": Beliefs about talk. In K. Bolton & H. Kwok (Eds.), *Sociolinguistics today: International perspectives* (pp. 218–243). London: Routledge & Kegan Paul.

Giles, H., & Franklyn-Stokes, A. (1989). Communicator characteristics. In M. K. Asante & W. B. Gudykunst (Eds.), *Handbook of international and intercultural communication* (pp. 117–144). Newbury Park, CA: Sage.

Gladwell, M. (2004). *Blink: The power of thinking without thinking*. Boston: Little, Brown.

Glanz, B. A. (2007). *What can I do? Ideas to help those who have experienced loss*. Minneapolis, MN: Augsburg Fortress.

Gleason, J. B., & Greif, E. B. (1983). Men's speech to young children. In B. Thorne, C. Kramarae, & N. Henley (Eds.), *Language, gender, and society* (pp. 140–150). Rowley, MA: Newbury House.

Global Publics Embrace Social Networking. (2010). Pew Internet & American Life Project. Retrieved from http://pewglobal.org/2010/12/15/global-publics-embrace-social-networking/

Gluszek, A., & Dovidio, J. F. (2010). Speaking with a nonnative accent: Perceptions of bias, communication difficulties, and belonging in the United States. *Journal of Language & Social Psychology, 29,* 224–234.

Gluszek, A., Newheiser, A.-K., & Dovidio, J. F. (2011). Social psychological orientations and accent strength. *Journal of Language and Social Psychology, 30,* 28–45.

Goetting, A. (1986). The developmental tasks of siblingship over the life cycle. *Journal of Marriage and the Family, 48,* 703–714.

Goffman, E. (1959). *The presentation of self in everyday life.* Garden City, NY: Doubleday.

Goffman, E. (1971). *Relations in public.* New York: Basic Books.

Golash-Boza, T., & Darity, W. (2008). Latino racial choices: The effects of skin colour and discrimination on Latinos' and Latinas' racial self-identifications. *Ethnic & Racial Studies, 31,* 899–934.

Gold, S. N., & Castillo, Y. (2010). Dealing with defenses and defensiveness in interviews. In D. L. Segal & M. Hersen (Eds.), *Diagnostic interviewing* (pp. 89–102). New York: Springer.

Goldschmidt, W. (1990). *The human career.* Cambridge, MA: Basil Blackman.

Goldsmith, D. J., & Fitch, K. (1997). The normative context of advice as social support. *Human Communication Research, 23,* 454–476.

Goldsmith, D. J., & Fulfs, P. A. (1999). "You just don't have the evidence": An analysis of claims and evidence in Deborah Tannen's *You just don't understand.* In M. E. Roloff (Ed.), *Communication yearbook 22* (pp. 1–49). Thousand Oaks, CA: Sage.

Goldstein, S. (2008). Current literature in ADHD. *Journal of Attention Disorders, 11,* 614–616.

Goleman, D. (1995). *Emotional intelligence: Why it can matter more than I.Q.* New York: Bantam.

Golen, S. (1990). A factor analysis of barriers to effective listening. *Journal of Business Communication, 27,* 25–36.

Golish, T. D. (2000). Is openness always better? Exploring the role of topic avoidance, satisfaction, and parenting styles of stepparents. *Communication Quarterly, 48,* 137–158.

Golish, T. D., & Caughlin, J. P. (2002). "I'd rather not talk about it": Adolescents' and young adults' use of topic avoidance in stepfamilies. *Journal of Applied Communication Research, 30,* 78–106.

Gonzaga, G. G., Haselton, M. G., Smurda J., Davies, M. & Poore, J. C. (2008). Love, desire, and the suppression of thoughts of romantic alternatives. *Evolution and Human Behavior, 29,* 119–126.

Good, G. E., Porter, M. J., & Dillon, M. G. (2002). When men divulge: Men's self-disclosure on prime time situation comedies. *Sex Roles, 46,* 419–427.

Goodboy, A. K., & Myers, S. A. (2008). The effect of teacher confirmation on student communication and learning outcomes. *Communication Education, 57,* 153–179.

Goodman, C. R., & Shippy, R. A. (2002). Is it contagious? Affect similarity among spouses. *Aging and Mental Health, 6,* 266–274.

Goodman, G., & Esterly, G. (1990). Questions—The most popular piece of language. In J. Stewart (Ed.), *Bridges not walls* (5th ed., pp. 69–77). New York: McGraw-Hill.

Goodman, K. L., & Southam-Gerow, M. A. (2010). The regulating role of negative emotions in children's coping with peer rejection. *Child Psychiatry & Human Development, 41,* 515–534.

Gordon, T. (1970). *P.E.T.: Parent effectiveness training.* New York: Wyden.

Gore, J. S. (2009). The interaction of sex, verbal, and nonverbal cues in same-sex first encounters. *Journal of Nonverbal Behavior, 33,* 279–299.

Gottman, J. (1994). *Why marriages succeed or fail and how you can make yours last.* New York: Simon & Schuster.

Gottman, J. (2000, September). Welcome to the love lab. *Psychology Today Online.*

Retrieved from http://www.findarticles.com/m1175/5_33/66380417/p1/article.jhtml

Gottman, J. (2003). Why marriages fail. In K. M. Galvin & P. J. Cooper (Eds.), *Making connections: Readings in relational communication* (pp. 258–266). Los Angeles: Roxbury.

Gottman, J. M., & Driver, J. L. (2005). Dysfunctional marital conflict and everyday marital interaction. *Journal of Divorce & Remarriage, 43*(3–4), 63–78.

Gottman, J. M., Katz, L. F., & Hooven, C. (1997). *Meta-emotion: How families communicate emotionally.* Mahwah, NJ: Erlbaum.

Gottman, J. M., & Levenson, R. W. (1999). Rebound for marital conflict and divorce prediction. *Family Process, 38,* 287–292.

Gottman, J. M., & Silver, N. (1999). *The seven principles for making marriages work.* New York: Three Rivers Press.

Graham, S. M., Huang, J. Y., Clark, M. S., & Helgeson, V. S. (2008). The positives of negative emotions: Willingness to express negative emotions promotes relationships. *Personality and Social Psychology Bulletin, 34,* 394–406.

Grant, C. H., III, Cissna, K. N., & Rosenfeld, L. B. (2000). Patients' perceptions of physicians' communication and outcomes of the accrual to trial process. *Health Communication, 12*(1), 23–39.

Gray, F. E. (2010). Specific oral communication skills desired in new accountancy graduates. *Business Communication Quarterly, 73*(1), 40–67.

Gray, J. (1992). *Men are from Mars, women are from Venus: A practical guide for improving communication and getting what you want in your relationship.* New York: HarperCollins.

Gray, J. (2008). *Why Mars and Venus collide.* New York: HarperCollins.

Greenberg, L. S., & Goldman, R. N. (2008). Fear in couples therapy. In L. S. Greenberg & R. N. Goldman (Eds.), *Emotion-focused couples therapy: The dynamics of emotion, love, and power* (pp. 283–313). Washington, DC: American Psychological Association.

Greene, K., Derlega, V. J., & Mathews, A. (2006). Self-disclosure in personal relationships. In A. Vangelisti & D. Perlman (Eds.), *The Cambridge handbook of personal relationships* (pp. 409–428). New York: Cambridge University Press.

Greenwald, A. G. (1995). Getting (my) self into social psychology. In G. G. Brannigan & M. R. Merrens (Eds.), *The social psychologists: Research adventures* (pp. 3–16). New York: McGraw-Hill.

Grewal, D., & Salovey, P. (2005). Feeling smart: The science of emotional intelligence. *American Scientist, 93,* 330–339.

Griffin, E. A. (2006). *A first look at communication theory with conversations with communication theorists* (6th ed.). New York: McGraw-Hill.

Grob, L. M., Meyers, R. A., & Schuh, R. (1997). Powerful/powerless language use in group interactions: Sex differences or similarities? *Communication Quarterly, 45,* 282–303.

Gross, J. J., Sutton, S. K., & Ketelaar, T. V. (1998). Relations between affect and personality: Support for the affect-level and affective-reactivity views. *Personality and Social Psychology Bulletin, 24,* 279–288.

Gross, M. A., & Guerrero, L. K. (2000). Managing conflict appropriately and effectively: An application of the competence model to Rahim's organizational conflict styles. *International Journal of Conflict Management, 11,* 200–226.

Gross, M. A., Guerrero, L. K., & Alberts, J. K. (2004). Perceptions of conflict strategies and communication competence in task-oriented dyads. *Journal of Applied Communication Research, 32,* 249–270.

Gudykunst, W. B. (1993a). *Communication in Japan and the United States.* Albany: State University of New York Press.

Gudykunst, W. B. (1993b). Toward a theory of effective interpersonal and intergroup communication: An anxiety/uncertainty management (AUM) perspective. In J. Koester & R. L. Wiseman (Eds.), *Intercultural communication competence* (pp. 33–71). Thousand Oaks, CA: Sage.

Gudykunst, W. B. (2005). *Theorizing about intercultural communication.* Thousand Oaks, CA: Sage.

Gudykunst, W. B., & Kim, Y. Y. (2002). *Communicating with strangers: An approach to intercultural communication* (4th ed.). New York: McGraw-Hill.

Gudykunst, W. B., & Matsumoto, Y. (1996). Cross-cultural variability of communication in personal relationships. In W. B. Gudykunst, S. Ting-Toomey, & T. Nishida (Eds.), *Communication in personal relationships across cultures* (pp. 19–56). Newbury Park, CA: Sage.

Guéguen, N., & Fischer-Lokou, J. (2002). An evaluation of touch on a large request: A field setting. *Psychological Reports, 90,* 267–269.

Guéguen, N., & Jacob, C. (2005). The effect of touch on tipping: An evaluation in a French bar. *International Journal of Hospitality Management, 24,* 295–299.

Guéguen, N., Jacob, C., & Boulbry, G. (2007). The effect of touch on compliance with a restaurant's employee suggestion. *International Journal of Hospitality Management, 26,* 1019–1023.

Guéguen, N., Meineri, S., & Charles-Sire, V. (2010). Improving medication adherence by using practitioner nonverbal techniques: A field experiment on the effect of touch. *Journal of Behavioral Medicine, 33,* 466–473.

Guéguen, N., & Vion, M. (2009). The effect of a practitioner's touch on a patient's medication compliance. *Psychology, Health & Medicine, 14,* 689–694.

Guerin, B. (2003). Combating prejudice and racism: New interventions from a functional analysis of racist language. *Journal of Community and Applied Social Psychology, 13,* 29–45.

Guerrero, L. K., & Afifi, W. A. (1995). Some things are better left unsaid: Topic avoidance in family relationships. *Communication Quarterly, 43,* 276–296.

Guerrero, L. K., Anderson, P. A., & Afifi, W. A. (2007). *Close encounters: Communication in relationships* (2nd ed.). Thousand Oaks, CA: Sage.

Guerrero, L. K., & Bachman, G. F. (2010). Forgiveness and forgiving communication in dating relationships: An expectancy-investment explanation. *Journal of Social and Personal Relationships, 27,* 801–823.

Guerrero, L. K., & Chavez, A. (2005). Relational maintenance in cross-sex friendships characterized by different types of romantic intent: An exploratory study. *Western Journal of Communication, 69,* 339–358.

Guerrero, L. K., & Floyd, K. (2006). *Nonverbal communication in close relationships.* Mahwah, NJ: Erlbaum.

Guerrero, L. K., Jones, S. M., & Boburka, R. R. (2006). Sex differences in emotional communication. In K. Dindia & D. J. Canary (Eds.), *Sex differences and similarities in communication* (2nd ed., pp. 232–252). Mahwah, NJ: Erlbaum.

Günaydin, G., Zayas, V., Selcuk, E., & Hazan, C. (2011, May). *I like you but don't know why: Facial resemblance to significant others influences snap judgments.* Paper presented at the Annual Meeting of the Association for Psychological Science, Washington, DC.

Gunn, D. O., & Gunn, C. W. (2000, September). *The quality of electronically maintained relationships.* Paper presented at the annual conference of the Association of Internet Researchers, Lawrence, KS.

Guynn, J. (2008, March 31). Silicon Valley meetings go "topless." *Los Angeles Times.* Retrieved from http://www.latimes.com/business/la-fi-no laptops31mar31,0,7194079.story

Hackman, M., & Walker, K. (1990). Instructional communication in the televised classroom: The effects of system design and teacher immediacy. *Communication Education, 39,* 196–206.

Haferkamp, N., & Krämer, N. C. (2010). Social comparison 2.0: Examining the effects of online profiles on social-networking sites. *Cyberpsychology, Behavior, and Social Networking, 14,* 309–314. doi:10.1089/cyber.2010.0120

Haga, S., Kraft, P., & Corby, E. (2009). Emotion regulation: Antecedents and well-being outcomes of cognitive reappraisal and expressive suppression in cross-cultural samples. *Journal of Happiness Studies, 10,* 271–291.

Hahlweg, K., & Richter, D. (2010). Prevention of marital instability and distress. Results of an 11-year longitudinal follow-up study. *Behaviour Research and Therapy, 48,* 377–383.

Hajek, C., & Giles, H. (2003). New directions in intercultural communication competence: The process model. In B. R. Burleson & J. O. Greene (Eds.), *Handbook of communication and social interaction skills* (pp. 935–957). Mahwah, NJ: Erlbaum.

Halatsis, P., & Christakis, N. (2009). The challenge of sexual attraction within heterosexuals' cross-sex friendship. *Journal of Social and Personal Relationships, 26,* 919–937.

Halberstadt, A. G., & Lozada, F. T. (2011). Emotion development in infancy through the lens of culture. *Emotion Review, 3,* 158–168.

Hale, J. L., Tighe, M. R., & Mongeau, P. A. (1997). Effects of event type and sex on comforting messages. *Communication Research Reports, 14,* 214–220.

Hall, E. T. (1959). *Beyond culture.* New York: Doubleday.

Hall, E. T. (1969). *The hidden dimension.* Garden City, NY: Anchor.

Hall, J. A. (2006a). How big are nonverbal sex differences? The case of smiling and nonverbal sensitivity. In K. Dindia & D. J. Canary (Eds.), *Sex differences and similarities in communication* (2nd ed., pp. 55–81). Mahwah, NJ: Erlbaum.

Hall, J. A. (2006b). Women and men's nonverbal communication: Similarities, differences, stereotypes, and origins. In V. Manusov & M. L. Patterson (Eds.), *The Sage handbook of nonverbal communication* (pp. 201–218). Thousand Oaks, CA: Sage.

Hall, J. A., Coats, E. J., & Smith LeBeau, L. (2005). Nonverbal behavior and the vertical dimension of social relations: A meta-analysis. *Psychological Bulletin, 131,* 898–924.

Hall, J. A., & Matsumoto, D. (2004). Gender differences in judgments of multiple emotions from facial expressions. *Emotion, 4,* 201–206.

Halone, K. K., & Pecchioni, L. L. (2001). Relational listening: A grounded theoretical model. *Communication Reports, 14,* 59–65.

Hamachek, D. E. (1982). *Encounters with others: Interpersonal relationships and you.* New York: Holt, Rinehart & Winston.

Hamachek, D. E. (1992). *Encounters with the self* (3rd ed.). Fort Worth, TX: Harcourt Brace.

Hample, D. (2006). Anti-comforting messages. In K. M. Galvin & P. J. Cooper (Eds.), *Making connections: Readings in relational communication* (4th ed., pp. 222–227). Los Angeles: Roxbury.

Hample, D., Warner, B., & Norton, H. (2007, November). *The effects of arguing expectations and predispositions on perceptions of argument quality and playfulness.* Paper presented at the annual meeting of the International Communication Association, San Francisco.

Hampson, E., van Anders, S. M., & Mullin, L. I. (2006). A female advantage in the recognition of emotional facial expressions: Test of an evolutionary hypothesis. *Evolution and Human Behavior, 27,* 401–416.

Han, S. (2001). Gay identity disclosure to parents by Asian American gay men. *Dissertation Abstracts International: Section A. Humanities and Social Sciences, 62*(1-A), 329.

Hancock, J. T., & Dunham, P. J. (2001). Impression formation in computer-mediated communication revisited: An analysis of the breadth and intensity of impressions. *Communication Research, 28,* 325–347.

Hansen, F. C. B., Resnick, H., & Galea, J. (2002). Better listening: Paraphrasing and perception checking—A study of the effectiveness of a multimedia skills training program. *Journal of Technology in Human Services, 20,* 317–331.

Hansen, J. (2007). *24/7: How cell phones and the internet change the way we live, work, and play.* New York: Praeger.

Hanzal, A., Segrin, C., & Dorros, S. M. (2008). The role of marital status and age on men's and women's reactions to touch from a relational partner. *Journal of Nonverbal Behavior, 32,* 21–35.

Harding, J. R. (2007). Evaluative stance and counterfactuals in language and literature. *Language & Literature, 16,* 263–280.

Harper, M. S., & Welsh, D. P. (2007). Keeping quiet: Self-silencing and its association with relational and individual functioning among adolescent romantic couples. *Journal of Social & Personal Relationships, 24,* 99–116.

Harrison, K., & Hefner, V. (2006). Media exposure, current and future body ideals, and disordered eating among preadolescent girls: A longitudinal panel study. *Journal of Youth Adolescence, 35,* 153–163.

Harwood, J. (2005). Social identity. In G. J. Shepherd, J. St. John, & T. Striphas (Eds.), *Communication as . . . : Perspectives on theory* (pp. 84–90). Thousand Oaks, CA: Sage.

Harwood, J., Bouchard, E., Giles, H., & Tyoski, S. (1997). Evaluations of patronizing speech and three response styles in a non-service-providing context. *Journal of Applied Communication Research, 25,* 170–195.

Hatchett, G. T., & Park, H. L. (2004). Relationships among optimism, coping styles, psychopathology, and counseling outcome. *Personality and Individual Differences, 36,* 1755–1769.

Hatfield, E., Cacioppo, J. T., Rapson, R. L., & Oatley, K. (1994). *Emotional contagion.* Cambridge, England: Cambridge University Press.

Hatfield, E., & Rapson, R. L. (2006). Passionate love, sexual desire, and mate selection: Cross-cultural and historical perspectives. In P. Noller & J. A. Feeney (Eds.), *Close relationships: Functions, forms and processes* (pp. 227–243). Hove, England: Psychology Press/Taylor & Francis.

Hatzigeorgiadis, A., Zourbanos, N., Mpoumpaki, S., & Theodorakis, Y. (2009). Mechanisms underlying the self-talk-performance relationship: The effects of motivational self-talk on self-confidence and anxiety. *Psychology of Sport and Exercise, 10,* 185–192.

Hawken, L., Duran, R. L., & Kelly, L. (1991). The relationship of interpersonal communication variables to academic success and persistence in college. *Communication Quarterly, 39,* 297–308.

Hayes, H. (2006). *"Don't worry about a thing, dear": Why women need financial intimacy.* San Mateo, CA: Primelife.

Heard, H. E. (2007). The family structure trajectory and adolescent school performance: Differential effects by race and ethnicity. *Journal of Family Issues, 28,* 319–354.

Hecht, M. L., Collier, M. J., & Ribeau, S. A. (1993). *African American communication: Perspectives, principles, and pragmatics.* Hillsdale, NJ: Erlbaum.

Hegelson, V. S., & Gottlieb, B. H. (2000). Support groups. In S. Cohen, L. G. Underwood, & B. H. Gottlieb (Eds.), *Social support measurement and intervention* (pp. 221–245). New York: Oxford University Press.

Heim, P., & Murphy, S. A. (2001). *In the company of women: Indirect aggression among women: Why we hurt each other and how to stop.* New York: Tarcher/Putnam.

Helms, H. M., Proulx, C. M., Klute, M. M., McHale, S. M., & Crouter, A. C. (2006). Spouses' gender-typed attributes and their links with marital quality: A pattern analytic approach. *Journal of Social and Personal Relationships, 23,* 843–864.

Helsper, E. J., & Whitty, M. T. (2010). Netiquette within married couples: Agreement about acceptable online behavior and surveillance between partners. *Computers in Human Behavior, 26,* 916–926.

Helweg-Larsen, M., Cunningham, S. J., Carrico, A., & Pergram, A. M. (2004). To nod or not to nod: An observational study of nonverbal communication and status in female and male college students. *Psychology of Women Quarterly, 28,* 358–361.

Henderson, S., & Gilding, M. (2004). "I've never clicked this much with anyone in my life": Trust and hyperpersonal communication in online friendships. *New Media & Society, 6,* 487–506.

Henline, B. H., Lamke, L. K., & Howard, M. D. (2007). Exploring perceptions of online infidelity. *Personal Relationships, 14,* 113–128.

Herfst, S. L., van Oudenhoven, J. P., & Timmerman, M. E. (2008). Intercultural effectiveness training in three western immigrant countries: A cross-cultural evaluation of critical incidents. *International Journal of Intercultural Relations, 32*(1), 67–80.

Hergovitch, A., Sirsch, U., & Felinger, M. (2002). Self-appraisals, actual appraisals and reflected appraisals of preadolescent children. *Social Behavior and Personality, 30,* 603–612.

Hess, J. A. (2000). Maintaining nonvoluntary relationships with disliked partners: An investigation into the use of distancing behaviors. *Human Communication Research, 26,* 458–488.

Hess, J. A., Fannin, A. D., & Pollom, L. H. (2007). Creating closeness: Discerning and measuring strategies for fostering closer relationships. *Personal Relationships, 14,* 25–44.

Hess, N. H., & Hagen, E. H. (2006). Sex differences in indirect aggression: Psychological evidence from young adults. *Evolution and Human Behavior, 27,* 231–245.

Heydenberk, W., & Heydenberk, R. (2007). More than manners: Conflict resolution in primary level classrooms. *Early Childhood Education Journal, 35,* 119–126.

Hian, L. B., Chuan, S. L., Trevor, T. M. K., & Detenber, B. H. (2004). Getting to know you: Exploring the development of relational intimacy in computer-mediated communication. *Journal of Computer-Mediated Communication, 9*(3). Retrieved from http://jcmc.indiana.edu/vol9/issue3/detenber.html

Hidalgo, M. C., & Hernandez, B. (2001). Place attachment: Conceptual and empirical questions. *Journal of Environmental Psychology, 21,* 273–281.

Hill, C., Memon, A., & McGeorge, P. (2008). The role of confirmation bias in suspect interviews: A systematic evaluation. *Legal and Criminological Psychology, 13,* 357–371.

Hinde, R. A., Finkenauer, C., & Auhagen, A. E. (2001). Relationships and the self-concept. *Personal Relationships, 8,* 187–204.

Hoffman, L. (2010). Experiencing intimacy: Women's reports in same-sex and cross-sex relationships. *Dissertation Abstracts International: Section B. The Sciences and Engineering, 70*(9-B), 5895.

Hoffman, M. L. (1991). Empathy, social cognition, and moral action. In W. Kurtines & J. Gerwirtz (Eds.), *Moral behavior and development: Theory, research, and applications* (Vol. 1, pp. 275–301). Hillsdale, NJ: Erlbaum.

Hofstede, G. (1984). *Culture's consequences: International differences in work-related values.* Newbury Park, CA: Sage.

Hofstede, G. (2001). *Culture's consequences: Comparing values, behaviors, institutions, and organizations across nations* (2nd ed.). Thousand Oaks, CA: Sage.

Høgh-Olesen, H. (2008). Human spatial behaviour: The spacing of people, objects, and animals in six cross-cultural samples. *Journal of Cognition and Culture, 8,* 245–280.

Holman, T. B., & Jarvis, M. O. (2003). Hostile, volatile, avoiding, and validating couple-conflict types: An investigation of Gottman's couple-conflict types. *Personal Relationships, 10,* 267–282.

Holmstrom, A. J., Burleson, B., and Jones, S. (2005). Some consequences for helpers who deliver "cold comfort": Why it's worse for women than men to be inept when providing emotional support. *Sex Roles, 53,* 153–172.

Holt, J. L., & DeVore, C. J. (2005). Culture, gender, organizational role, and styles of conflict resolution: A meta-analysis. *International Journal of Intercultural Relations, 29,* 165–196.

Holt-Lunstad, J., Smith T. B., & Layton, J. B. (2010). Social relationships and mortality risk: A meta-analytic review. *PLoS Med, 7*(7), e1000316. Retrieved from http://www.plosmedicine.org/article/info%3Adoi%2F10.1371%2Fjournal.pmed.1000316

Homburg, C., & Fürst, A. (2007). See no evil, hear no evil, speak no evil: A study of defensive organizational behavior towards customer complaints. *Journal of the Academy of Marketing Science, 35,* 523–536.

Hopcke, R. H., & Rafaty, L. (2001). *Straight women, gay men: Absolutely fabulous friendships.* Berkeley, CA: Wildcat Canyon Press.

Hopp, H., Troy, A. S., & Mauss, I. B. (2011). The unconscious pursuit of emotion regulation: Implications for psychological health. *Cognition & Emotion, 25,* 532–545.

Horan, S. M., & Booth-Butterfield, M. (2010). Investing in affection: An investigation of affection exchange theory and relational qualities. *Communication Quarterly, 58,* 394–413.

Hornik, J. (1992). Effects of physical contact on customers' shopping time and behavior. *Marketing Letters, 3,* 49–55.

Hornsey, M. J., Oppes, T., & Svensson, A. (2002). "It's ok if we say it, but you can't": Responses to intergroup and intragroup criticism. *European Journal of Social Psychology, 32,* 293–307.

Hornsey, M. J., Robson, E., Smith, J., Esposo, S., & Sutton, R. M. (2008). Sugaring the pill: Assessing rhetorical strategies designed to minimize defensive reactions to group criticism. *Human Communication Research, 34,* 70–98.

Horrigan, J. B., Rainie, L., & Fox, S. (2001, October 31). *Online communities: Networks that nurture long-distance relationships and local ties.* Pew Internet and American Life Project. Retrieved from http://www.pewinternet.org/reports/pdfs/PIP_Communities_Report.pdf

Horwitz, B. N., Neiderhiser, J. M., Ganiban, J. M., Spotts, E. L., Lichtenstein, P., & Reiss, D. (2010). Genetic and environmental influences on global family conflict. *Journal of Family Psychology, 24,* 217–220.

Hosman, L. A., & Siltanen, S. A. (2006). Powerful and powerless language forms: Their consequences for impression formation, attributions of control of self and control of others, cognitive responses, and message memory. *Journal of Language & Social Psychology, 25,* 33–46.

Houghton, T. J. (2001). A study of communication among supervisors: The influence of supervisor/supervisee verbal aggressiveness on communication climate and organizational commitment. *Dissertation Abstracts International: Section A. Humanities and Social Sciences, 61*(10-A), 3826.

Hsu, C.-F. (2010). Acculturation and communication traits: A study of cross-cultural adaptation among Chinese in America. *Communication Monographs, 77,* 414–425.

Huang, L. (1999). Family communication patterns and personality characteristics. *Communication Quarterly, 47,* 230–243.

Huang, Y.-Y., & Chou, C. (2010). An analysis of multiple factors of cyberbullying among junior high school students in Taiwan. *Computers in Human Behavior, 26,* 1581–1590.

Hubbard, A., Aune, K., & Lee, H. E. (2009, May). *Communication qualities, quantity, satisfaction, and talk impact in newly developing relationships: A longitudinal analysis.* Paper presented at the Annual Meeting of the International Communication Association, Chicago.

Hughes, P. C., & Baldwin, J. R. (2002). Communication and stereotypical impressions. *Howard Journal of Communications, 13,* 113–128.

Hullman, G. A. (2007). Communicative Adaptability Scale: Evaluating its use as an "other-report" measure. *Communication Reports, 20,* 51–74.

Hullman, G. A., Planisek, A., McNally, J. S., & Rubin, R. B. (2010). Competence, personality, and self-efficacy: Relationships in an undergraduate interpersonal course. *Atlantic Journal of Communication, 18,* 36–49.

Human, L. J., & Biesanz, J. C. (2011). Through the looking glass clearly: Accuracy and assumed similarity in well-adjusted individuals' first impressions. *Journal of Personality and Social Psychology, 100,* 349–364.

Hummert, M. L. (2011). Age stereotypes and aging. In K. W. Schaie & S. L. Willis (Eds.), *Handbook of the psychology of aging* (7th ed., pp. 249–262). San Diego, CA: Elsevier Academic Press.

Huston, T. L., & Vangelisti, A. L. (1995). How parenthood affects marriage. In M. A. Fitzpatrick & A. L. Vangelisti (Eds.), *Explaining family interactions* (pp. 147–176). Thousand Oaks, CA: Sage.

Hyde, R. B. (1993). Council: Using a talking stick to teach listening. *Communication Teacher, 7*(2), 1–2.

Hyvarinen, L., Tanskanen, P., Katajavuori, N., & Isotalus, P. (2010). A method for teaching communication in pharmacy in authentic work situations. *Communication Education, 59,* 124–145.

Imhof, M. (2003). The social construction of the listener: Listening behavior across situations, perceived listening status, and cultures. *Communication Research Reports, 20,* 357–366.

Impett, E. A., & Peplau, L. A. (2006). "His" and "her" relationships? A review of the empirical evidence. In A. Vangelisti & D. Perlman (Eds.), *The Cambridge handbook of personal relationships* (pp. 273–292). New York: Cambridge University Press.

Infante, D. A. (1987). Aggressiveness. In J. C. McCroskey & J. A. Daly (Eds.), *Personality and interpersonal communication* (pp. 157–192). Newbury Park, CA: Sage.

Infante, D. A., Chandler, T. A., & Rudd, J. E. (1989). Test of an argumentative skill deficiency model of interspousal violence. *Communication Monographs, 56,* 163–177.

Infante, D. A., & Gorden, W. I. (1989). Argumentativeness and affirming communicator style as predictors of satisfaction/dissatisfaction with subordinates. *Communication Quarterly, 37,* 81–90.

Infante, D. A., & Rancer, A. S. (1982). A conceptualization and measure of argumentativeness. *Journal of Personality Assessment, 46,* 72–80.

Infante, D. A., & Rancer, A. S. (1996). Argumentativeness and verbal aggressiveness: A review of recent theory and research. *Communication Yearbook, 19,* 320–351.

Infante, D. A., Riddle, B. L., Horvath, C. L., & Tumlin, S. A. (1992). Verbal aggressiveness: Messages and reasons. *Communication Quarterly, 40,* 116–126.

Infante, D. A., & Wigley, C. J., III. (1986). Verbal aggressiveness: An interpersonal model and measure. *Communication Monographs, 53,* 61–69.

Ireland, M. E., Slatcher, R. B., Eastwick, P. W., Scissors, L. E., Finkel, E. J., & Pennebaker, J. W. (2011). Language style matching predicts relationship initiation and stability. *Psychological Science, 22*(1), 39–44.

Irizarry, C. A. (2004). Face and the female professional: A thematic analysis of face-threatening communication in the workplace. *Qualitative Research Reports in Communication, 5,* 15–21.

IT Facts. (2008). 56% of Internet users send e-mail every day. Retrieved from http://www.itfacts .biz/56-of-internet-users-send-e-mail-every -day/9964

Iwata, Y., Suzuki, K., Takei, N., Toulopoulou, T., Tsuchiya, K. J., Matsumoto, K., et al. (2011). Jiko-shisen-kyofu (fear of one's own glance), but not taijin-kyofusho (fear of interpersonal relations), is an east Asian culture-related specific syndrome. *Australian and New Zealand Journal of Psychiatry, 45,* 148–152.

Iyer, P. (1990). *The lady and the monk: Four seasons in Kyoto.* New York: Vintage.

Jackson, W. C. (1978, September 7). *Wisconsin State Journal,* UPI.

Janas, M. (2001). Getting a clear view. *Journal of Staff Development, 22*(2), 32–34.

Jaret, C., Reitzes, D., & Shapkina, N. (2005). Reflected appraisals and self-esteem. *Sociological Perspectives, 48,* 403–419.

Jay, T., & Janschewitz, K. (2008). The pragmatics of swearing. *Journal of Politeness Research: Language, Behavior, Culture, 4,* 267–288.

Jerome, E. M., & Liss, M. (2005). Relationships between sensory processing style, adult attachment, and coping. *Personality and Individual Differences, 38,* 1341–1352.

Jin, B., & Peña, J. F. (2010). Mobile communication in romantic relationships: Mobile phone use, relational uncertainty, love, commitment, and attachment styles. *Communication Reports, 23,* 39–51.

Johnson, A. J., Becker, A. H., Craig, E. A., Gilchrist, E. S., & Haigh, M. M. (2009). Changes in friendship commitment: Comparing geographically close and long-distance young-adult friendships. *Communication Quarterly, 57,* 395–415.

Johnson, A. J., Wittenberg, E., Haigh, M., Wigley, S., Becker, J., Brown, K., & Craig, E. (2004). The process of relationship development and deterioration: Turning points in friendships that have terminated. *Communication Quarterly, 52,* 54–67.

Johnson, C. S., & Stapel, D. A. (2010). It depends on how you look at it: Being versus becoming mindsets determine responses to social comparisons. *British Journal of Social Psychology, 49,* 703–723.

Johnson, D. I. (2009). Connected classroom climate: A validity study. *Communication Research Reports, 26,* 146–157.

Johnson, D. I., & Lewis, N. (2010). Perceptions of swearing in the work setting: An expectancy violations theory perspective. *Communication Reports, 23,* 106–118.

Johnson, K. R., & Holmes, B. M. (2009). Contradictory messages: A content analysis of Hollywood-produced romantic comedy feature films. *Communication Quarterly, 57,* 352–373.

Johnson, S. (1987). *Going out of our minds: The metaphysics of liberation.* Freedom, CA: Crossing.

Joint Commission on Accreditation of Healthcare. (2008). *Sentinel event statistics.* Oakbrook Terrace, IL: Author.

Joireman, J. (2004). Relationships between attributional complexity and empathy. *Individual Differences Research, 2,* 197–202.

Jones, C., Berry, L., & Stevens, C. (2007). Synthesized speech intelligibility and persuasion: Speech rate and non-native listeners. *Computer Speech & Language, 21,* 641–651.

Jones, J. T., Pelham, B. W., & Carvallo, M. (2004). How do I love thee? Let me count the Js: Implicit egotism and interpersonal attraction. *Journal of Personality and Social Psychology, 87,* 665–683.

Jones, S. E. (1986). Sex differences in touch behavior. *Western Journal of Speech Communication, 50,* 227–241.

Jones, S. M., & Burleson, B. R. (2003). Effects of helper and recipient sex on the experience and outcomes of comforting messages: An experimental investigation. *Sex Roles, 48,* 1–19.

Jones, S. M., & Wirtz, J. G. (2006). How does the comforting process work? An empirical test of an appraisal-based model of comforting. *Human Communication Research, 32,* 217–243.

Junghyun, K., & Haridakis, P. (2008, May). *The role of Internet user characteristics and motives in explaining three dimensions of Internet addiction.* Paper presented at the meeting of the International Communication Association, Montreal, Quebec, Canada.

Jussim, L., Robustelli, S. L., & Cain, T. R. (2009). Teacher expectations and self-fulfilling prophecies. In K. R. Wenzel & A. Wigfield (Eds.), *Handbook of motivation at school* (pp. 349–380). New York: Routledge/Taylor & Francis Group.

Just, M. A., Keller, T. A., & Cynkar, J. A. (2008). A decrease in brain activation associated with driving when listening to someone speak. *Brain Research, 1205,* 70–80.

Just, N. (2007, September). *The hamburger method of constructive criticism.* Retrieved from http://n8tip.com/the-hamburger-method-of-constructive-criticism-works-for-vegetarians-too

Kagan, J. (2007). *What is emotion? History, measures, and meanings.* New Haven, CT: Yale University Press.

Kahneman, D., Krueger, A. B., Schkade, D. A., Schwarz, N., & Stone, A. A. (2004). A daily measure. *Science, 306,* 1645.

Kalman, Y. M., & Rafaeli, S. (2011). Online pauses and silence: Chronemic expectancy violations in written computer-mediated communication. *Communication Research, 38,* 54–69.

Kalman, Y. M., Scissors, L. E., & Gergle, D. (2010). Chronemic aspects of chat, and their relationship to trust in a virtual team. *Proceedings of the 5th Mediterranean Conference on Information Systems,* Tel-Aviv, Israel.

Kanaga, K. R., & Flynn, M. (1981). The relationship between invasion of personal space and stress. *Human Relations, 34,* 239–248.

Kanten, A. B., & Teigen, K. H. (2008). Better than average and better with time: Relative evaluations of self and others in the past, present, and future. *European Journal of Social Psychology, 38,* 343–353.

Kassing, J. W. (1997). Development of the Intercultural Willingness to Communicate Scale. *Communication Research Reports, 14,* 399–407.

Katt, J., & Collins, S. (2009, November). *The effects of provisionalism and verbal immediacy in written student assessments on student motivation and affective learning.* Paper presented at the conference of the National Communication Association, Chicago.

Katzer, C., Fetchenhauer, D., & Belschak, F. (2009). Cyberbullying: Who are the victims?: A comparison of victimization in internet chatrooms and victimization in school. *Journal of Media Psychology: Theories, Methods, and Applications, 21,* 25–36.

Kaufman, D., & Mahoney, J. M. (1999). The effect of waitresses' touch on alcohol consumption in dyads. *Journal of Social Psychology, 139,* 261–267.

Kaufmann, P. J. (1993). *Sensible listening: The key to responsive interaction* (2nd ed.). Dubuque, IA: Kendall/Hunt.

Kaya, N., & Burgess, B. (2007). Territoriality: Seat preferences in different types of classroom arrangements. *Environment and Behavior, 39,* 859–876.

Keashly, L., & Neuman, J. H. (2009). Building a constructive communication climate: The Workplace Stress and Aggression Project. In P. Lutgen-Sandvik, & B. D. Sypher (Eds.), *Destructive organizational communication: Processes, consequences, and constructive ways of organizing* (pp. 339–362). New York: Routledge/Taylor & Francis Group.

Kees, N. L., Aberle, J. T., & Fruhauf, C. A. (2007). Aging parents and end-of-life decisions: Helping families negotiate difficult conversations. In D. Linville & K. M. Hertlein (Eds.), *The therapist's notebook for family health care: Homework, handouts, and activities for individuals, couples, and families coping with illness, loss, and disability* (pp. 211–216). New York: Haworth Press.

Kellas, J. K. (2005). Family ties: Communicating identity through jointly told family stories. *Communication Monographs, 72,* 365–389.

Kellermann, K. (1989). The negativity effect in interaction: It's all in your point of view. *Human Communication Research, 16,* 147–183.

Kellermann, K., Reynolds, R., & Chen, J. B. (1991). Strategies of conversational retreat: When parting is not sweet sorrow. *Communication Monographs, 58,* 362–383.

Kelley, D. (1998). The communication of forgiveness. *Communication Studies, 49,* 255–272.

Kelley, D. L., & Waldron, V. R. (2005). An investigation of forgiveness-seeking communication and relational outcomes. *Communication Quarterly, 53,* 339–358.

Kelly, L., & Watson, A. K. (1986). *Speaking with confidence and skill.* Lanham, MD: University Press of America.

Kennedy, K. A., & Pronin, E. (2008). When disagreement gets ugly: Perceptions of bias and the escalation of conflict. *Personality and Social Psychology Bulletin, 34,* 833–848.

Kennedy-Moore, E., & Watson, J. C. (1999). *Expressing emotion: Myths, realities, and therapeutic strategies.* New York: Guilford Press.

Kerem, E., Fishman, N., & Josselson, R. (2001). The experience of empathy in everyday relationships: Cognitive and affective elements. *Journal of Social and Personal Relationships, 18,* 709–729.

Kidwell, B., Hardesty, D. M., Murtha, B. R., & Sheng, S. (2011). Emotional intelligence in marketing exchanges. *Journal of Marketing, 75,* 78–95.

Kihlstrom, J. F., & Klein, S. B. (1994). The self as a knowledge structure. In R. S. Wyer & T. K. Srull (Eds.), *Handbook of social cognition: Volume 1. Basic processes* (2nd ed., pp. 153–208). Hillsdale, NJ: Erlbaum.

Kim, E. J., & Buschmann, M. T. (1999). The effect of expressive physical touch on patients with dementia. *International Journal of Nursing Studies, 36,* 235–243.

Kim, H. S., & Chu, T. Q. (2011). Cultural variation in the motivation of self-expression. In D. Dunning (Ed.), *Frontiers of social psychology: Social motivation* (pp. 57–77). New York: Psychology Press.

Kim, M. S., Hunter, J. E., Miyahara, A., Horvath, A. M., Bresnahan, M., & Yoon, H. (1996). Individual- vs. culture-level dimensions of individualism and collectivism: Effects on preferred conversational styles. *Communication Monographs, 63,* 28–49.

Kim, M. S., Shin, H. C., & Cai, D. (1998). Cultural influences on the preferred forms of requesting and re-requesting. *Communication Monographs, 65,* 47–66.

Kimmel, M. S. (2008) *The gendered society* (3rd ed.). New York: Oxford University Press.

Kim-Prieto, C., & Eid, M. (2004). Norms for experiencing emotions in Sub-Saharan Africa. *Journal of Happiness Studies, 5,* 241–268.

Kingsley Westerman, C. Y., & Westerman, D. (2010). Supervisor impression management: Message content and channel effects on impressions. *Communication Studies, 61,* 585–601.

Kinzler, K. D., Shutts, K., Dejesus, J., & Spelke, E. S. (2009). Accent trumps race in guiding children's social preferences. *Social Cognition, 27,* 623–634.

Kirchler, E. (1988). Marital happiness and interaction in everyday surroundings: A time-sample diary approach for couples. *Journal of Social and Personal Relationships, 5,* 375–382.

Kleinke, C. L., Peterson, T. R., & Rutledge, T. R. (1998). Effects of self-generated facial expressions on mood. *Journal of Personality and Social Psychology, 74,* 272–279.

Kleinke, C. R. (1977). Compliance to requests made by gazing and touching experimenters in field settings. *Journal of Experimental Social Psychology, 13,* 218–223.

Kleman, E. E. (2008). "May I interest you in today's special?": A pilot study of restaurant servers' compliance-gaining strategies. *Rocky Mountain Communication Review, 5*(1), 32–42.

Klimstra, T. A., Hale, W. W., III, Raaijmakers, Q. A. W., Branje, S. J. T., & Meeus, W. H. J. (2010). Identity formation in adolescence: Change or stability? *Journal of Youth and Adolescence, 39,* 150–162.

Klohnen, E. C., & Luo, S. (2003). Interpersonal attraction and personality: What is attractive—self similarity, ideal similarity, complementarity or attachment security? *Journal of Personality and Social Psychology, 85,* 709–722.

Klopf, D. (1984). Cross-cultural apprehension research: A summary of Pacific Basin studies. In J. Daly & J. McCroskey (Eds.), *Avoiding communication: Shyness, reticence, and communication apprehension* (pp. 157–169). Beverly Hills, CA: Sage.

Knapp, M. L. (2006). Lying and deception in close relationships. In A. Vangelisti & D. Perlman (Eds.), *The Cambridge handbook of personal relationships* (pp. 517–532). New York: Cambridge University Press.

Knapp, M. L., & Hall, J. A. (2006). *Nonverbal communication in human interaction* (6th ed.). Belmont, CA: Wadsworth.

Knapp, M. L., & Hall, J. A. (2010). *Nonverbal communication in human interaction* (7th ed.). Boston: Cengage.

Knapp, M. L., & Vangelisti, A. (2000). *Interpersonal communication and human relationships* (4th ed.). Boston: Allyn & Bacon.

Knapp, M. L., & Vangelisti, A. (2006). *Interpersonal communication and human relationships* (6th ed.). Boston: Allyn & Bacon.

Knobloch, L. K., & Solomon, D. H. (2002). Information seeking beyond initial interaction: Negotiating relational uncertainty within close relationships. *Human Communication Research, 28,* 243–257.

Knobloch, L. K., & Solomon, D. H. (2003). Manifestations of relationship conception in conversation. *Human Communication Research, 29,* 482–515.

Knobloch, L. K., Miller, L. E., Bond, B. J., & Mannone, S. E. (2007). Relational uncertainty and message processing in marriage. *Communication Monographs, 74,* 154–180.

Knobloch-Westerwick, S., & Alter, S. (2006). Mood adjustment to social situations through mass media use: How men ruminate and women dissipate angry moods. *Human Communication Research, 32,* 58–73.

Knöfler, T., & Imhof, M. (2007). Does sexual orientation have an impact on nonverbal behavior in interpersonal communication? *Journal of Nonverbal Behavior, 31,* 189–204.

Ko, C., Yen, J., Chen, C., Chen, S., & Yen, C. (2005). Proposed diagnostic criteria of Internet addiction for adolescents. *The Journal of Nervous and Mental Disease, 11,* 728–733.

Koerner, A. F., & Fitzpatrick, M. A. (2002). Toward a theory of family communication. *Communication Theory, 12,* 70–91.

Koerner, A. F., & Fitzpatrick, M. A. (2006a). Family communications patterns theory: A social cognitive approach. In D. O. Braithwaite & L. A. Baxter (Eds.), *Engaging theories in family communication: Multiple perspectives* (pp. 50–65). Thousand Oaks, CA: Sage.

Koerner, A. F., & Fitzpatrick, M. A. (2006b). Family conflict communication. In J. Oetzel & S. Ting-Toomey (Eds.), *Handbook of conflict communication* (pp. 159–184). Thousand Oaks, CA: Sage.

Koesten, J. (2004). Family communication patterns, sex of subject, and communication competence. *Communication Monographs, 71,* 226–244.

Kohn, S. E., & O'Connell, V. D. (2005). *Six habits of highly effective bosses.* Franklin Lakes, NJ: Career Press.

Kolligan, J., Jr. (1990). Perceived fraudulence as a dimension of perceived incompetence. In R. J. Sternberg & J. Kolligan, Jr. (Eds.), *Competence considered* (pp. 261–285). New Haven, CT: Yale University Press.

Kopacz, M. A. (2006). Nonverbal communication as a persuasion tool: Current status and future directions. *Rocky Mountain Communication Review, 3*(1), 1–19.

Korchmaros, J. D., & Kenny, D. A. (2006). An evolutionary and close-relationship model of helping. *Journal of Social and Personal Relationships, 23,* 21–43.

Korn, C. J., Morreale, S. R., & Boileau, D. M. (2000). Defining the field: Revisiting the ACA 1995 definition of Communication Studies. *Journal of the Association for Communication Administration, 29*(1), 40–52.

Korzybski, A. (1933). *Science and sanity.* Lancaster, PA: Science Press.

Kotchemidova, C. (2010). Emotion culture and cognitive constructions of reality. *Communication Quarterly, 58,* 207–234.

Kotowski, M. R., Levine, T. R., Baker, C. R., & Bolt, J. M. (2009). A multitrait-multimethod validity assessment of the Verbal Aggressiveness and Argumentativeness Scales. *Communication Monographs, 76,* 443–462.

Koukkari, W. L., & Sothern, R. B. (2006). *Introducing biological rhythms: a primer on the temporal organization of life, with implications for health, society, reproduction and the natural environment*. New York: Springer.

Koukounas, E., & Letch, N. M. (2001). Psychological correlates of perception of sexual intent in women. *Journal of Social Psychology, 141*, 443–456.

Kramer, M. W., & Hess, J. A. (2002). Communication rules for the display of emotions in organizational settings. *Management Communication Quarterly, 16*, 66–80.

Kraus, M. W., Huang, C., & Keltner, D. (2010). Tactile communication, cooperation, and performance: An ethological study of the NBA. *Emotion, 10*, 745–749.

Krause, R. (2010). An update on primary identification, introjection, and empathy. *International Forum of Psychoanalysis, 19*(3), 138–143.

Krcmar, M., Giles, S., & Helme, D. (2008). Understanding the process: How mediated and peer norms affect young women's body esteem. *Communication Quarterly, 56*, 111–130.

Krebs, V. (2008). Social capital: The key to success for the 21st century organization. *International Association for Human Resources Journal, 12*, 38–42.

Kroeber, A. L., & Kluckhohn, C. (1952). *Culture: A critical review of concepts and definitions* (Harvard University, Peabody Museum of American Archeology and Ethnology Papers 47).

Krumhuber, E., Manstead, A. S. R., Cosker, D., Marshall, D., & Rosin, P. L. (2009). Effects of dynamic attributes of smiles in human and synthetic faces: A simulated job interview setting. *Journal of Nonverbal Behavior, 33*, 1–15.

Kubany, E. S., Richard, D. C., Bauer, G. B., & Muraoka, M. Y. (1992). Impact of assertive and accusatory communication of distress and anger: A verbal component analysis. *Aggressive Behavior, 18*, 337–347.

Kubic, K. N., & Chory, R. M. (2007). Exposure to television makeover programs and perceptions of self. *Communication Research Reports, 24*, 283–291.

Kujath, C. L. (2011). Facebook and MySpace: Complement or substitute for face-to-face interaction? *Cyberpsychology, Behavior, and Social Networking, 14*, 75–78.

Kuntze, J., van der Molen, H. T., & Born, M. P. (2009). Increase in counseling communication skills after basic and advanced microskills training. *British Journal of Educational Psychology, 79*, 175–188.

Kuo, F. E., & Sullivan, W. C. (2001a). Aggression and violence in the inner city: Effects of environment via mental fatigue. *Environment and Behavior, 33*, 543–571.

Kuo, F. E., & Sullivan, W. C. (2001b). Environment and crime in the inner city: Does vegetation reduce crime? *Environment and Behavior, 33*, 343–367.

Kurzban, R., & Weeden, J. (2005). HurryDate: Mate preferences in action. *Evolution and Human Behavior, 26*, 227–244.

La France, B. H. (2010). What verbal and nonverbal communication cues lead to sex?: An analysis of the traditional sexual script. *Communication Quarterly, 58*, 297–318.

La France, B. H., Henningsen, D. D., Oates, A., & Shaw, C. M. (2009). Social-sexual interactions? Meta-analyses of sex differences in perceptions of flirtatiousness, seductiveness, and promiscuousness. *Communication Monographs, 76*, 263–285.

Lakin, J. L. (2006). Automatic cognitive processes and nonverbal communication. In V. Manusov & M. L. Patterson (Eds.), *The Sage handbook of nonverbal communication* (pp. 59–77). Thousand Oaks, CA: Sage.

Lamm, C., Batson, C. D., & Decety, J. (2007). The neural substrate of human empathy: Effects of perspective-taking and cognitive appraisal. *Journal of Cognitive Neuroscience, 19*, 42–58.

Landrum, R. E., & Harrold, R. (2003). What employers want from psychology graduates. *Teaching of Psychology, 30*, 131–133.

Lane, K., Balleweg, B. J., Suler, J. R., Fernald, P. S., & Goldstein, G. S. (2000). Acquiring skills—Undergraduate students. In M. E. Ware & D. E. Johnson (Eds.), *Handbook of demonstrations and activities in the teaching of psychology: Vol. 3. Personality, abnormal, clinical-counseling, and social* (2nd ed., pp. 109–124). Mahwah, NJ: Erlbaum.

Langellier, K. M., & Peterson, E. E. (2006). Narrative performance theory: Telling stories, doing family. In D. O. Braithwaite, & L. A. Baxter (Eds.), *Engaging theories in family communication: Multiple perspectives* (pp. 99–114). Thousand Oaks, CA: Sage.

Langer, E. (1990). *Mindfulness.* Reading, MA: Addison-Wesley.

Langlois, J. H., & Roggman, L. A. (1990). Attractive faces are only average. *Psychological Science, 1,* 115–121.

Lapakko, D. (1997). Three cheers for language: A closer examination of a widely cited study of nonverbal communication. *Communication Education, 46,* 63–67.

Larson, J. H., Crane, D. R., & Smith, C. W. (1991). Morning and night couples: The effect of wake and sleep patterns on marital adjustment. *Journal of Marital and Family Therapy, 17,* 53–65.

Latz, J. (2010, May 28). 4 steps to speak better in interviews. *Ladders.* Retrieved from http://www.theladders.com/career-advice/4-steps-speak-better-interviews

Laurenceau, J.-P., Barrett, L. F., & Rovine, M. J. (2005). The Interpersonal Process Model of intimacy in marriage: A daily-diary and multilevel modeling approach. *Journal of Family Psychology, 19,* 314–323.

Laurenceau, J.-P., & Kleinman, B. M. (2006). Intimacy in personal relationships. In A. Vangelisti & D. Perlman (Eds.), *The Cambridge handbook of personal relationships* (pp. 637–656). New York: Cambridge University Press.

Laursen, B., & Pursell, G. (2009). Conflict in peer relationships. In K. H. Rubin, W. M. Bukowski, & B. Laursen (Eds.), *Handbook of peer interactions, relationships, and groups* (pp. 267–286). New York: Guilford Press.

Lawler, K. A., Younger, J. W., Piferi, R. L., Billington, E., Jobe, R., Edmondson, K., & Jones, W. H. (2003). A change of heart: Cardiovascular correlates of forgiveness in response to interpersonal conflict. *Journal of Behavioral Medicine, 26,* 373–393.

Lawrence, E., Yoon, J., Langer, A., & Ro, E. (2009). Is psychological aggression as detrimental as physical aggression? The independent effects of psychological aggression on depression and anxiety symptoms. *Violence and Victims, 24,* 20–35.

Lebula, C., & Lucas, C. (1945). The effects of attitudes on descriptions of pictures. *Journal of Experimental Psychology, 35,* 517–524.

Ledbetter, A. M., Mazer, J. P., DeGroot, J. M., & Meyer, K. R. (2011). Attitudes toward online social connection and self-disclosure as predictors of Facebook communication and relational closeness. *Communication Research, 38,* 27–53.

Lee, J. A. (1973). *The colors of love: Exploration of the ways of loving.* Don Mills, Ontario, Canada: New Press.

Lehmiller, J. J., VanderDrift, L. E., & Kelly, J. R. (2011). Sex differences in approaching friends with benefits relationships. *Journal of Sex Research, 48,* 275–284.

Lei, X. (2006). Sexism in language. *Journal of Language and Linguistics, 5*(1), 87–94.

Leit, L. (2009). Conversational narcissism in marriage: Effects on partner mental health and marital quality over the transition to parenthood. *Dissertation Abstracts International: Section B. The Sciences and Engineering, 69*(7-B), 4465.

Lengel, R. H., & Daft, R. L. (1988). The selection of communication media as an executive skill. *Academy of Management Executive, 2,* 225–232.

Lenhart, A. (2009). *Teens and sexting.* Pew Internet & American Life Project. Retrieved from http://www.pewinternet.org/Reports/2009/Teens-and-Sexting.aspx

Lenhart, A., Madden, M., Macgill, A. R., & Smith, A. (2007). *Teens and social media.* Washington, DC: Pew Internet & American Life Project.

Lenhart, A., Madden M., & Smith A. (2010). *Teens and social media.* Pew Internet & American Life Project. Retrieved from http://www.pewinternet.org/Reports/2007/Teens-and-Social-Media/1-Summary-of-Findings.aspx?r=1

Lenhart A, & Purcell, K. (2010). *Social media and young adults.* Pew Internet & American Life Project. Retrieved from http://pewinternet.org/Reports/2010/Social-Media-and-Young-Adults

Lenhart, A., Rainie, L., & Lewis, O. (2001). *Teenage life online.* Pew Internet and American Life Project. Retrieved from http://www.pewinternet.org/reports/toc.asp?Report536

Lerner, R. M., Rothbaum, F., Boulos, S., & Castellino, D. R. (2002). Developmental systems perspective on parenting. In M. Bornstein (Ed.), *Handbook of parenting: Vol. 2. Biology and ecology of parenting* (2nd ed., pp. 315–344). Mahwah, NJ: Erlbaum.

Levenson, R. W., Ekman, P., & Friesen, W. V. (1990). Voluntary facial action generates emotion-specific autonomic nervous system activity. *Psychophysiology, 27*, 363–384.

Levine, D. (2000). Virtual attraction: What rocks your boat. *CyberPsychology and Behavior, 3*, 565–573.

Levine, R. V. (1988). The pace of life across cultures. In J. E. McGrath (Ed.), *The social psychology of time* (pp. 39–60). Newbury Park, CA: Sage.

Levine, R. V., & Norenzayan, A. (1999). The pace of life in 31 countries. *Journal of Cross-Cultural Psychology, 30*, 178–205.

Levine, R. V., Reysen, S., & Ganz, E. (2008). The kindness of strangers revisited: A comparison of 24 US cities. *Social Indicators Research, 85*, 461–481.

Levine, T. R. (2009). To catch a liar. *Communication Currents, 4*, 1–2.

Levinson, M. H. (2010). General Semantics and . . . . *ETC: A Review of General Semantics, 67*, 127–143.

Levitt, S. D., & Dubner, S. J. (2005). *Freakonomics: A rogue economist explores the hidden side of everything.* New York: William Morrow.

Lewandowski, G. W., Aron, A., & Gee, J. (2007). Personality goes a long way: The malleability of opposite-sex physical attractiveness. *Personal Relationships, 14*, 571–585.

Lewis, L. K. (2006). Collaborative interaction: Review of communication scholarship and a research agenda. *Communication Yearbook, 30*, 197–247.

Lewis, M. H., & Reinsch, N. L., Jr. (1988). Listening in organizational environments. *Journal of Business Communication, 25*, 49–67.

Lewis, T., & Manusov, V. (2009). Listening to another's distress in everyday relationships. *Communication Quarterly, 57*, 282–301.

Lev-On, A., & Chavez, A. (2010). Group and dyadic communication in trust games. *Rationality and Society, 22*, 37–54.

Lieberson, S. (2000). *A matter of taste: How names, fashions, and culture change.* New Haven, CT: Yale University Press.

Lillian, D. L. (2007). A thorn by any other name: Sexist discourse as hate speech. *Discourse & Society, 18*, 719–740.

Lim, G. Y., & Roloff, M. E. (1999). Attributing sexual consent. *Journal of Applied Communication Research, 27*, 1–23.

Lim, L. L. (2009). The influences of harmony motives and implicit beliefs on conflict styles of the collectivist. *International Journal of Psychology, 44*, 401–409.

Limon, M. S., & LaFrance, B. H. (2005). Communication traits and leadership emergence: Examining the impact of argumentativeness, communication apprehension, and verbal aggressiveness in work groups. *Southern Communication Journal, 70*, 123–133.

Lippard, P. V. (1988). Ask me no questions, I'll tell you no lies: Situational exigencies for interpersonal deception. *Western Journal of Speech Communication, 52*, 91–103.

Lippert, T., & Prager, K. J. (2001). Daily experiences of intimacy: A study of couples. *Personal Relationships, 8*, 283–298.

Littlejohn, S. W. (2008). *Theories of human communication* (9th ed.). Boston: Cengage.

Litwin, A. H., & Hallstein, L. O. (2007). Shadows and silences: How women's positioning and unspoken friendship rules in organizational settings cultivate difficulties among some women at work. *Women's Studies in Communication, 30*(1), 111–142.

Lobchuk, M. M. (2006). Concept analysis of perspective-taking: Meeting informal caregiver needs for communication competence and accurate perception. *Journal of Advanced Nursing, 54*, 330–341.

Lobet-Maris, C. (2003). Cell phone tribes: Youth and social identity. In L. Fortunati, J. E. Katz, & R. Riccini (Eds.), *Mediating the human body: Technology, communication, and fashion* (pp. 87–92). Mahwah, NJ: Erlbaum.

Locher, M. A. (2010). Relational work, politeness, and identity construction. In D. Matsumoto (Ed.), *APA handbook of interpersonal communication* (pp. 111–138). Washington, DC: American Psychological Association.

Lock, C. (2004, July 31). Deception detection: Psychologists try to learn how to spot a liar. *Science News, 16*, 72.

Lombardo, M. V., Chakrabarti, B., Bullmore, E. T., Wheelwright, S. J., Sadek, S. A., Suckling J., & Baron-Cohen S. (2010). Shared neural circuits for mentalizing about the self and others. *Journal of Cognitive Neuroscience, 22*, 1623–1635.

Long, E. C. J., Angera, J. J., Carter, S. J., Nakamoto, M., & Kalso, M. (1999). Understanding the one you love: A longitudinal assessment of an empathy training program for couples in romantic relationships. *Family Relations: Interdisciplinary Journal of Applied Family Studies, 48*, 235–242.

Lorenzo, G. L., Biesanz, J. C., & Human, L. J. (2010). What is beautiful is good and more accurately understood: Physical attractiveness and accuracy in first impressions of personality. *Psychological Science, 21*, 1777–1782.

Loyd, D. L., Phillips, K. W., Whitson, J., & Thomas-Hunt, M. C. (2010). Expertise in your midst: How congruence between status and speech style affects reactions to unique knowledge. *Group Processes & Intergroup Relations, 13*, 379–395.

Lozano-Reich, N. M., & Cloud, D. L. (2009). The uncivil tongue: Invitational rhetoric and the problem of inequality. *Western Journal of Communication, 73*, 220–226.

Lucas, R. E., Le, K., & Dyrenforth, P. S. (2008). Explaining the extraversion/positive affect relation: Sociability cannot account for extraverts' greater happiness. *Journal of Personality, 76*, 385–414.

Luft, J. (1969). *Of human interaction*. Palo Alto, CA: National Press Books.

Lundqvist, L.-O. (2008). The relationship between the biosocial model of personality and susceptibility to emotional contagion: A structural equation modeling approach. *Personality and Individual Differences, 45*, 89–95.

Lunkenheimer, E. S., Shields, A. M., & Cortina, K. S. (2007). Parental emotion coaching and dismissing in family interaction. *Social Development, 16*, 232–248.

Luo, S., & Klohnen, E. (2005). Assortive mating and marital quality in newlyweds; A couple-centered approach. *Journal of Personality and Social Psychology, 88*, 304–326.

Luo, S., & Zhang, G. (2009). What leads to romantic attraction: Similarity, reciprocity, security, or beauty? Evidence from a speed-dating study. *Journal of Personality, 77*, 933–964.

Luo, S., Zhang, G., Watson, D., & Snider, A. G. (2010). Using cross-sectional couple data to disentangle the causality between positive partner perceptions and marital satisfaction. *Journal of Research in Personality, 44*, 665–668.

Lustig, M. W., & Koester, J. (1999). *Intercultural competence: Interpersonal communication across cultures* (3rd ed.). New York: Longman.

Lustig, M. W., & Koester, J. (2005). *Intercultural competence: Interpersonal communication across cultures* (4th ed.). Upper Saddle River, NJ: Allyn & Bacon.

Lutgen-Sandvik, P., Riforgiate, S., & Fletcher, C. (2011). Work as a source of positive emotional experiences and the discourses informing positive assessment. *Western Journal of Communication, 75*, 2–27.

Ma, R., & Chuang, R. (2001). Persuasion strategies of Chinese college students in interpersonal contexts. *Southern Communication Journal, 66*, 267–278.

Ma, Z., & Jaeger, A. M. (2010). A comparative study of the influence of assertiveness on negotiation outcomes in Canada and China. *Cross Cultural Management, 17*, 333–346.

MacGeorge, E. L., Feng, B., & Thompson, E. R. (2008). "Good" and "bad" advice: How to advise more effectively. In M. T. Motley (Ed.), *Studies in applied interpersonal communication* (pp. 145–164). Thousand Oaks, CA: Sage.

MacGeorge, E. L., Samter, W., Feng, B., Gillihan, S. J., & Graves, A. R. (2004). Stress, social support, and health among college students after September 11, 2001. *Journal of College Student Development, 45*, 655–670.

MacIntyre, P. D., & Thivierge, K. A. (1995). The effects of speaker personality on anticipated reactions to public speaking. *Communication Research Reports, 12*, 125–133.

MacNeil, S., & Byers, E. S. (2009). Role of sexual self-disclosure in the sexual satisfaction of long-term heterosexual couples. *Journal of Sex Research, 46*, 3–14.

Macrae, C. N., & Bodenhausen, G. V. (2001). Social cognition: Categorical person perception. *British Journal of Psychology, 92,* 239–256.

Madden, M., & Smith, A. (2010, May 26). *Reputation management and social media.* Pew Internet & American Life Project. Retrieved from http://pewinternet.org/Reports/2010/Reputation-Management.aspx

Madlock, P. E., & Kennedy-Lightsey, C. (2010). The effects of supervisors' verbal aggressiveness and mentoring on their subordinates. *Journal of Business Communication, 47,* 42–62.

Magnusson, A. (2006). Nonverbal conversation-regulating signals of the blind adult. *Communication Studies, 57,* 421–433.

Maisel, N. C., Gable, S. L., & Strachman, A. (2008). Responsive behaviors in good times and bad. *Personal Relationships, 15,* 317–338.

Makin, V. S. (2004). Face management and the role of interpersonal politeness variables in euphemism production and comprehension. *Dissertation Abstracts International: Section B. The Sciences and Engineering, 64*(8-B), 4077.

Mallalieu, S. D., Hanton, S., & Jones, G. (2003). Emotional labeling and competitive anxiety in preparation and competition. *The Sport Psychologist, 17,* 157–174.

Malle, B. F., & Hodges, S. D. (Eds.). (2005). *Other minds: How humans bridge the divide between self and others.* New York: Guilford Press.

Malouf, D. (2003, November). Made in England: Australia's British inheritance. *Quarterly Essay, 12,* 1–66.

Malpede, J. M. (2003). What is the experience of shame and the impact of self-disclosure on the healing process of women involved in a gender-specific addiction treatment program? *Dissertation Abstracts International: Section B: The Sciences and Engineering, 64*(1-B), 425.

Mansson, D. H., & Myers, S. A. (2011). An initial examination of college students' expressions of affection through Facebook. *Southern Communication Journal, 76,* 155–168.

Manusov, V. (1993). It depends on your perspective: Effects of stance and beliefs about intent on person perception. *Western Journal of Communication, 57,* 27–41.

Marangoni, C., & Ickes, W. (1989). Loneliness: A theoretical review with implications for measurement. *Journal of Social and Personal Relationships, 6,* 93–128.

Marchant, V. (1999, June 28). Listen up! *Time, 153,* 74.

Marek, C. I., Wanzer, M. B., & Knapp, J. L. (2004). An exploratory investigation of the relationship between roommates' first impressions and subsequent communication patterns. *Communication Research Reports, 21,* 210–220.

Mares, S. H. W., de Leeuw, R. N. H., Scholte, R. H. J., & Engels, R. C. M. E. (2010). Facial attractiveness and self-esteem in adolescence. *Journal of Clinical Child and Adolescent Psychology, 39,* 627–637.

Maricchiolo, F., Gnisci, A., Bonaiuto, M., & Ficca, G. (2009). Effects of different types of hand gestures in persuasive speech on receivers' evaluations. *Language and Cognitive Processes, 24,* 239–266.

Marriott, M. (1998, July 2). The blossoming of Internet chat [online]. *The New York Times.* Retrieved from http://www.nytimes.com/library/tech/98/07/circuits/articles/02/chat.html

Marsh, A. A., Elfenbein, H. A., & Ambady, N. (2003). Nonverbal "accents": Cultural differences in facial expressions of emotion. *Psychological Science, 14,* 373–376.

Marshall, T. C. (2008). Cultural differences in intimacy: The influence of gender-role ideology and individualism-collectivism. *Journal of Social and Personal Relationships, 25,* 143–168.

Marshall, T. C. (2010). Love at the cultural crossroads: Intimacy and commitment in Chinese Canadian relationships. *Personal Relationships, 17,* 391–411.

Martin, M. M., Dunleavy, K. N., & Kennedy-Lightsey, C. (2010). Can verbally aggressive messages in the instructor-student relationship be constructive? *College Student Journal, 44,* 726–736.

Martz, J. M., Verette, J., Arriaga, X. B., Slovik, L. F., Cox, C. L., & Rusbult, C. E. (1998). Positive illusion in close relationships. *Personal Relationships, 5,* 159–181.

Mashek, D., & Sherman, M. (2004). Desiring less closeness with intimate others. In D. Mashek & A. Aron (Eds.), *The handbook of closeness and intimacy* (pp. 343–356). Mahwah, NJ: Erlbaum.

Maslow, A. H. (1968). *Toward a psychology of being.* New York: Van Nostrand Reinhold.

Maslow, A. H., & Mintz, N. L. (1956). Effects of aesthetic surroundings: I. Initial effects of those aesthetic surroundings upon perceiving "energy" and "well-being" in faces. *Journal of Psychology, 41,* 247–254.

Massengill, J., & Nash, M. (2009, May). *Ethnocentrism, intercultural willingness to communicate, and international interaction among U.S. college students.* Paper presented at the conference of the International Communication Association, Chicago.

Mast, M. S., & Hall, J. A. (2004). Who is the boss and who is not? Accuracy of judging status. *Journal of Nonverbal Behavior, 28,* 145–165.

Matsumoto, D. (1993). Ethnic differences in affect intensity, emotion judgments, display rule attitudes, and self-reported emotional expression in an American sample. *Motivation and Emotion, 17,* 107–123.

Matsumoto, D. (2006). Culture and nonverbal behavior. In V. Manusov & M. L. Patterson (Eds.), *The Sage handbook of nonverbal communication* (pp. 219–235). Thousand Oaks, CA: Sage.

Matsumoto, D., & Yoo, S. H. (2005). Culture and applied nonverbal communication. In R. S. Feldman & R. E. Riggio (Eds.), *Applications of nonverbal communication* (pp. 255–277). Mahwah, NJ: Erlbaum.

Matveev, A. V. (2004). Describing intercultural communication competence: In-depth interviews with American and Russian managers. *Qualitative Research Reports in Communication, 5,* 55–62.

Mayne, T. J. (1999). Negative affect and health: The importance of being earnest. *Cognition and Emotion, 13,* 601–635.

McBride, J. L. (2007). The family. In O. J. Z. Sahler & J. E. Carr (Eds.), *The behavioral sciences and health care* (2nd ed., rev. and updated, pp. 147–156). Ashland, OH: Hogrefe & Huber.

McCain, J. (1999). *Faith of my fathers.* New York: Random House.

McClure, J., Meyer, L. H., Garisch, J., Fischer, R., Weir, K. F., & Walkey, F. H. (2011). Students' attributions for their best and worst marks: Do they relate to achievement? *Contemporary Educational Psychology, 36,* 71–81.

McCornack, S. A., & Levine, T. R. (1990). When lies are uncovered: Emotional and relational outcomes of discovered deception. *Communication Monographs, 57,* 119–138.

McCroskey, J. C. (2009). Communication apprehension: What have we learned in the last four decades. *Human Communication, 12,* 157–171.

McCroskey, J. C., & Richmond, V. P. (1996). *Fundamentals of human communication: An interpersonal perspective.* Prospect Heights, IL: Waveland.

McCroskey, J. C., Richmond, V. P., Heisel, A. D., & Hayhurst, J. L. (2004). Eysenck's Big Three and communication traits: Communication traits as manifestations of temperament. *Communication Research Reports, 21,* 404–410.

McCroskey, J. C., & Wheeless, L. (1976). *Introduction to human communication.* Boston: Allyn & Bacon.

McCullough, M. E., Root, L. M., Tabak, B. A., & Witvliet, C. van O. (2009). Forgiveness. In S. J. Lopez & C. R. Snyder (Eds.), *Oxford handbook of positive psychology* (2nd ed., pp. 427–435). New York: Oxford University Press.

McEwan, B., & Guerrero, L. K. (2010). Freshman engagement through communication: Predicting friendship formation strategies and perceived availability of network resources from communication skills. *Communication Studies, 61,* 445–463.

McGinn, M. M., McFarland, P. T., & Christensen, A. (2009). Antecedents and consequences of demand/withdraw. *Journal of Family Psychology, 23,* 749–757.

McGlone, M. S., Beck, G., & Pfiester, A. (2006). Contamination and camouflage in euphemisms. *Communication Monographs, 73,* 261–282.

McGoldrick, M., Watson, M., & Benton, W. (1999). Siblings through the life cycle. In B. Carter & M. McGoldrick (Eds.), *The expanded family life cycle: Individual, family, and social perspectives* (3rd ed., pp. 153–168). Needham Heights, MA: Allyn & Bacon.

McIntire, R. (1999). *Raising good kids in tough times: 7 crucial habits for parent success.* Berkeley Springs, WV: Summit Crossroads Press.

McLuhan, M. (1962). *The Gutenberg galaxy.* Toronto, Ontario, Canada: University of Toronto Press.

McNaughton, D., Hamlin, D., McCarthy, J., Head-Reeves, D., & Schreiner, M. (2008). Learning to listen: Teaching an active listening strategy to preservice education professionals. *Topics in Early Childhood Special Education, 27,* 223–231.

Meade, J. M. (2003). What is the experience of shame and the impact of self-disclosure on the healing process of women involved in a gender-specific addiction treatment program? *Dissertation Abstracts International: Section B. The Sciences and Engineering, 64*(1-B), 425.

Mehdizadeh, S. (2010). Self-presentation 2.0: Narcissism and self-esteem on Facebook. *Cyberpsychology, Behavior, and Social Networking, 13,* 357–364.

Mehl, M. R., Vazire, S., Holleran, S. E., & Clark, C. S. (2010). Eavesdropping on happiness: Well-being is related to having less small talk and more substantive conversations. *Psychological Science, 21,* 539–541.

Mehl, M. R., Vazire, S., Ramírez-Esparza, N., Slatcher, R. B., & Pennebaker, J. W. (2007). Are women really more talkative than men? *Science, 317,* 82.

Mehrabian, A. (1972). *Nonverbal communication.* Chicago: Aldine-Atherton.

Mehrabian, A. (2001). Characteristics attributed to individuals on the basis of their first names. *Genetic, Social, and General Psychology Monographs, 127,* 59–88.

Mehrabian, A. (2008). Communication without words. In C. D. Mortensen (Ed.), *Communication theory* (2nd ed., pp. 193–2000). Piscataway, NJ: Transaction Publishers.

Mehrabian, A., & Blum, J. S. (2003). Physical appearance, attractiveness, and the mediating role of emotions. In N. J. Pallone (Ed.), *Love, romance, sexual interaction: Research perspectives from current psychology* (pp. 1–29). New Brunswick, NJ: Transaction.

Mehrabian, A., & Weiner, M. (1967). Decoding of inconsistent communications. *Journal of Personality and Social Psychology, 6,* 109–114.

Meir, I., Sandler, W., Padden, C., & Aronoff, M. (2010). Emerging sign languages. In M. Marshark & P. E. Spencer (Eds.), *The Oxford handbook of deaf studies, language, and education* (Vol. 2, pp. 267–280). New York: Oxford University Press.

Mendes de Leon, C. F. (2005). Why do friendships matter for survival? *Journal of Epidemiology and Community Health, 59,* 538–539.

Merkin, R. S. (2006). Uncertainty avoidance and facework: A test of the Hofstede model. *International Journal of Intercultural Relations, 30,* 213–228.

Merkin, R. S., & Ramadan, R. (2010). Facework in Syria and the United States: A cross-cultural comparison. *International Journal of Intercultural Relations, 34,* 661–669.

Merolla, A. J. (2008). Communicating forgiveness in friendships and dating relationships. *Communication Studies, 59,* 114–131.

Merolla, A. J., Weber, K. D., Myers, S. A., & Booth-Butterfield, M. (2004). The impact of past dating relationship solidarity on commitment, satisfaction, and investment in current relationships. *Communication Quarterly, 52,* 251–264.

Merrill, D. M. (1997). *Caring for elderly parents: Juggling work, family, and caregiving in middle and working class families.* Westport, CT: Auburn House/Greenwood.

Mesch, G. S., & Beker, G. (2010). Are norms of disclosure of online and offline personal information associated with the disclosure of personal information online? *Human Communication Research, 36,* 570–592.

Mesch, G. S., & Talmud, I. (2010). *Wired youth: The social world of adolescence in the information age.* New York: Routledge.

Messman, S. J., & Mikesell, R. L. (2000). Competition and interpersonal conflict in dating relationships. *Communication Reports, 13,* 21–34.

Metts, S., & Cupach, W. R. (1990). The influence of relationship beliefs and problem-solving relationships on satisfaction in romantic relationships. *Human Communication Research, 17,* 170–185.

Metts, S., Cupach, W. R., & Bejllovec, R. A. (1989). "I love you too much to ever start liking you": Redefining romantic relationships. *Journal of Social and Personal Relationships, 6,* 259–274.

Metts, S., Cupach, W. R., & Imahori, T. T. (1992). Perceptions of sexual compliance-resisting messages in three types of cross-sex relationships. *Western Journal of Communication, 56,* 1–17.

Metts, S., & Grohskopf, E. (2003). Impression management: Goals, strategies, and skills. In B. Burleson & J. O. Greene (Eds.), *Handbook of communication and social interaction skills* (pp. 357–399). Mahwah, NJ: Erlbaum.

Michel, F. (2008). *Assert yourself.* Perth, Western Australia: Centre for Clinical Interventions.

Miczo, N., & Burgoon, J. K. (2008). Facework and nonverbal behavior in social support interactions within romantic dyads. In M. T. Motley (Ed.), *Studies in applied interpersonal communication* (pp. 245–266). Thousand Oaks, CA: Sage.

Mignault, A., & Chaudhuri, A. (2003). The many faces of a neutral face: Head tilt and perception of dominance and emotion. *Journal of Nonverbal Behavior, 27,* 111–132.

Miller, K. I., Joseph, L., & Apker, J. (2000). Strategic ambiguity in the role development process. *Journal of Applied Communication Research, 28,* 193–214.

Miller, K. I., & Koesten, J. (2008). Financial feeling: An investigation of emotion and communication in the workplace. *Journal of Applied Communication Research, 36,* 8–32.

Miller, L. C., Cooke, L. L., Tsang, J., & Morgan, F. (1992). Should I brag? Nature and impact of positive and boastful disclosures for women and men. *Human Communication Research, 18,* 364–399.

Miller, P., Niehuis, S., & Huston, T. L. (2006). Positive illusions in marital relationships: A 13-year longitudinal study. *Personality and Social Psychology Bulletin, 32,* 1579–1594.

Miró, E., Cano, M. C., Espinoza-Fernández, L., & Beula-Casal, G. (2003). Time estimation during prolonged sleep deprivation and its relation to activation measures. *Human Factors, 45,* 148–159.

Miwa, Y., & Hanyu, K. (2006). The effects of interior design on communication and impressions of a counselor in a counseling room. *Environment and Behavior, 38,* 484–502.

Moffat, M., Cleland, J., van der Molen, T., & Price, D. (2007). Poor communication may impair optimal asthma care: A qualitative study. *Family Practice, 24*(1), 65–70.

Mongeau, P. A., & Henningsen, M. L. M. (2008). Stage theories of relationship development. In L. A. Baxter & D. O. Braithewaite (Eds.), *Engaging theories in interpersonal communication: Multiple perspectives* (pp. 363–375). Thousand Oaks, CA: Sage.

Montgomery, B. M. (1993). Relationship maintenance versus relationship change: A dialectical dilemma. *Journal of Social and Personal Relationships, 10,* 205–223.

Montoya, R. M., Horton, R. S., & Kirchner, J. (2008). Is actual similarity necessary for attraction? A meta-analysis of actual and perceived similarity. *Journal of Social and Personal Relationships, 25,* 889–922.

Moody, E. J. (2001). Internet use and its relationship to loneliness. *Cyber Psychology and Behavior, 4,* 393–401.

Moore, J., & Lauters, A. (2008, May). *Rules online: Coordinated management of meaning in chat rooms.* Conference paper presented at the meeting of the International Communication Association, Montreal, Quebec, Canada.

Moore, S. A., Zoellner, L. A., & Mollenholt, N. (2008). Are expressive suppression and cognitive reappraisal associated with stress-related symptoms? *Behaviour Research and Therapy, 46,* 993–1000.

Morman, M. T., & Floyd, K. (2002). A "changing culture of fatherhood": Effects of affectionate communication, closeness, and satisfaction in men's relationships with their fathers and their sons. *Western Journal of Communication, 66,* 395–411.

Morreale, S. P., & Pearson, J. C. (2008). Why communication education is important: The centrality of the discipline in the 21st century. *Communication Education, 57*(2), 224–240.

Morris, D. (1973). *Intimate behavior.* New York: Bantam.

Morris, T. L., Gorham, J., Cohen, S. H., & Huffman, D. (1996). Fashion in the classroom: Effects of attire on student perceptions of instructors in college classes. *Communication Education, 45,* 135–148.

Morrison, J. (2008). The relationship between emotional intelligence competencies and preferred conflict-handling styles. *Journal of Nursing Management, 16,* 974–983.

Morry, M. M., Kito, M., & Ortiz, L. (2011). The attraction–similarity model and dating couples: Projection, perceived similarity, and psychological benefits. *Personal Relationships, 18,* 125–143.

Morton, J. B., & Trehub, S. E. (2001). Children's understanding of emotion in speech. *Child Development, 72,* 834–843.

Motley, M. T. (1990). On whether one can(not) communicate: An examination via traditional communication postulates. *Western Journal of Speech Communication, 54,* 1–20.

Motley, M. T. (1992). Mindfulness in solving communicators' dilemmas. *Communication Monographs, 59,* 306–314.

MTV. (2009). *A thin line.* AP Digital Abuse Study. Retrieved from http://www.athinline.org/MTV-AP_Digital_Abuse_Study_Executive_Summary.pdf

Muise, A., Christofides, E., & Desmarais, S. (2009). More information than you ever wanted: Does Facebook bring out the green-eyed monster of jealousy? *CyberPsychology & Behavior, 12,* 441–444.

Mulac, A. (2006). The gender-linked language effect: Do language differences really make a difference? In K. Dindia & D. J. Canary (Eds.), *Sex differences and similarities in communication* (2nd ed., pp. 211–231). Mahwah, NJ: Erlbaum.

Muñoz-Rivas, M. J., Graña, J. L., O'Leary, K. D., & González, M. P. (2007). Aggression in adolescent dating relationships: Prevalence, justification, and health consequences. *Journal of Adolescent Health, 40,* 298–304.

Murdock, G. P. (1965). *Social structure.* New York: Free Press.

Murray, J. E., Jr. (2002). *The current state of marriage and family.* Pittsburgh, PA: Duquesne University Family Institute. Retrieved from http://www2.duq.edu/familyinstitute/templates/features/csmf/children.html

Mychalcewycz, P. (2009, February 12). *Breaking up via text message becoming commonplace, poll finds.* Retrieved from http://www.switched.com/2009/02/12/breaking-up-via-text-message-becoming-commonplace-poll-finds/

Myers, D. (1980, May). The inflated self. *Psychology Today, 14,* 16.

Myers, S. (2000). Empathic listening: Reports on the experience of being heard. *Journal of Humanistic Psychology, 40,* 148–173.

Myers, S., & Brann, M. (2009). College students' perceptions of how instructors establish and enhance credibility through self-disclosure. *Qualitative Research Reports in Communication, 10,* 9–16.

Myers, S. A. (1998). Students' self-disclosure in the college classroom. *Psychological Reports, 83*(3, Pt. 1), 1067–1070.

Myers, S. A. (2002). Perceived aggressive instructor communication and student state motivation, learning, and satisfaction. *Communication Reports, 15,* 113–121.

Myers, S. A. (2003). Sibling use of relational maintenance behaviors. In K. M. Galvin & P. J. Cooper (Eds.), *Making connections: Readings in relational communication* (pp. 300–308). Los Angeles: Roxbury.

Myers, S. A., & Bryant, L. E. (2008). The use of behavioral indicators of sibling commitment among emerging adults. *Journal of Family Communication, 8,* 101–125.

Myers, S. A., Edwards, C., Wahl, S. T., & Martin, M. M. (2007). The relationship between perceived instructor aggressive communication and college student involvement. *Communication Education, 56,* 495–508.

Myers, S. A., & Rocca, K. A. (2001). Perceived instructor argumentativeness and verbal aggressiveness in the college classroom: Effects on student perceptions of climate, apprehension, and state motivation. *Western Journal of Communication, 65,* 113–137.

Myers, S. A., & Weber, K. D. (2004). Preliminary development of a measure of sibling relational maintenance behavior: Scale development and initial findings. *Communication Quarterly, 52,* 334–346.

Nardone, G., & Watzlawick, P. (2005). *Brief strategic therapy: Philosophy, techniques, and research.* Lanham, MD: Jason Aronson.

National Association of Colleges and Employers. (2010). *Job outlook 2011*. Bethlehem, PA: Author.

National Communication Association. (1999). *How Americans communicate* [online]. Retrieved from http://www.natcom.org/research/Roper/how_americans_communicate.htm

National Crime Prevention Council. (2007, February 28). *Teens and cyberbullying*. Executive Summary of a Report on Research Conducted for National Crime Prevention Council (NCPC). Retrieved from http://surfsafety.net/Cyberbullying-Exec%20Summary-FINAL.htm

National Institute of Mental Health. (2008, April 3). *Attention deficit hyperactivity disorder*. Retrieved from http://www.nimh.nih.gov/health/publications/adhd/complete-publication.shtml

National Youth Violence Prevention Resource Center. (2007, December 20). *Gangs fact sheet*. Retrieved from http://www.safeyouth.org/scripts/facts/gangs.asp

Naumann, L. P., Vazire, S., Rentfrow, P. J., & Gosling, S. D. (2009). Personality judgments based on physical appearance. *Personality and Social Psychology Bulletin, 35*, 1661–1671.

Neenan, M., & Dryden, W. (2006). *Rational emotive behaviour therapy in a nutshell*. London: Sage.

Nellermoe, D. A., Weirich, T. R., & Reinstein, A. (1999). Using practitioners' viewpoints to improve accounting students' communications skills. *Business Communication Quarterly, 62*(2), 41–60.

Nelson, J. E., & Beggan, J. K. (2004). Self-serving judgments about winning the lottery. *Journal of Psychology: Interdisciplinary and Applied, 138*, 253–264.

Nelson, T. D. (2005). Ageism: Prejudice against our feared future self. *Journal of Social Issues, 61*, 207–221.

Nelton, S. (1996, February). Emotions in the workplace. *Nation's Business, 44*, pp. 25–30.

Nemati, A., & Bayer, J. M. (2007). Gender differences in the use of linguistic forms in the speech of men and women: A comparative study of Persian and English. *Language in India, 7*, 1–12. Retrieved from http://www.languageinindia.com/sep2007/genderstudy.pdf

Neuliep, J. W. (1996). The influence of theory X and Y management style on the perception of ethical behavior in organizations. *Journal of Social Behavior and Personality, 11*, 301–311.

Newton, D. A., & Burgoon, J. K. (1990). The use and consequences of verbal influence strategies during interpersonal disagreements. *Human Communication Research, 16*, 477–518.

Ng, S. H., & Bradac, J. J. (1993). *Power in language: Verbal communication and social influence*. Newbury Park, CA: Sage.

Nguyen, H.-H. D., Le, H., & Boles, T. (2010). Individualism-collectivism and co-operation: A cross-society and cross-level examination. *Negotiation and Conflict Management Research, 3*, 179–204.

Nichols, M. P. (2009). *The lost art of listening: How learning to listen can improve relationships* (2nd ed.). New York: Guilford Press.

Nichols, R. G. (1948). Factors in listening comprehension. *Speech Monographs, 1*, 154–163.

Nie, N. H. (2001). Sociability, interpersonal relations, and the Internet. *American Behavioral Scientist, 45*, 420–435.

Nie, N. H., & Erbring, L. (2000, February 17). *Internet and society: A preliminary report*. Stanford, CA: Stanford Institute for the Quantitative Study of Society (SIQSS). Retrieved from http://www.stanford.edu/group/siqss/Press_Release/Preliminary_Report.pdf

Noakes, M. A., & Rinaldi, C. M. (2006). Age and gender differences in peer conflict. *Journal of Youth and Adolescence, 35*, 881–891.

Noller, P. (1995). Parent-adolescent relationships. In M. A. Fitzpatrick & A. L. Vangelisti (Eds.), *Explaining family interactions* (pp. 77–111). Thousand Oaks, CA: Sage.

Noller, P. (2005). Sibling relationships in adolescence: Learning and growing together. *Personal Relationships, 12*, 1–22.

Noller, P., & Fitzpatrick, M. A. (1993). *Communication in family relationships*. Englewood Cliffs, NJ: Prentice-Hall.

Nosko, A., Wood, E., & Molema, S. (2010). All about me: Disclosure in online social networking profiles: The case of Facebook. *Computers in Human Behavior, 26*, 406–418.

Notarius, C. I., & Herrick, L. R. (1988). Listener response strategies to a distressed other. *Journal of Social and Personal Relationships, 5*, 97–108.

O'Barr, W. M. (1982). *Linguistic evidence: Language, power, and strategy in the courtroom.* New York: Academic Press.

O'Brien, J. (2005). What is real? In J. O'Brien (Ed.), *The production of reality: Essays and readings on social interaction* (4th ed.). Thousand Oaks, CA: Pine Forge Press.

Oduro-Frimpong, J. (2007). Semiotic silence: Its use as a conflict-management strategy in intimate relationships. *Semiotica, 167*, 283–308.

Oetzel, J. G. (1998). The effects of self-construals and ethnicity on self-reported conflict styles. *Communication Reports, 11*, 133–144.

Oetzel, J. G., & Ting-Toomey, S. (2003). Face concerns in interpersonal conflict: A cross-cultural empirical test of the face negotiation theory. *Communication Research, 30*, 599–625.

Officer, S. A., & Rosenfeld, L. B. (1985). Self-disclosure to male and female coaches by high school female athletes. *Journal of Sport Psychology, 7*, 360–370.

Ogden, C. K., & Richards, I. A. (1923). *The meaning of meaning.* New York: Harcourt Brace.

Ohse, D. M., & Stockdale, M. S. (2008). Age comparisons in workplace sexual harassment perceptions. *Sex Roles, 59*, 240–253.

Olson, D. H. (2000). Circumplex model of marital and family systems. *Journal of Family Therapy, 22*(2), 144–167.

Olson, D. H., & Lavee, Y. (1989). Family systems and family stress: A family life cycle perspective. In K. Kreppner & R. M. Lerner (Eds.), *Family systems and life-span development* (pp. 165–195). Hillsdale, NJ: Erlbaum.

Olson, L. N. (2002). "As ugly and painful as it was, it was effective." Individuals' unique assessment of communication competence during aggressive conflict episodes. *Communication Studies, 53*, 171–188.

Olson, L. N. (2003). "From lace teddies to flannel PJ's": An analysis of males' experience and expressions of love. *Qualitative Research Reports in Communication, 4*, 38–44.

Olson, L. N., & Braithwaite, D. O. (2004). "If you hit me again, I'll hit you back": Conflict management strategies of individuals experiencing aggression during conflicts. *Communication Studies, 55*, 271–285.

O'Meara, D. (1989). Cross-sex friendship: Four basic challenges of an ignored relationship. *Sex Roles, 21*, 525–543.

O'Neill, O. A. (2009). Workplace expression of emotions and escalation of commitment. *Journal of Applied Social Psychology, 39*, 2396–2424.

Oosterwijk, S., Rotteveel, M., Fischer, A. H., & Hess, U. (2009). Embodied emotion concepts: How generating words about pride and disappointment influences posture. *European Journal of Social Psychology, 39*, 457–466.

Orbe, M. P., & Everett, M. A. (2006). Interracial and interethnic conflict and communication in the United States. In J. G. Oetzel & S. Ting-Toomey (Eds.), *The Sage handbook of conflict communication* (pp. 575–626). Thousand Oaks, CA: Sage.

Orbe, M. P., & Groscurth, C. R. (2004). A co-cultural theoretical analysis of communicating on campus and at home: Exploring the negotiation strategies of first generation college (FGC) students. *Qualitative Research Reports in Communication, 5*, 41–47.

Orbe, M. P., & Spellers, R. E. (2005). From the margins to the center: Utilizing co-cultural theory in diverse contexts. In W. B. Gudykunst (Ed.), *Theorizing about intercultural communication* (pp. 173–192). Thousand Oaks, CA: Sage.

Orcutt, H. K. (2006). The prospective relationship of interpersonal forgiveness and psychological distress symptoms among college women. *Journal of Counseling Psychology, 53*, 350–361.

Orman, S. (2005). *The money book for the young, fabulous, and broke.* New York: Riverhead.

Ortony, A., & Turner, T. J. (1990). What's basic about basic emotions? *Psychological Review, 97*, 315–331.

Osterman, K. (2001). Students' need for belonging in the school community. *Review of Educational Research, 70*, 323–367.

O'Sullivan, P. B. (2000). What you don't know won't hurt me: Impression management functions of communication channels in relationships. *Human Communication Research, 26*, 403–431.

O'Sullivan, P. B., & Flanagin, A. J. (2003). Reconceptualizing "flaming" and other problematic messages. *New Media and Society, 5,* 69–94.

Overall, N. C., & Sibley, C. G. (2008). Attachment and attraction toward romantic partners versus relevant alternatives within daily interactions. *Personality and Individual Differences, 44,* 1126–1137.

Pachankis, J. E. (2007). The psychological implications of concealing a stigma: A cognitive-affective-behavioral model. *Psychological Bulletin, 133,* 328–345.

Pahl, S., & Eiser, J. R. (2007). How malleable is comparative self-positivity? The effects of manipulating judgmental focus and accessibility. *European Journal of Social Psychology, 37,* 617–627.

Pal, G. C. (2007). Is there a universal self-serving attribution bias? *Psychological Studies, 52,* 85–89.

Paleari, F. G., Regalia, C., & Fincham, F. D. (2009). Measuring offence-specific forgiveness in marriage: The Marital Offence-Specific Forgiveness Scale (MOFS). *Psychological Assessment, 21,* 194–209.

Palmer, M. T., & Simmons, K. B. (1995). Communicating intentions through nonverbal behaviors: Conscious and nonconscious encoding of liking. *Human Communication Research, 22,* 128–160.

Palomares, N. A. (2008). Explaining gender-based language use: Effects of gender identity salience on references to emotion and tentative language in intra- and intergroup contexts. *Human Communication Research, 34,* 263–286.

Palombo, J. (2006). *Nonverbal learning disabilities: A clinical perspective.* New York: W. W. Norton.

Pam, A., & Pearson, J. (1998). *Splitting up: Enmeshment and estrangement in the process of divorce.* New York: Guilford Press.

Panksepp, J. (2007). Criteria for basic emotions: Is DISGUST a primary "emotion"? *Cognition & Emotion, 21,* 1819–1828.

Papadakis, M. (2003). Data on family and the Internet: What do we know and how do we know it. In J. Turow & A. L. Kavanaugh (Eds.), *The wired homestead* (pp. 121–140). Cambridge, MA: MIT Press.

Parisse, C. (2005). New perspectives on language development and the innateness of grammatical knowledge. *Language Sciences, 27,* 383–401.

Park, H. S., Levine, T. R., McCornack, S. A., Morrison, K., & Ferrara, M. (2002). How people really detect lies. *Communication Monographs, 69,* 144–157.

Parker-Pope, T. (2010). *For better: The science of a good marriage.* New York: Dutton.

Parks, J. B., & Roberton, M. A. (2000). Development and validation of an instrument to measure attitudes toward sexist/nonsexist language. *Sex Roles, 42,* 415–438.

Parks, J. B., & Roberton, M. A. (2008). Generation gaps in attitudes toward sexist/nonsexist language. *Journal of Language & Social Psychology, 27,* 276–283.

Parton, S., Siltanen, S. A., Hosman, L. A., & Langenderfer, J. (2002). Employment interviews outcomes and speech style effects. *Journal of Language and Social Psychology, 21,* 144–161.

Pasupathi, M., Stallworth, L. M., & Murdoch, K. (1998). How what we tell becomes what we know: Listener effects on speakers' long-term memory for events. *Discourse Processes, 26,* 1–25.

Pausch, R. (2008). *The last lecture.* New York: Hyperion.

Pawlowski, D. R. (1998). Dialectical tensions in marital partners' accounts of their relationships. *Communication Quarterly, 46,* 396–416.

Pearce, W. B. (2005). The Coordinated Management of Meaning (CMM). In W. B. Gudykunst (Ed.), *Theorizing about intercultural communication* (pp. 35–54). London: Sage.

Pearce, W. B., & Cronen, V. (1980). *Communication, action, and meaning.* New York: Praeger.

Pearson, J. C. (2000). Positive distortion: "The most beautiful woman in the world." In K. M. Galvin & P. J. Cooper (Eds.), *Making connections: Readings in relational communication* (2nd ed., pp. 184–190). Los Angeles: Roxbury.

Pennebaker, J. (2004). *Writing to heal: A guided journal for recovering from trauma and emotional upheaval.* Oakland, CA: New Harbinger.

Pennebaker, J. W. (1997). *Opening up: The healing power of expressing emotions* (Rev. ed.). New York: Guilford Press.

Pennebaker, J. W., Rime, B., & Blankenship, V. E. (1996). Stereotypes of emotional expressiveness of northerners and southerners: A cross-cultural test of Montesquieu's hypotheses. *Journal of Personality and Social Psychology, 70,* 372–380.

Pentok-Voak, I. S., Cahill, S., Pound, N., Kempe, V., Schaeffler, S., & Schaeffler, F. (2007). Male facial attractiveness, perceived personality, and child-directed speech. *Evolution and Human Behavior, 28*(4), 253–259.

Peper, M. (2000). Awareness of emotions: A neuropsychological perspective. In R. D. Ellis & N. Newton (Eds.), *The caldron of consciousness: Motivation, affect and self-organization—An anthology* (pp. 243–269). Philadelphia: John Benjamins.

Peterson, C. (2006). *A primer in positive psychology.* New York: Oxford University Press.

Petronio, S. (2000). The boundaries of privacy: Praxis of everyday life. In S. Petronio (Ed.), *Balancing the secrets of private disclosures* (pp. 37–49). Mahwah, NJ: Erlbaum.

Petronio, S. (2002). *Boundaries of privacy: Dialectics of disclosure.* Albany, NY: State University of New York Press.

Petronio, S. (2007). Translational research endeavors and the practices of communication privacy management. *Journal of Applied Communication Research, 35,* 218–222.

Petronio, S., & Durham, W. T. (2008). Communication privacy management theory. In L. A. Baxter & D. O. Braithewaite, (Eds.), *Engaging theories in interpersonal communication: Multiple perspectives* (pp. 309–322). Thousand Oaks, CA: Sage.

Pflug, J. (2011). Contextuality and computer-mediated communication: A cross cultural comparison. *Computers in Human Behavior, 27,* 131–137.

Piaget, J. (1952). *The origins of intelligence in children.* New York: International Universities Press.

Piercey, M. (2000). Sexism in the English language. *TESL Canada Journal/La revue TESL du Canada, 17*(2), 110–115.

Pilgeram, R. (2007). "Ass-kicking" women: Doing and undoing gender in a US livestock auction. *Gender, Work and Organization, 14,* 572–595.

Planalp, S. (1998). Communicating emotion in everyday life: Cues, channels, and processes. In P. A. Anderson & L. A. Guerrero (Eds.), *Handbook of communication and emotion: Research, theory, applications, and contexts* (pp. 29–48). San Diego, CA: Academic Press.

Planalp, S., Fitness, J., & Fehr, B. (2006). Emotion in theories of close relationships. In A. L. Vangelisti & D. Perlman (Eds.), *The Cambridge handbook of personal relationships* (pp. 369–384). New York: Cambridge University Press.

Plax, T. G., & Rosenfeld, L. B. (1979). Receiver differences and the comprehension of spoken messages. *Journal of Experimental Education, 48,* 23–28.

Plutchik, R. (1984). Emotions: A general psychoevolutionary theory. In K. R. Scherer & P. Ekman (Eds.), *Approaches to emotion* (pp. 197–219). Hillsdale, NJ: Erlbaum.

Pollack, W. (1999). *Real boys: Rescuing our sons from the myths of boyhood.* New York: Owl Books.

Powell, J. (1969). *Why am I afraid to tell you who I am?* Niles, IL: Argus Communications.

Powers, W. G., & Witt, P. L. (2008). Expanding the theoretical framework of communication fidelity. *Communication Quarterly, 56,* 247–267.

Prager, K. J., & Buhrmester, D. (1998). Intimacy and need fulfillment in couple relationships. *Journal of Social and Personal Relationships, 15,* 435–469.

Pratt, L., Wiseman, R. L., Cody, M. J., & Wendt, P. F. (1999). Interrogative strategies and information exchange in computer-mediated communication. *Communication Quarterly, 47,* 46–66.

Precht, K. (2008). Sex similarities and differences in stance in informal American conversation. *Journal of Sociolinguistics, 12,* 89–111.

Prentice, C. M., & Kramer, M. W. (2006). Dialectical tensions in the classroom: Managing tensions through communication. *Southern Communication Journal, 71,* 339–361.

Prentice, W. E. (2005). *Therapeutic modalities in rehabilitation.* New York: McGraw-Hill.

Preparing the workers of today for the jobs of tomorrow. (2009, July). Executive Office of the President, Council of Economic Advisors.

Priest, P. J., & Dominick, J. R. (1994). Pulp pulpits: Self-disclosure on "Donahue." *Journal of Communication, 44,* 74–97.

Proctor, R. F. (1989). Responsibility or egocentrism? The paradox of owned messages. *Speech Association of Minnesota Journal, 26,* 57–69.

Proctor, R. F., & Wilcox, J. R. (1993). An exploratory analysis of responses to owned messages in interpersonal communication. *ETC: A Review of General Semantics, 50,* 201–220.

Putnam, R. D. (2000). *Bowling alone.* New York: Touchstone.

Quartana, P. J., & Burns, J. W. (2010). Emotion suppression affects cardiovascular responses to initial and subsequent laboratory stressors. *British Journal of Health Psychology, 15,* 511–528.

Quinto-Pozos, D. (2008). Sign language contact and interference: ASL and LSM. *Language in Society, 37,* 161–189.

Quist, P., & Jørgensen, J. N. (2010). Crossing-negotiating social boundaries. In D. Matsumoto (Ed.), *APA handbook of intercultural communication* (pp. 169–185). Washington, DC: American Psychological Association.

Rabby, M. K. (2007). Relational maintenance and the influence of commitment in online and offline relationships. *Communication Studies, 58,* 315–337.

Rabby, M. K., & Walther, J. B. (2003). Computer-mediated communication effects on relationship formation and maintenance. In D. J. Canary & M. Dainton (Eds.), *Maintaining relationships through communication: Relational, contextual, and cultural variations* (pp. 141–162). Mahwah, NJ: Erlbaum.

Radmacher, K., & Azmitia, M. (2006). Are there gendered pathways to intimacy in early adolescents' and emerging adults' friendships? *Journal of Adolescent Research, 21,* 415–448.

Ragins, B. R. (2008). Disclosure disconnects: Antecedents and consequences of disclosing invisible stigmas across life domains. *The Academy of Management Review, 33,* 194–215.

Ragins, B. R., & Singh, R. (2007). Making the invisible visible: Fear and disclosure of sexual orientation at work. *Journal of Applied Psychology, 92,* 1103–1118.

Raider, E., Coleman, S., & Gerson, J. (2006). Teaching conflict resolution skills in a workshop. In M. Deutsch, P. T. Coleman, & E. C. Marcus (Eds.), *The handbook of conflict resolution: Theory and practice* (2nd ed., pp. 695–725). Hoboken, NJ: Wiley.

Rakow, L. F. (1992). Don't hate me because I'm beautiful. *Southern Communication Journal, 57,* 132–142.

Ramirez, A., & Zhang, S. (2007). When online meets offline: The effect of modality switching on relational communication. *Communication Monographs, 74,* 287–310.

Ramirez-Ponce, A. I. (2005). The influence of social support on the well-being of Latinas living in poverty. *Dissertation Abstracts International: Section A. Humanities and Social Sciences, 65*(9-A), 3572.

Rancer, A. S., & Avtgis, T. A. (2006). *Argumentative and aggressive communication: Theory, research, and application.* Thousand Oaks, CA: Sage.

Rancer, A. S., Kosberg, R. L., & Baukus, R. A. (1992). Beliefs about arguing as predictors of trait argumentativeness: Implications for training in argument and conflict management. *Communication Education, 41,* 375–387.

Raskin, R., & Shaw, R. (1988). Narcissism and the use of personal pronouns. *Journal of Personality, 56,* 393–404.

Rawlins, W. K. (1992). *Friendship matters: Communication, dialectics, and the life course.* New York: Aldine De Gruyter.

Redmond, M. V. (1989). The functions of empathy (decentering) in human relations. *Human Relations, 42,* 593–605.

Redmond, M. V. (1995). Interpersonal communication: Definitions and conceptual approaches. In M. V. Redmond (Ed.), *Interpersonal communication: Readings in theory and research* (pp. 4–27). Fort Worth, TX: Harcourt Brace.

Reeves, T., Horne, S. G., Rostosky, S. S., Riggle, E. D. B., Baggett, L. R., & Aycock, R. A. (2010). Family members' support for GLBT issues: The role of family adaptability and cohesion. *Journal of GLBT Family Studies, 6,* 80–97.

Rehman, U. S., & Holtzworth-Munroe, A. (2007). A cross-cultural examination of the relation of marital communication behavior to marital satisfaction. *Journal of Family Psychology, 21,* 759–763.

Reid, L. D., & Foels, R. (2010). Cognitive complexity and the perception of subtle racism. *Basic and Applied Social Psychology, 32,* 291–301.

Reid, S. A., & Ng, S. H. (1999). Language, power, and intergroup relations. *Journal of Social Issues, 55*, 119–139.

Reissman, C. K. (1990). *Divorce talk: Women and men make sense of personal relationships.* New Brunswick, NJ: Rutgers University Press.

Renner, K.-H., & Schütz, A. (2008). The psychology of personal web sites. In S. Kelsey & K. Amant (Eds.), *Handbook of research on computer mediated communication* (Vols. 1–2, pp. 267–282). Hershey, PA: Information Science Reference/IGI Global.

Reyes, A. (2005). Appropriation of African American slang by Asian American youth. *Journal of Sociolinguistics, 9*, 509–532.

Reynolds, D. (2007). Restraining Golem and harnessing Pygmalion in the classroom: A laboratory study of managerial expectations and task design. *Academy of Management Learning & Education, 6*, 475–483.

Reznik, R. M., & Roloff, M. E. (2011). Getting off to a bad start: The relationship between communication during an initial episode of a serial argument and argument frequency. *Communication Studies, 62*, 291–306.

Rheingold, H. (1988). *They have a word for it.* New York: Tarcher/Putnam.

Richards, I. A. (1948). Emotive meaning again. *Philosophical Review, 57*, New York, 145–157.

Richman, J. (2002, September 16). The news journal of the life scientist. *The Scientist, 16*, 42.

Richmond, V., Gorham, J. S., & Furio, B. J. (1987). Affinity-seeking communication in collegiate female-male relationships. *Communication Quarterly, 35*, 334–348.

Richmond, V. P., & McCroskey, J. C. (2000). The impact of supervisor and subordinate immediacy on relational and organizational outcomes. *Communication Monographs, 67*, 85–95.

Richmond, V. P., McCroskey, J. C., & Johnson, A. D. (2003). Development of the Nonverbal Immediacy Scale (NIS): Measures of self- and other-perceived nonverbal immediacy. *Communication Quarterly, 51*, 504–517.

Rick, S. I., Small, D. A., & Finkel, E. J. (2011). Fatal (fiscal) attraction: Spendthrifts and tightwads in marriage. *Journal of Marketing Research, 48*, 228–237.

Ridley, C. A., Wilhelm, M. S., & Surra, C. A. (2001). Married couples' conflict responses and marital quality. *Journal of Social and Personal Relationships, 18*, 517–534.

Rifkin, J. (2009). The empathic civilization: The race to global consciousness in a world in crisis. New York: Tarcher.

Riggio, H. R., & Kwong, W. Y. (2009). Social skills, paranoid thinking, and social outcomes among young adults. *Personality and Individual Differences, 47*, 492–497.

Riggio, R. E. (2006). Nonverbal skills and abilities. In V. Manusov & M. L. Patterson (Eds.), *The Sage handbook of nonverbal communication* (pp. 79–95). Thousand Oaks, CA: Sage.

Riggio, R. E., & Friedman, H. S. (1983). Individual differences and cues to deception. *Journal of Personality and Social Psychology, 45*, 899–915.

Righetti, F., Rusbult, C., & Finkenauer, C. (2010). Regulatory focus and the Michelangelo phenomenon: How close partners promote one another's ideal selves. *Journal of Experimental Social Psychology, 46*, 972–985.

Rill, L., Baiocchi, E., Hopper, M., Denker, K., & Olson, L. N. (2009). Exploration of the relationship between self-esteem, commitment, and verbal aggressiveness in romantic dating relationships. *Communication Reports, 22*, 102–113.

Rittenour, C. E., Myers, S. A., & Brann, M. (2007). Commitment and emotional closeness in the sibling relationship. *Southern Communication Journal, 72*, 169–183.

Ritts, V., Patterson, M. L., & Tubbs, M. E. (1992). Expectations, impressions, and judgments of physically attractive students: A review. *Review of Educational Research, 62*, 413–426.

Roach, K. D. (1997). Effects of graduate teaching assistant attire on student learning, misbehaviors, and ratings of instruction. *Communication Quarterly, 45*, 125–141.

Robbins, J. E., & Rosenfeld, L. B. (2001). Athletes' perceptions of social support provided by their head coach, assistant coach, and athletic trainer, pre-injury and during rehabilitation. *Journal of Sport Behavior, 24*, 277–297.

Roberto, A. J., Carlyle, K. E., & Goodall, C. E. (2007). Communication and corporal punishment:

The relationship between self-report parent verbal and physical aggression. *Communication Research Reports, 24,* 103–111.

Robins, R. W., Mendelsohn, G. A., Connell, J. B., & Kwan, V. S. Y. (2004). Do people agree about the causes of behavior? A social relations analysis of behavior ratings and causal attributions. *Journal of Personality and Social Psychology, 86,* 334–344.

Robinshaw, H. (2007). Acquisition of hearing, listening and speech skills by and during key stage 1. *Early Child Development and Care, 177,* 661–678.

Robinson, W. P., Shepherd, A., & Heywood, J. (1998). Truth, equivocation/concealment, and lies in job applications and doctor-patient communication. *Journal of Language and Social Psychology, 17,* 149–164.

Rochat, P. (2001). Origins of self-concept. In G. Bremner & A. Fogel (Eds.), *Blackwell handbook of infant development* (pp. 191–212). Malden. MA: Blackwell.

Rochman, G. M., & Diamond, G. M. (2008). From unresolved anger to sadness: Identifying physiological correlates. *Journal of Counseling Psychology, 55,* 96–105.

Rochmis, J. (2000). Study: Humans do many things. *Wired* (online). Retrieved from http://www.wired.com/culture/lifestyle/news/2000/02/34387

Rockwell, P. (2007a). The effects of cognitive complexity and communication apprehension on the expression and recognition of sarcasm. In A. M. Columbus (Ed.), *Advances in psychology research* (Vol. 49, pp. 185–196). Hauppauge, NY: Nova Science Publishers.

Rockwell, P. (2007b). Vocal features of conversational sarcasm: A comparison of methods. *Journal of Psycholinguistic Research, 36,* 361–369.

Rodero, E. (2011). Intonation and emotion: Influence of pitch levels and contour type on creating emotions. *Journal of Voice, 25*(1), 25–34.

Rodriguez, H. P., Rodday, A. C., Marshall, R. E., Nelson, K. L., Rogers, W. H., & Safran, D. G. (2008). Relation of patients' experiences with individual physicians to malpractice risk. *International Journal for Quality in Health Care, 20,* 5–12.

Rogers, L. E. (2001). Relational communication in the context of family. *Journal of Family Communication, 1,* 25–35.

Roloff, M. E., Janiszewski, C. A., McGrath, M. A., Burns, C. S., & Manrai, L. A. (1988). Acquiring resources from intimates: When obligation substitutes for persuasion. *Human Communication Research, 14,* 364–396.

Romaine, S. (1999). *Communicating gender.* Mahwah, NJ: Erlbaum.

Rose, A. J., Carlson, W., & Waller, E. M. (2007). Prospective associations of co-rumination with friendship and emotional adjustment: Considering the socioemotional trade-offs of co-rumination. *Developmental Psychology, 43,* 1019–1031.

Rosenfeld, L. B. (1979). Self-disclosure avoidance: Why I am afraid to tell you who I am. *Communication Monographs, 46,* 63–74.

Rosenfeld, L. B. (2000). Overview of the ways privacy, secrecy, and disclosure are balanced in today's society. In S. Petronio (Ed.), *Balancing the secrets of private disclosures* (pp. 3–17). Mahwah, NJ: Erlbaum.

Rosenfeld, L. B., & Bowen, G. L. (1991). Marital disclosure and marital satisfaction: Direct-effect versus interaction-effect models. *Western Journal of Speech Communication, 55,* 69–84.

Rosenfeld, L. B., & Richman, J. M. (1999). Supportive communication and school outcomes: Part II. Academically at-risk low income high school students. *Communication Education, 48,* 294–307.

Rosenthal, R., & Jacobson, L. (1968). *Pygmalion in the classroom.* New York: Holt, Rinehart & Winston.

Ross, J. B., & McLaughlin, M. M. (Eds.). (1949). *A portable medieval reader.* New York: Viking.

Ruben, B. D. (1989). The study of cross-cultural competence: Traditions and contemporary issues. *International Journal of Intercultural Relationships, 13,* 229–240.

Rubin, L. B. (1983). *Intimate strangers.* San Francisco: Harper & Row.

Rubin, L. B. (1985). *Just friends: The role of friendship in our lives.* New York: Harper & Row.

Rubin, R. B., & Graham, E. E. (1988). Communication correlates of college success: An exploratory investigation. *Communication Education, 37*, 14–27.

Rubin, R. B., Perse, E. M., & Barbato, C. A. (1988). Conceptualization and measurement of interpersonal communication motives. *Human Communication Research, 14*, 602–628.

Rusbult, C. E., Finkel, E. J., & Kumashiro, M. (2009). The Michelangelo phenomenon. *Current Directions in Psychological Science, 18*(6), 305–309.

Rusbult, C. E., & Van Lange, P. A. M. (1996). Interdependence processes. In E. T. Higgins & A. W. Kruglanski (Eds.), *Social psychology: Handbook of basic principles* (pp. 564–596). New York: Guilford Press.

Rymer, R. (1993). *Genie: An abused child's flight from silence.* New York: HarperCollins.

Sadalla, E. (1987). Identity and symbolism in housing. *Environment and Behavior, 19*, 569–587.

Sagarian, E. (1976, March). The high cost of wearing a label. *Psychology Today, 10*, 25–27.

Sager, K. L. (2008). An exploratory study of the relationships between Theory X/Y assumptions and superior communicator style. *Management Communication Quarterly, 22*, 288–312.

Sahlstein, E. (2004). Relational maintenance research: A review of reviews. *PsycCRITIQUES, 49*(Suppl. 14), np. Retrieved from http://www.apa.org

Sahlstein, E., & Dun, T. (2008). "I wanted time to myself and he wanted to be together all the time": Constructing breakups as managing autonomy-connection. *Qualitative Research Reports in Communication, 9*, 37–45.

Salimi, S.-H., Mirzamani, S.-H., & Shahiri-Tabarestani, M. (2005). Association of parental self-esteem and expectations with adolescents' anxiety about career and education. *Psychological Reports, 96*, 569–578.

Salimkhan, G., Manago, A., & Greenfield, P. (2010). The construction of the virtual self on MySpace. *Cyberpsychology: Journal of Psychosocial Research on Cyberspace, 4*, article 1. Retrieved from http://cyberpsychology.eu/view.php?cisloclanku=2010050203&article=1

Samovar, L. A., & Porter, R. E. (2004). *Communication between cultures* (5th ed.). Belmont, CA: Wadsworth.

Samovar, L. A., Porter R. E., & McDaniel, E. R. (2007). *Communication between cultures* (6th ed.). Belmont, CA: Wadsworth.

Samovar, L. A., Porter R. E., & McDaniel, E. R. (2010). *Communication between cultures* (7th ed.). Belmont, CA: Wadsworth.

Samp, J. A., & Monahan, J. L. (2007). Expressing under the influence: Alcohol consumption, nonverbal behavior, and performance. *Communication Research Reports, 24*, 79–86.

Samp, J. A., & Monahan, J. L. (2009). Alcohol-influenced nonverbal behaviors during discussions about a relationship problem. *Journal of Nonverbal Behavior, 33*, 193–211.

Samp, J. A., Wittenberg, E., & Gillett, D. L. (2003). Presenting and monitoring a gender-defined self on the Internet. *Communication Research Reports, 20*, 1–12.

Samter, W., & Burleson, B. R. (2005). The role of communication in same-sex friendships: A comparison among African Americans, Asian Americans, and European Americans. *Communication Quarterly, 53*, 265–283.

Samter, W., & Cupach, W. R. (1998). Friendly fire: Topical variations in conflict among same- and cross-sex friends. *Communication Studies, 49*, 121–138.

Sanchez-Burks, J., Bartel, C. A., & Blount, S. (2009). Performance in intercultural interactions at work: Cross-cultural differences in response to behavioral mirroring. *Journal of Applied Psychology, 94*, 216–223.

Sandel, T. L. (2004). Narrated relationships: Mothers-in-law and daughters-in-law justifying conflicts in Taiwan's Chhan-chng. *Research on Language and Social Interaction, 37*, 265–299.

Sanderson, C. A., & Karetsky, K. H. (2002). Intimacy goals and strategies of conflict resolution in dating relationships: A mediational analysis. *Journal of Social and Personal Relationships, 19*, 317–337.

Sanford, A. A. (2010). "I can air my feelings instead of eating them": Blogging as social support for the morbidly obese. *Communication Studies, 61*, 567–584.

Santilli, V., & Miller, A. N. (2011). The effects of gender and power distance on nonverbal immediacy in symmetrical and asymmetrical power conditions: A cross-cultural study of classrooms and friendships. *Journal of International & Intercultural Communication, 4,* 3–22.

Sapadin, L. A. (1988). Friendship and gender: Perspectives of professional men and women. *Journal of Social and Personal Relationships, 5,* 387–403.

Sargent, J. (2002). Topic avoidance: Is this the way to a more satisfying relationship? *Communication Research Reports, 19,* 175–182.

Savin-Williams, R. C. (2001). *Mom, dad. I'm gay. How families negotiate coming out.* Washington, DC: American Psychological Association.

Schachter, S. (1959). *The psychology of affiliation.* Stanford, CA: Stanford University Press.

Schaefer, M. T., & Olson, D. H. (1981). Assessing intimacy: The PAIR Inventory. *Journal of Marital and Family Therapy, 7,* 47–60.

Scharlott, B. W., & Christ, W. G. (1995). Overcoming relationship-initiation barriers: The impact of a computer-dating system on sex role, shyness, and appearance inhibitions. *Computers in Human Behavior, 11,* 191–204.

Schiefenhövel, W. (1997). Universals in interpersonal interactions. In U. C. Segerstråle & P. Molnár (Eds.), *Nonverbal communication: Where nature meets culture* (pp. 61–85). Hillsdale, NJ: Erlbaum.

Schmidt, J. J. (2006). *Social and cultural foundations of counseling and human services: Multiple influences on self-concept development.* Boston: Pearson/Allyn and Bacon.

Scholz, M. (2005, June). A "simple" way to improve adherence. *RN, 68,* 82.

Schotter, E. R., Berry, R. W., McKenzie, C. R. M., & Rayner, K. (2010). Gaze bias: Selective encoding and liking effects. *Visual Cognition, 18,* 1113–1132.

Schrodt, P. (2005). Family communication schemata and the Circumplex Model of family functioning. *Western Journal of Communication, 69,* 359–376.

Schrodt, P., Turman, P. D., & Soliz, J. (2006). Perceived understanding as a mediator of perceived teacher confirmation and students' ratings of instruction. *Communication Education, 55,* 370–388.

Schubert, T. W., & Koole, S. L. (2009). The embodied self: Making a fist enhances men's power-related self-conceptions. *Journal of Experimental Social Psychology, 45,* 828–834.

Schütz, A. (1999). It was your fault! Self-serving biases in autobiographical accounts of conflicts in married couples. *Journal of Social and Personal Relationships, 16,* 193–208.

Scott, C., & Myers, K. K. (2005). The socialization of emotion: Learning emotion management at the fire station. *Journal of Applied Communication Research, 33,* 67–92.

Scott, G. G. (2010). *Playing the lying game: Detecting and dealing with lies and liars, from occasional fibbers to frequent fabricators.* Santa Barbara, CA: Praeger.

Scudder, J. N., & Andrews, P. H. (1995). A comparison of two alternative models of powerful speech: The impact of power and gender upon the use of threats. *Communication Research Reports, 12,* 25–33.

Seabrook, J. (1994, June 6). My first flame. *New Yorker, 71,* 70–79.

Sedikides, C., Campbell, W. K., Reeder, G. D., & Elliot, A. J. (1998). The self-serving bias in relational context. *Journal of Personality and Social Psychology, 74,* 378–386.

Sedikides, C., & Skowronski, J. J. (1995). On the sources of self-knowledge: The perceived primacy of self-reflection. *Journal of Social and Clinical Psychology, 14,* 244–270.

Segrin, C. (1993). The effects of nonverbal behavior on outcomes of compliance gaining attempts. *Communication Studies, 44,* 169–187.

Segrin, C., Hanzal, A., & Domschke, T. J. (2009). Accuracy and bias in newlywed couples' perceptions of conflict styles and the association with marital satisfaction. *Communication Monographs, 76,* 207–233.

Seider, B. H., Hirschberger, G., Nelson, K. L., & Levenson, R. W. (2009). We can work it out: Age differences in relational pronouns, physiology, and behavior in marital conflict. *Psychology and Aging, 24,* 604–613.

Self, W. R. (2009). Intercultural and nonverbal communication insights for international commercial arbitration. *Human Communication, 12,* 231–237.

Semmer, N. K., Elfering, A., Jacobshagen, N., Perrot, T., Beehr, T. A., & Boos, N. (2008). The emotional meaning of instrumental social support. *International Journal of Stress Management, 15*, 235–251.

Servaes, J. (1989). Cultural identity and modes of communication. In J. A. Anderson (Ed.), *Communication yearbook 12* (pp. 383–416). Newbury Park, CA: Sage.

Sezov, D. D. (2002). The contribution of empathy to harmony in interpersonal relationships. *Dissertation Abstracts International: Section B. The Sciences and Engineering, 63*(6-B), 3046.

Shafer, D. N. (2007). Hearing loss hinders relationships. *ASHA Leader, 12*(9), 5–7.

Shamay, S. G., Tomer, R., & Aharon-Peretz, J. (2002). Deficit in understanding sarcasm in patients with prefrontal lesion is related to impaired empathic ability. *Brain and Cognition, 48*, 558–563.

Shattuck, R. (1980). *The forbidden experiment: The story of the Wild Boy of Aveyron.* New York: Farrar, Straus & Giroux.

Shearman, S. M., Dumlao, R., & Kagawa, N. (2011). Cultural variations in accounts by American and Japanese young adults: Recalling a major conflict with parents. *Journal of Family Communication, 11*, 105–125.

Sheeks, M. S., & Birchmeier, Z. P. (2007). Shyness, sociability, and the use of computer-mediated communication in relationship development. *CyberPsychology & Behavior, 10*, 64–70.

Sheldon, P. (2010). Pressure to be perfect: Influences on college students' body esteem. *Southern Communication Journal, 75*, 277–298.

Sherman, S. M., & Dumlao, R. (2008) A cross-cultural comparison of family communication patterns and conflict between young adults and parents. *Journal of Family Communication, 8*, 186–211.

Shimanoff, S. B. (1984). Commonly named emotions in everyday conversations. *Perceptual and Motor Skills, 58*, 514.

Shimanoff, S. B. (1985). Rules governing the verbal expression of emotions between married couples. *Western Journal of Speech Communication, 49*, 149–165.

Shimanoff, S. B. (1988). Degree of emotional expressiveness as a function of face-needs, gender, and interpersonal relationship. *Communication Reports, 1*, 43–53.

Shiota, M. N., & Levenson, R. W. (2007). Birds of a feather don't always fly farthest: Similarity in big five personality predicts more negative marital satisfaction trajectories in long-term marriages. *Psychology and Aging, 22*, 666–675.

Shirley, J. A., Powers, W. G., & Sawyer, C. R. (2007). Psychologically abusive relationships and self-disclosure orientations. *Human Communication, 10*, 289–301.

Shonbeck, K. (2011). Communicating in a connected world. In K. M. Galvin (Ed.), *Making connections: Readings in relational communication* (5th ed., pp. 393–400). New York: Oxford University Press.

Shuler, S., & Sypher, B. D. (2000). Seeking emotional labor; When managing the heart enhances the work experience. *Management Communication Quarterly, 14*, 51–89.

Sieberg, E., & Larson, C. (1971, April). *Dimensions of interpersonal response.* Paper presented at the meeting of the International Communication Association, Phoenix, AZ.

Siegman, A. W., & Snow, S. C. (1997). The outward expression of anger, the inward experience of anger and CVR: The role of vocal expression. *Journal of Behavioral Medicine, 1*, 29–45.

Sigler, K., Burnett, A., & Child, J. T. (2008). A regional analysis of assertiveness. *Journal of Intercultural Communication Research, 37*, 89–104.

Sillars, A. L., Folwell, A. L., Hill, K. C., Maki, B. K., & Hurst, A. P. (1994). Marital communication and the persistence of misunderstanding. *Journal of Social and Personal Relationships, 11*, 611–617. doi:10.1177/0265407594114008

Sillars, A., Roberts, L. J., Leonard, K. E., & Dun, T. (2000). Cognition during marital conflict: The relationship of thought and talk. *Journal of Social and Personal Relationships, 17*, 479–502.

Simon, V. A., Kobielski, S. J., & Martin, S. (2008). Conflict beliefs, goals, and behavior in romantic relationships during late adolescence. *Journal of Youth and Adolescence, 37*, 324–335.

Singer, J. K., Miller, L. C., & Murphy, S. (1998, July). *Sexual harassment and memory: How repetition of behavior and personal experience relate to judgments of sexual harassment.* Paper presented at the annual conference of the International Communication Association, Jerusalem.

Singer, M. (1998). *Perception and identity in intercultural communication.* Yarmouth, ME: Intercultural Press.

Singh, M., & Woods, S. (2008). Predicting general well-being from emotional intelligence and three broad personality traits. *Journal of Applied Social Psychology, 38,* 635–646.

Singh, R., Simons, J. J. P., Young, D. P. C. Y., Sim, B. S. X., Chai, X. T., Singh, S., & Chiou, S. (2009). Trust and respect as mediators of the other- and self-profitable trait effects on interpersonal attraction. *European Journal of Social Psychology, 39,* 1021–1038.

Singleton, R. A., Jr., & Vacca, J. (2007). Interpersonal competition in friendships. *Sex Roles, 57,* 617–627.

Skowron, E., Stanley, K., & Shapiro, M. (2009). A longitudinal perspective on differentiation of self, interpersonal and psychological well-being in young adulthood. *Contemporary Family Therapy: An International Journal, 31,* 3–18.

Slatcher, R. B., Vazire, S., & Pennebaker, J. W. (2008). Am "I" more important than "we"? Couples' word use in instant messages. *Personal Relationships, 15,* 407–424.

Smith, D. E., Gier, J. A., & Willis, F. N. (1982). Interpersonal touch and compliance with a marketing request. *Basic and Applied Social Psychology, 3,* 35–38.

Smith, L., Heaven, P. C. L., & Ciarrochi, J. (2008). Trait emotional intelligence, conflict communication patterns, and relationship satisfaction. *Personality and Individual Differences, 44,* 1314–1325.

Smith, M. (2010). Hearing into being. *Women at Heart.* Retrieved from http://www.women-at-heart.com/effective-communication.html

Smith-McLallen, A., Johnson, B. T., Dovidio, J. F., & Pearson, A. R. (2006). Black and white: The role of color bias and implicit race bias. *Social Cognition, 24,* 46–73.

Snyder, M., & Klein, O. (2005). Construing and constructing others: On the reality and the generality of the behavioral confirmation scenario. *Interaction Studies, 6*(1), 53–67.

Social Security Administration. (2011). *Popular baby names.* Retrieved from http://www.ssa.gov/cgi-bin/popularnames.cgi

Solomon, D. H., & Knobloch, L. K. (2001). Relationship uncertainty, partner interference, and intimacy within dating relationships. *Journal of Social and Personal Relationships, 8,* 804–820.

Solomon, D. H., & Williams, M. L. M. (1997). Perceptions of social-sexual communication at work: The effects of message, situation, and observer characteristics on judgments of sexual harassment. *Journal of Applied Communication Research, 25,* 197–216.

Solomon, S., & Knafo, A. (2007). Value similarity in adolescent friendships. In T. C. Rhodes (Ed.), *Focus on adolescent behavior research* (pp. 133–155). Hauppauge, NY: Nova Science Publishers.

Sommer, K. L., Williams, K. D., Ciarocco, N. J., & Baumeister, R. F. (2001). When silence speaks louder than words: Explorations into the intrapsychic and interpersonal consequences of social ostracism. *Basic and Applied Social Psychology, 23*(4), 225–243.

Sommer, R. (1969). *Personal space: The behavioral basis of design.* Englewood Cliffs, NJ: Prentice-Hall.

Sommer, R. (2002). Personal space in a digital age. In R. B. Bechtel & A. Churchman (Eds.), *Handbook of environmental psychology* (pp. 647–660). New York: Wiley.

Sopow, E. (2008). The communication climate change at RCMP. *Strategic Communication Management, 12,* 20–23.

Sorensen, A. L. (2009). Developing personal competence in nursing students through international clinical practice: With emphasis on communication and empathy. *Journal of Intercultural Communication, 19,* 1–7.

Sousa, L. A. (2002). The medium is the message: The costs and benefits of writing, talking aloud, and thinking about life's triumphs and defeats.

Dissertation Abstracts International: Section B. The Sciences and Engineering, 62(7-B), 3397.

Spears, R. (2001). The interaction between the individual and the collective self: Self-categorization in context. In C. Sedikides & M. B. Brewer (Eds.), *Individual self, relational self, collective self* (pp. 171–198). New York: Psychology Press.

Speicher, H. (1999). Development and validation of intimacy capability and intimacy motivation measures. *Dissertation Abstracts International: Section B. The Sciences and Engineering 59*(9-B), 5172.

Spitzberg, B. H. (1991). An examination of trait measures of interpersonal competence. *Communication Reports, 4*, 22–29.

Spitzberg, B. H. (1994). The dark side of (in)competence. In W. R. Cupach & B. H. Spitzberg (Eds.), *The dark side of interpersonal communication* (pp. 25–50). Hillsdale, NJ: Erlbaum.

Spitzberg, B. H. (2000). What is good communication? *Journal of the Association for Communication Administration, 29*, 103–119.

Sporer, S. L., & Schwandt, B. (2007). Moderators of nonverbal indicators of deception: A meta-analytic synthesis. *Psychology, Public Policy, and Law, 13*(1), 1–34.

Sprecher, S., & Felmlee, D. (2008). Insider perspectives on attraction. In S. Sprecher, A. Wenzel, & J. Harvey (Eds.), *Handbook of relationship initiation* (pp. 297–313). New York: Psychology Press.

Stafford, L. (2008). Social exchange theories. In L. A. Baxter & D. O. Braithewaite (Eds.), *Engaging theories in interpersonal communication: Multiple perspectives* (pp. 377–389). Thousand Oaks, CA: Sage.

Stafford L., & Canary, D. J. (1991). Maintenance strategies and romantic relationship type, gender, and relational characteristics. *Journal of Social and Personal Relationships, 8*, 217–242.

Stafford, L., Dainton, M., & Haas, S. (2000). Measuring routine and strategic relational maintenance. *Communication Monographs, 67*, 306–323.

Stamp, G. H., Vangelisti, A. L., & Daly, J. A. (1992). The creation of defensiveness in social interaction. *Communication Quarterly, 40*, 177–190.

Steen, S., & Schwartz, P. (1995). Communication, gender, and power: Homosexual couples as a case study. In M. A. Fitzpatrick & A. L. Vangelisti (Eds.), *Explaining family interactions* (pp. 310–343). Thousand Oaks, CA: Sage.

Steil, L. K. (1996). Listening training: The key to success in today's organizations. In M. Purdy & D. Borisoff (Eds.), *Listening in everyday life: A personal and professional approach* (2nd ed., pp. 213–237). Lanham, MD: University Press of America.

Steinberg, L. (2010). A dual systems model of adolescent risk-taking. *Developmental Psychobiology, 52*, 216–224.

Stephens, C., & Long, N. (2000). Communication with police supervisors and peers as a buffer of work-related traumatic stress. *Journal of Organizational Behavior, 21*, 407–424.

Stephens, K. K., Houser, M. L., & Cowan, R. L. (2009). R U able to meat me: The impact of students' overly casual email messages to instructors. *Communication Education, 58*, 303–326.

Stets, J. E., & Cast, A. D. (2007). Resources and identity verification from an identity theory perspective. *Sociological Perspectives, 50*, 517–543.

Stevens, B. (2005). What communication skills do employers want? Silicon Valley recruiters respond. *Journal of Employment Counseling, 42*, 2–9.

Steves, R. (1996, May–September). Culture shock. *Europe through the Back Door Newsletter, 50*, 20.

Steves, R. (n.d.). Culture shock and wiggle room. *Rick Steves' Europe through the Back Door.* Retrieved from http://www.ricksteves.com/tms/article.cfm?id=131&extras=false

Stewart, G. L., Dustin, S. L., Barrick, M. R., & Darnold, T. C. (2008). Exploring the handshake in employment interviews. *Journal of Applied Psychology, 93*, 1139–1146.

Stewart, S., Stinnett, H., & Rosenfeld, L. B. (2000). Sex differences in desired characteristics of short-term and long-term relationship partners. *Journal of Personal and Social Relationships, 17*, 843–853.

Stier, J., & Kjellin, M. S. (2010). Communicative challenges in multinational project work:

Obstacles and tools for reaching common understandings. *Journal of Intercultural Communication, 24,* 1–12.

Stiff, J. B., Dillard, J. P., Somera, L., Kim, H., & Sleight, C. (1988). Empathy, communication, and prosocial behavior. *Communication Monographs, 55,* 198–213.

Stiles, W. B., Walz, N. C., Schroeder, M. A. B., Williams, L. L., & Ickes, W. (1996). Attractiveness and disclosure in initial encounters of mixed-sex dyads. *Journal of Social and Personal Relationships, 13,* 303–312.

Stocker, C. M., & McHale, S. M. (1992). The nature and family correlates of preadolescents' perceptions of their sibling relationships. *Journal of Social and Personal Relationships, 9,* 179–195.

Strachan, H. (2004). Communication. *Research and Theory for Nursing Practice: An International Journal, 18,* 7–10.

Straus, M. A., & Field, C. J. (2003). Psychological aggression by American parents: National data on prevalence, chronicity, and severity. *Journal of Marriage and Family, 65,* 795–808.

Street, R. L., Jr. (2003). Interpersonal communication skills in health care contexts. In B. R. Burleson & J. O. Greene (Eds.), *Handbook of communication and social interaction skills* (pp. 909–933). Mahwah, NJ: Erlbaum.

Stritzke, W. G. K., Nguyen, A., & Durkin, K. (2004). Shyness and computer-mediated communication: A self-presentational theory perspective. *Media Psychology, 6,* 1–22.

Strong, C. M. (2005). The role of exposure to media-idealized male physiques on men's body image. *Dissertation Abstracts International: Section B. The Sciences and Engineering, 65*(8-B), 4306.

Sturman, E. D., & Mongrain, M. (2008). The role of personality in defeat: A revised social rank model. *European Journal of Personality, 22,* 55–79.

Suler, J. R. (2002). Identity management in cyberspace. *Journal of Applied Psychoanalytic Studies, 4,* 455–459.

Sullins, E. S. (1991). Emotional contagion revisited: Effects of social comparison and expressive style on mood convergence. *Personality and Social Psychology Bulletin, 17,* 166–174.

Sullivan, C. F. (1996). Recipients' perceptions of support attempts across various stressful life events. *Communication Research Reports, 13,* 183–190.

Sullivan, P. (2004). Communication differences between male and female team sport athletes. *Communication Reports, 17,* 121–128.

Surinder, K. S., & Cooper, R. B. (2003). Exploring the core concepts of media richness theory: The impact of cue multiplicity and feedback immediacy on decision quality. *Journal of Management Information Systems, 20,* 263–299.

Suter, E. A., Bergen, K. M., Daas, K. L., & Durham, W. T. (2006). Lesbian couples' management of public-private dialectical contradictions. *Journal of Social & Personal Relationships, 23,* 349–365.

Suter, E. A., & Daas, K. L. (2007). Negotiating heteronormativity dialectically: Lesbian couples' display of symbols in culture. *Western Journal of Communication, 71,* 177–195.

Sutter, D. L., & Martin, M. M. (1999). Verbal aggression during disengagement of dating relationships. *Communication Research Reports, 15,* 318–326.

Sutton, R. I. (2010, June 18). Is it sometimes useful to cuss when you are at work?: The strategic use of swear words. *Psychology Today.* Retrieved from http://www.psychologytoday.com/blog/work-matters/201006/is-it-sometimes-useful-cuss-when-you-are-work

Swain, S. (1989). Covert intimacy in men's friendships: Closeness in men's friendships. In B. J. Risman & P. Schwartz (Eds.), *Gender in intimate relationships: A microstructural approach* (pp. 71–86). Belmont, CA: Wadsworth.

Swami, V., & Furnham, A. (2008). *The psychology of physical attraction.* New York: Routledge/Taylor & Francis.

Swann, W. B., Jr., Rentfrow, P. J., & Guinn, J. S. (2003). Self-verification: The search for coherence. In J. P. Tangney & M. R. Leary (Eds.), *Handbook of self and identity* (pp. 367–383). New York: Guilford Press.

Swart, H., Turner, R., Hewstone, M., & Voci, A. (2011). Achieving forgiveness and trust in postconflict societies: The importance of self-disclosure and empathy. In L. R. Tropp & R. K.

Mallett (Eds.), *Moving beyond prejudice reduction: Pathways to positive intergroup relations* (pp. 181–200). Washington, DC: American Psychological Association.

Takaku, S., Weiner, B., & Ohbuchi, K (2001). A cross-cultural examination of the effects of apology and perspective-taking on forgiveness. *Journal of Language & Social Psychology, 20,* 144–167.

Tanaka, A., Koizumi, A., Imai, H., Hiramatsu, S., Hiramoto, E., & de Gelder, B. (2010). I feel your voice: Cultural differences in the multisensory perception of emotion. *Psychological Science, 21,* 1259–1262.

Tannen, D. (1986). *That's not what I meant! How conversational style makes or breaks your relations with others.* New York: William Morrow.

Tannen, D. (1990). *You just don't understand: Women and men in conversation.* New York: William Morrow.

Tannen, D. (1994a). *Talking from 9 to 5: Women and men in the workplace: Language, sex and power.* New York: William Morrow.

Tannen, D. (1994b, May 16). Gender gap in cyberspace. *Newsweek, 125,* 52–53.

Tannen, D. (2001). But what do you mean? Women and men in conversation. In J. M. Henslin (Ed.), *Down to earth sociology: Introductory readings* (11th ed., pp. 168–173). New York: Free Press.

Tannen, D. (2003). Talking past one another: "But what do you mean?" Women and men in conversation. In J. M. Henslin (Ed.), *Down to earth sociology: Introductory readings* (12th ed., pp. 175–181). New York: Free Press.

Tashiro, T., & Frazier, P. (2003). "I'll never be in a relationship like that again": Personal growth following romantic relationship breakups. *Personal Relationships, 10,* 113–128.

Taylor, A. F., Wiley, A., Kuo, F. E., & Sullivan, W. C. (1998). Growing up in the inner city: Green spaces as places to grow. *Environment and Behavior, 30,* 3–27.

Taylor, D. A., & Altman, I. (1987). Communication in interpersonal relationships: Social penetration processes. In M. E. Roloff & G. R. Miller (Eds.), *Interpersonal processes: New directions in communication research* (pp. 257–277). Newbury Park, CA: Sage.

Taylor, S., & Mette, D. (1971). When similarity breeds contempt. *Journal of Personality and Social Psychology, 20,* 75–81.

Teven, J. J., & Comadena, M. E. (1996). The effects of office aesthetic quality on students' perceptions of teacher credibility and communicator style. *Communication Research Reports, 13,* 101–108.

Teven, J. J., Richmond, V. P., McCroskey, J. C., & McCroskey, L. L (2010). Updating relationships between communication traits and communication competence. *Communication Research Reports, 27,* 263–270.

Tezer, E., & Demir, A. (2001). Conflict behaviors toward same-sex and opposite-sex peers among male and female late adolescents. *Adolescence, 36*(143), 525–533.

Thibaut, J. W., & Kelley, H. H. (1959). *The social psychology of groups.* New York: Wiley.

Thomas, D. E., Bierman, K. L., & Powers, C. J. (2011). The influence of classroom aggression and classroom climate on aggressive–disruptive behavior. *Child Development, 82,* 751–757.

Thourlby, W. (1978). *You are what you wear.* New York: New American Library.

Tidwell, L. C., & Walther, J. B. (2002). Computer-mediated communication effects on disclosure, impressions, and interpersonal evaluations: Getting to know one another a bit at a time. *Human Communication Research, 28,* 317–348.

Timmerman, L. M. (2002). Comparing the production of power in language on the basis of sex. In M. Allen, R. W. Preiss, B. M. Gayle, & N. Burrell (Eds.), *Interpersonal communication research: Advances through meta-analysis* (pp. 73–88). Mahwah, NJ: Erlbaum.

Ting-Toomey, S. (1991). Intimacy expressions in three cultures: France, Japan, and the United States. *International Journal of Intercultural Relations, 15,* 29–46.

Ting-Toomey, S. (1999). *Communicating across cultures.* New York: Guilford Press.

Ting-Toomey, S., Oetzel, J., & Yee-Jung, K. (2001). Self-construal types and conflict management styles. *Communication Reports, 14,* 87–104.

Ting-Toomey, S., & Takai, J. (2006). Explaining intercultural conflict: Promising approaches and future directions. In J. G. Oetzel & S. Ting-Toomey (Eds.), *The Sage handbook of conflict communication* (pp. 691–723). Thousand Oaks, CA: Sage.

Todorov, A., Chaiken, S., & Henderson, M. D. (2002). The heuristic-systematic model of social information processing. In J. P. Dillard & M. Pfau (Eds.), *The persuasion handbook: Developments in theory and practice* (pp. 195–211). Thousand Oaks, CA: Sage.

Tohidian, I. (2009). Examining linguistic relativity hypothesis as one of the main views on the relationship between language and thought. *Journal of Psycholinguistic Research, 38*(1), 65–74.

Tolar, T. D., Lederberg, A. R., Gokhale, S., & Tomasello, M. (2008). The development of the ability to recognize the meaning of iconic signs. *Journal of Deaf Studies and Deaf Education, 13*(1), 71–86.

Tolhuizen, J. H. (1989). Communication strategies for intensifying dating relationships: Identification, use and structure. *Journal of Social and Personal Relationships, 6,* 413–434.

Toller, P. (2011). Bereaved parents' experiences of supportive and unsupportive communication. *Southern Communication Journal, 76,* 17–34.

Toma, C., & Hancock, J. (2009, May) *Self-presentation in online dating profiles: The role of physical attractiveness.* Paper presented at the Annual Meeting of the International Communication Association, Chicago.

Toma, C. L., Hancock, J. T., & Ellison, N. B. (2008). Separating fact from fiction: An examination of deceptive self-presentation in online dating profiles. *Personality and Social Psychology Bulletin, 34,* 1023–1036.

Tong, S. T., & Walther, J. B. (2011a). Just say "No thanks": The effects of romantic rejection across computer-mediated communication. *Journal of Personal and Social Relationships, 28,* 488–506.

Tong, S. T., & Walther, J. B. (2011b). Relational maintenance and computer-mediated communication. In K. B. Wright & L. M. Webb (Eds.), *Computer mediated communication and personal relationships* (pp. 98–118). New York: Peter Lang.

Tracy, L. (1991). *The secret between us: Competition among women.* Boston: Little, Brown.

Tracy, S. J. (2002). When questioning turns to face threat: An interactional sensitivity in 911 call-taking. *Western Journal of Communication, 66,* 129–157.

Tracy, S. J. (2005). Locking up emotion: Moving beyond dissonance for understanding emotion labor discomfort. *Communication Monographs, 72,* 261–283.

Trees, A. R., Kerssen-Griefp, J., & Hess, J. A. (2009). Earning influence by communicating respect: Facework's contributions to effective instructional feedback. *Communication Education, 58,* 397–416.

Triandis, H. C. (1975). Culture training, cognitive complexity and interpersonal attitudes. In R. Brislin, S. Bichner, & W. Lonner (Eds.), *Cross-cultural perspectives on learning* (pp. 39–77). New York: Wiley.

Triandis, H. C. (1990). Cross-cultural studies of individualism and collectivism. In J. Berman (Ed.), *Nebraska symposium on motivation* (pp. 41–133). Lincoln: University of Nebraska Press.

Triandis, H. C. (1994). *Culture and social behavior.* New York: McGraw-Hill.

Triandis, H. C. (1995). *Individualism and collectivism.* Boulder, CO: Westview.

Tripp, G., Schaughency, E. A., Lanlands, R., & Mouat, K. (2007). Family interactions in children with and without ADHD. *Journal of Child and Family Studies, 16,* 385–400.

Trosset, C. (1998, September/October). Obstacles to open discussion and critical thinking: The Grinnell College study. *Change Magazine, 30,* 44–49.

Tsang, J.-A. (2006). The effects of helper intention on gratitude and indebtedness. *Motivation and Emotion, 30,* 199–205.

Tseung, C. N., & Schott, G. (2004). The quality of sibling relationship during late adolescence: Are there links with other significant relationships? *Psychological Studies, 49,* 20–30.

Tuckett, A. G. (2005). The care encounter: Pondering caring, honest communication and control. *International Journal of Nursing Practice, 11*(2), 77–84.

Turk, D. R., & Monahan, J. L. (1999). "Here I go again": An examination of repetitive behaviors during interpersonal conflicts. *Southern Communication Journal, 64,* 232–244.

Turkle, S. (1996, January). Who am we? *Wired, 4,* 149–152, 194–199.

Turkle, S. (2011). *Alone together: Why we expect more from technology and less from each other.* New York: Basic Books.

Turman, P. D. (2008). Coaches' immediacy behaviors as predictors of athletes' perceptions of satisfaction and team cohesion. *Western Journal of Communication, 72,* 162–179.

Turnage, A. K. (2007). Email flaming behaviors and organizational conflict. *Journal of Computer-Mediated Communication, 13*(1), 43–59.

Turner, R. E., Edgely, C., & Olmstead, G. (1975). Information control in conversation: Honesty is not always the best policy. *Kansas Journal of Sociology, 11,* 69–89.

Turnley, W. H., & Bolino, M. C. (2001). Achieving desired images while avoiding undesired images: Exploring the role of the self-monitoring in impression management. *Journal of Applied Psychology, 86,* 351–360.

Tuval-Mashiach, R., & Shulman, S. (2006). Resolution of disagreements between romantic partners, among adolescents, and young adults: Qualitative analysis of interaction discourses. *Journal of Research on Adolescence, 16,* 561–588.

Uchino, B. N. (2004). *Social support and physical health: Understanding the health consequences of relationships.* New Haven, CT: Yale University Press.

Ulrey, K. L. (2001). Intercultural communication between patients and health care providers: An exploration of intercultural communication effectiveness, cultural sensitivity, stress, and anxiety. *Health Communication, 13,* 449–463.

Underwood, M. K. (2003). *Social aggression among girls.* New York: Guilford Press.

Updegraff, J. A., Emanuel, A. S., Suh, E. M., & Gallagher, K. M. (2010). Sheltering the self from the storm: Self-construal abstractness and the stability of self-esteem. *Personality and Social Psychology Bulletin, 36,* 97–108.

Urberg, K. A., Degirmencioglu, S. M., & Tolson, J. M. (1998). Adolescent friendship selection and termination: The role of similarity. *Journal of Social and Personal Relationships, 15,* 703–710.

Urista, M. A., Dong, Q., & Day, K. D. (2009). Explaining why young adults use MySpace and Facebook through uses and gratifications theory. *Human Communication, 12,* 215–230.

U.S. Department of Justice. (2002, February). *OJJDP fact sheet: Highlights of the 2000 National Youth Gang Survey.* Washington, DC: Office of Juvenile Justice and Delinquency Prevention. Retrieved from http://www.ncjrs.gov/pdffiles1/ojjdp/fs200204.pdf

Utz, S. (2007). Media use in long-distance friendships. *Information, Communication & Society, 10,* 694–713.

Valentine, C. A., & Saint Damian, B. (1988). Communicative power: Gender and culture as determinants of the ideal voice. In C. A. Valentine & N. Hoar (Eds.), *Women and communicative power: Theory, research, and practice* (pp. 42–68). Washington, DC: National Communication Association.

Vancleave, D. S. (2008). Empathy training for master's level social work students facilitating advanced empathy responding. *Dissertation Abstracts International: Section A. Humanities and Social Sciences, 68*(9-A), 4074.

vanDellen, M. R., Bradfield, E. K., & Hoyle, R. H. (2010). Self-regulation of state self-esteem following threat: Moderation by trait self-esteem. In R. H. Hoyle (Ed.)., *Handbook of personality and self-regulation* (pp. 430–446). Hoboken, NJ: Wiley-Blackwell.

van den Bos, K., Brockner, J., Stein, J. H., Steiner, D. D., Van Yperen, N. W., & Dekker, D. M. (2010). The psychology of voice and performance capabilities in masculine and feminine cultures and contexts. *Journal of Personality and Social Psychology, 99,* 638–648.

Van Gelder, L. (1996). The strange case of the electronic lover. In R. Kling (Ed.), *Computerization and controversy: Value conflicts and social choices* (2nd ed., pp. 533–546). New York: Academic Press.

Vangelisti, A. (Ed.). (2004). *Handbook of family communication.* Mahwah, NJ: Erlbaum.

Vangelisti, A. L. (1994). Couples' communication problems: The counselor's perspective. *Journal of Applied Communication Research, 22,* 106–126.

Vangelisti, A. L., & Beck, G. (2007). Intimacy and fear of intimacy. In L. L'Abate (Ed.), *Low-cost approaches to promote physical and mental health: Theory, research, and practice* (pp. 395–414). New York: Springer Science 1 Business Media.

Vangelisti, A. L., Caughlin, J. P., & Timmerman, L. (2001). Criteria for revealing family secrets. *Communication Monographs, 68,* 1–27.

Vangelisti, A. L., & Crumley, L. P. (1998). Reactions to messages that hurt: The influence of relational contexts. *Communication Monographs, 65,* 173–196.

Vangelisti, A. L., Knapp, M. L., & Daly, J. A. (1990). Conversational narcissism. *Communication Monographs, 57,* 251–274.

van Leeuwen, M. L., & Macrae, C. N. (2004). Is beautiful always good? Implicit benefits of facial attractiveness. *Social Cognition, 22,* 637–649.

van Meurs, N., & Spencer-Oatey, H. (2010). Multidisciplinary perspectives on intercultural conflict: The "Bermuda Triangle" of conflict, culture, and communication. In D. Matsumoto (Ed.), *APA handbook of intercultural communication* (pp. 59–77). Washington, DC: American Psychological Association.

Van Swol, L. M. (2003). The effects of nonverbal mirroring on perceived persuasiveness, agreement with an imitator, and reciprocity in a small group discussion. *Communication Research, 30,* 461–480.

Vaughn, D. (1987, July). The long goodbye. *Psychology Today, 21,* 37–42.

Veroff, J., Douvan, E., Orbuch, T. L., & Acitelli, L. K. (1998). Happiness in stable marriages: The early years. In T. N. Bradbury (Ed.), *The developmental course of marital dysfunction* (pp. 152–179). New York: Cambridge University Press.

Versalle, A., & McDowell, E. E. (2004–2005). The attitudes of men and women concerning gender differences in grief. *Omega: Journal of Death and Dying, 50,* 53–67.

Versfeld, N. J., & Dreschler, W. A. (2002). The relationship between the intelligibility of time-compressed speech and speech-in-noise in young and elderly listeners. *Journal of the Acoustical Society of America, 111*(1, Pt. 1), 401–408.

Vilhauer, R. P. (2009). Perceived benefits of online support groups for women with metastatic breast cancer. *Women & Health, 49,* 381–404.

Villadsen, L. S. (2008). Speaking on behalf of others: Rhetorical agency and epideictic functions in official apologies. *RSQ: Rhetoric Society Quarterly, 38,* 25–45.

Villaume, W. A., & Bodie, G. D. (2007). Discovering the listener within us: The impact of trait-like personality variables and communicator styles on preferences for listening style. *International Journal of Listening, 21,* 102–123.

Vitak, J., Ellison, N., & Steinfield, C. (2011). The ties that bond: Re-examining the relationship between Facebook use and bonding social capital. In *Proceedings of the 44th Annual Hawaii International Conference on System Sciences* [CD-ROM]. Computer Society Press. Retrieved from http://vitak.files.wordpress.com/2009/02/hicss-social-provisions-revised-final.pdf

Vocate, D. R. (1994). Self-talk and inner speech: Understanding the uniquely human aspects of intrapersonal communication. In D. R. Vocate (Ed.), *Intrapersonal communication: Different voices, different minds* (pp. 3–31). Hillsdale, NJ: Erlbaum.

Vohs, K. D., & Heatherton, T. F. (2004). Ego threats elicits different social comparison process among high and low self-esteem people: Implications for interpersonal perceptions. *Social Cognition, 22,* 168–191.

Von Briesen, P. D. (2007). Pragmatic language skills of adolescents with ADHD. *Dissertation Abstracts International: Section B, The Sciences and Engineering, 68*(5-B), 3430.

Voss, K., Markiewicz, D., & Doyle, A. B. (1999). Friendship, marriage and self-esteem. *Journal of Social and Personal Relationships, 16,* 103–122.

Vrij, A. (2006). Nonverbal communication and deception. In V. Manusov & M. L. Patterson (Eds.), *The Sage handbook of nonverbal communication* (pp. 341–360). Thousand Oaks, CA: Sage.

Vrij, A., & Akehurst, L. (1999). The existence of a black clothing stereotype: The impact of a victim's black clothing on impression formation. *Psychology, Crime and Law, 3*(3), 227–237.

Vrij, A., Edward, K., Roberts, K. P., & Bull, R. (2000). Detecting deceit via analysis of verbal and nonverbal behavior. *Journal of Nonverbal Behavior, 24*, 239–263.

Vuchinich, S. (1987). Starting and stopping spontaneous family conflicts. *Journal of Marriage and the Family, 49*, 591–601.

Waara, E., & Shaw, P. (2006). Male and female witnesses' speech in Swedish criminal trials. *Journal of Language and Communication Studies, 36*, 129–156.

Wade, A., & Beran, T. (2011). Cyberbullying: The new era of bullying. *Canadian Journal of School Psychology, 26*, 44–61.

Wade, N. G., & Worthington, E. L., Jr. (2005). In search of a common core: A content analysis of interventions to promote forgiveness. *Psychotherapy: Theory, Research, Practice, Training, 42*, 160–177.

Waldron, V. R., & Kelley, D. L (2005). Forgiving communication as a response to relational transgressions. *Journal of Social and Personal Relationships, 22*, 723–742.

Wallace, H. M., Exline, J. J., & Baumeister, R. F. (2008). Interpersonal consequences of forgiveness: Does forgiveness deter or encourage repeat offenses? *Journal of Experimental Social Psychology, 44*, 453–460.

Wallace, J. C., Edwards, B. D., Shull, A., & Finch, D. M. (2009). Examining the consequences in the tendency to suppress and reappraise emotions on task-related job performance. *Human Performance, 22*, 23–43.

Walster, E., Aronson, E., Abrahams, D., & Rottmann, L. (1966). Importance of physical attractiveness in dating behavior. *Journal of Personality and Social Psychology, 4*, 508–516.

Walther, J. B. (1996). Computer-mediated communication: Impersonal, interpersonal, and hyperpersonal interaction. *Communication Research, 23*, 3–43.

Walther, J. B. (2007). Selective self-presentation in computer-mediated communication: Hyperpersonal dimensions of technology, language, and cognition. *Computers in Human Behavior, 23*, 2538–2557.

Walther, J. B., & Ramirez, A., Jr. (2010). New technologies and new directions in online relating. In S. W. Smith & S. R. Wilson (Eds.), *New directions in interpersonal communication research* (pp. 264–284). Thousand Oaks, CA: Sage.

Waring, E. M. (1981). Facilitating marital intimacy through self-disclosure. *American Journal of Family Therapy, 9*, 33–42.

Warren, K., Schoppelrey, S., & Moberg, D. (2005). A model of contagion through competition in the aggressive behaviors of elementary school students. *Journal of Abnormal Child Psychology, 33*, 283–292.

Watkins, L., & Johnston, L. (2000). Screening job applicants: The impact of physical attractiveness and application quality. *International Journal of Selection and Assessment, 8*, 76–84.

Watt, D. (2007). Toward a neuroscience of empathy: Integrating affective and cognitive perspectives. *Neuro-Psychoanalysis, 9*, 119–140.

Watts, R. E., Peluso, P. R., Lewis, T. F., Anderson, R. N., & Rasmussen, P. R. (2005). Psychological strategies. *Journal of Individual Psychology, 61*, 380–387.

Watts, S. A. (2007). Evaluative feedback: Perspectives on media effects. *Journal of Computer-Mediated Communication, 12*, 50–77.

Watzlawick, P. (1984). *The invented reality: How do we know what we believe we know?* New York: Norton.

Watzlawick, P. (1990). Reality adaptation or adapted "reality"? Constructivism and psychotherapy. In P. Watzlawick (Ed.), *Münchausen's pigtail: Or psychotherapy and "reality." Essays and lectures.* New York: Norton.

Watzlawick, P. (2005). Self-fulfilling prophecies. In J. O'Brien & P. Kollock (Eds.), *The production of reality* (4th ed., pp. 382–394). Thousand Oaks, CA: Sage.

Watzlawick, P., Beavin, J., & Jackson, D. (1967). *Pragmatics of human communication: A study of interactional patterns, pathologies, and paradoxes.* New York: Norton.

Weaver, J. B., & Kirtley, M. D. (1995). Listening styles and empathy. *Southern Communication Journal, 60*, 131–140.

Weber, K., Goodboy, A. K., & Cayanus, J. L. (2010). Flirting competence: An experimental study on appropriate and effective opening lines. *Communication Research Reports, 27,* 184–191.

Weder, M. (2008). Form and function of meta-communication in CMC. In S. Kelsey & K. St. Amant (Eds.), *Handbook of research on computer mediated communication* (Vols 1–2, pp. 570–586). Hershey, PA: Information Science Reference/IGI Global.

Weger, H., Jr. (2005). Disconfirming communication and self-verification in marriage: Associations among the demand/withdraw interaction pattern, feeling understood, and marital satisfaction. *Journal of Social & Personal Relationships, 22,* 19–31.

Weger, H., Jr., Castle, G. R., & Emmett, M. C. (2010). Active listening in peer interviews: The influence of message paraphrasing on perceptions of listening skill. *International Journal of Listening, 24,* 34–49.

Wei, Y., & Li, Y. (2001). The experimental research on the influence of different empathy training methods on children's sharing behavior. *Psychological Science China, 24,* 557–562.

Weider-Hatfield, D. (1981). A unit in conflict management skills. *Communication Education, 30,* 265–273.

Weigel, D. J. (2008). Mutuality and the communication of commitment in romantic relationships. *Southern Communication Journal, 73,* 24–41.

Weigel, D. J., & Ballard-Reisch, D. S. (1999). Using paired data to test models of relational maintenance and marital quality. *Journal of Social and Personal Relationships, 16,* 175–191.

Weigert, A. J., & Gecas, V. (2003). Self. In N. J. Herman-Kinney & L. T. Reynolds (Eds.), *Handbook of symbolic interactionism* (pp. 267–288). Walnut Creek, CA: AltaMira Press.

Weisbuch, M., Ambady, N., Clarke, A. L., Achor, S., & Weele, J. V.-V. (2010). On being consistent: The role of verbal-nonverbal consistency in first impressions. *Basic and Applied Social Psychology, 32,* 261–268.

Welch, I. D. (2003). *The therapeutic relationship: Listening and responding in a multicultural world.* Westport, CT: Praeger Publishers/Greenwood.

Werking, K. (1997). *We're just good friends: Women and men in nonromantic relationships.* New York, Guilford.

Wester, S. R., Vogel, D. L., Pressly, P. K., & Heesacker, M. (2002). Sex differences in emotion: A critical review of the literature and implications for counseling psychology. *Counseling Psychologist, 30,* 630–652.

Whaley, L. J. (1997). *Introduction to typology: The unity and diversity of language.* Thousand Oaks, CA: Sage.

Whiffen, V. E, Foot, M. L., & Thompson, J. M. (2007). Self-silencing mediates the link between marital conflict and depression. *Journal of Social and Personal Relationships, 24,* 993–1006.

Whitchurch, G., & Constantine, L. L. (1993). Systems theory. In P. Boss, W. J. Doherty, R. LaRossa, W. R. Schumm, & S. K. Steinmetz (Eds.), *Sourcebook of family theories and methods: A contextual approach* (pp. 325–355). New York: Plenum Press.

Whited, M. C., Wheat, A. L., & Larkin, K. T. (2010). The influence of forgiveness and apology on cardiovascular reactivity and recovery in response to mental stress. *Journal of Behavioral Medicine, 33,* 293–304.

Whitty, M. T. (2005). The realness of cybercheating: Men's and women's representations of unfaithful Internet relationships. *Social Science Computer Review, 23,* 57–67.

Whitty, M. T. (2007). Manipulation of self in cyberspace. In B. H. Spitzberg & W. R. Cupach (Eds.), *The dark side of interpersonal communication* (2nd ed., pp. 93–120). London: Routledge.

Whorf, B. L. (1956). The relation of habitual thought and behavior to language. In J. B. Carroll (Ed.), *Language, thought, and reality: Selected writings of Benjamin Lee Whorf* (pp. 134–159). Cambridge, MA: MIT Press.

Wiemann, J. M., & Knapp, M. L. (2008). Turn-taking in conversations. In C. D. Mortensen (Ed.), *Communication theory* (2nd ed., pp. 226–245). Piscataway, NJ: Transaction Publishers.

Wiemann, J. M., Takai, J., Ota, H., & Wiemann, M. (1997). A relational model of communication competence. In B. Kovacic (Ed.), *Emerging theories of human communication* (pp. 25–44). Albany: State University of New York Press.

Wilkins, R., & Gareis, E. (2006). Emotion expression and the locution "I love you": A cross-cultural study. *International Journal of Intercultural Relations, 30*, 51–75.

Williams, B. (2008, May 3). *Listen to this: Hearing problems can stress relationships.* Retrieved from http://www.healthyhearing.com/content/news/Buying/Benefits/16759-Listen-to-this-hearing

Williams, C. T., & Johnson, L. R. (2011). Why can't we be friends?: Multicultural attitudes and friendships with international students. *International Journal of Intercultural Relations, 35*(1), 41–48.

Williams, K. D., & Dolnik, L. (2001). Revealing the worst first: Stealing thunder as a social influence strategy. In J. P. Forgas & K. D. Williams (Eds.), *Social influence: Direct and indirect processes* (pp. 213–231). Hove, England: Psychology Press.

Williams-Baucom, K. J., Atkins, D. C., Sevier, M., Eldridge, K. A., & Christensen, A. (2010). "You" and "I" need to talk about "us": Linguistic patterns in marital interactions. *Personal Relationships, 17*, 41–56.

Willis, F. N., & Hamm, H. K. (1980). The use of interpersonal touch in securing compliance. *Journal of Nonverbal Behavior, 5*, 49–55.

Wilmot, W. W. (1987). *Dyadic communication* (3rd ed.). New York: Random House.

Wilmot, W. W. (1995). *Relational communication* (5th ed.). New York: McGraw-Hill.

Wilmot, W. W., & Hocker, J. L. (2010). *Interpersonal conflict* (8th ed.). New York: McGraw-Hill.

Winer, S., & Majors, R. (1981). A research note on supportive and defensive communication: An empirical study of three verbal interpersonal communication variables. *Communication Quarterly, 29*, 166–172.

Winsor, J. L., Curtis, D. B., & Stephens, R. D. (1997). National preferences in business and communication education: An update. *Journal of the Association for Communication Administration, 3*, 170–179.

Wire, J. (2010, October 9). 20 awesomely untranslatable words from around the world. *Matador Abroad.* Retrieved from http://matadornetwork.com/abroad/20-awesomely-untranslatable-words-from-around-the-world/

Wiseman, R. (2003). *Queen bees and wannabes: Helping your daughter survive cliques, gossip, boyfriends, and other realities of adolescence.* New York: Three Rivers Press.

Wolf, A. (2000). Emotional expression online: Gender differences in emoticon use. *CyberPsychology & Behavior, 3*, 827–833.

Wolff, F. I., & Marsnik, N. C. (1993). Perceptive listening (2nd ed.). Fort Worth, TX: Harcourt.

Wolfram, W., & Schilling-Estes, N. (2005). *American English: Dialects and variation* (2nd ed.). Malden, MA: Blackwell.

Wolvin, A. D. (1984). Meeting the communication needs of the adult learner. *Communication Education, 33*, 267–271.

Wood, J. T. (2005a). Feminist standpoint theory and muted group theory: Commonalities and divergences. *Women and Language, 28*(2), 61–65.

Wood, J. T. (2005b). *Gendered lives: Communication, gender, and culture* (6th ed.). Belmont, CA: Wadsworth.

Wood, J. T. (2009). *Gendered lives: Communication, gender, and culture* (8th ed.). Belmont, CA: Wadsworth.

Wood, J. T. (2010). *Interpersonal communication: Everyday encounters* (6th ed.). Boston, MA: Wadsworth.

Wood, J. T., & Inman, C. C. (1993). In a different mode: Masculine styles of communicating closeness. *Journal of Applied Communication Research, 21*, 279–295.

Wood, J. V., Heimpel, S. A., Manwell, L. A., & Whittington, E. J. (2009). This mood is familiar and I don't deserve to feel better anyway: Mechanisms underlying self-esteem differences in motivation to repair sad moods. *Journal of Personality & Social Psychology, 96*, 363–380.

Woodin, E. M. (2011). A two-dimensional approach to relationship conflict: Meta-analytic findings. *Journal of Family Psychology, 25*, 325–335.

Woodward, M. S., Rosenfeld, L. B., & May, S. K. (1996). Sex differences in social support in sororities and fraternities. *Journal of Applied Communication Research, 24*, 260–272.

Wout, D. A., Murphy, M. C., & Steele, C. M. (2010). When your friends matter: The effect of White students' racial friendship networks on meta-perceptions and perceived identity contingencies. *Journal of Experimental Social Psychology, 46,* 1035–1041.

Wright, C. N., Holloway, A., & Roloff, M. E. (2007). The dark side of self-monitoring: How high self-monitors view their romantic relationships. *Communication Reports, 20,* 101–114.

Wright, C. N., & Roloff, M. E. (2009). Relational commitment and the silent treatment. *Communication Research Reports, 26,* 12–21.

Wu, S., & Keysar, B. (2007). Cultural effects on perspective taking. *Psychological Science, 18,* 600–606.

Yasir H., & Sajid M. (2010). Understanding constructive feedback: A commitment between teachers and students for academic and professional development. *Journal of the Pakistani Medical Association, 60,* 224–227. Retrieved from http://www.jpma.org.pk/PdfDownload/1960.pdf

Ybarra, M. L., & Mitchell, K. J. (2007). Prevalence and frequency of Internet harassment instigation: Implications for adolescent health. *Journal of Adolescent Health, 41,* 189–195.

Ybarra, O., Burnstein, E., Winkielman, P., Keller, M. C., Manis, M., Chan, E., & Rodriguez, J. (2008). Mental exercising through simple socializing: Social interaction promotes general cognitive functioning. *Personality and Social Psychology Bulletin, 34,* 248–259.

Ybarra, O., Rees, L., Kross, E., & Sanchez-Burks, J. (2011). Social context and the psychology of emotional intelligence: A key to creating positive organizations. In K. Cameron & G. Spreitzer (Eds.), *Handbook of positive organizational scholarship* (pp. 201–214). New York: Oxford University Press.

Yee, N., & Bailenson, J. N. (2006, August). Walk a mile in digital shoes: The impact of embodied perspective-taking on the reduction of negative stereotyping in immersive virtual environments. *Proceedings of PRESENCE 2006: The 8th Annual International Workshop on Presence.* Cleveland, OH. Retrieved from http://www.temple.edu/ispr/prev_conferences/proceedings/2006/confindex.html

Yeh, J. B. (2010). Relations matter: Redefining communication competence from a Chinese perspective. *Chinese Journal of Communication, 3,* 64–75.

Yingling, J. (1994). Constituting friendship in talk and metatalk. *Journal of Social and Personal Relationships, 11,* 411–426.

Yopyk, D. J. A., & Prentice, D. A. (2005). Am I an athlete or a student? Identity salience and stereotype threat in student-athletes. *Basic and Applied Social Psychology, 27,* 329–336.

Young, R. W., & Cates, C. M. (2004). Emotional and directive listening in peer mentoring. *International Journal of Listening, 18,* 21–33.

Young, S. L. (2004). What the ____ is your problem?: Attribution theory and perceived reasons for profanity usage during conflict. *Communication Research Reports, 21,* 338–447.

Young, S. L. (2009). The function of parental communication patterns: Reflection-enhancing and reflection-discouraging approaches. *Communication Quarterly, 57,* 379–394.

Yurtsever, G., & de Rivera, J. (2010). Measuring the emotional climate of an organization. *Perceptual and Motor Skills, 110,* 501–516.

Zahn, C. J. (1989). The bases for differing evaluations of male and female speech: Evidence from ratings of transcribed conversation. *Communication Monographs, 56,* 59–74.

Zapf, D., & Holz, M. (2006). On the positive and negative effects of emotion work in organizations. *European Journal of Work and Organizational Psychology, 15,* 1–28.

Zarankin, T. G. (2008). A new look at conflict styles: Goal orientation and outcome preferences. *International Journal of Conflict Management, 19,* 167–184.

Zebrowitz, L. A., & Montepare, J. M. (2008). First impressions from facial appearance cues. In N. Ambady & J. J. Skowronski (Eds.), *First impressions* (pp. 171–204). New York: Guilford.

Zenmore, S. E., Fiske, S. T., & Kim, H. J. (2000). Gender stereotypes and the dynamics of social interaction. In T. Eckes & H. M. Trautner (Eds.), *The developmental social psychology of gender* (pp. 207–241). Mahwah, NJ: Erlbaum.

Zhang, S. (2009). Sender-recipient perspectives of honest but hurtful evaluative messages in romantic relationships. *Communication Reports, 22,* 89–101.

Zhang, S., & Stafford, L. (2008). Perceived face threat of honest but hurtful evaluative messages in romantic relationships. *Western Journal of Communication, 72,* 19–39.

Zhang, S., & Stafford, L. (2009). Relational ramifications of honest but hurtful evaluative messages in close relationships. *Western Journal of Communication, 73,* 481–501.

Zhang, Y. B., Harwood, J., & Hummert, M. L. (2005). Perceptions of conflict management styles in Chinese intergenerational dyads. *Communication Monographs, 72,* 71–91.

Zhong, J., Wang, A., Qian, M., Zhang, L., Gao, J., Yang, J., et al. (2008). Shame, personality, and social anxiety symptoms in Chinese and American nonclinical samples: A cross-cultural study. *Depression and Anxiety, 25,* 449–460.

Zick, A., Granieri, M., & Makoul, G. (2007). First-year medical students' assessment of their own communication skills: A video-based, open-ended approach. *Patient Education and Counseling, 68,* 161–166.

Zickuhr, K. (2010). *Generations 2010.* Pew Internet & American Life Project. Retrieved from http://pewinternet.org/Reports/2010/Generations-2010/Overview.aspx

Zimbardo, P. G. (1971). *The psychological power and pathology of imprisonment.* Statement prepared for the U.S. House of Representatives Committee on the Judiciary, Subcommittee No. 3, Robert Kastemeyer, Chairman. Unpublished manuscript, Stanford University, Stanford, CA.

Zimbardo, P. G. (1977). *Shyness: What it is, what to do about it.* Reading, MA: Addison-Wesley.

Zimbardo, P. G. (2007, March 30). Revisiting the Stanford prison experiment: A lesson in the power of situation. *Chronicle of Higher Education, 53,* B6.

Zimmerman, B. J. (1995). Self-efficacy and educational development. In A. Bandura (Ed.), *Self-efficacy in changing societies* (pp. 202–231). New York: Cambridge University Press.

Zinner, J. (2009). Psychodynamic couples therapy: An object relations approach. In G. O. Gabbard (Ed.), *Textbook of psychotherapeutic treatments* (pp. 581–601). Arlington, VA: American Psychiatric Publishing.

Zorn, T. E., & Gregory, K. W. (2005). Learning the ropes together: Assimilation and friendship development among first-year male medical students. *Health Communication, 17,* 211–231.

Zuckerman, M., & Driver, R. E. (1989). What sounds beautiful is good: The vocal attractiveness stereotype. *Journal of Nonverbal Behavior, 13,* 67–82.

Zuckerman, M., Miserandino, M., Bernieri, F., Manusov, V., Axtell, R. E., Wiemann, J. M., Knapp, M. L., O'Leary, M. J., & Gallois, C. (1999). Creating impressions and managing interaction. In L. K. Guerrero, J. A. DeVito, & M. L. Hecht (Eds.), *The nonverbal communication reader: Classic and contemporary readings* (2nd ed., pp. 379–422). Prospect Heights, IL: Waveland Press.

◼ Subject Index

Preparing and Presenting Your Speech

11

Chapter Outline

LEARNING OBJECTIVES

1 Choose an effective speaking topic.

2 Formulate a purpose statement and thesis statement that will help you develop that topic.

3 Analyze both the audience and occasion in any speaking situation.

4 Gather information on your chosen topic from a variety of sources.

5 Overcome debilitative stage fright.

6 Choose the most effective type of delivery for a particular speech.

Diane Sawyer famously dubbed Adora Svitak a "tiny literary giant." Svitak published her first book at age 7, and within 5 years was a well-known public speaker. Her TED talk, "What Adults Can Learn from Kids," which she presented at age 12, has been viewed more than 2 million times. The demand for her public appearances is so great that Svitak's parents created a TV studio in their basement, from which she speaks daily to audiences (mostly students and teachers) around the world. Companies such as Microsoft pay her $10,000 per speaking engagement.

Svitak's speaking skills arise from several factors. One is that she loves demonstrating her message—that children have more to offer than adults usually give them credit for. Another is that she does her homework. Svitak doesn't just propose the opinion that children can make a difference. She offers well-researched examples. A third strength is that Svitak handles words with great care, choosing and arranging them in ways that are artistic and powerful.

It's clear that Svitak knows her stuff when it comes to public speaking. Her success is no accident but rather the result of enthusiasm, hard work, practice, and a desire to connect with her audiences. Perhaps the reason she feels comfortable with large audiences is that she believes in mutual respect. She admires adults but does not feel intimidated by them. In fact, in the nicest tones possible, she tells adults to listen more. "It shouldn't just be a teacher at the head of the classroom telling students 'do this, do that,'" she maintains. "The students should teach their teachers. Learning between grown-ups and kids should be reciprocal."

Watch Svitak's talk by typing her name into the search window at www.ted.com. Then consider how well she displays the principles of public speaking in this chapter and the ones that follow. If you're like most people, you'll agree that we have a lot to learn from Adora Svitak.

Adora Svitak chose to speak about the role of children in an adult society because she feels strongly about that topic. Imagine a topic that you feel so strongly about that you would talk about it in public without it being a speech assignment. Now think about these three questions:

- What is your objective in speaking about this topic?
- What is your main idea?
- What information do you need to gather to support that idea?

You don't have to be a child prodigy like Adora Svitak to face the prospect of giving a public speech. In fact, even if you never took a course in which speech giving was required, you would almost certainly face the challenge of giving a speech at some point. It might be a job-related presentation, or something more personal, such as a wedding toast or a eulogy. You might find yourself speaking in favor of a civic-improvement project in your hometown or trying to persuade members of your club to deal more effectively with global problems like war, religious strife, or environmental threats.

Despite the potential benefits of effective speeches, many people view the prospect of standing before an audience with the same enthusiasm they have for a trip to the dentist or the tax auditor. In fact, giving a speech seems to be one of the most anxiety-producing things we can do: When asked to list their common fears, research subjects mention public speaking more often than they do insects, heights, accidents, and even death.[1]

There's no guarantee that the following chapters will make you love the idea of giving speeches, but we can promise that the information these chapters contain will give you the tools to design and deliver remarks that will be clear, interesting, and effective. And it's very likely that, as your skill grows, your confidence will too. This chapter will deal with your first steps in that process, through careful speech planning.

Getting Started

Your first tasks are generally choosing a topic, determining your purpose, and finding information.

Choosing Your Topic

The first question many student speakers face is, "What should I talk about?" When you need to choose a topic, you should try to pick one that is right for you, your audience, and the situation. You should try to choose a topic that interests you and that your audience will care about. Decide on your topic as early as possible. Those who wait until the last possible moment usually find that they don't have enough time to research, outline, and practice their speech.

Defining Your Purpose

No one gives a speech—or expresses *any* kind of message—without having a reason to do so. Your first step in focusing your speech is to formulate a clear and precise statement of that purpose.

Writing a Purpose Statement

Your **purpose statement** should be expressed in the form of a complete sentence that describes your **specific purpose**—exactly what you want your speech to accomplish. It should stem from your **general purpose**, which might be to inform, persuade, or entertain. Beyond that, though, there are three criteria for an effective purpose statement:

1. **A purpose statement should be result oriented.** Having a *result orientation* means that your purpose is focused on the outcome you want to accomplish with your audience members. For example, if you were giving an informative talk on the high cost of college, this would be an inadequate purpose statement:

    My purpose is to tell my audience about high college costs.

    As that statement is worded, your purpose is "to tell" an audience something, which suggests that the speech could be successful even if no one listened! A result-oriented purpose statement should refer to the response you want from your audience: It should tell what the audience members will know or be able to do after listening to your speech.

2. **A purpose statement should be specific.** To be effective, a purpose statement should be worded specifically, with enough details so that you would be able to measure or test your audience, after your speech, to see if you had achieved your purpose. In the example given earlier, simply "knowing

about high college costs" is too vague; you need something more specific, such as:

After listening to my speech, my audience will be able to reduce college costs.

This is an improvement, but it can be made still better by applying a third criterion:

③ **A purpose statement should be realistic.** It's fine to be ambitious, but you need to design a purpose that has a reasonable chance of success. You can appreciate the importance of having a realistic goal by looking at some unrealistic ones, such as "My purpose is to convince my audience to make federal budget deficits illegal." Unless your audience happens to be a joint session of Congress, it won't have the power to change U.S. fiscal policy. But any audience can write its congressional representatives or sign a petition. In your speech on college costs, it would be impossible for your audience members to change the entire structure of college financing. So a better purpose statement for this speech might sound something like this:

After listening to my speech, my audience will be able to list four simple steps to lower their college expenses.

Consider the following sets of purpose statements:

LESS EFFECTIVE	MORE EFFECTIVE
To talk about professional wrestling (not receiver oriented)	After listening to my speech, my audience will understand that kids who imitate professional wrestlers can be seriously hurt.
To tell my audience about gun control (not specific)	After my speech, the audience will be able to list five ways to keep guns out of the hands of criminals.

You probably won't include your purpose statement word-for-word in your actual speech. Rather than being aimed at your listeners, a specific purpose statement usually is a tool to keep you focused on your goal as you plan your speech.

Stating Your Thesis

After you have defined the purpose, you are ready to start planning what is arguably the most important sentence in your entire speech. The **thesis statement** tells your listeners the central idea of your speech. It is the one idea that you want your audience to remember after it has forgotten everything else you had to say. The thesis statement for a speech about winning in small claims court might be worded like this:

Arguing a case on your own in small claims court is a simple, five-step process that can give you the same results you would achieve with a lawyer.

Unlike your purpose statement, your thesis statement is almost always delivered directly to your audience. The thesis statement is usually formulated later in the speech-making process, after you have done some research on your topic. The progression from topic to purpose to thesis is, therefore, another focusing process, as you can see in the following example:

Topic: Organ donation

Specific Purpose: After listening to my speech, audience members will recognize the importance of organ donation and will sign an organ donor's card for themselves.

Thesis: Because not enough of us choose to become organ donors, thousands of us needlessly die every year. You can help prevent this needless dying.

Describe someone you consider an effective public speaker. This could be someone you know personally, such as a teacher, or someone you know only through the media, such as a celebrity or other public figure. What is it about this person that makes him or her effective?

Analyzing the Speaking Situation

There are two components to analyze in any speaking situation: the audience and the occasion. To be successful, every choice you make in putting together your speech—your purpose, topic, and all the material you use to develop your speech—must be appropriate to both of these components.

The Listener: Audience Analysis

Audience analysis involves identifying and adapting your remarks to the most pertinent characteristics of your listeners.

Audience Purpose Just as you have a purpose for speaking, audience members have a reason for gathering. Sometimes virtually all the members of your audience will have the same, obvious goal. Expectant parents at a natural childbirth class are all seeking a healthy delivery, and people attending an investment seminar are looking for ways to increase their net worth.

There are other times, however, when audience purpose can't be so easily defined. In some instances, different listeners will have different goals, some of which might not be apparent to the speaker. Consider a church congregation, for example. Whereas most members might listen to a sermon with the hope of applying religious principles to their lives, a few might be interested in being entertained or in merely appearing pious. In the same way, the listeners in your speech class probably have a variety of motives for attending. Becoming aware of as many of these motives as possible will help you predict what will interest them. Observing audience demographics helps you make that prediction.

Demographics **Demographics** are characteristics of your audience that can be categorized, such as cultural differences, age, gender, group membership, number of people, and so on. Demographic characteristics might affect your speech planning in a number of ways.[2] For example:

In the film *Flight*, pilot Whip Whitaker (Denzel Washington) tries to salvage his career after managing a successful crash landing by convincing authorities that he can overcome his addictions. How might he define the purpose and thesis of his speech?

- **Cultural diversity.** Do audience members differ in terms of race, religion, or national origin? The guideline here might be, *Do not exclude or offend any portion of your audience on the basis of cultural differences.* If there is a dominant cultural group represented, you might decide to speak to it, but remember that the point is to analyze, not stereotype, your audience. If you talk down to any segment of your listeners, you have probably stereotyped them.

- **Gender.** Although masculine and feminine stereotypes are declining, it is still important to think about how gender can affect the way you choose and approach a topic. Every speech teacher has a horror story about a student getting up in front of a class composed primarily, but not entirely, of men and speaking on a subject such as "Picking Up Babes."

- **Age.** Our interests vary and change with our age. These differences may run relatively deep; our approach to literature, films, finance, health, and long-term success may change dramatically over just a few years, perhaps from graphic novels to serious literature, from punk to classical music, or from hip-hop to epic poetry.

- **Group membership.** Groups generally form around shared interests among the members. By examining the groups to which they belong, you can surmise audience members' political leanings (Campus Reform Party, College Democrats, Young Republicans), religious beliefs (Catholic Youth

> cultural idiom

talk down to:
speak to in a condescending way

> cultural idiom

picking up babes:
offensive term for making the acquaintance of women or girls with sexual purposes in mind

Organization, Hillel, or Muslim Students' Association), or occupation (Bartenders Union or National Communication Association). Group membership is often an important consideration in college classes. Consider the difference between a "typical" college day class and one that meets in the evening. At many colleges the evening students are generally older and tend to belong to civic groups, church clubs, and the local chamber of commerce. Daytime students are more likely to belong to sororities and fraternities, sports clubs, and social action groups.

- **Number of people.** Topic appropriateness varies with the size of an audience. With a small audience you can be less formal and more intimate; you can, for example, talk more about your feelings and personal experiences. If you gave a speech before 5 people as impersonally as if they were a standing-room-only crowd in a lecture hall, they would probably find you stuffy. On the other hand, if you talked to 300 people about your unhappy childhood, you'd probably make them uncomfortable.

> cultural idiom

stuffy:
impersonal, not relating to the audience

You have to decide which demographics of your audience are important for a particular speech. For example, when Sneha Polisetti, a student at James Madison University in Virginia, gave a speech on the loss of Native American culture, she knew she had to broaden the appeal of her topic beyond the small demographic referred to in her speech. She adapted to her broader audience this way:

When the Native American cultures that are tied closely to America's story are lost, we all lose a part of our identity and history, whether we're Native Americans or not.[3]

These five demographic characteristics are important examples, but the list goes on. Other demographic characteristics that might be important in a college classroom include the following:

- Educational level
- Economic status
- Hometown
- Year in school
- Major subject
- Ethnic background

A final factor to consider in audience analysis concerns members' attitudes, beliefs, and values.

Ethical Challenge

Adapting to
Speaking
Situations

How much adaptation is ethical? How far would you go to be effective with an audience? Try the following exercise with your classmates.

1. Prepare, in advance, three index cards: one with a possible topic for a speech, one with a possible audience, and one with a possible occasion.

2. Form groups of four members each. Mark the back of each card with "A" for "audience," "T" for "topic," or "O" for "occasion," and turn the cards face down.

3. Take one card from each of the other members.

4. Turn the cards over. For each set, decide which characteristics of the audience, topic, and occasion would most likely affect the way the speech was developed.

5. Discuss the adaptation that would be necessary in each situation and the role ethics would play in determining how far you would go.

Attitudes, Beliefs, and Values   Audience members' feelings about you, your subject, and your intentions for them are central issues in audience analysis. One way to approach these issues is through a consideration of attitudes, beliefs, and values.[4] Attitudes, beliefs, and values reside in human consciousness like layers of an onion (see Figure 11-1). **Attitudes** lie closest to the surface. They reflect a predisposition to view you or your topic in a favorable or unfavorable way. **Beliefs** lie a little deeper and deal with the truth of something. **Values** are deeply rooted feelings about a concept's inherent worth or worthiness. You can begin to appreciate the usefulness of these concepts by considering an example. Suppose you were a dentist trying to persuade a group of patients to floss their teeth more often. Consider how audience analysis would help you design the most promising approach:

> *Attitudes.* How do your listeners feel about the importance of dental hygiene? If they recognize its importance, you can proceed confidently, knowing they'll probably want to hear what you have to say. On the other hand, if they are vaguely disgusted by even thinking about the topic, you will need to begin by making them want to listen.

> *Beliefs.* Does your audience accept the relationship between regular flossing and dental health? Or do you need to inform them about the consequences of neglecting this daily ritual?

> *Values.* Which underlying values matter most to your listeners: Health? Attractiveness? Career success? The approach you'll use will depend on the answer to these questions.

Experts in audience analysis, such as professional speechwriters, often try to concentrate on values. As one team of researchers pointed out, "values have the advantage of being comparatively small in number, and owing to their abstract nature, are more likely to be shared by large numbers of people."[5] Stable American values include the ideas of good citizenship, a strong work ethic, tolerance of differing political views, individualism, and justice for all. Michael Kelley, a student at Kansas State University, appealed to his audience's values when he wanted to make the point that unemployment discrimination was unfair:

> Jobless discrimination occurs when a company or business refuses to employ an individual unless they are already employed elsewhere. This should alarm us for several reasons. The Bureau of Labor Statistics, as of April 6, 2012, points out that there are 5.3 million Americans who have been unemployed for seven months or more because of the recession. It's not fair to discriminate against them. . . . We need to make jobless discrimination just as illegal as refusing to hire someone because of their sex, race or religion.[6]

Kelley pointed out that discriminating against unemployed people was basically unfair; his analysis had suggested that the value of fairness would be important to his audience. You can often make an inference about audience members' attitudes by recognizing the beliefs and values they are likely to hold. In this example, Kelley knew that his audience, made up mostly of idealistic college students and professors, would dislike the idea of unfair discrimination.

"I'll tell you what this election is about. It's about homework, and pitiful allowances, and having to clean your room. It's also about candy, and ice cream, and staying up late."

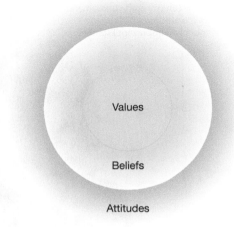

FIGURE 11-1 Structure of Values, Beliefs, and Attitudes

Attitudes, Beliefs, and Values

Find a persuasive appeal in an advertisement, newspaper editorial, or another source. Identify an attitude or value that the source of the message is appealing to. Explain why, in your opinion, this appeal is or is not effective.

The analysis of hidden psychological states can be extremely helpful in audience analysis. For example, a religious group might hold the value of "obeying God's word." For some fundamentalists this might lead to the belief, based on their religious training, that women are not meant to perform the same functions in society as men. This, in turn, might lead to the attitude that women ought not to pursue careers as firefighters, police officers, or construction workers.

You can also make a judgment about one attitude your audience members hold based on your knowledge of other attitudes they hold. If your audience is made up of undergraduates who have a positive attitude toward liberation movements, it is a good bet they also have a positive attitude toward civil rights and ecology. If they have a negative attitude toward collegiate sports, they may also have a negative attitude toward fraternities and sororities. This should suggest not only some appropriate topics for each audience but also ways that those topics could be developed.

The Occasion

The second phase in analyzing a speaking situation focuses on the occasion. The occasion of a speech is determined by the circumstances surrounding it. Three of these circumstances are time, place, and audience expectations.

Time Your speech occupies an interval of time that is surrounded by other events. For example, other speeches might be presented before or after yours, or comments might be made that set a certain tone or mood. External events such as elections, the start of a new semester, or even the weather can color the occasion in one way or another. The date on which you give your speech might have some historical significance. If that historical significance relates in some way to your topic, you can use it to help build audience interest.

The time available for your speech is also an essential consideration. You should choose a topic that is broad enough to say something worthwhile but brief enough to fit your limits. "Wealth," for example, might be an inherently interesting topic to some college students, but it would be difficult to cover such a broad topic in a 10-minute speech and still say anything significant. However, a topic like "How to Make Extra Money in Your Spare Time" could conceivably be covered in 10 minutes in enough depth to make it worthwhile. All speeches have limits, whether or not they are explicitly stated. If you are invited to say a few words, and you present a few volumes, you might not be invited back.

Former Alaska governor Sarah Palin delights in skewering political figures and viewpoints that conflict with her conservative beliefs and values. This motivates her supporters and antagonizes those who disagree with her. How successful is Palin at reaching her target audience? How can you craft your remarks to appeal to the attitudes, beliefs, and values of your most important listeners?

Place Your speech also occupies a physical space. The beauty or squalor of your surroundings and the noise or stuffiness of the room should all be taken into consideration. These physical surroundings can be referred to in your speech if appropriate. If you were talking about world poverty, for example, you could compare your surroundings to those that might be found in a poorer country.

Audience Expectations Finally, your speech is surrounded by audience expectations. A speech presented in a college class, or a TED talk like Adora Svitak's (which we mentioned at the beginning of this chapter), is usually expected to reflect a high level of thought and intelligence. This doesn't necessarily mean that it has to be boring or humorless; wit and humor are, after all, indicative of intelligence. But it does mean that you have to put a little more effort into your presentation than if you were discussing the same subject with friends over coffee.

In the movie *Bridesmaids*, Annie (Kristen Wiig) and Helen (Rose Byrne) try to outdo each other with dueling speeches (and breaking into song) instead of offering traditional engagement party toasts. Have you ever experienced a speech that didn't fit the occasion?

When you are considering the occasion of your speech, it pays to remember that every occasion is unique. Although there are obvious differences among the occasions of a college class, a church sermon, and a bachelor party "roast," there are also many subtle differences that will apply only to the circumstances of each unique event.

Gathering Information

This discussion about planning a speech purpose and analyzing the speech situation makes it apparent that it takes time, interest, and knowledge to develop a topic well. Setting aside a block of time to reflect on your own ideas is essential. However, you will also need to gather information from outside sources.

By this time you are probably familiar with both web searches and library research as forms of gathering information. Sometimes, however, speakers overlook interviewing, personal observation, and survey research as equally effective methods of gathering information. Let's review all these methods here and perhaps provide a new perspective on one or more of them.

Online Research

The ease of using search engines like Google has made them the popular favorite for speech research. But students are sometimes so grateful to have found a website dealing with their topic that they forget to evaluate it. Like any other written sources you would use, websites should be accurate and rational. Beyond that, there are three specific criteria that you can use to evaluate the quality of a website. They are listed in the checklist on page 335.

In the case of some special search engines, like Google Scholar, the criteria of credibility, objectivity, and currency will be practically guaranteed. However, these guidelines are especially important when accessing information from Wikipedia, the popular online encyclopedia. Because anyone can edit a Wikipedia article at any time, many professors forbid the use of it as a primary resource. Others allow

> cultural idiom

bachelor party:
a men-only gathering of the groom and his friends just prior to his wedding

roast:
an entertaining program in which the guest of honor is teased in an affectionate manner

@Work

Sample Analysis of a Speaking Situation

Audience: Employees in the Production Department of my company

Situation: Training session on sexual harassment

Management has realized that our company is at risk of being slapped with a harassment lawsuit. The most likely offenders are several "good old boys" who have worked in the Production Department a long time. They are really nice guys, and I know they view their jokes and comments as good-natured fun and not harassment. On the other hand, several female employees have complained about being offended by these men.

One of my duties as an intern in the Human Resources Department of my company is to share the latest information on sexual harassment with employees. My bosses know that this topic has been covered in my classes, and they decided I should pass it along.

Purpose: After I am finished speaking, I want audience members to view sexual harassment as a legitimate concern and to be careful to avoid communicating in a way that might be perceived as harassing.

Analysis: This is a tricky situation for me: First of all, these guys will be a captive audience, forced to listen to a subject that they find annoying. Also, I am younger than anyone in my audience, and I'm a woman. In fact, I've been the target of some of the behavior I'm being asked to discourage! There's a strong risk that the men who are the target of my remarks won't take me seriously, so I have to change their attitude about the subject and me.

I know that scolding and threatening these men would be a big mistake. Even if they didn't object out loud, they would probably regard me as some sort of chip-on-the-shoulder feminist and consider the advice I offered as "politically correct" and out of touch with the way the real world operates.

To avoid this sort of negative reaction, I need to separate myself from the law that they dislike, taking the position of sharing with them "here's what I've learned about how it works." I might even give them a few examples of harassment suits that I think were frivolous, so we can agree that some people are much too sensitive. That common ground will help put us on the same side. Then I can emphasize that they don't have to agree with the law to follow it. I'll tell stories of people like them who suffered as targets of harassment suits, pointing out that even an unfair accusation of harassment could make all of our lives miserable. My basic argument will be that potentially harassing behavior "isn't worth it."

I also hope to use my age and gender as advantages. A couple of the men have told me that they have daughters my age. I could ask the group to imagine how they would feel if their daughters were the targets of suggestive comments and sexual jokes. I'll tell them that I know how angry and protective my dad would feel, and I'll tell them that I know that, as good fathers, they'd feel the same way. I could also ask them to think about how they would feel if their wives, sisters, or mothers were the targets of jokes that made those women feel uncomfortable.

I don't think any speech will totally reverse attitudes that were built over these men's lifetimes, but I do think that getting on their side will be much more effective than labeling them as insensitive sexist pigs and threatening them with lawsuits. ●

Wikipedia to be used for general information and inspiration. Most will allow its use when articles have references to external sources (whether online or not) and the student reads the references and checks whether they really do support what the article says.

However you use the Web, remember that it is a good addition to, but *not* a substitute for, library research. Library experts help you make sense of and determine the validity of the information you find. And a library can be a great environment for concentration, a place of quiet with minimum distractions that is rare in our media age.

CHECKLIST > **Evaluating Websites**

Consider the following three criteria when choosing a website for online research:

☐ **Credibility.** Anyone can establish a website, so it is important to evaluate where your information is coming from. Who wrote the page? Anonymous sources should not be used. If the sources *are* listed, are their credentials listed? What institution publishes the document? Remember that a handsome site design doesn't guarantee high-quality information, but misspellings and grammatical mistakes are good signs of low quality.

☐ **Objectivity.** What opinions (if any) are expressed by the author? The domain names .edu, .gov, .org, or .net are generally preferable to .com, because if the page is a mask for advertising, the information might be biased.

☐ **Currency.** When was the page produced? When was it updated? How up-to-date are the links? If any of the links are dead, the information might not be current.

Library Research

Libraries, like people, tend to be unique. Although many of your library's resources will be available online through your school's website, it can be extremely rewarding to get to know your library in person, to see what kind of special collections and services it offers, and just to find out where everything is. There are, however, a few resources that are common to most libraries, including the library catalog, reference works, periodicals, nonprint materials, and databases.

The Library Catalog   The library catalog is an ancient and noble information-storing device. Once housed in long rows of oak drawers, catalogs are now computerized, but they remain your key to all the books and other materials in the library. Each work is filed according to subject, author, and title, so you can look for general topics as well as for specific books and authors.

Reference Works   Reference works will also be listed in the library catalog. There are encyclopedias galore, even specialized ones such as *The Historical Dictionary of American Slang* and *The Encyclopedia of American History*, and you can collect a lot of facts in a short time in the reference room. Reference works are good for uncovering basic information, definitions, descriptions, and sources for further investigation.

Periodicals   Magazines, journals, and newspapers are good resources for finding recently published material on interesting topics. Specialized indexes such as *Psychological Abstracts* can be used to find articles in specific fields, and newspaper indexes such as *The New York Times Index* can be used to find online newspaper articles. Periodicals are a good source of high-interest, up-to-date information on your topic.

Nonprint Materials   Most libraries are also treasuries of nonprint and audio-visual materials. Films, records, tapes, and videotapes can be used not only as research tools but also as aids during your presentation.

Databases   Libraries have access to databases that are not available to home users without hefty subscription fees. **Databases** are computerized collections of highly credible information from a wide variety of sources. One popular collection of databases is Lexis-Nexis, which contains millions of articles from news services, magazines, scholarly journals, conference papers, books, law journals, and other sources. Other popular databases include ProQuest, Factiva, and Academic Search Premier, and there are dozens of specialized databases, such as Communication and Mass Media Complete. Database searches are slightly different from web searches; they generally don't respond well to long strings of terms or searches worded as questions. With databases it is best to use one or two key terms with a connector such as AND, OR, or NOT.[7] Once you learn this technique and a few other rules (perhaps with a librarian's help), you will be able to locate dozens of articles on your topic in just a few minutes.

Interviewing

An information-gathering interview allows you to view your topic from an expert's perspective, to take advantage of that expert's experience, research, and thought. You can also use an interview to stimulate your own thinking. Often the interview will save you hours of Internet or library research and allow you to present ideas that you could not have uncovered any other way. And because an interview is an interaction with an expert, many ideas that otherwise might be unclear can become more understandable through questions and answers. Interviews can be conducted face-to-face, by telephone, or by e-mail. If you do use an interview for research, you might want to read the section on that type of interview in the appendix.

Survey Research

One advantage of **survey research**—the distribution of questionnaires for people to respond to—is that it can give you up-to-date answers concerning "the way things are" for a specific audience. For example, if you handed out questionnaires a week or so before presenting a speech on the possible dangers of body piercing, you could present information like this in your speech:

> According to a survey I conducted last week, 90 percent of the students in this class believe that body piercing is basically safe. Only 10 percent are familiar with the scarring and injury that can result from this practice. Two of you, in fact, have experienced serious infections from body piercing: one from a pierced tongue and one from a simple pierced ear.

That statement would be of immediate interest to your audience members because *they* were the ones who were surveyed. Another advantage of conducting your own survey is that it is one of the best ways to find out about your audience: It is, in fact, *the* best way to collect the demographic data mentioned earlier. The one disadvantage of conducting your own survey is that, if it is used as evidence, it might not have as much credibility as published evidence found in the library. But the advantages seem to outweigh the disadvantages of survey research in public speaking.

No matter how you gather your information, remember that it is the *quality* rather than the quantity of the research that is most important. The key is to determine carefully what type of research will answer the questions you need to have answered. Sometimes only one type of research will be necessary; at other times every type mentioned here will have to be used. Generally, you will collect far more information than you'll use in your speech, but the winnowing process will ensure that the research you do use is of high quality.

Along with improving the quality of what you say, effective research will also minimize the anxiety of actually giving a speech. Let's take a close look at that form of anxiety.

Managing Communication Apprehension

The terror that strikes the hearts of so many beginning speakers is commonly known as *stage fright* or *speech anxiety* and is called *communication apprehension* by communication scholars.[8] Whatever term you choose, the important point to realize is that fear about speaking can be managed in a way that works for you rather than against you.

Facilitative and Debilitative Communication Apprehension

Although communication apprehension is a very real problem for many speakers, it is definitely a problem that can be overcome. Interestingly enough, the first step in feeling less apprehensive about speaking is to realize that a certain amount of nervousness is not only natural but also facilitative. That is, **facilitative communication apprehension** is a factor that can help improve your performance. Just as totally relaxed actors or musicians aren't likely to perform at the top of their potential, speakers think more rapidly and express themselves more energetically when their level of tension is moderate.

It is only when the level of anxiety is intense that it becomes **debilitative**, inhibiting effective self-expression. Intense fear causes trouble in two ways. First, the strong emotion keeps you from thinking clearly.[9] This has been shown to be a problem even in the preparation process: Students who are highly anxious about giving a speech will find the preliminary steps, including research and organization, to be more difficult.[10] Second, intense fear leads to an urge to do something, anything, to make the problem go away. This urge to escape often causes a speaker to speed up delivery, which results in a rapid, almost machine-gun style. As you can imagine, this boost in speaking rate leads to even more mistakes, which only add to the speaker's anxiety. Thus, a relatively small amount of nervousness can begin to feed on itself until it grows into a serious problem.

Sources of Debilitative Communication Apprehension

Before we describe how to manage debilitative communication apprehension, let's consider why people are afflicted with the problem in the first place.[11]

Previous Negative Experience   People often feel apprehensive about speech giving because of unpleasant past experiences. Most of us are uncomfortable doing *anything* in public, especially if it is a form of performance in which our talents and abilities are being evaluated. An unpleasant experience in one type of performance can cause you to expect that a future similar situation will also be unpleasant.[12] These expectations can be realized through the self-fulfilling prophecies discussed in Chapter 3. A traumatic failure at an earlier speech and low self-esteem from critical parents during childhood are common examples of experiences that can cause later communication apprehension.

You might object to the idea that past experiences cause communication apprehension. After all, not everyone who has bungled a speech or had critical parents is debilitated in the future. To understand why some people are affected more strongly than others by past experiences, we need to consider another cause of communication apprehension.

Irrational Thinking   Cognitive psychologists argue that it is not events that cause people to feel nervous but rather the beliefs they have about those events. Certain irrational beliefs leave people feeling unnecessarily apprehensive. Psychologist

Actress Kim Basinger had such severe communication apprehension as a child that her parents had her tested for autism. The HBO film *Panic: A Film about Coping* features commentary from Basinger about her struggles with anxiety. How might Basinger have benefited from the advice in these pages? How can you use this advice to feel less anxious?

Albert Ellis lists several such beliefs, or examples of **irrational thinking**, which we will call "fallacies" because of their illogical nature.[13]

- **Catastrophic failure.** People who succumb to the **fallacy of catastrophic failure** operate on the assumption that if something bad can happen, it probably will. Their thoughts before a speech resemble these:

  "As soon as I stand up to speak, I'll forget everything I wanted to say."

  "Everyone will think my ideas are stupid."

  "Somebody will probably laugh at me."

  Although it is naive to imagine that all your speeches will be totally successful, it is equally naive to assume they will all fail miserably. One way to escape the fallacy of catastrophic failure is to take a more realistic look at the situation. Would your audience members really hoot you off the stage? Will they really think your ideas are stupid? Even if you did forget your remarks for a moment, would the results be a genuine disaster? It helps to remember that nervousness is more apparent to the speaker than to the audience.[14] Beginning public speakers, when congratulated for their poise during a speech, are apt to say, "Are you kidding? I was dying up there."

- **Perfection.** Speakers who succumb to the **fallacy of perfection** expect themselves to behave flawlessly. Whereas such a standard of perfection might serve as a target and a source of inspiration (like the desire to make a hole in one while golfing), it is totally unrealistic to expect that you will write and deliver a perfect speech, especially as a beginner. It helps to remember that audiences don't expect you to be perfect.

- **Approval.** The mistaken belief called the **fallacy of approval** is based on the idea that it is vital—not just desirable—to gain the approval of everyone in the audience. It is rare that even the best speakers please everyone, especially on topics that are at all controversial. To paraphrase Abraham Lincoln, you can't please all the people all the time, and it is irrational to expect you will.

- **Overgeneralization.** The **fallacy of overgeneralization** might also be labeled the fallacy of exaggeration, because it occurs when a person blows one poor experience out of proportion. Consider these examples:

  "I'm so stupid! I mispronounced that word."

  "I completely blew it—I forgot one of my supporting points."

  "My hands were shaking. The audience must have thought I was crazy."

  A second type of exaggeration occurs when a speaker treats occasional lapses as if they were the rule rather than the exception. This sort of mistake usually involves extreme labels, such as "always" or "never."

  "I always forget what I want to say."

  "I can never come up with a good topic."

  "I can't do anything right."

Overcoming Debilitative Communication Apprehension

There are five strategies that can help you manage debilitative communication apprehension:

> **cultural idiom**
> **hoot:**
> express rude and disparaging remarks

> **cultural idiom**
> **a hole in one:**
> hitting the golf ball in the hole with one swing of the club, a perfect shot

> **cultural idiom**
> **blows ... out of proportion:**
> exaggerates

Speech Anxiety

1. What is your overall level of anxiety about speech making?

   a. Nonexistent

   b. Moderate

   c. Severe

2. Are you in control of your speech anxiety, or is your speech anxiety in control of you?

   a. I'm in control

   b. Half and half

   c. Anxiety is in control

What level of the following do you experience while speaking?

3. Sweating/sweaty palms

   a. Nonexistent

   b. Moderate

   c. Severe

4. Rapid breathing

   a. Nonexistent

   b. Moderate

   c. Severe

5. Restless energy

   a. Nonexistent

   b. Moderate

   c. Severe

6. Forgetting what you wanted to say

   a. Nonexistent

   b. Moderate

   c. Severe

Give yourself one point for every "a," two points for every "b," and three points for every "c." If your score is:

6 to 9 You have nerves of steel. You're probably a natural public speaker.

10 to 13 You are the typical public speaker. Read the strategies discussed in the next section to learn how to improve your skills.

14 to 18 You tend to have significant apprehension about public speaking. You need to consider each strategy below carefully. Although you will benefit from the tips provided, you should keep in mind that some of the greatest speakers of all time have considered themselves highly anxious. ●

- **Use nervousness to your advantage.** Paralyzing fear is obviously a problem, but a little nervousness can actually help you deliver a successful speech. Being completely calm can take away the passion that is one element of a good speech. Use the strategies below to control your anxiety, but don't try to completely eliminate it.

- **Understand the difference between rational and irrational fears.** Some fears about speaking are rational. For example, you ought to be worried if you haven't properly prepared for your speech. But fears based on the fallacies you just read about aren't constructive. It's not realistic to expect that you'll deliver a perfect speech, and it's not rational to indulge in catastrophic fantasies about what might go wrong.

- **Maintain a receiver orientation.** Paying too much attention to your own feelings—even when you're feeling good about yourself—will take energy away from communicating with your listeners. Concentrate on your audience members rather than on yourself. Focus your energy on keeping them interested, and on making sure they understand you.

- **Keep a positive attitude.** Build and maintain a positive attitude toward your audience, your speech, and yourself as a speaker. Some communication consultants suggest that public speakers should concentrate on three statements immediately before speaking. The three statements are as follows:

  I'm glad I have the chance to talk about this topic.

  I know what I'm talking about.

  I care about my audience.

  Repeating these statements (until you believe them) can help you maintain a positive attitude.

  Another technique for building a positive attitude is known as **visualization.**[15] This technique has been used successfully with athletes. It requires you to use your imagination to visualize the successful completion of your speech. Visualization can help make the self-fulfilling prophecy discussed in Chapter 3 work in your favor.

- **Be prepared!** Preparation is the most important key to controlling communication apprehension. You can feel confident if you know from practice that your remarks are well organized and supported and your delivery is smooth. Researchers have determined that the highest level of communication apprehension occurs just before speaking, the second highest level at the time the assignment is announced and explained, and the lowest level during the time you spend preparing your speech.[16] You should take advantage of this relatively low-stress time to work through the problems that would tend to make you nervous during the actual speech. For example, if your anxiety is based on a fear of forgetting what you are going to say, make sure that your note cards are complete and effective, and that you have practiced your speech thoroughly (we'll go into speech practice in more detail in a moment). If, on the other hand, your great fear is "sounding stupid," then getting started early with lots of research and advance thinking is the key to relieving your communication apprehension.

One of the first things you'll want to consider is the type of delivery you will use.

Choosing a Type of Delivery

There are four basic types of delivery: extemporaneous, impromptu, manuscript, and memorized. Each type creates a different impression and is appropriate under different conditions. Any speech may incorporate more than one of these types of delivery. For purposes of discussion, however, it is best to consider them separately.

Extemporaneous

An **extemporaneous speech** is planned in advance but presented in a direct, spontaneous manner. Extemporaneous speeches are conversational in tone, which means that they give the audience members the impression that you are talking to them, directly and honestly. Extemporaneous speaking is the most common type of delivery in both the classroom and the "outside" world.

Impromptu

An **impromptu speech** is given off the top of one's head, without preparation. This type of speech is spontaneous by definition, but it is a delivery style that is necessary

> cultural idiom

off the top of one's head:
with little time to plan or think about

for informal talks, group discussions, and comments on others' speeches. It is also a highly effective training aid that teaches you to think on your feet and to organize your thoughts quickly.

Manuscript

Manuscript speeches are read word for word from a prepared text. They are necessary when you are speaking for the record, as when speaking at legal proceedings or when presenting scientific findings. The greatest disadvantage of a manuscript speech is the lack of spontaneity that may result.

Memorized

Memorized speeches—those learned by heart—are the most difficult and often the least effective. They often seem excessively formal. However, like manuscript speeches, they may be necessary on special occasions. They are used in oratory contests, and they are used as training devices for memory.

There is one guideline that is true for each type of speech: Practice.

> cultural idiom
> **for the record:**
> word-for-word documentation

What type of delivery do you prefer? Why?

Practicing the Speech

A smooth and natural delivery is the result of extensive practice. Get to know your material until you feel comfortable with your presentation. One way to do that is to go through some or all steps listed in the checklist on page 342.

Adora Svitak, whose profile appeared at the beginning of this chapter, practiced her speech while writing it:

> As far as preparation for the speech, I wrote a rough draft and actually practiced the speech even as I was making changes. I found that reading it aloud helped me find any structural/organizational errors or places where I could make my wording more effective. As someone who tends to write on the convoluted side, reading it aloud throughout the writing process was key to preparation.[19]

In each of these steps, critique your speech according to the guidelines that follow.

Guidelines for Delivery

Let's examine some nonverbal aspects of presenting a speech. As you read in Chapter 6, nonverbal behavior can change, or even contradict, the meaning of the words a speaker utters. If audience members want to interpret how you feel about something, they are likely to trust your nonverbal communication more than the words you speak. If you tell them, "It's great to be here today," but you stand before them slouched over with your hands in your pockets and an expression on your face like you're about to be shot, they are likely to discount what you say. This might cause your audience members to react negatively to your speech, and their negative reaction might make you even more nervous. This cycle of speaker and audience reinforcing each other's feelings can work for you, though, if you approach a subject with genuine enthusiasm. Enthusiasm is shown through both the visual and auditory aspects of your delivery.

Visual Aspects of Delivery

Visual aspects of delivery include appearance, movement, posture, facial expression, and eye contact.

In the timeless comedy *Bridget Jones's Diary*, Bridget (Renée Zellweger) delivers a hilariously awkward speech that manages to offend several audience members in only a few paragraphs. (To watch it, type "Bridget Jones speech" into your search engine.) How might Bridget have done a better (if less amusing) job? How can you avoid the kinds of mistakes Bridget makes?

CHECKLIST > **Practicing Your Presentation**

☐ First, present the speech to yourself. "Talk through" the entire speech, including your examples and forms of support. Don't skip through parts of your speech as you practice by using placeholders such as "This is where I present my statistics" or "This is where I explain about photosynthesis." Make sure you know how you plan to present your statistics and explanations.

☐ Tape-record the speech, and listen to it. Because we hear our own voices partially through our cranial bone structure, we are sometimes surprised at what we sound like to others. Videotaping has been proven to be an especially effective tool for rehearsals, giving you an idea of what you look like, as well as what you sound like.[17]

☐ Present the speech in front of a small group of friends or relatives.[18]

☐ Present the speech to at least one listener in the room in which you will present the final speech (or, if that room is not available, a similar room).

> cultural idiom

flashy:
showy, gaudy

Describe a speaker you have observed whose delivery is memorable—in either a good or a bad way. What visual and vocal elements of the speech do you recall that stood out, and how did they help or hinder the speaker from succeeding? How can you make your delivery more effective?

Appearance   Appearance is not a presentation variable as much as a preparation variable. Some communication consultants suggest new clothes, new glasses, and new hairstyles for their clients. In case you consider any of these, be forewarned that you should be attractive to your audience but not flashy. Research suggests that audiences like speakers who are similar to them, but they prefer the similarity to be shown conservatively.[20] Speakers, it seems, are perceived to be more credible when they look businesslike. Part of looking businesslike, of course, is looking like you took care in the preparation of your wardrobe and appearance.

Movement   The way you walk to the front of your audience will express your confidence and enthusiasm. And after you begin speaking, nervous energy can cause your body to shake and twitch, and that can be distressing both to you and to your audience. One way to control involuntary movement is to move voluntarily when you feel the need to move. Don't feel that you have to stand in one spot or that all your gestures need to be carefully planned. Simply get involved in your message, and let your involvement create the motivation for your movement. That way, when you move, you will emphasize what you are saying in the same way you would emphasize it if you were talking to a group of friends.

Movement can also help you maintain contact with all members of your audience. Those closest to you will feel the greatest contact. This creates what is known as the "action zone" in the typical classroom, within the area of the front and center of the room. Movement enables you to extend this action zone, to include in it people who would otherwise remain uninvolved. Without overdoing it, you should feel free to move toward, away from, or from side to side in front of your audience.

Remember: Move with the understanding that it will add to the meaning of the words you use. It is difficult to bang your fist on a podium or take a step without conveying emphasis. Make the emphasis natural by allowing your message to create your motivation to move.

Posture   Generally speaking, good posture means standing with your spine relatively straight, your shoulders relatively squared off, and your feet angled out to keep your body from falling over sideways. In other words, rather than standing at military attention, you should be comfortably erect.

Good posture can help you control nervousness by allowing your breathing apparatus to work properly; when your brain receives enough oxygen, it's easier for you to think clearly. Good posture also increases your audience contact because the audience members will feel that you are interested enough in them to stand formally, yet relaxed enough to be at ease with them.

Facial Expression The expression on your face can be more meaningful to an audience than the words you say. Try it yourself with a mirror. Say, "You're a terrific audience," for example, with a smirk, with a warm smile, with a deadpan expression, and then with a scowl. It just doesn't mean the same thing. But don't try to fake it. Like your movement, your facial expressions will reflect your genuine involvement with your message.

Eye Contact Eye contact is perhaps the most important nonverbal facet of delivery. Eye contact not only increases your direct contact with your audience but also can be used to help you control your nervousness. Direct eye contact is a form of reality testing. The most frightening aspect of speaking is the unknown. How will the audience react? What will it think? Direct eye contact allows you to test your perception of your audience as you speak. Usually, especially in a college class, you will find that your audience is more "with" you than you think. By deliberately establishing contact with any apparently bored audience members, you might find that they are interested, they just aren't showing that interest because they don't think anyone is looking.

To maintain eye contact, you could try to meet the eyes of each member of your audience squarely at least once during any given presentation. After you have made definite eye contact, move on to another audience member. You can learn to do this quickly, so you can visually latch on to every member of a good-sized class in a relatively short time.

The characteristics of appearance, movement, posture, facial expression, and eye contact are visual, nonverbal facets of delivery. Now consider the auditory nonverbal messages that you might send during a presentation.

Auditory Aspects of Delivery

As you read in Chapter 6, your paralanguage—the way you use your voice—says a good deal about you, especially about your sincerity and enthusiasm. In addition, using your voice well can help you control your nervousness. It's another cycle: Controlling your vocal characteristics will decrease your nervousness, which will enable you to control your voice even more. But this cycle can also work in the opposite direction. If your voice is out of control, your nerves will probably be in the same state. Controlling your voice is mostly a matter of recognizing and using appropriate volume, rate, pitch, and articulation.

Volume The loudness of your voice is determined by the amount of air you push past the vocal folds in your throat. The key to controlling volume, then, is controlling the amount of air you use. The key to determining the right volume is audience contact. Your delivery should be loud enough so that your audience members can hear everything you say but not so loud that they feel you are talking to someone in the next room. Too much volume is seldom the problem for beginning speakers. Usually they either are not loud enough or have a tendency to fade off at the end of a thought. Sometimes, when they lose faith in an idea in midsentence, they compromise by mumbling the end of the sentence so that it isn't quite coherent.

Rate There is a range of personal differences in speaking speed, or **rate**. Daniel Webster, for example, is said to have spoken at around 90 words per minute, whereas one actor who is known for his fast-talking commercials speaks at about 250. Normal speaking speed, however, is between 120 and 150 words per minute.

If you talk much more slowly than that, you may tend to lull your audience to sleep. Faster speaking rates are stereotypically associated with speaker competence,[21] but if you speak too rapidly, you will tend to be unintelligible. Once again, your involvement in your message is the key to achieving an effective rate.

Pitch   The highness or lowness of your voice—**pitch**—is controlled by the frequency at which your vocal folds vibrate as you push air through them. Because taut vocal folds vibrate at a greater frequency, pitch is influenced by muscular tension. This explains why nervous speakers have a tendency occasionally to "squeak," whereas relaxed speakers seem to be more in control. Pitch will tend to follow rate and volume. As you speed up or become louder, your pitch will have a tendency to rise. If your range in pitch is too narrow, your voice will have a singsong quality. If it is too wide, you may sound overly dramatic. You should control your pitch so that your listeners believe you are talking with them rather than performing in front of them. Once again, your involvement in your message should take care of this naturally for you.

When considering volume, rate, and pitch, keep emphasis in mind. Remember that a change in volume, pitch, or rate will result in emphasis. If you pause or speed up, your rate will suggest emphasis. Words you whisper or scream will be emphasized by their volume.

Articulation   The final auditory nonverbal behavior, articulation, is perhaps the most important. For our purposes here, **articulation** means pronouncing all the parts of all the necessary words and nothing else.

It is not our purpose to condemn regional or ethnic dialects within this discussion. It is true that a considerable amount of research suggests that regional dialects can cause negative impressions,[22] but our purpose here is to suggest careful, not standardized, articulation. Incorrect articulation is usually nothing more than careless articulation. It is caused by (1) leaving off parts of words (deletion), (2) replacing parts of words (substitution), (3) adding parts to words (addition), or (4) overlapping two or more words (slurring).

Deletion   The most common mistake in articulation is **deletion**, or leaving off part of a word. As you are thinking the complete word, it is often difficult to recognize that you are saying only part of it. The most common deletions occur at the ends of words, especially *-ing* words. *Going, doing,* and *stopping* become *goin', doin',* and *stoppin'.* Parts of words can be left off in the middle, too, as in *terr'iss* for *terrorist, Innernet* for *Internet,* and *asst* for *asked.*

Substitution   **Substitution** takes place when you replace part of a word with an incorrect sound. The ending *-th* is often replaced at the end of a word with a single *t,* as when *with* becomes *wit.* The *th-* sound is also a problem at the beginning of words, as *this, that,* and *those* have a tendency to become *dis, dat,* and *dose.* (This tendency is especially prevalent in many parts of the northeastern United States.)

Addition   The articulation problem of **addition** is caused by adding extra parts to words, such as *incentative* instead of *incentive, athalete* instead of *athlete,* and *orientated* instead of *oriented.* Sometimes this type of addition is caused by incorrect word choice, as when *irregardless* is used for *regardless.*

Another type of addition is the use of "tag questions," such as *you know?* or *you see?* or *right?* at the end of sentences. To have every other sentence punctuated with one of these barely audible superfluous phrases can be annoying.

Probably the worst type of addition, or at least the most common, is the use of *uh* and *anda* between words. *Anda* is often stuck between two words when *and* isn't even needed. If you find yourself doing that, you might want just to pause or swallow instead.[23]

Understanding Diversity

A Compendium of American Dialects

The following is a short glossary of examples of regionalized pronunciation (with apologies to all residents who find them exaggerated).

Appalachian Hill Country

Bile To bring water to 212 degrees

Cowcumber A vittle you make pickles out of

Hern Not his'n

Tard Exhausted

Bawlamerese (Spoken around Baltimore)

Arn What you do with an arnin board

Blow The opposite of above

Pleece Two or more po-leece

Torst Tourist

Boston

Back The outer covering of a tree trunk

Had licka Hard liquor

Moa The opposite of less

Pahk To leave your car somewhere, as in, "Pahk the cah in Haavaad Yahd"

NooYorkese

Huh The opposite of him

Mel pew? May I help you?

Reg you la caw fee Coffee with milk and sugar

Pock A place with trees and muggers

Philadelphia

Fluffya The name of the city

Mayan The opposite of yours

Pork A wooded recreational area

Tail What you use to dry off with after a shower

Southern

Abode A plank of wood

Bidness Such as, "Mistah Cottah's paynut bidness"

Shurf A local law enforcement officer

Watt The color of the Watt House in Wushinton

Texas

Ah stay Iced tea

Bayer A beverage made from hops

Pars A town in Texas. Also, the capital of France

Awful Tar The famous tall structure in Pars, France

Other interesting regionalisms can be found at the Slanguistics website, www.slanguage.com. ●

Slurring   **Slurring** is caused by trying to say two or more words at once—or at least overlapping the end of one word with the beginning of the next. Word pairs ending with *of* are the worst offenders in this category. *Sort of* becomes *sorta*, *kind of* becomes *kinda*, and *because of* becomes *becausa*. Word combinations ending with *to* are often slurred, as when *want to* becomes *wanna*. Sometimes even more than two words are blended together, as when *that is the way* becomes *thatsaway*. Careful articulation means using your lips, teeth, tongue, and jaw to bite off your words, cleanly and separately, one at a time.

Sample Speech

Adora Svitak was born in 1997. She was 12 years old when she gave the following speech at the TED conference in Long Beach, California, in 2010.

As a very young person planning to address an audience of older intellectuals, authors, and other notables who had paid $7,500 each to hear a 4-day series of speeches, Svitak had to do some serious analysis of her audience and occasion. In the end, she decided that no matter how distinguished her audience members were, they would still hold the universal human desire for a better future. She would refer to this in her speech:

> The goal is not to turn kids into your kind of adult, but rather better adults than you have been, which may be a little challenging considering your credentials.

Svitak also found another way to analyze the occasion of her speech:

> I also analyzed previous TED speakers. Indeed, you can get to know a lot about the ethos of a conference (and by extension, its audience) by considering past speeches.[24]

Svitak defined her speech purpose as follows:

> After listening to this speech, my audience members will be encouraged to listen and learn from kids, and to trust them and expect more from them.

She worded her thesis statement this way:

> Learning between grown-ups and kids should be reciprocal.

Svitak gathered information carefully and chose well-researched examples such as these:

> Now, what have kids done? Well, Anne Frank touched millions with her powerful account of the Holocaust, Ruby Bridges helped end segregation in the United States, and most recently, Charlie Simpson helped to raise 120,000 pounds for Haiti on his little bike.

She found visual aids to illustrate each of those examples, which she prepared in the form of Prezi slides (a dynamic form of PowerPoint that is available at www .prezi.com).

> She chose a combination of memorized and manuscript-style speaking:

> I chose to speak holding a manuscript mainly because the short preparation time before I went to the conference, as well as the number of changes I'd made the night before, made me want to have it on hand for the sake of confidence. I found the confidence I gained from holding the manuscript made me feel freer to improvise. However, in the future, I'd definitely prefer to memorize what I plan to say.

In terms of speech anxiety, Svitak felt she had an advantage over better-known speakers:

> Like probably anyone about to address an audience, I definitely felt some nervousness; luckily, it was tempered by the kindness of everyone at TED and the energy I felt as I ran onstage. You just have to realistically understand that you're giving a speech, not saving the world, but also just accept the nerves calmly instead of trying to fight them. However, it also helped that I was at this point pretty much a complete unknown to the audience, unburdened by too many prior expectations (versus a speaker like, say, James Cameron, who everyone probably knew a bit about).

Finally, Svitak said of her TED experience:

> I learned that the quality of an audience and the energy in the room can be amazing sources for the quality and energy in your speech. After speaking at a wide range of conferences, I realized that oftentimes if the crowd is a sleepy group around breakfast time, you have to work way harder to make people enthusiastic. Drawing energy from the crowd is great, but you also have to be prepared to create it.

SAMPLE SPEECH | What Adults Can Learn from Kids | **Adora Svitak**

1 Now, I want to start with a question: When was the last time you were called childish? For kids like me, being called childish can be a frequent occurrence. Every time we make irrational demands, exhibit irresponsible behavior, or display any other signs of being normal American citizens, we are called childish. Which really bothers me. After all, take a look at these events: imperialism and colonization, world wars, George W. Bush. Ask yourself, who's responsible? Adults.

The sharp focus of Svitak's introduction was made possible by her consideration of her purpose and the formation of her thesis statement. She shows Prezi slides illustrating each of her examples.

2 Now, what have kids done? Well, Anne Frank touched millions with her powerful account of the Holocaust, Ruby Bridges helped to end segregation in the United States, and, most recently, Charlie Simpson helped to raise 120,000 pounds for Haiti on his little bike.

She had researched her examples carefully, uncovering many more than we see here, but choosing just the ones that best fit her purpose. Again, she illustrates them with slides.

3 So, as you can see evidenced by such examples, age has absolutely nothing to do with it. The traits the word *childish* addresses are seen so often in adults that we should abolish this age-discriminatory word when it comes to criticizing behavior associated with irresponsibility and irrational thinking.

This was an applause line, and Svitak thanked her audience politely for it.

4 Then again, who's to say that certain types of irrational thinking aren't exactly what the world needs? Maybe you've had grand plans before but stopped yourself, thinking, "That's impossible," or, "That costs too much," or, "That won't benefit me." For better or worse, we kids aren't hampered as much when it comes to thinking about reasons why not to do things.

Again, she chooses specific examples to make her point.

5 Kids can be full of inspiring aspirations and hopeful thinking. Like my wish that no one went hungry or that everything were a free kind of utopia. How many of you still dream like that and believe in the possibilities? Sometimes a knowledge of history and the past failures of utopian ideals can be a burden because you know that if everything were free, then the food stocks would become depleted and scarce and lead to chaos. On the other hand, we kids still dream about perfection. And that's a good thing because in order to make anything a reality, you have to dream about it first.

She backs up her ideas about the advantages of children's ideas by recognizing the history of utopian ideals.

6 In many ways, our audacity to imagine helps push the boundaries of possibility. For instance, the Museum of Glass in Tacoma, Washington, my home state—yoo-hoo Washington!—has a program called Kids Design Glass, and kids draw their own ideas for glass art. Now, the resident artist said they got some of their best ideas through the program because kids don't think about the limitations of how hard it can be to blow glass into certain shapes; they just think of good ideas. Now, when you think of glass, you might think of colorful Chihuly designs or maybe Italian vases, but kids challenge glass artists to go beyond that into the realm of broken-hearted snakes and bacon boys, who you can see has meat vision.

Both "yoo-hoo Washington!" and "meat vision" are designed as laugh lines, and they are successful. Again, slides are used to illustrate.

7   Now, our inherent wisdom doesn't have to be insider's knowledge. Kids already do a lot of learning from adults, and we have a lot to share. I think that adults should start learning from kids. Now, I do most of my speaking in front of an education crowd, teachers and students, and I like this analogy: It shouldn't just be a teacher at the head of the classroom telling students, "Do this, do that." The students should teach their teachers. Learning between grown-ups and kids should be reciprocal. The reality, unfortunately, is a little different, and it has a lot to do with trust, or a lack of it.

8   Now, if you don't trust someone, you place restrictions on them, right? If I doubt my older sister's ability to pay back the 10 percent interest I established on her last loan, I'm going to withhold her ability to get more money from me until she pays it back. True story, by the way.

This well-chosen example from personal experience elicits a healthy laugh from her audience.

9   Now, adults seem to have a prevalently restrictive attitude towards kids from every "don't do that, don't do this" in the school handbook to restrictions on school Internet use. As history points out, regimes become oppressive when they're fearful about keeping control. And although adults may not be quite at the level of totalitarian regimes, kids have no, or very little, say in making the rules, when really the attitude should be reciprocal, meaning that the adult population should learn and take into account the wishes of the younger population.

A well-chosen historical truth that the audience can relate to.

10 Now, what's even worse than restriction is that adults often underestimate kids' abilities. We love challenges, but when expectations are low, trust me, we will sink to them. My own parents had anything but low expectations for me and my sister. Okay, so they didn't tell us to become doctors or lawyers or anything like that, but my dad did read to us about Aristotle and pioneer germ fighters when lots of other kids were hearing "The Wheels on the Bus Go Round and Round." Well, we heard that one too, but "Pioneer Germ Fighters" totally rules.

Another Prezi slide. Another laugh line.

11 I loved to write from the age of 4, and when I was 6 my mom bought me my own laptop equipped with Microsoft Word. Thank you Bill Gates and thank you Ma. I wrote over 300 short stories on that little laptop, and I wanted to get published. Instead of just scoffing at this heresy that a kid wanted to get published or saying wait until you're older, my parents were really supportive. Many publishers were not quite so encouraging, one large children's publisher ironically saying that they didn't work with children—children's publisher not working with children? I don't know, you're kind of alienating a large client there. Now, one publisher, Action Publishing, was willing to take that leap and trust me and to listen to what I had to say. They published my first book, *Flying Fingers*—you see it here—and from there on, it's gone to speaking at hundreds of schools, keynoting to thousands of educators and finally, today, speaking to you.

Again, a slide to show what her book looks like.

12 I appreciate your attention today, because to show that you truly care, you listen. But there's a problem with this rosy picture of kids being so much better than adults. Kids grow up and become adults just like you. (Laughter) Or just like you? Really? The goal is not to turn kids into your kind of adult, but rather better adults

than you have been, which may be a little challenging considering your credentials. (Laughter) But the way progress happens is because new generations and new eras grow and develop and become better than the previous ones. It's the reason we're not in the Dark Ages anymore. No matter your position or place in life, it is imperative to create opportunities for children so that we can grow up to blow you away. (Laughter)

Her audience analysis is manifested in her reference to the audience members' credentials.

13 Adults and fellow TEDsters, you need to listen and learn from kids and trust us and expect more from us. You must lend an ear today, because we are the leaders of tomorrow, which means we're going to be taking care of you when you're old and senile. No, just kidding. No, really, we are going to be the next generation, the ones who will bring this world forward. And in case you don't think that this really has meaning for you, remember that cloning is possible, and that involves going through childhood again, in which case you'll want to be heard just like my generation. Now, the world needs opportunities for new leaders and new ideas. Kids need opportunities to lead and succeed. Are you ready to make the match? Because the world's problems shouldn't be the human family's heirloom. Thank you.[25]

Shows slide: "You must lend an ear today, because we are the leaders of tomorrow."

Summary

This chapter dealt with your first tasks in preparing a speech: choosing and developing a topic. Some guidelines for choosing a topic include these: Look for a topic early and stick with it, choose a topic you find interesting, and choose a topic you already know something about.

One of your tasks is to understand your purpose so that you can stick to it as you prepare your speech. General purposes include entertaining, informing, and persuading. Specific purposes are expressed in the form of purpose statements, which must be result oriented, specific, and realistic.

Your next task is to formulate a thesis statement, which tells what the central idea of your speech is. Another early task is to analyze the speaking situation, including the audience and the occasion. When analyzing your audience, you should consider the audience purpose, demographics, attitudes, beliefs, and values. When analyzing the occasion, you should consider the time (and date) your speech will take place, the time available, the location, and audience expectations.

Although much of your speech will be based on personal reflection about your own ideas and experiences, it is usually necessary to gather some information from outside sources. Techniques for doing so include interviewing and surveys, as well as Internet and library research.

Carefully considering each of these preliminary tasks will enable you to avoid debilitative (as opposed to facilitative) communication apprehension. Sources of debilitative communication apprehension include irrational thinking, which might include a belief in one or more of the following fallacies: the fallacy of catastrophic failure (something is going to ruin this presentation), the fallacy of perfection (a good speaker never does anything wrong), the fallacy of absolute approval (everyone has to like you), and the fallacy of overgeneralization (you always mess up speeches). There are several methods of overcoming communication apprehension. The first is to remember that nervousness is natural, and to use it to your advantage. The others include being rational, receiver oriented, positive, and prepared.

There are four types of delivery: extemporaneous, impromptu, manuscript, and memorized. In each type, the speaker must be concerned with both visual and auditory aspects of the presentation. Visual aspects include appearance, movement, posture, facial expression, and eye contact. Auditory aspects include volume, rate, pitch, and articulation. The four most common articulation problems are deletion, substitution, addition, and slurring of word sounds.

Throughout all these preliminary tasks, you will be organizing information and choosing supporting material. These processes will be discussed in the next chapter.

Key Terms

addition The articulation error that involves adding extra parts to words. *p. 344*

articulation The process of pronouncing all the necessary parts of a word. *p. 344*

attitude The predisposition to respond to an idea, person, or thing favorably or unfavorably. *p. 331*

audience analysis A consideration of characteristics, including the type, goals, demographics, beliefs, attitudes, and values of listeners. *p. 329*

belief An underlying conviction about the truth of an idea, often based on cultural training. *p. 331*

database A computerized collection of information that can be searched in a variety of ways to locate information that the user is seeking. *p. 335*

debilitative communication apprehension An intense level of anxiety about speaking before an audience, resulting in poor performance. *p. 337*

deletion An articulation error that involves leaving off parts of words. *p. 344*

demographics Audience characteristics that can be analyzed statistically, such as age, gender, education, and group membership. *p. 329*

extemporaneous speech A speech that is planned in advance but presented in a direct, conversational manner. *p. 340*

facilitative communication apprehension A moderate level of anxiety about speaking before an audience that helps improve the speaker's performance. *p. 337*

fallacy of approval The irrational belief that it is vital to win the approval of virtually every person a communicator deals with. *p. 338*

fallacy of catastrophic failure The irrational belief that the worst possible outcome will probably occur. *p. 338*

fallacy of overgeneralization Irrational beliefs in which (1) conclusions (usually negative) are based on limited evidence or (2) communicators exaggerate their shortcomings. *p. 338*

fallacy of perfection The irrational belief that a worthwhile communicator should be able to handle every situation with complete confidence and skill. *p. 338*

general purpose One of three basic ways a speaker seeks to affect an audience: to entertain, inform, or persuade. *p. 327*

impromptu speech A speech given "off the top of one's head," without preparation. *p. 340*

irrational thinking Beliefs that have no basis in reality or logic; one source of debilitative communication apprehension. *p. 338*

manuscript speech A speech that is read word for word from a prepared text. *p. 341*

memorized speech A speech learned and delivered by rote without a written text. *p. 341*

pitch The highness or lowness of one's voice. *p. 344*

purpose statement A complete sentence that describes precisely what a speaker wants to accomplish. *p. 327*

rate The speed at which a speaker utters words. *p. 343*

slurring The articulation error that involves overlapping the end of one word with the beginning of the next. *p. 345*

specific purpose The precise effect that the speaker wants to have on an audience. It is expressed in the form of a purpose statement. *p. 327*

substitution The articulation error that involves replacing part of a word with an incorrect sound. *p. 344*

survey research Information gathering in which the responses of a sample of a population are collected to disclose information about the larger group. *p. 336*

thesis statement A complete sentence describing the central idea of a speech. *p. 328*

value A deeply rooted belief about a concept's inherent worth. *p. 331*

visualization A technique for behavior rehearsal (e.g., for a speech) that involves imagining the successful completion of the task. *p. 340*

Check Your Understanding

When it is time for you to prepare a speech assignment for your class, answer the following questions:

1. Why do you believe your topic has the potential to be effective for your specific audience?

2. Did your purpose statement and thesis statement follow the guidelines on pp. 327–328?

3. What characteristics of your audience and occasion made a difference in how you presented your speech?

4. What was the most effective piece of research that you found for your speech?

5. Would you consider yourself highly, moderately, or not particularly anxious about public speaking? What is the source of any anxiety you feel?

6. Why did you choose the type of delivery that you did?

Activities

1. **Formulating Purpose Statements** Write a specific purpose statement for each of the following speeches:

1. An after-dinner speech at an awards banquet in which you will honor a team who has a winning, but not championship, record. (You pick the team. For example: "After listening to my speech, my audience members will appreciate the individual sacrifices made by the members of the chess team.")

2. A classroom speech in which you explain how to do something. (Again, you choose the topic: "After listening to my speech, my audience members will know at least three ways to maximize their comfort and convenience on an economy class flight.")

3. A campaign speech in which you support the candidate of your choice. (For example: "After listening to my speech, my audience members will consider voting for Alexandra Rodman in order to clean up student government.")

Answer the following questions about each of the purpose statements you make up: Is it result oriented? Is it precise? Is it attainable?

2. **Formulating Thesis Statements** Turn each of the following purpose statements into a statement that expresses a possible thesis. For example, if you had a purpose statement such as this:

> After listening to my speech, my audience will recognize the primary advantages and disadvantages of home teeth bleaching.

you might turn it into a thesis statement such as this:

> Home bleaching your teeth can significantly improve your appearance, but watch out for injury to the gums and damaged teeth.

1. At the end of my speech, the audience members will be willing to sign my petition supporting the local needle exchange program for drug addicts.

2. After listening to my speech, the audience members will be able to list five disadvantages of tattoos.

3. During my speech on the trials and tribulations of writing a research paper, the audience members will show their interest by paying attention and their amusement by occasionally laughing.

3. **Gathering Information** Break up into groups of eight or fewer. Select a topic of your own choosing or one of the following:

1. Who came up with the idea of latitude and longitude lines, and how do they work?

2. College athletes are exploited by the schools they play for.

3. Our jury system does not work.

4. U.S. schools are not safe.

5. What are the steps in the design and construction of the Macy's Thanksgiving Day parade balloons?

6. What do modern-day witches believe?

7. What does it mean to be innumerate, and how many people suffer from this problem?

Assign each member of your group a different research source:

1. Internet search engine

2. Library catalog

3. Reference works

4. Periodicals

5. Databases

6. Talk to a librarian.

7. Talk to a professor.

8. Conduct a survey of your other class members.

During the next class period, report back to the class on which research sources were most productive.

4. **Communication Apprehension: A Personal Analysis** To analyze your own reaction to communication apprehension, think back to your last public speech, and rate yourself on how rational, receiver oriented, positive, and prepared you were. How did these attributes affect your anxiety level?

5. **Types of Delivery** Identify at least one speech you have seen presented using the four types of delivery: extemporaneous, impromptu, manuscript, or memorized. For this speech, decide whether the type of delivery was effective for the topic, speaker, and situation. Explain why or why not. If the speech was not effective, suggest a more appropriate type.

6. **Articulation Exercises** Tongue twisters can be used to practice careful articulation out loud. Try these two classics:

1. She sells seashells down by the seashore.

2. Peter Piper picked a peck of pickled peppers.

Now make up some of your own and try them out. Make twisters for both consonant sounds ("Frank's friendly face flushed furiously") and vowel sounds ("Oliver oiled the old annoying oddity").

For Further Exploration

For more resources about preliminary considerations in planning a speech, see the *Understanding Human Communication* website at www.oup.com/us/adler. There you will find a variety of resources: a list of books and articles, links to descriptions of feature films and television shows at the Now Playing website, study aids, and a self-test to check your understanding of the material in this chapter.

Organization and Support

Chapter Outline

LEARNING OBJECTIVES

1 Construct an effective speech outline using the organizing principles described in this chapter.

2 Develop an effective introduction, conclusion, and transitions.

3 Choose supporting material for a speech to make your points clear, interesting, memorable, and convincing.

Competing on a speech team has a lot in common with TV news reporting. Just ask Curt Casper, who has done both.

These days Casper is a sports and news reporter at KPTM-TV in Omaha, Nebraska. But he first honed his public speaking skills on the Hastings College forensics team. (Forensics is the process of considering evidence to reach a sound conclusion, whether it's making a speech or solving a crime.)

When Casper applied for the job at KPTM, the news director said he had never seen a résumé that included the words "speech/forensics." He asked Casper, "How would your experience in public speaking help you in this career?" Curt gave him examples, such as impromptu speaking competitions, in which he was given 2 minutes to prepare a 5-minute speech inspired by one quotation, and extemporaneous speaking competitions, in which he had 30 minutes to prepare a 7-minute answer to a question about national or world events using credible sources to back up his information. Casper explained the similarities between those competitions and news reporting. He got the job.

After Casper proved himself to be an effective newscaster, his news director praised the value of a background in public speaking, especially for a career in reporting.

"I use my speech skills every day," says Casper, who feels that public speaking has taught him to be a quick and effective researcher, to choose words carefully, and to speak within time limits. His two biggest lessons—as both a public speaker and a news reporter—have been to find strong supporting material and to organize it in a way that makes sense to an audience. As you'll see in the sample speech at the end of this chapter, Casper began making good use of these skills when he was still in college.

Public speaking skills helped Curt Casper attain his "dream job." See if you can answer the following questions about your own career aspirations.

- What is your dream job?
- What communication skills could help you attain that job?
- How would public speaking relate to such a career choice?

As Curt Casper learned as both a public speaker and a newscaster, *knowing* what you are talking about and *communicating* that knowledge aren't the same thing. It's frustrating to realize you aren't expressing your thoughts clearly, and it's equally unpleasant to be unable to follow what a speaker is saying because the material is too jumbled. In the following pages, you will learn methods of organizing and supporting your thoughts effectively.

Structuring Your Speech

As discussed in Chapter 2, people tend to arrange their perceptions in some meaningful way in order to make sense of the world. Being clear to your audience, however, isn't the only benefit of good organization: Structuring a message effectively will help you refine your own ideas and construct more persuasive messages.

A good speech is like a good building: Both grow from a careful plan. Chapter 11 showed you how to begin this planning by formulating a purpose, analyzing your audience, and conducting research. You apply that information to the structure of the speech through outlining. Like any other plan, a speech outline is the framework on which your message is built. It contains your main ideas and shows how they relate to one another and to your thesis. Virtually every speech outline ought to follow the basic structure outlined in Figure 12-1.

This **basic speech structure** demonstrates the old aphorism for speakers: "Tell what you're going to say, say it, and then tell what you said." Although this structure sounds redundant, the research on listening cited in Chapter 5 demonstrates that receivers forget much of what they hear. The clear, repetitive nature of the basic speech structure reduces the potential for memory loss, because audiences have a tendency to listen more carefully during the beginning and ending of a speech.[1] Your outline will reflect this basic speech structure.

Outlines come in all shapes and sizes, but the three types that are most important to us here are working outlines, formal outlines, and speaking notes.

Your Working Outline

A **working outline** is a construction tool used to map out your speech. The working outline will probably follow the basic speech structure, but only in rough form. It is for your eyes only, and you'll probably create several drafts as you refine your ideas. As your ideas solidify, your outline will change accordingly, becoming more polished as you go along.

Your Formal Outline

A **formal outline** such as the one shown on page 356 uses a consistent format and set of symbols to identify the structure of ideas.

A formal outline serves several purposes. In simplified form, it can be displayed as a visual aid or distributed as a handout. It can also serve as a record of a speech that was delivered; many organizations send outlines to members who miss meetings at which presentations were given. Finally, in speech classes, instructors often use speech outlines to analyze student speeches. When one is used for that purpose, it is usually a full-sentence outline and includes the purpose, thesis, and topic or title. Most instructors also require a bibliography of sources at the end of the outline. The bibliography should include full research citations, the correct form for which can be found in any style guide, such as *The Craft of Research*, by Wayne Booth et al.[2] There are at least six standard bibliographic styles. Whichever style you use, you should be consistent in form and remember the two primary functions of a bibliographic citation: to demonstrate the credibility of your source and to enable the readers—in this case, your professor or your fellow students—to find the source if they want to check its accuracy or explore your topic in more detail.

Another person should be able to understand the basic ideas included in your speech by reading the formal outline. In fact, that's one test of the effectiveness of your outline. See if the outline on page 356 passes this test for you.

Your Speaking Notes

Like your working outline, your speaking notes are for your use only, so the format is up to you. Many teachers suggest that speaking notes should be in the form of a brief keyword outline, with just enough information listed to jog your memory but not enough to get lost in.

Many teachers also suggest that you fit your notes on one side of one 3-by-5-inch note card. Other teachers recommend that you also have your introduction and conclusion on note cards, and still others recommend that your longer quotations be written out on note cards. Curt Casper's notes for his speech on suicide survivors (see the sample outline, page 356) might look like the ones in Figure 12-2.

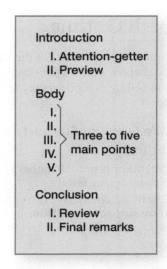

FIGURE 12-1 **Basic Speech Structure**

Do you usually make outlines for term papers, essay responses on exams, and class presentations? If not, how could you benefit from outlining more often?

537

Speech Outline

The following outline is for the sample speech at the end of this chapter, which Curt Casper presented at a national event in college. A bibliography for this speech can be found on page 373.

Suicide Survivor Support

INTRODUCTION

I. Attention-getter: My father's suicide had a powerful impact on my family.

II. Thesis statement: We can change the stigma of suicide if we stop survivors from suffering alone.

III. Preview main points.

BODY

I. We need to recognize the reasons suicide survivors (family and friends of those who commit suicide) do not receive the help they deserve.

    A. The deficiencies in survivor support can be found on a societal level.

        1. Society's refusal to use the word *suicide* sets up a social stigma.

        2. Religious doctrine increases this social stigma.

        3. Even media guidelines increase the stigma.

    B. The deficiencies in survivor support can be found on an economic level.

        1. Survivors are left with funeral, counseling, and living expenses.

        2. Survivors might not be eligible for life insurance payouts.

        3. Survivors might not use the money they do receive wisely.

II. We need to examine the impact of that lack of help.

    A. A suicide can cause more grief than most normal deaths.

    B. A suicide can cause post-traumatic stress disorder.

III. We need to examine some possible solutions.

    A. Survivor support solutions can and should be facilitated on a societal level.

        1. One part of the solution would be to require insurance companies to give back the premiums that were paid before the suicide.

        2. Another part of the solution would be to use the word *suicide* when talking to survivors.

    B. Survivor support solutions can and should be facilitated on an individual level.

        1. If you have a friend who is a survivor, just be there for him or her.

        2. If you are a survivor yourself, share your story with others in similar situations.

            a. Make survivors realize that they are not at fault for what happened.

            b. Become part of a LOSS team.

            c. Make sure you also get the help you need.

Conclusion

I. Review main points.

II. I have seen firsthand how a suicide can destroy a family.

III. I know my dad would have wanted us to move on and know that everything is okay.

Principles of Outlining

Over the years, a series of rules or principles for the construction of outlines has evolved. These rules are based on the use of the standard symbols and format discussed next.

Standard Symbols

A speech outline generally uses the following symbols:

    I. Main point (roman numeral)

      A. Subpoint (capital letter)

        1. Sub-subpoint (standard number)

          a. Sub-subsubpoint (lowercase letter)

In the examples in this chapter, the major divisions of the speech—introduction, body, and conclusion—are not given in symbols. They are listed by name, and the roman numerals for their main points begin anew in each division. An alternative form is to list these major divisions with roman numerals, main points with capital letters, and so on.

538

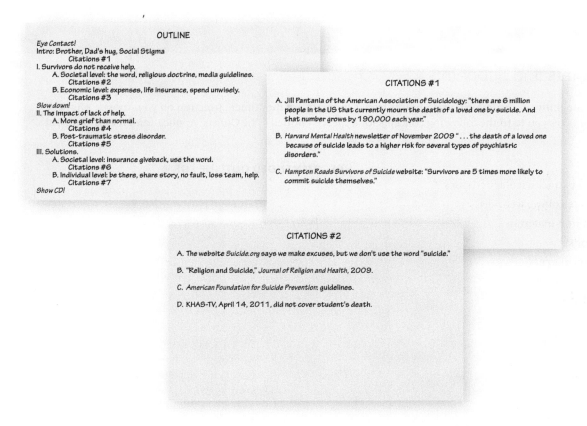

OUTLINE

Eye Contact!
Intro: Brother, Dad's hug, Social Stigma
        Citations #1
I. Survivors do not receive help.
    A. Societal level: the word, religious doctrine, media guidelines.
        Citations #2
    B. Economic level: expenses, life insurance, spend unwisely.
        Citations #3
Slow down!
II. The impact of lack of help.
    A. More grief than normal.
        Citations #4
    B. Post-traumatic stress disorder.
        Citations #5
III. Solutions.
    A. Societal level: insurance giveback, use the word.
        Citations #6
    B. Individual level: be there, share story, no fault, loss team, help.
        Citations #7
Show CD!

CITATIONS #1

A. Jill Pantania of the American Association of Suicidology: "there are 6 million people in the US that currently mourn the death of a loved one by suicide. And that number grows by 190,000 each year."

B. Harvard Mental Health newsletter of November 2009 "...the death of a loved one because of suicide leads to a higher risk for several types of psychiatric disorders."

C. Hampton Roads Survivors of Suicide website: "Survivors are 5 times more likely to commit suicide themselves."

CITATIONS #2

A. The website Suicide.org says we make excuses, but we don't use the word "suicide."

B. "Religion and Suicide," Journal of Religion and Health, 2009.

C. American Foundation for Suicide Prevention: guidelines.

D. KHAS-TV, April 14, 2011, did not cover student's death.

FIGURE 12-2 Speaking Notes These speaking notes are based on the outline on page 356. The entire set would be eight cards, including one for the outline and seven for citations.

Standard Format

In the sample outlines in this chapter, notice that each symbol is indented a number of spaces from the symbol above it. Besides keeping the outline neat, the indentation of different-order ideas is actually the key to the technique of outlining; it enables you to coordinate and order ideas in the form in which they are most comprehensible to the human mind. If the standard format is used in your working outline, it will help you create a well-organized speech. If it is used in speaking notes, it will help you remember everything you want to say.

Proper outline form is based on a few rules and guidelines, the first of which is the rule of division.

The Rule of Division

In formal outlines, main points and subpoints always represent a division of a whole. Because it is impossible to divide something into fewer than two parts, you always have at least two main points for every topic. Then, if your main points are divided, you will always have at least two subpoints, and so on. Thus, the rule for formal outlines is as follows: Never a "I" without a "II," never an "A" without a "B," and so on.

Three to five is considered to be the ideal number of main points. It is also considered best to divide those main points into three to five subpoints, when necessary and possible. Notice how Curt Casper divided the body of his topic as shown in the sample outline on page 356.

Main Points and Subpoints

To get an idea of your ability to distinguish main points from subpoints, set the "timer" function on your mobile phone and see how long it takes you to fit the following concepts for a speech entitled "The College Application Process" into outline form:

CONCEPTS	RECOMMENDED OUTLINE FORM
Participation in extracurricular activities	I.
Visit and evaluate college websites	A.
Prepare application materials	B.
Career ambitions	II.
Choose desired college	A.
Letters of recommendation	B.
Write personal statement	C.
Visit and evaluate college campuses	III.
Choose interesting topic	A.
Test scores	B.
Include important personal details	1.
Volunteer work	2.
Transcripts	3.

You can score yourself as follows:

    30 seconds or less: Congratulations, organization comes naturally to you.

    31 to 60 seconds: You have typical skills in this area.

    61 to 90 seconds: Give yourself extra time while building your speech outline. ●

The Rule of Parallel Wording

Your main points should be worded in a similar, or "parallel," manner. For example, if you are developing a speech against capital punishment, your main points might look like this:

    I. Capital punishment is not effective: It is not a deterrent to crime.

   II. Capital punishment is not constitutional: It does not comply with the Eighth Amendment.

  III. Capital punishment is not civilized: It does not allow for a reverence for life.

Whenever possible, subpoints should also be worded in a parallel manner. For your points to be worded in a parallel manner, they should each contain one, and only one, idea. (After all, they can't really be parallel if one is longer or contains more ideas than the others.) This will enable you to completely develop one idea before moving on to another one in your speech. If you were discussing cures for indigestion, your topic might be divided incorrectly if your main points looked like this:

    I. "Preventive cures" help you before eating.

   II. "Participation cures" help you during and after eating.

540

You might actually have three ideas there and thus three main points:

I. Prevention cures (before eating)
II. Participation cures (during eating)
III. Postparticipation cures (after eating)

Organizing Your Outline into a Logical Pattern

ON YOUR FEET

Outlining
Present a 1-minute talk on the principles of outlining. Use only a formal outline for your presentation.

An outline should reflect a logical order for your points. You might arrange them from newest to oldest, largest to smallest, best to worst, or in a number of other ways that follow. The organizing pattern you choose ought to be the one that best develops your thesis.

Time Patterns

Arrangement according to **time patterns**, or chronology, is one of the most common patterns of organization. The period of time could be anything from centuries to seconds. In a speech on airline food, a time pattern might look like this:

I. Early airline food: a gourmet treat
II. The middle period: institutional food at 30,000 feet
III. Today's airline food: the passenger starves

Arranging points according to the steps that make up a process is another form of time patterning. The topic "Recording a Hit Song" might use this type of patterning:

I. Record the demo CD.
II. Tape a YouTube video.
III. Get a recording company to listen and view.

Time patterns are also the basis of **climax patterns**, which are used to create suspense. For example, if you wanted to create suspense in a speech about military intervention, you could chronologically trace the steps that eventually led us into Afghanistan or Iraq in such a way that you build up your audience's curiosity. If you told of these steps through the eyes of a soldier who entered military service right before one of those wars, you would be building suspense as your audience wonders what will become of that soldier.

The climax pattern can also be reversed. When it is, it is called *anticlimactic* organization. If you started your military intervention speech by telling the audience that you were going to explain why a specific soldier was killed in a specific war, and then you went on to explain the things that caused that soldier to become involved in that war, you would be using anticlimactic organization. This pattern is helpful when you have an essentially uninterested audience, and you need to build interest early in your speech to get the audience to listen to the rest of it.

Space Patterns

Space patterns are organized according to area. The area could be stated in terms of continents or centimeters or anything in between. If you were discussing the Great Lakes, for example, you could arrange them from west to east:

I. Superior
II. Michigan
III. Huron
IV. Erie
V. Ontario

Topic Patterns

A topical arrangement or **topic pattern** is based on types or categories. These categories could be either well known or original; both have their advantages. For example, a division of college students according to well-known categories might look like this:

I. Freshmen

II. Sophomores

III. Juniors

IV. Seniors

Well-known categories are advantageous because audiences quickly understand them. But familiarity also has its disadvantages. One disadvantage is the "Oh, this again" syndrome. If the members of an audience feel they have nothing new to learn about the components of your topic, they might not listen to you. To avoid this, you could invent original categories that freshen up your topic by suggesting an original analysis. For example, original categories for "college students" might look like this:

I. Grinds: Students who go to every class and read every assignment before it is due.

II. Renaissance students: Students who find a satisfying balance of scholarly and social pursuits.

III. Burnouts: Students who have a difficult time finding the classroom, let alone doing the work.

Sometimes topics are arranged in the order that will be easiest for your audience to remember. To return to our Great Lakes example, the names of the lakes could be arranged so their first letters spell the word "HOMES." Words used in this way are known as *mnemonics*. Carol Koehler, a professor of communication and medicine, uses the mnemonic "CARE" to describe the characteristics of a caring doctor:

C stands for *concentrate*. Physicians should pay attention with their eyes and ears . . .

A stands for *acknowledge*. Show them that you are listening . . .

R stands for *response*. Clarify issues by asking questions, providing periodic recaps . . .

E stands for *exercise emotional control*. When your "hot buttons" are pushed . . .[3]

Problem-Solution Patterns

The **problem-solution pattern**, as you might guess from its no-nonsense name, describes what's wrong and proposes a way to make things better. It is usually (but not always) divisible into two distinct parts, as in this example:

I. The Problem: Addiction (which could then be broken down into addiction to cigarettes, alcohol, prescribed drugs, and street drugs)

II. The Solution: A national addiction institute (which would study the root causes of addiction in the same way that the National Cancer Institute studies the root causes of cancer)

We will discuss this pattern in more detail in Chapter 14.

One of the greatest speakers of the 20th century, Dr. Martin Luther King Jr., knew well how to construct a speech and how to conclude with passion. What best practices can you use to boost the impact when organizing your speeches?

> **Understanding Diversity**

Nontraditional Patterns of Organization

In addition to the traditional patterns usually taught in public speaking classes, researchers are looking at other organizational patterns commonly used by women and ethnic speakers. For example, Cheryl Jorgenson-Earp is exploring a number of alternative patterns that women have used historically. She argues that many speakers are uncomfortable with the standard organization patterns because of cultural backgrounds or personal inclinations. As alternatives, she proposes several less direct and more "organic" patterns that provide a clear structure for a speech but have a less linear form.

One of these is the wave pattern. In this pattern the speaker uses repetitions and variations of themes and ideas. The major points of the speech come at the crest of the wave. The speaker follows these with a variety of examples leading up to another crest, where she repeats the theme or makes another major point.

Perhaps the most famous speech that illustrates this pattern is the Reverend Martin Luther King Jr.'s "I Have a Dream." King used this memorable line as the crest of a wave that he followed with examples of what he saw in his dream; then he repeated the line. He ended with a "peak" conclusion that emerged from the final wave in the speech—repetition and variation on the phrase "Let freedom ring."

An excerpt from Sojourner Truth's "Ain't I a Woman?" speech also illustrates this pattern:

That man over there says that women need to be helped into carriages, and lifted over ditches, and to have the best place everywhere. Nobody ever helps me into carriages, or over mud-puddles, or gives me any best place!

And ain't I a woman?

Look at me! Look at my arm! I have ploughed and planted, and gathered into barns, and no man could head me!

And ain't I a woman?

I could work as much and eat as much as a man—when I could get it—and bear the lash as well!

And ain't I a woman?

I have borne thirteen children and seen them most all sold off to slavery, and when I cried out with my mother's grief, none but Jesus heard me!

And ain't I a woman? ●

Jaffe, C. (2007). *Public speaking*: *Concepts and skills for a diverse society* (5th ed.). Boston: Wadsworth, © 2007. Reprinted with permission of Wadsworth, an imprint of the Wadsworth Group, a division of Thomson Learning.

Why is diversity important in the messages you send and receive? Why is message organization such an important factor?

Cause-Effect Patterns

Cause-effect patterns are similar to problem-solution patterns in that they are basically two-part patterns: First you discuss something that happened, and then you discuss its effects.

A variation of this pattern reverses the order and presents the effects first and then the causes. Persuasive speeches often have effect-cause or cause-effect as the first two main points. Elizabeth Hallum, a student at Arizona State University, organized the first two points of a speech on "workplace revenge"[4] like this:

I. The effects of the problem
   A. Lost productivity
   B. Costs of sabotage
II. The causes of the problem
   A. Employees feeling alienated
   B. Employers' light treatment of incidents of revenge

The third main point in this type of persuasive speech is often "solutions," and the fourth main point is often "the desired audience behavior." Hallum's final points were as follows:

III. Solutions: Support the National Employee Rights Institute.
IV. Desired Audience Response: Log on to www.disgruntled.com.

Cause-effect and problem-solution patterns are often combined in various arrangements. In the sample speech at the end of this chapter, Curt Casper uses a problem-effect-solution pattern. One extension of the problem-solution organizational pattern is Monroe's Motivated Sequence.

Monroe's Motivated Sequence

The Motivated Sequence was proposed by a scholar named Alan Monroe in the 1930s.[5] In this persuasive pattern, the problem is broken down into an attention step and a need step, and the solution is broken down into a satisfaction step, a visualization step, and an action step. In a speech on "random acts of kindness,"[6] the Motivated Sequence might break down like this:

I. The attention step draws attention to your subject. ("Just the other day Ron saved George's life with a small, random, seemingly unimportant act of kindness.")
II. The need step establishes the problem. ("Millions of Americans suffer from depression, a life-threatening disease.")
III. The satisfaction step proposes a solution. ("One random act of kindness can lift a person from depression.")
IV. The visualization step describes the results of the solution. ("Imagine yourself having that kind of effect on another person.")
V. The action step is a direct appeal for the audience to do something. ("Try a random act of kindness today!")

Chapter 14 has more to say about the organization of persuasive speeches.

Using Transitions

Transitions keep your message moving forward. They perform the following functions:

They tell how the introduction relates to the body of the speech.
They tell how one main point relates to the next main point.
They tell how your subpoints relate to the points they are part of.
They tell how your supporting points relate to the points they support.

Transitions, to be effective, should refer to the previous point and to the upcoming point, showing how they relate to each other and to the thesis. They usually sound something like this:

"Like [previous point], another important consideration in [topic] is [upcoming point]."

"But _____ isn't the only thing we have to worry about. _____ is even more potentially dangerous."

"Yes, the problem is obvious. But what are the solutions? Well, one possible solution is . . ."

Sometimes a transition includes an internal review (a restatement of preceding points), an internal preview (a look ahead to upcoming points), or both:

> Think of an idea that you could present to your class. Which pattern of organization would be most effective for that presentation?

ON YOUR FEET

Motivated Sequence
Outline a persuasive topic in just five sentences, one for each step of the Motivated Sequence.

544

"So far we've discussed _____ , _____ , and _____ . Our next points are _____ , _____ , and _____ .

You can find several examples of transitions in the sample speech at the end of this chapter.

Beginning and Ending the Speech

The **introduction** and **conclusion** of a speech are vitally important, although they usually will occupy less than 20 percent of your speaking time. Listeners form their impression of a speaker early, and they remember what they hear last; it is, therefore, vital to make those few moments at the beginning and end of your speech work to your advantage.

The Introduction

There are four functions of a speech introduction. It serves to capture the audience's attention, preview the main points, set the mood and tone of the speech, and demonstrate the importance of the topic.

Capturing Attention   There are several ways to capture an audience's attention. The checklist on this page shows how some of these ways might be used in a speech entitled "Communication Between Plants and Humans."

Previewing Main Points   After you capture the attention of the audience, an effective introduction will almost always state the speaker's thesis and give the

 ON YOUR FEET

Grabbing Attention
Introduce any idea to your class in no more than 30 seconds. Then ask for a show of hands: Who would like to hear more?

CHECKLIST > Capturing Audience Attention

☐ **Refer to the audience.** The technique of referring to the audience is especially effective if it is complimentary: "Julio's speech last week about how animals communicate was so interesting that I decided to explore a related topic: Whether people can communicate with plants!"

☐ **Refer to the occasion.** A reference to the occasion could allude to the event of your speech: "Our assignment is to focus on an aspect of *human* communication. Given this guideline, it seems appropriate to talk about whether humans can communicate with plants."

☐ **Refer to the relationship between the audience and the subject.** "It's fair to say that all of us here believe it's important to care for our environment. What you'll learn today will make you care about that environment in a whole new way."

☐ **Refer to something familiar to the audience.** "Most of us have talked to our pets. Today, you'll learn that there are other conversational partners around the house."

☐ **Cite a startling fact or opinion.** "See that lilac bush outside the window? At this very moment it might be reacting to the joys and anxieties that you are experiencing in this classroom." *Or,* "There is now actual scientific evidence that plants appreciate human company, kind words, and classical music."

☐ **Ask a question.** "Have you ever wondered why some people seem able to grow beautiful, healthy plants effortlessly, whereas others couldn't make a weed grow in the best soil? Perhaps it's because they have better relationships with those plants."

☐ **Tell an anecdote.** "The other night, while taking a walk in the country, I happened on a small garden that was rich with vegetation. But it wasn't the lushness of the plants that caught my eye. There, in the middle of the garden, was a man who was talking quite animatedly to a giant sunflower."

☐ **Use a quotation.** "Max Thornton, the naturalist, recently said, 'Psychobiology has proven that plants can communicate. Now humans need to learn how to listen to them.'"

☐ **Tell an (appropriate) joke.** "We once worried about people who talked to plants, but that's no longer the case. Now we only worry if the plants talk back."

listeners an idea of the upcoming main points. Katherine Graham, the former publisher of the *Washington Post*, addressed a group of businessmen and their wives in this way:

> I am delighted to be here. It is a privilege to address you. And I am especially glad the rules have been bent for tonight, allowing so many of you to bring along your husbands. I think it's nice for them to get out once in a while and see how the other half lives. Gentlemen, we welcome you.
>
> Actually, I have other reasons for appreciating this chance to talk with you tonight. It gives me an opportunity to address some current questions about the press and its responsibilities—whom we are responsible to, what we are responsible for, and generally how responsible our performance has been.[7]

Thus, Graham previewed her main points:

(1) To explain whom the press is responsible to

(2) To explain what the press is responsible for

(3) To explain how responsible the press has been

Sometimes your preview of main points will be even more straightforward:

"I have three points to discuss: They are _____ , _____ , and _____ ."

Sometimes you will not want to refer directly to your main points in your introduction. Your reasons for not doing so might be based on a plan calling for suspense, humorous effect, or stalling for time to win over a hostile audience. In that case, you might preview only your thesis:

"I am going to say a few words about _____ ."

"Did you ever wonder about _____ ?"

"_____ is one of the most important issues facing us today."

Setting the Mood and Tone of Your Speech Notice, in the example just given, how Katherine Graham began her speech by joking with her audience. She was a powerful woman speaking before an all-male organization; the only women in the audience were the members' wives. That is why Ms. Graham felt it necessary to put her audience members at ease by joking with them about women's traditional role in society. By beginning in this manner, she assured the men that she would not berate them for the sexist bylaws of their organization. She also showed them that she was going to approach her topic with wit and intelligence. Thus, she set the mood and tone for her entire speech. Imagine how different that mood and tone would have been if she had begun this way:

> Before I start today, I would just like to say that I would never have accepted your invitation to speak here had I known that your organization does not accept women as members. Just where do you Cro-Magnons get off, excluding more than half the human race from your little club?

Demonstrating the Importance of Your Topic to Your Audience Your audience members will listen to you more carefully if your speech relates to them as individuals. Based on your audience analysis, you should state directly *why* your topic is of importance to your audience members. This importance should be related as closely as possible to their specific needs at that specific time. For example, Stephanie Hamilton, a student at North Dakota State University, presented a speech

ON YOUR FEET

Setting the Tone

Present a brief introduction for a speech, but alter the tone you set by preparing three different versions.

about loopholes in the justice system when crimes of violence occur on cruise ships. After telling the story of a rape aboard ship, she established the importance of her topic this way:

> Each year, millions of people take to the seas on cruises. Many of us have taken cruises of our own or plan to take one someday, and practically everyone knows at least someone who has taken a cruise. Even if we will never take a cruise, we are a part of society and a possible target for crime. If someone were found guilty of a crime, would we want them free? That is exactly what is happening without laws of recourse in place for our protection. We don't need to let our family, friends, neighbors or ourselves be taken advantage of and never given justice.[8]

Establishing Credibility   One final consideration for your introduction is to establish your credibility to speak on your topic. One way to do this is to be *well prepared*. Another is to *appear confident* as soon as you face your audience. A third technique is to *tell your audience about your personal experience* with the topic, in order to establish why it is important to you. Curt Casper, in the sample speech found at the end of this chapter, used all three of these techniques. His first sentence says it all: "It is the four-year anniversary since my dad decided to drive in front of a train, dying by suicide."

In the *Anchorman* comedies, newscaster Ron Burgundy (Will Ferrell) reads the same opening and closing statements every night. Even if you haven't seen the films, it's easy to imagine the effect of his approach. How can you make your delivery most authentic?

The Conclusion

The conclusion, like the introduction, is an especially important part of your speech. The conclusion has three essential functions: to restate the thesis, to review your main points, and to provide a memorable final remark.

You can review your thesis either by repeating it or by paraphrasing it. Or you might devise a striking summary statement for your conclusion to help your audience remember your thesis. Grant Anderson, a student at Minnesota State University, gave a speech against the policy of rejecting blood donations from homosexuals. He ended his conclusion with this statement: "The gay community still has a whole host of issues to contend with, but together all of us can all take a step forward by recognizing this unjust and discriminatory measure. So stand up and raise whatever arm they poke you in to draw blood and say 'Blood is Blood' no matter who you are."[9] Grant's statement was concise but memorable.

Your main points can also be reviewed artistically. For example, first look back at that example introduction by Katherine Graham, and then read her conclusion to that speech:

> So instead of seeking flat and absolute answers to the kinds of problems I have discussed tonight, what we should be trying to foster is respect for one another's conception of where duty lies, and understanding of the real worlds in which we try to do our best. And we should be hoping for the energy and sense to keep on arguing and questioning, because there is no better sign that our society is healthy and strong.

Let's take a closer look at how and why this conclusion was effective. Graham posed three questions in her introduction. She dealt with those questions in her speech and reminded her audience, in her conclusion, that she had answered the questions.

PREVIEW (FROM INTRODUCTION OF SPEECH)	REVIEW (FROM CONCLUSION)
1. To whom is the press responsible?	1. To its own conception of where its duty lies
2. What is the press responsible for?	2. For doing its best in the "real world"
3. How responsible has the press been?	3. It has done its best

CHECKLIST > Effective Conclusions

You can make your final remarks most effective by avoiding the following mistakes:

☐ **Do not end abruptly.** Make sure that your conclusion accomplishes everything it is supposed to accomplish. Develop it fully. You might want to use signposts such as "Finally . . . ," "In conclusion . . . ," or "To sum up what I've been talking about here . . ." to let your audience know that you have reached the conclusion of the speech.

☐ **Don't ramble, either.** Prepare a definite conclusion, and never, never end by mumbling something like "Well, I guess that's about all I wanted to say . . ."

☐ **Don't introduce new points.** The worst kind of rambling is "Oh, yes, and something I forgot to mention is . . ."

☐ **Don't apologize.** Don't say, "I'm sorry I didn't have more time to research this subject," or use any of those sad songs. They will only highlight the possible weaknesses of your speech, and there's a good chance those weaknesses were far more apparent to you than to your audience. It's best to end strong. You can use any of the attention-getters suggested for the introduction to make the conclusion memorable. In fact, one kind of effective closing is to refer to the attention-getter you used in your introduction and remind your audience how it applies to the points you made in your speech.

> cultural idiom

sad songs:
statements meant to elicit sympathy

Supporting Material

It is important to organize ideas clearly and logically. But clarity and logic by themselves won't guarantee that you'll interest, enlighten, or persuade others; these results call for the use of supporting materials. These materials—the facts and information that back up and prove your ideas and opinions—are the flesh that fills out the skeleton of your speech.

Functions of Supporting Material

There are four functions of supporting material.

To Clarify   As explained in Chapter 4, people of different backgrounds tend to attach different meanings to words. Supporting material can help you overcome this potential source of confusion by helping you clarify key terms and ideas. For example, when Jacoby Cochran, a student at Bradley University in Illinois, spoke on the dangers of "special administrative measures," or SAMs, he needed to clarify what he meant by his key term. He used supporting material in this way:

> AlterNet of June 13, 2011, explains that SAMs are measures including limited communication, solitary confinement, the withholding of evidence and enhanced interrogation, enacted against individuals convicted or suspected of mob or terrorist ties. In the most extreme circumstances, such as keeping a known mob boss from running an organization from inside prison, SAMs have

@Work

Organizing Business Presentations

When top business executives plan an important speech, they often call in a communication consultant to help organize their remarks. Even though they are experts, executives are so close to the topic of their message that they may have difficulty arranging their ideas so others will understand or be motivated by them.

Consultants stress how important organization and message structure are in giving presentations. Seminar leader and corporate trainer T. Stephen Eggleston sums up the basic approach: "Any presentation . . . regardless of complexity . . . should consist of the same four basic parts: an opening, body, summary and closing."[10]

Ethel Cook, a Massachusetts consultant, is very specific about how much time should be spent on each section of a speech. "In timing your presentation," she says, "an ideal breakdown would be:

Opening–10 to 20 percent
Body–65 to 75 percent
Closing–10 to 20 percent."[11]

Within the body of a presentation, business coach Vadim Kotelnikov gives his clients a step-by-step procedure to organize their ideas. "List all the points you plan to cover," he advises. "Group them in sections and put your list of sections in the order that best achieves your objectives. Begin with the most important topics."[12]

Toastmasters International, an organization that runs training programs for business professionals, suggests alternative organizational patterns:

To organize your ideas into an effective proposal, use an approach developed in the field of journalism—the "inverted pyramid." In the "inverted pyramid" format, the most important information is given in the first few paragraphs. As you present the pitch, the information becomes less and less crucial. This way, your presentation can be cut short, yet remain effective.[13]

While each consultant may offer specific tips, all agree that clear organization is essential when a business speaker wants his or her ideas to be understood and appreciated. ●

Imagine a business presentation you might have to make in your future career. Why would organization be important in such a presentation?

See the appendix of this book for more on work-related communication.

---

proven beneficial, but their recent expansions have elevated them from a rarely used, extreme holding measure to a legal basis for torture, detentions without charge or trial, and the shredding of constitutional rights.[14]

To Prove   A second function of support is to be used as evidence, to prove the truth of what you are saying. If you were giving a speech on what is known as the immigration crisis, you might want to point out that concerns about immigration are nothing new. The following could be used to prove that point:

A prominent American once said about immigrants, "Few of their children in the country learn English. . . . The signs in our streets have inscriptions in both languages. . . . Unless the stream of their importation could be turned they will soon so outnumber us that all the advantages we have will not be able to preserve our language, and even our government will become precarious." This sentiment did not emerge from the rancorous debate over the immigration bill defeated not long ago in the Senate. It was not the lament of some . . . candidate intent on wooing bedrock conservative votes. Guess again. Voicing this grievance was Benjamin Franklin. And the language so vexing to him was the German spoken by new arrivals to Pennsylvania in the 1750s, a wave of immigrants whom Franklin viewed as the "most stupid of their nation."[15]

To Make Interesting   A third function of support is to make an idea interesting or to catch your audience's attention. For example, when Nathan Dunn, a student at Oklahoma City College, spoke about how special education students are sometimes treated, he started with this concrete example:

> For most high school seniors, their biggest problems revolve around getting into college, getting a job, or finding a date to the prom. Unfortunately, Andre McCollins of Canton, Massachusetts, is not most high school seniors. In October 2002, Andre was an 18-year-old student at the Judge Rotenberg Educational Center, a residential school for students with developmental disabilities less than 20 miles from where we are right now. One morning, Andre did not respond to a staff member asking him to take off his coat. In response, staff members tied him to a board face down, for 7 hours, with no breaks for food, water, or bathroom use. More horrifying, though, was that staff members electrically shocked Andre 31 times while he was tied down. The school's classroom cameras captured the whole day on a video the school fought to keep secret for years.[16]

To Make Memorable   A final function of supporting materials, related to the preceding one, is to make a point memorable. We have already mentioned the importance of "memorable" statements in a speech conclusion; use of supporting material in the introduction and body of the speech provides another way to help your audience retain important information. When Chris Griesinger of Eastern Michigan University spoke about the importance of pain management, he wanted his audience to remember the severity of the problem, so he used the following as supporting material:

> Every year the National Committee on Treatment of Intractable Pain receives letters from people sharing their stories of loved ones who died in pain. One letter reads, "I lost my mother to cancer. Her pain was so horrid that she lost her mind and ate her bottom lip completely off from clenching her top teeth so tightly. My 13-year-old sister and I watched this for 6 weeks."[17]

Types of Supporting Material

As you may have noted, each function of support could be fulfilled by several different types of material. Let's take a look at these different types of supporting material.

Definitions   It's a good idea to give your audience members definitions of your key terms, especially if those terms are unfamiliar to them or are being used in an unusual way. A good definition is simple and concise. When Elizabeth Hobbs, a student at Truman State University in Missouri, gave a speech on U.S. torture policy, she needed to define a key term, *extraordinary rendition*:

> "Extraordinary rendition" is the phrase used by the CIA to describe the U.S. practice of secretly sending terrorist suspects to countries where torture is routine.[18]

Examples   An **example** is a specific case that is used to demonstrate a general idea. Examples can be either factual or hypothetical, personal or borrowed. In Elizabeth Hobbs's speech on U.S. torture policy, she used the following example:

> He was kidnapped while making a business trip to Macedonia. To be transported to a secret prison in Afghanistan, he was beaten, his underwear was forcibly removed and he was put into a diaper, and chained spread eagle inside the plane. In Afghanistan he was beaten, interrogated and put into solitary confinement. To get out, he started a hunger strike, but after 37 days without food, a feeding

tube was forced through his nose and into his stomach. Nearly 5 months later he was released, with no explanation of his imprisonment.

Does this sound like Chile under the Pinochet regime? Prisoner abuse in Uzbekistan? A Russian gulag? It wasn't. This is a story of a victim of America's War on Terror.[19]

Hypothetical examples can often be more powerful than factual examples, because hypothetical examples ask audience members to imagine something, thus causing them to become active participants in the thought. Stephanie Wideman of the University of West Florida used a hypothetical example to start off her speech on oil prices:

The year is 2020. One day you are asked not to come into work, not because of a holiday, but instead because there is not enough energy available to power your office. You see, it is not that the power is out, but that they are out of power.[20]

Statistics   Statistics are numbers that are arranged or organized to show that a fact or principle is true for a large percentage of cases. Statistics are actually collections of examples, which is why they are often more effective as proof than are isolated examples. Here's the way a newspaper columnist used statistics to prove a point about gun violence:

I had coffee the other day with Marian Wright Edelman, president of the Children's Defense Fund, and she mentioned that since the murders of Robert Kennedy and the Rev. Martin Luther King Jr. in 1968, well over a million Americans have been killed by firearms in the United States. That's more than the combined U.S. combat deaths in all the wars in all of American history. "We're losing eight children and teenagers a day to gun violence," she said. "As far as young people are concerned, we lose the equivalent of the massacre at Virginia Tech about every 4 days."[21]

Because statistics can be powerful proof, you have certain rules to follow when using them. You should make sure that they make sense and that they come from a credible source. You should also cite the source of the statistic when you use it. A final rule is based on effectiveness rather than ethics. You should reduce the statistic to a concrete image if possible. For example, $1 billion in $100 bills would be about the same height as a 60-story building. Using concrete images such as this will make your statistics more than "just numbers" when you use them. For example, one observer expressed the idea of Bill Gates's wealth this way:

Examine Bill Gates' wealth compared to yours: Consider the average American of reasonable but modest wealth. Perhaps he has a net worth of $100,000. Mr. Gates' worth is 400,000 times larger. Which means that if something costs $100,000 to him, to Bill it's as though it costs 25 cents. So for example, you might think a new Lamborghini Diablo would cost $250,000, but in Bill Gates dollars that's 63 cents.[22]

> Recall a recent occasion in which you tried to change the mind of one or more people. What were your arguments? Which forms of support did you use to back them up?

Analogies/Comparison-Contrast   We use **analogies**, or comparisons, all the time, often in the form of figures of speech, such as similes and metaphors. A simile is a direct comparison that usually uses *like* or *as*, whereas a metaphor is an implied comparison that does not use *like* or *as*. So if you said that the rush of refugees from a war-torn country was "like a tidal wave," you would be using a simile. If you used the expression "a tidal wave of refugees," you would be using a metaphor.

Source: DILBERT: Scott Adams, Inc./Dist. by United Feature Syndicate, Inc.

Analogies are extended metaphors. They can be used to compare or contrast an unknown concept with a known one. For example, here's how one writer made her point against separate Academy Awards for men and women:

> Many hours into the 82nd Academy Awards ceremony this Sunday, the Oscar for best actor will go to Morgan Freeman, Jeff Bridges, George Clooney, Colin Firth, or Jeremy Renner. Suppose, however, that the Academy of Motion Picture Arts and Sciences presented separate honors for best white actor and best non-white actor, and that Mr. Freeman was prohibited from competing against the likes of Mr. Clooney and Mr. Bridges. Surely, the Academy would be derided as intolerant and out of touch; public outcry would swiftly ensure that Oscar nominations never again fell along racial lines.
>
> Why, then, is it considered acceptable to segregate nominations by sex, offering different Oscars for best actor and best actress?[23]

Anecdotes   An **anecdote** is a brief story with a point, often (but not always) based on personal experience. (The word *anecdote* comes from the Greek, meaning "unpublished item.") Ronald Reagan was famous for his use of anecdotes. In his farewell address, when he wanted to make the point that America stood as a symbol of freedom to people in other lands, he used the following anecdote:

> It was back in the early eighties, at the height of the boat people, and a sailor was hard at work on the carrier *Midway*, which was patrolling the South China sea. The sailor, like most American servicemen, was young, smart and fiercely observant. The crew spied on the horizon a leaky little boat—and crammed inside were refugees from Indochina hoping to get to America. The *Midway* sent a small launch to bring them to the ship, and safety. As the refugees made their way through the choppy seas, one spied the sailor on deck, and stood up and called out to him. He yelled, "Hello American Sailor—Hello Freedom Man."
>
> A small moment with a big meaning, a moment the sailor, who wrote it in a letter, couldn't get out of his mind. And when I saw it, neither could I.[24]

Quotations/Testimonies   Using a familiar, artistically stated saying will enable you to take advantage of someone else's memorable wording. For example, if you were giving a speech on personal integrity, you might quote Mark Twain, who said, "Always do right. This will gratify some people, and astonish the rest." A quotation like that fits Alexander Pope's definition of "true wit": "What was often thought, but ne'er so well expressed."

You can also use quotations as **testimony**, to prove a point by using the support of someone who is more authoritative or experienced on the subject than you are. When Rajiv Khanna, a student at Newman University in Kansas, wanted to prove that the distortion of history was a serious problem, he used testimony this way:

> Eugene Genovese, Professor Emeritus of History at Emory University, states in the July 11 issue of the *Chronicle of Higher Education*, "The distortion of history remains a serious problem to the academic community and the country at large." He continues, "As individuals who are history-making animals, we remain rooted in the past, and we are shaped by our society's version of its history."[25]

Sometimes testimony can be paraphrased. For example, when one business executive was talking on the subject of diversity, he used a conversation he had with Jesse Jackson Sr., an African American leader, as testimony:

In the film *Lincoln*, Daniel Day-Lewis captures the 16th U.S. president's use of folksy anecdotes to clarify ideas for his listeners. How can you use stories effectively to get your points across?

> At one point in our conversation, Jesse talked about the stages of advancement toward a society where diversity is fully valued. He said the first stage was emancipation—the end of slavery. The second stage was the right to vote and the third stage was the political power to actively participate in government—to be part of city hall, the Governor's office and Capitol Hill. Jesse was clearly focused, though, on the fourth stage—which he described as the ability to participate fully in the prosperity that this nation enjoys. In other words, economic power.[26]

Ethical Challenge

The Ethics of Support

Have you ever "stretched" supporting material to help it conform to a point you were trying to make? (An example might be citing an "expert" for an idea of your own when discussing a social issue with a friend.) How far can you stretch the facts without violating ethical standards?

Styles of Support: Narration and Citation

Most of the forms of support discussed in the preceding section could be presented in either of two ways: through narration or through citation. **Narration** involves telling a story with your information. You put it in the form of a small drama, with a beginning, middle, and end. For example, Evan McCarley of the University of Mississippi narrated the following example in his speech on the importance of drug courts:

> Oakland contractor Josef Corbin has a lot to be proud of. Last year his firm, Corbin Building Inc., posted revenue of over 3 million dollars after funding dozens of urban restoration projects. His company was ranked as one of the 800 fastest-growing companies in the country, all due to what his friends call his motivation for success. Unfortunately, until 1996 Corbin used this motivation to rob and steal on the streets of San Francisco to support a heroin and cocaine habit. But when he was charged with possession in 1996, Josef was given the option to participate in a state drug court, a program targeted at those recently charged with drug use, possession, or distribution. The drug court offers

offenders free drug treatment, therapy, employment, education, and weekly meetings with a judge, parole officer and other accused drug offenders.[27]

Citation, unlike narration, is a simple statement of the facts. Citation is shorter and more precise than narration, in the sense that the source is carefully stated. Citation will always include such phrases as, "According to the July 25, 2010, edition of *Time* magazine," or, "As Mr. Smith made clear in an interview last April 24." Evan McCarley cited statistics later in his speech on drug courts:

> Fortunately, Corbin's story, as reported in the May 30th *San Francisco Chronicle*, is not unique, since there are currently over 300 drug courts operating in 21 states, turning first-time and repeat offenders into successful citizens with a 70% success rate.[29]

Some forms of support, such as anecdotes, are inherently more likely to be expressed as narration. Statistics, on the other hand, are nearly always cited rather than narrated. However, when you are using examples, quotation/testimony, definitions, and analogies, you often have a choice.

Sample Speech

The following sample speech was presented by Curt Casper, whose story began this chapter. When Curt was a senior at Hastings College in 2011, he presented this speech at the Interstate Oratorical Association Annual Contest, hosted by James Madison University. He won second place in the tournament, but the speech was important to him for more than that.

Curt chose his topic because of his intimate experience with it:

> My dad committed suicide when I was a senior in high school. I strongly believed my voice and speech mattered through showing others what my family went

---

Understanding Communication Technology

Plagiarism in a Digital Age

Some experts believe that the Web is redefining how students understand the concept of authorship and originality. After all, the Internet is the home of file sharing that allows us to download music, movies, and TV programs without payment. Google and Wikipedia are our main portals to random free information, also. It all seems to belong to us, residing on our computer as it does. Information wants to be free.

According to one expert on the topic, "Now we have a whole generation of students who've grown up with information that just seems to be hanging out there in cyberspace and doesn't seem to have an author. It's possible to believe this information is just out there for anyone to take."[28] Other experts beg to differ. They say students are fully aware of what plagiarism is, online or off, and they know it's cheating. It's just that it's so easy to copy and paste online material, and students like to save time wherever they can.

Public speaking instructors are on the front lines of those fighting plagiarism, because it's so important for successful student speakers to speak from the heart, in their own words and with their own voice. Plus, citing research enhances credibility. Plagiarism in public speaking isn't just cheating, it's ineffective.

The general rule for the digital age is as follows: Thou shalt not cut and paste into a final draft—not for a paper, and not for a speech. Cutting and pasting is fine for research, but everything that's cut and pasted should be placed in a separate "research" file, complete with a full citation for the website you found it in. Then switch to your "draft" file to put everything in your own words, and go back to the research file to find the attribution information when you need to cite facts and ideas that you got from those sources. ●

Have you ever had a problem with online plagiarism? What was the outcome?

through when my dad did this. I wanted people in my shoes to have the opportunity to get help, the opportunity to know there is hope, and that it will get better.[30]

Curt used a simple problem-effect-solution organizational structure, as seen in his outline, presented on page 356.

Curt collected his supporting material from a wide range of sources, as seen in the following bibliography:

Bibliography

American Association of Suicidology. (2009). *Survivors of suicide fact sheet.* Washington, D.C.: American Association of Suicidology.

American Foundation for Suicide Prevention. (2011). *For the media.* Retrieved March 15, 2011, from American Foundation for Suicide Prevention: http://www.afsp.org/media

American Foundation for Suicide Prevention. (2011). *Out of the darkness community walks.* (EABnet.) Retrieved March 15, 2011, from SOS-walk.org: http://www.sos-walk.org/sos/index.htm

Belau, D. (2011, March 16). LOSS team. (C. Casper, E-mail)

Caruso, K. (2011). *Suicide survivors: Coping with rumors and gossip.* Retrieved March 15, 2011, from suicide.org: http://www.suicide.org/suicide-survivors-coping-with-rumors-and-gossip.html

Cerel, J., Jordan, J. R., & Duberstein, P. R. (2008). The impact of suicide on the family. *Crisis Intervention and Suicide Prevention, 29*(1), 38–44.

Evans, D. (2011, February 28). Accidental death becomes suicide when insurers dodge payouts. *Bloomberg Markets Magazine.* http://www.bloomberg.com/news/2011-03-01/accidental-death-becomes-suicide-when-insurers-dodge-paying-life-benefits.html

Gearing, R. E., & Lizardi, D. (2009, October). Religion and suicide. *Journal of Religion and Health, 48*(3), 332–341.

Hudenko, D., & Crenshaw, D. (2010, October 5). *The relationship between PTSD and suicide.* Retrieved March 15, 2011, from National Center for PTSD: http://www.ptsd.va.gov/professional/pages/ptsd-suicide.asp

Harvard Mental Health. (2009, November). Supporting survivors of suicide loss. *Harvard Mental Health Letter, 4,* 5.

Hopkins, K. (2010, July 15). Suicides, attempts spike again in western Alaska villages. *Anchorage Daily News,* 1.

Insurance.com. (2007, May 17). *Will mental illness affect your life insurance cost?* Retrieved March 15, 2011, from insurance.com: http://www.insurance.com/life-insurance/health-and-life-insurance/will-mental-illness-affect-your-life-insurance-cost.aspx

Johnson, C. (2011, March 15). Compensability clauses. (C. Casper, Interviewer)

KHAS-TV. (2011, April 17). Suicide coverage. (C. Casper, Interviewer)

National Endowment for Financial Education. (2011). *Surviving a suicide loss: A financial guide.* New York: American Foundation for Suicide Prevention.

Patania, J. (2011, March 16). Program assistant for American Association Suicidology. (C. Casper, Interviewer)

University of Nebraska Public Policy Center. (2010). *2010 Nebraska State Suicide Prevention Summit.* Hastings: University of Nebraska-Lincoln.

As you read Curt's speech below, notice how he carefully chooses various types of supporting material to back up what he has to say.

SAMPLE SPEECH | Survivor Support   **Curt Casper**

1 It is the 4-year anniversary since my dad decided to drive in front of a train, dying by suicide. My family has never been the same. My little brother, Blake, who was 10 at the time, has now been in more than a dozen different homes and has been diagnosed with post-traumatic stress syndrome three times. While there was initial help from friends and relatives, the support system quickly went away, and there was nowhere my family could turn to for help.

> Curt begins with a startling statement about his personal experience. This sets the tone for the speech.

2 Three days before my dad killed himself, I received a hug asking for help. I refused to see the pain that my dad was suffering and kept it to myself. Six months later, I wanted to drive in front of a train, because I blamed myself.

> He expands on his personal experience with another powerful statement.

3 My brother and I are not alone. Jill Pantania of the American Association of Suicidology recently told me, "There are 6 million people in the U.S. that currently mourn the death of a loved one by suicide. And that number grows by 190,000 each year."

> He backs up his personal experience with statistics from an interview.

4 Our society is suffering from a mental health stigma. We cannot change this stigma until we stop suicide survivors from suffering alone. Suicide survivors include friends, families, and loved ones who are left behind to deal with a suicide. The *Harvard Mental Health* newsletter of November 2009 notes that the death of a loved one because of suicide leads to a higher risk for several types of psychiatric disorders. According to the Hampton Roads Survivors of Suicide website, "survivors are five times more likely to commit suicide themselves." In other words, suicide isn't the end of a problem for anyone—it's often the starting point for more crises. We all have to become the support that survivors so desperately need.

> Here Curt states his thesis, defines a key term ("suicide survivors"), and provides statistics.

5 Today, I'd like to tell you how we can all facilitate survivor support. First, though, we need to recognize the reasons suicide survivors do not receive the help they deserve. Second, we need to examine the impact of that lack of help. And then finally, we can consider some possible solutions to give survivors the hope they deserve.

> A transition in the form of a preview of main points.

6 The deficiencies in survivor support can be found on both a societal and economic level.

> Another transition, in the form of a preview of two subpoints.

7 First, it can take a while to get over a suicide because our society refuses to use the word *suicide*. The website suicide.org says we as a society make up excuses for the suicide, like "it was his time to go"; yet we don't use the word *suicide*.

> He backs up his first subpoint with information from a website . . .

8 This negative connotation regarding suicide is furthered by religious doctrine, because some religions believe that suicide is a one-way ticket to hell. This is confirmed in the essay "Religion and Suicide," published in the *Journal of Religion and Health* in 2009.

> . . . and a printed essay . . .

9 There are even guidelines in place restricting the use of the word in the media, according to the American Foundation for Suicide Prevention. For instance, KHAS-TV said in a personal correspondence on April 14, 2011, that they did not cover a student's death in December because it was suicide, yet in March they covered a student's death because she died from a skiing accident and not from suicide. These guidelines are in place to prevent other suicides. However, these same guidelines implicitly affirm the messages of guilt and stigma for the family and other survivors.

> . . . and an example that he found in an e-mail interview.

10 Second, as the National Endowment for Financial Education states, "someone getting over a suicide will face financial turmoil." Life insurance companies do not provide benefits if a suicide occurs within 24 months of signing with the company. This is known as the "suicide clause." In some cases, this makes it difficult to pay for the funeral arrangements and other financial obligations. For example, one mother in Nebraska lost her husband to suicide 10 months after

> He introduces his second subpoint with a citation and then backs it up with an example.

signing with the insurance company. She could not even afford to send her son, who witnessed his father shooting himself, to counseling. In other cases the money *is* received, but it is received in one large sum, and survivors feel guilty about receiving it. They might not want to touch the money, or they might just waste it, rather than saving it for a time of need.

11 With an understanding of the causes that undermine survivor support, we can consider the impact of this lack of support, including profound grief and post-traumatic stress disorder on the part of the survivor.

A clearly stated transition from his first to his second main point.

12 First, a suicide causes more grief than most normal deaths, as there are unanswered questions. Survivors wonder, "why" and "what could I have done," which can lead to depression and further suicides, as noted by the *Journal of Crisis Intervention and Suicide Prevention* in 2008. For example, a small community in Alaska, Yukon-Kuskwim Delta, saw nine people between the ages of 17 and 22 commit suicide within only a few weeks of each other. According to the *Anchorage Daily News* of July 15, 2010, there was a chain reaction as each person was affected by the previous death. Alaska is not alone; my campus experienced the suicide cycle back in December.

Several examples, from research and personal experience.

13 Second, because denial and shock are often the first emotions felt by survivors, it can take years for bereavement, creating a condition known as post-traumatic stress disorder, or PTSD. On average, it takes 4.5 years after a suicide before a survivor seeks help. I learned that from Dr. Dan Belau, a mental health advocate, in personal correspondence during March 2011. According to Dr. Belau, PTSD leads to nightmares and flashbacks, ultimately making it difficult for a survivor to effectively function in society. We have all seen the effects of post-traumatic stress on soldiers fighting overseas, but often people don't realize that we are at war *here* with suicide.

His next subpoint.

14 The National Center for PTSD website, which I accessed in October 2010, says there is a "direct link between survivors of suicide and PTSD." Even small events, like seeing someone else's dad come to watch your sports event or come to a birthday party can result in a paralysis of emotions for survivors—even many years after the suicide.

Although Curt words this example as a generality, his audience knows he is referring to personal experience here, which provides a sort of transition to his next, personal statement.

15 I was eventually able to get help, and I no longer blame myself. I have not contemplated suicide since I got the help I needed. However, many survivors simply do not get help. Survivor support solutions can and should be facilitated on two levels: through survivor supporters and through survivors themselves.

A transition in the form of a preview of final subpoints.

16 First, our lawmakers could be survivor supporters by easing the red tape on insurance policies. Insurance agent Caleb Johnson, in a personal interview on March 15, 2011, says, "A simple solution would be to set a standard that insurance companies give back the premiums that were paid before the suicide." If someone is willing to spend money on insurance, they should know their loved ones would be taken care of if a suicide occurs. If you wanted to become a survivor supporter, you could encourage insurance reform by sending a brief e-mail about this issue to your local lawmakers.

First subpoint is developed with a quotation.

17 On a more personal level, if you have a friend who is a survivor, just be there for them by giving them a list of resources. I've prepared a CD with this type of resources, such as inexpensive but effective counselors, along with a list of websites that can help supporters and survivors. I'd be glad to give you a copy of this CD after my speech.

Direct statement of next subpoint.

18 As a survivor supporter, you need to use the word *suicide* when talking to survivors. This will ease their grief, because it will help make suicide visible. While attending an Active Minds Conference, I was able to see a display of 1,100 backpacks that represents the number of collegiate suicides annually. The display,

A subpoint developed with a descriptive anecdote.

entitled *Send Silence Packing*, travels across the nation to show the effects suicide has on all. There are stories of survivors who have dealt with a suicide in each backpack. In addition, the cool part is, you can get the backpacks in your communities—that information will also be available at the end of my speech.

19 Second, I urge survivors to share their stories to help others in similar situations. I use my story, because I know I cannot change what happened to my dad, but by sharing my story I can help other families.

20 The first step is for survivors to realize that they are not at fault for what happened. Yes, the grief is going to be difficult to handle, but it can get easier. We as a community of survivors need to be there for each other. I am currently a member of a LOSS team, which is a group of individuals who are survivors and want to help other survivors. When there is a suicide in the area, the team is dispatched to the family. Dr. Dan Belau, the mental health advocate I mentioned earlier, told me, "The time it takes for a survivor to seek help changes from 4.5 years to 39 days" when resources like the LOSS team are provided.

LOSS stands for Local Outreach to Suicide Survivors. Curt felt the acronym was intuitive and did not require an explanation. Do you agree?

21 Finally, survivors, remember it's never too late to request the help you deserve. If it takes 4.5 years to get the courage and seek unsolicited help, how long might it take before we come to terms with the event? Survivor support cannot be rushed; there is no statute of limitations on grief.

22 I realize this is a tough topic to talk about. That's why I have created this CD with a list of resources that can help you and survivors. Please take one of these. In fact, take a few of them so you can give them to others, because while a survivor will never know the reasons why a suicide occurs, having a better understanding of how to deal with the loss will help ease the grieving mind.

Curt picks up the CD here so audience members can see it.

23 I have seen firsthand how a suicide can destroy a family. In light of the 4-year anniversary of my father's death, I hope that my brother, Blake, and the rest of my family will be able to pick up the pieces and begin to rebuild our family. And, while the road to recovery will still be tough and has been tough, I know my dad would have wanted us to move on and know that everything is okay.[31]

Powerful personal experience is used as supporting material in this conclusion.

Summary

This chapter dealt with speech organization and supporting material. Speech organization is a process that begins with the formulation of a thesis statement to express the central idea of a speech. The thesis is established in the introduction, developed in the body, and reviewed in the conclusion of a structured speech. The introduction will also gain the audience's attention, preview the main points, set the mood and tone of the speech, and demonstrate the importance of the topic to the audience. The conclusion will review your thesis and/or main points and supply the audience with a memory aid.

Organizing the body of the speech will begin with a list of points you might want to make. These points are then organized according to the principles of outlining. They are divided, coordinated, and placed in a logical order. Transitions from point to point help make this order apparent to your audience. Organization follows a pattern, such as time, space, topic, problem-solution, cause-effect, Motivated Sequence, or climax arrangements.

Supporting materials are the facts and information you use to back up what you say. Supporting material has four purposes: to clarify, to make interesting, to make memorable, and to prove.

Types of support include *definitions* of key terms; *examples*, which can be real or hypothetical; *statistics*, which show that a fact or principle is true for a large percentage of cases; *analogies*, which compare or contrast an unknown or unfamiliar concept with a known or familiar one; *anecdotes*, which add a lively, personal touch; and *quotations and testimony*, which are used for memorable wording as well as ideas from a well-known or authoritative source. Any piece of support might combine two or more of these types. Support may be narrated (told in story form) or cited (stated briefly).

Key Terms

analogy An extended comparison that can be used as supporting material in a speech. *p. 369*

anecdote A brief, personal story used to illustrate or support a point in a speech. *p. 370*

basic speech structure The division of a speech into introduction, body, and conclusion. *p. 355*

cause-effect pattern An organizing plan for a speech that demonstrates how one or more events result in another event or events. *p. 361*

citation A brief statement of supporting material in a speech. *p. 372*

climax pattern An organizing plan for a speech that builds ideas to the point of maximum interest or tension. *p. 359*

conclusion (of a speech) The final structural unit of a speech, in which the main points are reviewed and final remarks are made to motivate the audience to act or help listeners remember key ideas. *p. 363*

example A specific case that is used to demonstrate a general idea. *p. 368*

formal outline A consistent format and set of symbols used to identify the structure of ideas. *p. 355*

hypothetical example An example that asks an audience to imagine an object or event. *p. 369*

introduction (of a speech) The first structural unit of a speech, in which the speaker captures the audience's attention and previews the main points to be covered. *p. 363*

narration The presentation of speech supporting material as a story with a beginning, middle, and end. *p. 371*

problem-solution pattern An organizing pattern for a speech that describes an unsatisfactory state of affairs and then proposes a plan to remedy the problem. *p. 360*

space pattern An organizing plan in a speech that arranges points according to their physical location. *p. 359*

statistic Numbers arranged or organized to show how a fact or principle is true for a large percentage of cases. *p. 369*

testimony Supporting material that proves or illustrates a point by citing an authoritative source. *p. 370*

time pattern An organizing plan for a speech based on chronology. *p. 359*

topic pattern An organizing plan for a speech that arranges points according to logical types or categories. *p. 360*

transition A phrase that connects ideas in a speech by showing how one relates to the other. *p. 362*

working outline A constantly changing organizational aid used in planning a speech. *p. 355*

Check Your Understanding

1. Which of the organizing principles for outlining from pages 356–359 do you need to work on in your own outlining? Which ones come naturally to you?

2. What are the primary characteristics of introductions, conclusions, and transitions? Why is each important?

3. Which one of the goals of supporting material, as outlined on pages 366–368, do you consider most important? Why?

Activities

1. **Dividing Ideas** For practice in the principle of division, divide each of the following into three to five subcategories:

   1. Clothing
   2. Academic studies
   3. Crime
   4. Health care
   5. Fun
   6. Charities

2. **Organizational Effectiveness** Take any written statement at least three paragraphs long that you consider effective. This statement might be an editorial in your local newspaper, a short magazine article, or even a section of one of your textbooks. Outline this statement according to the rules discussed here. Was the statement well organized? Did its organization contribute to its effectiveness?

3. **The Functions of Support** For practice in recognizing the functions of support, identify three instances of support in each of the speeches at the end of Chapters 13 and 14. Explain the function of each instance of support. (Keep in mind that any instance of support *could* perform more than one function.)

For Further Exploration

For more resources about organization and support, see the *Understanding Human Communication* website at www.oup.com/us/adler. There you will find a variety of resources: "Media Room" clips from popular films and television shows to further illustrate important concepts, a list of books and articles, links to descriptions of feature films and television shows at the *Now Playing* website, study aids, and a self-test to check your understanding of the material in this chapter.

Informative Speaking

Chapter Outline

LEARNING OBJECTIVES

1 Create information hunger by stressing the relevance of your material to your listeners' needs.

2 Use the strategies outlined in this chapter to organize unfamiliar information in an understandable manner.

3 Emphasize important points in your speech.

4 Generate audience involvement.

5 Use visual aids effectively.

ShaoLan Hsueh is a radical. Or rather, her approach to teaching Chinese is.

As the daughter of a calligrapher in Taiwan, Hsueh spent 15 years mastering the symbols that represent Chinese words. Because there are more than 20,000 of these symbols in all, many people consider Chinese the most difficult language in the world.

"It must seem as impenetrable as the Great Wall of China," Hsueh acknowledges. "Over the years I often wondered if I could find a way to break down this wall."[1] She may have done just that.

Hsueh has designed an easy-to-learn system she calls Chineasy. It's based on eight simple characters for words such as *person*, *tree*, *sun*, and *moon*. Once people understand them, the meaning of 30 or 40 additional symbols becomes apparent, and so on. Soon, Hsueh says, people can quickly learn enough to read Chinese road signs, menus, and newspapers.

The idea is catching on. Chineasy has achieved worldwide attention, and Hsueh is in demand as a public speaker. You will find her TED talk, which has been viewed more than 700,000 times, at the end of this chapter.

ShaoLan Hsueh's TED talk demonstrates that even complicated topics can be explained clearly.

- What speakers have you encountered who have the ability to present difficult concepts in a clear and interesting way? What lessons can you learn from them?

- What complicated topics would you like to explain in a clearer and more interesting way? How can you do so by applying the information in this chapter?

Have you noticed that there's a lot of information going around these days? Some people call it the age of information; others call it the age of information glut, data smog, and clutter. There are, in fact, a hundred names for it, but they all deal with the same idea: There is just too much information. And the amount of information is increasing exponentially. One information expert estimates that every 2 days now we create as much information as we did from the dawn of civilization up until 2003.[2]

Social scientists tell us that the information glut leads to **information overload**, which is a form of psychological stress that occurs when people become confused and have trouble sorting through all the information that is available to them.[3] Some experts use another term, **information anxiety**, for the same phenomenon. To check on how information overload affects you personally, do the self-assessment on p. 381.

As ShaoLan Hsueh discovered when planning her speech on the Chineasy method, the informative speaker's responsibility is not just to provide new information. Informative speaking, when it's done effectively, seeks to relieve information overload by turning information into **knowledge** for an audience. Information is the raw materials, the sometimes-contradictory facts and competing claims that rain down on public consciousness. Knowledge is what you get when you are able to make sense of and use those raw materials. Effective public

> cultural idiom
> **rain down on:**
> fall like rain, overwhelm

speakers filter, organize, and illustrate information in order to reach small audiences with messages tailored for them, in an environment in which they can see if the audience is "getting it." If they aren't, the speaker can adjust the message and work with the audience until they do.

Informative speaking goes on all around you: in your professors' lectures or in a mechanic's explanation of how to keep your car from breaking down. You engage in this type of speaking frequently whether you realize it or not. Sometimes it is formal, as when you give a report in class. At other times, it is more casual, as when you tell a friend how to prepare your favorite dish. The main objective of this chapter is to give you the skills you need to enhance all of your informative speaking.

SELF-ASSESSMENT

Are You Overloaded with Information?

Problems in informative speaking are often the result of information overload—on the part of both the speaker and the audience. For each statement to the right, select "often," "sometimes," or "seldom" to assess your level of information overload.

1. I forget information I need to know.

   Often   Sometimes   Seldom

2. I have difficulty concentrating on important tasks.

   Often   Sometimes   Seldom

3. When I go online, I feel anxious about the work that I don't have time to do.

   Often   Sometimes   Seldom

4. I have e-mail messages sitting in my inbox that are more than 2 weeks old.

   Often   Sometimes   Seldom

5. I constantly check my online services because I am afraid that if I don't, I will never catch up.

   Often   Sometimes   Seldom

6. I find myself easily distracted by things that allow me to avoid work I need to do.

   Often   Sometimes   Seldom

7. I feel fatigued by the amount of information I encounter.

   Often   Sometimes   Seldom

8. I delay making decisions because of too many choices.

   Often   Sometimes   Seldom

9. I make wrong decisions because of too many choices.

   Often   Sometimes   Seldom

10. I spend too much time seeking information that is *nice to know* rather than information that I *need to know*.

    Often   Sometimes   Seldom

Scoring: Give yourself 3 points for each "often," 2 points for each "sometimes," and 1 point for each "seldom." If your score is:

10–15: Information overload is not a big problem for you. However, it's probably still a significant problem for at least some members of your audience, so try to follow the guidelines for informative speaking outlined in this chapter.

16–24: You have a normal level of information overload. The guidelines in this chapter will help you be a more effective speaker.

25–30: You have a high level of information overload. Along with observing the guidelines in this chapter, you might also want to search online for guidelines to help you overcome this problem. ●

Types of Informative Speaking

There are several types of informative speaking. The primary types have to do with the content and purpose of the speech.

By Content

Informative speeches are generally categorized according to their content, including the following types:

Speeches About Objects   This type of informative speech is about anything that is tangible (that is, capable of being seen or touched). Speeches about objects might include an appreciation of the Grand Canyon (or any other natural wonder) or a demonstration of the newest smartphone (or any other product).

Speeches About Processes   A process is any series of actions that leads to a specific result. If you spoke on the process of aging, the process of learning to juggle, or the process of breaking into a social networking business, you would be giving this type of speech.

Speeches About Events   You would be giving this type of informative speech if your topic dealt with anything notable that happened, was happening, or might happen: an upcoming protest against hydraulic fracturing ("fracking"), for example, or the prospects of your favorite baseball team winning the national championship.

Speeches About Concepts   Concepts include intangible ideas, such as beliefs, theories, ideas, and principles. If you gave an informative speech about postmodernism, vegetarianism, or any other "ism," you would be giving this type of speech. Other topics would include everything from New Age religions to theories about extraterrestrial life to rules for making millions of dollars.

By Purpose

We also distinguish among types of informative speeches depending on the speaker's purpose. We ask, "Does the speaker seek to describe, explain, or instruct?"

Descriptions   A speech of **description** is the most straightforward type of informative speech. You might introduce a new product like a wearable computer to a group of customers, or you might describe what a career in nursing would be like. Whatever its topic, a descriptive speech uses details to create a "word picture" of the essential factors that make that thing what it is.

Explanations   **Explanations** clarify ideas and concepts that are already known but not understood by an audience. For example, your audience members might already know that a U.S. national debt exists, but they might be baffled by the reasons why it has become so large. Explanations often deal with the question of *why* or *how*. Why do we have to wait until the age of 21 to drink legally? How did China evolve from an impoverished economy to a world power in a single generation? Why did tuition need to be increased this semester?

Instructions   **Instructions** teach something to the audience in a logical, step-by-step manner. They are the basis of training programs and orientations. They often deal with the question of *how to*. This type of speech sometimes features a demonstration or a visual aid. Thus, if you were giving instructions on "how to promote your career via social networking sites," you might demonstrate by showing the

ON YOUR FEET

Content and Purpose

Choose a topic for an informative speech. Briefly explain to your classmates why you have chosen this topic and what you hope to accomplish by presenting it. Listen carefully to their reactions and see if you need to adjust your idea.

social media profile of successful people. For instructions on "how to perform CPR," you could use a volunteer or a dummy.

These types of informative speeches aren't mutually exclusive. As you'll see in the sample speech at the end of this chapter, there is considerable overlap, as when you give a speech about objects that has the purpose of explaining them. Still, even this imperfect categorization demonstrates how wide a range of informative topics is available. One final distinction we need to make, however, is the difference between an informative and a persuasive speech topic.

Sushi chef Toshio Suzuki presents a training session on preparing raw fish at Oceana in New York. Even when an audience is interested in a topic, it takes skill for a speaker to present material in a way that is understandable.

Informative Versus Persuasive Topics

There are many similarities between an informative and a persuasive speech. In an informative speech, for example, you are constantly trying to "persuade" your audience to listen, understand, and remember. In a persuasive speech, you "inform" your audience about your arguments, your evidence, and so on. However, two basic characteristics differentiate an informative topic from a persuasive topic.

An Informative Topic Tends to Be Noncontroversial

In an informative speech, you generally do not present information that your audience is likely to disagree with. Again, this is a matter of degree. For example, you might want to give a purely informative talk on the differences between hospital births and home-based midwife births by simply describing what the practitioners of each method believe and do. By contrast, a talk either boosting or criticizing one method over the other would clearly be persuasive.

The noncontroversial nature of informative speaking does not mean that your speech topic should be uninteresting to your audience; rather, it means that your approach to it should not engender conflict. You could speak about the animal rights movement, for example, by explaining the points of view of both sides in an interesting but objective manner.

Find an interesting informative speech online. (For example, see www.ted.com.) How would you categorize this speech by content and purpose?

The Informative Speaker Does Not Intend to Change Audience Attitudes

The informative speaker does seek a response (such as attention and interest) from the listener and does try to make the topic important to the audience. But the speaker's primary intent is not to change attitudes or to make the audience members *feel* differently about the topic. For example, an informative speaker might explain how a microwave oven works but will not try to "sell" a specific brand of oven to the audience.

The speaker's intent is best expressed in a specific informative purpose statement, which brings us to the first of our techniques of informative speaking.

 ON YOUR FEET

Informative vs. Persuasive Approaches

Pick a speech topic that interests you. Describe two speeches on this topic, one informative and the other persuasive.

How Culture Affects Information

Cultural background is always a part of informative speaking, although it's not always easy to spot. Sometimes this is because of ethnocentrism, the belief in the inherent superiority of one's own ethnic group or culture. According to communication scholars Larry Samovar and Richard Porter, ethnocentrism is exemplified by what is taught in schools.

Each culture, whether consciously or unconsciously, tends to glorify its historical, scientific, and artistic accomplishments while frequently minimizing the accomplishments of other cultures. In this way, schools in all cultures, whether or not they intend to, teach ethnocentrism. For instance, the next time you look at a world map, notice that the United States is prominently located in the center—unless, of course, you

are looking at a Chinese or Russian map. Many students in the United States, if asked to identify the great books of the world, would likely produce a list of books mainly by Western, white, male authors. This attitude of subtle ethnocentrism, or the reinforcing of the values, beliefs, and prejudices of the culture, is not a uniquely American phenomenon. Studying only the Koran in Iranian schools or only the Old Testament in Israeli classrooms is also a quiet form of ethnocentrism. ●

How would culture affect the informative topic you have chosen?

From Samovar, L., & Porter, R. (2010) *Communication between cultures* (5th ed.). Boston: Wadsworth. ©2010. Reprinted with permission of Wadsworth, an imprint of the Wadsworth Group, a division of Cengage Learning.

Techniques of Informative Speaking

The techniques of informative speaking are based on a number of principles of human communication in general, and public speaking specifically, that we have discussed in earlier chapters. The most important principles to apply to informative speaking include those that help an audience understand and care about your speech. Let's look at how these principles apply to specific techniques.

Define a Specific Informative Purpose

As Chapter 11 explained, any good speech must be based on a purpose statement that is audience oriented, precise, and attainable. When you are preparing an informative speech, it is especially important to define in advance, for yourself, a clear informative purpose. An **informative purpose statement** will generally be worded to stress audience knowledge, ability, or both:

> After listening to my speech, my audience will be able to recall the three most important questions to ask when shopping for a smartphone.

> After listening to my speech, my audience will be able to identify the four reasons that online memes go viral.

> After listening to my speech, my audience will be able to discuss the pros and cons of using drones in warfare.

Notice that in each of these purpose statements a specific verb such as *to recall*, *to identify*, or *to discuss* points out what the audience will be able to do after hearing the speech. Other key verbs for informative purpose statements include these:

"I know so much that I don't know where to begin."

Accomplish	Choose	Explain	Name	Recognize
Analyze	Contrast	Integrate	Operate	Review
Apply	Describe	List	Perform	Summarize

CHECKLIST > **Techniques of Informative Speaking**

☐ Define a specific informative purpose.

☐ Create information hunger by relating to audience needs.

☐ Make it easy for audience members to listen.
- Limit the amount of information presented.
- Use familiar information to introduce unfamiliar information.
- Start with simple information before moving to more complex ideas.

☐ Use clear, simple language.

☐ Use clear organization and structure.

☐ Support and illustrate your points.
- Provide interesting, relevant facts and examples, citing your sources.
- Use visual aids that help make your points clear, interesting, and memorable.

☐ Emphasize important points.
- Repeat key information in more than one way.
- Use signposts: words or phrases that highlight what you are about to say.

☐ Generate audience involvement.
- Personalize the speech.
- Use audience participation.
- Use volunteers.
- Have a question-and-answer period at the end.

A clear purpose statement will lead to a clear thesis statement. As you remember from Chapter 11, a thesis statement presents the central idea of your speech. Sometimes your thesis statement for an informative speech will just preview the central idea:

> Today's smartphones have so many features that it is difficult for the uninformed consumer to make a choice.

> Understanding how memes go viral could make you very wealthy someday.

> Soldiers and civilians have different views on the morality of drones.

At other times, the thesis statement for an informative speech will delineate the main points of that speech:

> When shopping for a smartphone, the informed consumer seeks to balance price, dependability, and user friendliness.

> The four basic principles of aerodynamics—lift, thrust, drag, and gravity—can explain why memes go viral.

> Drones can save warrior lives but cost the lives of civilians.

Setting a clear informative purpose will help keep you focused as you prepare and present your speech.

Create Information Hunger

An effective informative speech creates **information hunger**: a reason for your audience members to want to listen to and learn from your speech. To do so, you can use the analysis of communication functions discussed in Chapter 1 as a guide. You read there that communication of all types helps us meet our physical needs, identity needs, social needs, and practical needs. In informative speaking, you could tap into your audience members' physical needs by relating your topic to their survival or to the improvement of their living conditions. If you gave a speech on food (eating it, cooking it, or shopping for it), you would be dealing with that basic physical need. In the same way, you could appeal to identity needs by showing your audience members how to be respected—or simply by showing them that you respect them. You could relate to social needs by showing them how your topic could help them be well liked. Finally, you can relate your topic to practical audience needs by telling your audience members how to succeed in their courses, their job search, or their quest for the perfect outfit.

> Think about an effective informative presentation you've seen recently. How did it connect with your needs?

Make It Easy to Listen

Keep in mind the complex nature of listening, discussed in Chapter 5, and make it easy for your audience members to hear, pay attention, understand, and remember. This means first that you should speak clearly and with enough volume to be heard by all your listeners. It also means that as you put your speech together you should take into consideration techniques that recognize the way human beings process information.

Limit the Amount of Information You Present   Remember that you probably won't have enough time to transmit all your research to your audience in one sitting. It's better to make careful choices about the three to five main ideas you want to get across and then develop those ideas fully. Remember, too much information leads to overload, anxiety, and a lack of attention on the part of your audience. You will notice in the sample speech at the end of this chapter that ShaoLan Hsueh bases her system of learning Chinese on just eight simple characters.

Use Familiar Information to Increase Understanding of the Unfamiliar   Move your audience members from familiar information (on the basis of your audience analysis) to your newer information. For example, if you are giving a speech about how the stock market works, you could compare the daily activity of a broker with that of a salesperson in a retail store, or you could compare the idea of capital growth (a new concept to some listeners) with interest earned in a savings account (a more familiar concept). In the sample speech at the end of this chapter, you'll notice that ShaoLan Hsueh connects Chinese characters with common images that her audience is familiar with.

Ethical Challenge

The Ethics of Simplicity

Often, persuasive speakers use language that is purposely complicated or obscure in order to keep the audience uninformed about some idea or piece of information. Informative rather than persuasive intent can often help clear the air. Find any sales message (a print ad or television commercial, for example) or political message (a campaign speech, perhaps) and see if you can transform it into an informative speech. What are the differences?

Use Simple Information to Build Up Understanding of Complex Information
Just as you move your audience members from the familiar to the unfamiliar, you can move them from the simple to the complex. An average college audience, for example, can understand the complexities of genetic modification if you begin with the concept of inherited characteristics. Again, ShaoLan Hsueh's sample speech begins with simple images and moves on to more complex characters.

Use Clear, Simple Language

Another technique for effective informative speaking is to use clear language, which means using precise, simple wording and avoiding jargon. As you plan your speech, consult online dictionaries such as Dictionary.com to make sure you are selecting precise vocabulary. Remember that picking the right word seldom means using a word that is unfamiliar to your audience; in fact, just the opposite is true. Important ideas do not have to sound complicated. Along with simple, precise vocabulary, you should also strive for direct, short sentence structure. For example, when Warren Buffet, one of the world's most successful investors, wanted to explain the impact of taxes on investing, he didn't use unusual vocabulary or complicated sentences. He explained it like this:

> Suppose that an investor you admire and trust comes to you with an investment idea. "This is a good one," he says enthusiastically. "I'm in it, and I think you should be, too." Would your reply possibly be this? "Well, it all depends on what my tax rate will be on the gain you're saying we're going to make. If the taxes are too high, I would rather leave the money in my savings account, earning a quarter of 1 percent." So let's forget about the rich and ultrarich going on strike and stuffing their ample funds under their mattresses if—gasp—capital gains rates and ordinary income rates are increased. The ultrarich, including me, will forever pursue investment opportunities.[4]

Each idea within that explanation is stated directly, using simple, clear language.

Use a Clear Organization and Structure

Because of the way humans process information (that is, in a limited number of chunks at any one time),[5] organization is extremely important in an informative speech. Rules for structure may be mere suggestions for other types of speeches, but for informative speeches they are ironclad.

Chapter 12 discusses some of these rules:

- Limit your speech to three to five main points.
- Divide, coordinate, and order those main points.
- Use a strong introduction that previews your ideas.
- Use a conclusion that reviews your ideas and makes them memorable.
- Use transitions, internal summaries, and internal previews.

The repetition that is inherent in strong organization will help your audience members understand and remember those points. This will be especially true if you use a well-organized introduction, body, and conclusion.

The Introduction   The following principles of organization from Chapter 12 become especially important in the introduction of an informative speech:

1. Establish the importance of your topic to your audience.
2. Preview the thesis, the one central idea you want your audience to remember.
3. Preview your main points.

For example, Kevin Allocca, the trends manager at YouTube, began his TED talk "Why Videos Go Viral" with the following introduction:

> I professionally watch YouTube videos. It's true. So we're going to talk a little bit today about how videos go viral and then why that even matters. Web video has

Sheryl Sandberg, chief operating officer and member of the board of Facebook, has earned a reputation for exploring socially important topics in a way that holds the attention of a mass audience.

> cultural idiom
> **ironclad:**
> mandatory

made it so that any of us or any of the creative things that we do can become completely famous in a part of our world's culture. Any one of you could be famous on the Internet by next Saturday. But there are over 48 hours of video uploaded to YouTube every minute. And of that, only a tiny percentage ever goes viral and gets tons of views and becomes a cultural moment. So how does it happen? Three things: tastemakers, communities of participation, and unexpectedness.[6]

The Body   In the body of an informative speech, the following organizational principles take on special importance:

1. Limit your division of main points to three to five subpoints.
2. Use transitions, internal summaries, and internal previews.
3. Order your points in the way that they will be easiest to understand and remember.

Kevin Allocca followed these principles for organizing his speech on why some videos go viral and some do not. He developed his speech with the following three main points:

   I. Tastemakers: Tastemakers like Jimmy Kimmel introduce us to new and interesting things and bring them to a larger audience.

  II. Communities of participation: A community of people who share this big inside joke start talking about it and doing things with it.

 III. Unexpectedness: In a world where more than 2 days of video get uploaded every minute, only those that are truly unique can go viral.

The Conclusion   Organizational principles are also important in the conclusion of an informative speech:

1. Review your main points.
2. Remind your audience members of the importance of your topic to them.
3. Provide your audience with a memory aid.

For example, this is how Kevin Allocca concluded his speech on viral videos:

Tastemakers, creative participating communities, complete unexpectedness, these are characteristics of a new kind of media and a new kind of culture where anyone has access and the audience defines the popularity. One of the biggest stars in the world right now, Justin Bieber, got his start on YouTube. No one has to green-light your idea. And we all now feel some ownership in our own pop culture. And these are not characteristics of old media, and they're barely true of the media of today, but they will define the entertainment of the future.

Use Supporting Material Effectively

Some instructors point out that students naturally organize ideas in the order in which those ideas occurred to them, rather than for strategic effect. Do you agree?

Another technique for effective informative speaking has to do with the supporting material discussed in Chapter 12. All of the purposes of support (to clarify, to prove, to make interesting, to make memorable) are essential to informative speaking. Therefore, you should be careful to support your thesis in every way possible. Notice the way in which ShaoLan Hsueh uses solid supporting material in the sample speech at the end of this chapter. In particular, notice her use of visuals, which can grab your audience members' attention and keep them attuned to your topic throughout your speech.

You should also try to briefly explain where your supporting material came from. These **vocal citations** build the credibility of your explanations and increase audience trust in the accuracy of what you are saying. For example, when Kerry Konda of Northern State University in South Dakota gave a speech on post-traumatic stress disorder, he used the following vocal citation:

The *Journal of the American Medical Association* published a report on a study conducted by Charles Hoge, Jennifer Auchterlonie, and Charles Milliken which found 1 in 5 soldiers returning from Iraq and Afghanistan suffered from post-traumatic stress disorder, a statistic that rivals the Vietnam experience.[7]

By telling concisely and simply where his information came from, Konda reassured his audience that his statistics were credible.

Emphasize Important Points

One specific principle of informative speaking is to stress the important points in your speech through repetition and the use of signposts.

Repetition   Repetition is one of the age-old rules of learning. Human beings are more likely to comprehend information that is stated more than once. This is especially true in a speaking situation, because, unlike a written paper, your audience members cannot go back to reread something they have missed. If their minds have wandered the first time you say something, they just might pick it up the second time.

Of course, simply repeating something in the same words might bore the audience members who actually are paying attention, so effective speakers learn to say the same thing in more than one way. Kathy Levine, a student at Oregon State University, used this technique in her speech on contaminated dental water:

> The problem of dirty dental water is widespread. In a nationwide *20/20* investigation, the water used in approximately 90% of dental offices is dirtier than the water found in public toilets. This means that 9 out of 10 dental offices are using dirty water on their patients.[8]

Redundancy can be effective when you use it to emphasize important points.[9] It is ineffective only when (1) you are redundant with obvious, trivial, or boring points or (2) you run an important point into the ground. There is no sure rule for making certain you have not overemphasized a point. You just have to use your best judgment to make sure that you have stated the point enough that your audience members get it without repeating it so often that they want to give it back.

Signposts   Another way to emphasize important material is by using **signposts**: words or phrases that emphasize the importance of what you are about to say. You can state, simply enough, "What I'm about to say is important," or you can use some variation of that statement: "But listen to this . . . ," or "The most important thing to remember is . . . ," or "The three keys to this situation are . . . ," and so on.

Generate Audience Involvement

The final technique for effective informative speaking is to get your audience involved in your speech. **Audience involvement** is the level of commitment and attention that listeners devote to a speech. Educational psychologists have long known that the best way to teach people something is to have them do it; social psychologists have added to this rule by proving, in many studies, that involvement in a message increases audience comprehension of, and agreement with, that message.

There are many ways to encourage audience involvement in your speech. One way is by following the rules for good delivery by maintaining enthusiasm, energy, eye contact, and so on. Other ways include personalizing your speech, using audience participation, using volunteers, and having a question-and-answer period.

Personalize Your Speech   One way to encourage audience involvement is to give audience members a human being to connect to. In other words, don't be afraid to be yourself and to inject a little of your own personality into the speech. If you happen to be good at storytelling, make a narration part of your speech. If humor is a personal strength, be funny. If you feel passion about your topic, show it. Certainly if you have any experience that relates to your topic, use it.

Kathryn Schulz, author of *Being Wrong* and a self-proclaimed "wrongologist," personalized her TED speech, "Being Wrong," this way:

> So it's 1995, I'm in college, and a friend and I go on a road trip from Providence, Rhode Island, to Portland, Oregon. And you know, we're young and unemployed, so we do the whole thing on back roads through state parks and national forests—basically the longest route we can possibly take. And somewhere in the middle of South Dakota, I turn to my friend and I ask her a question that's been bothering me for 2,000 miles. "What's up with the Chinese character I keep seeing by the side of the road?"
>
> My friend looks at me totally blankly. There's actually a gentleman in the front row who's doing a perfect imitation of her look. (Laughter) And I'm like, "You know, all the signs we keep seeing with the Chinese character on them." She just stares at me for a few moments, and then she cracks up, because she figures out what I'm talking about. And what I'm talking about is this:

> (Laughter) Right, the famous Chinese character for picnic area.[10]

Another way to personalize your speech is to link it to the experience of audience members . . . maybe even naming one or more.

Use Audience Participation Audience participation, having your listeners actually do something during your speech, is another way to increase their involvement in your message. For example, if you were giving a demonstration on isometric exercises (which don't require too much room for movement), you could have the entire audience stand up and do one or two sample exercises. If you were explaining how to fill out a federal income-tax form, you could give each class member a sample form to fill out as you explain it. Outlines and checklists can be used in a similar manner for just about any speech. Here's how one student organization used audience participation to demonstrate the various restrictions that were once placed on voting rights:

> Voting is something that a lot of us may take for granted. Today, the only requirements for voting are that you are a U.S. citizen aged 18 or older who has lived in the same place for at least 30 days and that you have registered. But it hasn't always been that way. Americans have had to struggle for the right to vote. I'd like to illustrate this by asking everyone to please stand.
>
> [Wait, prod class to stand.]
>
> I'm going to ask some questions. If you answer no to any question, please sit down.
>
> Have you resided at the same address for at least 1 year? If not, sit down. Residency requirements of more than 30 days weren't abolished until 1970.

Are you white? If not, sit down. The 15th Amendment gave non-whites the right to vote in 1870, but many states didn't enforce it until the late 1960s.

Are you male? If not, sit down. The 19th Amendment only gave women the right to vote in 1920.

Do you own a home? If not, sit down. Through the mid-1800s only property owners could vote.

Are you Protestant? If not, sit down. That's right. Religious requirements existed in the early days throughout the country.[11]

Use Volunteers   Some points or actions are more easily demonstrated with one or two volunteers. Selecting volunteers from the audience will increase the psychological involvement of all audience members, because they will tend to identify with the volunteers.

Kathryn Schulz, in her speech on being wrong, subtly enlisted volunteers when she wanted to impress an important point on her audience. She began by addressing a rhetorical question to her entire audience but then directed it to a few individuals in the front row:

> So let me ask you guys something—or actually, let me ask you guys something, because you're right here: How does it feel—emotionally—how does it feel to be wrong?

Schulz then listened to the responses and repeated them for the rest of the audience:

> Dreadful. Thumbs down. Embarrassing. . . . Thank you, these are great answers, but they're answers to a different question. You guys are answering the question: How does it feel to *realize* you're wrong? When we're wrong about something—not when we realize it, but before that—*it feels like being right*.

Have a Question-and-Answer Period   One way to increase audience involvement that is nearly always appropriate if time allows is to answer questions at the end of your speech. You should encourage your audience to ask questions. Solicit questions and be patient waiting for the first one. Often no one wants to ask the first question. When the questions do start coming, the following suggestions might increase your effectiveness in answering them:

(1) Listen to the substance of the question. Don't zero in on irrelevant details; listen for the big picture, the basic, overall question that is being asked. If you are not really sure what the substance of a question is, ask the questioner to paraphrase it. Don't be afraid to let the questioners do their share of the work.

(2) Paraphrase confusing or quietly asked questions. Use the active listening skills described in Chapter 5. You can paraphrase the question in just a few words: "If I understand your question, you are asking _____. Is that right?"

(3) Avoid defensive reactions to questions. Even if the questioner seems to be calling you a liar or stupid or biased, try to listen to the substance of the question and not to the possible personality attack.

Rubes®   **By Leigh Rubin**

"In order to adequately demonstrate just how many ways there are to skin a cat, I'll need a volunteer from the audience."

Source: "Rubes" by Leigh Rubin. By permission of Leigh Rubin and Creators Syndicate.

> cultural idiom
> **zero in on:**
> focus directly on

▽ **ON YOUR FEET**

Using Audience Participation
Present one point from the informative speech you are preparing. To demonstrate your point, find a way to use audience participation from your entire class or from a volunteer or two. After this demonstration, invite suggestions for improvement.

④ Answer the question briefly. Then check the questioner's comprehension of your answer by observing his or her nonverbal response or by asking, "Does that answer your question?"

Using Visual Aids

Visual aids are graphic devices used in a speech to illustrate or support ideas. Although they can be used in any type of speech, they are especially important in informative speeches. For example, they can be extremely useful when you want to show how things look (photos of your trek to Nepal or the effects of malnutrition) or how things work (a demonstration of a new ski binding or a diagram of how seawater is made drinkable). Visual aids can also show how things relate to one another (a graph showing the relationships among gender, education, and income). In the sample speech at the end of this chapter, ShaoLan Hsueh demonstrates how effective visual aids can be.

Types of Visual Aids

There is a wide variety of types of visual aids. The most common types include the following.

Objects and Models   Sometimes the most effective visual aid is the actual thing you are talking about. This is true when the thing you are talking about is portable enough to carry and simple enough to use during a demonstration before an audience: a piece of sports equipment such as a lacrosse racket or a small piece of weight-training equipment. **Models** are scaled representations of the object you are discussing and are used when that object is too large (the new campus arts complex) or too small (a DNA molecule) or simply don't exist anymore (a *Tyrannosaurus rex*).

Diagrams   A **diagram** is any kind of line drawing that shows the most important properties of an object. Diagrams do not try to show everything but just those parts of a thing that the audience most needs to be aware of and understand. Blueprints and architectural plans are common types of diagrams, as are maps and organizational charts. A diagram is most appropriate when you need to simplify a complex object or phenomenon and make it more understandable to the audience. Figure 13-1 shows a humorous depiction of one student's perception of what was covered on a final exam, in the form of a Venn diagram.

Word and Number Charts   **Word charts** and **number charts** are visual depictions of key facts or statistics. Your audience will understand and remember these facts and numbers better if you show them than if you just talk about them. Many speakers arrange the main points of their speech, often in outline form, as a word chart. Other speakers list their main statistics. In the sample speech at the end of this chapter, ShaoLan Hsueh uses a number chart in her sample speech to allow her audience to keep track visually of an important point: that 20,000 characters are needed for Chinese language scholarship, 1,000 characters are needed for basic literacy, and 200 are needed to read road signs and restaurant menus—but you can build up to all these numbers from eight basic characters (see Figure 13-2).

Pie Charts   **Pie charts** are shaped as circles with wedges cut into them. They are used to show divisions of any whole: where your tax dollars go, the percentage of the population involved in various occupations, and so

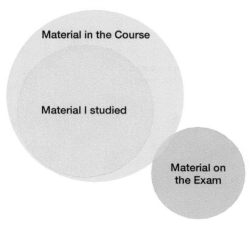

FINAL EXAMS

Material in the Course

Material I studied

Material on the Exam

FIGURE 13-1 Venn Diagram: Student Perception of Final Exam

on. Pie charts are often made up of percentages that add up to 100 percent. Usually, the wedges of the pie are organized from largest to smallest. The pie chart in Figure 13-3 represents one's person's perception of "people who find you on Facebook," and Figure 13-4 shows how the U.S. government adapted a pie chart for a new nutrition diagram. Coincidentally, Figure 13-4 is also a **pictogram**, which is a visual aid that conveys its meaning through images of an actual object.

Bar and Column Charts   **Bar charts**, such as the one shown in Figure 13-5, compare two or more values by stretching them out in the form of horizontal rectangles. **Column charts**, such as the one shown in Figure 13-6, perform the same function as bar charts but use vertical rectangles.

Line Charts   A **line chart** maps out the direction of a moving point; it is ideally suited for showing changes over time. The time element is usually placed on the horizontal axis so that the line visually represents the trend over time. Figure 13-7 is a line chart.

Media for Presenting Visual Aids

Obviously, many types and variations of visual aids can be used in any speech. And a variety of materials can be used to present these aids.

FIGURE 13-2 Number Chart

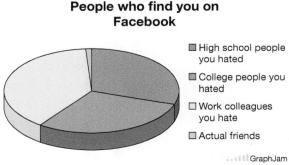

FIGURE 13-3 Pie Chart

FIGURE 13-4 Adaptation of a Pie Chart

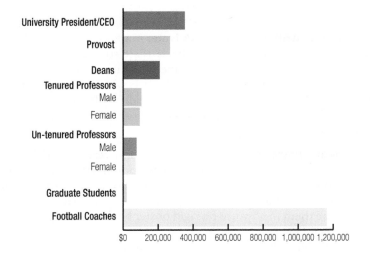

FIGURE 13-5 Bar Chart: College Salaries

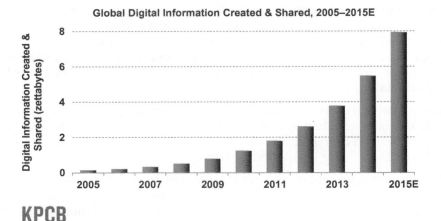

FIGURE 13-6 Column Chart: Global Digital Information Created and Shared
Source: IDC report "Extracting Value from Chaos" 6/11.

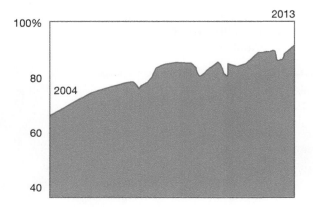

FIGURE 13-7 Line Chart: Percentage of American Adults Who Own a Cell Phone, 2004–2013

Chalkboards, Whiteboards, and Polymer Marking Surfaces The major advantage of these write-as-you-go media is their spontaneity. With them you can create your visual aid as you speak, including items generated from audience responses. Along with the odor of whiteboard markers and the squeaking of chalk, a major disadvantage of these media is the difficulty of preparing visual aids on them in advance, especially if several speeches are scheduled in the same room at the same hour.

Flip Pads and Poster Board Flip pads are like oversized writing tablets attached to a portable easel. Flip pads enable you to combine the spontaneity of the chalkboard (you can write on them as you go) with portability, which enables you to prepare them in advance. If you plan to use your visuals more than once, you can prepare them in advance on rigid poster board and display them on the same type of easel.

Despite their advantages, flip pads and poster boards are bulky, and preparing professional-looking exhibits on them requires a fair amount of artistic ability.

Handouts   The major advantage of handouts is that audience members can take away the information they contain after your speech. For this reason, handouts are excellent memory and reference aids. The major disadvantage is that they are distracting when handed out during a speech: First, there is the distraction of passing them out, and second, there is the distraction of having them in front of the audience members while you have gone on to something else. It's best, therefore, to pass them out at the end of the speech so audience members can use them as take-aways.

Projectors   When your audience is too large to view handheld images, projectors are an ideal tool. *Digital projectors* allow you to use screen images directly from a computer screen, making them the most direct way to use computer software presentations. Projectors allow you to use room-sized images, rather than displaying images on screens that are too small for audiences to see well, such as laptops.

In this photo director James Cameron uses digital projectors to enhance the ideas he presents at iEX 2013 (idea Exchange 2013), a conference to explore the intersection of creativity with technology for storytelling.

Other Electronic Media   A wide range of other electronic media are available as presentation aids. Audio aids such as CDs can supply information that could not be presented any other way (comparing musical styles, for example, or demonstrating the differences in the sounds of gas and diesel engines), but in most cases you should use them sparingly. Remember that your presentation already relies heavily on your audience's sense of hearing; it's better to use a visual aid, if possible, than to overwork the audio.

Of course, there are audiovisual aids, including DVDs. These should also be used sparingly, however, because they allow audience members to receive information passively, thus relieving them of the responsibility of becoming active participants in the presentation. The general rule when using these media is *Don't let them get in the way of the direct, person-to-person contact that is the primary advantage of public speaking.*

Rules for Using Visual Aids

It's easy to see that each type of visual aid and each medium for its presentation have their own advantages and disadvantages. No matter which type you use, however, there are a few rules to follow.

Simplicity   Keep your visual aids simple. Your goal is to clarify, not confuse. Use only key words or phrases, not sentences. The "rule of seven" states that each exhibit you use should contain no more than seven lines of text, each with no more than seven words. Keep all printing horizontal. Omit all nonessential details.

Size   Visual aids should be large enough for your entire audience to see them at one time but portable enough for you to get them out of the way when they no longer pertain to the point you are making.

Attractiveness   Visual aids should be visually interesting and as neat as possible. If you don't have the necessary artistic or computer skills, try to get help from a friend or at the computer or audiovisual center on your campus.

The Pros and Cons of Presentation Software

PowerPoint is by far the most popular form of work presentation today. In fact, as one expert points out, "Today there are great tracts of corporate America where to appear at a meeting without PowerPoint would be unwelcome and vaguely pretentious, like wearing no shoes."[12] Prezi, as an enhanced form of PowerPoint, is subject to many of the same advantages and criticisms.

The Pros   The advantages of PowerPoint are well known. Proponents say that PowerPoint slides can focus the attention of audience members on important information at the appropriate time. The slides also help listeners appreciate the relationship between different pieces of information. By doing so, they make the logical structure of an argument more transparent.

Some experts think the primary advantage of PowerPoint is that it forces otherwise befuddled speakers to organize their thoughts in advance. Most, however, insist that its primary benefit is in providing two channels of information rather than just one. This gives audiences a visual source of information that is a more efficient way to learn than just by listening. One psychology professor puts it this way: "We are visual creatures. Visual things stay put, whereas sounds fade. If you zone out for 30 seconds—and who doesn't?—it is nice to be able to glance up on the screen and see what you missed."[13]

The Cons   For all its popularity, PowerPoint has been receiving some bad press lately, being featured in articles with such downbeat titles as "PowerPoint Is Evil"[14] and "Does PowerPoint Make You Stupid?"[15] But the statement that truly put the anti-PowerPoint argument on the map was a 23-page pamphlet with a less dramatic title, *The Cognitive Style of PowerPoint*,[16] because it was authored by Edward R. Tufte, a well-respected author of several influential books on the effective design of visual aids.

According to Tufte, the use of low-content PowerPoint slides trivializes important information. It encourages oversimplification by asking the presenter to summarize key concepts in as few words as possible—the ever-present bullet points.

Tufte also insists that PowerPoint makes it easier for a speaker to hide lies and logical fallacies. When dazzling slides are used, the audience stays respectfully still, and a speaker can quickly move past gross generalizations, imprecise logic, superficial reasoning, and misleading conclusions.

Perhaps most seriously, opponents of PowerPoint say that it is an enemy of interaction, that it interferes with the spontaneous give-and-take that is so important in effective public speaking. One expert summarized this effect by saying, "Instead of human contact, we are given human display."[17]

The Middle Ground?   PowerPoint proponents say that it is just a tool, one that can be used effectively or ineffectively. They are the first to admit that a poorly done PowerPoint presentation can be boring and ineffective, such as the infamous "triple delivery," in which precisely the same text is seen on the screen, spoken aloud, and printed on the handout in front of you. One proponent insists, "Tufte is correct in that most talks are horrible and most PowerPoint slides are bad—but that's not PowerPoint's fault. Most writing is awful, too, but I don't go railing against pencils or chalk."[18]

PowerPoint proponents say that PowerPoint should not be allowed to overpower a presentation—it should be just one element of a speech, not the whole thing. They point out that even before the advent of the personal computer, some people argued that speeches with visual aids stressed format over content. PowerPoint just makes it extremely easy to stress impressive format over less-than-impressive content, but that's a tendency that the effective speaker recognizes and works against. Thus, proponents say, the arguments for and against PowerPoint are really the arguments for and against visual aids. These arguments are merely accentuated now that they apply to one of the most influential media technologies of our day. Opponents shake their heads sadly at this explanation and insist that every technology changes the humans that use it in some way, and sometimes those changes are subtle and dangerous. ●

After reviewing the pros and cons of PowerPoint, would you say that PowerPoint is a benefit or detriment to effective public speaking? Why?

578

Appropriateness Visuals must be appropriate to all the components of the speaking situation—you, your audience, and your topic—and they must emphasize the point you are trying to make. Don't make the mistake of using a visual aid that looks good but has only a weak link to the point you want to make—such as showing a map of a city transit system while talking about the condition of the individual cars.

Reliability You must be in control of your visual aid at all times. Test all electronic media (projectors, computers, and so on) in advance, preferably in the room where you will speak. Just to be safe, have nonelectronic backups ready in case of disaster. Be conservative when you choose demonstrations: Wild animals, chemical reactions, and gimmicks meant to shock a crowd can often backfire.

When it comes time for you to use the visual aid, remember one more point: Talk to your audience, not to your visual aid. Some speakers become so wrapped up in their props that they turn their backs on their audience and sacrifice all their eye contact.

> cultural idiom

gimmicks:
clever means of drawing attention

wrapped up in:
giving all one's attention to something

Using Presentation Software

Several specialized programs exist just to produce visual aids. Among the most popular of these programs are Microsoft PowerPoint, Apple's Keynote, and Prezi.

In its simplest form, presentation software lets you build an effective slide show out of your basic outline. You can choose color-coordinated backgrounds and consistent formatting that match the tone and purpose of your presentation. Most presentation software programs contain a clip art library that allows you to choose images to accompany your words. They also allow you to import images from outside sources and to build your own charts.

If you would like to learn more about using PowerPoint, Keynote, and Prezi, there are several Web-based tutorial programs, which you can find easily by typing the name of your preferred program into your favorite search engine.

Sample Speech

The sample speech for this chapter was presented by ShaoLan Hsueh, whose profile began this chapter. The speech was presented at a TED conference in 2013.[19] Her purpose is to introduce a method of learning to read Chinese and to demonstrate that method's efficiency. Her purpose statement could be worded like this:

> After listening to my speech, my audience will be able to identify eight basic characters of the Chinese language.

Her thesis statement might be worded this way:

> Eight basic characters can be used to build a workable vocabulary for reading Chinese.

Throughout this speech Hsueh makes it easy for her audience members to hear, pay attention, understand, and remember. She does this by limiting the amount of information she presents, by using information and images to increase understanding of the unfamiliar, and by using simple information to build up an understanding of more complex information.

Her organization is based on a limited number of fundamental characters; she then demonstrates how these characters can be used to exponentially increase one's knowledge of Chinese. She does this efficiently by using a series of well-designed visuals and effective analogies throughout. You can find her complete set of slides on this book's companion website, www.oup.com/us/adler.

SAMPLE SPEECH | Learn to Read Chinese . . . with Ease! **ShaoLan Hsueh**

1   Growing up in Taiwan as the daughter of a calligrapher, one of my most treasured memories was my mother showing me the beauty, the shape, and the form of Chinese characters. Ever since then, I was fascinated by this incredible language.

Her introduction personalizes the speech, while establishing her credibility at the same time.

2   But to an outsider, it seems to be as impenetrable as the Great Wall of China. Over the past few years, I've been wondering if I can break down this wall, so anyone who wants to understand and appreciate the beauty of this sophisticated language could do so. I started thinking about how a new, fast method of learning Chinese might be useful.

3   Since the age of 5, I started to learn how to draw every single stroke for each character in the correct sequence. I learned new characters every day during the course of the next 15 years. Since we only have 5 minutes, it's better that we have a fast and simpler way.

4   [Slide; see p. 393] A Chinese scholar would understand 20,000 characters. You only need 1,000 to understand the basic literacy. The top 200 will allow you to comprehend 40 percent of basic literature—enough to read road signs, restaurant menus, to understand the basic idea of the Web pages or the newspapers. Today I'm going to start with eight to show you how the method works. You are ready?

5   [Slide] Open your mouth as wide as possible until it's square. You get a mouth.

[Slide] This is a person going for a walk. Person.

[Slide] If the shape of the fire is a person with two arms on both sides, as if she was yelling frantically, "Help! I'm on fire!"—this symbol actually is originally from the shape of the flame, but I like to think that way. Whichever works for you.

[Slide] This is a tree. Tree.

[Slide] This is a mountain.

[Slide] The sun.

[Slide] The moon.

[Slide] The symbol of the door looks like a pair of saloon doors in the Wild West.

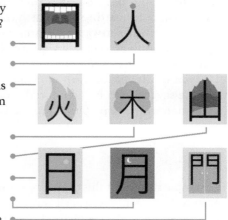

Radicals is used here in its most basic sense, meaning "fundamentals" or "roots." Considering the level of her audience, ShaoLan did not believe she had to define this term beyond her reference to "building blocks."

6   I call these eight characters radicals. They are the building blocks for you to create lots more characters.

[Slide] A person.

[Slide] If someone walks behind, that is "to follow."

[Slide] As the old saying goes, two is company, three is a crowd.

[Slide] If a person stretched their arms wide, this person is saying, "It was this big."

7   [Slide] The person inside the mouth, the person is trapped. He's a prisoner, just like Jonah inside the whale.

[Slide] One tree is a tree. Two trees together, we have the woods. Three trees together, we create the forest.

[Slide] Put a plank underneath the tree, we have the foundation.

[Slide] Put a mouth on the top of the tree, that's "idiot." (Laughter) Easy to remember, since a talking tree is pretty idiotic.

[Slide] Remember fire? Two fires together, I get really hot. Three fires together, that's a lot of flames.

[Slide] Set the fire underneath the two trees, it's burning.

8   . . . So we have gone through almost 30 characters. By using this method, the first 8 radicals will allow you to build 32. The next group of 8 characters will build an extra 32. So with very little effort, you will be able to learn a couple hundred characters, which is the same as a Chinese 8-year-old.

9   So after we know the characters, we start building phrases. [Slide] For example, the mountain and the fire together, we have fire mountain. It's a volcano.

[Slide] A mouth which tells you where to get out is an exit. This is a slide to remind me that I should stop talking and get off of the stage. Thank you.

person

follow
(two people)

crowd
(three people)

big
(person with arms wide)

prisoner
(person inside a mouth)

tree

woods
(two trees)

forest
(three trees)

foundation
(plank below a tree)

idiot
(mouth above a tree)

fire

hot (two fires)

flame (three fires)

burning
(fire under two trees)

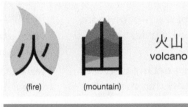

(fire)

(mountain)

火山
volcano

Her mission accomplished, she ends quickly. For a different audience, this might have seemed abrupt. For a TED audience, it was perfect.

Summary

This chapter classified informative speaking based on content (speeches about objects, processes, events, and concepts) and purpose (descriptions, explanations, and instructions). Next, it discussed the differences between informative and persuasive speaking. It then suggested techniques for effective informative speaking. These techniques include using a specific informative purpose that stresses audience knowledge and/or ability, creating information hunger by tapping into audience needs, and making it easy to listen by limiting the amount of information you present, by using familiar information to increase understanding of the unfamiliar, and by using simple information to build up understanding of complex information. Other techniques include emphasizing important points through repetition and signposts; using clear organization and structure; using effective supporting materials, including visual aids; using clear language (language that uses precise, simple vocabulary and avoids jargon); and involving the audience through audience participation, the use of volunteers, and a question-and-answer period.

Key Terms

audience involvement The level of commitment and attention that listeners devote to a speech. *p. 389*

audience participation Listener activity during a speech; a technique to increase audience involvement. *p. 390*

bar chart A visual aid that compares two or more values by showing them as elongated horizontal rectangles. *p. 393*

column chart A visual aid that compares two or more values by showing them as elongated vertical rectangles. *p. 393*

description A type of speech that uses details to create a "word picture" of the essential factors that make that thing what it is. *p. 382*

diagram A line drawing that shows the most important components of an object. *p. 392*

explanations Speeches or presentations that clarify ideas and concepts already known but not understood by an audience. *p. 382*

information anxiety The psychological stress that occurs when dealing with too much information. *p. 380*

information hunger Audience desire, created by a speaker, to learn information. *p. 385*

information overload The decline in efficiency that occurs when the rate of complexity of material is too great to manage. *p. 380*

informative purpose statement A complete statement of the objective of a speech, worded to stress audience knowledge and/or ability. *p. 384*

instructions Remarks that teach something to an audience in a logical, step-by-step manner. *p. 382*

knowledge The understanding acquired by making sense of the raw material of information. *p. 380*

line chart A visual aid consisting of a grid that maps out the direction of a trend by plotting a series of points. *p. 393*

model (in speeches and presentations) A replica of an object being discussed. It is usually used when it would be difficult or impossible to use the actual object. *p. 392*

number chart A visual aid that lists numbers in tabular form in order to clarify information. *p. 392*

pictogram A visual aid that conveys its meaning through an image of an actual object. *p. 393*

pie chart A visual aid that divides a circle into wedges, representing percentages of the whole. *p. 392*

signpost A phrase that emphasizes the importance of upcoming material in a speech. *p. 389*

visual aids Graphic devices used in a speech to illustrate or support ideas. *p. 392*

vocal citation A simple, concise, spoken statement of the source of your evidence. *p. 388*

word chart A visual aid that lists words or terms in tabular form in order to clarify information. *p. 392*

Check Your Understanding

For each of the following questions, please refer to your informative speech topic.

1. What are the ways in which you can generate information hunger with this topic?

2. Give examples of the strategies that can be used to organize unfamiliar information.

3. Identify ways of emphasizing important points in your speech.

4. How could you generate audience involvement?

5. What visual aids would you use for your speech?

Activities

1. **Informative Purpose Statements** For practice in defining informative speech purposes, reword the following statements so that they specifically point out what the audience will be able to do after hearing the speech.

   1. My talk today is about building a wood deck.

   2. My purpose is to tell you about vintage car restoration.

   3. I am going to talk about toilet training.

   4. I'd like to talk to you today about sexist language.

   5. There are six basic types of machines.

   6. The two sides of the brain have different functions.

   7. Do you realize that many of you are sleep deprived?

2. **Effective Repetition** Create a list of three statements, or use the three that follow. Restate each of these ideas in three different ways.

   1. The magazine *Modern Maturity* has a circulation of more than 20 million readers.

   2. Before buying a used car, you should have it checked out by an independent mechanic.

   3. One hundred thousand pounds of dandelions are imported into the United States annually for medical purposes.

3. **Using Clear Language** For practice in using clear language, select an article from any issue of a professional journal in your major field. Using the suggestions in this chapter, rewrite a paragraph from the article so that it will be clear and interesting to a layperson.

4. **Inventing Visual Aids** Take any sample speech. Analyze it for where visual aids might be effective. Describe the visual aids that you think will work best. Compare the visuals you devise with those of your classmates.

For Further Exploration

For more resources about informative speaking, see the *Understanding Human Communication* website at www .oup.com/us/adler. There you will find a variety of resources: "Media Room" clips from popular films and television shows to further illustrate important concepts, a list of books and articles, links to descriptions of feature films and television shows at the *Now Playing* website, study aids, and a self-test to check your understanding of the material in this chapter.

CHAPTER 14

Persuasive Speaking

Chapter Outline

LEARNING OBJECTIVES

1 Formulate an effective persuasive strategy to convince or actuate an audience.

2 Formulate your persuasive strategy based on ethical guidelines.

3 Bolster your credibility as a speaker by enhancing your competence, character, and charisma.

4 Build persuasive arguments through audience analysis, solid evidence, and careful reasoning.

5 Organize a persuasive speech for greatest audience effect.

"I want my 2-year-old to be a rapper," proclaims Tunette Powell.[1]

The 27-year-old mother of two acknowledges that she might change her mind about that career choice down the road. But for now, she says, the idea that rapping gives the toddler a "freestyle" way to express himself is sweet indeed.

She should know. Although Powell is now a published author and a nationally recognized speaker, it took many years to find her own voice. She was born to a mother with limited education and a father who was addicted to crack cocaine and often in trouble with the law. Growing up, Powell felt silently trapped in a "room" she didn't create. Eventually, she says, she realized that the door wasn't locked.

These days Powell inspires audiences and readers to unlock the barriers that hold them back. "We can't change what room we were born into. . . . We can't change who our parents are. We can't change what city we were born into, what home we were born into," she tells an audience at the University of Nebraska–Omaha (UNO).[2] "But we can choose to leave that room. We can choose to open doors and open possibilities."

Powell's door opener was self-expression. But she didn't know that at first. In her first semester of college, she was an unmotivated student who often skipped class and made low grades. There seemed to be a locked door between her and the degree she hoped to earn. "I had to change," she says, "to adapt myself to fit into that lock."[3]

A transformative moment in Powell's life occurred when—in a moment of deep distress—she started to put her feelings on paper. The effort blossomed into a place on the university's forensics team and, eventually, a national title as a persuasive speaker.[4] She graduated with a degree in speech communication in 2012 and recently published her critically acclaimed first book, *The Other Woman*, about her life and her father's struggles.

Powell's style combines the power of a polished and passionate storyteller, a rap lyricist, and a been-there-and-survived adult who isn't afraid of life's darker moments and knows how to connect with audiences who have experienced a few of their own. She acknowledges that doors don't always open easily but encourages people to not be afraid of that. "It's just going to take a little bit more work," she says. "And every time the door gets tougher, the rewards are greater."[5]

Powell now travels the country talking about growing up with a father addicted to drugs. One of her speeches appears at the end of this chapter.

Tunette Powell is a model of how persuasive speaking can change lives.

- What persuasive messages have moved you?

- What audiences would you hope to reach through your own public speaking? How would you like to change the way they think and act?

How persuasion works and how to accomplish it successfully are complex topics. Our understanding of persuasion begins with classical wisdom and extends to the latest psychological research. We begin by looking at what we really mean by the term.

Characteristics of Persuasion

Persuasion is the process of motivating someone, through communication, to change a particular belief, attitude, or behavior. Implicit in this definition are several characteristics of persuasion.

Persuasion Is Not Coercive

Persuasion is not the same thing as coercion. If you put someone in a headlock and said, "Do this, or I'll choke you," you would be acting coercively. Besides being illegal, this approach would be ineffective. As soon as the authorities came and took you away, the person would stop following your demands.

The failure of coercion to achieve lasting results is also apparent in less dramatic circumstances. Children whose parents are coercive often rebel as soon as they can; students who perform from fear of an instructor's threats rarely appreciate the subject matter; and employees who work for abusive and demanding employers are often unproductive and eager to switch jobs as soon as possible. Persuasion, by contrast, makes a listener *want* to think or act differently.

Persuasion Is Usually Incremental

Attitudes do not normally change instantly or dramatically. Persuasion is a process. When it is successful, it generally succeeds over time, in increments, and usually small increments at that. The realistic speaker, therefore, establishes goals and expectations that reflect this characteristic of persuasion.

Communication scientists explain this characteristic of persuasion through **social judgment theory**.[6] This theory tells us that when members of an audience hear a persuasive appeal, they compare it to opinions that they already hold. The preexisting opinion is called an **anchor**, but around this anchor there exist what are called **latitudes of acceptance**, **latitudes of rejection**, and **latitudes of noncommitment**. A diagram of any opinion, therefore, might look something like Figure 14-1.

People who care very strongly about a particular point of view will have a very narrow latitude of noncommitment. People who care less strongly will have a wider latitude of noncommitment. Research suggests that audience members simply will not respond to appeals that fall within their latitude of rejection. This means that persuasion in the real world takes place in a series of small movements. One persuasive speech may be but a single step in an overall persuasive

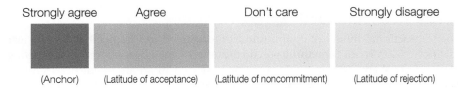

Strongly agree	Agree	Don't care	Strongly disagree
(Anchor)	(Latitude of acceptance)	(Latitude of noncommitment)	(Latitude of rejection)

FIGURE 14-1 Latitudes of Acceptance, Rejection, and Noncommitment

campaign. The best example of this is the various communications that take place during the months of a political campaign. Candidates watch the opinion polls carefully, adjusting their appeals to the latitudes of acceptance and noncommitment of the uncommitted voters.

Public speakers who heed the principle of social judgment theory tend to seek realistic, if modest, goals in their speeches. For example, if you were hoping to change audience views on the pro-life/pro-choice question, social judgment theory suggests that the first step would be to consider a range of arguments such as this:

Abortion is a sin.

Abortion should be absolutely illegal.

Abortion should be allowed only in cases of rape and incest.

A woman should be required to have her husband's permission to have an abortion.

A girl under the age of 18 should be required to have a parent's permission before she has an abortion.

Abortion should be allowed during the first 3 months of pregnancy.

A girl under the age of 18 should not be required to have a parent's permission before she has an abortion.

A woman should not be required to have her husband's permission to have an abortion.

Abortion is a woman's personal decision.

Abortion should be discouraged but legal.

Abortion should be available anytime to anyone.

Abortion should be considered simply a form of birth control.

You could then arrange these positions on a continuum and estimate how listeners would react to each one. The statement that best represented the listeners' point of view would be their anchor. Other items that might also seem reasonable to them would make up their latitude of acceptance. Opinions that they would reject would make up their latitude of rejection. Those statements that are left would be the listeners' latitude of noncommitment.

Social judgment theory suggests that the best chance of changing audience attitudes would come by presenting an argument based on a position that fell somewhere within the listeners' latitude of noncommitment—even if this wasn't the position that you ultimately wanted them to accept. If you pushed too hard by arguing a position in your audience's latitude of rejection, your appeals would probably backfire, making your audience *more* opposed to you than before.

> cultural idiom

backfire:
produce a result opposite of the one
intended

Persuasion Is Interactive

The transactional model of communication described in Chapter 1 makes it clear that persuasion is not something you do *to* audience members but rather something you do *with* them. This mutual activity is best seen in an argument between two people, in which an openness to opposing arguments is essential to resolution. As one observer has pointed out,

Arguments are not won by shouting down opponents. They are won by changing opponents' minds—something that can happen only if we give opposing arguments a respectful hearing and still persuade their advocates that there is something wrong with those arguments. In the course of this activity, we may well decide that there is something wrong with our own.[7]

Even in public communication, both speaker and audience are active. This might be manifested in the speaker taking an audience survey *before* a speech, a sensitivity to audience reactions *during* a speech, or an open-minded question-and-answer period *after* a speech.

Persuasion Can Be Ethical

Even when they understand the difference between persuasion and coercion, some people are still uncomfortable with the idea of persuasive speaking. They see it as the work of high-pressure hucksters: salespeople with their feet stuck in the door, unscrupulous politicians taking advantage of beleaguered taxpayers, and so on. Indeed, many of the principles we are about to discuss have been used by unethical speakers for unethical purposes, but that is not what all—or even most—persuasion is about. Ethical persuasion plays a necessary and worthwhile role in everyone's life.

It is through ethical persuasion that we influence others' lives in worthwhile ways. The person who says, "I do not want to influence other people," is really saying, "I do not want to get involved with other people," and that is an abandonment of one's responsibilities as a human being. Look at the good you can accomplish through persuasion: You can convince a loved one to give up smoking or to not keep a firearm in the house; you can get members of your community to conserve energy or to join together to refurbish a park; you can persuade an employer to hire you for a job in which your own talents, interests, and abilities will be put to their best use.

> What does an ethical persuasive speaker need to do to ensure that he or she is sharing a well-founded message?

Persuasion is considered ethical if it conforms to accepted standards. But what are the standards today? If your plan is selfish and not in the best interest of your audience members, but you are honest about your motives—is that ethical? If your plan is in the best interest of your audience members, yet you lie to them to get them to accept the plan—is that ethical? Philosophers and rhetoricians have argued for centuries over questions like these.

There are many ways to define **ethical persuasion**.[8] For our purpose, we will consider it as *communication in the best interest of the audience that does not depend on false or misleading information to change an audience's attitude or behavior.* The best way to appreciate the value of this simple definition is to consider the many strategies listed in Table 14-1 that do not fit it. For example, faking enthusiasm about a speech topic, plagiarizing material from another source and passing it off as your own, and making up statistics to support your case are clearly unethical.

Besides being wrong on moral grounds, unethical attempts at persuasion have a major practical disadvantage: If your deception is uncovered, your credibility will suffer. If, for example, prospective buyers uncover your attempt to withhold a structural flaw in the condominium you are trying to sell, they will probably suspect that the property has other hidden problems. Likewise, if your speech instructor suspects that you are lifting material from other sources without giving credit, your entire presentation will be suspect. One unethical act can cast doubt on future truthful statements. Thus, for pragmatic as well as moral reasons, honesty really is the best policy.

> cultural idiom

lifting material:
using another's words or ideas as one's own

Tunette Powell's speech at the end of this chapter is an example of an honest, ethical speech.

589

Table 14-1   **Unethical Communication Behaviors**

1. Committing Plagiarism
   a. Claiming someone else's ideas as your own
   b. Quoting without citing the source

2. Relaying False Information
   a. Deliberate lying
   b. Ignorant misstatement
   c. Deliberate distortion and suppression of material
   d. Fallacious reasoning to misrepresent truth

3. Withholding Information; Suppression
   a. About self (speaker); not disclosing private motives or special interests
   b. About speech purpose
   c. About sources (not revealing sources; plagiarism)
   d. About evidence; omission of certain evidence (card stacking)
   e. About opposing arguments; presenting only one side

4. Appearing to Be What One Is Not; Insincerity
   a. In words, saying what one does not mean or believe
   b. In delivery (for example, feigning enthusiasm)

5. Using Emotional Appeals to Hinder Truth
   a. Using emotional appeals as a substitute or cover-up for lack of sound reasoning and valid evidence
   b. Failing to use balanced appeals

Source: Adapted from Andersen, M. K. (1979). *An analysis of the treatment of ethos in selected speech communication textbooks* (Unpublished dissertation). University of Michigan, Ann Arbor, pp. 244–247.

Ethical Challenge

Analyzing Communication Behaviors

Read Table 14-1 carefully. The behaviors listed there are presented in what some (but certainly not all) communication experts would describe as "most serious to least serious" ethical faults. Do you agree or disagree with the order of this list? Explain your answer, and whether or not you would change the order of any of these behaviors. Are there any other behaviors that you would add to this list?

Categorizing Types of Persuasion

There are several ways to categorize the types of persuasive attempts you will make as a speaker. What kinds of subjects will you focus on? What results will you be seeking? How will you go about getting those results? In the following pages we will look at each of these questions.

By Types of Proposition

Persuasive topics fall into one of three categories, depending on the type of thesis statement (referred to as a "proposition" in persuasion) that you are advancing. The three categories are propositions of fact, propositions of value, and propositions of policy.

Propositions of Fact   Some persuasive messages focus on **propositions of fact**: issues in which there are two or more sides about conflicting information, in which listeners are required to choose the truth for themselves. Some questions of fact are these:

The National Security Agency was/was not justified in listening in to the phone calls of everyday citizens.

Windmills are/are not a practical way for the private homeowner to create clean energy.

Bottled water is/is not healthier for you than tap water.

These examples show that many questions of fact can't be settled with a simple "yes" or "no" or with an objective piece of information. Rather, they are open to debate, and answering them requires careful examination and interpretation of evidence, usually collected from a variety of sources. That's why it is possible to debate questions of fact, and that's why these propositions form the basis of persuasive speeches and not informative ones.

Propositions of Value   **Propositions of value** go beyond issues of truth or falsity and explore the worth of some idea, person, or object. Propositions of value include the following:

Cheerleaders are/are not just as valuable as the athletes on the field.

The United States is/is not justified in attacking countries that harbor terrorist organizations.

The use of laboratory animals for scientific experiments is/is not cruel and immoral.

In order to deal with most propositions of value, you will have to explore certain propositions of fact. For example, you won't be able to debate whether the experimental use of animals in research is immoral—a proposition of value—until you have dealt with propositions of fact such as how many animals are used in experiments and whether experts believe they actually suffer.

Propositions of Policy   **Propositions of policy** go one step beyond questions of fact or value: They recommend a specific course of action (a "policy"). Some questions of policy are these:

The World Bank should/should not create a program of microloans for citizens of impoverished nations.

The Electoral College should/should not be abolished.

Genetic engineering of plants and livestock is/is not an appropriate way to increase the food supply.

Looking at persuasion according to the type of proposition is a convenient way to generate topics for a persuasive speech, because each type of proposition suggests different topics. Selected topics could also be handled differently depending on how they are approached. For example, a campaign speech could be approached as a proposition of fact ("Candidate X has done more for this community than the opponent"), a proposition of value ("Candidate X is a better person than the opponent"), or a proposition of policy ("We should get out and vote for Candidate X"). Remember, however, that a fully developed persuasive speech is likely to contain all three types of propositions. If you were preparing a speech advocating that college athletes should be paid in cash for their talents

591

(a proposition of policy), you might want to first prove that the practice is already widespread (a proposition of fact) and that it is unfair to athletes from other schools (a proposition of value).

By Desired Outcome

We can also categorize persuasion according to two major outcomes: convincing and actuating.

Convincing When you set about to **convince** an audience, you want to change the way its members think. When we say that convincing an audience changes the way its members think, we do not mean that you have to swing them from one belief or attitude to a completely different one. Sometimes audience members will already think the way you want them to, but they will not be firmly enough committed to that way of thinking. When that is the case, you reinforce, or strengthen, their opinions. For example, if your audience already believed that the federal budget should be balanced but did not consider the idea important, your job would be to reinforce members' current beliefs. Reinforcing is still a type of change, however, because you are causing an audience to adhere more strongly to a belief or attitude. In other cases, a speech to convince will begin to shift attitudes without bringing about a total change of thinking. For example, an effective speech to convince might get a group of skeptics to consider the possibility that bilingual education is/isn't a good idea.

Actuating When you set about to **actuate** an audience, you want to move its members to a specific behavior. Whereas a speech to convince might move an audience to action, it won't be any specific action that you have recommended. In a speech to actuate, you do recommend that specific action.

There are two types of action you can ask for—adoption or discontinuance. The former asks an audience to engage in a new behavior; the latter asks an audience to stop behaving in an established way.

? persuasion when he spoke in support of Barack Obama Convention. Will you be direct or indirect in your next

If you gave a speech for a political candidate and then asked for contributions to that candidate's campaign, you would be asking your audience to adopt a new behavior. If you gave a speech against smoking and then asked your audience members to sign a pledge to quit, you would be asking them to discontinue an established behavior.

By Directness of Approach

We can also categorize persuasion according to the directness of approach employed by the speaker.

Direct Persuasion In **direct persuasion** the speaker will make his or her purpose clear, usually by stating it outright early in the speech. This is the best strategy to use with a friendly audience, especially when you are asking for a response that the audience is reasonably likely to give you. Direct persuasion is the kind we hear in most academic situations. Eugene Nemirovskiy, a student at Glendale Community College in California, used direct persuasion in his speech about America's mental health care system. Part of his introduction announced his intention to persuade in this way:

> The Virginia Tech shooter, Seung-Hui Cho, was released from a psychiatric hospital and ordered by the court to go to an outpatient treatment center. He never received care and no one enforced the court order. In Brooklyn, this past June, Esmin Green keeled over and died on the floor of a psychiatric emergency room while she waited for help. She waited for more than 24 hours. . . . In fixing health care we've forgotten mental health care. There's no parallel thing happening in other health care fields. People are not languishing or being neglected in cardiology wards across America. . . . In order to cure our mental health care systems we must first uncover what needs to be fixed, then, second, why the problems occur, and finally offer some viable solutions.[9]

Indirect Persuasion   **Indirect persuasion** disguises or deemphasizes the speaker's persuasive purpose in some way. The question, "Is a season ticket to the symphony worth the money?" (when you intend to prove that it is) is based on indirect persuasion, as is any strategy that does not express the speaker's purpose at the outset.

Indirect persuasion is sometimes easy to spot. A television commercial that shows us attractive young men and women romping in the surf on a beautiful day and then flashes the product name on the screen is pretty indisputably indirect persuasion. Political oratory also is sometimes indirect persuasion, and it is sometimes more difficult to identify as such. A political hopeful might be ostensibly speaking on some great social issue when the real persuasive message is "Please remember my name, and vote for me in the next election."

In public speaking, indirect persuasion is usually disguised as informative speaking, but this approach isn't necessarily unethical. In fact, it is probably the best approach to use when your audience is hostile to either you or your topic. It is also often necessary to use the indirect approach to get a hearing from listeners who would tune you out if you took a more direct approach. Under such circumstances, you might want to ease into your speech slowly.[10] You might take some time to make your audience feel good about you or the social action you are advocating. If you are speaking in favor of your candidacy for city council, but you are in favor of a tax increase and your audience is not, you might talk for a while about the benefits that a well-financed city council can provide to the community. You might even want to change your desired audience response. Rather than trying to get audience members to rush out to vote for you, you might want them simply to read a policy statement that you have written or become more informed on a particular issue. The one thing you cannot do in this instance is to begin by saying, "My appearance here today has nothing to do with my candidacy for city council." That would be a false statement. It is more than indirect; it is untrue and therefore unethical.

The test of the ethics of an indirect approach would be whether you would express your persuasive purpose directly if asked to do so. In other words, if someone in the audience stopped you and asked, "Don't you want us to vote for you for city council?" You would admit to it rather than deny your true purpose, if you were ethical.

Creating the Persuasive Message

Persuasive speaking has been defined as "reason-giving discourse." Its principal technique, therefore, involves proposing claims and then backing those claims up with reasons that are true. Preparing an effective persuasive speech isn't easy, but

> cultural idiom

tune you out:
stop listening to you

 ON YOUR FEET

Direct or Indirect Persuasion?
Find a current political speech online and give a brief summary of its persuasive appeal. Would you categorize the speech as direct or indirect persuasion? Why?

it can be made easier by observing a few simple rules. These include the following: Set a clear, persuasive purpose; structure the message carefully; use solid evidence; and avoid fallacies.

Set a Clear, Persuasive Purpose

Remember that your objective in a persuasive speech is to move the audience to a specific, attainable attitude or behavior. In a speech to convince, the purpose statement will probably stress an attitude:

> After listening to my speech, my audience members will agree that steps should be taken to save whales from extinction.

In a speech to actuate, the purpose statement will stress behavior:

> After listening to my speech, my audience members will sign my petition.

As Chapter 11 explained, your purpose statement should always be specific, attainable, and worded from the audience's point of view. "The purpose of my speech is to save the whales" is not a purpose statement that has been carefully thought out. Your audience members wouldn't be able to jump into the ocean and save the whales, even if your speech motivated them into a frenzy. They might, however, be able to support a specific piece of legislation.

A clear, specific purpose statement will help you stay on track throughout all the stages of preparation of your persuasive speech. Because the main purpose of your speech is to have an effect on your audience, you have a continual test that you can use for every idea, every piece of evidence, and every organizational structure that you think of using. The question you ask is "Will this help me to get the audience members to think/feel/behave in the manner I have described in my purpose statement?" If the answer is "yes," you forge ahead.

Structure the Message Carefully

A sample structure of the body of a persuasive speech is outlined in Figure 14-2. With this structure, if your objective is to convince, you concentrate on the first two components: establishing the problem and describing the solution. If your objective is to actuate, you add the third component, describing the desired audience reaction.

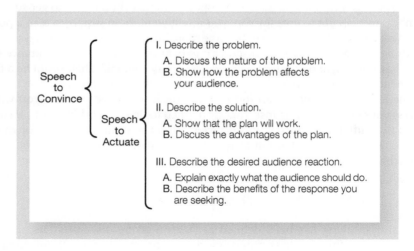

FIGURE 14-2 Sample Structure for a Persuasive Speech

There are, of course, other structures for persuasive speeches. This one can be used as a basic model, however, because it is easily applied to most persuasive topics.

Describe the Problem   In order to convince an audience that something needs to be changed, you have to show members that a problem exists. After all, if your listeners don't recognize the problem, they won't find your arguments for a solution very important. An effective description of the problem will answer two questions, either directly or indirectly.

What Is the Nature of the Problem?   Your audience members might not recognize that the topic you are discussing is a problem at all, so your first task is to convince them that there is something wrong with the present state of affairs. For example, if your thesis were "This town needs a shelter for homeless families," you would need to show that there are, indeed, homeless families and that the plight of these homeless families is serious.

Your approach to defining your problem will depend largely on your audience analysis, as discussed in Chapter 11. If your prespeech analysis shows that your audience may not feel sympathetic to your topic, you will need to explain why your topic is, indeed, a problem that your audience should recognize. In a speech about the plight of the homeless, you might need to establish that most homeless people are not lazy, able-bodied drifters who choose to panhandle and steal instead of work. You could cite respected authorities, give examples, and maybe even show photographs to demonstrate that some homeless people are hardworking but unlucky parents and innocent children who lack shelter owing to forces beyond their control.

How Does the Problem Affect Your Audience?   It's not enough to prove that a problem exists. Your next challenge is to show your listeners that the problem affects them in some way. This is relatively easy in some cases: the high cost of tuition, the lack of convenient parking near campus, the quality of food in the student center. In other cases, you will need to spell out the impact to your listeners more clearly. Hope Stallings, a student at Berry College in Georgia, presented a speech on deferred prosecution agreements for large corporations. She connected this topic to her audience in the following way:

> What do Morgan Stanley, Wachovia, Fannie Mae, Merrill Lynch, and AIG all have in common? You might say that they all contributed to the credit crisis in September, and according to the *Washington Post* of March 5, 2009, the ensuing $787 billion government bailout of big business. And you'd be right—partially. You see, these corporations have something else in common. In the past 5 years, each has been indicted on criminal charges like fraud. Never heard about the trials or verdict? That's because in spite of their fraudulent behavior, these corporations never went to court. They avoided the media spotlight, investor scrutiny, and public outrage by entering into deferred prosecution agreements. The *Record* of July 21, 2008, explains that deferred prosecution agreements allow corporations to avoid criminal convictions by paying a small fine out of court. In other words, these companies paid our government to ensure that we remain ignorant, and we have, right up to the collapse of our economy and our personal financial security.[11]

The problem section of a persuasive speech is often broken up into segments discussing the cause and the effect of the problem. (The sample speech at the end of this chapter is an example of this type of organization.)

Describe the Solution   Your next step in persuading your audience members is to convince them that there is an answer to the problem you have just introduced. To describe your solution, you should answer two questions:

Will the Solution Work?   A skeptical audience might agree with the desirability of your solution but still not believe that it has a chance of succeeding. In the homeless speech discussed previously, you would need to prove that the establishment of a shelter can help unlucky families get back on their feet—especially if your audience analysis shows that some listeners might view such a shelter as a way of coddling people who are too lazy to work.

What Advantages Will Result from Your Solution?   You need to describe in specific terms how your solution will lead to the desired changes. This is the step in which you will paint a vivid picture of the benefits of your proposal. In the speech proposing a shelter for homeless families, the benefits you describe would probably include these:

(1) Families will have a safe place to stay, free of the danger of living on the street.

(2) Parents will have the resources that will help them find jobs: an address, telephone, clothes washers, and showers.

(3) The police won't have to apply antivagrancy laws (such as prohibitions against sleeping in cars) to people who aren't the intended target of those laws.

(4) The community (including your listeners) won't need to feel guilty about ignoring the plight of unfortunate citizens.

Describe the Desired Audience Response   When you want to go beyond simply a strategy to convince your audience members and use a strategy to actuate them to follow your solution, you need to describe exactly what you want them to do. This action step, like the previous ones, should answer two questions:

What Can the Audience Do to Put Your Solution into Action?   Make the behavior you are asking your audience members to adopt as clear and simple as possible for them. If you want them to vote in a referendum, tell them when and where to go to vote and how to go about registering, if necessary (some activists even provide transportation). If you're asking them to support a legislative change, don't expect them to write their congressional representative. *You* write the letter or draft a petition and ask them to sign it. If you're asking for a donation, pass the hat at the conclusion of your speech, or give audience members a stamped, addressed envelope and simple forms that they can return easily.

What Are the Direct Rewards of This Response?   Your solution might be important to society, but your audience members will be most likely to adopt it if you can show that they will get a personal payoff. Show that supporting legislation to reduce acid rain will produce a wide range of benefits, from reduced lung damage to healthier forests to longer life for their car's paint. Explain that saying "no" to a second drink before driving will not only save lives but also help your listeners avoid expensive court costs, keep their insurance rates low, and prevent personal humiliation. Show how helping to establish and staff a homeless shelter can lead to personal feelings of satisfaction and provide an impressive demonstration of community service on a job-seeking résumé.

On the reality TV series *Shark Tank*, budding entrepreneurs pitch their ideas to potential investors. What persuasive strategies distinguish successful contestants from unsuccessful ones? How can you adapt these strategies to your persuasive appeals?

Adapt the Model Persuasive Structure   Describing the problem and the solution makes up the basic structure for any persuasive speech. However, you don't have to analyze too many successful persuasive speeches to realize that the best of them do far more than the basic minimum. In one adaptation of the basic model, the speaker will combine the solution with the desired audience response. Another adaptation is known as the Motivated Sequence.

The **Motivated Sequence**, mentioned in Chapter 12 as a persuasive organization pattern (see Table 14.2), was proposed by a scholar named Alan Monroe in the 1930s and is still widely in use today.[12] In the Motivated Sequence, the problem is broken down into an attention step and a need step, and the solution is broken down into a satisfaction step, a visualization step, and an action step. In a speech on "organ donation," the Motivated Sequence might break down like this:

I. The attention step draws attention to your subject. ("Someday, someone you know may be on an organ donation list; it might even be you.")
II. The need step establishes the problem. ("There is a lack of life-saving organs.")
III. The satisfaction step proposes a solution. ("Organ donation benefits both the donor's family and the recipient.")
IV. The visualization step describes the results of the solution. ("Donating an organ could be one of the greatest gifts you could ever give.")
V. The action step is a direct appeal for the audience to do something. ("Sign an organ donor card today.")

Use Solid Evidence

All the forms of support discussed in Chapter 12 can be used to back up your persuasive arguments.[13] Your objective here is not to find supporting material that just clarifies your ideas, but rather to find the perfect example, statistic, definition, analogy, anecdote, or testimony to establish the truth of your claim in the mind of this specific audience.

You choose **evidence** that strongly supports your claim, and you should feel free to use **emotional evidence**, which is supporting material that evokes audience feelings such as fear, anger, sympathy, pride, or reverence. Emotional evidence is an ethical fault only when it is used to obscure the truth (see Table 14-1, page 408). It is ethical, however, to use emotion to give impact to a truth.

Whatever type of evidence you use, you should cite your sources carefully. It is important that your audience know that your sources are credible, unbiased, and current. If you are quoting the source of an interview, give a full statement of the source's credentials:

> According to Sean Wilentz, Dayton–Stockton Professor of History, Director of American Studies at Princeton University, and the author of several books on this topic . . .

Table 14-2   **Monroe's Motivated Sequence—The Five Steps**

STEP	FUNCTION	IDEAL AUDIENCE RESPONSE
_____ 1. Attention	To get the audience to listen	"I want to hear what you have to say."
_____ 2. Need	To get the audience to feel a need or want	"I agree. I have that need/want."
_____ 3. Satisfaction	To tell the audience how to fill a need or want	"I see your solution will work."
_____ 4. Visualization	To get the audience to see the benefits of a solution	"This is a great idea."
_____ 5. Action	To get the audience to take action	"I want it."

If the currency of the interview is important, you might add, "I spoke to Professor Wilentz just last week . . ." If you are quoting an article, give a quick statement of the author's credentials and the full date and title of the magazine:

> According to Professor Sean Wilentz of Princeton University, in an article in the April 21, 2006, *Rolling Stone Magazine . . .*

You do not need to give the title of the article (although you may, if it helps in any way) or the page number. If you are quoting from a book, include a quick statement of the author's credentials:

> According to Professor Sean Wilentz of Princeton University, in his book *The Rise of American Democracy . . .*

How can you tell if evidence will be effective?

You don't need to include the copyright date unless it's important to authenticate the currency of the quotation, and you don't have to mention the publisher or city of publication unless it's relevant to your topic. Generally, if you're unsure about how to cite your sources in a speech, you should err in the direction of too much information rather than too little.

Carefully cited sources are part of a well-reasoned argument. This brings us to our next step in creating a persuasive message.

Avoid Fallacies

A **fallacy** (from the Latin word meaning "false") is an error in logic. Although the original meaning of the term implied purposeful deception, most logical fallacies are not recognized as such by those who use them. Scholars have devoted lives and volumes to the description of various types of logical fallacies.[14] Here are some of the most common ones to keep in mind when building your persuasive argument:[15]

Attack on the Person Instead of the Argument (*Ad Hominem*)   In an *ad hominem* **fallacy** the speaker attacks the integrity of a person in order to weaken the argument. At its crudest level, an *ad hominem* argument is easy to detect. "How can you believe that fat slob?" is hardly persuasive. It takes critical thinking to catch more subtle *ad hominem* arguments, however. Consider this one: "All this talk about 'family values' is hypocritical. Take Senator _____, who made a speech about the 'sanctity of marriage' last year. Now it turns out he was having an affair with his secretary, and his wife is suing him for divorce." Although the senator certainly does seem to be a hypocrite, his behavior doesn't necessarily weaken the merits of family values.

Reduction to the Absurd (*Reductio Ad Absurdum*)   A *reductio ad absurdum* **fallacy** unfairly attacks an argument by extending it to such extreme lengths that it looks ridiculous. "If we allow developers to build homes in one section of this area, soon we will have no open spaces left. Fresh air and wildlife will be a thing of the past." "If we allow the administration to raise tuition this year, soon they will be raising it every year, and before we know it only the wealthiest students will be able to go to school here." This extension of reasoning doesn't make any sense: Developing one area doesn't necessarily mean that other areas have to be developed, and one tuition increase doesn't mean that others will occur. Any of these policies might be unwise or unfair, but the *ad absurdum* reasoning doesn't prove it.

Either-Or   An **either-or fallacy** sets up false alternatives, suggesting that if the inferior one must be rejected, then the other must be accepted. An angry citizen used either-or thinking to support a proposed city ordinance: "Either we outlaw alcohol in city parks, or there will be no way to get rid of drunks." This reasoning overlooks the possibility that there may be other ways to control public

ON YOUR FEET

Logical Fallacies

Choose one of the logical fallacies discussed here and give an example of how it might be used in an argument. Then show how it could be corrected with more effective reasoning.

drunkenness besides banning all alcoholic beverages. The old saying "America, love it or leave it" provides another example of either-or reasoning. For instance, when an Asian-born college professor pointed out examples of lingering discrimination in the United States, some suggested that if she didn't like her adopted country, she should return to her native home—ignoring that it is possible to admire a country and still envision ways to make it a better place.

False Cause (*Post Hoc Ergo Propter Hoc*)   A *post hoc* **fallacy** mistakenly assumes that one event causes another because they occur sequentially. An old (and not especially funny) joke illustrates the *post hoc* fallacy. Mac approaches Jack and asks, "Hey, why are you snapping your fingers?" Jack replies, "To keep the elephants away." Mac is incredulous: "What are you talking about? There aren't any elephants within a thousand miles of here." Jack smiles and keeps on snapping: "I know. Works pretty well, doesn't it?"

In real life, *post hoc* fallacies aren't always so easy to detect. For example, one critic of education pointed out that the increase in sexual promiscuity among adolescents began about the same time as prayer in public schools was prohibited by the courts. A causal link in this case may exist: Decreased emphasis on spirituality could contribute to promiscuity. But it would take evidence to establish a *definite* connection between the two phenomena.

Appeal to Authority (*Argumentum Ad Verecundiam*)   An *argumentum ad verecundiam* **fallacy** involves relying on the testimony of someone who is not an authority in the case being argued. Relying on experts is not a fallacy, of course. A movie star might be just the right person to offer advice on how to seem more glamorous, and a professional athlete could be the best person to comment on what it takes to succeed in organized sports. But an *ad verecundiam* fallacy occurs when the movie star promotes a political candidate or the athlete tells us why we should buy a certain kind of automobile. When considering endorsements and claims, it's smart to ask yourself whether the source is qualified to make them.

Understanding Diversity

Cultural Differences in Persuasion

Different individuals have a tendency to view persuasion differently, and often these differences are based on cultural background. Even the ability to recognize logical argument is, to a certain extent, culturally determined. Not all cultures use logic in the same way that the European-American culture does. The influence of the dominant culture is seen even in the way we talk about argumentation. When we talk about "defending" ideas and "attacking our opponent's position," we are using male-oriented militaristic/aggressive terms. Logic is also based on a trust in objective reality, on information that is verifiable through our senses. As one researcher points out, such a perspective can be culturally influenced:

> Western culture assumes a reality that is materialist and limited to comprehension via the five senses. African

culture assumes a reality that is both material and spiritual viewed as one and the same.[16]

The way logic is viewed differs between Eastern and Western Hemisphere cultures, also. As Larry A. Samovar and Richard E. Porter point out:

> Westerners discover truth by active searching and the application of Aristotelian modes of reasoning. On the contrary, many Easterners wait patiently, and if truth is to be known it will make itself apparent.[17]

It is because of cultural differences such as these that speech experts have always recommended a blending of logical and emotional evidence. ●

Bandwagon Appeal (*Argumentum Ad Populum*)   An *argumentum ad populum fallacy* is based on the often-dubious notion that, just because many people favor an idea, you should, too. Sometimes, of course, the mass appeal of an idea can be a sign of its merit. If most of your friends have enjoyed a film or a new book, there is probably a good chance that you will, too. But in other cases widespread acceptance of an idea is no guarantee of its validity. In the face of almost universal belief to the contrary, Galileo reasoned accurately that the earth is not the center of the universe, and he suffered for his convictions. The lesson here is simple to comprehend but often difficult to follow: When faced with an idea, don't just follow the crowd. Consider the facts carefully and make up your own mind.

> cultural idiom
> **follow the crowd:**
> do what the majority does

Adapting to the Audience

It is important to know as much as possible about your audience for a persuasive speech. For one thing, you should appeal to the values of your audience whenever possible, even if they are not *your* strongest values. This advice does not mean you should pretend to believe in something. According to our definition of *ethical persuasion*, pretense is against the rules. It does mean, however, that you have to stress those values that are felt most forcefully by the members of your audience.[18]

In addition, you should analyze your audience carefully to predict the type of response you will get. Sometimes you have to pick out one part of your audience—a **target audience**, the subgroup you must persuade to reach your goal—and aim your speech mostly at those members. Some of your audience members might be so opposed to what you are advocating that you have no hope of reaching them. Still others might already agree with you, so they do not need to be persuaded. A middle portion of your audience members might be undecided or uncommitted, and they would be the most productive target for your appeals.

Of course, you need not ignore that portion of your audience that does not fit your target. For example, if you were giving a speech against smoking, your target might be the smokers in your class. Your main purpose would be to get them to quit, but at the same time, you could convince the nonsmokers not to start and to use their influence to help their smoking friends quit.

All of the methods of audience analysis described in Chapter 11—surveys, observation, interviews, and research—are valuable in collecting information about your audience for a persuasive speech.

Establish Common Ground

It helps to stress as many similarities as possible between yourself and your audience members. This technique helps prove that you understand them: If not, why should they listen to you? Also, if you share a lot of common ground, it shows you agree on many things; therefore, it should be easy to settle one disagreement—the one related to the attitude or behavior you would like them to change.

Celebrities such as Angelina Jolie and George Clooney regularly speak out on issues they feel strongly about. Here, as a special envoy for refugees, Angelina Jolie speaks before the Security Council at the United Nations to urge the world's nations to prioritize the fight against war zone rape. What characteristics of her audience did she have to consider to make her speech effective?

The manager of public affairs for *Playboy* magazine gave a good demonstration of establishing common ground when he reminded a group of Southern Baptists that they shared some important values with him:

> I am sure we are all aware of the seeming incongruity of a representative of *Playboy* magazine speaking to an assemblage of representatives of the Southern Baptist convention. I was intrigued by the invitation when it came last fall, though I was not surprised. I am grateful for your genuine and warm hospitality, and I am flattered (although again not surprised) by the implication that I would have something to say that could have meaning to you people. Both *Playboy* and the Baptists have indeed been considering many of the same issues and ethical problems; and even if we have not arrived at the same conclusions, I am impressed and gratified by your openness and willingness to listen to our views.[19]

Organize According to the Expected Response

It is much easier to get an audience to agree with you if the members have already agreed with you on a previous point. Therefore, you should arrange your points in a persuasive speech so you develop a "yes" response. In effect, you get your audience into the habit of agreeing with you. For example, if you were giving a speech on the donation of body organs, you might begin by asking the audience members if they would like to be able to get a kidney if they needed one. Then you might ask them if they would like to have a major role in curbing tragic and needless dying. The presumed response to both questions is "yes." It is only when you have built a pattern of "yes" responses that you would ask the audience to sign organ donor cards.

An example of a speaker who was careful to organize material according to expected audience response is the late Robert Kennedy. Kennedy, when speaking on civil rights before a group of South Africans who believed in racial discrimination, arranged his ideas so that he spoke first on values that he and his audience shared—values like independence and freedom.[20]

If audience members are already basically in agreement with you, you can organize your material to reinforce their attitudes quickly and then spend most of your time convincing them to take a specific course of action. If, on the other hand, they are hostile to your ideas, you have to spend more time getting the first "yes" out of them.

Neutralize Potential Hostility

One of the trickier problems in audience adaptation occurs when you face an audience hostile to you or your ideas. Hostile audiences are those who have a significant number of members who feel adversely about you, your topic, or the speech situation. Members of a hostile audience could range from unfriendly to violent. Two guidelines for handling this type of audience are (1) show that you understand their point of view and (2) if possible, use appropriate humor. A good example of a speaker who observed these guidelines was First Lady and literacy activist Barbara Bush when she was invited to speak at the commencement exercises at Wellesley College in 1990. After the invitation was announced, 150 graduating seniors at the prestigious women's college signed a petition in protest. They wrote, in part:

> We are outraged by this choice and feel it is important to make ourselves heard immediately. Wellesley teaches us that we will be rewarded on the basis of our own work, not on that of a spouse. To honor Barbara Bush as a commencement speaker is to honor a woman who has gained recognition through the achievements of her husband.[21]

Bush decided to honor her speaking obligation, knowing that these 150 students and others who shared their view would be in the audience of 5,000 people. Bush diffused most of this hostility by presenting a speech that stressed that everyone should follow her personal dream and be tolerant of the dreams of others:

> For over 50 years, it was said that the winner of Wellesley's annual hoop race would be the first to get married. Now they say the winner will be the first to become a C.E.O. Both of these stereotypes show too little tolerance. . . . So I offer you today a new legend: the winner of the hoop race will be the first to realize her dream, not society's dream, her own personal dream.[22]

Ethical Challenge

Adapting to a Hostile Audience

How far would you go in adapting to a hostile audience? What forms would that adaptation take? Discuss this question with your classmates, using a specific speech situation as an example. You can make up the speech situation or choose one of the following:

1. Speaking before a group of advertising executives about your firm belief that there should be heavy governmental penalties for false or deceptive advertising

2. Speaking before a group of Catholic bishops about your belief in reproductive choice

3. Speaking before a group of animal rights advocates about advances in interspecies (animal to human) organ transplants

---

Building Credibility as a Speaker

Credibility refers to the believability of a speaker. Credibility isn't an objective quality; rather, it is a perception in the minds of the audience. In a class such as the one you're taking now, students often wonder how they can build their credibility. After all, the members of the class tend to know one another well by the time the speech assignments roll around. This familiarity illustrates why it's important to earn a good reputation before you speak, through your class comments and the general attitude you've shown.

> cultural idiom
>
> **roll around:**
> occur, arrive

It is also possible for credibility to change during a speaking event. In fact, researchers speak in terms of initial credibility (what you have when you first get up to speak), derived credibility (what you acquire while speaking), and terminal credibility (what you have after you finish speaking). It is not uncommon for a student with low initial credibility to earn increased credibility while speaking and to finish with much higher terminal credibility.

Without credibility, you won't be able to convince your listeners that your ideas are worth accepting, even if your material is outstanding. On the other hand, if you can develop a high degree of credibility in the eyes of your listeners, they will be likely to open up to ideas they wouldn't otherwise accept. Members of an audience form judgments about the credibility of a speaker based on their perception of many characteristics, the most important of which might be called the "three Cs" of credibility: competence, character, and charisma.[23]

Competence

Competence refers to the speaker's expertise on the topic. Sometimes this competence can come from personal experience that will lead your audience to regard you as an authority on the topic you are discussing. If everyone in the audience knows you've earned big profits in the stock market, they will probably take your investment advice seriously. If you say that you lost 25 pounds from a

Persuasive Speech

Use the following self-assessment for a persuasive speech you have presented or plan to present.

1. Have you set a clear, persuasive purpose?

    I've done my best.   I've got work to do.   I've barely started.

2. Is your purpose in the best interest of the audience?

    I've done my best.   I've got work to do.   I've barely started.

3. Have you structured the message to achieve a "yes" response?

    I've done my best.   I've got work to do.   I've barely started.

4. Have you used solid evidence for each point?

    I've done my best.   I've got work to do.   I've barely started.

5. Have you used solid reasoning for each point?

    I've done my best.   I've got work to do.   I've barely started.

6. Have you adapted to your audience?

    I've done my best.   I've got work to do.   I've barely started.

7. Have you built your own credibility?

    I've done my best.   I've got work to do.   I've barely started.

8. Is your information true to the best of your knowledge?

    I've done my best.   I've got work to do.   I've barely started.

Scoring on this assessment is self-evident: For every area in which you've got work left to do, do it.

---

diet-and-exercise program, most audience members will be likely to respect your opinions on weight loss.

The other way to be seen as competent is to be well prepared for speaking. A speech that is well researched, organized, and presented will greatly increase the audience's perception of the speaker's competence. Your personal credibility will therefore be enhanced by the credibility of your evidence, including the sources you cite, the examples you choose, the way you present statistics, the quality of your visual aids, and the precision of your language.

Character

Competence is the first component of being believed by an audience. The second is being trusted, which is a matter of character. *Character* involves the audience's perception of at least two ingredients: honesty and impartiality. You should try to find ways to talk about yourself (without boasting, of course) that demonstrate your integrity. You might describe how much time you spent researching the subject or demonstrate your open-mindedness by telling your audience that you changed your mind after your investigation. For example, if you were giving a speech arguing against a proposed tax cut in your community, you might begin this way:

You might say I'm an expert on the municipal services of this town. As a lifelong resident, I owe a debt to its schools and recreation programs. I've been protected by its police and firefighters and served by its hospitals, roads, and sanitation crews.

I'm also a taxpayer who's on a tight budget. When I first heard about the tax cut that's been proposed, I liked the idea. But then I did some in-depth

@Work

Persuasion Skills in the World of Sales

The skills you develop while learning to prepare persuasive speeches are generalizable to a number of important skills in the world of work. The advice of business consultant George Rodriguez makes it clear that the process of developing a successful sales plan is very much like the planning involved in building a persuasive speech.

"A sales plan is basically your strategic and tactical plan for achieving your marketing objectives," Rodriguez explains. "It is a step-by-step and detailed process that will show how you will acquire new business; and how you will gain more business from your existing customer base."[24]

The process of audience analysis is as important in sales-plan development as it is in persuasive speaking. "The first step is to clearly identify your target markets," Rodriguez says. "Who are more likely to buy your product? The more defined your target market, the better. Your target market can be defined as high-income men ages 30–60 who love to buy the latest electronic gadgets; or mothers with babies 0–12 months old living in urban areas."

And don't forget the guideline that persuasion is interactive. "Prospects are more likely to purchase if you can talk to them about solving their problems," Rodriguez points out.

Rodriguez is far from alone in pointing out the importance of thinking in terms of problems and solutions. Business consultant Barbara Sanfilippo advises her clients to "prepare, prepare, and plan your calls. Today's customers and prospects have very little time to waste. They want solutions. A sales consultant who demonstrates a keen understanding of customers' needs and shows up prepared will earn the business."[25] Sanfilippo suggests reviewing the customer's website and interviewing key people in advance of the meeting.

Sanfilippo also points out the importance of building credibility: "How can you stand out from the pack of sales professionals and consultants all offering similar services?" she asks rhetorically. "Establish Credibility and Differentiate!"

But George Rodriguez probably has the last word in how valuable training in persuasive speaking is to the sales professional. Before you make that first sales call, he says, "You may want to take courses on how to improve your confidence and presentation skills." ●

---

investigation into the possible effects, not just to my tax bill but to the quality of life of our entire community. I looked into our municipal expenses and into the expenses of similar communities where tax cuts have been mandated by law.

Charisma

Charisma is spoken about in the popular press as an almost indefinable, mystical quality. Even the dictionary defines it as "a special quality of leadership that captures the popular imagination and inspires unswerving allegiance and devotion." Luckily, communication scholars favor a more down-to-earth definition. For them, charisma is the audience's perception of two factors: the speaker's enthusiasm and likability. Whatever the definition, history and research have both shown us that audiences are more likely to be persuaded by a charismatic speaker than by a less charismatic one who delivers the same information.

Enthusiasm is sometimes called "dynamism" by communication scholars. Your enthusiasm will mostly be perceived from how you deliver your remarks, not from what you say. The nonverbal parts of your speech will show far better than your words that you believe in what you are saying. Is your voice animated and sincere? Do your gestures reflect your enthusiasm? Do your facial expression and eye contact show you care about your audience?

You can boost your likability by showing that you like and respect your audience. Insincere flattery will probably boomerang, but if you can find a way to give your listeners a genuine compliment, they'll be more receptive to your ideas.

> cultural idiom

down-to-earth:
practical

> cultural idiom

boomerang:
create a negative effect

Building your personal credibility through a recognition of the roles of competence, character, and charisma is an important component of your persuasive strategy. When combined with a careful consideration of audience adaptation, persuasive structure, and persuasive purpose, it will enable you to formulate the most effective strategy possible.

CHECKLIST > Ethos, Pathos, and Logos

The Greek philosopher Aristotle divided the means of persuasion into three types of appeal: **ethos**, **pathos**, and **logos**. Use the following checklist to make sure you are using all three means in your persuasive speeches.

☐ **Ethos (credibility), or ethical appeal:** Have you established your credibility as a speaker so that your audience believes you to be trustworthy?

☐ **Pathos (emotions):** Have you used emotional appeals effectively to make your case?

☐ **Logos (logic):** Have you made logical arguments to appeal to the audience's sense of reasoning? This was Aristotle's favorite, and the most important form of appeal we have discussed in this chapter.

Sample Speech

The sample speech for this chapter was presented by Tunette Powell, who was profiled at the beginning of this chapter. When Powell gave this speech, she was a student and member of the forensics team at the University of Nebraska–Omaha. She was coached by Abbie Syrek and Vanessa Hatfield-Reeker. With this speech, Powell won first place at the Interstate Oratorical Association Annual Contest, hosted by Emerson College in 2012.

Powell's thesis statement could be worded this way:

The U.S. government should change the focus of its war on drugs.

Her purpose statement could be worded as follows:

After listening to my speech, my audience members will agree that the government should decriminalize drug addiction.

Powell carefully organized her argument in a problem-effects-solution format, arranging her points for maximum persuasive impact. Her persuasive organization can be seen in the following outline. (Parenthetical numbers refer to paragraphs in the speech.)

INTRODUCTION

  I. Attention-getter (1)

 II. Statement of thesis (2–4)

III. Preview of main points (5–6)

BODY

  I. We are the problem, for two reasons. (7–9)

    A. We demonize addiction as a moral rather than a public health issue. (8)

    B. We put addicts behind bars rather than giving them treatment. (9)

 II. This problem has a number of serious negative effects on the addict and society. (10–15)

    A. When addicts go to prison, they go from being sick to being criminals. (12)
      1. They are released without treatment. (12)
      2. They are released without employment prospects. (13)
    B. When addicts go to prison, society's tax dollars are wasted. (14–15)

III. Solutions can be found on personal, organizational, and governmental levels. (16–18)
    A. Personal solutions involve both attitudes and actions. (17)
      1. Each of us must change our attitudes about addiction.
      2. Each of us should get involved to promote rehabilitation.
    B. Organizational solutions include A New Path. (18)
    C. Governmental solutions involve a needed change of policy. (19)
      1. Government policy should change to reflect the differences between possession and distribution. (19)
      2. Government policy should change to decriminalize the use of drugs. (20)

CONCLUSION (21)

  I. Review of main points
  II. Restatement of thesis
  III. Final remarks

As you read Powell's speech, notice how she expands on this outline as she develops her argument point by point. Notice also how she uses solid evidence throughout, including emotional evidence. Her research was culled from the following bibliography:

Bibliography

Addiction a brain disorder, not just bad behavior. (2011, August 16). *USA Today.*

Amen, H. (2011, July 1). 10 years of drug decriminalization in Portugal has reduced addiction, crime. *Matador Magazine.*

Carmichael, M. (2010, June 28). The case for treating drug addicts in prison. *News Weekly.*

Herman, C., & Whalen, K. (Filmmakers). (2010). *Tulia Texas: The war on drugs* [Documentary]. United States: PBS.

Jackson, S. (2011, May 6). Beyond prisons. *Yes Magazine, 58. 1–75.*

A New Path. (2012, February 17). Retrieved from http://anewpathsite.org/

Office of National Drug Control Policy. (2011). Retrieved from http://www.drugsense.org/cms/wodclock

Public Safety Performance Project. (2011). *Pew Research Center.* Retrieved from http://www.pewcenteronthestates.org/topic_category.aspx?category=528

Reinberg, S. (2011, September 10). Study: More U.S. adults using illegal drugs. *USA Today.*

Schuessler, J. (2012, March 7). Drug policy as race policy: Best seller galvanizes the debate. *The New York Times,* p. 1C.

The science of drug abuse and addiction. (2011). *National Institute on Drug Abuse.* Retrieved from http://www.drugabuse.gov/

Southern Center for Human Rights. (2011, October 6). Retrieved from http://www.schr.org/safety/criminalization

Skolnick, A. (2011, February 9). Runaway prison costs trash state budgets. *The Fiscal Times.*

Szalavitz, M. (2011, September 27). Drugs, risk and the myth of the "evil" addict. *New York Times.* Retrieved from http://opinionator.blogs.nytimes.com/2011/09/27/drugs-risk-and-the-myth-of-the-evil-addict/?scp=2&sq=Maia%20Szalavitz&st=cse

Uniform crime report. (2011, October). *Federal Bureau of Investigation.* Retrieved from http://www.fbi.gov/about-us/cjis/ucr/ucr

Williams, K. (2011, October 3). Recovery month 2011: Getting rid of addiction stigma. *Huffington Post.* Retrieved from http://www.huffingtonpost.com/kimberly-williams/the-problem-is-not-the-pe_b_989742.html

SAMPLE SPEECH It's Not the Addict, It's the Drug: Redefining America's War on Drugs **Tunette Powell**

1 Bruce Callis grew up in one of the poorest projects in San Antonio, Texas. His mother was a housekeeper; his father, a full-time alcoholic. Bruce downed his first beer at age 13, smoked marijuana at 14, and at 21 he was addicted to crack cocaine. By the time he was 30 Bruce was convicted of possession of crack cocaine and sentenced to 15 years behind bars.

Attention-getter: A high-impact introduction uses an example that personalizes the problem.

2 Forty years ago, Richard Nixon launched the "War on Drugs" to eliminate drug use and the illegal drug trade in our country. Sadly, Nixon and presidents after him waged the wrong war. This 40-year fight has become less about preventing drug distribution and more about the criminalization of addiction. According to the *New York Times* of March 7, 2012, the United States currently incarcerates 2.3 million people, of which 23 percent are nonviolent drug offenders.

Direct statement of the thesis, demonstrating that this is direct persuasion. Statistics from trustworthy sources increase Powell's credibility on this topic.

3 Yes, drug distribution in our country is a serious concern, but according to the Law Office for the Southern Center for Human Rights, our misguided attitudes and policies toward drugs has created a culture that is intolerant of addiction. Although many people recognize addiction as a disease, we are still more likely to punish people for it than to help them with recovery.

Here Powell expands on her thesis statement, explaining the basic problem she will address in the rest of her speech.

4 According to the Office of National Drug Control Policy, "The U.S. federal government spent over $15 billion dollars in 2010 on the War on Drugs, at a rate of about $500 per second." But the cost of criminalizing addiction isn't just paid in dollars, it is paid in lives. According to the summer 2011 issue of *YES* magazine, only one-fifth of addicts behind bars have adequate access to rehabilitation programs, making it almost impossible for them to recover and become functioning members of society, which hurts not only them but society as a whole.

Powell could have also broken down this statistic to $41 million a day, $1.7 million an hour, or $28.5 thousand a minute. Which is more memorable?

5 Today, let's set aside what we've previously been told about drug use in America and focus on the person behind the addiction by discussing the problems, impacts, and solutions of criminalizing addiction. Attitude is the paint that can change the color of any room. And the walls of America are in dire need of a touch-up.

Preview of main points.

6 According to the *USA Today* of September 10, 2011, over 20 million Americans struggling with addictions never receive help with recovery. Let's ask ourselves not *what* the problem is, but *who* the problem is.

Powell continues to establish the problem with solid evidence from a reliable source.

7 *We* are the problem for two reasons. One, we demonize addiction as dirty and morally wrong, and, two, our policies reinforce this by putting addicts behind bars without rehabilitation.

Statement of the first main point, preview of the first two subpoints.

8 First, we are guilty of branding addiction as morally wrong when it is really an issue of public health. Maia Szalavitz wrote in the *New York Times* on September 27, 2011, "Prejudice against people based on the substances they use is one of the few remaining acceptable biases." She explains that we are blinded by a cultural perception that addicts are expendable; that they "*deserve* to die because they have violated the law and aren't taking responsibility for the consequences of their actions." Just proving her point further, in response to the article one reader exclaimed, "Is it really in the social interest to save the lives of junkies who overdose?"

She chooses powerful quotations from a reliable source to develop her first subpoint.

9 Unfortunately, this voice is only one in a chorus of intolerance toward addicts, which leads to our second problem: We incarcerate addicts instead of giving them treatment. As we discussed earlier, the United States currently incarcerates over 500,000 nonviolent drug users, all despite this: As *USA Today* explained on August 16, 2011, two decades of neuroscience have uncovered how addiction hijacks different parts of the brain and changes the cognitive and behavioral functions of drug users.

Development of the second subpoint.

10 According to the National Institute on Drug Abuse in 2011, "addiction is a chronic disease similar to other chronic diseases such as type II diabetes, cancer, and cardiovascular disease." If cancer were treated the same as addiction, we would refuse treatment to inmates suffering from lung cancer simply because they had a history of smoking cigarettes. According to *News Weekly* on June 28, 2010, only one-fifth of prison inmates get any form of drug treatment, and nowhere does our public health policy stipulate that such treatment has to be "effective."

A powerful analogy used as proof.

11 Bruce Callis was in and out of prison from his early 20s to his late 40s. Most prisons didn't offer him treatment, and the ones that did were ineffective. Criminalizing addictions results in two alarming impacts: on the addict and society.

A return to her personal example and a preview of the next main point.

12 According to a 2011 Public Safety Performance Project conducted by the Pew Research Center, 4 out of 10 drug offenders returned to state prison within 3 years of their release. And with little treatment available, this shouldn't surprise us. A cycle is created the first time an addict goes to prison. They go from a sick person to a criminal. The addict is then released back into society. The sickness is ignored, and the cycle repeats itself all over again.

The first subpoint of the second main point.

13 As previously cited, neuroscience journalist Maia Szalavitz points out, "Even when drug users are released, their criminal record makes it impossible for them to find meaningful employment." So not only are many addicts fighting disease without medical assistance, but many do so as unemployed, sometimes homeless, members of our society.

Evidence from a reliable source.

14 This leads to startling social impacts. According to *Uniform Crime Reports*, published by the FBI in October of 2011, every 20 seconds someone in America is arrested for violating a drug law. However, many of these arrests are for drug possession with no intent to distribute. For example, according to that same report, approximately 900,000 people in 2009 were arrested for marijuana, of which 89 percent were charged with possession with no intent to distribute.

Transition to the next point.

15 Our economy is in a state of emergency, yet our eagerness to criminalize drugs and put users behind bars is costing us billions of dollars a year. *The Fiscal Times* reported on February 9th, 2011, that in California alone it costs about $45,000 per year to incarcerate a drug user; the same price as one year at Harvard University with room and board. By contrast, rehabilitation would cost less than $5,000 per year. Our tax dollars continue to be wasted on room and board for inmates who will never benefit or recover as long as they're incarcerated.

Another powerful analogy, with statistics.

16 Bruce Callis was released from prison for the final time when he was 47 years old. After 1 week his son found him slumped over at a bus station, high on crack and barely able to walk. Notice that nowhere in Callis's story have I mentioned drug

Return to the personal example; a preview of the final main point.

treatment, only incarceration. What can we do to help people like him? Let's look at personal, organizational, and governmental solutions.

17 Our personal solution comes first, because it is the foundation for all other solutions: We must change our attitudes about addiction. Dr. Ellen Friedman, a psychologist, told the *Huffington Post* on October 3, 2011, "The profile of the addict as an amoral thrill-seeker is . . . scientifically wrong." We don't shame people for cancer diagnoses; we cannot continue to demonize drug users.

Again, an excellent coupling of an analogy with statistical evidence.

18 Second, we have to get involved to promote rehabilitation and fight incarceration for nonviolent drug users. There are existing organizations that need our support, such as A New Path, an organization that is dedicated to reducing the stigma of addictive illness and advocates for therapeutic rather than punitive drug policies. Visit their website at anewpathsite.org. This organization publishes updates on national drug legislation; check it out to learn more about legislation in your area.

Desired audience behavior.

19 On a governmental level, the first step is for policy to reflect the differences between possession and distribution, which would greatly reduce the number of drug users behind bars. This would help law enforcement distinguish between the *crime* of distributing drugs and the *person* who is addicted to them.

20 Finally, perhaps our government can look to Portugal, which has set a noble example. Ten years ago, Portugal decriminalized the use of drugs, according to *Matador Magazine* in July 2011. People caught using illegal substances are sent before a panel of psychologists and social workers instead of a judge in a criminal court. *Matador Magazine* reported that since the 2001 law was enacted, the number of addicts has been cut in half. Portugal is a real-life example of what happens when a country treats drug addiction as a health issue and not a criminal one.

Example/analogy used as evidence.

21 Now is the time to separate the War on Drugs from the war on addiction. Today you've heard the problems, impacts, and solutions of criminalizing addictions. Bruce Callis is 50 years old now. And he is still struggling with his addiction. While you all are sitting out there listening to this, I'm living it. Bruce Callis is my father, and for my entire life, I have watched our misguided system destroy him. The irony here is that we live in a society where we are told to recycle. We recycle paper, aluminum, and old electronics. But why don't we ever consider recycling the most precious thing on earth—the human life.[26]

A review of the main points and a restatement of the thesis.

Summary

Persuasion—the act of moving someone, through communication, toward a belief, attitude, or behavior—can be both worthwhile and ethical. Ethical persuasion requires that the speaker be sincere and honest and avoid such behaviors as plagiarism. It also requires that the persuasion be in the best interest of the audience.

Persuasion can be categorized according to the type of proposition (fact, value, or policy), outcome (convincing or actuating), or approach (direct or indirect). A persuasive strategy is put into effect through the use of several techniques.

These include setting a specific, clear persuasive purpose, structuring the message carefully, using solid evidence (including emotional evidence), using careful reasoning, adapting to the audience, and building credibility as a speaker.

A typical structure for a speech to convince requires you to explain what the problem is and then propose a solution. For a speech to actuate, you also have to ask for a desired audience response. The basic three-pronged structure can be adapted to more elaborate persuasive plans, but the basic components will remain a part of any persuasive strategy.

For each of these components, you need to analyze the arguments your audience will have against accepting what you say and then answer those arguments.

In adapting to your audience, you should establish common ground, organize your speech in such a way that you can expect a "yes" response along each step of your persuasive plan, and take special care with a hostile audience. In building credibility, you should keep in mind the audience's perception of your competence, character, and charisma.

Key Terms

actuate To move members of an audience toward a specific behavior. *p. 410*

ad hominem fallacy A fallacious argument that attacks the integrity of a person to weaken his or her position. *p. 416*

anchor The position supported by audience members before a persuasion attempt. *p. 405*

argumentum ad populum fallacy Fallacious reasoning based on the dubious notion that because many people favor an idea, you should, too. *p. 418*

argumentum ad verecundiam fallacy Fallacious reasoning that tries to support a belief by relying on the testimony of someone who is not an authority on the issue being argued. *p. 417*

convincing A speech goal that aims at changing audience members' beliefs, values, or attitudes. *p. 410*

credibility The believability of a speaker or other source of information. *p. 420*

direct persuasion Persuasion that does not try to hide or disguise the speaker's persuasive purpose. *p. 410*

either-or fallacy Fallacious reasoning that sets up false alternatives, suggesting that if the inferior one must be rejected, then the other must be accepted. *p. 416*

emotional evidence Evidence that arouses emotional reactions in an audience. *p. 415*

ethical persuasion Persuasion in an audience's best interest that does not depend on false or misleading information to induce change in that audience. *p. 407*

ethos A speaker's credibility or ethical appeal. *p. 423*

evidence Material used to prove a point, such as testimony, statistics, and examples. *p. 415*

fallacy An error in logic. *p. 416*

indirect persuasion Persuasion that disguises or deemphasizes the speaker's persuasive goal. *p. 411*

latitude of acceptance In social judgment theory, statements that a receiver would not reject. *p. 405*

latitude of noncommitment In social judgment theory, statements that a receiver would not care strongly about one way or another. *p. 405*

latitude of rejection In social judgment theory, statements that a receiver could not possibly accept. *p. 405*

logos A speaker's use of logical arguments to appeal to an audience's sense of reasoning. *p. 423*

Motivated Sequence A five-step plan used in persuasive speaking; also known as Monroe's Motivated Sequence. *p. 415*

pathos A speaker's use of emotional appeals to persuade an audience. *p. 423*

persuasion The act of motivating a listener, through communication, to change a particular belief, attitude, value, or behavior. *p. 405*

post hoc fallacy Fallacious reasoning that mistakenly assumes that one event causes another because they occur sequentially. *p. 417*

proposition of fact A claim bearing on issue in which there are two or more sides of conflicting factual evidence. *p. 409*

proposition of policy A claim bearing on issue that involves adopting or rejecting a specific course of action. *p. 409*

proposition of value A claim bearing on issue involving the worth of some idea, person, or object. *p. 409*

reductio ad absurdum fallacy Fallacious reasoning that unfairly attacks an argument by extending it to such extreme lengths that it looks ridiculous. *p. 416*

social judgment theory An explanation of attitude change that posits that opinions will change only in small increments and only when the target opinions lie within the receiver's latitudes of acceptance and noncommitment. *p. 405*

target audience That part of an audience that must be influenced in order to achieve a persuasive goal. *p. 418*

Check Your Understanding

Answer the following for a persuasive speech you have presented or plan to present:

1. What was your persuasive strategy for this speech?

2. Which guidelines did you use to make sure your speech was ethical?

3. How did you bolster your credibility as a speaker? Give specific examples.

4. Which guidelines did you use to check the effectiveness of your persuasive arguments?

5. How did you organize your speech for the desired effect on your audience?

Activities

1. **Audience Latitudes of Acceptance** To better understand the concept of latitudes of acceptance, rejection, and noncommitment, formulate a list of perspectives on a topic of your choice. This list should contain 8 to 10 statements that represent a variety of attitudes, such as the list pertaining to the pro-life/pro-choice issue on page 406. Arrange this list from your own point of view, from most

acceptable to least acceptable. Then circle the single statement that best represents your own point of view. This will be your "anchor." Underline those items that also seem reasonable. These make up your latitude of acceptance on this issue. Then cross out the numbers in front of any items that express opinions that you cannot accept. These make up your latitude of rejection. Those statements that are left would be your latitude of noncommitment. Do you agree that someone seeking to persuade you on this issue would do best by advancing propositions that fall within this latitude of noncommitment?

2. **Personal Persuasion** When was the last time you changed your attitude about something after discussing it with someone? In your opinion, was this persuasion interactive? Not coercive? Incremental? Ethical? Explain your answer.

3. **Propositions of Fact, Value, and Policy** Which of the following are propositions of fact, propositions of value, and propositions of policy?

   1. "Three Strikes" laws that put felons away for life after their third conviction are/are not fair.

   2. Elder care should/should not be the responsibility of the government.

   3. The mercury in dental fillings is/is not healthy for the dental patient.

   4. Congressional pay raises should/should not be delayed until an election has intervened.

   5. Third-party candidates strengthen/weaken American democracy.

   6. National medical insurance should/should not be provided to all citizens of the United States.

   7. Elderly people who are wealthy do/do not receive too many Social Security benefits.

   8. Tobacco advertising should/should not be banned from all media.

   9. Domestic violence is/is not on the rise.

   10. Pit bulls are/are not dangerous animals.

4. **Structuring Persuasive Speeches** For practice in structuring persuasive speeches, choose one of the following topics, and provide a full-sentence outline that conforms to the outline in Figure 14-2, page 412.

   1. It should/should not be more difficult to purchase a handgun.

   2. Public relations messages that appear in news reports should/should not be labeled as advertising.

   3. Newspaper recycling is/is not important for the environment.

   4. Police should/should not be required to carry nonlethal weapons only.

   5. Parole should/should not be abolished.

6. The capital of the United States should/should not be moved to a more central location.

7. We should/should not ban capital punishment.

8. Bilingual education should/should not be offered in all schools in which students speak English as a second language.

5. **Find the Fallacy** Test your ability to detect shaky reasoning by identifying which fallacy is exhibited in each of the following statements.

   a. *Ad hominem*   d. *Post hoc*

   b. *Ad absurdum*   e. *Ad verecundiam*

   c. Either-or   f. *Ad populum*

   1. Some companies claim to be in favor of protecting the environment, but you can't trust them. Businesses exist to make a profit, and the cost of saving the earth is just another expense to be cut.

   2. Take it from me, imported cars are much better than domestics. I used to buy only American, but the cars made here are all junk.

   3. Rap music ought to be boycotted. After all, the number of assaults on police officers went up right after rap became popular.

   4. Carpooling to cut down on the parking problem is a stupid idea. Look around—nobody carpools!

   5. I know that staying in the sun can cause cancer, but if I start worrying about every environmental risk I'll have to stay inside a bomb shelter breathing filtered air, never drive a car or ride my bike, and I won't be able to eat anything.

   6. The biblical account of creation is just another fairy tale. You can't seriously consider the arguments of those Bible-thumping, know-nothing fundamentalists, can you?

6. **The Credibility of Persuaders** Identify someone who tries to persuade you via public speaking or mass communication. This person might be a politician, a teacher, a member of the clergy, a coach, a boss, or anyone else. Analyze this person's credibility in terms of the three dimensions discussed in the chapter. Which dimension is most important in terms of this person's effectiveness?

For Further Exploration

For more resources about persuasive speaking, see the *Understanding Human Communication* **website at www .oup.com/us/adler.** There you will find a variety of resources: "Media Room" clips from popular films and television shows to further illustrate important concepts, a list of books and articles, links to descriptions of feature films and television shows at the *Now Playing* website, study aids, and a self-test to check your understanding of the material in this chapter.

Propositions of Fact   Some persuasive messages focus on **propositions of fact**: issues in which there are two or more sides about conflicting information, in which listeners are required to choose the truth for themselves. Some questions of fact are these:

The National Security Agency was/was not justified in listening in to the phone calls of everyday citizens.

Windmills are/are not a practical way for the private homeowner to create clean energy.

Bottled water is/is not healthier for you than tap water.

These examples show that many questions of fact can't be settled with a simple "yes" or "no" or with an objective piece of information. Rather, they are open to debate, and answering them requires careful examination and interpretation of evidence, usually collected from a variety of sources. That's why it is possible to debate questions of fact, and that's why these propositions form the basis of persuasive speeches and not informative ones.

Propositions of Value   **Propositions of value** go beyond issues of truth or falsity and explore the worth of some idea, person, or object. Propositions of value include the following:

Cheerleaders are/are not just as valuable as the athletes on the field.

The United States is/is not justified in attacking countries that harbor terrorist organizations.

The use of laboratory animals for scientific experiments is/is not cruel and immoral.

In order to deal with most propositions of value, you will have to explore certain propositions of fact. For example, you won't be able to debate whether the experimental use of animals in research is immoral—a proposition of value— until you have dealt with propositions of fact such as how many animals are used in experiments and whether experts believe they actually suffer.

Propositions of Policy   **Propositions of policy** go one step beyond questions of fact or value: They recommend a specific course of action (a "policy"). Some questions of policy are these:

The World Bank should/should not create a program of microloans for citizens of impoverished nations.

The Electoral College should/should not be abolished.

Genetic engineering of plants and livestock is/is not an appropriate way to increase the food supply.

Looking at persuasion according to the type of proposition is a convenient way to generate topics for a persuasive speech, because each type of proposition suggests different topics. Selected topics could also be handled differently depending on how they are approached. For example, a campaign speech could be approached as a proposition of fact ("Candidate X has done more for this community than the opponent"), a proposition of value ("Candidate X is a better person than the opponent"), or a proposition of policy ("We should get out and vote for Candidate X"). Remember, however, that a fully developed persuasive speech is likely to contain all three types of propositions. If you were preparing a speech advocating that college athletes should be paid in cash for their talents (a proposition of policy), you might want to first prove that the practice is already widespread (a proposition of fact) and that it is unfair to athletes from other schools (a proposition of value).

By Desired Outcome

We can also categorize persuasion according to two major outcomes: convincing and actuating.

Convincing   When you set about to **convince** an audience, you want to change the way its members think. When we say that convincing an audience changes the way its members think, we do not mean that you have to swing them from one belief or attitude to a completely different one. Sometimes audience members will already think the way you want them to, but they will not be firmly enough committed to that way of thinking. When that is the case, you reinforce, or strengthen, their opinions. For example, if your audience already believed that the federal budget should be balanced but did not consider the idea important, your job would be to reinforce members' current beliefs. Reinforcing is still a type of change, however, because you are causing an audience to adhere more strongly to a belief or attitude. In other cases, a speech to convince will begin to shift attitudes without bringing about a total change of thinking. For example, an effective speech to convince might get a group of skeptics to consider the possibility that bilingual education is/isn't a good idea.

Actuating   When you set about to **actuate** an audience, you want to move its members to a specific behavior. Whereas a speech to convince might move an audience to action, it won't be any specific action that you have recommended. In a speech to actuate, you do recommend that specific action.

There are two types of action you can ask for—adoption or discontinuance. The former asks an audience to engage in a new behavior; the latter asks an audience to stop behaving in an established way. If you gave a speech for a political candidate and then asked for contributions to that candidate's campaign, you would be asking your audience to adopt a new behavior. If you gave a speech against smoking and then asked your audience members to sign a pledge to quit, you would be asking them to discontinue an established behavior.

By Directness of Approach

We can also categorize persuasion according to the directness of approach employed by the speaker.

Direct Persuasion   In **direct persuasion** the speaker will make his or her purpose clear, usually by stating it outright early in the speech. This is the best strategy to use with a friendly audience, especially when you are asking for a response that the audience is reasonably likely to give you. Direct persuasion is the kind we hear in most academic situations. Eugene Nemirovskiy, a student at Glendale Community College in California, used direct

Bill Clinton used a direct form of persuasion when he spoke in support of Barack Obama at the 2012 Democratic National Convention. Will you be direct or indirect in your next persuasive speech?